Freedom in a Slave Society
Stories from the Antebellum South

Before the Civil War, most Southern white people were as strongly committed to freedom for their kind as to slavery for African Americans. This study views that tragic reality through the lens of eight authors – representatives of a South that seemed, to them, destined for greatness but was, we know, on the brink of destruction. Exceptionally able and ambitious, these men and women won repute among the educated middle classes in the Southwest, South, and the nation, even amid sectional tensions. Although they sometimes described liberty in the abstract, more often these authors discussed its practical significance: what it meant for people to make life's important choices freely and to be responsible for the results. They publically insisted that freedom caused progress, but hidden doubts clouded this optimistic vision. Ultimately, their association with the oppression of slavery dimmed their hopes for human improvement, and fear distorted their responses to the sectional crisis.

Johanna Nicol Shields holds a BA, MA, and PhD from the University of Alabama. She taught at the University of Alabama in Huntsville (UAH) between 1967 and 2007 and is the founding director of the UAH Humanities Center. She has won numerous awards for teaching and research, including UAH's Alumni Association Distinguished Faculty Award. Shields has held research awards from the American Association of University Women and the National Endowment for the Humanities. Her work has been published in the *Journal of the Early Republic*, the *Journal of Southern History*, *Southern Cultures*, *Alabama Review*, and *Mississippi Quarterly*. She is the author of *The Line of Duty: Maverick Congressmen and the Development of American Political Culture, 1836–1860* (1985), which won the Ralph Gabriel Prize awarded by the American Studies Association and Greenwood Press.

CAMBRIDGE STUDIES ON THE AMERICAN SOUTH

Mark M. Smith, University of South Carolina, Columbia
David Moltke-Hansen, Center for the Study of the American South,
 University of North Carolina at Chapel Hill

Interdisciplinary in its scope and intent, this series builds on and extends Cambridge University Press's long-standing commitment to studies on the American South. The series not only will offer the best new work on the South's distinctive institutional, social, economic, and cultural history but also will feature works in national, comparative, and transnational perspectives.

Robert E. Bonner, *Southern Slaveholders and the Crisis of American Nationhood*
Peter McCandless, *Slavery, Disease, and Suffering in the Southern Lowcountry*
Christopher Michael Curtis, *Jefferson's Freeholders and the Politics of Ownership in the Old Dominion*
Johanna Nicol Shields, *Freedom in a Slave Society: Stories from the Antebellum South*

Freedom in a Slave Society

Stories from the Antebellum South

JOHANNA NICOL SHIELDS
University of Alabama in Huntsville

CAMBRIDGE UNIVERSITY PRESS
Cambridge, New York, Melbourne, Madrid, Cape Town,
Singapore, São Paulo, Delhi, Mexico City

Cambridge University Press
32 Avenue of the Americas, New York, NY 10013-2473, USA

www.cambridge.org
Information on this title: www.cambridge.org/9781107013377

© Johanna Nicol Shields 2012

This publication is in copyright. Subject to statutory exception
and to the provisions of relevant collective licensing agreements,
no reproduction of any part may take place without the written
permission of Cambridge University Press.

First published 2012

Printed in the United States of America

A catalog record for this publication is available from the British Library.

Library of Congress Cataloging in Publication data
Shields, Johanna Nicol.
　Freedom in a slave society : stories from the antebellum South / Johanna Nicol Shields,
　University of Alabama in Huntsville.
　　p.　cm. – (Cambridge studies on the American South)
　Includes index.
　ISBN 978-1-107-01337-7 (hardback)
　1. Southern States – Intellectual life – 19th century.　2. American literature – Southern
States – History and criticism.　3. Authors, American – Southern States – Political
and social views.　4. Politics and literature – Southern States – History – 19th
century.　5. Whites – Southern States – Attitudes – History – 19th century.　6. Liberty in
literature.　7. Slavery in literature.　I. Title.
F214.S55　2012
973.5–dc23　　　2012003302

ISBN 978-1-107-01337-7 Hardback

Cambridge University Press has no responsibility for the persistence or accuracy of URLs
for external or third-party Internet Web sites referred to in this publication and does not
guarantee that any content on such Web sites is, or will remain, accurate or appropriate.

For Nick, Anna, and Katherine – the heart of my life

Contents

List of Figures	*page* xi
Preface	xiii
Acknowledgments	xxi
List of Abbreviations	xxiii

1. Regarding a "Weird Utopia" — 1
   The Promise of a Rising South — 2
   The Idea of Freedom with Slavery — 15

   PART ONE: THE SOCIAL ORIGINS OF INDIVIDUAL FREEDOM

2. Self-Making in Southwestern Towns — 25
   A Sociable Spokesman for Southern Literature — 29
   An Enterprising Woman from the North — 39
   Not Quite a Literary Man — 47

3. The Domestic Foundations of Self-Determination — 61
   A Myth-Making Individual and the Changing Family — 65
   A Lonely Striver — 71
   An Ambivalent Patriarch — 75
   A Proud Young Moralist — 83

4. The Voluntary Bonds of Friendship — 95
   A Pair of Competitive Friends — 99
   A New Englander's Alliance with the Rising South — 106
   The Tangled Friendships of a Controversial Man — 115

   PART TWO: WRITING FREEDOM, WITH SLAVES

5. Southwestern Histories for a Divided Market — 133
   An Anxious Planter's History — 136
   The Historian of Unfettered Intellect — 147
   One Romantic, Two Skeptics, and the Aftermath
   of Pickett's History — 157

6.	Slave Characters and the Problem of Human Nature	173
	The Darkest Kind of Humor	180
	A Sentimental View of Slavery	189
	The Mysterious Slave	199

PART THREE: THE CRISIS OF THE RISING SOUTH

7.	Slavery and Political Trust	215
	The Psychology of Tyranny	219
	Mastery and Self-Mastery	228
	The Failure of Self-Determination and the Politics of Hate	239
8.	Self-Determination and Slavery in Conflict	251
	Fate and Freedom	254
	Independence and the Politics of War	265
	The Lessons of War	276

Epilogue: The Remains of a Rising South	291
Index	299

Figures

1.1. Alabama in 1820	*page* 5
1.2. Antebellum Alabama	6
2.1. Captain Simon Suggs	55
3.1. Albert Pickett	77
3.2. Augusta Evans	89
4.1. Alexander Meek	104
4.2. "Gladiators of the Senate; Bulley's of the House"	123
5.1. Dedication page of Pickett's *History*	143
5.2. Simon Suggs, Jr.	151
6.1. Distribution of slaves in Alabama, 1860	178
6.2. Mr. and Mrs. Moreland and Albert, from *The Planter's Northern Bride* (1854)	194
8.1. Georgia Cottage	265
E.1. William Russell Smith	295

Preface

The Abraham Lincoln Presidential Library in Springfield, Illinois, owns a copy of *The Flush Times of Alabama and Mississippi* in its collection of the president's memorabilia. Written by Joseph Baldwin, a southerner just a few years younger than Lincoln, this book chronicles the comic misadventures of lawyers, and Lincoln liked it very much. One summer's day, I turned the book's pages under the watchful eye of the library's curator, looking for notes in the great leader's hand. Sadly, there were none. But, halfway through the book, smudges from fingers marked the margins of about twenty pages, where a reader held the book open. I felt a thrill – almost a shiver – when I realized that my hands probably were touching Abraham Lincoln's fingerprints.[1]

This copy of *Flush Times* came to the Presidential Library by way of its later owner, Henry Whitney, who explained how Lincoln made those marks. A lawyer, Whitney rode circuit with Lincoln in Illinois, seeking clients. Many years later, Whitney recalled that Lincoln often sat in his hotel room with friends and read aloud from *Flush Times*, a "series of sketches" by a lawyer who also rode circuit in the West. The book was published in 1853, but Lincoln's copy was from the ninth printing, issued in 1854 in both New York and London. The fingerprints I saw plainly marked Lincoln's favorite tale, "The Earthquake Story." According to Whitney, Lincoln read this hilarious story so many times that he loosened the pages where it lay. Lincoln himself told Baldwin, when they met during the Civil War, that *Flush Times* was "one of his classics," which pleased the ambitious author a great deal.[2]

---

[1] The curator, James M. Cornelius, was responsible for supervising anyone who handled Lincoln's book. Without his generous assistance, I would not have realized that the smudges I was seeing appeared at Lincoln's favorite story. The most useful recent version is *The Flush Times of Alabama and Mississippi: A Series of Sketches*, intro. by James Justus (Baton Rouge: Louisiana State University Press, 1987, c. 1853).

[2] Baldwin wrote his friend and son-in-law John Felton that "Abe and I grew very pleasant and spent an hour together in the White House very cosily.... He says he is always quoting me when he gets facetious (probably to restore gravity to his guests." Baldwin to Felton, November 1, 1863, in Lester-Gray Collection of Documents filmed from material loaned by Robert M.

Holding Lincoln's book was exciting but unsettling. As a historian, I knew that Baldwin subtly defended the South and slavery, while Lincoln defeated the South and ended slavery. Rather typically, Baldwin had inserted slavery into "The Earthquake Story," where a "servant" Jo uttered a key line before a group of lawyers. The African American called one lawyer "Mas" (for master) and he spoke in crude dialect.[3] Why would Lincoln, who hated slavery, find Baldwin's work so funny that he read it aloud many times?

That is an important question without an easy answer. Because people laugh quickly, without thinking, Lincoln may not have reflected about his amusement. Nonetheless, Baldwin and Lincoln shared many ideas. They were both inspired by American possibilities. Convinced that free men were making a great society, they saw western lawyers as crucial to the process. Lawyers, however, were not angels, and Baldwin constantly made fun of the way they aimed high and fell short. Because their aspirations were generally constructive, and they were persistent, the lawyers' foibles were amusing. Baldwin and Lincoln had abiding faith in the civilizing mission of the law, so they laughed at temporary setbacks.[4]

Although Baldwin meant to amuse, "The Earthquake Story" used wild exaggeration to teach an ethical lesson: how lawyers could correct one another without diminishing any man's freedom. The story was a brilliant fragment within a sketch called "Cave Burton, Esq., of Kentucky" in which circuit-riding lawyers played an instructive practical joke on the title character. Burton was a loudmouth, a "monstrous demagogue" who told juries long-winded stories that appealed to their emotions rather than the facts of law. He

---

Lester (film made by the New York Public Library in 1949). Baldwin went to the White House to get a pass to visit in Virginia, which he was denied. Whitney apparently got Lincoln's book from William Hearndon, and Whitney's son passed it on to the state of Illinois. Whitney's account is in his *Life on the Circuit with Lincoln* (Boston: Estes and Lauriat, 1892; reprint, Caldwell, ID: Caxton Printers, 1940), 185; he also writes that Baldwin was one of Lincoln's favorite authors; ibid., 177. M. L. Houser and Esther Cowles Cushman, *Abraham Lincoln, Student: His Books* (Peoria, IL: Priv. Print. by E. J. Jacob, 1932), 24, note that the book was in the collection of the governor when they wrote and that the pages of Lincoln's favorite story showed its "hard usage."

[3] "The Earthquake Story" begins on page 162 of *Flush Times* and, rather than ending, fades into the larger story that frames it. His fingerprints indicate that Lincoln read to the end of the larger story, "Cave Burton, Esq., of Kentucky"; Jo speaks, 175.

[4] See Robert A. Ferguson, *Law and Letters in American Culture* (Cambridge, MA: Harvard University Press, 1984) for a discussion of how Lincoln, Baldwin, and others of their generation represented a Ciceronian model of the law in a changing era. Long before I saw Lincoln's copy of *Flush Times*, I was struck by the similarities between his legal experiences and those of Baldwin when reading David H. Donald's prize-winning biography *Lincoln* (New York: Simon & Schuster, 1995). A more recent prize-winning study that links Lincoln to his southern heritage, but contrasts his ideas with those of slaveholding southerners, is Orville Vernon Burton, *The Age of Lincoln* (New York: Hill and Wang, 2007). An extended discussion that places Burton's claims in the context of southern intellectual history is Eric Arnesen, Bertram Wyatt-Brown, Stephen Berry, David Moltke-Hansen, and Vernon Burton, "Forum on *The Age of Lincoln*," *JHS* 9 (September 2009): 309–372.

also had "animal appetites" and never got enough to eat or drink. While he and other lawyers were at a hotel one night, Burton's friends ordered a feast: three barrels of fresh oysters, condiments, and whiskey. They told Burton the treat was being prepared in the kitchen, then they tricked him into telling an extravagant tale while they slipped, one at a time, from the room. During "The Earthquake Story," they ate every last oyster. Baldwin entertained with a moral. Taking advantage of Burton's gluttony and demagoguery, his friends taught him to attend to facts.[5]

In one simple line, Baldwin's slave revealed what Burton's friends were up to. When Burton realized that one of them was eating oysters, he rushed to the door and told Jo to "get mine ready this minute.... Be quick, Jo, old fel." "Hat in hand, Jo said, 'Why, Mas Cave, dey's all gone dis hour past; de gem'men eat ebery one up.'" In a quick stroke, Baldwin put a black waiter where he belonged, making slavery seem natural. But Jo's name signaled his significance, because Baldwin signed his letters "Jo," an abbreviation for Joseph and an alternate spelling for his nickname, Joe. Jo told the truth, yet he served the purposes of free men. So, to answer my own question: Lincoln laughed at the antics of circuit-riding lawyers, and he probably did not pause when he spoke, in dialect, the line of a black slave.[6]

Freedom in a Slave Society: Stories from the Antebellum South treats eight white writers who, like Joe Baldwin, deliberately placed themselves between a changing region and a nation of readers. I explore pervasive tensions within their world. I want to answer questions like the ones that bothered me when I held Lincoln's copy of *Flush Times*. How did these writers incorporate slavery into freedom so well as to satisfy readers around the country? What do their intellectual accomplishments, and their failures, say about the sectional cultures that produced the Civil War? To answer such questions, I examine six men and two women, each of whom lived at least a dozen years in Alabama between the 1830s and the Civil War. Historians call their rapidly growing region the Old Southwest. In order to emphasize these writers' belief in their society's great potential, I have chosen to call it the rising South. All of these women and men believed in liberty, especially their own, but slavery stunted their freedom to choose. Hoping to fathom the deep ethical dilemmas of a modernizing slave society, I study them and the stories they told.

Like Lincoln, each of these men and women was ambitious. Like him, they lived in towns, mingling with middle-class citizens. Five of the male writers were lawyers and journalists, each of whom held public office. The one planter also wrote for newspapers, and friends tried to make him Alabama's governor. The two women, a teacher and a single person who lived with her parents, relied on writing because custom limited their public speaking. But print was the common medium through which all of these individuals exercised influence. Like Baldwin, they expressed themselves, entertained readers, offered

[5] "Cave Burton," in *Flush Times*, 155.
[6] *Ibid.*, 172.

lessons, and, hopefully, made money. They wrote fiction, poetry, and history, publishing in the Southwest, the Southeast, or the North. Although unfamiliar in the twenty-first century, Caroline Hentz, Johnson Hooper, Augusta Evans, and Joseph Baldwin sold thousands of books in the nineteenth century. Albert Pickett, Alexander Meek, William Russell Smith, and Jeremiah Clemens were best known in the South, but they, too, were widely read.

In *Freedom in a Slave Society*, I argue that these writers expressed a variation on a familiar American theme of individual liberty. Like most middle-class people, they understood freedom to mean self-determination – the ability to make choices about their lives. Investing mostly their talents, they sought personal, professional, and political independence as other ambitious people around the country did. Along the way, they advocated middle-class values to improve their slave society, and they applied the same values in explaining the Southwest to outsiders. Their popularity suggests that many American readers found inequality an acceptable product of freedom, despite sectional differences about slavery. In the end, however, these authors exposed profound tensions between freedom and slavery, and those tensions had self-destructive consequences. Although their successes were impressive, these men and women also showed the ethical dilemmas of their class.

These eight authors described how the white people of the rising South built good lives. They laughed at their shortcomings or moralized about errant folk who should mend their ways. Only one author, the northern-born Hentz, wrote a long defense of slavery, and she knew its opposition. Time and again, the others extolled freedom's possibilities and minimized slavery, despite their commitment to it. Like Lincoln, they were influenced by a West that seemed to have a stunning future. Only by grasping their wholly American hope – and its powerful undertow of anxiety – can we know writers like Baldwin, comprehend why northerners like Lincoln read their books, and recognize the impulses that led them into war.

This book asks readers to take seriously the ideas of people who lived in pre–Civil War Alabama, where no one much expects to find worthwhile literature. For years, Alabama's auto license plates carried "Heart of Dixie," taking their cue from the old song "Dixie", a minstrel tune that Lincoln loved.[7] In truth, antebellum Alabama was the "land of cotton," but it held more than planters and their slaves. Increasingly, historians of the Old South study the middle classes and intellectuals and find evidence of modernity in the region. This book adds to that scholarship by integrating the social history of popular writers with their ideas, which were more like those of other Americans than Alabama's reputation suggests.[8]

---

[7] On the popularity of "Dixie" in the North and South, see Coleman Hutchison, "Whistling 'Dixie' for the Union (Nation, Anthem, Revision)," *ALH* 19 (Autumn 2007): 603–628, but it was David Moltke-Hansen who first alerted me to Lincoln's fondness for the song.

[8] The notion that southern writing was the product of the planter class has been closely related to historical interpretations that stress the hegemony of slaveholding planters. For a clear statement of this view, see the essay by Eugene D. Genovese and Elizabeth Fox-Genovese,

METHODS AND ORGANIZATION

In selecting writers for this book, I made judgments that readers should know. Because I wanted to examine people who reached a broad public, I selected men and women who published at least one book of poetry, fiction, or history – genres generally understood as literature – and I excluded authors who primarily wrote polemics or who principally published scientific or religious works. These standards left out interesting characters like the erudite educator F. A. P. Barnard, humorist John Gorman Barr, racial theorist Josiah Nott, and the influential Baptist cleric Basil Manly. But eight subjects seemed right for credible generalizations without sacrificing depth. Popular literature required authors to attempt coherence, for readers expected motives and action, character and conduct to be connected. Particularly in fiction and history, writers created human beings. Inevitably, authors transcribed more of their inner subjectivity than they knew. By the same token, they revealed more than they intended about their surroundings.

My decision to study popular authors had unintended consequences. Class was never a criterion, but it turned out that only one of these eight people was a planter, that none came from the lower class, and that all of them lived in towns. That all of them were white was unsurprising: there was almost no chance for a black person living in Alabama to produce a book. In 1833, not too long before Joe Baldwin migrated from the Shenandoah Valley, an enslaved man named James Williams was forced to leave his family in Virginia and move to Alabama, where he served as driver to more than a hundred of his absentee master's slaves. At one point, Williams lived not far from Baldwin, but they inhabited different social universes. The enslaved man was abused by a drunken overseer and made to beat his fellow slaves. In 1838, after Williams escaped, he narrated his experiences for the American Anti-Slavery Society in Boston. He could not write, but his editor copied "his manner, and in many instances his precise language." Williams's narrative underscores the unconscious omissions and deliberate erasures of southern white writers.[9] Stories like his found an audience, but an educated white woman, Harriet Beecher

---

"The Cultural History of Southern Slave Society: Reflections on the Work of Lewis P. Simpson," in J. Gerald Kennedy and Daniel Mark Fogel, eds., *American Letters and the Historical Consciousness: Essays in Honor of Lewis P. Simpson* (Baton Rouge: Louisiana State University Press, 1987). The historian most responsible for disentangling the study of southern intellectual history from claims that the South was not modern is Michael O'Brien, most importantly, his *Conjectures of Order: Intellectual Life and the American South, 1810–1860*, 2 vols. (Chapel Hill: University of North Carolina Press, 2004), but also the earlier statements in *Rethinking the South: Essays in Intellectual History* (Baltimore: Johns Hopkins University Press, 1988). The most forceful assertion of the importance of the town-dwelling middle class is Jonathan Daniel Wells, *The Origins of the Southern Middle Class, 1800–1861* (Chapel Hill: University of North Carolina Press, 2004).

[9] *Narrative of James Williams, an American Slave, Who Was for Several Years a Driver on a Cotton Plantation in Alabama* (New York: Published by the American Anti-Slavery Society, 1838), xix; Electronic Edition, http://docsouth.unc.edu/fpn/williams/williams.html.

Stowe, converted them into a best-seller. By studying popular authors, my selections reflected the market's bias.

I did not deliberately select writers for race, or class, or gender, but I did choose a geographical setting, for I was curious about the understudied intellectual life of the Southwest. That choice evolved. Originally intending to draw from several states, I modified the design when finding unexpectedly prolific authors from Alabama. Moreover, these eight represent other states, because early Alabama, like Illinois, was a crossroads. Hooper, Baldwin, and Hentz migrated as adults from North Carolina, Virginia, and Ohio, respectively; a New Englander until her marriage, Hentz also lived in North Carolina, Kentucky, Georgia, and Florida; born in South Carolina, Meek lived during the Civil War in Mississippi; born in Georgia, Evans lived there and in Texas until she was an adolescent. Clemens was the only native-born Alabamian among these writers, and only three died in the state. These writers illuminate a complex social reality.

Some practical considerations influenced my composition. To avoid a text too littered with unfamiliar people, I put scholars' names only in the notes. I quote writers at greater length than historians usually do, because, ultimately, writing was an art, and, without knowing the art, commentary hangs in thin air. Compared to, say, *Moby Dick* or *Uncle Tom's Cabin*, *Flush Times* is no longer a famous book. As a historian, I ground my interpretations of literary texts in writers' experiences more than I rely on theory (although the curious may find some theoretical issues in the notes).

This book traces how writers put abstract ideas to work, trying to pin down the slippery meanings they assigned to freedom. By mixing biography and history with literary analysis, I show the interaction of events and ideas. These writers interpreted individual motives and social conduct in an informal way. They meant to be accessible, which is why Lincoln was happy to read *Flush Times* aloud. Because they were talented, if not great, writers, they made their world come alive. In thousands of pages, they observed the short life of a rising South. I exploit their creativity while measuring their successes and their failures.

Eight authors do not appear alone in this book; they are surrounded by a large cast of town-dwelling southern white people. My purpose in discussing these others was to show how authors' ideas reflected experiences that were shared. Moreover, in order to make a reasonable claim that these eight writers represent other southerners in ways that transcend authorship, I want to show how much their experiences and ideas were rooted in social existence. So, to an unusual extent, writers' parents, spouses, children, cousins, friends, and even a few enemies appear as subjects in this book. They are not my primary concern, but they are more than minor figures in the complex social fabric of the rising South I portray.

Freedom in a Slave Society has an introductory chapter that introduces key ideas and summarizes important influences on the writers of the rising South. It sets the stage for the braided narrative that follows. Like all braided narratives, this one combines stories with analysis, but I treat eight subjects, each of whom, with family and friends, gets roughly equal attention in at least two, and more often three, different chapters. In each instance, I have tried to give a writer's experience and his or her work sufficient depth for a reader to retain a sense of the subject's individuality. Partly because this method runs the risk that the reader can't see the forest for the trees, the opening chapter focuses on the forest.

Part One considers how Alabama's writers understood middle-class ethical standards about self-determination and applied them to real and imaginary relations with community, family, and friends. Mentioning slavery mainly where they did, I focus on the social relations of white people and on writers' efforts to advance themselves. Chapter 2 introduces three writers as they launched their careers using talent as a social asset. Convinced that persuasion produced public action through voluntary commitments, they saw themselves leading a free people. Chapter 3 discusses four more writers, focusing on how families bred independence despite the inequalities within them. And Chapter 4 analyzes writers' friendships as evidence of their conviction that voluntary relations best connected free people.

Part Two considers writing as a form of public discourse about the past and future of a rising South. It treats the challenges of writing for a print medium where self-determination and slavery often clashed, rhetorically. Chapter 5 analyzes the competition among several authors to write histories reconciling freedom and slavery, and it assesses how the effort to attract northern and/or southern readers affected their writing. Chapter 6 analyzes three writers' portrayals of slavery as they faced a divided readership. Treating the dialogue between white and black characters, I unearth writers' anxieties about freedom and slavery.

Part Three shows the destructive results of these anxieties in the late antebellum political crisis and war. Chapter 7 considers self-determination and democracy in three writers' assessments of politics. Unspoken fears that slaveholders' desires for mastery might run amok increased these writers' sensitivity to antislavery politicians, but those fears also exaggerated their response to other southerners. They debated who was most dangerous: radical southern nationalists or conservative Unionists. Using writers who supported or opposed the Confederacy, Chapter 8 shows them reevaluating the possibilities for self-determination as events spiraled out of control during the Civil War. An Epilogue briefly suggests the postwar influence of the writers of the once rising South.

Writing was action that connected Alabama's authors to other people. Because these writers were respected in their communities – elected to office or honored with material and symbolic rewards – I argue from strong evidence that their town-dwelling neighbors accepted their ideas. I suspect, but can less conclusively demonstrate, that many other educated southerners – planters and prosperous farmers, and townspeople across the South – also admired them and shared their ideas. Certainly, many thousand sympathetic consumers bought their books. I began here by wondering what Lincoln thought when he read *Flush Times* aloud. In recent years, scholars have learned much about publishing, and they have learned something about books' circulation. But we may never know just where nineteenth-century books were bought and which ordinary people read them. After considering sales, reviews, and notices, I make careful claims about readers, aware that evidence is missing except in exceptional cases – like that of Abraham Lincoln.

The idea of a rising South did not entirely die when slavery did, but it was significantly changed, and these popular writers anticipated the terms of that transformation. As white Americans resumed the business of self-determination after the Civil War, economic issues displaced social reform, and the northern majority eventually abandoned the former slaves to a southern fate. Shaken by war, middle-class optimism about self-determination diminished when evolutionary theory raised questions about human nature. And, in the 1870s, industrial labor conflict and agrarian unrest began to disturb middle-class hopes for harmony among classes. Racism and fear of big government played a role in the retreat of northern reformers, but the logic of self-determination was also at play, for, given freedom, black people were supposed to take care of themselves. When white southerners called for a "New South" in the late nineteenth century, the ideas of Alabama's writers were reborn. Once again, southerners joined self-determination with inequality – this time in ways that northern Americans accepted.

Acknowledgments

I am indebted to a great many people who helped me sustain this project over time. I must begin with my colleagues in the History Department at the University of Alabama in Huntsville. I am grateful for the support of the late Frances Roberts, John White, Carolyn White, Philip Boucher, Lee Williams, Andrew Dunar, Stephen Waring, Richard Gerberding, and John Severn. They made a small university with a technological focus a rewarding place to work. Sue Kirkpatrick and Brian Martine brought insights from psychology and philosophy, respectively, to stimulating conversations. In countless ways, Beverly Gentry and Deborah Nelson allowed me to keep research alive in the face of administrative tasks. Sharon Watkins (now Lang) was an indispensable graduate assistant in the formative stages of this project. I thank the staff of the Salmon Library at UAH, especially Anne Coleman, Lelon Oliver, Wilson Luquire, and the entire Interlibrary Loan department.

In a time when the Internet connects researchers around the world to scattered collections, I am thankful for the librarians and archivists who know their sources and share them enthusiastically. I am particularly grateful to the staff of the Southern Historical Collection, University of North Carolina at Chapel Hill; of the Perkins Library at Duke; of the Alabama Department of Archives and History; of the Hoole Special Collections Library at the University of Alabama; and of the Manuscripts Division at the Library of Congress.

A number of colleagues lent their talents to the development of this book, and I am deeply grateful for their friendship and support. Anne C. Rose is the best possible critic one could have. She read every page of the manuscript, asked probing questions, and never failed to encourage my progress. Lawrence F. Kohl talked with me endlessly about ideas and read portions of the manuscript more times than anyone should have to. His forceful and always engaged critiques sharpened my arguments. John Mayfield's superb literary insights repeatedly improved my reading and my writing about antebellum southern literature. Daniel Dupre offered encouragement and useful suggestions for the chapter on Alabama's early historians. John Quist fielded several questions about Tuscaloosa that only he could have answered. Bertram Wyatt-Brown provided sympathetic criticism about earlier portions of this work. Ann Webb gave me the benefit of her scholarship on Alabama's planter families, usually sandwiched into conversations about our own families.

Two groups of scholars have been a source of intellectual stimulation for many years. Through Michael O'Brien's unique brand of leadership, the Southern Intellectual History Circle became a seedbed of ideas and a site of good fellowship. The founders of the St. George Tucker Society, Eugene D. Genovese and the late Elizabeth Fox-Genovese, welcomed me graciously to the society's wide-ranging discussions of critical issues when I was just beginning to study southern history.

As the manuscript became a book, I accumulated new debts. David Moltke-Hansen has been a superb editor: astoundingly knowledgeable, thorough, flexible, and patient. His suggestions improved the final product in dozens of ways. By insisting that I pay more attention to the importance of property, Mark Smith led me to fruitful reconsiderations of changing class relations. Mills Thornton, an anonymous reviewer for Cambridge, could not remain anonymous to me because no one else knows what he knows about antebellum Alabama's politics. Not only did he catch a few embarrassing errors; he pushed me to rethink some overgeneralized interpretations. Another anonymous reviewer prodded me to clarify my claims about the representative character of literary figures. I also thank Anne Lovering Rounds for critical assistance in assembling the manuscript in appropriate form and Lewis Bateman for his encouragement and support. All of these individuals helped me greatly, and the shortcomings that inevitably remain in this book belong to me alone.

My final, and greatest, gratitude is reserved for my family. My parents, Rene and Thomas Nicol, did not live to see the conclusion of a project they had lovingly supported. They gave me food, drink, a comfortable (and free) room at their lake home, and interested conversation during my research trips to Montgomery. My husband, Nick, who works in the space and defense industries, has cheerfully learned more southern history than he could have imagined when he married me. He repeatedly helped me work through difficult intellectual problems and never once even hinted that my intense preoccupation with history interfered with our family's life. Our daughter Anna Shields, a fine scholar of medieval Chinese literature, said, as we discussed our work while floating in the pool one summer afternoon: "Why don't you take a serious look at friendship? I think it would help you." And that suggestion led to Chapter 4 of this book. Our daughter Katherine Shields Tarica provided a different perspective on my work, reminding me that my subjects (like ourselves) have lives filled with meaning quite apart from what is intellectualized or put in writing. Along with Stephen, Tommy, Michael, and Jack Hegarty, and Ian, Albert, and Margaret Tarica, Nick, Anna, and Katherine are the heart of my life. This book is for them.

Abbreviations

ADAH	Alabama Department of Archives and History
AHR	*American Historical Review*
AL	*American Literature*
ALHist	*American Literary History*
AQ	*American Quarterly*
AR	*Alabama Review*
DBR	De Bow's Review
DUL	Duke University Library
HEH	Henry E. Huntington Library, San Marino, California
HSP	Historical Society of Pennsylvania, Philadelphia
JDBH	John De Berniere Hooper Papers
JER	*Journal of the Early Republic*
JHS	*Journal of the Historical Society*
JSH	*Journal of Southern History*
LC	Library of Congress
MDAH	Mississippi Department of Archives and History
MissQ	Mississippi Quarterly
NYHS	New York Historical Society
SLM	Southern Literary Messenger
SQR	Southern Quarterly Review
UA	University of Alabama
UNC	University of North Carolina (Chapel Hill)
USAHI	United States Army Military History Institute, Carlisle Barracks, Pennsylvania
UVA	University of Virginia

I

Regarding a "Weird Utopia"

> A weird Utopia drew me on,
> To rend the most sublime connection,
> That ever civil man had known.
> "Proem," Alexander Meek

In 1865, one of the rising South's best-known poets, Alexander Meek, lamented the mistakes he and his fellow writers had made before the Civil War. In promoting a "weird Utopia" – a slave society that would surpass the United States in freedom's perfections – they had made an error of monumental proportions. Meek had been an influential politician, which was not unusual among antebellum Alabama's writers. As a member of his state's contingent at the 1860 Democratic national convention in Charleston, he had walked out when northern delegates failed to meet southern demands, and this turned out to be a fateful step in the path to secession and war.[1] Unlike many other Confederates, Meek regretted that he had ever advanced utopian notions about his society. Yet, more or less, he had.

"Weird Utopia," is, at first glance, a jarring image for a South that seems weird enough but hardly utopian. Utopias construct a new reality, and Meek's particular utopia had a short life, at best, so it has been easily misunderstood. He believed, however, that it had promised a free and progressive society for white citizens, alongside black slavery. This possibility seemed most alluring in the towns of the Southwest, places in Alabama like Tuscaloosa and Mobile, where Meek lived. In recent years, historians have explored the developments that moved American slave society in modern directions, and they have demonstrated that southerners responded thoughtfully to the crosscurrents of tradition and modernity that characterized Europe in the nineteenth century. To date, however, few historians have described the sudden advent of modern life

---

[1] The phrase appears in a rough draft of a poem that was never published; "Proem," in A. B. Meek Papers, DUL. The draft is undated but was written between the end of the war and Meek's death in 1865.

in the western South; thus this chapter summarizes those features that mattered most to writers like Meek.

It also summarizes the conception of freedom that propelled a weirdly modernizing society toward conflict. Meek and his friends thought liberty a defining condition of everyday existence, and ideas about it appeared everywhere in their writing. As Joseph Baldwin put it in *The Flush Times of Alabama and Mississippi*, the "law of liberty" constantly "refreshes and vivifies and vitalizes thought and gives freedom, range and energy to action."[2] Clearly, Baldwin did not think that this powerful "law of liberty" merely meant the freedom to own slaves, as some critics asserted. He and his literary compatriots shared with other Americans and Europeans an ancient philosophical tradition in which the very idea of freedom hinged on its apparent opposite, slavery.[3] But they brought distinctly modern ideas about human nature and society to this tradition.

Utterly convinced that their society was the best the world had known, Alabama's writers shared with other Americans a faith in progress shaped by freedom. In 1860, therefore, they could not believe that Abraham Lincoln and the Republican Party were honest when they claimed that ordinary white southerners were made less than free by the existence of slavery. In her vehemently Confederate novel *Macaria*, Augusta Evans had one heroine proclaim: "I am a free-born American, thank God."[4] And Evans believed her statement described all white southerners. Not all of Alabama's writers were as militant as Evans or as utopian as Meek, but they shared a vision for the rising South that rested on individual freedom – for one race. Weird or not, that vision had empirical foundations, to which this chapter now turns.

THE PROMISE OF A RISING SOUTH

Profound historical changes lay beneath the idea of freedom in the rising South, and they related Alabama's townspeople to other Americans. First, a booming economy bred tremendous excitement about the future. Second, economic changes spurred the rapid ascent of the middle class. Third, a dramatically expanding print culture gave these writers and other educated people fresh opportunities. Without these changes, which occurred in the forty-year period between statehood and the Civil War, Meek's "weird Utopia" would never have been conceived.

---

[2] *The Flush Times of Alabama and Mississippi: A Series of Sketches*, intro. by James Justus (Baton Rouge: Louisiana State University Press, 1987, c. 1853), 229.

[3] The ancient lineage was brilliantly explored by Orlando Patterson in *Freedom in the Making of Western Culture* (New York: Basic Books, 1991) and in other of his works, but it has also been a major theme in the influential works of David Brion Davis, beginning with *The Problem of Slavery in Western Culture* (Ithaca: Cornell University Press, 1966).

[4] *Macaria, or, Altars of Sacrifice*, ed. with intro. by Drew Gilpin Faust (Baton Rouge: Louisiana State University Press, 1992, c. 1864), 200.

Regarding a "Weird Utopia" 3

The idea of a rising South grew, first, when economic changes produced a forward-looking mentality in the midst of a slave society. Alabama's writers spoke for those people who believed that their civilization would share equally in a prosperous American future. Although such hopes lived elsewhere in the South, and in much of the North, they were very strong within the town-dwelling minority in Alabama. The state was the epicenter of the changing Southwest because, there, territorial expansion, massive shifts in the transatlantic economy, and huge demographic movements had radically altered the landscape in a few decades. Informed by science, Augusta Evans imagined sentient beings on other planets in a universe millions of years old, and she expected endless change. To the beneficiaries of a modernizing Alabama, almost anything seemed possible.[5]

The Old Southwest emerged from an extraordinarily rapid appropriation of land. Although the United States acquired much of the trans-Appalachian region at the end of the Revolution, it did not gain the coast of the Gulf of Mexico, and growth was stymied by continuing conflict among Europeans and Native Americans. Then, in 1803, President Thomas Jefferson bought Louisiana, which held New Orleans and a large, undefined area to its west. Soon, aggressive southwesterners seized the central Gulf coast. Following a preemptive invasion by General Andrew Jackson, an 1819 treaty with Spain added East Florida (the present state) and drew the western boundary of the Louisiana Purchase. In its first forty years, the nation had gained an inland empire that extended to the Rocky Mountains. Within it, a Black Belt, named for its fertile soils, crossed from western Georgia through central Alabama into Mississippi. Lured by "Alabama fever," white settlers poured in. Many brought slaves or bought them from interstate traders. By 1840, there were 590,756 residents of Alabama, 43 percent of them slaves.[6] Most of the writers discussed in this book migrated alone or came with families between the

---

[5] An illuminating overview of how differently modernization affected various parts of the South is in William W. Freehling, *The Road to Disunion. Vol. 1, Secessionists at Bay, 1776–1854* (New York: Oxford University Press, 1990), "Part I: A Swing around the Southern Circle." Daniel S. Dupre emphasizes that conflicting conceptions of growth marked northern Alabama's early settlers in *Transforming the Cotton Frontier: Madison County, Alabama, 1800–1840* (Baton Rouge: Louisiana State University Press, 1997). J. Mills Thornton, *Politics and Power in a Slave Society: Alabama, 1800–1860* (Baton Rouge: Louisiana State University Press, 1977) summarizes modernization in the late antebellum period, with an emphasis on the political consequences. Evans's comments on life on other planets are in *Macaria*, 179. The best one-volume history of the state is William Warren Rogers et al., *Alabama: The History of a Deep South State* (Tuscaloosa: University of Alabama Press, 1994). A readable study of the period that emphasizes the optimistic spirit is Daniel Feller, *The Jacksonian Promise: America, 1815–1840* (Baltimore: Johns Hopkins University Press, 1995).

[6] A recent analysis of these developments is Adam Rothman, *Slave Country: American Expansion and the Origins of the Deep South* (Cambridge, MA: Harvard University Press, 2005). Unless otherwise noted, census data here and elsewhere are taken from the wonderfully helpful Historical Census Browser of the University of Virginia Alderman Library at http://mapserver.lib.virginia.edu.

organization of the Mississippi Territory in 1804 and 1837, when a depression interrupted the flow. The spirit of the boom marked their thought.

The writers of the rising South claimed that its white inhabitants carved it suddenly from a wilderness. But, like Abraham Lincoln's Illinois, which entered the Union at about the same time, Alabama had been home to Native Americans who fiercely resisted white encroachment. During the War of 1812, Jackson broke the back of the powerful Creek confederation at Horseshoe Bend. Sporadic wars and treaties produced the removal of most of the Indians in the 1830s. The last of Alabama's Indian wars, the Creek War of 1836, occurred just four years after the Black Hawk War in which Lincoln participated. Whites claimed that Native Americans could not effectively use land, although farming Indians lived among them. While sometimes regretting the bloody conquest, these authors were mesmerized by the progress of those who reaped its rewards.[7]

Crucially, they expected progress to continue unabated. The forces that created the rising South originated in the most modern sectors of the world, for England's textile industries, and soon American ones as well, created an insatiable demand for cotton. By the 1820s, newly invented steamboats began moving crops. Much of the lower Southwest was drained by big rivers that flowed together across the Black Belt and into Mobile Bay. In northern Alabama, the Tennessee River linked fertile valley soils to the upper South. Local entrepreneurs demanded transportation – first roads, then railroads – but, ironically, navigable rivers and proximity to the Gulf let the Southwest lag behind the Northwest in improvements. Yet scientists mapped abundant coal and iron deposits in north-central Alabama, and famous British geologist Sir Charles Lyell, who visited in 1842, publicized them internationally. By the 1850s, the state planned railroads to join lower Alabama to the Tennessee, Ohio, and Mississippi rivers. With splendid resources, Alabama's prospects fed excitement about change that was unusual in older slave societies.[8]

---

[7] Jackson's role in the acquisition of the Southwest is told in Robert V. Remini, *Andrew Jackson and the Course of American Empire, 1767–1821* (New York: Harper & Row, 1977). Although there are numerous histories of the early encounters between white settlers and Native Americans in Alabama, none is as evocative as the account for Lincoln's Sangamon County in the opening chapters of John Mack Faragher's *Sugar Creek: Life on the Illinois Prairie* (New Haven: Yale University Press, 1986). As I show in Chapter 6, Alabama's writers helped establish the historical tradition that focused on white conquests and accomplishments.

[8] The changes in the national economy are detailed in Charles Grier Sellers, *The Market Revolution: Jacksonian America, 1815–1846* (New York: Oxford University Press, 1991), but scholars disagree about how much the Deep South was affected. An account that emphasizes the fundamental economic differences between North and South is John Ashworth, *Slavery, Capitalism, and Politics in the Antebellum Republic*, Vol. 1, *Commerce and Compromise, 1820–1850*, and Vol. 2, *The Coming of the Civil War, 1850–1861* (Cambridge: Cambridge University Press, 1995 and 2007). Despite Alabama's late-nineteenth-century industrialization, little has been written about goals established before the war. More remarkably, there is no comprehensive study of the state's cotton economy, and the only study of slavery is badly outdated; see James Benson Sellers, *Slavery in Alabama*, (Tuscaloosa: University of Alabama Press, 1994, c. 1950). The most up-to-date evidence for the state's interest in economic

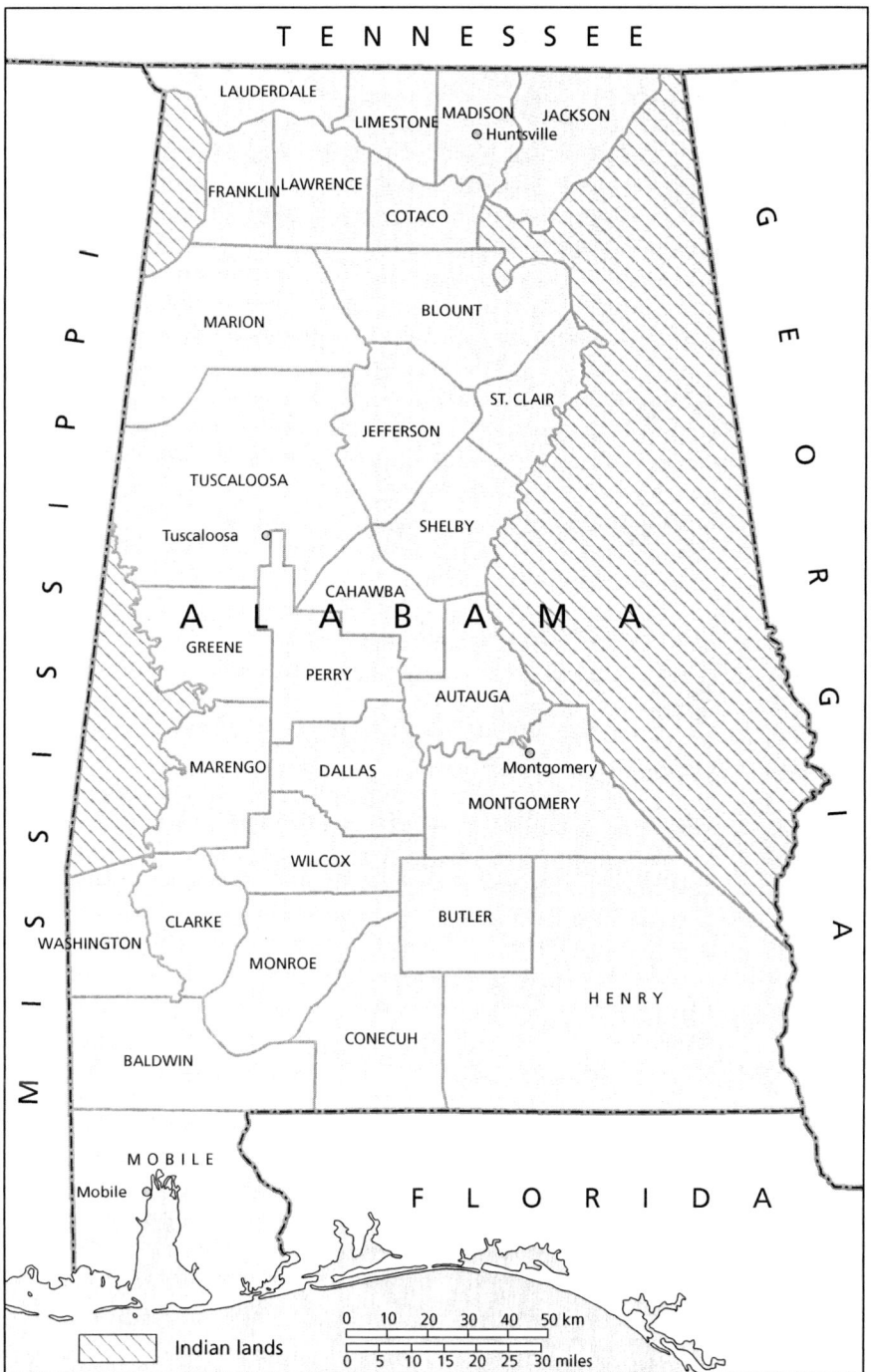

FIGURE 1.1. Alabama in 1820.
The year after statehood in 1819, Alabama had only a few large counties, and much of the eastern half of the state was still in the possession of the Creek Indians. Map by Cox Cartographic, Ltd.

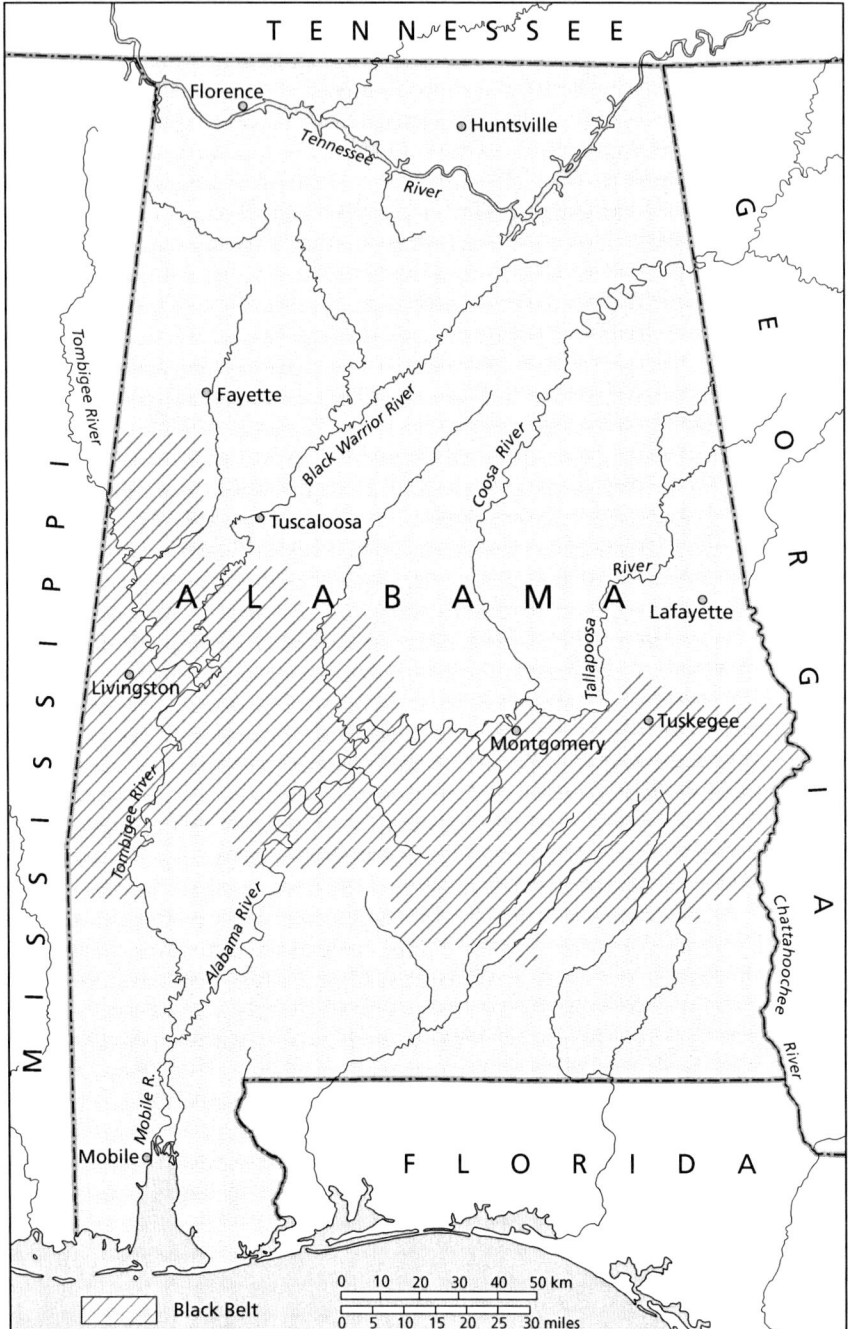

FIGURE 1.2 Antebellum Alabama.
Alabama benefited from major rivers that were navigable from the Gulf of Mexico across the central plantation district of the Black Belt. Although towns were often located along the rivers, writers lived in small towns and cities across the state. Map by Cox Cartographic, Ltd.

The backbreaking labor that enriched the region's planters affected most writers and other middle-class professionals indirectly. The thousands of slaves in Alabama lived mainly on farms, especially the plantations of the Black Belt. In 1850, when all of the rising South's eight writers but Evans were working adults, Meek, Jeremiah ("Jere") Clemens, and Caroline Hentz owned no slaves; Johnson Hooper owned one, William Smith four, and Baldwin seven. Only Albert Pickett worked dozens in his fields. Hentz, who never owned a slave, rented them. In Baldwin's "The Earthquake Story," which Lincoln often read aloud, the "servant" Jo reflected town slavery. Slaves were assets, but writers used them to secure comfort, not to create new wealth.[9] Pickett aside, writers did not command slaves like planters did.

Alabama's writers shared a commitment to slavery but differed about how to develop the state. This issue divided citizens politically when an international depression after 1837 reduced cotton prices, crippled banks, and slowed commerce. Writers supported the Democrats or the Whigs, national parties that differed about the role of government in the economy. Baldwin was a Whig who, like Lincoln, attended his party's 1848 convention in Philadelphia. In Alabama, small farmers made the Democrats dominant, while town dwellers and commercial farmers supported the Whigs. In general, Whigs advocated government aid for development and Democrats favored laissez faire, but these differences became muted over time. Hooper, a Whig, was cautious

---

development is found in Curtis J. Evans, *The Conquest of Labor: Daniel Pratt and Southern Industrialization* (Baton Rouge: Louisiana State University Press, 2001), but Thornton's summary of the "economic miracle of the 1850s" in *Politics and Power* (268–291, quote p. 291) has not been superseded. On Lyell's visit, with a convenient list of his publications about it, see Daniel B. Arden, "Charles Lyell's Observations on Southeastern Geology," in James X. Corgan, ed., *The Geological Sciences in the Antebellum South* (Tuscaloosa: University of Alabama Press, 1982), 1130–1141. As Thornton notes, the more thorough explorations of geologist Michael Toumey received great attention later (*Politics and Power*, 190), but Lyell gave the issue international recognition. A provocative study of the politics of modernization is Donna M. Castellano, "A Promise Delayed: The Politics of Banking, Railroad, and Mineral Development in Alabama, 1846–1860" (M.A. thesis, University of Alabama in Huntsville, 2001).

[9] The status of slavery in towns is a relatively neglected subject in an otherwise thriving field. On cities, the standard studies are Richard C. Wade, *Slavery in the Cities: The South, 1820–1860* (New York: Oxford University Press, 1964) and Claudia Dale Goldin, *Urban Slavery in the American South, 1820–1860* (Chicago: University of Chicago Press, 1976). A suggestive study that compares slavery in different demographic settings is Barbara J. Fields, *Slavery and Freedom on the Middle Ground: Maryland during the Nineteenth-Century* (New Haven: Yale University Press, 1985). Perhaps the most useful summary of scholarship on slavery is Peter Kolchin, *American Slavery, 1619–1877* (New York: Hill and Wang, 2nd. ed., 2003). A creative study about towns just across the border from Alabama is Lisa C. Tolbert, *Constructing Townscapes: Space and Society in Antebellum Tennessee* (Chapel Hill: University of North Carolina Press, 1999), which integrates slaves' lives into town society. A discussion of the neglect of town slavery within the context of a fascinating analysis of a small town in Georgia is David E. Paterson, "Slavery, Slaves, and Cash in a Georgia Village, 1825–1865," *JSH* 75 (November 2009): 879–930.

about tariffs, and Meek, a Democrat, wrote Alabama's first public education law. In towns, both parties had hopes for the rising South.[10]

The second essential condition for a rising South was the ascent of the middle class in southwestern towns. Antebellum census data were notoriously unreliable, and most towns were tallied with counties, but one careful scholar estimates that Alabama's towns grew about twice as fast as rural areas. Subsistence farms existed without towns, but commercial farming required lawyers to make land a commodity, merchants to exchange crops for manufactures, and teachers to provide essential skills. The rough categories of the census reflected these facts, with the percentage of farmers steadily shrinking compared to the learned professions, manufacturers, and merchants. In 1860, about a quarter of the state's free adult males belonged to these nonfarming categories. In that year, the capital at Montgomery had almost ten thousand people (about half enslaved), and it was the largest town besides Mobile, which had not quite thirty thousand residents. Tuscaloosa had fewer than four thousand people. Because writers usually lived in county seats that focused politics, law, education, and trade, they knew that their influence exceeded their numbers.[11]

Alabama's writers also saw that the middle class increasingly relied on consumer goods. Although manufacturing grew slowly, towns like Huntsville and Tuscaloosa contained textile mills by the 1840s, and many more manufactured goods were imported. Newspapers advertised hats and gloves, bolts of fancy and plain textiles, household goods like cooking utensils and rugs, and the ubiquitous patent medicines. Writers understood the culture of consumption. In Johnson Hooper's 1845 fiction, when a backwoodsman visited Tuscaloosa, he marveled at the displays in windows of a drugstore and a booksellers' shop.

---

[10] The most compelling analysis of antebellum Alabama politics is Thornton, *Politics and Power*, but also indispensable are the relevant essays in Samuel L. Webb and Margaret E. Armbrester, *Alabama Governors: A Political History of the State* (Tuscaloosa: University of Alabama Press, 2001).

[11] The careful scholar is Thornton, *Politics and Power*, 292. The only South-wide analysis of the middle classes is Jonathan D. Wells, *The Origins of the Southern Middle Class, 1800–1861* (Chapel Hill: University of North Carolina Press, 2004). There are local histories of varying quality for Alabama towns, but the best scholarly works are four, and each was important in shaping my understanding of how townspeople lived: for Mobile, Harriet E. Amos Doss, *Cotton City: Urban Development in Antebellum Mobile* (Tuscaloosa: University of Alabama Press, 1985); for Huntsville (and Madison County) Dupre, *Transforming the Cotton Frontier*; for a Black Belt town, the first chapters in G. Ward Hubbs, *Guarding Greensboro: A Confederate Company in the Making of a Southern Community* (Athens: University of Georgia Press, 2003); for Tuscaloosa, John W. Quist, *Restless Visionaries: The Social Roots of Antebellum Reform in Alabama and Michigan* (Baton Rouge: Louisiana State University Press, 1998). In addition to the work of Lisa Tolbert, two other excellent studies helped me appreciate the pace of changes in southwestern towns: Christopher Morris, *Becoming Southern: The Evolution of a Way of Life, Warren County and Vicksburg, Mississippi, 1770–1860* (New York: Oxford University Press, 1995), and Edward E. Baptist, *Creating an Old South: Middle Florida's Plantation Frontier before the Civil War* (Chapel Hill: University of North Carolina Press, 2002), which, despite its title, also deals with towns.

He observed the "koniac" and "rot-gut" at a "grocery" before visiting a tavern with chandeliers, fine wines, and fancy "viands." Discriminating between country and town, he disparaged liquor made in local stills and chose to drink the imports.[12]

Southwestern towns were like those of Lincoln's Illinois in the voluntary associations that were the hallmark of the middle class. In the countryside, churches and kin connected scattered people. Where neighbors were close, folks formed all sorts of associations to improve themselves. Local governments were manned by middle-class people, and open meetings promoted railroads and schools. Citizens in Clemens's town of Huntsville organized the Haydn Society, and Hentz joined a literary club in Florence. Meek was president of a temperance society in Tuscaloosa (even though he was known for imbibing). Hooper was a Mason, which linked him to upwardly mobile men across the nation. Pickett and Meek were founders of Alabama's first historical society at Tuscaloosa. These writers believed that progress demanded cooperation.[13]

One index to the importance of Alabama's middle classes was the growing influence of lawyers. Although farmers greatly outnumbered them, lawyers were overrepresented in the legislature. As early as 1840, 12 percent of the state's legislators were lawyers; and the fatal convention that voted Alabama out of the Union contained 37 percent lawyers. Just as Lincoln represented railroads because they had money, lawyers in Alabama represented planters and townsmen – or almost anyone with cash. Like Lincoln, they rode circuit, but they also served their towns. When Hooper first practiced law in the county seat of Chambers County, he often represented his father-in-law. While living in a Black Belt river port, Baldwin wrote contracts for land and slaves, but *Flush Times* mostly put lawyers in towns.[14]

---

[12] Johnson Jones Hooper, *Adventures of Captain Simon Suggs, Late of the Tallapoosa Volunteers: Together with "Taking the Census" and Other Alabama Sketches*, intro. by Johanna Nicol Shields (Tuscaloosa: University of Alabama Press, 1993), 53, 55. No one has done for the South what Catherine E. Kelly has done for New England, *In The New England Fashion: Reshaping Women's Lives in the Nineteenth Century* (Ithaca: Cornell University Press, 1999). In the absence of scholarly studies, I am relying on impressionistic analysis of newspapers, inventories of estates, and family financial records as well as literary sources. An example of southern enthusiasm for one particular consumer good (timepieces) is detailed in the first chapter of Mark M. Smith, *Mastered by the Clock: Time, Place, and Freedom in the American South* (Chapel Hill: University of North Carolina Press, 1992). Tolbert, *Constructing Townscapes*, deals with consumption in the Southwest, albeit indirectly, where she links it with women's domesticity. Influential studies that evaluate the changing culture of the middle classes are Richard L. Bushman, *The Refinement of America: Persons, Houses, Cities* (New York: Knopf, 1992), and Karen Halttunen, *Confidence Men and Painted Women: A Study of Middle-Class Culture in America, 1830–1870* (New Haven: Yale University Press, 1982).

[13] Here I am indebted to Quist, *Restless Visionaries*, which details both the extent to which associations were typical of one Alabama town and how widespread was the middle class's participation.

[14] Figures on lawyers from Thornton, *Politics and Power*, 64–66, 426.

Class affiliation changed as individuals rose or fell. Nonetheless, by the objective standards of income and occupation, all writers except Pickett lived middle-class lives. Subjectively, rich relatives brought status and, occasionally, material advantages. Clemens's father owned a plantation by the time Jere became an adult, and the erratic lawyer moved in and out of his father's town home. Before the Panic of 1837, Evans's father owned a store, a fine home, and slaves, but, grossly overextended, he lost his fortune and worked as a middling merchant until the Civil War. Like Lincoln, some of these writers were upwardly mobile. Orphaned and raised in an artisan's household, Smith acquired property from his legal practice and good marriages, but he never counted himself rich. Perhaps most importantly, the only writer to own a plantation was Pickett, although Clemens inherited a portion of his father's plantation in 1860. They all worried about how people saw them. Pickett's wariness toward powerful families, Evans's sermonizing about the idle rich, and Smith's anxieties about poverty suggest class tensions where status was fragile.[15]

Like other successful Americans, the writers of the rising South displayed their status with servants. Touring Lincoln's pleasant Victorian house in Springfield, I was surprised to see a servant's room at the rear of the second story. Our guide commented that Lincoln saw domestic service as a way for poor people, often immigrants, to improve themselves. Alabamians did not expect

---

[15] Historians' attempts to evaluate class formation are marked by theoretical and definitional disputes. A recent discussion of some of those is in Gary Kornblith, Seth Rockman, Jennifer Goloboy, Andrew Schocket, and Christopher Clark, "Symposium on Class in the Early Republic," *JER* 25 (Winter 2005): 523–564. For the American middle classes, with comments on theoretical issues, see Stuart M. Blumin, *The Emergence of the Middle Class: Social Experience in the American City, 1760–1900* (Cambridge: Cambridge University Press, 1989); Stuart M. Blumin, "The Hypothesis of Middle-Class Formation in Nineteenth-Century America: A Critique and Some Proposals," *AHR* 90 (April 1985): 775–809; Burton J. Bledstein and Robert D. Johnston, *The Middling Sorts: Explorations in the History of the American Middle Class* (New York: Routledge, 2001); Maris A. Vinovskis, "Stalking the Elusive Middle Class in Nineteenth-Century America: A Review," *Comparative Studies in Society and History* 33 (July 1991): 582–587. In addition to Wells, for the southern middle classes see Frank J. Byrne, *Becoming Bourgeois: Merchant Culture in the South, 1820–1865* (Lexington: University Press of Kentucky, 2006); Jennifer R. Green, *Military Education and the Emerging Middle Class in the Old South* (Cambridge: Cambridge University Press, 2008); Tom Downey, *Planting a Capitalist South: Masters, Merchants, and Manufacturers in the Southern Interior, 1790–1860* (Baton Rouge: Louisiana State University Press, 2006). One of the rare works to consider northern and southern middle classes together is Anne C. Rose, *Victorian America and the Civil War* (New York: Cambridge University Press, 1992), which has shaped my thinking about middle-class ethics.
  Class formation cannot be measured by eight writers, but the material, experiential, and intellectual evidence suggests that most of these people belonged to an assertive southwestern middle class. Whatever wealth they lost or gained, regardless of their relatives, and despite their common desire to be seen as superior, it strains credulity to call any of these men and women aristocrats, with the arguable exception of Albert Pickett, who was, at least, a wealthy planter. For an exhaustive depiction of those people whom some might call aristocratic, see William K. Scarborough, *Masters of the Big House: Elite Slaveholders of the Mid-Nineteenth-Century South* (Baton Rouge: Louisiana State University Press, 2003), although Scarborough

their servants to move up, and they may or may not have given them comfortable rooms. But white northerners and black southerners provided similar services: laid fires before dawn, tended gardens, cooked meals, cleaned houses and barns, cared for animals, and nursed children. They distinguished middle from lower classes and gave privileged families the leisure to develop social capital. In that respect, Mary Todd Lincoln was not very different from Sidney White Baldwin, Joseph's wife. But the Baldwins could sell servants and probably did when they left Alabama for free California in 1854, while the Lincolns could only relieve theirs of employment if one created problems. Comfort and capital were advantages middle-class writers did not intend to yield.[16]

A third essential ingredient in the development of a rising South was the increasing importance of print. As much as a modernizing economy created towns and the middle classes, the writers of the rising South knew an expanding print culture offered them unique opportunities. Yet scholars have failed to examine changes that must have seemed revolutionary to people who lived through them. As an old man, William Smith recalled a story about the salience of print in his career. At the end of a political campaign, an opponent attacked him too late for Smith to answer in his party's newspaper. Smith therefore persuaded a Tuscaloosa printer to open his office at night so he could make himself a handbill. Using rusty skills, the former editor printed single sheets with "HEAD THAT LIE" in large type at the top of his explanation. He then had supporters distribute the handbills. Smith implied that victory rested on his wit and skills – the quintessential advantages of the middle-class writer. But a local printing press and his constituents' literacy were just as important, and Smith suggested as much when he closed his story: "Heaven bless the man that first invented types!"[17]

---

makes them thoroughgoing capitalists. For a delightful discussion that considers problems with defining the bourgeoisie across the Atlantic world, see Peter Gay, *Schnitzler's Century: The Making of Middle-Class Culture, 1815–1914* (New York: W. W. Norton, 2002), chapter 1, "Bourgeoisie(s)."

[16] The standard works are Faye E. Dudden, *Serving Women: Household Service in Nineteenth-Century America* (Middletown, CT: Wesleyan University Press, distributed by Harper & Row, 1983), and Jeanne Boydston, *Home and Work: Housework, Wages, and the Ideology of Labor in the Early Republic* (New York: Oxford University Press, 1990). For a literary analysis, see Barbara Ryan, *Love, Wages, Slavery: The Literature of Servitude in the United States* (Chicago: University of Illinois Press, 2006). Mary Cathryn Cain links the growth of a republican ideology of whiteness with middle-class northern women's anxieties about domestic servants in "Race, Republicanism, and Domestic Service in the Antebellum United States," *Left History*, 12 (Fall/Winter 2007): 64–83. On southerners, see Stephanie Cole, "'A White Woman, of Middle Age, Would be Preferred': Children's Nurses in the Old South," in Susanna Delfino and Michele Gillespie, eds., *Neither Lady nor Slaves: Working Women in the Old South* (Chapel Hill: University of North Carolina Press, 2002), 75–101.

[17] Smith's anecdote is in William Russell Smith, *Reminiscences of a Long Life; Historical, Political, Personal and Literary.* (Washington, DC: W. R. Smith, Sr., 1889), quoted passages 172, 178. The paucity of studies in antebellum southern print culture is puzzling, but there is important information about print in Michael O'Brien's work (cited in Preface, n. 8) and

Without print and a literate public, middle-class people could not have imagined a modern Southwest. For lawyers, merchants, teachers, and newspaper editors, printed materials mediated the flow of information across the Atlantic, between North and South, across states, and in towns. In the 1840s, small-town newspapers like Hooper's Lafayette *East Alabamian* were studded with legal notices, advertisements, descriptions of school programs, and accounts of public meetings for every kind of civic and religious purpose. Newspapers had a growing market. In Alabama, as in Illinois, more than 90 percent of the white population could read and write by 1840. In that same year, however, there was one school or college for every 444 people in Alabama but one for every 367 in Illinois. Meek wrote Alabama's first public school law in 1854, and, between 1850 and 1860, the number of students climbed from 62,846 to 98,204 (all of them, of course, white).

An increase in local printing accompanied rising education. In 1840, there were only 28 newspapers in Alabama (in Illinois there were 43, serving a larger white population). Twenty years later, the number for Alabama had reached 96. Other forms of print grew, too. The year 1820 saw only 11 imprints, most of them from the brand new government. In 1859, however, the more than 50 imprints of book, pamphlets, and broadsides from the state's presses included publications by Baptists, Methodists, Presbyterians, and Masons; records of government; promotional materials for railroads and schools; speeches before college fraternities; and eulogies. In addition, more than 20 literary magazines came and went before 1860. All of these issued from towns, mostly from the presses of partisan newspapers. Until S. H. Goetzel of Mobile opened in the late 1850s, however, there was no real publishing firm in Alabama. Hooper bragged that his newspaper's steam press could publish books, and it did issue a few. But he published most of his own books in New York.[18]

---

the essays in O'Brien and David Moltke-Hansen, *Intellectual Life in Antebellum Charleston* (Knoxville: University of Tennessee Press, 1986). For the antebellum period, the most extensive quantitative information is in Wells, *Origins of the Middle-Class*. For Alabama, the most important sources are two older, very reliable, descriptive studies, Rhoda Coleman Ellison, *Early Alabama Publications, A Study in Literary Interests* (Tuscaloosa: University of Alabama Press, 1947), and Rhoda Coleman Ellison, *A Check List of Alabama Imprints, 1807–1870* (Tuscaloosa: University of Alabama Press, 1976). See also my "Writers in the Old Southwest and the Commercialization of American Letters," *JER* 27 (Fall 2007): 471–505, where I criticize a history of scholarship that insists, without much in the way of empirical evidence, that the South lay outside of the modernizing influences of print. Inspired by the ideas of Benedict Anderson, scholars of Confederate nationalism have been among the first to discuss the significance of print in the Old South. See, for example, Drew Gilpin Faust, *The Creation of Confederate Nationalism: Ideology and Identity in the Civil War South* (Baton Rouge: Louisiana State University Press, 1988), and Anne Sarah Rubin, *A Shattered Nation: The Rise and Fall of the Confederacy, 1861–1868* (Chapel Hill: University of North Carolina Press, 2005). See also Alice Fahs, *The Imagined Civil War: Popular Literature of the North & South, 1861–1865* (Chapel Hill: University of North Carolina Press, 2001).

[18] All figures except the number of imprints are from the census; I counted the imprints in Ellison, *A Check List*.

As Hooper understood, an information revolution was altering the relationship between writers, publishers, and readers. Books came mostly from the Northeast, where mass production lowered costs and converted authors into producers in a long chain of print capitalism. From hiring labor, to making paper (sometimes from cotton rags), to using rotary steam presses, to the binding and distribution of books, urban publishers had advantages that small-town printers could not match. The postal service cheaply carried magazines and newspapers, shipping them by stagecoaches, boats, and railroads. Churches and religious societies exploited the new development. National reform organizations and their branches distributed free materials to poor people or sold them to those who could pay. In 1827, for example, the Bible Society sent Meek's father, a minister who owned a drug store, 100 Bibles and 75 Testaments. According to a survey of the American Tract Society, fewer than 10 percent of the free households in Alabama lacked a Bible in the 1850s.[19]

Town-dwelling Alabamians also imported secular materials. As one diligent scholar has discovered, a count by the postmaster in Montgomery County for one month in the fall of 1857 revealed that almost 25 percent of the hundreds of newspapers he tallied and 77 percent of the magazines came from the North. In a county where, in 1850, there were 1,881 dwellings, there were 440 subscribers to Alabama newspapers and 190 to New York papers. There were 120 subscribers to *Harper's Magazine,* 70 to *Harper's Weekly,* and 40 to *Godey's Lady's Book.* In contrast, there were no subscribers to in-state magazines (perhaps there were none then). A thorough student of literature in newspapers found that Alabamians paid far more attention to authors from England and the North than local writers.[20]

---

[19] The foundational study of publishing is John Tebbel, *A History of Book Publishing in the United States, Vol. I, The Creation of an Industry, 1639–1865,* 2 vols. (New York and London: R. R. Bowker Co., 1972); see also Tebbel's *Between Covers: The Rise and Transformation of Book Publishing in America* (New York: Oxford University Press, 1987); William Charvat, *Literary Publishing in America, 1790–1850* (Philadelphia: University of Pennsylvania Press, 1959). For more recent perspectives, see the useful introductory handbook, Scott E. Casper, Joanne D. Chaison, and Jeffrey D. Groves, *Perspectives on American Book History: Artifacts and Commentary* (Amherst and Worcester, MA; Washington, DC: University of Massachusetts Press; American Antiquarian Society; Center for the Book, Library of Congress, 2002); Scott E. Casper, *The Industrial Book, 1840–1880, A History of the Book in America,* Vol. 3 (Chapel Hill: Published in association with the American Antiquarian Society by the University of North Carolina Press, 2007). Ronald J. Zboray, *A Fictive People: Antebellum Economic Development and the American Reading Public* (New York: Oxford University Press, 1993) is essential for connecting the new patterns of publishing with changes in readership. On the role of the postal service, see Richard R. John, *Spreading the News: The American Postal System from Franklin to Morse* (Cambridge, MA: Harvard University Press, 1995). The close description of the Bible and Tract Societies' activities is in Quist, *Restless Visionaries,* 32–47.

[20] Figures for Montgomery in Wells, *Origins of the Middle Class,* 48–49 (number of dwellings, however, from the census). Ellison argues that Alabama's readers favored nonsouthern authors throughout *Early Alabama Publications.*

Although evidence is spotty, studies suggest that commercial publishers devoted only a small percentage of their advertising budgets to the South and West, for the northeastern market was more accessible and more concentrated. Even though there were booksellers in towns like Tuscaloosa, Huntsville, and Montgomery, it is likely that many of Alabama's readers borrowed books from friends. As late as 1850, there were only 4 public libraries in the state, in contrast to Illinois, where there were 33; but there were more libraries in schools in Alabama than in Illinois (32, as opposed to 29). Meek began collecting a library when he was in college, and he loaned books to his friends Smith, Hentz, and Cyrus Baldwin, Joe's brother, among others. When Baldwin visited New York to publish *Flush Times*, he came home with books for his family by Longfellow, Hawthorne, and other popular writers. In the 1850s, Hooper's Montgomery *Mail* regularly reviewed books that were locally available, and he favored southern writing. He told his readers that he had received a copy of *Walden* and simply had not had time to read it (which may or may not have been true). As libraries grew with the number of schools, readers in most counties had access to at least some books. But reading required leisure, if not much money, and the middle classes were still advantaged.[21]

Printed materials taught middle-class Alabamians to think like readers elsewhere. Religious literature preached ethics. Secular magazines defined respectable conduct; Hooper claimed that no gentleman could miss the influential British magazine *Blackwood's*. *Godey's* stressed manners, clothing, and household décor as well as the uses of feminine leisure. It also noted the publications of Alabama's writers, even masculine humor that was too crude to print in its pages. All newspapers carried speeches from partisans around the nation, merging the interests of local activists with those of loose national organizations. And advertisements encouraged common fashions. Although editors reported local news and information about crops, cotton prices, and slavery, they deliberately connected readers with the outside world and, in so doing, promoted similarities.[22]

But the publications that homogenized the middle classes also alerted them to sectional differences. In the 1830s, antislavery organizations sent thousands

---

[21] On sectional distribution (based on limited data), Zboray, *Fictive People*, 65–68; see also his appendix on "Regionalism, Literacy, and Economic Development," 196–201. His research focused on the urban Northeast. A catalog of Meek's books (many of which were destroyed before his death) listed 642 volumes; Meek Papers, UA. There are notes about his lending habits throughout his papers; see one list for 1839 that includes Smith and Baldwin, Meek Papers, ADAH. For Joseph Baldwin's purchase, see Chapter 3, n. 18. Hooper's comments on *Walden*, Montgomery *Mail*, September 7, 1854.

[22] Hooper's comments on *Blackwood's*, Montgomery *Mail*, April 12, 1854. Trish Loughran, *The Republic in Print: Print Culture in the Age of U.S. Nation Building, 1770–1870* (New York: Columbia University Press, 2007) argues that proslavery and antislavery publishing made print culture divisive, not nationalistic. But middle-class readers had many cultural similarities in spite of political differences. See Glenn C. Altschuler and Stuart M. Blumin, "Where Is the Real America?: Politics and Popular Consciousness in the Antebellum Era," *AQ* 49, no. 2 (1997): 225–267, which uses literary and political sources to get at middle-class opinion.

of pamphlets southward, provoking a hot dispute about the postal service. Many scholars have accurately described antislavery literature and the proslavery response, but, significantly, writing about slavery was a very small part of what people read. Often, when Ralph Waldo Emerson in Massachusetts and Alexander Meek in Alabama spoke to local audiences, each man followed his speeches with essays for wider readership. Knowing Meek personally, Augusta Evans quoted Emerson, who was more famous. Although they differed radically about slavery, these authors shared many interests. Both Emerson's "American Scholar" and Meek's "Americanism in Literature" proclaimed that freedom would make the nation's literature great.[23]

Like Emerson and other transcendentalists, Alabama's writers described changes that swept their world, eyeing people's gains or the mistakes they must correct. Because some of them defended slavery, it is tempting to think it inspired them to write, and it did. But that was only part of their story, and it was the lesser part because they cared more about freedom. Alabama lagged behind its sister state of Illinois, but the southern state's writers thought the future was theirs to make. Like their bourgeois counterparts around the Atlantic world, they expected to thrive in an inegalitarian world where inferior people yielded to their betters. Through these writers, we apprehend a strange mentality, for they thought that a progressive freedom for white people, with slaves, formed the promise of a rising South.

THE IDEA OF FREEDOM WITH SLAVERY

Although Abraham Lincoln liked to read aloud to his friends from *Flush Times,* during the Civil War he described the conflict between North and South as if he had forgotten Joseph Baldwin's enthusiasm for freedom. In 1864, Lincoln complained that "the world has never had a good definition of the word liberty." Northerners thought liberty meant "for each man to do as he pleases with himself, and the product of his labor," while southerners thought it meant "for some men to do as they please with other men, and the product of other men's labor." To Lincoln, the southern conception was "tyranny." Historians obscure the ethical dilemmas of the nineteenth century when they adopt Lincoln's stark contrast, for, as his fondness for *Flush Times* suggests, he exaggerated the real differences between North and South.[24]

[23] Both authors had Romantic views of the relationship between national culture and art; both called for literary independence; both saw nature as inspiring; both were ostensibly democratic but revered genius; and both used literary nationalism to boost their careers. Meek's address was one of his better efforts but not, of course, the philosophical equal of Emerson's. Emerson's widely reprinted address is readily accessible at http://www.rwe.org/complete-works/i---nature,-addresses-&-lectures/addresses-&-lectures/the-american-scholar, and Meek's was reprinted in his *Romantic Passages in Southwestern History* (New York and Mobile, AL: S. H. Goetzel & Co., 1857).

[24] From his speech to a Sanitary Fair at Baltimore, April 14, 1864, in vol. 7 of *Collected Works of Abraham Lincoln*, Roy Basler et al. eds. (New Brunswick: Rutgers University Press, 1953),

Lincoln justifiably complained, however, about inadequate definitions, so it seems wise to spell out here what the writers of the rising South meant by liberty and how they nestled slavery within it. Like Lincoln, these eight authors believed that freedom existed so that individuals could better themselves through their own choices. There were serious flaws in their conception. We know, for example, that much of the prosperity of white Americans originated in legalized coercion – in the appropriation of Native American land and the exploitation of slaves' labor. Nonetheless, middle-class Americans in the North and South believed their well-being came from the self-determined efforts of free people.[25]

In one of the best pieces in *Flush Times*, Baldwin explained how the "law of liberty" operated among lawyers. Tongue in cheek, he detailed the "opportunities and advantages for improvement" in the Southwest. And he began with contests over property, joking about disputes between Indians and whites and between speculators who were quick to sue. As usual, Baldwin mentioned slaves, who "furnished an important addition to the litigation," having been imported "in large numbers," sometimes with "no title" at all. Whether land or slaves, property was up for grabs. As much as Baldwin regretted westerners' recklessness, he saw unparalleled "opportunities and advantages for improvement" in wholesale freedom. His point was that the "law of liberty" fostered a first-rate legal fraternity.[26]

Like Lincoln, Baldwin respected property rights, but their thinking departed from early American republicanism, which had privileged landholding as the basis of freedom. Farmers had been the moral muscle of the republic – "god's

---

302–303, reproduced at http://quod.lib.umich.edu/cgi/t/text/text-idx?c=lincoln;cc=lincoln;view=text;idno=lincoln7;rgn=div1;node=lincoln7%3A665. For Republicans' contrast of slave and free societies (by scholars of different perspectives), see Eric Foner, *Free Soil, Free Labor, Free Men: The Ideology of the Republican Party before the Civil War* (New York: Oxford University Press, 1970), and William E. Gienapp, *The Origins of the Republican Party, 1852–1856* (New York: Oxford University Press, 1987).

[25] These ideas about freedom correspond to what philosopher Isaiah Berlin called positive (in contrast to negative) freedom, a distinction some historians have used. See Isaiah Berlin, *Four Essays on Liberty* (London and New York: Oxford University Press, 1969); Gerald C. MacCallum, "Negative and Positive Freedom," *Philosophical Review* 76, no. 3 (1967): 312–334; [anon], "Positive and Negative Liberty," in *Stanford Encyclopedia of Philosophy* (Stanford: Stanford University Press, 2003), http://plato.stanford.edu. See also a particularly emphatic usage of positive liberty in James M. McPherson, *Abraham Lincoln and the Second American Revolution* (New York: Oxford University Press, 1990), 62–64. I have been influenced by Lawrence Frederick Kohl, *The Politics of Individualism: Parties and the American Character in the Jacksonian Era* (New York: Oxford University Press, 1989), which argues that Democrats and Whigs accepted individualism differently. In his account, the Whigs' conception resembled what Berlin called positive freedom, with the Democrats more nearly negative, and Mills Thornton found a similar distinction for Alabama's Whigs and Democrats; but neither scholar relied explicitly on Berlin. Among writers in Alabama there was a broad consensus, transcending parties, that freedom existed so that people could, cooperatively, make their society better.

[26] *Flush Times*, 229, 236, 237.

chosen people," Jefferson called them. He and his contemporaries relied on those Enlightenment philosophers who had updated classical republicanism. John Locke, for one, argued in the *Second Treatise of Civil Government* that property originated from the application of individual reason to the "common stock of Nature." That made property rights essential to personal liberty and entitled to protection from government. From Jefferson on, Americans linked widespread property with the nation's destiny. But a change in the character of property was occurring as Lincoln and Baldwin grew to manhood. It altered the way middle-class people thought about freedom, and, not at all incidentally, it affected how they thought about slavery.[27]

Many forces contributed to this transformation. As Baldwin saw, the forcible seizure of Indian lands mocked the premise that reason created property. The constant turnover in western property holding made land fungible, one more contractual relationship and commodity among many. General laws of incorporation obscured personal responsibility. Paper money and wildcat banking dissociated the material and moral status of property. The legal right to property became substantive – at once vague and broad. With all of this, Locke's ideas got a common-sense extension: property's value came from brainpower and land lost its unique moral status. When Baldwin wrote "opportunities and advantages for improvement," he did not denote the material world. As the human uses of nature changed, intellectual, even psychological, traits joined land as the pillars of free government.

These changes were especially felt in towns. Well-to-do merchants owned their stores, but many professionals owned only their homes, if that. Some goods were produced in town homes – women or slaves sewed, tended gardens, and made food – but, across an emerging bourgeois world, homes were settings for the putative pleasures of domesticity, and they were becoming centers of consumption as much as production. In the towns of the Southwest, land and slaves were important property. Every day, however, their instrumental purposes were apparent. They furnished "opportunities and advantages" for middle-class townspeople to improve themselves, at home as well as in the market.

---

[27] Jefferson's famous line from Query XIX of *Notes on the State of Virginia*, conveniently available, in the 1787 edition, at http://books.google.com. Locke's justification of property rights is in chapter 5, "Of Property," in the *Second Treatise of Civil Government*. There is an extensive literature on early American republicanism. The most complete discussion is Gordon S. Wood, *The Creation of the American Republic, 1776–1787* (Chapel Hill: University of North Carolina Press, 1969), but an especially useful slant on the southern significance of land is Drew R. McCoy, *The Elusive Republic: Political Economy in Jeffersonian America* (Chapel Hill: University of North Carolina Press, 1980), and an account of how economic changes began unraveling the republican ideal is Steven Watts, *The Republic Reborn: War and the Making of Liberal America, 1790–1820* (Baltimore: Johns Hopkins University Press, 1987). Joyce Appleby has consistently argued that the early tradition was more liberal than republican, most recently in *Inheriting the Revolution: The First Generation of Americans* (Cambridge, MA: Harvard University Press, 2000). Christopher M. Curtis has observed that, in Virginia, the transformation

And improvement was the key to middle-class ideas about freedom. In this book, I frequently use the term *self-determination* to denote what Alabama's writers meant by liberty. Self-determination is the ability of individuals to make decisions about their lives without coercion – to do as they please, in Lincoln's terms. Freedom lets people make choices, and these writers assumed that choices could be wise. Specifically, they thought self-determination used two traits of human nature: reason and sympathy. By the former, they meant logical thinking; by the latter, they meant helpful responses to other people's feelings. While they often emphasized rationality, which allowed people to plan ahead, they thought that feeling for others, certainly family and friends, entered any sensible person's calculations. These ideas had classical foundations, and they were modified by Enlightenment philosophers. They were strengthened by evangelical faith, which stressed free will and self-reform, by Romanticism, which glorified emotion, and by the success of the United States, which showed that freedom worked, whatever it was.[28]

For Lincoln and the authors of the rising South, self-determination was heavily weighted with middle-class ethics. Mostly studying the North, scholars have described a mentality they label Victorian, or bourgeois, or simply middle class. Generally Protestant, middle-class people insisted that men and women were responsible for controlling their feelings and their actions. They thought that good folks voluntarily created long-term ties like friendship and marriage. They valued property, respected contracts, advocated hard work, and believed in the rule of law. They thought that education improved everyone and made children into good citizens. Like most of their peers, Alabama's writers thought reasonable adults more often than not agreed about right and wrong, even if they disagreed about particular actions. Given that confidence, they thought that freedom brought personal and social progress.[29]

---

of property created a substantial legal debate that elevated the significance of slavery; see his "Jefferson's Chosen People: Legal and Political Conceptions of the Freehold in the Old Dominion from Revolution to Reform" (Ph.D. dissertation, Emory University, 2002). I am grateful to Professor Curtis for sharing his forthcoming book on this subject.

[28] I do not suggest that most of Alabama's writers actually explored the metaphysical assumptions on which their ideas of freedom rested. Although Augusta Evans was concerned about metaphysical issues, and certainly Clemens, Meek, and Smith encountered ethics as a discipline in college, these writers' ideas reflected the general tenets of the Scottish Enlightenment, which had infiltrated popular literature as well as the college curriculum. The formal influence of European ideas in southern intellectual life is a major theme in O'Brien's *Conjectures of Order* and in many works by Eugene D. Genovese and Elizabeth Fox-Genovese, especially in *The Mind of the Master Class: History and Faith in the Southern Slaveholders' Worldview* (Cambridge: Cambridge University Press, 2005). Although, in his earlier work, Genovese regarded southerners as premodern, the later work – clearly as early as with *The Slaveholders' Dilemma: Freedom and Progress in Southern Conservative Thought, 1820–1860* (Columbia: University of South Carolina Press, 1992) – has related contemporary intellectual influences to proslavery ideas.

[29] In addition to the works cited previously that address these issues, a succinct summary of the relationship between the economic, religious, and political ideas of middle-class Americans is

Scholars have identified Lincoln with free-labor theory, a bias Alabama's writers implicitly shared, so long as it was applied to whites. They saw their enterprising society as filled with individuals who improved themselves economically, or who could improve if they wanted to. Like other free-labor thinkers, they often attributed inequality to lack of effort or innate deficiencies. They admired wealthy people who worked for their status and did not flaunt it, and they suspected that poor whites needed to work harder. They feared that Native Americans and immigrants (among others) were not ready for freedom. They did not think that black people could use freedom – but not all of them ruled the possibility out.

It is important, however, that these writers thought that the pursuit of happiness transcended wealth, and they applied the ethics of self-determination to many issues besides economic ones. They expected people to make independent decisions about their homes, faiths, spouses, friends, and political leaders. They especially wanted Americans to think, speak, and write freely (except on such taboo subjects as slavery). Although they pursued economic success, Alabama's writers valued the emotional, spiritual, and intellectual content of freedom. In that, too, they were like Lincoln.[30]

The writers of the rising South were much respected, but I do not claim that all southwesterners, much less all southerners, thought like them. There is solid historical evidence that some powerful planters and ideologues doubted the value of freedom, or, at least, thought that poor whites did not fully deserve it. And I agree with those historians who argue that the habit of commanding slaves was not easily suppressed in white/white relations. When, in his "House Divided" speech, Lincoln warned northern voters that the United States would be all slave or all free, he evoked fear of such undemocratic southerners. Historians also offer some evidence that poor whites had a negative conception of freedom – that they wanted the powerful to leave them alone – though evidence for people who wrote little is hard to come by. Certainly, Alabama's writers worried that some people disliked their zeal for improvement, and they tried to shape opinion. If the warmth of their arguments suggests anxiety, their attempt to persuade the doubtful

---

Anne C. Rose, *Voices of the Marketplace: American Thought and Culture, 1830–1860* (New York: Twayne Publishers, 1995), xv–xxiii.

[30] Very influentially, C. B. Macpherson has insisted that the essence of liberty in the modern Anglo-American tradition has been economic – a derivative of capitalism; see Macpherson, *The Political Theory of Possessive Individualism: Hobbes to Locke* (Oxford: Clarendon Press, 1962). Among the many literary interpretations that argue similarly are Joseph Fichtelberg, *Critical Fictions: Sentiment and the American Market, 1780–1870* (Athens: University of Georgia Press, 2003); Gillian Brown, *Domestic Individualism: Imagining Self in Nineteenth-Century America* (Berkeley: University of California Press, 1990); Lori Merish, *Sentimental Materialism: Gender, Commodity Culture, and Nineteenth-Century American Literature* (Durham: Duke University Press, 2000). As I see it, class influenced but did not control writers' ideas, and I would distinguish the ideas of individuals from the ideology of any group. On ideology, see the influential essay by Quentin Skinner, "Some Problems in the Analysis of Political Thought and Action," *Political Theory* 2 (August 1974): 277–303.

was a token of faith. They believed progress was pushing the world in their direction.[31]

They thought progress should only go so far, however, and the writers of the rising South did not think it promised a predictable end to slavery. Here, quite obviously, they differed from Lincoln, who wanted black people to have self-determination. They knew that racial prejudice was national and that black people lacked full rights where they were free.[32] Into the early 1850s, these facts misled the Southwest's writers into thinking they had more northern allies than they did. By the mid-1850s, however, they realized that their commitment to slavery distinguished their faith in freedom from that of most northerners. When Baldwin quietly wove slavery into his stories, he expected some readers to disapprove. Wanting a wide audience, he and most of his fellow writers rarely tackled slavery head on in their literary works.

When the writers of the rising South did defend slavery, however briefly, they relied on principles of self-determination. They sketched black people deficient in reason and morality, the two crucial traits that made freedom good. They implied, or said outright, that capable white people had a responsibility to take care of helpless slaves, and they sometimes compared slavery

---

[31] The most comprehensive statement of the idea that proslavery advocates were thinking about, if not exactly advocating, limits on white men's freedom is Genovese and Fox-Genovese, *Slavery in Black and White: Class and Race in the Southern Slaveholders' New World Order* (Cambridge: Cambridge University Press, 2008), although the general nature of their claim is longstanding. In influential state studies, several historians suggested that ordinary white men believed the rich were up to no good. See, for example, Harry L. Watson, *Jacksonian Politics and Community Conflict: The Emergence of the Second American Party System in Cumberland County, North Carolina* (Baton Rouge: Louisiana State University Press, 1981); Lacy K. Ford, *Origins of Southern Radicalism: The South Carolina Upcountry, 1800–1860* (New York: Oxford University Press, 1988); Thornton, *Politics and Power*. Early on, Genovese tried to suggest that his understanding of slaveholders' hegemony in southern society could be made to fit with the resistance of white farmers in his essay "Yeoman Farmers in a Slaveholders' Democracy," in *Fruits of Merchant Capital: Slavery and Bourgeois Property in the Rise and Expansion of Capitalism* (New York: Oxford University Press, 1983), 249–264. A creative attempt to explain similar tensions is that of William H. Freehling, see especially part II, "Social Control in a Despots' Democracy," in *The Road to Disunion: Secessionists at Bay*, which makes the tension between *herrenvolk* democracy and slaveholder's paternalism a constant source of anxiety and, ultimately, political insecurity. See also Lacy Ford's appreciative review of Freehling's two-volume study in "Democracy, Despotism, and Disunion: A Review Essay," *JSH* 76 (February 2010): 107–120, with which I generally concur.

[32] So many historians, literary critics, and interdisciplinary scholars in whiteness studies have documented the pervasiveness of racism across the United States, even within the ranks of antislavery activists, that it seems almost superfluous to cite sources. Among those that are most important for literary issues are Arthur Riss, *Race, Slavery, and Liberalism in Nineteenth-Century American Literature* (Cambridge: Cambridge University Press, 2006); Joseph Boskin, *Sambo: The Rise and Demise of an American Jester* (New York: Oxford University Press, 1986); Thomas F. Gossett, *Uncle Tom's Cabin and American Culture* (Dallas: Southern Methodist University Press, 1985); Eric J. Sundquist, *To Wake the Nations: Race in the Making of American Literature* (Cambridge, MA: Belknap Press of Harvard University Press, 1993).

to the beneficial inequality within families. They claimed that sympathy was greater between master and slave than between employer and employee. They suggested that white people had to restrain African Americans in order to protect civilization, which depended on brainpower. None of this was systematic, for Alabama's writers borrowed haphazardly from proslavery theory. On occasion, there were aggressive defenses of slavery in the political arena: by Jere Clemens, on the floor of the Senate, for example. But brief, ad hoc references were most common. To oversimplify, if not by much: the rising South's writers suggested that a biracial civilization required the enslavement of blacks, who could not be self-determined, by whites, who must be free.[33]

Perhaps more instructive than fleeting proslavery remarks, however, were writers' remarkable (if infrequent) use of slaves as fictional characters. There, the frequent resort to familial analogies underscores how changes in property affected slavery. Slaves were, as southerners insisted, portable property – legal chattel. With land and labor becoming fluid commodities, however, homes were sanctified as the site of security, and the application of domestic ideals to slavery followed suit. Alabama's writers incorporated slaves into white homes, placing them where inequality seemed as natural as sex and age. They made slaves "servants," like the hired help readers everywhere knew and often found useful.

The recourse to domesticity did not, however, allay writers' anxieties about the ethical consequences of slavery. If their model was domestic slavery, productive slavery – on farms and plantations – was the dominant reality, and that did not easily fit into middle-class ideals of self-determination. Planters might (or might not) be patriarchs, in the classical sense, but extreme hierarchy hardly fit the domestic model. Like other forward-looking southerners, writers preferred not to think about forced migrations and the relentless labor of cultivating cotton, especially on new soils, but these were economic realities that were discomfiting, and the slave trade was even more distressing. With open disapproval, Alabama's authors occasionally described people managing slaves through coercion, deceit, or abuse. Although they claimed these

---

[33] For many years, historians debated whether a racist (but liberal) *herrenvolk* democracy or a class-based (and conservative) paternalism dominated proslavery ideology, but recent scholarship has found that both were widespread justifications for slavery. A summary of proslavery arguments (with a bibliography that cites scholarship) is in Kolchin, *American Slavery*, 189–197. A cogent essay that places proslavery thought in the context of changing intellectual currents is Wyatt-Brown, "From Piety to Fantasy: Proslavery's Troubled Evolution," in *Yankee Saints and Southern Sinners* (Baton Rouge: Louisiana State University Press, 1985), 155–182. By emphasizing self-determination, I place writers' understanding of slavery in the bourgeois middle, neither as democratic, libertarian, and racist as *herrenvolk* nor as aristocratic, authoritarian, and classist as paternalism, but capable of reconciliation with either, in a pinch. The popular modes in which they wrote enabled literary men and women to evade rigorous logic – perhaps gratefully, when it came to slavery. Lacy K. Ford, *Deliver Us from Evil: The Slavery Question in the Old South* (Oxford and New York: Oxford University Press, 2009), treats the evolution of proslavery ideas as the South moved westward, finding paternalism ultimately persuasive everywhere, but influenced by *herrenvolk* ideas.

occurrences were atypical, they frequently spotted mastery and slavishness in white society when, for example, husbands tyrannized wives or politicians duped the people. Were the habits of slavery contagious? Such fears fed antislavery politics in the North, as Lincoln knew. But these writers did not admit slavery caused their anxiety. The fateful mixture of slavery and freedom had built their society, and they were not about to challenge it.

Instead, they turned their anxieties into doubts about human nature, which produced more unfocused fears. Living in homes where black and white people interacted all day, every day, Alabama's writers described slaves using reason and sympathy to judge whites, influence their conduct, and resist wrongs. They invariably made slaves seem inferior but not a great deal worse than poor, uneducated whites. And more than one writer made a slave the moral superior of a white man or woman. Similarities across racial lines undercut all claims that freedom only suited white people and slavery only blacks. In writers' worst moments, such similarities suggested that white people might be enslaved, making self-determination all the more imperative. Unwilling to be, as Clemens once said, "slaves instead of masters," writers revealed irrepressible fears.[34]

In sum, the eight writers of the rising South exposed both the common ground and the one great fault line in American ideas about freedom. Writing for the middle classes, they insisted that free people could make good choices for themselves and their society. Emphasizing individualism, they expected diminishing inequality among white men but thought that some inequalities would persist. While they defended slavery, it sapped their confidence in freedom. And yet, as slavery was more threatened, they made self-determination more essential. By the time of the Civil War, these writers had what I would call an existential idea of freedom. That is, they admitted their uncertainty about human nature, and they advocated self-determination without a clear grasp of their goals. When they relinquished slavery, they retained racism. In that regard, and in their tendency to blame inequality on those who suffered from it, they were like the middle-class people who read their books. A flawed idea of freedom remained a transcendent ethical value long after it had undermined a rising South.

---

[34] Speech at Huntsville, August 6, 1860, from a typescript copy of the speech printed in the Montgomery *Weekly Post*, September 5, 1860, in the Jeremiah Clemens folder, ADAH. Although he does not consider southern white writers, I think that Maurice S. Lee, in *Slavery, Philosophy, and American Literature, 1830–1860* (Cambridge: Cambridge University Press, 2005), makes an essentially correct point when he argues that the debate over slavery reshaped American philosophy and literature. Slavery challenged existing assumptions so fundamentally that it moved intellectual writers toward new conceptions of human nature and human society and, ultimately, shook the implicit metaphysical foundations of nineteenth-century thought. As O'Brien writes of southern intellectuals' attempts to understand the concept of race, "Intended to demonstrate order, race had a singular gift for creating intellectual disorder"; *Conjectures of Order*, 1: 239.

PART ONE

THE SOCIAL ORIGINS OF INDIVIDUAL FREEDOM

From the perspective of its writers, early Alabama was a wide-open field of personal opportunity. In the absence of substantial assets in land or slaves, most authors used their talents to achieve success. They developed social capital by making connections in the growing towns of the Southwest. Building families and friendships, they allied with other middle-class people. In the process, they came to believe not only that they were making themselves but that self-reliant individuals created their society's progress. Often ignoring slavery, these authors advocated the middle-class ethics of self-determination because it seemed to explain their experiences in a developing region. Although their society had relied on coercion since its inception, the writers of the rising South created a literature that celebrated individual freedom.

2

Self-Making in Southwestern Towns

> Well, mother-wit kin beat book-larning at *any* game.... Human natur' and the human family is *my* books, and I never seed many but what I could hold my own with.
>
> Johnson Hooper, *Adventures of Captain Simon Suggs*

In the nineteenth century, educated Americans saw the frontier as a place where brave pioneers tamed a wilderness. It was one thing to imagine the West, however, and another for an author to live there, for there were not a great many readers on the edge of civilized society. Abraham Lincoln learned to read without much formal education, and Illinois was ahead of the other western states to its south. As of 1840, more than 40 percent of Alabama's residents were African American slaves whose schooling was prohibited. Native Americans were colorful subjects but not citizens. Most white people lived in farm families with little money for books or time to read them, and there was no statewide public education. Among the educated, planters were scattered and townspeople still were relatively few. Although some towns had literary societies by the 1830s, nothing resembled the intellectual life of Charleston, much less Boston. No wonder Simon Suggs, a comic hero in the region's fiction, bragged that "mother wit" could "beat book-larning at *any* game."[1] With so few readers, a cunning man might find books useless.

---

[1] Johnson Jones Hooper, *Adventures of Simon Suggs, Late of the Tallapoosa Volunteers; Together with "Taking the Census" and Other Alabama Sketches*, intro. by Johanna Nicol Shields (Tuscaloosa: University of Alabama Press, 1993), 53. I have explored some of these themes in "Writers in the Old Southwest and the Commercialization of American Letters," *JER* 27 (Fall 2007): 471–505, but literary production in the Southwest has been understudied; Michael O'Brien, *Conjectures of Order: Intellectual Life and the American South, 1810–1860*, 2 vols. (Chapel Hill: University of North Carolina Press, 2004), is attentive to differences within the South's subregions; on the vitality of Charleston, see Michael O'Brien and David Moltke-Hansen, *Intellectual Life in Antebellum Charleston* (Knoxville: University of Tennessee Press, 1986); for an earlier period in which southern cities developed intellectual urbanity, see David S. Shields, *Civil Tongues & Polite Letters in British America* (Chapel

Given this setting, it may seem strange that men and women in early Alabama dreamed of literary fame. Yet, beginning in the 1830s, a few individuals exploited the ambiguous freedom of the Southwest to make themselves. Simon Suggs's motto – "it is good to be shifty in a new country" – parodied their initiative. The early careers of Alexander Meek, Caroline Hentz, and Johnson Hooper, Suggs's creator, illustrate the tactics middle-class writers used to get ahead. Each of them enjoyed self-expression, played with ideas, and used an expanding print medium to gain income. With sharp eyes on their interests, they criticized the Southwest, urged its improvement, and celebrated its progress. In trying to attract readers, they were like anyone who sells books in a capitalist market. But they lived in small towns such as Tuscaloosa, Florence, and Lafayette, and they sought to please friends and neighbors, too. In that, they were like other middle-class Americans who simultaneously sought independence and respect.[2]

While they were pursuing individual agendas, Meek, Hentz, and Hooper helped build communities and define a southern middle class. They knew that economic competition was replacing warfare in Alabama, and brainpower counted. Opportunities for professional people multiplied as citizens relied on lawyers, teachers, and merchants. Although these writers realized the significance of farmers, planters, and slaves, they represented a town-dwelling minority that wanted a modern society. By insisting on the primacy of self-

---

Hill: Published for the Institute of Early American History and Culture, Williamsburg, Virginia, by University of North Carolina Press, 1997); for a contrast between intellectual centers, see William H. Pease and Jane H. Pease, *The Web of Progress: Private Values and Public Styles in Boston and Charleston, 1828–1843* (New York: Oxford University Press, 1985), esp. ch. 8, "Education, Work, and Cultural Values."

[2] A fine study that broke with the long-standing literary argument that southern writers were too embedded in their communities to feel alienation is Scott Romine, *The Narrative Forms of Southern Community* (Baton Rouge: Louisiana State University Press, 1999); for frontal assaults on the older argument, see Michael O'Brien, *Rethinking the South: Essays in Intellectual History* (Baltimore: Johns Hopkins University Press, 1988) and Michael Kreyling, *Inventing Southern Literature* (Jackson: University Press of Mississippi, 1998). A study that shows how thoroughly northern authors were embedded in their communities is Ronald J. Zboray and Mary Saracino Zboray, *Literary Dollars and Social Sense: A People's History of the Mass Market Book* (New York: Routledge, 2005). A theoretically helpful and thoughtful exploration of the different ways in which authors approached the market is Leon Jackson, *The Business of Letters: Authorial Economies in Antebellum America* (Stanford: Stanford University Press, 2008). Other important studies are Susan L. Albertine, *A Living of Words: American Women in Print Culture* (Knoxville: University of Tennessee Press, 1995); Susan Coultrap-McQuin, *Doing Literary Business: American Women Authors in the Nineteenth Century* (Chapel Hill: University of North Carolina Press, 1990); Michael Newbury, *Figuring Authorship in Antebellum America* (Stanford: Stanford University Press, 1997); and David Dowling, *Capital Letters: Authorship in the Antebellum Literary Market* (Iowa City: University of Iowa Press, 2009). Particular attention to the social context of authorship is in Ronald J. Zboray and Mary Saracino Zboray, *Everyday Ideas: Socioliterary Experience Among Antebellum New Englanders* (Knoxville: University of Tennessee Press, 2006), and David Dowling, *The Business of Literary Circles in Nineteenth-Century America* (New York: Palgrave Macmillan, 2011).

determination, they explained their success and justified the values of middle-class people. Across the state, everyone was anxious about who would set the course of change.[3] Almost instinctively, Meek, Hentz, and Hooper converted uncertainties into personal assets.

They knew that theirs was not a sophisticated civilization. Paradoxically, however, both the Southwest's backwardness and its rapid development offered opportunity. Although writers usually praised pioneers, critics lamented "barbarism and Bowie-Knives," as Meek put it, and outsiders condemned the Southwest for its brutal slavery. Understandably, educated residents wanted to assert their merits, and writers helped them do it. They celebrated educational progress such as the anniversaries of schools, observed holidays such as the Fourth of July, and welcomed famous visitors such as Andrew Jackson. Among Americans in general, a reflexive defensiveness suggested anxieties about their inferiority to Europeans. As he launched his career, Ralph Waldo Emerson began "The American Scholar" (1837) by criticizing the nation's "sluggard spirit" and summoning a "free and brave" man to voice its cultural independence.[4] But recurring violence, instability, and slavery made the angst of the Old Southwest more severe. Hopeful that a dark past was receding and that slavery could buttress freedom, Alabama's writers spoke for a rising South.

Their methods revealed important values they shared with other middle-class Americans. Like Emerson, most writers relied on persuasion, the linchpin of American freedom. In republican theory – the heritage of the Revolution – reasonable individuals aired their differences to establish common goals. Persuasion made democratic politics and the market economy work. It united

---

[3] For sources that treat the significance of towns in the western South, see Chapter 1, n. 9 and n. 11; see also Weymouth T. Jordan, *Ante-Bellum Alabama: Town and Country* (Tallahassee: Florida State University, 1957). On the shifting status of professionals, see Samuel Haber, *The Quest for Authority and Honor in the American Professions, 1750–1900* (Chicago: University of Chicago Press, 1991). The most comprehensive discussion for the entire South is Jonathan D. Wells, *The Origins of the Southern Middle Class, 1800–1861* (Chapel Hill: University of North Carolina Press, 2004).

[4] Characterization of the Southwest from Alexander B. Meek, "Jack-Cadeism and the Fine Arts: An Oration Before the Literary Societies of La-Grange College, Alabama, June 16, 1841," in *Romantic Passages in Southwestern History* (New York: S. H. Goetzel & Co., 1857; repr. Spartanburg, SC: The Reprint Company, 1975), 182. Ralph Waldo Emerson, "The American Scholar," in *Selected Writings* (New York: Random House, 1950), 45, 57; address is online at http://www.rwe.org/complete-works/i---nature,-addresses-&-lectures/addresses-&-lectures/the-american-scholar. The contrast between the Southwest and older societies is developed in Joan E. Cashin, *A Family Venture: Men and Women on the Southern Frontier* (New York: Oxford University Press, 1991), which should be compared with James David Miller, *South by Southwest: Planter Emigration and Identity in the Slave South* (Charlottesville: University of Virginia Press, published in cooperation with the William P. Clements Center for Southwest Studies, Southern Methodist University, 2002). Both of these studies, however, focus on the planter class rather than town-dwelling people. A perceptive analysis of literary and popular responses to southwestern violence is Dickson D. Bruce, *The Kentucky Tragedy: A Story of Conflict and Change in Antebellum America* (Baton Rouge: Louisiana State University Press, 2006).

sympathetic citizens in civic causes such as temperance or educational reform. Supposedly, persuasion distinguished American decision making from the hierarchal operations of monarchies and aristocracies, but it subtly obscured inequality. When Meek, Hentz, and Hooper addressed their neighbors, they condescended, often implying that their efforts reflected genius (to use one of Meek's favorite words). And beneath their condescension was the routine middle-class belief that educated people were superior, not only to benighted savages but to illiterate whites, which is to say, the poor. While these writers preached self-improvement, they drew a line between the educated and those who, for whatever reason, did not read books.[5]

To be sure, Alabama's writers also distinguished between the self-reliant and the idle rich, who did not do honest work. Like other middle-class southerners, authors saw that the masters of many slaves controlled wealth, and they did not dispute its legitimacy. But they scorned conspicuous consumption and presumptuous manners. And they insisted that only diligence, talent, and good character qualified individuals for leadership. Like most middle-class people, writers insisted that education enabled the talented to rise. Although only three of Alabama's most prominent writers went to college – Meek actually had a master's degree – all had schooling. When Hooper derided "book-larning," he was joking, for it was his strong suit. He resented his lack of college education but thought he was as smart as anybody, and his good friend Meek agreed.

Education was necessary but not sufficient to realize literary ambitions because the print medium entangled authorship with money. Unless a writer had independent wealth, and not many did, there were very few ways to avoid the market economy, although groups such as literary societies occasionally paid for publications. In little towns, presses struggled to stay afloat; magazines and newspapers begged for subscribers and often failed to get them. Ignoring copyright laws, newspaper editors freely swapped materials that they had not paid for to begin with. By the 1830s, some northern magazines paid contributors, and a handful of authors – James Fenimore Cooper and William Gilmore Simms, for example – made money from book sales. But, when they began writing, Meek, Hentz, and Hooper sold themselves in another way: advertising their intelligence to gain employment, win clients, or enhance their future options.

Regardless of where it occurred – in Benjamin Franklin's Philadelphia, Lincoln's Springfield, or Alabama – self-making took a lot of effort, but it

---

[5] Three theoretical studies that helped me appreciate how persuasion and print bolstered the Southwest's middle classes are Walter J. Ong, *Orality and Literacy: The Technologizing of the World* (London: Routledge, 2007, c. 1982); Benedict R. Anderson, *Imagined Communities: Reflections on the Origin and Spread of Nationalism* (London: Verso, 1990, c. 1983); Jürgen Habermas, *The Structural Transformation of the Public Sphere: An Inquiry into a Category of Bourgeois Society* (Cambridge, MA: MIT Press, 1989). A political scientist applies theory to the nineteenth-century American context, with somewhat ahistorical but provocative results, in Kimberly K. Smith, *The Dominion of Voice: Riot, Reason, and Romance in Antebellum Politics* (Lawrence: University Press of Kansas, 1999).

was the creed of an ascending middle class. At some level, Meek, Hentz, and Hooper knew their efforts compromised their independence. While they made themselves authors through talent, work, and a fair amount of self-promotion, their success had unexpected costs. Meek mobilized his fellow townsmen behind his literary goals but felt uncomfortable about losing his independent identity. The northern-born Hentz found ways to express her opinions to southwesterners yet felt anxious seeking approval from unfamiliar people. Hooper became an overnight sensation with a popular book about the likeable scoundrel Simon Suggs. But he exposed the dangers as well as the possibilities of freedom, and, more clearly than the rest, Hooper saw hidden traps in the art of persuasion.[6]

For Alabama's writers, self-determination was a personal goal that reflected the values of people they cared about. The Old Southwest offered writers unique literary material and allowed them upward mobility. Even as they preached self-reliance, they attached their destinies to those of their friends and neighbors and aligned themselves with readers, wherever they were. Most of those readers were middle class, and only some of them belonged to a slave society that was on the defense. Meek, Hentz, and Hooper sometimes worried about needing public approval, but they did not realize that they wed themselves to impossible goals. Ironically, however, the greater their success, the more controlled they were by the moral dilemma of black slavery in the midst of white freedom. Their self-entrapment began when they first wooed the public in a rising South, but it seemed, at the outset, a small price to pay for making themselves.

A SOCIABLE SPOKESMAN FOR SOUTHERN LITERATURE

No writer was more adept at using public ceremonies to promote his reputation than Alexander Meek, who had large literary ambitions. There was no intellectual establishment in Alabama in the late 1830s, when Meek began to make his mark, but he operated at the edge of what passed for one in Tuscaloosa, home to the state's capital and its first public university. Without a prominent family, Meek improvised ways of getting attention. He used his literary skills

---

[6] Relations of some southwestern writers with their societies are explored in Bertram Wyatt-Brown, *Hearts of Darkness: Wellsprings of a Southern Literary Tradition*, (Baton Rouge: Louisiana State University Press, 2003); Wyatt-Brown, *The Literary Percys: Family History, Gender, and the Southern Imagination* (Athens: University of Georgia Press, 1994); Wyatt-Brown, *The House of Percy: Honor, Melancholy, and Imagination in a Southern Family* (New York: Oxford University Press, 1994); Philip D. Beidler, *First Books: The Printed Word and Cultural Formation in Early Alabama* (Tuscaloosa: University of Alabama Press, 1999). An application of Wyatt-Brown's interpretation of honor is Ritchie Devon Watson, *Yeoman Versus Cavalier: The Old Southwest's Fictional Road to Rebellion* (Baton Rouge: Louisiana State University Press, 1993). An influential study that relates writers' alienation to their espousal of proslavery ideas is Drew Gilpin Faust, *A Sacred Circle: The Dilemma of the Intellectual in the Old South, 1840–1860* (Baltimore: Johns Hopkins University Press, 1977), though her focus is on the Southeast.

in several occupations and in politics, forging useful alliances. Equally important in Meek's advancement was his role as advocate for southern literature, a cause that he, more than anyone else, brought to Alabama. Even as he succeeded, however, Meek suspected that readers limited his self-determination. They awarded reputation but defined it on their terms, not his.

As a young man, Meek was something of a dilettante. Samuel Meek, his Irish-American father, was a Methodist minister, pharmacist, doctor, and farmer, who brought his family to Tuscaloosa a few years after Alex's birth in Columbia, South Carolina, in 1814. Alexander was among the first graduates of the University of Alabama, which opened in 1831. Imposing at six-feet-four inches tall, blue-eyed, and very handsome, Meek was utterly sociable, compensating for his lack of money with constant flirtation, conviviality, and graceful self-promotion. Before he reached thirty, he had been a lawyer, volunteer in the Creek War, legislator, judge, interim attorney general of the state, and editor of the local Democratic newspaper, *The Flag of the Union*. A gifted orator, he also wrote poetry and history, but Meek admitted he was chronically lazy and without the discipline to match his ambition.[7] He faulted himself, but he did not reform.

Instead, the young bachelor used his charm. With an impressive speaking voice, he exploited public events to further his ambitions. Because the state's government patronized presses, Meek found publishers for such orations as his address to the university's society of alumni in December of 1836 and his poem on the Fourth of July before the "Ciceronian Club, and other Citizens" in 1838. He befriended women: his diary recorded his attendance at the "Circle of Industry," which had men and women, and his first public speech was at a Temperance Society meeting, where he supported the organization of a ladies' society. He noted romance in his diaries, remarking that he sought a girl with money, for "love is like the chameleon; it cannot live on air," but also admitting his preference for women who were beautiful and able to converse.[8] Meek made the social, political, and intellectual aspects of life inseparable.

---

[7] There is no comprehensive scholarly biography of Meek, but see Herman Clarence Nixon, *Alexander Beaufort Meek: Poet, Orator, Journalist, Historian, Statesman* (Auburn: Alabama Polytechnic Institute Historical Studies, 1910); Benjamin Buford Williams, *A Literary History of Alabama: The Nineteenth Century* (Rutherford, NJ: Fairleigh Dickinson University Press, 1979), 39–57; and, for a literary analysis of Meek's most notable work, Beidler, *First Books*, ch. 6 (76–86). There are scattered but, in the aggregate, extensive Meek papers at DUL, UA, ADAH, and MDAH (see subsequent notes for specific citations). Meek's laziness must have been far above the ordinary, for it was even mentioned in his eulogy and obituaries; see Rev. Phillip P. Neely, *Address Delivered at the Funeral of Hon. Alexander B. Meek* (Columbus, MS: Printed at the Sentinel Job Office, 1866), 3, 7. Meek's own admissions riddle the pages of his diaries; see, for example, the Diary entry of May 6, 1840, in Meek Papers, DUL.

[8] *A Poem Pronounced before the Ciceronian Club and Other Citizens of Tuscaloosa, Alabama, July 4, 1838* (Tuscaloosa: Published by the Ciceronian Club, 1838); "Circle of Industry," Diary for 1840, entry for May 22, DUL; "woman like chameleon," *ibid.*, entry for Apr. 28. The impact of government patronage of the press can be traced in Rhoda Coleman Ellison, *A Check List of Alabama Imprints, 1807–1870* (Tuscaloosa: University of Alabama Press,

The most ambitious literary project of Meek's early adulthood began in 1839, when he became editor of a magazine he named *The Southron*. This was the second magazine founded by Tuscaloosa's literati; the first, *Bachelor's Button: A Monthly Museum of Southern Literature*, had been edited by Meek's friend William Smith in 1836–1837, but it quickly expired. The magazines were similar, and the editors wrote for each other, just as they and other writers took turns composing newspaper copy. Meek's friends contributed to *The Southron*, identified by their names (or by transparent pseudonyms like Buford Keem for Alexander Beaufort Meek). Women were quite visible: the editor listed individuals as contributors and subscribers, and a women's school was advertised on the back cover of the first number. Most importantly, *The Southron* aggressively aligned itself with the South and Southwest.[9]

The new venture revealed Meek's anxiety about his reception. Launching *The Southron* with a statement of principle, the editor included an edgy bit of humor about his handsome appearance and the common notion that writing was a little unmanly. Meek compared his feelings about his subscribers to those of a debutante, who, "with a fluttering heart and undisguised anxiety," offered herself for "partiality and patronage." Playing on the Southwest's reputation for tough competition, he described how "her blue eyes – blue eyes are always beautiful! – fill with suppressed tears, as she anticipates the boisterous crowd, into which she is about to enter." He assessed her chances:

There are cynic lips, she knows, which will sneer, even at her perfections; envious rivals, who will attempt to detract from her merits; and, more than all, fond friends, who look anxiously for her success. Her heart is pained, and palpitates uneasily, as she gazes upon the opening vista of her career.

Abruptly, however, Meek switched to a safer trope – he was a "PIONEER" in a new field – and he appealed to the common good. The task of "promoting the Literature of the South," he claimed, should please "every intelligent and patriotic mind within our borders."[10] In case his readers thought literature was effeminate, Meek reminded them that his cause was very manly.

Because literary magazines more often than not failed, Meek used persuasive tactics. Drawing on Romanticism, he identified his project with American and southern destinies. Suggesting a global mission, he claimed that slavery would make southerners "the richest people on earth" and provide leisure

---

1946). Meek, *An Oration before the Society of the Alumni of the University of Alabama* (Tuscaloosa: M. D. J. Slade, 1837).

[9] If Smith's magazine contained a statement of principle, it was in the first number, which is not extant, but Meek's opening to *The Southron* suggests that his was the first to espouse such principles in Alabama; *The Southron: A Monthly Magazine and Review* 1 (January 1839): 1–8. Descriptions of these and other literary magazines are in Rhoda Coleman Ellison, *Early Alabama Publications: A Study in Literary Interests* (Tuscaloosa: University of Alabama Press, 1947), esp. chapter 3 (88–132).

[10] *Southron*, 1 (January 1839): 1.

for art. To attract a wide readership, he disavowed partisanship and ignored contemporary politics. He requested contributions from anyone who lived in the South or wrote on undefined southern themes. Long residence was not a standard, for the first contribution after Meek's in his opening number was a poem by Caroline Hentz, who was raised in New England and was not yet a southerner. Meek's longest piece was an essay on southwestern history, including his favorite subject, the Native Americans now displaced by white Americans.[11]

As part of his attempt to attract readers, Meek identified with what passed for a literary establishment in the South. Like Meek himself, the idea of a distinctive Southern literature originated in South Carolina, and the southwesterner regularly paid homage to the best known of the region's literati, Charleston's William Gilmore Simms, currently editing *The Magnolia*. Simms was an early proponent of a southern literature, and Meek made him a model. Meek printed a message of congratulations, unsigned but obviously from Simms; he published one of Simms's poems and the tale "A Story of the Sea," and he named the South Carolinian as a contributor.[12] Despite Meek's effort to identify with the region, however, *The Southron* died in early 1840, like most such ventures.

A year later, Meek bitterly expressed his disappointment, blaming his failure on a defective society. Addressing students at La Grange College near Florence, Alabama, the orator sarcastically attacked materialism, citing the failure of literary magazines as evidence of American and southern decadence. The Southwest, he claimed, was "thoroughly engrossed" in the quest for money: its "greatest proficiency" was "the limited philosophy of the ploughshare and the jackplane." Instead of education that taught "moral or intellectual greatness," southwesterners got utilitarian lessons in money making, which engendered "ignorant vanity." Such "self-chuckling and deaf" self-regard "besets and debases" a man's "whole moral nature." Although they learned the useful ethics of honesty and industry, Alabamians lacked kindness, courtesy, patriotism, and religion. A good society had to produce

---

[11] *Ibid.*, 7. Meek was Union Democrat, in opposition to the politics of John C. Calhoun, and he was a supporter of Martin Van Buren in 1936. Hentz's poem, "The Father's Vow," *ibid.*, 9–11. Meek's "Sketches of the History of Alabama, and Incidentally, of the Adjacent States," *ibid.*, 17–26.

[12] "A Story of the Sea," in *The Southron*, 6 (June 1839): 329–335; the message of congratulations and the poem "River Serenade" are in *The Southron*, 3 (March 1839): 192, 138. In *The Southron*'s first issue, Meek had also reviewed Simms's anonymously published romance, *Richard Hurdis; or, The Avenger of Blood. A Tale of Alabama* (Philadelphia: Carey & Hart, 1838). Simms's lurid account of southwestern life had offended some readers, and Meek regretted the low "moral tone" of the work, criticized its lack of humor, and lamented the author's shallow portrayal of women. Mostly, however, he praised the author, concluding that he could become "the first of America's fictitious writers." It does not appear from the context that Meek knew Simms was the author whose work he reviewed; *The Southron*, 1 (January 1839): 61–62. The most balanced discussion of the movement to encourage a distinctly Southern literature is O'Brien, *Conjectures of Order*, esp. 2: 700–706.

more than wealth. Decent people "must have some other catechism than Poor Richard's Almanac."[13]

Meek's Romantic jeremiad urged salvation, and, predictably, he insisted that "one true, generous, unflinching, uncompromising, right-onward scholar" could change society. Drawing from German idealists such as Frederick von Schlegel, who used "imaginative culture" to prevent "the lowest dregs of society welling up, and muddying the whole social system," he asked his listeners to promote the fine arts. Meek assailed the anti-intellectualism of the masses, who made it the "fate of genius" to be "suspected if not despised." With himself no doubt in mind, he insisted that scholars "in all our village streets" often heard "the sneering prophecies of the dunce and dotard – those human moles who ridge the footpath – that such a one will never be of any account in life; for he is a literary man!" But Meek also criticized wealthy people who wasted themselves in "idle follies or flagrant dissipation."[14] He wanted to change people's minds about culture and class, and his frustration showed – a certain amount of posturing notwithstanding.

Meek's whole oration identified his cause with the common good. He insisted that literature would "redeem and illustrate this mighty sugar-cane and cotton-growing region," so that it would "no longer be mapped in the moral geography, as the land of barbarism and Bowie-knives!" He called for leadership by intellectuals, not a moneyed elite, for he wanted to preserve "our plain democratic patrimony" instead of the "tawdry furniture and gilded trappings of aristocratic institutions." Finally, he sketched his vision of a rising South: the "domes and turrets of a mighty people" who "joined intellectual and religious excellence" with "social and domestic beauty" in steady "improvement" and "rapid strides" to "perfection." Such an exalted vision would not, he hoped, be like the "wild dreams" or "Utopian fancies" of European philosophers but something a democratic society led by scholars could produce.[15] Little in this oration hinted at the presence of slavery, for he described the magnificent destiny of white men.

Meek's youthful efforts at literary self-determination had mixed results. His vision of a modernizing slave society rested on persuasion, and not everyone thought democratic means adequate. Meek had already run afoul of one southerner who wanted to ally upper-class power with persuasion to civilize the frontier. Since moving from a prestigious Baptist pulpit in Charleston

---

[13] "Jack-Cadism and the Fine Arts," engrossment in money, 150; moral debasement, 152; Poor Richard, 157.

[14] "Jack-Cadism and the Fine Arts," scholar, 182; Germans, 173; fate of genius, 152; dissipated wealth, 177.

[15] Ibid., region's ills, 178, 182; antiaristocratic tone and vision, 190. Sam Hale, who had followed Meek as editor of the Flag of the Union, saw the demise of The Southron differently. Although he regretted its failure, he thought it had printed too much that was not original (and he mentioned Simms). But he identified Meek's motives in quitting; no one should wonder that he gave up the journal when similar energy "bestowed upon other pursuits is found to be so much more profitable" (Flag, October 16, 1839).

to become president of the University of Alabama in 1837, Basil Manly had tried to impose order through exhortation and tight discipline. Dedicated to patriarchal principles, he battled constantly with the disorder of a town where legislators and college men cavorted together. Despite Meek's occasional leadership in the temperance society, he was a convivial soul, as was his good friend, fellow writer, and faculty member Frederick A. P. Barnard, a serious drinker and a northerner. Manly categorically mistrusted northerners: "Very few of these Yankees will do – take my word for it. I find them out more & more, every year," he wrote in 1841. And Meek's friendship with Barnard helped make the writer, in Manly's words, "no friend to the university."[16]

Manly had the power to impede Meek's ambitions, and the young writer knew it. When the university's chair in literature had become vacant in 1840, Meek's friends had petitioned Manly in his behalf. They stressed not only the writer's morality and accomplishments but the fact that his "birth place education & future destiny are all identified with & locked in the cause of Southern rights." The petitioners noted that "there has been an attempt to produce an impression that the appointment of Mr. Meek would not be agreeable to the citizens of Tuscaloosa," and they specified their intent to "undo that impression."[17] But Meek did not get the chair. The moralizing president admired literature when it bespoke conservative principles, and he did not trust sociable scholars.

An unlikely event showed the tension between Meek's democratic and Manly's patriarchal approaches to civilizing the Southwest when Manly chose Simms, Meek's favorite southern writer, to speak at commencement in December of 1842. Meek was not included in the official ceremonies, although he and Simms had corresponded about the region's writing. Manly anxiously monitored the formalities. "The number and quality of the Audience, on such occasions, are manifestly improving," he wrote in his dairy, "and the

---

[16] Manly's comment on Yankees is in a letter to E. B. League, Sept. 2, 1841; comment on Meek in Manly's diary on the occasion of an event from which the president had excluded Meek, Diary 2 (1834–1846), entry for June 24, 1839, Basil Manly Papers, UA. An excellent account of Manly's years at the university is in A. James Fuller, *Chaplain to the Confederacy: Basil Manly and Baptist Life in the Old South* (Baton Rouge: Louisiana State University Press, 2000); discussion of Manly's conflicts with Barnard, 170–174. Manly had been a nullifier and State Rights Democrat while Meek was a Union Democrat, another probable source of discord between the two men. A biography of Barnard is William J. Chute, *Damn Yankee! The First Career of Frederick A. P. Barnard, Educator, Scientist, Idealist* (Port Washington, NY: National University Publications, Kennikat Press, 1978). John Quist, in *Restless Visionaries: The Social Roots of Antebellum Reform in Alabama and Michigan* (Baton Rouge: Louisiana State University Press, 1998), 7, finds a "largely similar climate of reform" existing in Ann Arbor, Michigan, and Tuscaloosa; and he argues that slaveholding and reform sentiments were compatible, as Manly's temperance activities suggest.

[17] Petition in Meek Family Papers, MDAH; undated, but internal references place it in 1840 or 1841. Meek recorded in his daybook for 1840 that he wanted a faculty position, entry for August 12, 1840, in Meek Papers, ADAH.

attention, order and interest likewise." Held in the huge classical rotunda that dominated the tiny campus, the event gathered the full panoply of the state's power. As the editor of the Whig *Independent Monitor* wrote, Manly, Simms, and Governor Benjamin Fitzpatrick (who had excellent Carolina relations) sat before townspeople, students, trustees, and lawmakers. No doubt, Manly thought that Simms would enhance the university's prestige and link it with the conservative order of Charleston.[18]

Simms was no aristocrat, but he shared elite Charlestonians' negative view of the Southwest. Set in Alabama, his 1838 novel *Richard Hurdis* had vividly described the region's criminality. Now, he bade planters to lead its moral progress. His "eloquent and polished" oration, *The Social Principle: The Source of National Permanence*, addressed the patriarchal responsibilities of planters, offering the model of the British landed gentry and, at least by implication, South Carolina's resident aristocracy. He warned that the greatest threat to American order was "the wandering habit of our people," wretchedly embodied in the Southwest. Greedy young men, free from "controlling" parents, acquired "presumption, insubordination and insolence – looseness of principle – recklessness of conduct – levity of manners, excess in indulgence, brutality in habit, drunkenness and debauchery, beastliness the most loathsome, and, frequently, crimes the most atrocious." Simms asked his listeners to rescue the Southwest by enacting patriarchal principles. It is easy to imagine Basil Manly nodding "Amen."[19]

Meek was more democratic than Simms, and the mobility the South Carolinian decried almost defined the southwesterner's hopes for self-determination. Although Simms's views were less rigid than Manly's, they were not Meek's, which stressed freedom. In Meek's view, patriarchy "must and will resolve itself into Despotism." Having long since rejected the idea of migrating westward, Simms prescribed reverence for the land while Meek wrote (in his diary): "*I heartily hate country life....* Give me the bustling

---

[18] Manly comment, Diary 2, December 14, 1842, Manly Papers, UA. The *Monitor*'s account appeared on December 21. As the *Monitor* described it, the event must have attracted a fair proportion of the town's less than fifteen hundred white inhabitants, swelled temporarily by the fact that the state legislature was in session. The editor emphasized both the dignitaries who sat in the front of the Rotunda and the "numerous audience," which included the legislature's members (in a body), other dignitaries, and "the fair sex from the city, as well as other parts of the State, and of fashion and intelligence generally." See William Stanley Hoole, "Alabama and W. Gilmore Simms," *AR* 16 (April and July 1965): 83–107. Neither the *Monitor* nor Manly mentioned Meek, although surely he was present at Simms's speech.

[19] Characterization of oration, *Monitor*, December 21, 1842. Simms, *The Social Principle: The Source of National Permanence* (Tuscaloosa: Published by the Erosophic Society, 1843), 35, 45. There are accounts of Simms's address in David Moltke-Hansen, "Between Plantation and Frontier: The South of William Gilmore Simms," in John Caldwell Guilds and Caroline Collins, eds., *William Gilmore Simms and the American Frontier* (Athens: University of Georgia Press, 1997), 3–26; and in Miller, *South by Southwest*, 87–99, where he compares Simms's views with those of Meek and finds more similarities than differences.

town – the crowded city!"[20] The two writers shared Romantic ideas, however, and they both believed that literature and refined culture were redemptive. Simms himself, moreover, was a newcomer to the establishment. The differences between the two writers did not inhibit their literary friendship, which now turned to Meek's advantage. Meek was a host for the final event of Simms's visit – a public dinner in his honor. It prominently displayed the flexible values of townsmen rather than the conservative morality of the university's president, who did not attend.[21]

Outside of Manly's control, Meek worked to convert Simms's visit to his advantage, demonstrating the handy fit between his sociability and his literary aspirations. Meek, Manly's nemesis Barnard, and three other local young professionals had issued Simms an invitation in advance of his trip, and they planned the dinner. Because the *Independent Monitor* closely reported the festivities, its account underscores the importance of male writers' access to the press. It gave the dinner twice as much space as commencement or Simms's formal address. The planners surely provided the *Monitor*'s editor an outline (probably a good bit more), for the town's editors often wrote for each other anonymously despite their partisan differences. The article quoted by name only Simms, Meek, Barnard, and one other member of the planning group.[22] The *Monitor*'s reporting demonstrated the way literary men influenced the rising South, and in the absence of formal power.

[20] Meek on patriarchy, ms. address on July 4th, 1833, in Meek Papers, ADAH; Meek on "country life," entry for July 15, Diary for 1840, DUL. Meek's family was comfortably middle class; an inventory of his father's will describes a small farm and some property, with six slaves (including two children); Orphans' Court Records for 1847, Tuscaloosa County Court House. The most comprehensive discussion of Simms's attitudes to the frontier is contained in the various essays in Guilds and Collins, eds., *Simms and the Frontier*.

[21] In addition to Simms's participation in Meek's magazine, Simms wrote Benjamin Perry on October 30, 1842, that he had heard from Meek, who suggested a plan for writing a series of literary biographies; in *The Letters of William Gilmore Simms*, collected and edited by Mary C. Simms Oliphant, Alfred Taylor Odell, and T. C. Duncan Eaves, 5 vols. (Columbia: University of South Carolina Press, 1952), vol 1: 328–330. The *Monitor* noted Simms's arrival in town on December 14, then reported the commencement, his address, and the dinner on the 21st. *The Flag of the Union*, Meek's former paper, also noted that Simms would speak, but the editor observed that he missed the lecture; *Flag*, November 30, December 14, 1842.

[22] In addition to Meek, Barnard, and the third member of the planning group, Frederick Porter, the *Monitor*'s article named John Cochrane, W. R. Smith, D. Woodruff, Thos. Maxwell, and Dr. W. A. Cochrane as people who delivered toasts, but the paper did not specify which toasts each man delivered; Tuscaloosa *Independent Monitor*, December 21, 1842, contains all of the quotes from the dinner. In a friendly biography for which Barnard's wife gathered materials, John Fulton claimed that Barnard was the "active but unavowed" editor of the *Monitor* for some years; see John Fulton, *Memoirs of Frederick A. P. Barnard* (New York: Macmillan and Co., 1896), 91. A discussion of the town's newspapermen is in Robert McKenzie, "Newspapers and Newspaper Men during Tuscaloosa's Capital Period, 1826–1846," *Alabama Historical Quarterly* 44 (Fall-Winter 1982): 187–202. See also the recollections of a former journalist, W. W. Screws, "Alabama Journalism," in *Memorial Record of Alabama* (Madison, WI, 1893).

Unlike the dignified hierarchy of commencement, the freer form of the dinner revealed a society organized by middle-class people who used a competitive form of persuasion. Held at a hotel, the banquet was an all-male gathering of townsmen at which Simms was repeatedly toasted. After the dinner table was cleared, the ceremonies began with ten "regular" toasts that were planned in advance – all of which the *Monitor* quoted verbatim. Next were "many voluntary toasts" and still more speeches, some impromptu, others perhaps expected. Toasting was a kind of contest of honor in which the audience chose winners and losers with applause, and short speeches had a similar character, so that a speaker's wit was required to read the audience and gain its approval. In a way, then, the give and take of the dinner created a semispontaneous, ostensibly democratic definition of the local pecking order among educated men. As was often the case when spirits were high, the festivities lasted late into the night, but the *Monitor*'s writer assured his readers that the "utmost harmony and pleasure" prevailed.[23]

The theme of the "regular" toasts was the significance of literature for American, southern, and southwestern society. Although the planners must have assigned the toasts, a competitive spirit prevented any one person's control. In any case, the toasts perfectly suited Meek – at least in the version reported by the *Monitor*. The first two toasts evoked a national perspective, proclaiming that America's literature should be as great as its government and making writers equal to statesmen. The third toast applied those ideas to Simms, who had "shed honor upon our country's literature" and shown "the world" that South Carolina deserves "the high place in Letters which she has ever held in the Field and Forum." "After enthusiastic applause," Simms spoke for forty-five minutes, eliciting more "loud and continuous applause by the company." The regular toasts continued to favor the South, paying tribute to writers from William Wirt, biographer of Patrick Henry, to Augustus Baldwin Longstreet, author of the humorous work *Georgia Scenes* – not a model for orthodox literature but a popular form.

The eighth toast – to the university, the "hope and pride of our state" – betrayed the tension between Manly's managed order and the looser associations of middle-class men like Meek. The *Monitor* quoted it and the comments that followed it "substantially" as if to sanction the speaker, F. A. P. Barnard, for his were the only impromptu remarks it quoted. And Barnard began by claiming that "circumstances seem to have deprived us of the presence" of

---

[23] Quotes from *Monitor*, December 21, 1842. Quist describes the ups and downs of Tuscaloosa's temperance movement, *Restless Visionaries*, ch. 3, "Toward the Sober Slaveholder: Temperance in Tuscaloosa County," noting that Meek and some of his friends were active in the movement but had relapsed by 1843; Meek's relapse, n. 126, p. 233. Although some of the *Monitor*'s comments imply that alcohol was served, the event could have been alcohol-free, or there could have been choices allowed. I appreciate Quist's advice on this issue. Some of the participants were temperance advocates. Without the influence of temperance, such all-male events would normally have contained drinking. All quotes in the passages that follow are from the *Monitor* article.

the president.[24] Playing his audience, he insisted he was pressured to speak in behalf of the university: "at least friends around me seem determined not to be content, unless I do." Then the Yankee intensified the sectionalism of the previous toasts. After noting his northern birth, he added an unscheduled toast, "Southern Colleges for Southern Men," and urged southwesterners to educate their own. Since Barnard was one of the planners, perhaps he spoke for them, or maybe he was trying to mollify critics like Manly by flagging his southern allegiance. For sure, someone thought it important to put Barnard's joking remarks and the unscheduled toast in the newspaper.

If Barnard's comments obliquely targeted Manly, what followed favored Meek, whom Manly had rejected. After Barnard's little show, the planned toasts resumed and Meek took the podium to toast Simms again. The regular toasts concluded with the obligatory tribute to women as "the soul of society and the inspiration of the poet." Then began the spontaneous toasts, which the newspaper omitted, but it did not omit the moment when Simms turned the spotlight on Meek. The famous man not only acknowledged his friendship with Meek, which conferred honor, but also promoted Meek's standing among his fellows: "May the State honor him whose genius has honored her." The company responded with "strong approbation," and Meek was visibly moved, according to the *Monitor*. The townsmen had asserted themselves, and Simms had implicitly (and probably unintentionally) rebuked Manly (who represented "the State"). Regardless, the great man had anointed Meek a genius, and that was a significant victory.[25] Meek and his cronies had engineered the banquet, and the newspaper made it count.

The *Monitor*'s account of the banquet showed how persuasion in print could compete with the power of a nascent establishment, although the competition was very polite. Through print, the effect of Simms's visit on Alexander Meek rippled outward. Simms mentioned his visit in the *Magnolia*, modestly failing to comment on the honors tendered him at the dinner. He praised Meek's as-yet-to-be published epic poem about the Creek Indian hero *Red Eagle*, which the young author had shared with him. Simms also wrote a close friend about his visit, enclosing a clipping with a "meagre account of the dinner." In a small-town newspaper, the "meagre account" loomed pretty large.[26] The public dinner resembled hundreds of other social occasions where

---

[24] Manly probably saw no reason to attend. He commented in his diary that forty people "partook of dinner, at my expense, after the exercises," calling his event a "sumptuous affair." From his perspective, a reception that same evening in Steward's Hall "closed" the "festivities" of commencement. See Manly Diary 2, December 14, 1842, UA.

[25] Meek's toast was to Simms as author of *Richard Hurdis*, and he did not mention his earlier review.

[26] Simms to James Lawson, January 7, 1843, in *Letters*, 1: 339, 340. Comments in *The Magnolia*, II.n.s. (May 1843): 366. When *Red Eagle: A Poem of the South* (New York: D. Appleton & Co., 1855) was eventually published, it was dedicated to Simms. The copy of the poem in the Duke Library, interestingly, is inscribed to F. de B. Hooper from C. M. Hooper, the niece and sister-in-law, respectively, of Meek's friend Johnson Hooper (F. was Fanny, the daughter of DeBerniere Hooper, and C. M. was Caroline Mallet, wife of George Hooper).

Self-Making in Southwestern Towns 39

literary activities were featured. Such events were essential to the establishment of writers' status, insofar as their efforts rested on face-to-face influence. For the larger public, however, newspapers intervened between what was said and what was known, and newspapers let literary townspeople – men and women – spread their ideas.

The newspapers and presses that writers relied on were not primarily concerned with literature. In Tuscaloosa, printing flourished because of the government's patronage, and in that sense papers served the establishment – such as it was. Yet middle-class editors might tweak the noses of the powerful, and sometimes they simply advanced their own interests. Editors like the *Monitor*'s Stephen Miller, Meek, and their friends boasted about the cultural accomplishments of their villages. They published what they thought popular, whether it was news of circuses, scandals, or murders, and they sought to be useful, running ads for consumer goods, lawyers, and runaway slaves. They pled for subscribers. Under these circumstances, it is no wonder that the ebb and flow of an informal public dinner got more space than the proprieties of commencement. The account of the banquet had entertainment value, and it suggested that there was more behind the scenes than could be reported. In that sense, the editors' work was as literary as any fiction.

Nonetheless, Alexander Meek knew that newspapers were not to be confused with literature even if they required art in writing, for, above all, newspapers served their parties. They printed speeches, notices of public meetings, descriptions of parades and barbecues, and sometimes slashing editorials. Editing was a job that attracted talent, but articles were rarely signed. As spokesmen for political parties, most editors were pens for hire, and they knew it. Meek, for one, did not like the resulting anonymity. As he once wrote, editors "are considered the channels through which 'all things' are to be done by any means, the path which is to communicate to the world all that is bad in prose and worse in poetry." Readers, he wailed, granted editors "no actual existing identity."[27] Because every kind of print had an audience, or a market, a writer's self-determination was always compromised by the need for approval. A free press relied on persuasion, and in the small towns of the Southwest that meant addressing the mentality of people one knew. A newspaper only exaggerated the problem, and the dependence it required was sometimes too much, even for a man who courted the public at every turn.

AN ENTERPRISING WOMAN FROM THE NORTH

In the summer of 1834, Caroline Hentz, a native of New England, arrived with her family in Florence, a village in the northwestern corner of Alabama.

---

[27] Undated fragment ms. in the Meek Papers, ADAH. The passage is on the reverse of a statement written for the *Flag* on the occasion of its being purchased by a new publisher, James Warren, who took over the newspaper in 1846, but it is not entirely clear that the two sides of the paper are part of the same text. The handwriting is, however, Meek's, in both cases.

She would live there almost nine years, longer than any other place in her adult life. Hentz faced real barriers to literary success: as a woman, she could not speak in public without harming her reputation; as a Yankee, she reminded southerners of abolitionists; and, as a schoolteacher and mother, she had to snatch moments to write. Nonetheless, Hentz won audiences by playing on their hopes. She displayed her knowledge to emphasize the importance of education, and she dramatized her virtues to explain how work, self-control, and sentiment could tame the Southwest. Along the way, she found ways to circumvent the constraints on women, and print was chief among them. One of her admirers called her a "rare, magnetic woman," but she worked as hard to establish herself as did men who more obviously promoted themselves.[28] Obstacles did not prevent Hentz's self-determination, which slowly connected her to the rising South.

Caroline's appearance in Florence marked one more in a long series of moves that characterized her marriage to Nicholas Hentz, a French-born artist, entomologist, and teacher. Born in 1800 to a respectable family, Caroline had married Nicholas in Massachusetts in 1824, and the next year they migrated southward. As his son Charles later recalled, Nicholas was a "rolling stone" who rarely settled down. A growing Hentz family lived first in Chapel Hill, where Nicholas taught at the University of North Carolina, then moved to Covington, Kentucky, and then across the river to Cincinnati. There, Nicholas and Caroline were active members of a regular literary club that at some point included Harriet Beecher Stowe, years before she became famous. From Cincinnati, Caroline had published her first novel, *Lovell's Folly*, though the poorly written book quickly vanished from the market.[29]

---

[28] The admirer was Octavia Walton Le Vert, herself an author from Mobile; quoted in Mary Forrest, *Women of the South, Distinguished in Literature* (New York, 1866) 265. There is no full-length biography of Hentz. The best extended treatments are in Elizabeth Moss, *Domestic Novelists in the Old South: Defenders of Southern Culture* (Baton Rouge: Louisiana State University Press, 1992), which argues that Hentz always felt an outsider in the South (74); and in Mary Kelley, *Private Women, Public Stage: Literary Domesticity in Nineteenth-Century America* (New York: Oxford University Press, 1984), which finds similarities between northern and southern writers.

[29] Charles A. Hentz, *A Southern Practice: The Diary and Autobiography of Charles A. Hentz, M.D.*, ed. with an intro. by Stephen M. Stowe (Charlottesville: Published for the Southern Texts Society by the University Press of Virginia, 2000), 405. Charles's sketches of his parents' life in Cincinnati rely on family memory, since he was a small child. A brief account of Nicholas Hentz's scientific interests is in Collier Cobb, "Nicholas Marcellus Hentz," *Journal of the Elisha Mitchell Scientific Society* 47 (January, 1932): 47–51. For concise biographical sketches of both Hentzes, see Mary Kelley, "Caroline Lee Hentz" and Richard Walser, "Nicholas Marcellus Hentz," in William S. Powell, ed., *Dictionary of North Carolina Biography*, 6 vols. (Chapel Hill: University of North Carolina Press, 1988), 3: 115–117. *Lovell's Folly; a Novel* (Cincinnati: Hubbard and Edmands, 1833) drew from Hentz's experiences in New England and the South, and it reflects her early ambivalence about slaves and slavery. There is no solid evidence about why the novel was withdrawn, but the *New England Magazine* 6 (January 1834): 84–85, panned it, concluding that "It has one general fault, – it is silly." http://cdl.library.cornell.edu.

Although Caroline had literary ambitions before she came to Alabama, her family's needs displaced them. In her new home, she focused initially on mundane tasks. Not long after they moved to Florence, the couple established a girls' school Caroline named Locust Dell. They bought a small building and expanded it into a large facility where the family lived and both parents taught. As its name suggested, Florence had hopes of becoming a commercial metropolis. Such ambitions were common in the fertile Tennessee Valley, where cotton thrived in the speculative boom before the Panic of 1837. Although Florence contained fewer than a thousand people, perhaps a third of them slaves, Hentz was determined to make it a good home.[30]

Hentz faced unfamiliar neighbors, however, from an insecure base, for her marriage was shaky. Nicholas was an unreasonably jealous husband, and he had provoked a conflict over Caroline's friendship – apparently harmless enough – with a male admirer in their Cincinnati circle. The confrontation had led to their sudden departure from Cincinnati and hasty relocation in Alabama. Perhaps to steady herself, Hentz kept a diary in 1836, and it reveals the strain of her unsettled relationship with Nicholas as well as her desire to reconcile her literary ambitions with her husband's mistrust. Understandably, she was sensitive to how people saw her, and the combination of anxiety and ambition kept her on edge. She mocked "a sour, vinegar old maid – who has been venting her spleen on me." And she complained that the woman talked about "'the bold atmosphere of Mrs. Hentz.'" Caroline despised her dependence on the good opinion of others: "I would rather earn my living by the sweat of my brow – than by such bondage of the spirit," she wrote dejectedly.[31]

Prudently, Hentz restricted her ambitions to avoid more conflict with Nicholas, but they did not abate. When she got a Philadelphia newspaper containing one of her poems with "some flattering remarks," she ruefully noted that her writing was "one link that still binds me to the great world" but affirmed her acceptance of the simple life in Florence. She reminded herself that happiness at home was her overriding goal, and she recorded small signs that her relationship with Nicholas was improving. He brought her a pair

---

[30] The population of Lauderdale County, where Florence was located, was nearly 12,000, roughly a third of whom were slaves, so Locust Dell could draw on a nearby body of middle- and upper-class farmers in the county.

[31] Entries for May 13 and March 19, 1836, in her Diary, Hentz Family Papers, UNC. The first careful exploration of the diary was Rhoda Coleman Ellison in "Caroline Lee Hentz's Alabama Diary, 1936," *AR* (October, 1951): 254–269. Charles recalls his father's jealousy and the episode in Cincinnati, *Diary and Autobiography*, 406, 411; Locust Dell, 412–415. An account that emphasizes Hentz's bad marriage is Helen Waite Papashvily, *All the Happy Endings: A Study of the Domestic Novel in America, the Women Who Wrote It, the Women Who Read It, in the Nineteenth Century* (New York: Harper & Brothers, 1956). An illustrated account that also treats the Hentz's troubled relations is Philip D. Beidler, "Caroline Lee Hentz's Long Journey," *Alabama Heritage* (Winter 2005): 24–31. As their son recalled, the Hentz parents joined the local lyceum, "gotten up amongst the intelligent and literary citizens of Florence," which met every week or two; *Diary and Autobiography*, 422.

of vases with "remember me" inscribed in gold on them and, another time, a silver pencil. Nicholas acquired a small farm, hired two slaves (one was a woman who helped Caroline with domestic chores), and experimented futilely with raising silkworms. The family and servants helped him hunt bugs and spiders for his large collection, which traveled around with him. Enrollments in Locust Dell grew. And despite the limitations of "this secluded spot" and the loneliness of life in a "cold, strange land," Caroline's talent slowly found outlets beyond the classrooms in which she taught.[32]

In February of 1836, she converted western warfare into literary opportunity. Patriotic events let women make silent appearances while serving the public, and Hentz's patriotism was sincere. Her father, a Revolutionary veteran, had been an officer during the early nineteenth century, and one of her brothers was later a Brigadier General. In 1836, when war broke out with the Creek Indians, the governor of Alabama called out the militia. In a fit of martial spirit, the men around Florence responded, and the Hentzes joined in a celebration. After Nicholas bought red, white, and blue satin, Caroline helped students sew a banner, and she made an eagle from golden foil. Describing her "difficult task," she prodded herself not to "despair of making at last – a resemblance of our country's emblem." She claimed "quite a flow of inspiration" as she composed a poem for a student to read at the gathering – the job was less tedious than needlework. After three days of sewing, she produced a gilded eagle surrounded by stars, wryly observing that she was "with all my love for stars & passion for soaring ... very glad to leave them."[33]

Hentz's work paid off. The "morning dark and drear" of the event featured snow, sleet, and rain, so the school's delegation rode to the Methodist church "through a deluge of mud." They joined two or three hundred other people, which was a very large crowd for a village. At the program's climax, Caroline and Nicholas held her satin banner over the head of the girl who recited Caroline's poem, which, she happily noted, got "much applause." It was a lot of trouble for a brief triumph, but Hentz satisfied her "passion for soaring." Her efforts produced more than applause, however, for the same troops visited Locust Dell a month later, and her public favor persisted. Nicholas was away when the troops rode out to the school, and Caroline thought momentarily that she might have to make a speech, but, instead, the males honored the females. She noted that "the Captain made quite a complimentary address," and the soldiers hoisted her star-studded banner, which they "waved gallantly before us."[34]

Although Caroline was delighted with the approval she won, she was displeased with the crudity of her town. Fears of further conflict with the Creeks prompted more musters, and Hentz recorded their darker side. Three months

---

[32] Caroline Hentz Diary, Hentz Family Papers, UNC; Flattering remarks, Feb. 20; vases, May 26; (pencil, June 1); "secluded spot," Feb. 22; "cold, strange land," June 10, 1836.
[33] Ibid., "Difficult task," Feb. 25; "flow of inspiration," Feb. 26; love of stars, Feb. 27.
[34] Ibid., day of ceremonies, Mar. 1, 1836, visit of the volunteers, Apr. 4.

after the first celebration, the "whole school" attended a muster where the officers once more saluted the females as an "*inspiring* presence." This time, however, it was terribly hot, the school's delegation sat on a hard rail, and there were few volunteers for service. After the girls left, the officers "plied" potential recruits with "whiskey & they came briskly out of the ranks," filling the muster requirement. Hentz's patriotism dimmed after the shoddy performance, and she complained "Oh! That we were far removed from the red man of the wilderness, as well as the children of Africa." No doubt, she kept her dissatisfaction to herself.[35]

Now the leading lights of Florence recognized the luster the Hentzes brought to their town, so Caroline found new opportunities to shine. At the top of the social heap were the family of General John Coffee. Coffee had been a planter and land speculator who was a friend of President Andrew Jackson and brother-in-law to Jackson's wife, Rachel. Coffee's widow had a "grand old plantation" where the Hentz family visited, and their children attended Locust Dell.[36] When President Jackson visited Florence, Caroline wrote a poem for the festivities and, again, appeared silently as it was read. Hentz enjoyed the approval of her neighbors, but this kind of prominence exposed her to audiences she could not evaluate, for the bridge between oral performance and a printed poem was a short one if newspapers entered the picture, as at least one did on the occasion of Jackson's visit.

In towns like Florence, newspapers were the only local publications – the main chance for writers to appear in print. To boost circulation, editors reported special occasions, often quoting poems or addresses that were delivered. When the Hentzes appeared, therefore, they got free publicity for their school as well as a showcase for Caroline's talent. Newspaper accounts often praised participants and the audience because editors were inveterate boosters. Description invited criticism, however, for communal feeling was lost in black and white, and a brief poem suffered when separated from the performer's style – a particular handicap to Hentz, who had, her son recalled, "one of the most lovely, sunny dispositions that ever existed."[37] In a way, a newspaper might expand an author's reputation and also constrain it. It could promote reputation a Yankee schoolteacher might otherwise not attain, calling attention to the writer as a writer, but it could also spotlight transgressions.

Because President Jackson's visit was truly printworthy, Hentz's tribute circulated more widely than the streets of Florence. It caught the attention of one Philip Alston, a young Episcopal minister in nearby Tennessee, who relayed it to his friend De Berniere Hooper in Chapel Hill, where both men had known

---

[35] Ibid., Second muster day, May 29.
[36] Charles Hentz recalled the Coffee's plantation, and Caroline recorded fishing trips there in her diary. Charles also recalled that although Locust Dell was a school for girls, he and a few other males attended, including two of the Coffee boys; *Diary and Autobiography*, 416–417.
[37] Ibid., 406.

the Hentzes. Hooper was interested in news from Alabama because his two brothers, George and Johnson, had migrated there. Not very kindly, Alston satirized the Hentzes' performance:

> I saved a newspaper a long time for your benefit, which I can't now lay my hands upon. – It contained a piece of poetry laudatory of the President, written by Mrs. Hentz, and read by Monsieur to the old General in a large company at Florence, – his wife leaning on his arm.... Imagine the Old Hero, standing stiff as a poker, his iron features relaxed into an expression of sheepish embarrassment: imagine the complacent smile of the Monsieur, the paper held close before his spectacles, – with one hand, while the other waves with graceful emphasis, as his lips are rhyming "sage" and "Hermitage" and so on, through seven or eight mortal stanzas! – imagine the lady's downcast look of modesty, as she leans upon her lord, – and fill up the background with amused spectators – and there is a picture worthy of Cruickshank himself.[38]

In print, Hentz's modesty was transparent; her "mortal stanzas" earned ridicule. She used the great man's visit to show her talents, but the newspaper exposed her in ways she could not blunt with charm. Hentz's anxiety about public approval was warranted.

Anxiety did not, however, inhibit Hentz's determination. The appearance in 1837 of Alabama's first literary magazine, *Bachelor's Button: A Monthly Museum of Southern Literature*, offered Hentz a new venue. Despite the title's emphasis on masculinity and region, the journal imposed fewer constraints than a polite gathering, and it gave Hentz more control over her image than did a newspaper. *Bachelor's Button* was first published in Mobile, at the opposite end of Alabama, though it aimed at a state-wide circulation. The magazine's male editor, William Smith, wrote most of it using pseudonyms, and Hentz simply initialed her contribution. With some distance from her neighbors, she offered her values as a corrective to southwestern flaws. Without specifying its setting, Hentz's story "A Nice Sense of Honor" modified the regional ideal of manliness by adding middle-class virtues: industry, frugality, selflessness, and studiousness. Where dizzying speculations were the rule, Hentz asked for restraint.[39]

Specifically, "A Nice Sense of Honor" moralized that hard work, self-restraint, and talent were more important than wealth. A "false sense of honor" belonged to a man who committed suicide in shame after his speculations ruined his family and (worse) an orphaned ward whose money he risked. The story's hero was the villain's eighteen year-old son, whose "nice sense of honor" redeemed his family's name. To repay the ward's losses, the youth left

---

[38] Philip W. Alston to J. D. B. Hooper, Jan. 20, 1837, in John De Berniere Hooper Papers, UNC; hereinafter cited as JDBH Papers. De Berniere was a long-time professor of classical languages at UNC and was referred to within his family as D. B.

[39] "A Nice Sense of Honor," *Bachelor's Button: A Monthly Museum of Southern Literature* 5 (October 1837): 170–180. The magazine was published first in Mobile and then in Tuscaloosa, but the line "Mobile, May 1, 1837," appears at the bottom of Hentz's story. Copies of the magazine are rare; numbers 2 and 5 are both available at UA.

his brilliant studies at the university for a life of "self-denial," spending three years in "ceaseless efforts" as a lowly clerk – "enterprising, industrious, and economical." Having met his selfless goal, the hero abjured wealth (Hentz commented: "We see the very lowest grade of talent subserve the purpose of money making"). Returning to his studies, he earned public esteem as a writer – a model of self-determination and talent. Hentz's ethical perspective had northern roots, and the story's setting was vague, but it suggested her hope that southwesterners shared her ideas.[40]

"A Nice Sense of Honor" criticized speculation that was a national woe, and Hentz inched closer to criticism of her new region with another story published in the state's second literary magazine: Meek's venture, *The Southron*. Although most of the writing in *The Southron* was by men, this time Hentz signed her work "Mrs. Caroline Lee Hentz," and she contributed short poetry and prose. "A Legend of the Silver Wave," an eight-page story, contrasted western violence with middle-class, womanly virtues. Set during the American Revolution, her romance was not about "*hair-breadth* events," or "fictitious" woe, but "that elevation of feeling," that "all-pervading, life-giving, yet self-annihilating principle, which imparts its own light and energy to every thing around and about it." Hentz's grossly overwrought "legend" treated the collision of Indians and Anglo-Saxons near the Ohio River, gently suggesting wrongs done to Native Americans.[41]

By making a woman's genteel ethics reform the character of a Native American man, Hentz simultaneously displayed derogatory stereotypes about Indians and their possibility for civilization. Amidst the upheaval of war, an impetuous American – seeking revenge for his brother's death – mistakenly murdered a noble Indian couple and orphaned their infant son. A benevolent soldier and his wife adopted the boy, bestowing Christianity and education on him. Quickly jumping forward, Hentz made the grown-up Indian boy the lover of his benefactors' "virgin" daughter after he saved her from drowning during a steamboat fire (her father died trying to rescue the girl). Although the steamboat suggested a new and common kind of western violence, the lovers escaped its wreckage. Through the white girl's influence, the brave Indian boy became as "gentle and mild as the gentlest of his sex," softening "all the harsher traits of the aboriginal character."[42] The havoc of the frontier gave way to civilized progress.

By setting her story in a distant place and time (too distant for a steamboat to have been there) Hentz removed herself from Alabama's "red men of the wilderness." Like the distance created by the print medium, her historical setting let her criticize white men's aggression in a way she could hardly have suggested to Florence's militia, while the presence of her name in a journal

---

[40] Ibid., 173, 175, 180.
[41] "A Legend of the Silver Wave," *The Southron* 1 (February 1839): 97–104, quoted passage 100. Emphasis in the original.
[42] Ibid., 103.

with those of male writers gave her a symbolic equality no personal appearance could afford. Indeed, her story implied Hentz's superiority as the author of the "life-giving, yet self-annihilating principle" of sentimental romance. But there was not much self-annihilation in Hentz's stance, which identified her with the progress of the rising South.

Despite her reservations about manly aggression, Hentz returned in 1842 to heroic themes in a poem written at the invitation of the young men of the La Fayette [sic] Society of La Grange College, where Alexander Meek had spoken the year before. Once more, Hentz did not actually speak, but a member delivered, and the society quickly printed, her "address." Evoking the American Revolution, she eulogized the Marquis de Lafayette, for whom the society was named. Perhaps unconsciously, she drew on the militia celebration in 1836, depicting a female icon of American freedom who "flings / Her banner o'er" the Frenchman, "while her eagle's wings, / Dipped in the sun, with golden plumes unfurl'd / Send their far shadows to an elder world." Hentz qualified her praise of heroism by urging the young men not only to emulate Lafayette but also to pursue "science, art, and religion."[43] By connecting her little audience with an American freedom that inspired the "elder world," Hentz promoted herself and her civilizing mission.

Meanwhile, using her own "link" to the "great world," Hentz also began publishing in magazines like *Godey's Lady's Book*, increasing her repute in Florence. In 1843, however, Nicholas suddenly abandoned the little town. This time he moved his family to Tuscaloosa, where the Hentzes had a new school, the Alabama Female Institute. Because Hentz had published in the magazines of the town's literati, her reputation preceded her. A local press published her *De Lara; or, The Moorish Bride*, a poetic drama, the year she arrived. In 1844, she wrote a long poem for the Erosophic Society, one of the University of Alabama's two literary clubs. Naturally, she did not speak, but the Society published her poem, noting in the title that a male member read it. Despite this kind of welcome, however, the Hentzes were not fully accepted. Their oldest son, Charles, recalled later that a schoolmate mocked him with the rhyme "'Charles Arnould Hentz pally boo fanzy & yankee too'" – referring to his French father and New England–born mother. Charles called the child "half-witted, a big dunce, too," but the taunts showed that some southwesterners found the Hentzes a little odd.[44]

---

[43] *An Address: Written, by Request, for the La Fayette Society of La Grange College* (Florence, AL: Printed at the Florence Gazette Office, 1842), 6, 9.

[44] Charles Hentz, *Diary and Autobiography*, 431. An early example of Hentz's publication in *Godey's* is "The Shaker Girl," excerpt from *Lady's Book* (Feb. 1839): 49–58. The activities of the Tuscaloosa circle are described in Williams, *Literary History of Alabama*, 21–24. *De Lara: or, the Moorish Bride: A Tragedy in Five Acts* (Tuscaloosa: Woodruff & Olcott, 1843). Hentz wrote De Lara while she was in Covington, Kentucky, won a prize in Philadelphia for it, and it was "enacted for many successive nights" at the Arch Street Theater in that city, according to Forrest, *Women of the South*, 267; see also Beidler, "Hentz's Long Journey," 27–28. Hentz, *Human and Divine Philosophy. A Poem Written for the Erosophic Society*

Self-Making in Southwestern Towns   47

When her peripatetic husband decided in 1845 to move on to Tuskegee – a smaller town than Tuscaloosa – Caroline left behind a growing printed record of her presence. In Tuskegee, the Hentzes ran Glen Alpine, another school for girls, but they would stay there less than two years, and the family's security diminished. As usual, Caroline labored at many tasks, yet she increased her writing as her husband's emotional and economic well-being declined. Charles recalled his amusement at seeing his mother, "the authoress ... with her sleeves rolled up, kneading dough." Although she was making a reputation in Alabama, she was soon to learn that there was money in the "great world."[45] Whatever her disadvantages, Caroline Hentz was becoming an author. By linking her talent to the opportunity of the Southwest, she demonstrated the self-determination of a woman who was still a Yankee, but not for much longer.

NOT QUITE A LITERARY MAN

The formal ceremonies where Meek and Hentz appeared – even the convivial dinner for Simms – encouraged refinement. Outside the pale of respectability, where mother wit beat book learning, unlettered farmers governed themselves, and if, as Meek said, they sneered at genius, they could cripple writers' efforts to civilize the Southwest. Few men described this predicament better than Meek's friend Johnson Hooper, who created a southwestern icon in the

---

of the University of Alabama, by Caroline Lee Hentz and Recited by A. W. Richardson (Tuscaloosa: Journal & Flag Office, 1844). In Tuscaloosa, Hentz also gave "An Address Delivered before the Total Abstinence Society of Alabama, at Tuscaloosa, on the Anniversary of American Independence," noted in the *Southern Literary Messenger* (December 1843): 745. Charles recalls that the Hentzes did not own the academy in Tuscaloosa but rented it, and he also remembers that his father regularly played chess with Alexander Meek. Early in 1843, Meek wrote Simms that he was preparing biographical sketches (for a project that never materialized) of Hentz and Smith, suggesting that she was already considered part of their circle; Alexander Meek to William Gilmore Simms, April 14, 1843, in Gratz Collection, HSP.

[45] Charles Hentz, *Diary and Autobiography*, Diary entry for December 12, 1845, 75. According to Charles's recollection, his father owned $600 of the $2,600 stock in the new school, for which his mother once again chose the name; *ibid.*, 448. He describes her (in the diary) as authoress of "The Mob Cap," a story collected eventually in a book with that title; the only edition of *The Mob Cap, and Other Tales* was published by T. B. Peterson, but the publication date is unknown, and Peterson did not publish any other of Hentz's works until the 1850s. Charles could be referring to an earlier version of the title story, or the Peterson edition could have been 1844 or 1845. On the other hand, Charles does not refer to *Aunt Patty's Scrap-Bag* (Philadelphia: Getz and Buck, 1845) which appeared from a small press in 1845 but was picked up by Carey and Hart and later reprinted many times. Carey and Hart records first 1,000 and then 300 copies printed of *Aunt Patty's Scrap Bag* (Record Book, Vol. 3, 1845, August 23, 103, and December 13, 136; HSP), at a cost for the first thousand of $66.40, but it does not record how much Hentz was paid. Although she was already writing for *Godey's* and *McMakin's Saturday Courier*, at this point, Hentz could only have begun to realize how much she could produce for the mass market; Charles describes her as a "regular contributor" to the magazines while they were in Tuskegee; *Diary and Autobiography*, 451.

vulgar confidence man Simon Suggs. Because Hooper's fiction was impolite, he gained an unorthodox reputation, yet he avidly promoted southern literature. Hooper saw that writers depended on their readers, and he found it liberating because he reveled in his talent and loved to show it off. Capturing the social dynamics of persuasion, his stories featured constant conversation – much of it manipulative – and they revealed the links between speaking, writing, and print. While expressing his peculiar genius and winning repute, Hooper hinted there was danger in the self-determination of southwestern men.

On the whole, Hooper thought southwestern society beneath him, for he was a man of inordinate pride, more blue-blooded than Meek or most other people. Born in 1815 in Wilmington, North Carolina, Hooper had a large and distinguished clan that included a signer of the Declaration of Independence. Erudition was a family trait: one cousin, William Hooper, was a classical scholar who moved in Basil Manly's circles as a professor (at the University of North Carolina and South Carolina College) and college president (at Furman and Wake Forest); and Johnson's older brother De Berniere (a name denoting the French nobility in their family) was also on the faculty at North Carolina. With his background and intelligence, Johnson should have become a lettered man, but he did not. Having exhausted an inheritance, Johnson's father became a newspaper editor in Wilmington; then, when Johnson was a teenager, the family drifted to the brink of poverty in the port town. With the help of kin, the Hoopers scraped together a classical education for Johnson in North Carolina and Charleston, but the boy had to work while he went to school, and the circumstances were humiliating.[46]

[46] There are two full-length biographies of Hooper: William Stanley Hoole, *Alias Simon Suggs: The Life and Times of Johnson Jones Hooper* (Tuscaloosa: University of Alabama Press, 1952), and Paul Somers, Jr., *Johnson J. Hooper* (Boston: Twayne Press, 1984). The former is more complete but badly out of date, almost Confederate in its sympathies, and done without benefit of the Hooper family papers; the latter is more balanced, but it, too, does not reflect the materials in the family papers. More accurate on Hooper's early years is my introduction to Johnson Hooper, *Adventures of Captain Simon Suggs* (Tuscaloosa: University of Alabama Press, 1993), vii–lxiv. The collections for the Hooper family are JDBH Papers and Caroline Mallet Hooper Papers (Johnson's sister-in-law), UNC (hereinafter referred to as CMH papers). Family history is recounted in a biographical sketch of William (the signer) Hooper by Johnson's father Archibald Maclaine (A. M.) Hooper, taken from his Hillsboro *Recorder* of November and December 1822; a sketch of "The Late Archibald Maclaine Hooper," by Griffith McRee (a cousin), in *The North Carolina University Magazine* 4 (1855): 57–62, and a family history by Fanny de Berniere Hooper Whitaker (De Berniere's daughter) reprinted in *The North Carolina Booklet* 5 (July 1905): 39–71. Manly describes a visit with William Hooper (the educator) in his diary for Monday, December 29, 1834, when he was in Charleston; Diary 2, Manly papers, UA. W. Hooper describes an offer to teach at the University of Alabama (before Manly was there) in a letter to Charles Manly (Basil's brother), February 8, 1830, in JDBH papers. Family letters detail Johnson's youth and their poverty; see, for example, August 22 [1832]; George to D. B., February 3, 1833; Charlotte (Johnson's mother) to D. B., March 29 (in which she notes that Johnson is "the best Latin scholar in school but there are 2 or 3 better in Greek") and December 30, 1833; A. M. (Johnson's father) to D. B., June 12, 1834; all in JDBH papers. See also Edward McCrady (a cousin) to William Porcher Miles, for a note that Johnson was educated for a time in Charleston by his relatives,

Hooper understood his future depended on his efforts, but he had trouble focusing them. He followed his oldest brother George to Alabama in 1834, and, with his family's help, he got a short-lived job in Tuscaloosa, hoping to attend the university. Instead, frustrated by poverty and continuing dependence on his family, he began roaming about the Southwest. He had been "wild" in Wilmington, and his bad habits persisted. When Hooper tried to establish a store in Dadeville, he floundered. On a buying trip to Charleston he found himself without credit and wrote a friend: "God damn the goods to Hell.... When you do go to Texas, I will go with you by God." Perhaps predictably, he was sued for debts. Finally, in 1842 he moved to the tiny town of Lafayette near the Georgia border, where George lived. He practiced law a little, married sixteen-year old Mary Brantley, and became the editor of the *East Alabamian*, the local Whig paper. Despite his heritage, Hooper had to scramble just like the crudest social climber. His pride was terribly bruised, and he disguised it with jokes.[47]

Hooper hid a lot behind humor. In a period when Americans in general and southerners in particular judged men by their stature and physiognomy, Hooper's appearance was a public joke. Of medium height, he was scrawny and thin-shouldered, and the protruding bones in his skinny face overshadowed a small chin. In a literary series for a Black Belt newspaper, one "Captain Cuttle" argued that, in "marring" Hooper's face, "Nature" thought "she was clipping his wings and precluding his rise to fame." But she was only partly right, for while "his homeliness" blocked Hooper from one route to success, it opened another, contributing "fully as much to his success as his mental resources and efforts." Instead of talking, Hooper's "principal delight" was to watch the people around him, "always on the look out for eccentricities of manner, thought, and expression" that he could portray on his "canvass." Like his character Suggs, Johnson Hooper sensed

> including the wife of John Johnson, the brother of Associate Justice of the Supreme Court William Johnson. The family's pride shows plainly in A. M.'s comments about Johnson to D. B., as Johnson left Charleston for Alabama. Hoping that Johnson will soon "astonish the young pettifoggers of the West," he added "I believed him to possess superior talents and yet I apprehended that circumstances would keep him in an inferior & subordinate position;" A. M. to D. B., June 12, 1834, in JDBH papers.

[47] Charlotte calls Johnson "wild" in her letter of August 22 [1832], but her complaints about him were constant and apparently warranted. The "damn" goods letter is from Johnson to Joseph Johnson, October 3, 1838, reprinted in Edgar E. Thompson, "The Literary Career of Johnson Jones Hooper: A Bibliographical Study of Primary and Secondary Material (With a Collection of Hooper's Letters)" (M.A. thesis, Mississippi State College, 1971): 74. Hoole is inaccurate about the early years in Alabama. Many letters within the family document Johnson's wanderings and his failure to settle down; see, for example, George to A. M., April 16, 1838, and August 12, 1839, in JDBH papers. The records of the legal action against Johnson and his partner may be traced through the Circuit Court Trial Dockets and Minutes, Tallapoosa County, 1839–1841 (Tallapoosa County Courthouse, Dadeville, AL). Although letters within the family suggest that Johnson wrote home occasionally, few of his letters survive. See, for an example of his humiliation about dependence, Johnson to D. B., August 23, 1836, in JDBH papers.

people's "soft spots" because he looked beneath appearance and listened to the voices he heard.[48]

Hooper wanted an audience and found it in his little town. With his usual bite, Hooper once admitted that respectable folk thought journalism a "sort of tolerated loaferism," but he was perfectly matched to the emerging profession. Whereas Meek resented the obscurity of editing, Hooper saw it as a means of influence, and his newspapers became a vehicle for expressing his personal opinions as well as the political views he was obliged to provide. Although Hooper's style was always direct, often colloquial, and sometimes inflammatory, he was a town booster who promoted middle-class refinement. The *East Alabamian* printed, for example, an address on "The Science of Music" by the head of the local academy, a Frenchman with the unlikely name of La Taste. Hooper reported on a lecture at the lyceum, published poetry (some of it funny), and reprinted an account of a visit to the home of William Wordsworth. In these respects, Hooper's *East Alabamian* was a typical small-town newspaper.[49]

But Hooper made his newspaper atypical and gained an "actual existing identity" like no other editor. As was customary across the United States, he pirated materials from other papers, but he also wrote his own fiction: a satiric humor that used vernacular language to describe the antics of commoners from the perspective of educated observers. Longstreet's *Georgia Scenes* was a prototype, and the toast to him at the banquet for Simms testified that this humor was somewhere within the realm of literature. Like other humorists, Hooper parodied the speech of common folk, but his cast of speakers came from all classes, and he set them talking with vital energy. His style reflected the influence of picaresque fiction and satire (*Don Quixote* was his favorite), and it had oral ancestry in competitive stories among men, but Hooper made it utterly reliant on print, even in its use of italics and capitals for emphasis.[50]

---

[48] "Captain Cuttle," in the Livingston (AL) *Sumter Democrat*, July 3, 1852. For the significance of personal appearance in the South, see Bertram Wyatt-Brown, *Southern Honor: Ethics and Behavior in the Old South* (New York: Oxford University Press, 1982), esp. 48–49.

[49] In noting that the public's opinion of journalists had improved over the previous ten years, Hooper also commented that "with this change in social footing" they had no more money; Montgomery *Weekly Mail*, August 10, 1854. On the insulting character of the term "loaferism," see Michael Zakim, "The Business Clerk as Social Revolutionary; or, a Labor History of the Nonproducing Classes," *JER* 26 (Winter 2006): 563–564. There are only a few numbers of the *East Alabamian* extant, but Hooper's Whig politics, his basic style, and his civic boosting are evident. He reported the address by La Taste on the front page of the paper, *East Alabamian*, August 19, 1843, along with a one-column song about Henry Clay; he noted a second address by La Taste, November 4, 1844, this one focusing on education as a sign of progress; the article on visiting Wordsworth was August 11, 1843.

[50] There is a large body of scholarly writing about what was customarily called southwestern humor, though that label is less frequently used than it once was. The best recent scholarship is James H. Justus's comprehensive analysis, *Fetching the Old Southwest: Humorous Writing from Longstreet to Twain* (Columbia: University of Missouri Press, 2004); excellent essays in M. Thomas Inge and Edward J. Piacentino, eds. *The Humor of the Old South* (Lexington: University of Kentucky Press, 2001), and John Mayfield's splendid study

Hooper's zest jumped off the pages. He was not just telling stories; he was displaying himself.

At first, Hooper aimed his stories at readers in Lafayette, but the locale did not circumscribe his ambitions for long. In 1843, he published in the *East Alabamian* "Taking the Census," a satire of rural folks' resistance to being counted, based on his experience as an agent in 1840. Somehow it attracted the attention of William T. Porter, editor of the New York sporting newspaper *Spirit of the Times*, which reprinted the story for thousands of readers. Other stories followed, and during the winter of 1844–1845 the character Simon Suggs began to appear in the *East Alabamian*, in the *Spirit*, and in southern papers. Porter put notes from Hooper in the *Spirit*, letting the writer puff his work by mail. Encouraged, Hooper organized more stories of Suggs into a book, which Porter marketed to the publishing firm of Carey and Hart. *Adventures of Captain Simon Suggs* appeared in 1845 and went through more than a dozen printings before the Civil War. Individual stories were widely pirated – even in faraway England, in *Bentley's Miscellany*.[51]

The *Adventures* revealed Hooper's raw talent. They masqueraded as a campaign biography about a vulgar rascal running for sheriff. As the putative biographer narrated Simon Suggs's exploits, he ridiculed ignorant common people, shady speculators, ambitious legislators, and miscellaneous other venal types who populated the Southwest. Obviously, Hooper the Whig satirized Andrew Jackson and his Democrats, for the narrator compared his biography to Amos Kendall's famous one of Jackson. But Hooper wove much of southwestern history into Suggs's life story: from such specific things as Jackson's

---

Counterfeit Gentlemen: Manhood and Humor in the Old South (Gainesville: University Press of Florida, 2009). For older scholarship, see Nancy Snell Griffith, compiler, *Humor of the Old Southwest: An Annotated Bibliography of Primary and Secondary Sources* (New York: Greenwood Press, 1989). Hooper's copy of *Don Quixote* is in the Evans Memorial Library, Aberdeen, Mississippi, along with an original paperback of the Simon Suggs stories that has a strikingly racist cover (which, unfortunately, is too faded to reproduce here). On continuities with European satire, see Howard Winston Smith, "Simon Suggs and the Satiric Tradition," in Howard Creed, ed., *Essays in Honor of Richebourg Gaillard McWilliams* (Birmingham: Birmingham Southern College Press, 1970). Justus discusses the relationship between vernacular speech and print in "The Languages of Southwest Humor," in *Fetching the Frontier*.

[51] *Adventures of Captain Simon Suggs, Late of the Tallapoosa Volunteers; Together with "Taking the Census" and Other Alabama Sketches* (New York: Carey and Hart, 1845). Hoole discusses the early publications and Porter's discovery of Hooper in *Alias Simon Suggs*, 45–65. Porter negotiated with Carey and Hart in Hooper's behalf; see William T. Porter to Mssrs. Carey & Hart, March 3 and 13, 1845, NYHS. Porter's broader role in promoting humor is in Norris W. Yates, *William T. Porter and the Spirit of the Times* (Baton Rouge: Louisiana State University Press, 1957). Thompson, "Literary Career," helpfully reprints most of the notes from Hooper to the *Spirit*; Griffith, *Bibliography*, provides lists of stories and some of the places they were reprinted. On the reception abroad, see Milton Rickels, "The Humorists of the Old Southwest in the London Bentley's Miscellany," *AL* 27 (1956): 557–560; Louis Fraiberg, "The Westminster Review and American Literature, 1824–1885," *AL* 24 (1952–1953): 310–329.

victory over the Creeks at Horseshoe Bend (on the Tallapoosa River); to the generic economic problems of wildcat banking, land speculation, and gambling; to the psychology between fathers and sons and the emotions of religious revival. Suggs was a con man who inhabited the zone between petty criminality and splendid fraud – one of the prototypes for a figure increasingly visible in American fiction, as much a symbol of rampant capitalism as of the Southwest.[52]

Suggs was self-determined to a fault, a predator who exploited the "soft spots" in human nature for profit and for fun. His "whole ethical system" lay in his motto "IT IS GOOD TO BE SHIFTY IN A NEW COUNTRY." But Suggs was more amusing than terrifying, and Hooper celebrated his character's creativity as much as he criticized Suggs's immorality. Although Hooper's satire suggested the need for restraint through the Whiggish means of persuasion and cooperation, Suggs could only have been born where men were free to make themselves. Suggs was a "genius" because he made something from nothing; and Hooper flaunted his own genius. As his preface said, he first wrote "to amuse a community unpretending in its tastes," and now he created a book for the "Great Public." Inspired by the rising South and the burgeoning literary market, Hooper created a symbol of freedom's possibilities, which were his own.[53]

In the process of asserting himself, moreover, Hooper bared the complex ties between writers and their middle-class communities. Although his style was rude, Hooper affirmed the refinement of his readers by asking them to laugh at uneducated people. Yet he demonstrated that freedom empowered crude talent, and, time and again, he showed that Suggs made himself through the mastery of words. And Suggs depended on his audience, deriving his force not only from his ability but from the visceral responses of his listeners. Although Suggs was smarter than the crowd, everyone was morally flawed. A true democratic rhetorician, Suggs demonstrated that persuasion rested not only on reason and sympathy but also on power and passion, for he tapped feelings that lay beneath words. Through Suggs and the people he conned, Hooper revealed a profound ambivalence about his society. He covered it, however, with the anarchic spirit of humor, which gave him license to show truths others might ignore.

Every one of Suggs's many scams turned on his extraordinary ability to read his audiences and match his words to their expectations. The powers of observation that "Captain Cuttle" attributed to Hooper were nowhere more evident than in the tale of how Suggs was chosen Captain of the Tallapoosa Volunteers. The fake campaign biography turned on this story, which proved that Suggs was electable. It partly satirized Jackson at Horseshoe Bend in

---

[52] I have discussed Hooper and the Suggs stories at greater length in "A Sadder Simon Suggs: Freedom and Slavery in the Humor of Johnson Hooper," *JSH* 56 (Nov. 1990): 641–664; reprinted in Inge and Piacentino, eds., *Humor of the Old South*, 130–153.

[53] *Simon Suggs*, 12, 35, preface, iv.

1814, but the setting was the Creek War of 1836 – the same war for which Hentz extolled the militia and for which Meek had volunteered. In the story, Suggs knew that there were no hostile Creeks nearby, but he manipulated public fears to win repute. As refugees from the nonexistent violence gathered in a tavern, Suggs enjoyed "the noise and confusion, the fun and the free drinking" and he made petty profits from scaring ignorant folk.[54] His election as a militia officer was pointless: without a war, the people did not need a captain, but no matter. Suggs relished his game.

The pure play of Hooper's imagination coursed through this story. To get elected, Suggs had to engineer opinion, and Hooper's scene brilliantly exposed the volatile dynamics of public speaking. He satirized a long tradition of warriors, as Suggs manipulated men who wanted to be heroes to their women. Suggs's voice dominated the scene as he demonstrated his mastery to the crowd. While Suggs addressed the men, he watched the women, whose fear inspired him as he fueled it. Hooper punctuated Suggs's crude language with the narrator's more refined descriptions:

"Gentlemen," said he impressively, "this here is a critercle time; the wild savage of the forest are beginnin' of a bloody, hostile war, which they're not a-goin' to spar nither age nor sek – not even to the women and children!"

"Gracious Lord above! what is a body to do!" exclaimed the portly widow Haycock, who was accounted wealthy, in consideration of the fact that she had a hundred dollars in money, and was the undisputed owner of one entire negro – "we shall all be skelped, and our truck all burnt up and destr'yed! What shall we do?"

"That's the question," remarked Simon, as he stooped to draw a glass of whiskey from a barrel of that article – the only thing on sale in the "store" – "that's the question. Now, as for you women folks" – here Suggs dropped a lump of brown sugar in his whiskey, and began to stir it with his finger, looking intently in the tumbler, the while – "as for you women-folks, it's plain enough what you've got to do" – here Simon tasted the liquor and added a little more sugar – "plain enough! You've only got to look to the Lord and hold your jaws; for that's all you kin do! But what's the 'sponsible men" – taking his finger out of the tumbler and drawing it through his mouth – "of this crowd to do? The inemy will be down upon us right away, and before mornin'" – Simon drank half the whiskey – "blood will flow like – like" – the Captain was bothered for a simile, and looked around the room for one, but finding none, continued – "like all the world! Yes, like all the world" – an idea suggested itself – "and the Tallapusssey river! It'll pour out," he continued, as his fancy got rightly to work, "like a great gulgin ocean! – d – – – – d ef it don't!" And then Simon swallowed the

---

[54] *Ibid.*, 85. Hooper joined his brother George in Alabama as the Creek War of 1836 was frightening Alabamians. George Hooper, according to his mother, "fought in a battle;" he wrote that he attended a muster at the home of Albert J. Pickett, but in his reassuring letters to his fiancé he made fun of all of the fuss; Charlotte Hooper to D. B., June 10, 1836, JDBH papers; George to Caroline Mallet, February 21, 28, May 11, 22, 1836, in CMH papers. Johnson was, at this time, in Perry County (west of Montgomery, in the Black Belt) living with a cousin; see Mary Hooper to D. B., April (n.d.), 1836, JDBH papers. June 10, 1836, in JDBH papers. There is no evidence that Hooper saw anything of the action involved in the Creek War, though he could hardly have avoided the general excitement.

rest of the whiskey, threw the tumbler down, and looked around to observe the effect of this brilliant exordium.

The effect was tremendous!

As Suggs paused, the narrator described the terrified women, hugging each other, "sobbing hysterically," rolling their eyes, and wringing their hands.

Hooper made Suggs self-conscious about his persuasion. After his pause let the crowd's emotions build, he returned to his work and set the stage for his election:

"My apinion," continued Simon, as he stooped to draw another tumbler of whiskey; "my apinion, folks, is this here. We ought to form a company right away, and make some man capting that aint afeard to fight – mind what I say, now – that-aint afeard-to-fight! – some sober, stiddy feller" – here he sipped a little from the tumbler – "that's a good hand to manage women and keep 'em from hollering – which they're a-needin' somethin' of the sort most damdibly, and I eech to git holt o' that one a-making the devilish racket in the corner, thar" – the noise in the corner was suddenly suspended – "and more'n all, a man that's acquainted with the country and the ways of the Injuns!" Having thus spoken, Suggs drank off the rest of the whiskey, threw himself into a military attitude, and awaited a reply.

As he stood before them, a chorus of men shouted "Suggs is the man," making him their Captain. Using only his talent and his instinct for "soft spots," Suggs prevailed.[55] While Suggs's voice controlled the crowd, however, the voice of the biographer/narrator cued the reader about Suggs's drinking and the women's fear, and it was he who noted the "owner of one entire negro." Like similar narrators in a long tradition of picaresque literature, the educated biographer enjoyed the action without getting involved.

Through the narrator, Hooper also drew attention to himself and his creativity, making his satire self-reflexive – as much about the manipulations of authorship as Suggs's speech. Because the biographer was trying to get a scoundrel elected to public office, it was clear from the start of the *Adventures* that the educated man was managing opinion like Suggs was. For most of the book, Hooper gave his biographer/narrator distance from Suggs, having him namelessly comment on the action, clearly bemused. Moreover, Hooper had appeared, also nameless, in his Preface, where he claimed he was "induced" to create his book. He did not name William Porter as the person who "induced" him (though he dedicated the book to Porter, identified as editor of the *Spirit of the Times*). And, while leaving the preface unsigned, Hooper put its "unpretending" place of origin at the bottom of the page: "La Fayette, Chambers County, Ala." Not until the last story did Hooper identify himself as the man who was selling Suggs to the public.[56]

There, in a wildly complicated, deftly executed exchange between Suggs and the narrator, Hooper collapsed the distance between his crude subject,

---

[55] The long scene from which both of these excerpts are taken in is *Simon Suggs*, 85–87.
[56] *Ibid.*, 6.

"A paleness more ghastly than that of death came over the widow's face as she heard the sentence. Falling to the earth, she grovelled at the feet of Captain Suggs."—*Page* 104.

FIGURE 2.1. Captain Simon Suggs.
After his oration about the dangers of war with the Creeks, Simon Suggs was elected captain of the Tallapoosa Volunteers, exploiting the fears of women like the one bowing before him in this illustration by F. O. C. Darley in *Adventures of Captain Simon Suggs* (1845), by Johnson Hooper. Courtesy of the W. S. Hoole Special Collections Library, The University of Alabama.

his readers in Alabama, and educated readers around the nation. He suggested that Suggs's speech, his own *East Alabamian*, and books like the *Adventures* were related forms of persuasion – all creative and all suspect. Throughout this final story, the bold juxtaposition of three modes of communication – speaking, handwriting, and print – established Hooper's complicity. "CONCLUSION – AUTOGRAPHIC LETTER FROM SUGGS" began innocently with the biographer telling his readers that he had received from Suggs a handwritten letter containing a new story. What followed, he claimed, was a "faithful transcript" except that he had "altered – or rather added" – punctuation. Suggs sent his "letter" to the "edditur of the eest Allybammyun, la Fait, chambers Kounty, Al.," and he addressed the biographer as "Johns," which was Hooper's nickname. With this stroke, Hooper united the narrator and himself, and this redefined persona began interjecting parenthetical comments into Suggs's letter.[57]

In effect, Hooper created a dialogue between the editor/narrator/biographer Johns (who was himself) and Suggs. He inserted into the transcript of Suggs's letter five parenthetical comments that fixed readers' attention on Johns. They referred to real people and actual publications. Once Johns puffed Porter's *Spirit of the Times*, and, twice, he advertised another of Porter's projects – the just-published collection *The Big Bear of Arkansas*, which also contained one of Hooper's stories. Johns addressed a fourth comment to F. O. C. Darley, the illustrator of both volumes. Then, having mentioned national publications, Hooper used Suggs's voice to comment on the local medium. Suggs implied that Johns was not entirely honest: he "useter be a nicety a dimmikrat as ever drinkt whiskey" but now he was a Whig editor. Because of Johns's dubious honesty, he could easily make Suggs's letter into a tall tale – "fix it up to the best advantage" for the voters. Johns's fifth parenthetical comment was a disgusted "(Tell your own story, Cap*ting!)*"[58] By giving the story to his lower-class scoundrel, Hooper winked at his readers and excused himself from what followed.

Letting Suggs tell his own story allowed Hooper to flaunt his racism. With Suggs speaking for him, Hooper repeated the epithet "nigger" ten times. In a story about Suggs floating paper dollars so worthless that "even the niggers knowd they warn't no 'count," Hooper made fun of black slaves and white southwesterners. Clearly, the tactic of having Suggs tell the story let Hooper sanitize himself a bit. Still, as Suggs finished his story, the rascal took a final swipe at Hooper: "Quit ritin lies for the d – d feddul whigs, and come back to your ole prinsippels." With that parting shot, Suggs closed his letter, and Johns returned to being narrator for the remaining lines of the *Adventures*, urging readers to vote for Suggs "at the polls!"[59] Hooper wanted his readers to see his cleverness and yet to know he laughed at himself, for he really was a partisan editor (who,

[57] Ibid., 141–142.
[58] Ibid.
[59] Ibid., 142–148. Suggs's misspelling of principles is obscured in the original text, so the letters "sip" are my best guess.

Self-Making in Southwestern Towns 57

in fact, had been a Democrat and drank a lot). Counting on the biases of readers everywhere, he pursued the racial and class agenda of a rising South.

In *Adventures*, Hooper asserted his mission as a writer. Offering himself as a model, he showed readers they could civilize their society and channel human energy through persuasion. And he suggested that the Southwest had great potential because it was a free society with slaves. Hooper deliberately mingled realities and scams, implicating readers of campaign biographies and citizens everywhere along with men like Suggs and authors like himself. When he dramatized the relationship between the narrator and his crude subject and obfuscated the issue of narrative control, he revealed himself as the genius behind his book. All along, he was writing for educated readers: townspeople who read the *East Alabamian*, the sporting subscribers to the *Spirit*, and the consumers who bought the *Adventures*. He asked them to accept the creative freedom of the Southwest – its energy and its dubious morality – and to see its relationship to a nation that would improve itself. He addressed northern and southern readers as if they had the same values, and he believed he was right.

Because he did it all with humor, however, he reduced the risk of personal embarrassment if his book should fail before the "Great Public." Happily for him, multiple printings marked a success. Hooper thought he was on his way to a self-determination earned by his talent, and he thought his sales indicated the popularity of his ideas. A short review in Edgar Allan Poe's journal *Aristidean* suggests the readers' response – albeit a Southern one – to the "true, indigenous humor" of Simon Suggs: "We sat down to this book quietly; read, laughed – read, and laughed again." Emboldened by success, Hooper moved within a year of his first book's publication to Alabama's new capital at Montgomery and began editing the *Alabama Journal*, soon the leading Whig paper in the state. He continued his efforts to mold public opinion when he began publishing other southern writers' books, the first a proslavery tract. Hooper was cultivating different readers – local and national – but his feet were planted firmly in the Old Southwest, and there was a chilling consistency in his vision of a middle-class society, with slaves.[60]

* * *

A growing mythology about the American West exaggerated its opportunities, but it is easy to appreciate the excitement these budding writers felt as they

---

[60] From the *Aristidean*, October 1845, 320–322. The following explanation is from a Web site: "This item is the fourth installment of the series 'Our Bookshelves,' printed in the *Aristidean*. W. D. Hull, 1941, attributes this installment (and installment III) to Poe;" from the Web site of the E. A. Poe Society of Baltimore, http://www.eapoe.org/works/criticsm/bkshlvs4.htm. Hooper was anxious about his reputation. In noting that the *Spirit* had reprinted "Taking the Census," Hooper dismissed Porter's praise by saying "we suspect that we know our own calibre pretty well – and we are small in the bore;" *East Alabamian*, September 23, 1843. I have described more fully the publishing of the proslavery tract in "Writers in the Old Southwest and the Commercialization of Letters," 487–490.

won repute. Caroline Hentz, Alexander Meek, and Johnson Hooper believed that self-determination was real in the Southwest because they were proving it. With flexible tactics, all three writers relied on their talents to establish themselves. Deploying literary skills where they were scarce, all of them appealed to the individuality of their readers and reminded them that they, too, possessed the power to make themselves. Confident that their values were useful and good, they intended to make the Southwest better.

If their experiences confirmed to Meek, Hentz, and Hooper that hard work and talent produced results, their interaction with local audiences suggests their faith in middle-class townspeople. Unlike planters, who commanded black slaves, these writers were demonstrating the power of persuasion to move free men and women. There probably was a smattering of planters in the Methodist church where Hentz appeared in Florence, perhaps more at Simms's speech in Tuscaloosa. But at Hentz's school, at the banquet in Tuscaloosa, and among the readers of the Lafayette *East Alabamian*, middle-class people were managing themselves. When these three writers addressed the public, they demonstrated their confidence that educated southwesterners could make wise choices about the shape of their society. Simms had suggested that patriarchal principles should organize the Southwest, and Basil Manly adopted them. As Meek, Hentz, and Hooper flattered, criticized, cajoled, and poked fun, they fully expected their audiences to determine their own futures.

They had little interest in people who, as they saw it, did not want to make themselves. In this early work, Meek, Hentz, and Hooper barely mentioned slavery, although it was certainly relevant to their public goals. Still identified with the North, Hentz had little to say about slaves; Hooper included a few in the first tales that he wrote for the *East Alabamian*, and he added more when he made the Suggs stories into a book; Meek acknowledged the centrality of slavery to southwestern society and then moved on, as if it were hardly worth discussing. Significantly, however, none of these writers paid much attention to wealthy planters, either. They concentrated, instead, on those white people who improved themselves through individual initiative. At the center of their vision was, as Meek put it, the "true, generous, unflinching, uncompromising, right-onward scholar," his image of the self-made man. They did not ignore the farming people of the Southwest – white or black – but they did not identify with any of them.

Where social relations were in flux and individuals were supposedly responsible for themselves, writers worried about their status. Hentz saw the seedy side of musters; her diary's sarcasm about the reluctance of men to volunteer until they were "plied" with whiskey anticipated the drinking in Hooper's sketch of the Tallapoosa Volunteers. Neither writer liked drunken commoners. Hentz relished the applause at the Methodist church where she celebrated the militia, but she felt disgust at a less-refined event with a similar purpose. A woman with a "life-giving, self-annihilating principle" might elevate the feeling of frontier people, but it was no easy task for either male or female because too much hung on the character of the audience. Like the celebrants

Self-Making in Southwestern Towns 59

at the banquet for Simms or Hooper drawing Suggs, Hentz knew there must be a close fit between speaker and listeners. When one addressed a diverse audience, finding the fit could tax the spirit.

As much as Meek, Hentz, and Hooper valued their "uncompromising" independence, they were uneasy about being judged. In revealing terms, Hentz called public scrutiny "bondage of the spirit," and she saw that neighbors gossiped about her boldness. Meek joked when comparing his anxieties about *The Southron* to those of a debutante, and his image of a brave pioneer suggested greater self-reliance. Hooper preempted the attention of the "Great Public" to his shortcomings by referring to a "community unpretending in its tastes," and even the masterful Suggs "looked around to observe the effect" of his "brilliant exordium." Writers walked a fine line between self-assertion and self-promotion, between expressing themselves and currying favor.

Facing that challenge in person was a qualitatively different experience than approaching readers through print, which ignored the nonreading poor. Highly literate people in a society that still relied on orality, Meek, Hooper, and Hentz distrusted the illiterate. They understood print to be a unique communication – "her one link" Hentz called it – that opened up a larger world than the one they encountered daily. Meek compared people who scrutinized a debutante in person with the critics of his magazine. He complained that newspaper readers granted him "no actual existing identity" when he had to write what his party expected. When he failed to sell his literary magazine, however, he learned that the market for print had its own kind of dependency.

More perceptively than Hentz or Meek, Hooper saw psychological implications in print. He recognized that words could alter what people thought of as reality. He also realized that power flowed from speaker to audience or writer to reader, and back again, and that gave him pause. Believing that persuasion could be deployed as readily for evil as for good, he knew that books reached further than speech. In his phony biography, Hooper suggested that the power of persuasion could corrupt anyone who used it – Amos Kendall, or Simon Suggs, or Johns Hooper – or anyone who felt its force – American voters, Suggs's Volunteers, or the readers of the "eest Allybammyun." If the same predatory "human natur'" lay behind both "mother wit" and "book-larning," what might the future hold? When he questioned the trustworthiness of print, Hooper interrogated the foundation of modernity. Without answers, the journalist hoped to muster rational men behind a rising South, but he had glimpsed a serious problem.

In order to make themselves, Hooper, Meek, and Hentz exploited the anxieties of southwestern people about a modernizing world. Regardless of its vulgarity, Hooper's book touted civilization as much as Hentz's poetry or Meek's orations. In *Simon Suggs*, Hooper achieved the same objective as in his newspaper's reporting of La Taste's lecture on music: he asked readers to be proud of their refinement. And his relentless condescension was not unlike Hentz's fleeting reference to the "harsher traits of the aboriginal character" or Meek's anger about the "moles" who sneered at genius. Meek, Hentz, and Hooper wished to encourage civilization. It was no coincidence that the La Fayette Society, where Hentz appeared, and the town of Lafayette, where Hooper lived, bore the same Frenchman's name.[61] The American landscape was studded with inflated names – Troy, or Athens, or Rome – that conjured up a splendid past to suggest a glorious future. The Southwest was extreme because it was so very raw, but it was not unique.

As Hooper first discovered, and other writers would soon find, northern readers shared their interests, slavery notwithstanding. Just as Hentz learned that her middle-class values resonated with southwestern audiences, Hooper realized that his hopes and fears about the Southwest were as funny to readers around the country as they were to the readers of the *East Alabamian*. Self-determination was a core ideal, equally applicable to the middle classes in the North, South, East, and West. Both the opportunities for self-reliance and its strains were a national preoccupation. When they made themselves models, writers exposed themselves, revealing the mentality that committed middle-class people across America to the project of self-determination.

Hooper, Meek, and Hentz bound themselves to their society, relying on it to affirm their self-images as creative, intelligent people. In their search for readers, they communicated about the purposes and possibilities of their world. They no doubt felt responsible for what they said, but they required approval and they found it. This meant that they, like Suggs, kept their eyes on the chorus around them. One by one, they found readers outside of the Southwest. When that happened, the sectional implications of their roles surfaced, with scary results that Hooper barely glimpsed in 1845. Writing was, however, only part of what bound authors to their communities. They had unusual talents, but their ideas were rooted in experiences common to other middle-class people. Had that not been so, they would have had few readers, anywhere.

---

[61] All of the quoted passages in this concluding analysis appear earlier in this chapter. Simon Suggs's phonetic misspelling of La Fayette as "la Fait" suggests that Hooper thought the pretensions of his town as amusing as the inability of ordinary people to pronounce the Frenchman's name. Hooper called attention to the mispronunciation because it was, in fact, the way the town's name was (and is) said in Alabama, where it sounds like le-fay-it, with stress on the middle syllable. Shields, "Introduction," *Simon Suggs*, xi–xii.

3

The Domestic Foundations of Self-Determination

> The cabin is a real home; the fields
> Blossom with foreign vines; the babbling rill,
> Familiar, answers now the prattling tongues,
> And laves the uncovered feet, of boys and girls
> Native and destined round about to see
> The city spread its paved avenues ...
>
> <div align="right">William Russell Smith, <i>The Uses of Solitude</i></div>

Like the novels of James Fenimore Cooper or the histories of Francis Parkman, southwestern literature had frontier heroes. The rising South's writers knew, however, that families made civilization. William Smith acknowledged it when he praised the "hardy pioneer," Daniel Boone, in the poem *The Uses of Solitude* (1860). Boone was the "monarch in the wilderness," while his wife, a "great spirited woman and American," followed him "for weal or woe" to a simple cabin. Smith saw the future when he scanned the past, for their barefooted children would "see / The city spread its paved streets." The writer admitted that men's adventures produced "woe" as well as "weal." But his tribute to self-reliance in *The Uses of Solitude* was of a piece with most American literature. Families formed a backdrop to the feats of self-determined men.[1]

---

[1] Smith, *The Uses of Solitude* (Tuscaloosa: Printed for the Alabama Alpha of the Phi Beta Kappa Society of the University of Alabama at Tuskaloosa, 1860), 30–31. Among the many scholars who have treated, in broad terms, the relationship between self-determined manhood and families are Cindy Weinstein, *Family, Kinship, and Sympathy in Nineteenth-Century American Literature* (Cambridge: Cambridge University Press, 2004); Andrew Burstein, *Sentimental Democracy: The Evolution of America's Romantic Self-image* (New York: Hill and Wang, 1999). More focused on peculiarly southern relations are Stephen W. Berry, *All That Makes a Man: Love and Ambition in the Civil War South* (New York: Oxford University Press, 2003); Bertram Wyatt-Brown, *Southern Honor: Ethics and Behavior in the Old South* (New York: Oxford University Press, 1982). A work that explores the tensions between aggressive manhood and more modern conceptions (and treats both North and South) is Amy S. Greenberg, *Manifest Manhood and Antebellum American Empire* (New York: Cambridge University Press, 2005).

The stories of Smith, Joseph Baldwin, Augusta Evans, and Albert Pickett dramatize the relationship between individual accomplishment and family life in the rising South. All of them expressed middle-class ideals and thought families should teach independence, but they learned these values differently. Like Johnson Hooper, Smith and Evans came from troubled families, and they learned self-reliance the hard way. Like Alexander Meek and Caroline Hentz, Baldwin grew up in middle-class security, and his family taught him to balance self-interest with cooperation. In contrast, Pickett was raised with wealth, though his father was a pioneer who had advanced himself in Alabama's society. Each of these writers had some advantages, but they all expected to make their way through individual initiative. Striving was their common creed.

Several features distinguished writers' families from the patriarchal model that William Gilmore Simms had recommended in Tuscaloosa. Their families pooled resources and shared them in a roughly egalitarian way (Pickett, not surprisingly, was something of an exception). Some fathers helped their children, but many children helped their parents, brothers, sisters, and in-laws; and cousins leaned on one another. In addition, writers sought marriages that were partnerships in mobility. They tried to choose mates with backgrounds similar to theirs; spouses supported each other and shared responsibilities. Finally, writers sought and received emotional satisfaction from families in which relative equality promoted interdependence. They recorded – in letters and in literature – shared affection and mutual attempts to find happiness. Writers' families aided them more often by providing safety nets than by restraining their choices. Families sheltered strivers who wanted to belong but also wanted to choose their associations. In the rising South, families abetted middle-class aspirations.[2]

---

[2] I am drawing here from evidence gleaned from my reconstruction of writers' families, for there is little scholarly work on town-dwelling families in Alabama or the larger Southwest. For comparative purposes, the most useful works are Mary P. Ryan, *Cradle of the Middle Class: The Family in Oneida County, New York, 1790–1865* (Cambridge: Cambridge University Press, 1981); Stuart M. Blumin, *The Emergence of the Middle Class: Social Experience in the American City, 1760–1900* (Cambridge: Cambridge University Press, 1989); Anne Rose, *Victorian America and the Civil War* (New York: Cambridge University Press, 1992). Works that are more directly relevant to Alabama are Joan Cashin, *A Family Venture: Men and Women on the Southern Frontier*; Lisa C. Tolbert, *Constructing Townscapes: Space and Society in Antebellum Tennessee* (Chapel Hill: University of North Carolina Press, 1999); Jane Turner Censer, *North Carolina Planters and Their Children, 1800–1860*; Jonathan Daniel Wells, *The Origins of the Southern Middle Class, 1800–1861* (Chapel Hill: University of North Carolina Press, 2004). I have learned from Steven Ruggles, *Prolonged Connections: The Rise of the Extended Family in Nineteenth-Century England and America* (Madison: University of Wisconsin Press, 1987), which analyzes a variety of family patterns and finds that middle-class families were very likely to rely on kin and co-resident relatives, in contrast to the stereotype that large families were an older pattern associated with the peasantry. A fine study of planter families in Alabama that emphasizes the impact of modern patterns is Ann Williams Boucher [Webb], "Wealthy Planter Families in Nineteenth-Century Alabama" (Ph.D. dissertation, University of Connecticut, 1978).

Because Smith, Baldwin, Pickett, and Evans believed that self-determined individuals were shaped in childhood, families were central to their long-term hopes for their society. When they found faults in it, they often urged reform through family life. In this, they were influenced by an idealization of families they shared with middle-class Americans who never saw the Southwest. Anyone who read newspapers, magazines, or popular fiction knew this ideal. At its heart was romantic love, which made the creation of families a matter of free choice. Wives deferred to husbands, and they supposedly chose roles according to their natures. Children were to be obedient, but parents – especially mothers – guided through persuasion more than physical punishment. They bred independence by teaching self-control and work habits. Although, in business, fathers pursued self-interest, sympathy with their families checked their self-aggrandizement. Like the concept of self-determination, this model of the family merged economic and social ethics, and it was supported by religion. With its insistence on voluntary ties, it was supposed to nurture autonomous individuals and social progress.[3]

Geographical mobility tested these assumptions, for families stretched, and sometimes broke, with the drive for self-determination. Nonetheless, Alabama's writers believed that migration let out-of-luck rich folks like Evans's parents recover or a middle-class man like Baldwin improve himself. In 1834, George Hooper explained to his brother why he wanted their younger sibling Johnson to join him: "if he can be made steady" he will advance in Alabama, where "a fluent tongue & abundant assurance invariably succeed with any modicum of talent." Writers' families sometimes suffered, however, when men pursued the main chance. In search of pleasure and literary work, Alexander Meek left his five younger siblings in Tuscaloosa. His brother Samuel wrote a sister that "from Brother, we hardly *ever hear*." The neglect pained Sam, who complained that "for the family, if he has any affection, he has a very bad way of showing it."[4] Sam hoped Alex would marry (preferably well) and settle down instead of chasing literary fame.

Openly marrying for money was as noxious in the Southwest as it was elsewhere in the United States, but love was not incompatible with economic and social motives. Almost all of Alabama's writers chose spouses who were as well off as they were, and most of them improved their prospects with marriage. This was not uncommon among ambitious people. Whatever Abraham Lincoln's attraction to Mary Todd, he surely knew that her prominent family might be useful. Jeremiah Clemens married the daughter of his father's business partner – a girl Meek rejected because she was not rich. But Clemens's father had more money than Meek's, and Jere could afford to marry the girl he adored. Nearly penniless, Hooper married the daughter of a prosperous farmer; Mary

---

[3] For exploration of these ideas, see sources in previous note, esp. Rose, *Victorian America and the Civil War*, and Ryan, *Cradle of the Middle Class*.
[4] George to De Berniere Hooper, October 3, 1834, JDBH Papers, UNC; Samuel Meek to Dr. J. M. Meek, October 25, 1850, in Samuel Mills Meek, Jr., Papers, UA.

brought to the match a female slave and her father's legal business. Not long thereafter, Hooper satirized conniving men who used women to gain wealth.[5]

For families to be incubators of freedom, adults had to cooperate by choice. As was normal, males controlled economic resources in writers' families, but they preferred to rely on persuasion rather than command. To be sure, appeals to reason and sympathy sometimes disguised self-interest. So Sam Meek faulted Alex's lack of affection instead of his failure to send his family money. And Smith characterized Boone's wife as a "great-spirited woman and American" for following her husband to the wilds, as if she helped choose their destination. Accustomed to controlling his slaves, Pickett barely hid his desire to dominate his family's choices. Quite sincerely, however, he assured his wife that his goal was their "domestic happiness." In spite of inequalities, middle-class standards emphasized voluntary relations. These writers preached them as the source of harmony and tried to behave accordingly.

Baldwin, Smith, Pickett, and Evans penned stories of individual accomplishment with their own families in mind. Blessed with families that seem actually to have combined self-determination with responsibility, Baldwin praised manly independence and mocked men who let it hurt their families. After a harrowing childhood, Smith was always edgy about autonomy, and he wrote a pensive story about the immorality a haughty family taught a small boy. In his family and in his history of the Southwest, Pickett uneasily mixed habits of command with middle-class values of work and domesticity. Evans's proud family nurtured her talent, but her father's risk taking limited her chances; and she struggled to reconcile self-determination with feminine inequality in her novels. Observing the inevitable tensions between individual autonomy and collective welfare, these writers suggested that middle-class families could merge them if they really tried.

Families reflected both the similarities and the differences between middle-class southwesterners and other Americans. Writers shared a widespread turn toward more democratic and egalitarian relations, and they thought middle-class families represented progress. They described the problems within families as valuable lessons, insisting that challenges taught individuals to be self-reliant, just as the wilderness made Daniel Boone a hero. In part, writers reasoned backward from their personal success to conclude that obstacles were instructive. Like white Americans in the Northwest, they knew the violence of the frontier and the instability of migration, and they saw those passing away. But only southwesterners combined these pioneering experiences with slavery, and it tainted their families in subtle ways. Writers preferred to minimize the influence of slavery on free people, but, all the while, the psychological investments they made in slaveholding families tied them firmly to the rising South.

---

[5] I dealt with patterns of family relations for seven male writers in "A Social History of Antebellum Alabama Writers," *Alabama Review* (July 1989): 163–191; a table comparing the status of writers to that of their bride's families at the time of marriage, 178–179.

A MYTH-MAKING INDIVIDUAL AND THE CHANGING FAMILY

Joseph Baldwin's *The Flush Times in Alabama and Mississippi* was a myth-making classic of antebellum literature.[6] It made the erosion of tradition by southwestern freedom an evolutionary phenomenon – a sign of progress – and it captured the drive for autonomy in unforgettable images. *Flush Times* depicted its author as the quintessential self-made man, born to a good Virginia family but impelled by economic necessity to make his way alone in the West. Baldwin wrote as if migration separated him from family and friends, but, in fact, his family had helped him advance in Alabama. Mediating between the disruptions of mobility and the comfort of close relationships, the Baldwins encouraged autonomy and interdependence at the same time. The good humor and gentle irony of *Flush Times* grew from a sturdy and flexible familial foundation. Exuding confidence, Baldwin suggested that self-determination flourished in the rising South without harming families and with a mere trace of slavery's influence.

Baldwin grew up in a family that was comfortable but not wealthy, and he learned a steadfast will to achieve. He was born in 1815 in the Shenandoah Valley of Virginia, where his father had founded the first textile mills and his mother sometimes taught school. She encouraged his talents, and Joe got a good foundation for classical learning; but the family could not afford college, so Joe read law with his prominent uncle, Judge Briscoe Baldwin (to whom he dedicated *Flush Times*), and his close cousin, Alexander H. H. Stuart, a future Whig congressman. Joe wrote a little for small-town newspapers, one belonging to his brother, got involved in politics, then, just as he turned twenty-one, migrated westward with Alexander Garber, a close friend. Joe's brothers, Cyrus and Cornelius, followed him to Alabama. Cyrus briefly worked as a printer in Tuscaloosa, where he became a favorite member of Alexander Meek's convivial circle before moving on to Mississippi. Cornelius returned to Virginia.[7]

[6] Baldwin, *The Flush Times of Alabama and Mississippi: A Series of Sketches*, intro. and notes by James H. Justus (Baton Rouge: Louisiana State University Press, 1987). Justus emphasizes Baldwin's construction of a transcendent masculine identity as the center of *Flush Times*. See also Justus's fine discussions of Baldwin's work in *Fetching the Old Southwest: Humorous Writing from Longstreet to Twain* (Columbia: University of Missouri Press, 2004). An insightful study that discusses Baldwin with Hooper is John Mayfield, *Counterfeit Gentlemen: Manhood and Humor in the Old South* (Gainesville: University Press of Florida, 2009), 48–66.

[7] The most important information on Baldwin's life is in the Lester-Gray Collection of Documents filmed from material loaned by Robert M. Lester (film made by the New York Public Library in 1849), which is available on microfilm. The Lester-Gray Collection not only contains Baldwin family letters, but a biographical sketch by Joseph's brother Cornelius that draws from other letters no longer available. Samuel B. Stewart, "Joseph Glover Baldwin" (Ph.D. dissertation, Vanderbilt University, 1942) makes careful use of these biographical materials, but there is no full biography in published form. Cornelius attributes Joe's intellect and moral balance to his mother in his manuscript remembrances of Joe in the Lester-Gray Collection. Three studies that explore Baldwin's ideas in some depth are Adam L. Tate, *Conservatism and Southern*

With and without his family's help, Baldwin began to prosper. Riding the legal circuits of the Alabama-Mississippi Black Belt, and getting to know Alabama's capital himself, Joe settled at Gainesville, a river port town about sixty miles south of Tuscaloosa. There, in January of 1840, he brought his bride Sidney White. Joe's younger sister Cornelia moved in with them in 1844. By 1850, the Baldwins had five children, they had slowly gained a modest prosperity, and they had joined the ranks of small slaveholders. His family continued to advance Joe's prospects, and he returned the help as he could.

Baldwin's marriage to Sidney White increased the importance of his family. She brought Joe helpful local connections, for her father had been a circuit judge in northern Alabama before becoming a small-scale planter in Talladega. She also strengthened her husband's ties to Virginia. Joe told Sidney his mother was pleased "that you come of a good family, even connected with the Baker-Briscoe-Baldwin family," though he added his mild disapproval: "Heaven help the old lady's family pride which I have not reverence enough to regard as anything but weakness." More important than her connections, however, was Sidney's role in a relationship that helped Joe seek fame and money without losing his emotional center. She was, in that sense, a perfect example of the virtues of domesticity in middle-class households. A eulogist once wrote of Baldwin that "had he been less happy at home, he would have been more renowned abroad," a remarkable claim about a man whose public reputation epitomized self-making.[8] But the Baldwins seem to have been unusually happy.

They were both lovers and companions – a model of middle-class ideals. From the beginning of their courtship, Joe shared his ambitions with Sidney. In letters, he recognized her intellectuality and constantly expressed his love, signing one letter "yours wholly and soully." He also acknowledged his faults with the kind of openness that often bespeaks security. A few weeks before their wedding, Joe joked with Sidney about his egotism. After she scolded him for not writing, he expressed surprise at her "premature perversion." "I always suspected that you would turn out to be a shrew," he claimed, "but thought that your characteristic tact would cause you to postpone the

---

Intellectuals, 1789–186: Liberty, Tradition, and the Good Society (Columbia: University of Missouri Press, 2005); John M. Grammer, *Pastoral and Politics in the Old South* (Baton Rouge: Louisiana State University Press, 1996); Philip D. Beidler, *First Books: The Printed Word and Cultural Formation in Early Alabama* (Tuscaloosa: University of Alabama Press, 1999). All three scholars (Tate, a historian, and Grammer and Beidler, literary scholars) find Baldwin more conservative than I do, though Tate sees Baldwin diverging from his conservative predecessors.

[8] Joseph Baldwin to Sidney White, September 20, 1839; eulogy is from an unidentified newspaper clipping dated October 9, 1867; both in Lester-Gray Collection. The family connections between Baldwin and Sidney had political significance, too, as her uncle was U.S. Senator Ephriam Foster of Tennessee, a Whig who had just resigned rather than accepting instructions from the state legislature (he would serve again, 1843–1845). Sidney's brother Alexander would become a U.S. Congressman (a Whig in the 32d Congress, 1851–1853, and a Republican in the 43d Congress, 1873–1874).

manifestation of your stiffnecked tendencies until you were legally entitled to henpeck your devoted slave, whose meekness of disposition you have so long imposed upon."[9] Baldwin knew he was not meek, and he certainly did not think himself slavish. Instead of shrewish wife and henpecked husband, he expected they would be relative equals.

As this same letter continued, Baldwin made more fun of himself, shifting quickly from the imagery of slavery to Christian selflessness. "Ah, it is indeed a misfortune to be humble and lowly in spirit," he insisted; "from this self-deprecating and self-denying principle I have derived most of the evils that have thronged my path through life." Light-hearted self-criticism was a signature pattern in Baldwin's writing. He was eager to achieve, but he wanted to restrain his selfishness. Instead of worrying too much about what other people thought, he laughed with self-awareness. A slight man, Baldwin rarely commented on his appearance, although at thirty-five he wrote Sidney that he was pleased when the exercise of swimming made him more "robust" because it offset the "effeminacy" of his face, which appeared "delicate" in his youth. In frank exchanges with Sidney, Joe used humor to address his imperfections.[10]

Baldwin had learned to take his familial obligations seriously in a home where cooperation was required. His male relatives depended on talents and family connections rather than inheritance, while family responsibility bound generations of striving men and women together. Certainly the Baldwins made distinctions between the sexes, but reciprocity, more than authority, characterized their relations. From several homes, Joe and Sidney provided encouragement, advice, and material support to other family members for twenty-five years. When the couple married, Sidney's family had given her a female slave, their first servant, but two years later the Whites were in financial trouble. Sidney's mother was teaching school; her father borrowed money from Joe.[11] When no single person's resources were adequate, this family shared.

Baldwin knew that family responsibilities constrained his ambition. Writing Sidney in 1843, when the death of his father required him to send "a good deal of money" to Virginia, Joe did not ask Sidney's permission, but he explained why their sacrifice was important to his siblings. Joe's younger brother, Cyrus,

---

[9] Closing in Joe to Sidney White, August 11, 1839; Joe to "Dearest Sid," New Year's Eve, 1839, only weeks before their marriage; both in Lester-Gray Collection.

[10] Joseph Baldwin to Sidney White, December 31, 1839; comments about his delicate features in Joseph to Sidney Baldwin, July 26, 1850; another love letter written just after the birth of their first child refers to Sidney's "poetic temperament;" Joseph to Sidney Baldwin, December 21, 1840; all in Lester-Gray Collection. My interpretation here might be compared to that of Steven M. Stowe, *Intimacy and Power in the Old South: Ritual in the Lives of the Planters* (Baltimore: Johns Hopkins University Press, 1987), esp. 121, although, again, the emphasis there is on planter families. Baldwin's brother Cornelius notes that Joe was so nervous that he bit his fingernails all of his life, which seems to suggest both his nervous energy and an inattention to appearances; biographical sketch in Lester-Gray Collection.

[11] Sidney's mother wrote her about her teaching in February 1841 (letter incorrectly dated 1840), and John White, her father, wrote Baldwin asking for a loan on February 25, 1842, expressing his "feelings of mortification and distress"; both in Lester-Gray Collection.

needed money to buy books, his younger sister Cornelia required an education, and Cornelius, his older brother, was "in dire straits." In addition, "sacred and imperative duty" required him to honor a large debt his father had made. (The brother of Baldwin's friend Alex Garber was married to Joe's older sister and had loaned $2,500 to Joe's father but was now "desperate.") Joe wrote Sidney forthrightly: "I thought, with a foolish presumption ... that I was on the high road to fortune; but these events have thrown me back and will keep me back."[12] Baldwin's eventual success was built on a resilient network that checked self-aggrandizement while promoting self-determination.

Baldwin's remarkable emotional poise pervaded *Flush Times*, which was a genteel effort at self-promotion in the form of stories about other lawyers. He began writing to boost his reputation, but making money also figured into his plans. Although his first stories appeared in the Richmond-based *Southern Literary Messenger*, he immediately expanded them into a book for the national market in 1853. Recalling the Southwest's boom days, Baldwin starkly contrasted East and West, placing himself on a middle ground that was more psychological than geographic, somewhere between Virginia gentlemen and southwestern rowdies. Consistently ironic, Baldwin praised Virginians for their oratory, sociability, and hospitality and mocked their ineptitude at practical living; he celebrated the creativity of southwestern lawyers and ridiculed their constant battles to outdo one another by any means. Baldwin judged the situation from the perspective of one who survived flush times, suggesting that he was one of the "modest, unobtrusive, retiring men of worth and character" whose talents let him climb to the top of the southwestern pile.[13]

Baldwin neglected families in *Flush Times* because he made the Southwest a crucible of manly independence. He highlighted the absence of families: "where else," he wrote, "can a man get this self-reliance so well as in a new country, where he is thrown upon his own resources; where his only friends are his talents; where those only are above him whose talents are above his; where there is no *prestige* of rank, or ancestry, or wealth, or past reputation – and no family influence, or dependants, or patrons."[14] In this environment, men made themselves, or they did not survive. Foolishly inept aristocrats with poor self-control littered the pages of *Flush Times*, their complacent disregard for practicality dooming them to failure. Some moved on to Texas, others returned to Virginia, and still others hung on in one or another state of dependence. Baldwin made hard-working lawyers – men like himself – intellectual pioneers who were fully self-determined, rarely mentioning the families behind them.

---

[12] Joseph to Sidney Baldwin, February 9, 1843, Lester-Gray Collection. Baldwin's emphasis on familial responsibilities might be read as highly traditional, which his language "sacred and imperative" suggests. But, if so, such elements of family responsibility disappeared very slowly, for bourgeois families were, as Mary Ryan suggests, at the heart of middle-class life.
[13] *Flush Times*, 89.
[14] Ibid., 228.

Baldwin believed that the Southwest swept patriarchy away. In a brilliant little sketch within "How the Times Served the Virginians," Baldwin revealed the depth and breadth of the social changes he experienced, and he folded a man's family into the story. Major Wormly was "the noblest of the noble, the best of the good" Virginians of the "old school." The Major's happy Alabama plantation contained a cheerful wife and four wonderful daughters ("not beauties, but good housewife girls"). And Wormly was so benevolent to his slaves that "it was enough to convert an abolitionist." But he overdid his liberality, entertaining anyone who came within sight of his home and signing friends' notes at the drop of a hat. For a time, his kin helped, and the "fortunate death of a few Aunts, for whom the girls were named," delayed his bankruptcy.[15] When the inevitable occurred, the Major was too honorable to repudiate his debts, and he faced utter ruin.

Baldwin's feckless patriarch was saved, however, by the female members of his family and by his human property. While the Wormly women took over the household economy, an acquaintance relieved the Major of all slaves but his "house-servants" and put them to work. Baldwin joked that the Major's "heart pained him at the thought of the negroes going off," but he ridiculed slaves when the Major "consoled himself with the idea of the discipline and exercise being good for the health of sundry of them who had contracted sedentary disease." Without slave labor, Wormly converted his home into a tavern, completely transforming agricultural property into a business. He simply "put up a sign, and three weeks afterwards, you couldn't have told that any thing had happened." His daughters "were as cheerful, as bustling, as light-hearted as ever, and seemed to think of the duties of hostesses a mere bagatelles." In the new regime, the Major's job was telling stories about Virginia – the same ones over and over, "and not one of them under the legal age of twenty-one."[16] His failure to work rendered him irrelevant.

Baldwin's story asserted a twisted work ethic for the rising South. He insisted that "if the Major had worked his negroes as he had those anecdotes," he could have paid his debts. But Baldwin did not explain how slavery fit within a work ethic because he observed white people. The working Wormly women tolerated the Virginian's idleness and laughed at stories they had heard "at least a thousand times."[17] With women hiding his helplessness, the Major only masqueraded as head of the household, yet Baldwin's humor revealed the man's dependence with amusement instead of scorn. In the modernizing Southwest, men and women revised traditional roles. People had to work – women as well as men. Skimming quickly over the hard labor of enslaved people and ignoring how their status as Wormly's chattel altered slaves' families, Baldwin ruefully acknowledged that women paid for men's incompetence.

[15] Ibid., 100–103.
[16] Ibid., 104–105.
[17] Ibid., 105.

On the whole, though, he saw constructive change in an environment that required self-reliance.

For all of his indifference to slaves, Baldwin made the Wormly women perfectly at ease in their new circumstances, and his humor reflected his confidence that he and his family would succeed. With his unrelenting determination to make himself, Baldwin left Sidney for long periods of time to care for their family, but he believed she shared his hopes. When he traveled to Richmond and New York to market *Flush Times*, his letters detailed his adventures. He described the gifts he was buying: "some jewelry" and books "for all of us": a good sampling of English and American writers from William Thackeray, who had praised Baldwin's stories in the *Messenger*, to Nathaniel Hawthorne and Henry Wadsworth Longfellow. Once he slipped, describing a former sweetheart. When Sidney bristled, he assured her distress was unwarranted, for she could not make a tragedy out of an affectionate relationship in their "railway, sausage-chopping, machine age."[18] Like work, marriage evolved under beneficial change.

Baldwin sought genteel reputation – "to claim my place as modestly as becomes a diffident man, but firmly." Yet he also tried to persuade Sidney that his aspirations served his family as well as him. "Money," he wrote critically, "is the only title to respect or it is certainly the only sure dependence against the ills of life." This was a pragmatic moralist's conclusion, one dictated by "this selfish world." Baldwin knew that the "scramble and scratching to keep up appearances" was not independence. When he wrote Sidney about the favorable reception of his book, he assured her that he was not caught up in the game. Pleased to achieve literary repute, he purred that "I am quite a lion – at least a cat."[19] The humorous juxtaposition was typical; he shared his pride but deflated his puffery, certain she would appreciate both meanings.

Baldwin knew the difficulty of gaining economic autonomy, but he also benefitted from a new kind of emotional dependence in which men and women shared the effort to get ahead. *Flush Times* became more popular than anything before written from the Old Southwest. Like *Simon Suggs*, it linked the region's opportunity with individual drive, intelligence, and ingenuity, but it lacked the undercurrents of fear that marked Hooper's testament to western freedom. More persuasively than most southwestern fiction,

---

[18] He describes the gifts, Joseph to Sidney Baldwin, July 30, 1853 (and wrote earlier about bringing her a watch, or, if she preferred, dedicating the book to her, which seems to have been a joke; July 12, 1853); funny and affectionate letter about their differences over his former sweetheart, Joseph to Sidney Baldwin, August 4, 1853; all in Lester-Gray Collection. In his second letter from Richmond (the first, unfortunately, described the former sweetheart), Baldwin wrote that Thackeray had visited with *SLM* editor John R. Thompson, who showed him Baldwin's work and told Baldwin that the Englishman thought it "of the right stuff"; July 5, 1853, in *ibid*.

[19] His modest ambition, Joseph to Sidney Baldwin, August 3, 1853; the importance of money and scrambling, Joseph to Sidney Baldwin, December 11, 1853; a lion, Joseph to Sidney Baldwin, December 30, 1853; all in *ibid*.

Flush Times connected individual self-determination to progress, celebrating middle-class virtues and what they could achieve. Baldwin's private life suggested that southwestern families might harness individualism for collective good, and perhaps he thought that slavery could be domesticated, too. But those were not his main concerns. When Baldwin asked "where else" but in the Southwest could a man make himself, he knew that families like his were important, but it was the end result that fascinated him.

A LONELY STRIVER

Although no writer in the rising South more endlessly preached self-determination, William Smith's experience demonstrated how much instability could blight the family life and scar the psyche of a talented man. Born to privilege, Smith was forced to acquire independent habits as a child because his family collapsed around him. He worked steadily to recover from their problems, and ultimately he did. In the process, however, he acquired profound anxieties about dependence and a formidable urge to exercise self-control. Smith displayed his scars in a self-revelatory story that exposed the corrosive effect of slavery on a child's development – the single most negative description of southwestern family life among any that these eight writers produced. Smith realized that extreme inequality harmed both dominant and subordinate people, yet his concern was always for the character of free white men rather than black slaves. Fearing that southern families might breed dangerous habits of mastery rather than the healthy psychology of self-determination, he advised readers to avoid the threat.

Smith's family history was unusually troubled, even for the Southwest. Born to comfort in Kentucky in 1815, young William's good fortune began crumbling shortly after his birth when his father died from wounds received in Indian warfare. Following a quarrel with her husband's family, Smith's mother Elizabeth took her "ample" inheritance, including slaves, and fled to Alabama with her six children. They lived well for a few years in Huntsville, near her brother, but when he died Elizabeth moved the family to Tuscaloosa, where, when William was eight, she, too, died.[20] In a crude village, the orphans were scattered among several families. Smith recalled that guardians robbed them

---

[20] Two versions of this story concur in the general outline. See the biographical sketch "William Russell Smith," by Thomas McAdory Owen in *The Library of Southern Literature*, Edwin Alderman et al., eds., 13 vols. (Atlanta: Martin and Hoyt, 1908–1913), 11: 4985–4986, and the biography by Smith's daughter, Anne Easby-Smith, *William Russell Smith of Alabama* (Philadelphia: Dolphin Press, 1931), 13–15. Eliza Smith died owing debts of $556.84 and holding assets of $254.12, according to the Orphans' Court Minutes, 1824–1831, July 7, 1824, Probate Records, Tuscaloosa County Court House. Because the record is from the year after her death, it may not reflect the slaves William later recalled being lost to neglect by the putative guardians of the children. There is no scholarly study of Smith, who deserves more attention than he has received. The children of William and Wilhemine carried the name Easby-Smith at the will of their paternal grandfather.

of their remaining resources and let their slaves run away. William was so abused that he, too, fled, returning only to live with his only brother, Sidney, who was not yet a man. Still, when a member of their father's family came to return them to Kentucky, the children chose to stay in Tuscaloosa, where adolescent siblings supported the others. When his older sister married a tailor, William worked in his shop.

Faced with a situation that demanded self-help, William made an impressive recovery, dazzling his schoolmasters with his precocious intellect and attracting the patronage of a prominent attorney who sent him to the university and helped him become a lawyer. Joining the convivial circle of local literati, he published his first long poem, *College Musings*, while he was still in school, and he gained repute as a writer. At twenty, Smith set up legal practice in Greensboro, just south of Tuscaloosa in the Black Belt. Law was briefly interrupted when he enlisted as a Captain in the Creek War. But Smith soon faced more tragedy. His beloved brother, Sidney, who had volunteered for the Texas War for Independence, was killed in the massacre at Goliad when Mexican General Santa Anna had several hundred unarmed American prisoners shot. Eager for revenge, William recruited volunteers to join the war in Texas, but at its end his company was in Mobile.[21] Able but alone, he had to be truly self-reliant.

Smith's miserable childhood left indelible marks on his character. Mistrusting other people, he developed inordinate ambition and a compulsive work ethic. He was introspective and sometimes depressed. Smith's writing promised reputation he could convert to income, and he always used it to improve his standing, but he also wrote to cure his sadness. During the year in Mobile after Sidney Smith's death, the twenty-one year-old wrote his first drama, "Aaron Burr," and began *Bachelor's Button*, the state's first literary journal. Hard pressed for contributors, Smith did like most beginning editors and wrote much of his magazine, although other literati like Meek and Hentz contributed. In the second number of *Bachelor's Button*, in January of 1837, he published "The Memoirs of an Ambitious Man." Although Smith's daughter later called the story "partly fanciful, partly true," it was in fact bizarre, for it revealed Smith's horror at dependence.[22] Through a damning depiction of a southwestern family, Smith showed the lessons in self-determination a proper home should teach.

---

[21] Owen provides details about the abusive guardians that Easby-Smith, who rarely mentions negative aspects of her father's life, omits; See Owen, "William Russell Smith," 4986, and Easby-Smith, *William Russell Smith*, 16. Smith's patron was George Crabb, a Whig lawyer and congressman (1837–1840), whom Smith described in his *Reminiscences of a Long Life* (Washington, DC: Published by William R. Smith, 1889) 73–79.

[22] Easby-Smith, quote p. 15. "The Memoirs of an Ambitious Man," *Bachelor's Button* 1 (January, 1837) 2: 24–31. The story was written anonymously, like many others in *Bachelor's Button*, but Smith's daughter used sections of it to begin her biography of her father, and the style is manifestly her father's. A brief portion of Smith's drama about Burr also appeared in *The Southron*, 1 (February 1839) 2: 84–89.

The Domestic Foundations of Self-Determination

Smith's tale suggested frightening influences in the life of a planter's child and condemned the privilege that crippled him psychologically. Opening with the narrator's memories of his childhood home, the story recalled his pleasure at wandering through the woods like "a little Caesar," with a "train of sooty adherents." But this casual analogy denoted the defective character the boy acquired from his mother:

> I was her pet. She denied me nothing. I was, by nature, an amiable and a gentle boy, but I was nurtured into a tyrant by her fond indulgence. Having yielded to my will once, she thereby made that *will* my *right*, and there is something even in a boy's mind that makes him cling to his privileges. I will not moralize. I am going to write my life. Be the moral with the wise.

His mother's unwitting perversion of nurture produced a small monster, whose depravity the narrator detailed. If slaves refused to gratify his whims, he screamed to get them flogged, yet he blamed them for their misfortune. He was "a tyrant of their own making, and it was well for them to suffer the inconveniences resulting from their imprudences."[23]

Overindulgence led the little tyrant to commit "a crime of the deepest die" when, annoyed at a petty issue, he blinded his nurse by sticking a fork in her eye. Smith's narrator recognized his wrong: the slave was "a good old woman; always so kind to me and so indulgent." He loved her afterward, when "she used to carry the keys of the closet, and she gave me raisins, and sugar plumbs, and preserves." Although the boy's "career of wickedness" began with this event, the ambitious man assured his readers that he "repented, even unto tears," his evil deed. The memory still sat on his heart, he claimed, "like an incubus" that would not go away.[24] It created at least some conscience about slavery and a fear of his own mastery that nothing would erase. Still, while the ambitious man recognized his youthful cruelty, he worried more about his faulty character than the harm he did the slave.

Smith's story got darker still. Having blamed his mother and her slaves for his tyranny, the narrator suggested that his father encouraged his love of money and increased his tendency to violence. Smith's attempt at humor quickly deteriorated:

> I was born – yes – I have said that once before. I think I had a father.... [He] took me on his knee and kissed me. I remember his whiskers; they were rough, and large, and black, and they scratched my tender face. But I liked his purse. He rattled the silver it contained in my ear, and he gave it to me.... I soon threw aside the purse, but my heart naturally yearned towards the silver. I believe the love of money is born with us!

The episode ended badly when the boy pulled his father's whiskers, and "he slapped me!" The effects of "the blow" lasted. The boy "brooded over it" later, for "many an hour"; and he would have "slain" his father if his "strength" had

---

[23] "Memoirs of an Ambitious Man," 24.
[24] Ibid., 24–25.

equaled his "will." Moreover, he copied his father's violence. When an infant sister usurped his mother's love, the four-year-old boy kidnapped her and left her to be killed by a "passing animal," while he got off scot-free and remained his mother's pet: "I congratulated myself on my ingenuity; and I was again the wild, happy and ungovernable boy which I had been."[25] Indulgence and violence had prevented the growth of self-control.

At this low point, Smith's story began to turn. The boy became even more his mother's idol when his father died fighting Indians, leaving the child "the tomahawk of a chief" he had killed. The narrator called the weapon "a sanctified relic" of his father's courage. But the tomahawk was the father's only bequest because his "improvidence" had caused the family's "beggary." Thus Smith's bizarre tale morphed into a story of self-determination, a fragment of a *bildungsroman* like Johann Wolfgang von Goethe's *Wilhelm Meister*, one of Smith's favorite novels. Without their "princely estate" to indulge her son, his mother corrected her errors and wrote the word "*ambition*" on his heart. When he entered school, her lesson worked. By cultivating his excellent mind ("a garden" that "must be carefully weeded") and learning to work diligently, the boy saved himself from his awful beginning.[26]

Smith wrote this strange little story for a regional audience, but the "moral to the wise" could have been that of Baldwin or the northern-born Hentz. Indeed, Smith's ideas about self-reliance resembled the lesson of popular American success stories from Benjamin Franklin's autobiography forward. Smith's version made a family with slaves an obstacle. It displayed the writer's dismay at the psychological dependence created for white children by wealth and slavery, and it expressed his fear of inbred tyranny. Indulgence and violence made a little monster, but Smith's moral was simple: to accomplish anything significant, "an ambitious man" must cast off his "ungovernable nature" and work. The effort made Smith's "*whole* life" like that of the "ambitious man," an "interesting, but a miserable one." It took constant striving to overcome the destructive environment Smith's readers surely recognized.[27]

Smith's story cannot be read literally, although its emotional currents confirm his daughter's description of it as "partly true." One hopes that Smith did not blind one of his family's slaves (though a child might do so accidentally), much less kill a sister (though his daughter recalled that the death of an infant made William "the dearest child"). If Smith's mother did both spoil him and create his ambition, he remembered her with gratitude and love (though probably not with clarity, since he was eight when she died). No doubt Smith's family suffered poverty after his parents' death, and he actually owned his father's tomahawk. Something unusual caused his mother's decision to leave Kentucky

---

[25] Ibid., 25.
[26] Ibid., 27–28. Through the main characters in Smith's novel *As It Is* (Albany, NY: Munsell and Rowland, 1860), the author gave a four-page explanation about why *Wilhelm Meister* was a masterpiece and how it influenced young intellectuals; 160–163.
[27] "Memoirs of an Ambitious Man," 29.

and her children's refusal to return there when invited. Smith's daughter confirmed that he was abused, but by his guardians. Certainly few sons, much less one with Smith's ambition, would denounce a father who had died from war wounds.[28]

Smith's story was less a confession, then, than an object lesson in what families should not be, and the story's focus was the "ambitious man," the author. Repeatedly, in poetry and prose, Smith asserted that a man could make himself with intellect, hard work, and ambition, just as he believed he had done. He touted self-control, conscience, and responsibility. Bereft in a strange city, the orphaned young man's story anticipated his future, for he was bent on success and he had acquired the tools to achieve it. In Smith's story, his desire to determine his own fate proved the boy's practical salvation. Whether Smith learned self-reliance from his mother or his brother and sisters, he understood its value and knew the effort it took.

During these difficult years, Smith continued his rise in the world, and he wrote primarily to advance his political goals. He was elected to Congress in 1851 for the first of three terms. In 1853, he met eighteen-year-old Wilhemine Easby at the White House, and the next year they were married, when William was thirty-nine. Wilhemine brought William wealth, love, and an independent character to match his own. Their daughter Anne wrote that "to fail to understand Judge Smith's life with his family, would be to miss more than half the breadth and depth of his character. It never interfered with his public life, but by its deep reality, enriched his being."[29] The wreckage of his family had encouraged Smith to prescribe middle-class values and produced his acute fears about the dangers of dependence. By fixing his ambitions to a slave society, however, he deepened the tension between self-determination and inequality that was born in his family. It dogged him for decades and lent anxiety to everything he wrote.

AN AMBIVALENT PATRIARCH

Easily the wealthiest among them, Albert Pickett was driven by the desire for gain like the poorest of southwestern writers. Born in North Carolina in 1810, Pickett benefitted from mobility. After two years alone, William R. Pickett brought eight-year-old Albert and the rest of his family to the Black Belt region just before Alabama's statehood. Albert saw his father win prosperity through

---

[28] Easby-Smith, 15, 29; Smith wrote his wife during the Civil War that poverty was "the ruling and controlling demon of my life;" William R. Smith to Wilhemine Easby-Smith, Sept. 10, 1862, in Easby-Smith Family Papers, LC. Smith did not name a child for his father, but he named his first-born for his brother Sidney. Ezekial Smith left his family a tomahawk that the family said he used to kill the Shawnee chief Tecumseh in the War of 1812; he died, however, from wounds received in the Seminole War; Easby-Smith, 14.

[29] Easby-Smith, 89. Easby-Smith records many details of her parents' marriage, drawing from letters and family records, some of which are available in the Easby-Smith Family Papers, LC, and in the William Russell Smith Papers, UNC.

the tough businesses of western planting and selling goods to settlers and Creek Indians. By the time Albert reached manhood, his father owned a large plantation and more than sixty slaves. Albert was enriched when he married Sarah Alston Harris in March of 1832. Her family was more prominent in North Carolina than Pickett's, and her ailing mother had a plantation near his father's. Sarah and her sister soon inherited land and slaves, and Albert managed Sarah's portion. Ironically, its locale became known as Pickett's Springs. By 1840, Albert controlled more than eighty slaves, giving him some standing among the hundreds of planters in the rich area. His growing family divided its time between plantations and their nearby town house in Montgomery.[30]

Albert Pickett showed patriarchal tendencies when he was only in his twenties, while his father was still alive. William R. had two sons: Albert and William Dickson Pickett. In 1837, Albert's brother died shortly after his wife's death, leaving an orphaned child, Eliza, under the guardianship of her grandfather. Albert helped care for Eliza and the family's interests in her estate when the Picketts' sole control of the seven-year-old girl was questioned by her mother's sister, a New Englander. Before his death, William D. had written to his wife's family that he wanted Eliza educated in the North. Albert was skeptical. Writing Eliza's aunt in behalf of his family, Pickett agreed that "little Dick" should eventually be educated with her northern relatives. He worried, however, that men would one day pursue her riches, for she already had a large estate and would inherit more from her grandfather. He insisted that Eliza needed supervision.[31]

In a more aggressive, later letter, Albert revealed his close identification with the rising South. At first he emphasized his parents' feelings. Eliza, he wrote, was the joy of her "poor old" grandparents' life and was far too young to be sent away from them. He had found her a place near their home where the wife of a "respectable attorney" (George Hooper, Johnson's brother) would teach her for a year or two. Then she might go North – but she might not. Pickett wasted no words about the reason for his hesitation. Eliza's property was in Alabama, where she should marry, and a New England education might pollute her mind, as "a *large majority* of the people at the North would desire to see our throats and those of our wifes and children cut by our own slaves." To protect her from that ideological contamination, he demanded assurances that Eliza's northern relatives lived among no such people.[32]

[30] Genealogical information in Albert J. Pickett Papers, ADAH; slaveholding information from U.S. Censuses, 1830, 1840, and 1850, schedules for Montgomery and Autauga County. Sarah Harris's mother, an Alston, was a member of one of North Carolina's wealthiest families. Jane Turner Censer, *North Carolina Planters and Their Children*, 155, 159, treats the history of four Alston families. Sarah and Albert Pickett named two children for her North Carolina families.

[31] "Little Dick" in Albert Pickett to Mrs. Jane Keely, January 24, 1838; see also letters of William Dickson Pickett to William Bailey, August 24, 1836, November 10, 1836, December 28, 1836, May 27, 1837, and July 30, 1837; all in Pickett Papers, ADAH.

[32] Pickett to Mrs. Jane Keely, January 24, 1838, and February 15, 1839, in *ibid*. George Hooper lived in Lafayette, roughly fifty miles from the Picketts, and he and William D. Pickett had

The Domestic Foundations of Self-Determination

FIGURE 3.1. Albert Pickett.
This portrait of a young Albert Pickett shows his status, both in the quality of the art and the clothing he wears. But the portrait also displays a quill pen that suggests Pickett's literary propensities. Courtesy of the W. S. Hoole Special Collections Library, The University of Alabama.

Later events suggest Pickett's self-interest in Eliza's fate. When she was eighteen, Pickett's niece found an excellent match in Huntsville's Leroy Pope Walker, a member of an enterprising clan of planters that originated in Virginia and dominated Alabama's politics at the time of statehood. Albert was proud of the marital alliance, but the dynasty's power made him nervous. Apparently

> been friends. Eliza's schooling would provide the Hoopers with income and assure their further friendship with a prominent family, and Albert could rest easy. Eliza would not be exposed to antislavery ideas in the Hoopers' household. George's letters to his future wife, Caroline Mallet, describe the teaching arrangement, his friendship with William D., and a small debt he owed the family; see letters of February 21, 1836, March 9, 1838, March 20, 1838, and April 15, 1838, in Caroline Mallet Hooper Papers, UNC. Eliza Pickett also made a lasting friendship with another resident of Lafayette, Mary Brantley, who was soon to marry George's brother Johnson.

the anxieties were mutual, for "the Walkers" required a complete accounting of Eliza's estate. Albert's father formally consented to the marriage, and the accounting occurred just before his death in 1850. Albert wrote his wife early in 1851 about a narrowly averted clash of interests: "Are you not glad that a settlement was made with the Walkers, at the time that it was? If it had been put off, Father's estate would have been ruined."[33] Instead, Albert received a thousand acres of land and much of his father's remaining property to add to his already substantial holdings. Pickett's possessiveness showed the grasping side of patriarchy, and his wariness revealed how hard it was to secure wealth and status in the Southwest.

Pickett began writing to acquire repute in a way that would demonstrate his personal worth rather than his wealth. He first wrote for Montgomery's newspapers while he was in his twenties, perhaps encouraged by the fact that his sister's husband edited the *Alabama Journal*. An enthusiastic Jacksonian, Pickett boosted the state's prospects. And, despite his agricultural interests, he was a modernizer, urging railroads and an improved banking system. Then, when he was in his mid-thirties, Pickett began to write a history of Alabama, gathering a large private library. After publishing short pieces, Pickett completed his work by 1851 and decided to supervise its publication. He travelled to New York for illustrations and went to Charleston for the printing of the two-volume text. Pickett's trip was his first long absence from Sarah, who now had seven children, the youngest an infant. Despite the fact that Sarah had many servants, Pickett found that his literary aspirations collided with his family responsibilities.

The family of Albert and Sarah reflected tensions between the planter's need for love and his habits of domination. Often eased by humor, the tensions showed in Albert's letters while he was supervising the publication of his history in Charleston. Although he competed with peers like the Walkers and condescended to outsiders like Eliza's New England aunt, Albert indulged, and clearly loved, his wife and children. Some proslavery ideologues claimed that patriarchy bred harmony by eliminating competition, but Pickett's letters revealed more egalitarian ideals of romantic love and domesticity as often as they issued commands. It was hard for the best paternalist to balance persuasion and power, however, and Albert's desire for both affection and obedience made his conduct inconsistent.

Pickett treated Sarah as a junior partner in slave management. When she let him know that the slaves on one plantation had inadequate meat, he sent a letter for her to "seal and hand to" the overseers. He asked her to visit the plantation and "see the negroes." "Sorry" that they did not "get enough to eat," he hoped his letter would solve the problem. "I am glad you wrote to me about it," he noted approvingly: "Never keep any bad news from me that, by knowing it, I could remedy." And he added a mildly self-critical line: "I am

---

[33] Quoted passages, Albert to Sarah Pickett, March 25, 1851; see also William R. Pickett to Leroy Pope Walker, February 20, 1850; both in Pickett Papers, ADAH.

now not like I used to be," he insisted, obviously referring to an impatient temper. He assured Sarah that he had "I hope much more philosophy & take things with much more composure than I formerly did." Perhaps relieved by the fact that Albert appreciated her involvement, Sarah continued it, and a few weeks later he wrote that he was "glad that you sent the bacon to the negroes, for if I had been at home I should have done exactly as you did." Nonetheless, he again enclosed a letter for the overseer, as "it will make him more particular in the future."[34] Ill-tempered or not, Pickett expected obedience, but he honestly tried to persuade his wife that he meant well.

Pickett shared his power over slaves with his wife, and he recognized that Sarah had special authority in their home, but he was not completely at ease with it. In a speech at a local church gathering, he explained that women should teach their children morality: "if Mothers had the exclusive control of their children and exercised their authority," the young would behave better than they did – a frank expression of the kind of middle-class values that were eroding patriarchy. Nonetheless, Pickett directed his family by mail in a playful way that subverted Sarah's authority. His letters show how much he loved his children. He teased his daughter Sooky about the newest baby Albert: "You say he is sweeter than cologne & sugar. I am proud to hear it, & if he is as sweet as sugar, I don't want you to suck him away, till I see him." But then he undermined Sarah: "You say your Ma won't give you any dimes. You shall have plenty when I come home and never be without them."[35] It was not easy for the master to share power.

At once persuasive and directive, Pickett's teasing letters indicated some self-awareness. He wrote his daughter Lida about her baby brother Albert, who was "fat & can spit & can make blubbering noise with his mouth." That pleased the planter, who saw himself in his namesake, and he told Lida to "let him continue to spit, for his father spits a good deal. If he spits on the floor don't scold him." Most babies spit, and Lida could not have stopped her brother had she wanted to, but Pickett's banter reminded her of male prerogatives. Pickett truly missed his family, telling Sarah of his "constant anxiety to see you & the children." He was happy that the owners of his Charleston boarding house had a young family, "the first children I have heard cry since I last saw Albert, & you do not know how much good it does me." He played with the landlords' children often, for they reminded him of his "own."[36] Although Sarah was probably less delighted when children cried, she knew the feeling behind this reference and may scarcely have noticed the ego that saw his "good" in the tears of a child.

[34] Albert to Sarah Pickett, April 12, 1851, and May 5, 1851, in *ibid*.
[35] Pickett's comment on mothers' control in "Address at Asbury Church;" Albert to Sooky, Marcy 24, 1851; Albert to Lida, March 24, 1851; all in *ibid*. Sooky is probably Sarah, who was eight, and Lida is probably Eliza, who was ten. The notes for the girls and those for two other children, including the baby, were in the same envelope with a note for Sarah Pickett, who presumably read the notes to the younger children.
[36] Albert to Sarah Pickett, April 4, 1851, in *ibid*.

The planter's ego showed plainly on other subjects, with somewhat less self-awareness. As a young man, Albert had a chubby face; when older, he carried some weight but took pride in his looks. He wrote Sarah that he was "treated with much attention" in New York and described clothes that he and her brother-in-law, John Gindrat, had bought. People "stare at us with admiration," he joked, claiming that "many Persons have told us ... that we are the finest looking men that had visited the North in a great while." Albert laughed that "this was news to me, but none to John. He said he knew before, that he was good looking." But when Albert asked Sarah to send his "summer vests" to Charleston, he warned: "Unless the vests are very good ones, I don't want you to send them." Ironically, Pickett thought Gindrat self-centered, and perhaps he was. When the Gindrats failed to keep in touch, Pickett called them "two very selfish people" and carped: "I don't know who John is wrapped up with, unless it is with money. I expect that if any one was to ask them if they were acquainted with Albert Pickett they would hesitate sometime, & finally say that they once *slightly* knew such a man."[37] Annoyed at neglect, the materialistic planter criticized the Gindrats for loving money.

While Pickett regretted his absence from his family, he worried more about his reputation. He claimed he must supervise the printing of his *History of Alabama* or it would be done wrong. Besides, he told Sarah, it would cost too much money ($50) for him to commute to Charleston. As his trip stretched into months, Sarah apparently wrote to suggest that she needed Albert at home, for she had seven teeth extracted. His response revealed sympathy and a sense of responsibility, but he also implied that her nerves were part of the problem. "I did not know, until you mentioned it, that your health was bad," he insisted. "Do write me immediately how you are, and if you are still nervous and weak, I will come immediately home to see you." He excused himself, moreover, by reference to his work. As if readers were eagerly awaiting his book, he explained that "I hate to return home & tell people, who will be continually asking, that the *history of Alabama is not done*. I wish to have it to say that it *is* done."[38] Clearly, Pickett weighed his anxiety about reputation against his concern for Sarah and expected her to share his priorities. The planter and his wife were partners like the Baldwins.

Still, Pickett's self-centeredness infected his message to Sarah, even as he assured her that "when I get this disagreeable job off of my hands, I anticipate that we shall have a great deal of domestic happiness as long as we live." For he closed by telling her how she should feel: "So cheer up – you have all the children to keep you company & I have none of them. You ought to be

---

[37] Albert to Sarah from New York, Feb. 13, 1851; on vests, March 27, 1851; on the in-laws, May 15, 1851, in *ibid*. Pickett weighed 175 pounds at 5'9", according to his son-in-law's recollections; Woods, *Personal Reminiscences*, 610, but his portraits suggest a heavier man. He must have forgiven his in-laws' selfishness, for Pickett's last child was named John Gindrat Pickett.

[38] Sarah's teeth, May 15, 1851; figure it would cost to travel, April 12, 1851, in Pickett Papers, ADAH.

happy, especially when you hear from me so often." Was Pickett's light tone designed to suggest that he wanted Sarah to suffer quietly, or to discourage her from asking him to return without denying her outright? His cavalier "cheer up ... you ought to be happy" was the phrase of a man accustomed to command, whatever its intent. Maybe he realized that, however, for he added a postscript: "I had rather see you than any, or all other persons of this wide world – than all the sweets of Arabia, the diamonds of Peru, or the gold of California."[39] Knowing his love of money, Sarah surely recognized the compliment and valued the feeling behind it.

The publication of his *History* revealed Pickett's fixation with his image, and the authorial posture he adopted in the preface showed how deeply he was influenced by his family's wealth. Pickett located his historical inspiration in his childhood, when he knew the white traders and Creek Indians, "hundreds of whom came almost daily" to his father's trading house. He pictured himself as a childish patriarch, appropriating knowledge from the Native Americans "while they were seated in the shades of the spreading mulberry and walnut, upon the banks of the beautiful Tallapoosa" and "leisurely smoked their pipes." In an unusually reflective tone, Pickett wrote that his interest in history had "no particular object in view." He wanted to gratify his "curiosity," which led him "for my own satisfaction alone" to learn Alabama's history.[40] His curiosity was genuine, but Pickett's history was also an extension of his ego – a way of claiming, intellectually, the land that he owned.

The mixed motives behind his writing – a dissonance between his patriarchal posture and an intellectual's work ethic – marked Pickett's *History*. His preface observed his wealth and status: he had many "leisure hours" to gratify his curiosity because planting "did not occupy one-fourth of my time." Believing it the "duty of every man" to be "useful to his race," he undertook his research. Speaking before an audience at a local church, he had echoed this preface and immodestly reminded his neighbors that he had done his "duty" in a way that also emphasized his desire for accomplishment. If he died immediately, he said, "the remembrance of this achievement" would be satisfying. Pickett's speech emphasized his effort, as did his preface. His history was "the hardest work of my life," so hard that he "almost resolved to abandon the attempt."[41] Pickett projected a hybrid image: a wealthy man of leisure and a hard-working historian. In short, he was a gentleman who was also self-made.

---

[39] *Ibid.*
[40] *History of Alabama, and Incidentally of Georgia and Mississippi, from the Earliest Period*, 2 vols. (Charleston: Walker and James, 1851), 1: ix–x.
[41] *Ibid.*, viii; Pickett's self-description from his "Address, Delivered at Asbury Church, in Autaugaville, AL, on Saturday, September 17, 1853, by Col. A. J. Pickett, typescript, 11–12, in Pickett Papers, ADAH (the state's first archivist, Thomas McAdory Owen, made typescripts of some of Pickett's manuscripts and newspaper clippings, not all of which are extant); almost abandoned the work, *History*, ix.

Written mainly for southern readers, Pickett's *History* focused on the period of exploration and conquest – prior to the author's arrival in the Southwest – and both the content of his text and his historical style reflected a patriarch's mentality. The *History* treated the conquest of brave but savage Indians by heroic white men, often accompanied by slaves. Although Pickett sketched pioneer families and explained Creek folkways, he extensively dramatized battles or skirmishes and featured brave and dashing males of diverse races and nationalities. Romantic historians such as Alexander Meek stressed the importance of the genius that interpreted his culture, but Pickett would have none of that, claiming to be the narrator of objective reality. Insisting that his evidence was reliable, he minimized the mentality that assembled it, for to reveal his mind's operations would be to open them to question. Pickett's historical writing asserted his authority, absent self-awareness. He intended command as much as persuasion.[42]

Pickett paid for his history out of his own pocket, and it may have added to financial pressures that turned his thoughts to further migration. Although he had diversified his investments, Pickett depended on cotton sales for income, and low prices had strained his resources. Concerned for his future and that of his (now nine) children, Albert went to Texas in 1856 to scout out new lands. In an attempt to persuade Sarah that migration would be wise, he sent her glowing previews of the wonders of Texas, claiming that the new place would make them "young & energetic." He wrote about people she knew from Alabama, knowing she would value them in a strange home. To help make his case, he assured her that the people he had met were "far superior in intelligence to most of the planters in our region," and that he had "many pressing invitations" to visit them, implying that they recognized his superiority. And, very improbably, he insisted that Texas was "the only state in the South where people can travel peaceably without fire arms. No one carries them in Texas." Fortunately for Pickett's slaves – perhaps for Sarah and the children – the migration never occurred.[43]

Pickett's plans for migration and his *History* reflected, in different ways, his desire for self-determination, and his family relations showed that middle-class domestic values reached the upper ranks of southwestern families. Because he had more land, slaves, and children than any other of Alabama's writers, it is not surprising he was more aggressively patriarchal. Not long after his Texas trip, Pickett wrote his grandson Albert a note that revealed the mixture in his character. Transmitting his mixed legacy of prerogative and self-making, Pickett wrote that he would make the boy "a heap of money"

---

[42] Pickett detailed his views on writing history in "The Claims and Characteristics of Alabama History. An Address before the Historical Society of that State, at its Anniversary at Tuscaloosa, July 9, 1855"; in Pickett Papers, ADAH. A fuller discussion of the *History* is in Chapter 5.

[43] Albert to Sarah Pickett, December 5, 1856. This letter and a second one (December 10, 1856) contain long passages with economic information for William and detailed accounts of the new country for the whole family; in Pickett Papers, ADAH.

The Domestic Foundations of Self-Determination

so he could go to West Point and become a general. Next, the planter jokingly subverted his daughter's authority, telling his grandson, "Every time your ma puts you in the bathing tub I want you to kick & scuffle till you get out."[44] While encouraging such assertion, however, Pickett assumed that his daughter – not one of her slaves – bathed the child. In his family and writing, Pickett left an ambiguous legacy: tensions between command and persuasion, honor and work, and power and love that tracked the spreading influence of bourgeois ideas in the rising South.

A PROUD YOUNG MORALIST

Most writers believed that women's generous morality compensated for the cold economic world beyond middle-class homes. Without power, however, women did not always inhibit men's ambition, and not all women checked their self-aggrandizing impulses. In an environment where opportunities loomed large, economic influences invaded quiet homes. One of the rising South's most famous writers, Augusta Evans, learned self-determination at home when her father's risk taking required it. Her intense desire to control her future conflicted with womanly subordination, which she thought proper but troubling. Her famous images of strong-willed but deferential females revealed more stress in the Southwest's families than did the also famous males of Hooper's *Simon Suggs* or Joseph Baldwin's *Flush Times*. Wary of men's self-interest, Evans hoped that women could domesticate it. For her, however, the family was a site of conflict between self-determination and inequality in ways few men could appreciate.

Evans's childhood taught a rough lesson about a man's failure during flush times. Her father, Matthew Evans, migrated in 1830 from South Carolina to the new western town of Columbus, Georgia, where he plunged into land speculation and a mercantile business with a nest of like-minded relatives and in-laws. In 1834, he made an excellent marriage to Sarah Howard, a planter's daughter who, it was rumored, brought him a $30,000 dowry. Whether this good fortune occurred or not, Matt soon built a mansion, replete with mahogany woodwork, silver door fixtures, and Italian marble fireplaces. Augusta was born in 1835. During the depression after 1837, Matt Evans was a loser: to pay his debts, he mortgaged his home, town properties, and thirty-three slaves, and he moved his growing family to a small farm just across the river in Russell County, Alabama. Finally, in 1845, Evans sought what Baldwin called a "means of escape ... the nearest and best route to Texas."[45]

---

[44] Albert Pickett to Albert Pickett Harris, June 13, 1857, in *ibid*.
[45] Baldwin quotation from *Flush Times*, 90–91. The most complete biographical treatment of Evans is *William Perry Fidler, Augusta Evans Wilson, 1835–1809, A Biography* (Tuscaloosa: University of Alabama Press, 1951). Fidler drew from family materials and recollections that are no longer available, and, although all scholars since have drawn from his work, it reflects family and local pride in the famous author. Thanks to a new interest in women's writing, a number of scholars have more recently discussed Evans's work. Among the best are Mary

Matt Evans's risk was not rewarded, and, because of the Mexican War, he subjected his family of seven to a setting at least as unstable as that of earlier Alabama. After a brief stop in Houston, the family settled in San Antonio, which served as a depot for American armies invading Mexico. Matt again became a merchant, with no better results. In 1848, the family left Texas for a rented home outside of Mobile, where Matt found employment with a cotton merchant.[46] Not long thereafter, the house burned, destroying most of their possessions. Then his health declined. By 1850, Augusta at fifteen was the oldest of eight children in a proud family with scanty means. The girl had limited options for improving her circumstances beyond the usual choice of marriage.

Instead of marrying, Evans began writing, trying to convert her southwestern experience into money. Augusta's mother had cultivated her child's formidable intellect with extensive reading, and the result appeared in *Inez: A Tale of the Alamo*, published in New York in 1855, just as Augusta turned twenty.[47] Although Hentz had by then shown how widely women's fiction from the Southwest could sell, Augusta knew her writing defied her family's standards for femininity. According to family legend, she won approval by presenting the manuscript to her father as a Christmas gift. Although *Inez* sold poorly at first, and Evans was correctly dissatisfied with it, it began to explore the problem that shaped her more successful novels: how a woman could assert independence from within a conservative social order. In a novel where men's choices produced disaster, Evans made young girls uphold the Protestant faith and find true love, even if they crossed their fathers. Reflecting a problem that she was living, Evans wrote about girls trying to become self-determined but unequal adults.[48]

However fruitless Matt Evans's Texas experiment had been, Evans escaped within an intact family, but her heroines had no such luck. In *Inez*, three motherless girls confronted the "numerous hardships" of frontier living and the chaos of war. In a contorted plot that showed Evans's inexperience,

---

Kelley, *Private Woman, Public Stage: Literary Domesticity in Nineteenth-Century America* (New York: Oxford University Press, 1984); Anne Goodwyn Jones, *Tomorrow Is Another Day: The Woman Writer in the South, 1859–1936* (Baton Rouge: Louisiana State University Press, 1981); Elizabeth Moss, *Domestic Novelists in the Old South: Defenders of Southern Culture* (Baton Rouge: Louisiana State University Press, 1992). Also helpful are the introductions to paperback editions of Evans's second and third novels: *Beulah*, ed. with intro. by Elizabeth Fox-Genovese (Baton Rouge: Louisiana State University Press, 1992), and *Macaria*, ed. with intro. by Drew Gilpin Faust (Baton Rouge: Louisiana State University Press, 1992).

[46] According to family recollections, the "discomforts of frontier life and the numerous instances of violence" caused Matt Evans to return to Mobile; Fidler, 31.

[47] *Inez: A Tale of the Alamo* (New York: Harper & Bros., 1855).

[48] Critics differ about how far Evans's independent streak carried her. Fox-Genovese has emphasized how religion provided Evans with intellectual and spiritual autonomy while forming the basis for her conservative social views; *Beulah*, xix. Jones stresses Evans's ambivalence about her independence, arguing that she finally capitulates to social convention; *Tomorrow Is Another Day*, 91.

the novel alternated between copious bloodshed, religious discussions, and romance as a group of Americans became entangled in the war for Texas independence and eventually fled eastward for safety. Written in the midst of Mobile's nativist controversies, *Inez* assaulted Catholicism through tedious conversations that advanced Protestant doctrines of religious freedom. Evans assigned contrasting spirits to her main characters – Florry, Mary, and Inez – and, through them, she probed the opportunities for and limitations to women's self-determination.[49]

Of the three girls, Florry was most like Evans and the most important character. Florry was born to wealth, but her father's speculations cost him his plantation and slaves, and he took Florry and his orphaned niece, Mary, to Texas. Although loving, Florry was excessively proud and her religious convictions were shaky until the "blessed" Mary convinced her to accept Protestant beliefs (in doctrinal debates that showed Evans's erudition). Gentle, kind, and selfless, Mary evangelized everyone. Eager to be useful, she persuaded Florry to join her in teaching Mexican children, and the girls did household chores together. Unlike Florry, however, Mary was too angelic to have an earthly destiny, so she died of consumption in her sweetheart's arms.

Evans named her novel for the most fully autonomous of her three characters, yet Inez revealed her author's uncertainty about women's capabilities. The child of a wealthy, domineering Mexican of Spanish descent, Inez was beautiful and passionate. She was also bold, like male frontier heroes, which Evans conveyed by having Inez don a man's clothing, escape kidnappers, and warn the Americans of impending danger. Inez had a feminine backbone, too: she defied her autocratic father by refusing to marry a rich cousin and by rejecting Catholicism. Nonetheless, Inez rejected Mary's efforts to convert her. Writing dialogue for Inez that demonstrated her courage and wit, Evans showed her admiration for the girl's self-reliance. Heroic as she was, however, Inez illustrated the dangers of manly conduct, for bravery earned her death in the wake of the massacre at Goliad. And Inez died alone.[50]

Evans gave Florry a much more seemly kind of feminine independence than Inez's. Nonetheless, Florry overcame the influence of two men who would prevent her self-determination: her father, the "cold, proud man of the world" who dragged her to Texas; and Father Mazzolin, a wicked priest who was, improbably, Florry's half-brother by an illicit liaison of her father. Father Mazzolin thirsted for wealth and power over his flock, and he sought revenge

---

[49] Evans specifically addresses the issue of women's suffering from migration through the character of Mrs. Carlton, a woman who followed her husband, who had lost his wealth, "to seek his fortune" in Texas, where they met "the numerous hardships which those who have not endured can never fully realize." *Inez*, 54.

[50] Michael O'Brien observes that Evans's religious ideas in *Beulah* were far more intellectually venturesome than her faith might suggest; *Conjectures of Order*, 2: 1166–1170. It is not lack of faith that condemns Inez to death, and Evans asks her readers to sympathize with her character when she dies: "Peace, Inez, to thy memory, and may the sod lie lightly on thy early grave." *Inez*, 248.

on the father who had deserted him. As Evans's baroque plot developed, Father Mazzolin converted his/Florry's father to Catholicism and made the ruined man extract a deathbed promise from Florry that she would follow his example. But Mary soon convinced Florry to renounce her father's dictation. Throwing away the rosary her father gave her – symbolically casting off her dependence on him and a hierarchal church – Florry achieved self-reliance.[51]

Despite her murky plot, Evans clearly demonstrated that men's selfish decisions harmed their families, and she moralized about work, responsibility, and restraint. Perhaps she had her father in mind when she described Florry's father's mistakes. Still, the writer was much harsher in judging powerful men like Mazzolin and Inez's father, who deliberately misused their dependents. Across the board, she made the angelic Mary's morality correct weak or evil men. Even the best man needed her advice. Although Mary's sweetheart Frank was a physician and a hard-working, nurturing, thoroughly admirable Christian, Mary guided him. Indeed, shortly before she died in Frank's arms, Mary counseled him not to seek fame or riches. He would, she told him, need "some employment to draw forth every faculty: in a life of active benevolence and usefulness, this will be supplied."[52] The dying girl explained the path to middle-class morality as if Frank could not find it without a woman.

Evans's hope that self-determination and some degree of equality could coexist within a marriage showed in Florry, who refused to subordinate her morality to a man's. Like Mary's sweetheart Frank, Florry's sweetheart Dudley was an earnestly religious professional, a dedicated teacher who was nurturing rather than commanding. Dudley appeared briefly in the novel's opening, only to return (inexplicably and with little warning) as the Americans fled from Texas. When he announced his love for Florry, however, she failed to say immediately that she had very briefly been a Catholic; when he learned it, Dudley accused Florry of deception. But Evans did not submit her heroine to masculine judgment, for Florry staunchly defended her morality. She told Dudley: "Your love or indifference would have not weighed an atom in my decision to act according to my sense of right and wrong."[53] Florry's firm language indicated that romance did not reduce her moral autonomy.

Evans showed, however, that families inhibited crucial life decisions for women, and she briefly portrayed slaves as even more dependent on white families. Her novel's women regretted the West's "numerous hardships," but they followed men "without a murmur," and slaves came along, too. Florry's father's devoted slave, Aunt Fanny, loved her owner's family, and Evans insisted that Aunt Fanny's "tidy appearance, and honest, happy smiling face presented the best refutation of the gross slanders of our northern brethren." When the white Americans fled the war, however, they left servants behind.

---

[51] *Inez*, "Cold, proud," 62.
[52] *Ibid.*, 222. Jones speculates that Evans's treatment of men reflects a "certain ambivalence" about her father; *Tomorrow Is Another Day*, 58, and I agree.
[53] *Inez*, 232.

While Mary felt sure they would "incur no danger," she regretted leaving them, "particularly should they object." Evans staged a sentimental scene of the departure, with the "true-hearted negress," Aunt Fanny, sobbing that she would never see her "old friend" Mary again. With that, Aunt Fanny disappeared from *Inez*.[54]

Familial images of slavery did not disappear from the novel, however, as Evans tied her heroine's self-determination to an improbable ending that placed middle-class domesticity on a southern plantation and permanently rescued Florry from the perils of the Southwest. To Florry's delight (and the reader's surprise), her new husband Dudley had inherited from an uncle the same plantation that her father had lost to speculation, and her own family's slaves (apparently minus Fanny) joyously welcomed her return. In fact, Matt Evans had sold at least two slaves, including one five-year-old boy, when he faced ruin, but probably he left others with his family in Georgia. And one slave woman seems to have stayed with the Evans family through Matt's misadventures. Augusta put a good face on a problem she knew firsthand, for she knew that white men's poor choices harmed the families of enslaved people.

Nonetheless, her happy ending glossed over slaves' risky status as property and focused on the bliss of the newly wedded white couple. Dudley promised Florry a life of "perfect confidence" and pledged that the two would "strive to guide and cheer each other" as partners in their marriage. Florry, in turn, asked Dudley to help her to "break down my pride and to be more like Mary."[55] While their elegant home and loving slaves symbolized the reconstruction of a southern family, Florry and Dudley's union suggested middle-class ideas about work, romance, and self-determination. Like William Smith's "Memoirs of an Ambitious Man," *Inez* used a child's family as a bad model. But Evans did no more than imply – if that – that the abusive power of masters over slaves and the power of fathers over children had something in common. The self-appointed moralist took her criticisms only so far.

In *Inez*, Evans associated disorder with the newest Southwest and hinted that masculine adventures in self-making could be offset by women's morality. For, along with her wariness, Augusta had learned self-determination, and her

---

[54] *Ibid.*, "numerous hardships," and no "murmer," 67; Aunt Fanny's appearance, 42; Mary's comments, 134; sobbing departure, 190.

[55] *Ibid.*, Dudley and Florry's remarks, 295–296. It is possible that Evans's father left some servants with his brother-in-law, who held a mortgage on his Georgia properties, but there is no direct evidence about the fate of most of the slaves he left behind. It seems likely that some of the slaves Matt Evans and his daughter held by 1860 were from the same group. There are relevant materials in the papers of Evans's most prominent brother-in-law: Henry Benning-Seaborn Jones Collection at Columbus State University, Columbus, GA. I am indebted to the library's archival assistant, Giselle Remy-Bratcher, for invaluable help in sorting through these papers and for assistance in finding local histories that illuminated them. A search of the probate records from Muscogee County, Georgia, and Russell County, Alabama, revealed that Evans sold some slaves, perhaps to Jones and others, and Jones's papers show that he regularly managed slaves for other people.

well-born parents gave the young woman an abiding confidence that she could overcome disadvantages. Later in her life, Evans answered a query about herself with a generous tribute to her "blessed *father* and *mother*." Remembering their difficulties, she asked rhetorically: "What did they not deny themselves – to guide me aright!"[56] Beneath Evans's customary hyperbole lay a genuine gratitude, for while her parents could not protect her from the consequences of Matt Evans's foolhardy decisions, they did teach her how to work and use her mind. She believed she could create her own security.

The work ethic Evans learned at home combined women's customary labor with intellectual exercise. As the oldest child, Augusta helped her mother manage. In the 1850s in Mobile, Matt Evans's large household contained several slaves. Nonetheless, late in the decade, Augusta peppered her correspondence with references to her responsibilities: nursing other family members (and one "servant"), being the family's "sewing machine," and teaching her sisters. The latter was no trivial tutoring, for she wrote a friend that her two sisters were "reading to me a course of History and Philosophy, which requires at least *half the day*," that they were "deep in Grote's Greece (12 volumes)," and that she was reading them the *Iliad*.[57] Although Evans meant to imply she carried a load – excusing her failure to write letters – she described her duties affectionately. Her work ethic and domesticity reflected national middle-class values, but her experience at home built self-determination into Augusta's character.

Ideally, women chose to marry, and the marriage of Florry in *Inez* suggested that Evans thought it desirable. She loved her family and wanted to form a new one, but marriage was a challenge for the unusual young woman. Augusta's history did not fully prepare her for the high society of Mobile, a port city with wealth that flowed from cotton. Although she could belong to the best circles by virtue of kinship, she had little money behind her. A portrait from the late 1850s showed an attractive but not pretty woman with a serious gaze and high forehead that, to contemporaries, bespoke intelligence. Dedicated to work, Evans fiercely criticized social-climbing belles and idle men. Her family's standards were high and her intellect intimidating. Finding a suitable partner had to be difficult.[58]

---

[56] Augusta Evans to Mrs. Crawford (the mother of a friend), April 8, 1887, in Rebecca Grant Sexton, ed., *A Southern Woman of Letters: The Correspondence of Augusta Jane Evans Wilson* (Columbia: University of South Carolina Press, 2002), 166; hereinafter referred to as *Correspondence*. Evans referred in the same letter to the fact that her "precious mother" was in heaven and did not mention her deceased father. Perhaps Evans simply meant to indicate the bond between mothers and daughters, because she was consoling Mrs. Crawford about the death of her daughter.

[57] Nursing the "servant," in a letter of April 22, 1856, quoted in full in Sara S. Frear, "'You My Brother Will be Glad with Me': The Letters of Augusta Jane Evans to Walter Clopton Harris, January 29, 1856, to October 29, 185[8?]," in "Notes and Documents," *AR* 60 (April 2007): 131; "sewing machine," Augusta Evans to Rachel Lyons, December 8, 1859, in *Correspondence*, 4; teaching, Evans to Rachel Lyons, May 29, 1860, in *ibid*.

[58] The portrait is at ADAH.

FIGURE 3.2. Augusta Evans.
This portrait of Evans appeared in *Women of the South, Distinguished in Literature* (New York, 1861), which also contained biographical sketches of Evans and Caroline Hentz. Original in possession of the author.

Just as she finished *Inez*, moreover, the proud young intellectual strengthened her self-determination with an identity crisis that ended in a leap of faith. Describing it in letters to a young Methodist minister in 1856, Evans recalled periods of doubt, speculation, depression, and prayer. She explained to him that her new faith called her to a life of love and duty, but it also sanctioned her writing. As she wrote the minister, one must *"Trust God,* and be at *peace*"; but one must also act. Suggesting that she was in a class with Shakespeare, whose morality she criticized, she wrote "I want to soar." Evans's writing would display her intellectual superiority along with her faith, for art "should elevate, should refine, should sanctify the heart!" No matter if people disliked her ideas, she wrote defiantly: "'n'importe!' I only want the truth, whether old or new, popular or scorned."[59] This was an exaggeration, however, because Evans knew that authorship made a woman financially independent only if she sold her books.

This new sense of mission and Evans's need for money produced *Beulah*, which was published in New York in 1859. With this much better novel, Evans figuratively moved beyond the Old Southwest and relocated her anxieties about women's self-determination in the modern South, but the novel aimed at universal appeal. Unlike *Inez*, with its trio of heroines and convoluted plot, *Beulah* was one woman's *bildungsroman*, the equivalent of a man's quest for a place in the world. Nevertheless, the new novel repeated Evans's ambivalence about women's autonomy. *Beulah* described an orphaned girl's search for happiness and ultimate marriage to her wealthy, older guardian – another physician, Dr. Guy Hartwell. No ordinary female, Beulah was obsessed with independence. She represented Inez's boldness and passion, Florry's pride and her doubts, Mary's faith, and Augusta's searching intellect. Beulah's efforts to find some autonomy in a conservative society formed the backbone of Evans's plot.

Despite her desire to "soar," Evans's discomfort about literary success appeared in *Beulah*. In many respects, she asserted women's capabilities. Where *Inez* had assaulted Catholicism, *Beulah* attacked pantheism, and her relentless speculations displayed Evans's philosophical knowledge. As Beulah's autonomy emerged, she became an author, supporting herself. At first, she was "ambitious, and labored to obtain distinction as a writer; and this, under various fictitious signatures, was hers." But then Evans used religion to constrain Beulah, describing an emotional struggle like the one Augusta herself had experienced. When Beulah found faith, her aspirations changed. The new Beulah "still studied and wrote, but with another aim, now, than mere desire of literary fame; wrote to warn others of the snares in which she had so long been entangled, and to point young seekers after truth to the only sure fountain."[60] In the end, Beulah might use her power to persuade– about one truth.

Evans's anxieties about marriage also appeared in *Beulah's* conclusion. For most of the novel, Beulah identified economic independence with emotional autonomy and refused to marry her guardian. Finally, however, she accepted her feelings and married Hartwell. She assured him that love mattered more than fame, ambition, and her literary work. But she did not flatly promise to give up writing. When Hartwell asked his bride if she had

---

[59] "Trust God," Evans to Walter Clopton Harris, January 29, 1856, in "'You My Brother,'" 129; other quotes, Evans to Harris, October 12, 1856, in *ibid.*, 137–138.
[60] Evans, *Beulah*, 379.

abandoned her "faith" in genius, she answered: "I have not lost it all. I hope I never shall," and she explained that true genius could reconcile religious and secular knowledge. While the novel closed with Beulah's deference to her husband, it left her literary future open.[61] This ending suggested that Evans wanted to marry, but she might continue to write, with or without a man.

And Evans did continue to write, while *Beulah* sold very well, but the author remained anxious about her vocation. She vented to a friend, Rachel Lyons, in 1860. Rachel had literary ambitions, and Augusta briskly encouraged them: "What do you suppose your Creator gave you 'good gifts' for?" She warned, however, that "literary women have trials that the world knows not of." These trials produced a paralyzing mood: "There come hours to *all of us*, when hope folds her wings, and we sit listlessly holding our hands, despairing of success; well-nigh careless, indifferent to the future, asking nothing, hoping nothing, and immeasurably worse than all, doing nothing." This depression of "*all*" literary women was fear of failure, which Evans recognized: "I know what this disease is; am too familiar with each of its symptoms not to sympathize with the victim writhing in its grasp." But, she insisted, "*work*: *work* is the only medicine."[62] Evans was defining herself. Work transformed women into authors who could shape their world.

Nonetheless, Evans knew that inequality narrowed her options. Admitting she shared Rachel's sense of futility, Augusta wrote that she found no solace in a "weary round of fashion and gayety," for "no *true* woman ever yet fed contentedly on these husks." Because most paid work was taboo for a lady, she proclaimed either marriage or writing as moral alternatives. Women must choose "holier idols than the world can erect; – they must have either *Love* or *Duty*. The fortunate and happiest women have *both*; but the *last* can give great comfort, pure joy, perfect serenity." In the absence of romantic love, a talented woman should "faithfully begin God's work" and pursue the writer's mission.[63] The construction of a family would have to wait.

Beulah won Evans a wide readership, and the author's melding of regional and national cultures typified a rising South. It also reflected a family that was fortunate in spite of its trials. In an all-too-normal way, Matt Evans had risked his wife and children. Augusta remembered, even as she absorbed his desire to take bold action. And she would often claim that poverty spurred effort. Taught by her mother, she knew that women's work counted. With the profits from her writing, Evans helped her father buy a house. The property held his family and his slaves, along with slaves she had acquired. It was a large cottage rather than the mansion they left in Georgia, but it seemed a step in the right

---

[61] Ibid., 418.
[62] *Correspondence*, 18–20, first two quotes, Evans to Rachel Lyons, July 20, 1860; second two from a second letter on the same themes, Evans to Lyons, August 28, 1860. These letters were written in the wake of a broken engagement; see Chapter 8.
[63] Ibid., 20, Evans to Lyons, August 28, 1860.

direction.[64] In the shadow of the Old Southwest, Evans was gaining a practical self-determination in which inequality had an unclear but important role.

* * *

A fascination with the autonomous self was well-nigh universal among middle-class Americans, and many authors exaggerated the extent to which families engendered self-reliance. Like other heroes and heroines in mid-century literature, Evans's Beulah was an orphan, and most southwestern writers were not – William Smith's terrible experience notwithstanding. But when writers deprived their characters of parents or gave them dreadful ones, they stressed the strength autonomy required. Like Joe Baldwin's claim that he came alone to the Southwest, when he did not, orphaned characters affirmed self-determination. Although Pickett claimed his father's wealth, he understood, and perhaps shared, a suspicion that too many advantages sapped an individual's strength. Indeed, Baldwin and Smith both made planters the antithesis of self-making. Too idle to save himself from ruin, Baldwin's Wormly depended on his wife and daughters; and Smith's little tyrant had to learn self-control to overcome his rich family's influence. Although Evans ended *Inez* with Florry on a plantation, overbearing patriarchs threatened her heroines. Each of these writers made good families the source of self-reliance.

Moreover, Baldwin, Smith, Pickett, and Evans practiced the domestic virtues of the middle classes. In the absence of inherited wealth, they shared resources, and, without patriarchal power, they divided responsibilities. Baldwin sent money to his father and his father-in-law, and he felt morally obliged to buy books for his brother and schooling for his sister. Smith depended on his siblings after his parents' death, working for a time in the shop of his sister's husband, a tailor. For all of his wealth and power, Pickett urged mothers to have "exclusive control" of their children. And he tried to persuade Sarah that he acted with his family in mind when he stayed in Charleston to supervise his book's printing. Evans was her family's "sewing machine," and she tutored her siblings at home, where she herself was taught. These were families that valued cooperation,

[64] See Figure 8.1. Evans's home was named "Georgia Cottage" by its builder, not the Evans family, according to Fidler, n. 43, p. 232. The best source of information on the cottage is in the National Park Service's Historical American Buildings Survey (HABS), which was written in August of 1972 by Park Service architectural historian Charles A Herrington. He summarizes some of the history of the house as well as its most significant architectural features. He establishes the 1857 purchase date from Deed Books in the Probate Office in Mobile, although he also repeats the idea that Evans purchased the home for her father, who, however, owned the house himself, and he seems to be drawing from Fidler and local mythology about Evans. If Evans did buy Georgia Cottage when she was twenty-three, all previous historians' assessments about the poor sales of *Inez* must be revisited. "Hardaway-Wilson House" ("Georgia Cottage"), photographs, written historical and descriptive date at http://memory.loc.gov/pnp/habshaer/al/al10400/al10461/data/al10461.pdf. I suspect that it is possible that Evans himself paid for much of the cottage with money from his job, or by selling some of his remaining slaves, but the record is hazy.

The Domestic Foundations of Self-Determination

affection, and work. If they did not always achieve, in Pickett's words, "domestic happiness," it was not because writers misunderstood their responsibilities.

Whether or not they frankly discussed their families in public, writers knew their homes shaped their work. Like William Smith, Augusta Evans deliberately mined her family life for literary materials. As deliberately, Joseph Baldwin slighted families in his sketches of the Old Southwest. It seems likely that all three wrote popular fiction, however, partly because their families could not support advanced education, serious research, large libraries, and the leisure for frequent intellectual exchange or systematic analysis. According to family lore, Evans wrote at night when her family was asleep. A friend recalled Baldwin writing as his children played around him. Pickett wrote history, which required extensive research, largely because he had the time and money to gather materials and many slaves to care for his wife and children. Withal, these were men and women who worked and cared for families, and their busyness explains a sometimes hurried, always immediate quality to their writing. Families did not always warrant much literary attention, but they were not easily set aside.

Families incorporated self-determination into the marrow of writers' identities: psychologically, practically, and emotionally. By emphasizing voluntary ties, and by making women and children seem willingly subordinate, writers palliated the inequalities within families. They rightly understood that domestic persuasion improved on the kind of patriarchy that Smith recalled in the parent who slapped him. There was genuine affection in Pickett's family letters, even as he cheerily subverted his wife's authority. But the strains within families also became part of the visceral center from which these men and women wrote. Although writers believed that families should nurture, rather than control, their members, they knew it was not always the case, for not everyone was equally self-determined. Smith and his siblings suffered from his mother's decision to flee Kentucky, Pickett felt the conflict between his work and his wife's welfare, and Evans hid her writing from her father. Idealization did not hide structural inequalities or their different weight for men and women.

Idealizations and inequalities affected middle-class families everywhere, but southwestern writers felt peculiar tensions because they relied so much on slaves. Authors noted but rarely examined that dependence – not necessarily because they did not know it as dependence, as Smith's "Memoirs" revealed, but because it was unpleasant to consider, as his story also proved. Through his anecdote of a blinded nurse whose indulgences gratified a little tyrant's ego, Smith cast a harsh light on Pickett's inflated sense of self and Major Wormly's endless jokes. But most writers shrunk from illuminating a much-criticized institution. No doubt, as Meek observed, slaves helped them find time to write. And, as some history, poetry, and fiction revealed (and later chapters more fully discuss), slaves were entering writers' consciousness. However vaguely, these authors sensed that slavery was kin to other familial inequalities, and fears of dependence fed their literary imaginations.

With greater self-awareness than they showed about slaves, writers depended on southern white men and women. If they could, migrants moved with familiar people when they ventured into unknown territory. In Lincoln's Northwest, for example, this pattern marked politics and society. In southern Illinois, friends and relatives from the Upper South had moved together – Lincoln and his family from Kentucky – and in the northern part of the state, native-born immigrants came from New England and the Middle Atlantic states. As a result, the two halves of Illinois voted differently about slavery issues, right down to the Civil War. In the Old Southwest, where most migrants came from the coastal South, they still clung to familiar people. Albert Pickett feared that his niece's mind would be poisoned by northern relatives, and he mistrusted the Walkers, who came from Virginia and Georgia. His decision to educate the girl with family friends from North Carolina (his father's and his mother's home) was both typical and deliberate. Joe Baldwin's mother was pleased that he married a Virginian, and Smith's mother followed her brother from Kentucky to Huntsville. Multiplied many times, such free choices repeatedly connected writers' families to a slave society. The general principles that governed their families resembled those of middle-class northerners, but ties of blood and marriage bound Alabama's authors to the rising South.

4

The Voluntary Bonds of Friendship

> The claims of true friendship are imperative.
>
> Augusta Evans, *Beulah*

Friends attached writers to the Southwest in webs of relations that were binding, like families, which is why Augusta Evans called true friendship's requirements "imperative." Yet friendships were made by choice, and, like other educated Americans, the rising South's writers believed that the voluntary bonds of friendship enriched the lives of autonomous individuals. Through the real and imaginary friendships they constructed, writers let affection guide self-determination. Their friendships strengthened writers' conviction that free people like themselves were building a progressive slave society.

Although friendship has universal meaning, it had particular import for middle-class people in an increasingly individualistic America. Friendships created social capital in a fluid society. In towns, where people organized to share knowledge or accomplish social goals, they found friends. Friendships increased individual opportunity because they offset more traditional relations based on inherited status or family ties. Friendships built community among migrants from different areas of the country, and they gradually integrated European immigrants like Nicholas Hentz into American society. Friendships brought emotional satisfactions – companionship and a sense of belonging – to people who moved about. When they worked, friendships served self-interest, psychological needs, and collective welfare at the same time.[1]

---

[1] Evans, *Beulah* (Baton Rouge: Louisiana State University Press, 1992, c. 1859), 361. Most studies of American friendships have focused exclusively on either males or females. The foundational study for women is Carroll Smith-Rosenberg, "The Female World of Love and Ritual: Relations between Women in Nineteenth-Century America," originally published in 1975 but reprinted in her collection *Disorderly Conduct: Visions of Gender in Victorian America* (New York: A. A. Knopf, 1985); for men, see Anthony Rotundo, *American Manhood: Transformations in Masculinity from the Revolution to the Modern Era* (New York: Basic Books, 1993). A useful collection that attempts to relate studies of masculine and feminine

American friendship had a distinguished ethical pedigree. In classical literature, Aristotle offered an influential typology classifying friendships of utility, pleasure, and virtue. Biblical friendships like that of Ruth and Naomi taught timeless lessons of affection. And Shakespeare had frequently evoked the security of lasting friendships or the tragedy of broken ones. The rise of individual freedom in European society produced new concepts of friendship that came from the same Enlightenment thinkers, especially Scottish moral philosophers, who developed liberal political and economic ideas. In their conception, the sympathy that built friendship was a fundamental human trait that made self-interest and social harmony coexist.[2] Because friendship connected people of their own volition, it reinforced self-determination. Because it required the toleration of difference, it encouraged individuality. Unlike family members, friends could be shed, yet, while it stood, friendship required trust, sharing, and open communication. It fixed moral obligations to relations that were

patterns of relationships is Laura McCall and Donald Yacone, eds., *A Shared Experience: Men, Women, and the History of Gender* (New York: New York University Press, 1998). Particularly insightful is Caleb Crain, *American Sympathy: Men, Friendship, and Literature in the New Nation* (New Haven: Yale University Press, 2001), even though it focuses entirely on the North. Excellent on women's intellectual friendships around the nation is Mary Kelley, *Learning to Stand & Speak: Women, Education, and Public Life in America's Republic* (Chapel Hill: University of North Carolina Press, 2006). On the lack of study about southern males, see Anya Jabour, "Male Friendship and Masculinity in the Early National South: William Wirt and His Friends," *JER* 20 (Spring, 2000): 82–111, and she treats young women's friendships in *Scarlett's Sisters: Young Women in the Old South* (Chapel Hill: University of North Carolina Press, 2007). Charlene Boyer-Lewis, *Ladies and Gentlemen on Display: Planter Society at the Virginia Springs* (Charlottesville: University of Virginia Press, 2001), emphasizes upper-class habits, as do Christie Anne Farnham, *The Education of the Southern Belle: Higher Education and Student Socialization in the Antebellum South* (New York: New York University Press, 1994), and Stephen Stowe, *Intimacy and Power in the Old South: Ritual in the Life of Planters* (Baltimore: Johns Hopkins University Press, 1987).

[2] Ivy Schweitzer, in *Perfecting Friendship: Politics and Affiliation in Early American Literature* (Chapel Hill: University of North Carolina Press, 2006), 6–71, offers an excellent explanation of historical conceptions, and she does so in a helpful discussion of the scholarly literature on friendship in the early national period. Two important essays by Allan Silver, "Friendship and Trust as Moral Ideals: A Historical Approach," *European Journal of Sociology* 30 (1989): 274–297, and "Friendship in Commercial Society: Eighteenth-Century Social Theory and Modern Sociology," *American Journal of Sociology* 95 (1989): 1474–1504, contrast premodern and modern friendships and relate the modern conception to the British Enlightenment. Useful introductory explanations to the interdisciplinary study of friendship include Rosemary Blieszner and Rebecca G. Adams, *Adult Friendship* (Newbury Park, CA: Sage Publications, 1992), which includes a good chapter on the history of friendship and friendship research. See also Stacey J. Oliker, "The Modernization of Friendship: Individualism, Intimacy, and Gender in the Nineteenth Century," in Rebecca G. Adams and Graham Allan, eds., *Placing Friendship in Context* (Cambridge: Cambridge University Press, 1998). A number of other collections have historical dimensions, including Peter M. Nardi, ed., *Men's Friendships* (Newbury Park, CA: Sage Publications, 1992). An excellent, readable overview that blends contemporary theory, philosophical insights, and historical patterns is Ray Pahl, *On Friendship* (Cambridge: Cambridge University Press, 2000). For a discussion of conceptions of friendship throughout the Western tradition, see Jacques Derrida, *The Politics of Friendship*, trans. George Collins (London: Verso, 1997).

freely chosen rather than inherited or rigidly prescribed. This modern ideal of friendship was enshrined in fiction, poetry, and didactic literature on both sides of the Atlantic, in the American North and South.

It was especially well-suited to the West, where friends were often the equivalent of relatives in more stable societies. In a state with few banks, friends made loans such as that of William D. Pickett to George Hooper. When Alexander Meek's friends petitioned Basil Manly to make him a professor, they supported the young writer's ambitions. Lawyers made friends for company when circuit riding, as Joe Baldwin described in *Flush Times*, and they made useful business connections as well. Young men and women discussed their marriage prospects with friends, as Meek did with William Smith and Evans did with Rachel Lyons. In ways such as these, Alabama's writers acted like other middle-class people who had to improvise new relations. Abraham Lincoln made good friends riding circuit in Illinois, and he shared the trials of choosing a wife with his intimate friend, Joshua Speed, whom he had only known a few years. Friendships were the glue of towns where people came and went frequently.[3]

For would-be writers in the Southwest, friendships also provided a congenial testing ground for ideas. Evans, for example, thanked Lyons for her critique of *Beulah*: "There are numbers to flatter me, but *very few*, sufficiently *my friend* to tell me honestly of my faults." One acquaintance remembered that Baldwin's lawyer friends criticized his stories as he wrote. Their writing habits distinguished townspeople from the uneducated farmers and slaves around them. When they wrote poetic inscriptions in albums, held debates, and organized for social reforms, educated men and women developed intellectual skills, with or without profound exchange.[4] In this way, as in others, middle-class friendships depended on how easily like-minded townspeople could meet. If such frequent contacts promoted conformity – and surely they did – they also encouraged the exchange of ideas in a congenial setting.

These habits of friendship encouraged a moderate social criticism. Alabama's writers insisted that true friendship mitigated class differences – "soaring

---

[3] For Lincoln, see David Donald, *We Are Lincoln Men: Abraham Lincoln and His Friends* (New York: Simon and Schuster, 2003), which explores the relationship between various kinds of friendship Lincoln experienced in Illinois, and makes distinctions similar to those drawn here between sociability and serious friendships.

[4] Evans to Rachel Lyons, October 17, 1859, in *A Southern Woman of Letters: The Correspondence of Augusta Jane Evans Wilson*, Rebecca Grant Sexton, ed. (Columbia: University of South Carolina Press, 2002), 2. The relationship between friendships and literary interests in the Northeast are emphasized in Ronald J. Zboray and Mary Saracino Zboray, *Everyday Ideas: Socioliterary Experience among Antebellum New Englanders* (Knoxville: University of Tennessee Press, 2006). David Dowling argues that the economic interests mixed with friendship in *The Business of Literary Circles in Nineteenth-Century America* (New York: Palgrave Macmillan, 2011). For middle-class southerners, the connection between associations and intellectual culture is discussed in Jonathan Daniel Wells, *The Origins of the Southern Middle Class, 1800–1861* (Chapel Hill: University of North Carolina Press, 2004), 89–110, but he does not discuss close friendships.

above the dross and dust of worldly conventionalities," as Evans once wrote. They frequently described friendships overcoming the barriers between the rich and the poor. And Alabama's writers were especially sensitive to inequalities within the ranks of the respectable. They contrasted democratic friendships with aristocratic hierarchies of kin and patronage. They criticized the ethics of honor, which required men to outdo one another and establish their rank. And they also complained about the harsh competition of capitalism, which ranked people in a slightly different way. Baldwin, for one, made these two competitive modes indistinguishable, for both of them complicated men's sociability. But competition also distorted the friendships of women, whose clothing, jewelry, and homes marked status. "Empty husks," Evans called their displays. Unable to keep pace with the truly rich and unwilling to attack property, these writers derided ostentatious consumption and presumptuous manners as impediments to social harmony.[5]

Despite the fact that Alabama's writers portrayed friendships crossing class lines, they forged their friendships with people of roughly similar standing.[6] Pickett's best friends came from among Autauga County's planters, though he also counted the middle-class brothers George and Johnson Hooper among his less intimate friends. Most of Baldwin's friends were lawyers, and Meek, who had planters' sons for friends in college, associated with professionals in Mobile. Middle-class writers did not often befriend the truly poor, but some of them mingled with the rich. After they won repute, both Meek and Caroline Hentz made friends with a very prominent socialite, Octavia Walton Le Vert, who also had literary ambitions. A literary reputation could, in fact, be useful, as Baldwin noticed when he became a cat, if not a lion, in Mobile.

Four writers shed light on friendships in the rising South, using the ideal of true friendship to measure their conduct and criticizing people (real and fictional) who betrayed its ethical obligations. Lifelong friends, Alexander Meek

---

[5] Stephen W. Berry argues that competition impeded men's friendships in *All That Makes a Man: Love and Ambition in the Civil War South* (New York: Oxford University Press, 2003), 39–40. The negative impact of competition on the trust and cooperation among Alabama's men is also a theme of Daniel S. Dupre, *Transforming the Cotton Frontier: Madison County, Alabama, 1800–1840* (Baton Rouge: Louisiana State University Press, 1997), which traces the conflict between traditional and more modern conceptions of social relations. For the corrosive effect of capitalism, see Karen Halttunen, *Confidence Men and Painted Women: A Study of Middle-Class Culture in America, 1830–1870* (New Haven: Yale University Press, 1982).

[6] John Quist found that Tuscaloosa's Whiggish reformers contained a minority of artisans and lower-middle-class people and a majority of elite professionals and planters, and that slaveholders were influential in all reform societies. This suggests that town society mixed people across class lines. His analysis did not distinguish between upper- and middle-class townspeople (he used occupation and slaveholding but did not generalize to class), and he studied association rather than friendship; *Restless Visionaries: The Social Roots of Antebellum Reform in Alabama and Michigan* (Baton Rouge: Louisiana State University Press, 1998), esp. ch. 1, "Slaveholding Operative of the Benevolent Empire." His reformers "perceived their efforts as liberating for individuals and believed that they provided a progressive course for American society," 21.

and William Smith overcame the damaging effects of competition by applying similar standards of friendship, and each described the results in poetry about the South. Caroline Hentz developed friendships that effectively made the northern-born woman a southerner, albeit with divided sympathies. Jeremiah Clemens entangled his friendships in a quest for status, yet he showed his alienation from upper-class southwesterners when his novels applied the ethics of friendship to ordinary Mexicans. Like many other middle-class Americans, Smith, Meek, Hentz, and Clemens believed that friendships brought pleasure, satisfaction, and security to all free people who chose them.

People everywhere anchor themselves in the world through friendship, but the ethics of friendship also belong to specific cultures. It is thus significant that southwestern writers asked friendships to reflect a middle-class ideal of self-determination, which challenged older traditions of honor, hierarchy, and rank. Their expectations demonstrated their belief that voluntary relations suited their slave society. Friendships reconciled autonomy and dependence, helping these writers believe they were choosing their lives. As such, they were central to writers' hopes for a better future. But even the ideal of friendship hid problems. Friendship aggravated the differences among people by sorting them into groups. It lent inequalities an innocent air by making them seem more voluntary than they were. When friendship spilled over into broader relationships – especially into politics – it had public ramifications. And friendship created conformity if the human need for acceptance became an incessant search for approval. At bottom, the philosophy of friendship assumed the harmony between individual and social well-being, and practice did not always conform to theory. That dilemma was inescapable in the free society of the rising South.

A PAIR OF COMPETITIVE FRIENDS

Born less than a year apart, Alexander Meek and William Smith grew up friends in Tuscaloosa. Meek was by far the more sociable of the two men. The minister officiating at his funeral in 1865 described what made Meek "so charming in the circle of friendship":

He sought the happiness of others, rather than his own. His whole nature seemed womanly in all the finer and more delicate components of its organization, so that, whether in the forum, the halls of legislation, the literary circle, or around the fireside at home, gentleness of manner and a most winning refinement and grace drew all hearts to him irresistibly.[7]

As this clergyman saw Meek, the writer was not inured to his "womanly" nature like most men of the world. Yet Meek's relations with Smith sometimes belied the warmth his eulogist praised. Smith was a somber man who worried

---

[7] Rev. Phillip P. Neely, *Address Delivered at the Funeral of Hon. Alexander B. Meek* (Columbus, MS: Printed at the Sentinel Office, 1866), 4.

about relying on other people. He and Meek were close, however, and they wrote about each other in ways that show the modern ideal of friendship shaping more traditional masculine relations. In a society noted for bare-knuckled competition, both men achieved literary success. Their friendship formed a common ground from which they could observe, and sometimes criticize, their world.

Meek revealed the tension between ethical ideals and his daily conduct in diaries he kept when he was in his twenties, living with his parents or in a boarding house. Meek wrote in a breezy style, saying a little about work and a lot about the leisure of a middle-class young townsman. He recorded walks around Tuscaloosa or along the Black Warrior River, late-night chats in his room, his search for a wife, his membership in debate clubs and reform societies, his attendance at political meetings, churches, and parties, and the progress (or lack of it) in his studies. He sometimes wrote in the company of men like Smith or Cyrus Baldwin, Joe's brother, who was a printer in town. Meek was not always sober when he wrote. His remarks were never deeply reflective, rarely religious. Occasionally he noted reading or inserted poetry into his diary. He also made lists of the books he loaned friends like Smith, Baldwin, and Caroline Hentz. Cheerfully engrossed in himself, Meek also analyzed his relations with friends – mostly other young men, sometimes older family acquaintances, and once in a while, a woman.[8]

Meek liked women but not always as friends. He vied for the attentions of eligible women, whose names and traits he recorded. He also noted the men who prowled the town with him in search of flirtation. He offered variations on the theme of sex. Meek's attitude toward women was often crass. Like a connoisseur, he appraised their appearance, manners, intelligence, and wealth. He noticed Miss Mary Read of Huntsville, the amber-haired, blue-eyed sister of a friend and "truly a pretty girl!" He cataloged her virtues: she was "beautiful in person, & elegant and pleasing in manners"; she played the piano and sang; she was "small but well-shaped." She was, in sum "such a girl as I could fall in love with, if – if – she were – rich," but she was not. "I can love her, but cannot marry poverty," he wrote playfully. But he also described his "desperate" search at a party for a "woman who could say something more than Yes or No!" He found one, only to discover that she was a northerner, a teacher, a blue-stocking, and too old.[9]

Also a bachelor, Smith was a frequent companion in Meek's quest for a mate. Meek spent too much time "visiting the Society and thinking of the Ladies," habits that were "vitiating" because they prevented work. But the strategy had advantages because he was trying to get ahead, and he assessed them with Smith. Smith consoled Meek about his "love scrapes" and identified potential matches. Meek and his friends joked mercilessly about women.

---

[8] Generalizations drawn from Meek's diaries, the largest parts of which are at DUL (1834) and ADAH (1838 and 1840).
[9] July 17, 1834, and January 21, 1834, in Diary, 1834, A. B. Meek Papers, DUL.

The Voluntary Bonds of Friendship

In Cyrus Baldwin's presence, Alex punned about visiting a woman who asked him to ring for her servant. Instead, he took a ring from his finger and put it on hers, "thus ringing the belle." Baldwin responded that Meek "should have used his *clapper*!" Smith did not like puns. When the men gathered in Meek's room several nights later, he asked Meek to transcribe a rhyme that satirized puns. When Meek dutifully wrote the poem in his diary, he joked that he was its target, adding, however, "Smith swears he means 'nothing personal.'"[10]

Given the salience of honor in southern society, tension marked male bonding, which is why Smith assured Meek that he meant "nothing personal." Competitive banter put a bite in friendships, as young men tested themselves. It is perhaps no wonder that they drank freely, for alcohol relaxed tension; but it also decreased rationality and released aggression. Insults and wounded feelings followed. Meek learned how to manage a pistol, just in case it ever became "necessary to fight a duel," though he vowed he would never kill. Where honor mattered, a man could not forget that verbal sparring might escalate.[11] Ideally, friendship reduced the risk.

Meek and his circle could be exclusive – and mean about it. In his 1840 diary, Meek described a "good hit" on a "loafer," one John Cochrane who was "forcing his company upon a set at my room." One of the men punned that Cochrane reminded him of a friend who had "lost a part of his *penis*," for Cochrane was only "*half-cocked*." Meek retorted that he wished Cochrane was "whole *cocked*" so there "would be some chance of his *going-off*!" Proud of his pun, Meek noted that Cochrane quickly left the room.[12] Most of Meek's crude jokes aimed at women *in absentia*, and they seem to have been routine within the circle. If men propped up their egos by putting women down, however, verbal play also exposed them to hits from one another.

Not surprisingly, competition marred the literary friendship between Meek and Smith. By the time they were twenty, they were planning a publication called "Tales and Legends of the South," which never materialized, although it anticipated the journals – *Bachelor's Button* and *The Southron* – that they eventually edited. Meek was a harsh critic of his friend, perhaps jealous because Smith could write better. But Meek outshone Smith as a speaker. On Independence Day in 1834, Meek heard his friend's public oration and penned a scathing evaluation: Smith's speech was "*weak, flimsy,* bombastic &

---

[10] May 6, 1834; May 5, 1834; Diary, 1834, Meek Papers, DUL; puns with Baldwin, January 3, and with Smith on January 10, 1840; in Diary, 1840, Meek Papers, ADAH. Although Meek's comments about his "vitiating" habits were about himself, he says much the same of Smith; January 21, 1834, Diary, 1834, Meek Papers, DUL.

[11] Comment on his marksmanship and dueling, n.d., Diary, 1834, Meek Papers, DUL. Meek also commented on the more formal competition of debating clubs, noting one about the merits of slavery, January 2, 1838, Diary, 1838, Meek Papers, ADAH, and another about the benefits of early marriage, March 7, 1834, Diary, 1834, Meek Papers, DUL.

[12] January 3, 1840, Diary, 1840, Meek Papers, ADAH. It is possible that this is the New Yorker Meek mentioned in his diary on January 1, 1838, Diary, 1838, Meek Papers, ADAH.

disgusting. One continued concatenation of turgid, butterfly, tinsel, syllabub declamation." As if to justify his spite, Meek added that Smith "disappointed the expectations of all."[13] He did not identify the "all," but the phrase suggests that a gossiping circle of townsmen turned on one of their own.

Knowing that friendship required trust, Meek later judged himself. When he reviewed a draft of Smith's work *The Bridal Eve*, he ridiculed the "poor, uninteresting, and bad-written tale." He insisted that "the plot is *no plot* at all," that the work has "no mystery or engaging interest – combining neither beauty of style, sentiment [n]or character," adding that "the poetry is worse than the prose and that is bad enough in all conscience." But Meek recognized that his "*private opinion*" conflicted with his friendship for Smith, and he pledged that he "would not utter it in public for any consideration." Remembering their long friendship, Meek reflected that Smith had become "somewhat cold," which he attributed to "a want of adulation and flattery of his works on my part." He caught himself again, however: "I may be mistaken – Suspicion is the mother of a thousand abortions – I wish Smith *well*." Meek was checking his competitive instincts by the standard of friendship.[14]

Meek also expected emotional satisfaction from his friendship with Smith. Several months later, when Smith presented him with the printed version of *The Bridal Eve*, Meek was grateful for the "token of friendship from one of my earliest & now one of my warmest friends." That night, the young men apparently celebrated with a "champagne frolic, & all got *drunk*," which, unremarkably, produced a "headache & nauseous stomach."[15] Meek wanted warmth as well as intellectual stimulation from his friends, and the literary and social aspects of his relations overlapped unpredictably. He and Smith shared the desire to encourage southern literature, but it created problems as well as satisfactions when ambitions intervened.

Ambitions led the friends in different directions in the mid-1840s. An increasingly prominent Democrat, Meek became an editor of the Mobile *Register*, while Smith plunged into Whig politics and was elected to Congress in 1851. Literary friendships continued significant in Meek's life after he left Tuscaloosa. He continued writing through a variety of jobs, and eventually, when he finally married a wealthy woman, he found publishers for his works. *Songs and Poems of the South* (1857) abundantly demonstrated Meek's sociability.[16] Written from the late 1830s onward, many of the poems were originally read to local audiences, but some first saw print in magazines or newspapers. Meek aimed his collection at regional and national readers, publishing the volume in Mobile and New York. With only hints of the bourgeoning sectional conflict, Meek placed a South of romance, friendship, beauty, and pleasure

---

[13] Discussion of "Tales and Legends," January 26, 1834; evaluation, July 21, 1834; both in Diary, 1834, Meek Papers, DUL.
[14] January 21, 1834, *ibid.*
[15] June 18, 1834, *ibid.*
[16] *Songs and Poems of the South* (New York: B. F. Goetzel, 1857).

within the context of American ideals. He described the rising South at its finest, as he saw it.

Meek's light rhymes epitomized the social function of literature. Many of them were written to entertain, and others were inscriptions to particular friends or former lovers. A number carried dedications to other writers – to William Smith, Texas's Mirabeau Lamar, and Georgia's Richard Wilde. A few were brief epitaphs and others public commemorations at the death of famous men such as Daniel Webster, Henry Clay, and Andrew Jackson. Some glorified Alabama's people, scenery, flowers, and birds – even its smells. Meek's poems casually treated appearances and rarely aimed at complexity. Only occasional humor betrayed a critical moment beneath the sentiment. Pleasant to scan – it is easy to imagine them read or sung – they would not win Meek lasting repute, but they confirmed his status as a popular poet.

Perhaps most importantly, in the context of political hatreds that would not be healed, *Songs and Poems of the South* celebrated communities of convivial friendship. "Song at the Bar Dinner," for example, reflected an all-male gathering in Mobile that was probably similar to the dinner in Tuscaloosa for William Gilmore Simms. Read aloud at the event, the poem was full of puns about the law. Meek urged his hearers to "Exchange *your cases* for this *case* / Of wines, cigars, and capers" and invited them to "Put by your summons, writs and pleas, / Your briefs and declarations, / And for a season, take your ease / In feastings and libations!" Less masculine in tenor, "The Nuptial Féte" described a party of beautiful women and dashing men on a steamboat decorated with wedding banners. As they cruised down the Black Warrior, amid rousing dances and flirtations in every corner of the boat, the men drank champagne "in showers."[17] Whether sentimental or frivolous, Meek's poems about his friends showed only the happy South he wanted American readers to appreciate.

Songs and Poems of the South only hinted at the defects in men's friendships. In a poetic tribute to his deceased mother, Meek waxed nostalgic (though he was only thirty when he wrote). Recalling the feelings he enjoyed in her lifetime, Meek insisted that "the dear friends, I loved so fondly then, / Have left my side, or grown to cold-browed men, / And I now mingle in life's fever-fray, / With little lingering of that better day."[18] Here he suggested a brief moral lesson. Friendship represented the emotional comfort that "cold-browed men" lost when they pursued self-interest, and Meek acknowledged he made regrettable choices when he joined "life's fever-fray." Despite the sentimental gloss, he no doubt had Smith and their circle in mind.

Whether he wrote his poetry for his friends' albums, for local audiences, or for national publication, Meek usually (but not always) ignored his society's

---

[17] "Song at the Bar Dinner," 37, 36; "The Nuptial Féte," 277, in *ibid*. The latter poem had appeared in the *SLM* 10 (October, 1841): 685–690, as "The Nuptial Fete. An Irregular Poem."

[18] "My Mother," *Songs and Poems of the South*, 116.

ALEXANDER B. MEEK.

FIGURE 4.1. Alexander Meek.
This portrait of Alexander Meek suggests why he was called handsome, and it reinforces the romantic image he adopted in his oratory and writing. Courtesy of the W. S. Hoole Special Collections Library, The University of Alabama.

deficiencies. Only his diaries show the tensions within southwestern friendships, and it is not clear that those troubled him very much. But his friend Smith did not share Meek's reluctance to write for the public about their friendship. Smith was as prone to self-analysis as Meek was to superficial cheer, and that contrast informed their friendship in his account. Smith understood his relationship with Meek within the broader framework of southern sociability, and he criticized the conviviality his friend celebrated. His recollection of their youthful friendship suggested that it grew from the sympathetic communication of their similarities and their real differences.

Written to be read in Tuscaloosa in 1860, Smith's Phi Beta Kappa poem *The Uses of Solitude* was a blank verse counterpoint to Meek's lyrics. While Meek's collected poetry lauded sociability, Smith's forty-five-page poem idealized self-reliance. Although the friendly rivalry between the two friends may have diminished with the distance between them, it lingered in Smith's poem. Meek's 1857 volume had dedicated a long poem to Smith, yet *The Uses of Solitude* cast Meek in an unflattering role – not by name, but so vividly sketched that no well-informed listener could have missed it. Smith addressed his poem to the college men who listened before him, urging them to be independent. Placing an evocative description of two youthful friends at the end of his poem, Smith used Meek as an illustration of the dangers awaiting young men who failed to achieve self-reliance.[19]

The Uses of Solitude placed Smith's ethical lessons within tales of great leaders – "shadows of mighty men" – across the history of the western world, and behind it lurked the fearsome crisis of 1860. And Smith used Meek not only to express his ideas about friendship but to suggest his deeper anxieties about the South's future. All along, Meek and Smith had shared a vision of a modernizing slave society, while differing about particular policies. Now, Smith adamantly opposed secession, which he thought would destroy slavery and the rising South. While he was not a radical, Meek accepted secession. He was a political friend of the state's leading fire-eater, William Lowndes Yancey, whom Smith thought a reckless demagogue. Yancey epitomized honor *in extremis*, and Meek did not; but, in his use of Meek, Smith cautioned men against the search for approval. As he declaimed early in the poem: "who waits on others / Loses his time and dies without a name."[20]

Smith's extended description of two young writers illustrated the ideal of friendship resting on individuality, for they shared their differences – their "thoughts, ambitions, hopes, and fears" – with confidence. Smith's tone was both affectionate and reflective as he compared the two writers in appearance, character, and habits: the "majestical," handsome orator was clearly Meek and the "dark-browed" intellectual was just as plainly Smith. The "fond" friends were talented and ambitious: "each lofty in his aims, / Each gifted beyond mortals of his type / With some peculiar excellence; each bent / In his fond dreams on Immortality." Nonetheless, Smith made Meek a crowd-pleasing dilettante and himself a disciplined, introspective artist.[21] While the "two, so

[19] William R. Smith, *The Uses of Solitude* (Tuscaloosa: Printed for the Alabama Alpha of the Phi Beta Kappa Society, 1860).

[20] Ibid., 5–6. For an account of Meek's youthful role in a duel involving Yancey and North Carolinian Thomas L. Clingman, see Eric H. Walther, *William Lowndes Yancey and the Coming of the Civil War* (Chapel Hill: University of North Carolina Press, 2006), 77–78. More recently, Meek had been a member, with Yancey, of the Alabama delegation that walked out of the Democratic national convention at Charleston, so he was, as Smith knew, in the midst of the movement that would disrupt the Union.

[21] *Uses of Solitude*, 38–39. Smith described Meek as "First in the ring of pleasure; in the race / Of frolic, foremost ever; apt of wit; / Rapid and smooth-tongued, even eloquent; / Well fashioned and of shape majestical," 39. The stanzas comparing the two friends run for six pages (38–44) just before the conclusion of the long poem. Smith's daughter quotes from this poem repeatedly in her biography of her father, and she includes the full text in an appendix. She describes its composition (claiming, no doubt from his recollection, that it took only a few days). She

different" men walked one morning "arm in arm," along the river's edge, they discussed what each had done the night before. The Meek-like character raved about a splendid ball where "'The wit and fashion of the city came'" and added (as Meek might have done), "'O! the wine!'" The "graver youth" spent his time better: "'I held a festival myself, last night; / In my own closet, with my books alone. / My little chamber thronged with visitors'" – the authors and subjects of his solitary reading.[22] After the intimate friends recalled their evenings, Smith drew his lesson from their differences.

Smith's moral lesson connected the Meek-like character's sociability with a pointless quest for honor and made social conformity a deadly trap. Continuing his contrast of the two friends, Smith explained that their futures diverged. Displaying his "genius," Smith's Meek-like orator won applause, and the acclaim fed an insatiable appetite for more approval. But when he chased fame, he earned a sad fate: people said that he "*'left great signs / Of Genius'* – but he labored not and died." The Smith-like man, on the other hand, applied himself in solitude, crafted literature for the ages, "shunning for Learning's sake a life of pleasure."[23] Smith used poetic license, for Meek was not dead and the author courted public favor like his friend. Older listeners in Tuscaloosa and later readers of the published poem knew that. Smith spoke, however, to the men of Phi Beta Kappa, who surely strolled on that river's bank, "arm in arm" with their friends, and might see themselves in his poem. And he wrote to persuade men – perhaps Meek among them – that self-reliance was more important than pleasing a crowd.

Smith's poem was not an epitaph for this friendship, which survived the political strains of 1860. Smith had little use for the many casual relations Meek enjoyed, but their friendship was important to him. Despite their differences, Smith understood Meek – perhaps better than anyone else. Smith recognized traits that Meek preferred to ignore, though his diary indicated that he knew them. The idealization of true friendship minimized the difficulties of maintaining affection in the face of difference, but its claims were "imperative," as Augusta Evans wrote, and Smith and Meek met that requirement. Competition damaged friendship but did not destroy the bonds that joined Alexander Meek and William Smith to each other and the rising South.

A NEW ENGLANDER'S ALLIANCE WITH THE RISING SOUTH

Although the temperamental differences between William Smith and Alexander Meek were at least as large as the ones Smith sketched in *The Uses of Solitude*, their friendship reflected a middle-class ideal of friendship that stretched across the Atlantic. The experience of Massachusetts-born Caroline

---

also notes that he considered it "his most inspired poem"; Anne Easby-Smith, *William Russell Smith of Alabama; His Life and Works* (Philadelphia: Dolphin Press, 1931), 90.

[22] *Uses of Solitude*, 39–40.
[23] Ibid., 43.

Hentz complicates the sharp contrast Smith drew between sociability and self-reliance. Hentz, too, thought friends benefitted from sharing their differences, and she tried to maintain an independent view, yet she found that friends encouraged common values. Too strong-willed to jettison the social ethics she brought from New England, she discovered that many of her ideas about white society fit very well in the rising South. As Hentz made good friends in Alabama, and later in Georgia, she became a literary advocate for a modern slave society.

Hentz gained her southern friends slowly, hindered at first not only by her northern origins but by the terms of her marriage. Nicholas had psychological problems that grew more serious as he aged, and unreasoning jealousy was one manifestation of his disorder. In theory, the values of trust, sympathy, honesty, and respect for differences applied to all friendships. Most nineteenth-century writers believed, however, that women were more amply endowed by nature with sympathy (when his eulogist spoke of Alexander Meek's "charming" friendship, he said his nature was "womanly"). Respectable women had to exercise caution, for some sympathies were out of bounds.[24] And Nicholas drew Caroline's boundaries more narrowly than respectability required.

Hentz relied on friends for intellectual companionship, and her unstable husband's choices diminished hers. Their Cincinnati literary club, run by New Englanders, had mixed and men and women. But, after Caroline's friendship with a man in the circle prompted her husband to move the family to Florence, Nicholas forbade his wife to have male friends. After hearing from her friend Elizabeth Drake, whose husband was a leader in the Cincinnati group, Hentz complained to her diary: "I sometimes fall into hypochondriac fits – I feel as if there were no one in the world to love me, as if I were removed from all that were once interested in my happiness & that those around me were alienated from me." For good reason, she worried that Nicholas, her only "anchor" in Florence, would fail her. When the Drakes visited, she found it "delightful to meet old friends once more, in a cold, strange land." Despite the fact that the town's most eminent woman, Mrs. John Coffee, entertained Caroline and her northern visitors at the family's plantation, Hentz felt excluded.[25]

---

[24] Meek characterization in the eulogy quoted *supra*, n. 7.

[25] Diary entries: "hypochondriac fit," April 27; "cold, strange land," June 10 or 20 (unclear); all in Caroline's Diary for 1836, Hentz Family Papers, UNC. Hentz noted the visit to Mrs. Coffee's on July 5, *ibid*. The Cincinnati circle is described in Louis L. Tucker, "The Semi-Colon Club of Cincinnati," *Ohio History* 73 (Winter 1964): 13–26. It included, for example, Lyman Beecher, his two daughters, Harriet and Catharine, and Harriet's husband, Calvin Stowe; and it combined sociability – the moderate consumption of alcohol was allowed – with literary criticism of the members' works. Hentz repeatedly showed her ambivalence about her isolation in Florence and its causes in her diary. On Washington's birthday, she recalled a ball in Boston many years earlier from the perspective of her life in "this secluded spot," insisting that she was now convinced of the "emptiness of all these glittering vanities," and concluding: "Had I always valued the blessings allotted me in the domestic circle as I now do, I might still have mingled with a world I no longer love too well"; February 22, 1836, in Diary for 1836, UNC.

To be sure, Caroline felt more than equal to her neighbors, even if her Puritan ancestry carried no great distinction in Alabama. She knew she ranked a notch below women who did not have to earn money, but she scorned some southerners with an undisguised pride. She wrote acidly in her diary about parents who treated the school-teaching Hentzes high-handedly. She emphasized their arrogance: one galling incident "was not the first time Mr. H. has received such a *gentlemanly* mark of attention in Florence." Understanding status in the cotton town, she complained after calling on a local bride: "She is not handsome – not even pretty, – nor witty but her father has 4 or 500 slaves and that makes her lovely in this Southern land."[26] Hentz had standards for rank, but they did not conform to the local ones – at least not yet. Not surprisingly, she hoped her family would move again.

In spite of Caroline's initial loneliness, the Hentzes began to make friends. Although the family visited the Coffees' plantation for fishing, bug-hunting, and picnics, most of Caroline's friends were townspeople. The Hentzes became active Presbyterians and joined a lyceum "amongst the intelligent & literary citizens of Florence," their son recalled. When the family finally moved on, after nearly nine years, Caroline celebrated her friendships in a poem. "Farewell to Florence" bade "Adieu to the friends who have twined round the hours / Of social enjoyment, affection's sweet flowers; / Whose hearts and whose spirits have mingled with mine; / Round the fireside of home and the prayer-hallowed shrine." Although Hentz was chronically sentimental, her mingling of "hearts and spirits" indicated that the people of Florence had met her standards for friendship. Moreover, as Charles recalled, the family of five stayed a week at the Coffees' plantation while their things were packed for shipment to Tuscaloosa.[27] Caroline had made good friends.

In Tuscaloosa, where the Hentzes lived only two years, Caroline had more options in choosing friends, for the college town's diversity allowed her to cultivate her talent, enjoy fellow northerners, and still connect with respectable southerners. The Hentzes became friends with their neighbors, the family of ex-Governor Joshua Martin. The less prominent Meek family provided friendships for Nicholas, who played chess with Alex, for Caroline, who shared literary tastes, and for young Charles, who liked Alex's sisters. Another of Nicholas's chess opponents was Professor Samuel Stafford, and Caroline became friends with Stafford's wife Maria, herself a New Englander and former teacher – "a handsome Lady, and an accomplished woman." The

---

[26] Diary entry complaining about parents, February 11; on the bride's assets, May 20; both in Diary for 1836, UNC. For comments on Hentz's Puritan "pedigree," see the eulogy in *New England Historical and Genealogical Register* 10 (January 1856): 194–195.

[27] Characterization of the lyceum, Charles A. Hentz, *A Southern Practice: The Diary and Autobiography of Charles A. Hentz, M.D.*, ed. with an intro. by Stephen M. Stowe (Charlottesville: Published for the Southern Texts Society by the University Press of Virginia, 2000), 422. "Farewell to Florence," reprinted in the Muscle Shoals *Sunday News*, March 2, 1924; Charles recalled that the family "spent a week or so of delightful visit" at Mrs. Coffee's; *Diary and Autobiography*, 428.

The Voluntary Bonds of Friendship

Hentzes grew roots, for when Nicholas moved them again in 1845, young Thaddeus stayed in Tuscaloosa for school. Charles soon returned to work in a doctor's office, and his parents sent "little bundles of presents for Tuscaloosa friends," a token of the affections they left behind.[28]

A letter Caroline wrote to Maria Stafford in 1846 showed how friendships were binding her to the South. Her note rambled like a conversation between close friends, sharing literary progress, gossip, family events, and political opinions. Caroline was pleased to have renovated her parlor with money from her writing. Although teaching kept her busy, she promised to send Stafford new stories – evidence of an interested reviewer. Accustomed now to African American servants, Caroline appreciated the low cost of renting a slave, "one of the best workers I ever knew & a very good cook." She asked about the potential impact of the relocation of the state's capital, snapping that it would not hurt the university because the "legislators manifested so little interest in the cause of education" – a familiar gripe among townspeople who wanted the rural state to move forward.[29]

Her dig at the legislature was not the only comment that Hentz expected Stafford to keep confidential. She also repeated an anecdote about a young woman's encounter with their mutual friend Alexander Meek. She warned Maria: "You know how everything said about him is repeated & it might come back to his ears – so only, *entre nous*." She wondered if Meek would join the university faculty, adding: "I am told he is greatly improved, though in mind and manners I thought there was little room for it. I always thought him one of the most interesting men I ever knew."[30] Clearly, Hentz now enjoyed the kind of chatter that formed social consensus. Although Stafford, too, was New England born, Hentz's brief evaluation of a slave and her casual gossip suggest that the outsider was becoming an insider.

Another sign of Hentz's increasing acceptance was the friendship she made with Mobile's reigning socialite, Octavia Le Vert. Noted for her beauty, wealth, hospitality, and intelligence, Le Vert collected famous people. She befriended Caroline when the Hentzes visited Mobile in 1845, before Nicholas chose Tuskegee as their next home. Several years later, Le Vert described the "mystic tie" between the two women. Mourning the sudden death of two

---

[28] Charles's description of Mrs. Stafford, *Diary and Autobiography*, 442; the presents he took back with him are noted in his diary for June 9, 1846, *ibid.*, 102. Both his diary and autobiography are littered with references to the friends the family made in Tuscaloosa. Virginia Clay-Clopton recalled Mrs. Stafford's educational influence in Tuscaloosa and her New England roots; *A Belle of the Fifties: Memoirs of Mrs. Clay of Alabama*, with intro., annotations, and index by Leah Rawls Atkins, Joseph H. Harrison, Jr., and Sara A. Hudson (Tuscaloosa: University of Alabama Press, 1999, c. 1905), 9.

[29] Hentz to Maria Stafford, June 2, 1846, Hentz Family Papers, UNC.

[30] *Ibid.* It is not clear when Hentz met Meek. As early as 1843, he was writing W. Gilmore Simms about her and sent Simms, then editing the *Magnolia*, a sketch of her that he had written; Meek to Simms, April 14, 1843, HSP; several months later he passed on to Simms the information that she occasionally wrote a story or poem for *Bachelor's Button*; Meek to Simms, October 20, 1843, HSP.

of her children, Le Vert confided to Hentz "a depth of Desolation" beyond "the power of written words or of speech." Although she could not speak her children's names to her mother, she could use the literary language of sentiment with Hentz. Indeed, she found "a strange pleasure in leaning upon your sympathy & dwelling upon my sorrows." Sure that Hentz would "appreciate the intensity of my anguish," she probably knew that Caroline had lost a toddler in a freak household accident.[31] Le Vert's expression of feeling ignored the differences in the women's backgrounds. It made the ideal of friendship seem real.

The growing ease in Hentz's female friendships was accompanied by a new freedom with men. After three years in Tuskegee, the Hentz family moved just across the Chattahoochee River to Columbus, Georgia, where Nicholas's mind unraveled. Caroline wrote Maria Stafford in 1851 that Nicholas, sick with "nerves," was taking "laudamen & morphine constantly." Showing her new independence and obvious relief, she added: "At least now he does tolerate my having male friends." Perhaps men's friendships were appealing because they had been long forbidden, but there were other reasons they were attractive. Men in her Cincinnati circle had encouraged Caroline; men were useful because they controlled the public sphere; and they did not have to disguise their intelligence. Her comments to Maria Stafford about Meek had illustrated some of this. Hentz knew people's qualms about Meek's morality, but she liked his "mind and manners," and she found him "interesting."[32] She did not need to mention that he had published her work, for that was common knowledge.

In any case, Hentz resented the limitations on women's choices, for she knew that friendships encouraged intellectual growth. She suggested a relationship between women's options and the advantages of male friendships in her short but blunt essay "The Sex of the Soul." She argued that a man could improve himself to the very limit of his ability because he gained mental discipline from broad education. A woman, she angrily wrote, was "told to hold down the aspirations of her intellect" because thinking might make her "spurn the bondage" society imposed. An intellectual woman, she observed sarcastically, might "repel and alienate the being whom she was created to charm."[33] Although Hentz closed her essay by agreeing that an essential inequality intertwined men and women in marriage, she had gained confidence. Now freed by her husband's malady, Hentz had greater license to choose her friends.

She exercised her freedom carefully. Nicholas would "tolerate" Caroline's male friendships because, in his lucid periods, he saw the responsibilities she

---

[31] Letter to Hentz copied into Le Vert's daybook, DUL, 79–80, dated September 5, 1852. The only biography of Le Vert is Frances Gibson Satterfield, *Madame Le Vert: A Biography of Octavia Walton Le Vert* (Edisto Island, SC: Edisto Press, 1987). Charles recalled the friendship in his *Autobiography*, 447.

[32] Hentz to Maria Stafford, March 5, 1851, UNC.

[33] "The Sex of the Soul," in *The Banished Son; and Other Stories of the Heart* (Philadelphia: T. B. Peterson, 1856), 267.

carried. Increasingly, she produced her family's income with writing that had grown in popularity after the publication of *Aunt Patty's Scrap-Bag* in 1846. Work limited Caroline's social life, however, and she remained conscious that she was a Yankee among southerners. She also understood that any friendships between men and women required self-restraint. After visiting New England in 1850, Hentz wrote an old friend, "Mr. Willard," that her trip had "closed up" a "great chasm." Using "poetry in expression," she assured him that no one felt "a deeper, warmer interest in their friends." And she asked Willard to consult his wife about the "privilege of expressing my friendship for her husband," calling it "pure, unadulterated friendship." Even as she pledged not to "encroach" on his wife's "peculiar rights and feelings," she said that her "*friendship*" was "as ardent as the *love* of most women."[34] Hentz seemed eager to feel deeply.

New England was far away, however, and Hentz knew that attenuated ties could not fully sustain her. A year later, she suggested this concern to the same "dear Friends," this time writing both Mr. and Mrs. Willard. Memories of her "beloved New England" were "cheering and sustaining," she wrote, implying she was a "prisoner" of Nicholas's "nervous malady." But most of her friends in Columbus had gone for the summer, and only "some very dear and kind ones" remained to "scatter the sunbeams of sociability" around her. Plaintively, but without whining, she asked her distant friends to imagine her "white house with green trees before it & a pure breeze rustling through the foliage." Maybe they could "catch a glimpse of a figure through the parlor window curtains, scribbling as is her wont to do, trying but in vain to express half the kind thoughts that fill her heart, when she thinks of her New England friends."[35] Hentz's letter connected friends in Georgia and Massachusetts, for people in each place gave her comfort. This matched the strategy of sectional reconciliation she had begun to implement in her fiction.

Despite attempts to balance her loyalties, Hentz's writing was increasingly southern, and it sold well. She began the new regional emphasis in *Linda; or, The Pilot of the Belle Creole* (1850), which was quickly followed by four more southern novels in six years. During the same time, she set two novels in New England.[36] Although all of Hentz's novels featured women's friendships,

---

[34] Hentz to Mr. Williard, October 25, 1850, Barrett Collection, UVA. Mr. Willard is apparently Paul Willard, with whom she visited again in 1854; see Hentz to Abraham Hart, Feb. 13 [1854], written from Charleston and asking him to direct any immediate response to Charleston in care of Willard; letter is at HEH. *Aunt Patty's Scrap-Bag* (Philadelphia: Carey & Hart, 1846).

[35] Hentz to Mr. and Mrs. Willard, August 21, 1851, UVA.

[36] *Linda; or, The Young Pilot of Belle Creole* (Philadelphia: A. Hart, 1850); *The Planter's Northern Bride*, 2 vols. (Philadelphia: Parry & McMillan, 1854). All of Hentz's fiction was repeatedly published, often with two printings by different publishers in the same year, and some of it appeared in serial form. T. B. Peterson reprinted all of her works in the late 1850s in inexpensive form. *Linda* was serialized in the Philadelphia *American Courier* (1846). *Rena; or, The Snowbird* (Philadelphia: A. Hart, 1851) and *Helen and Arthur; or, Miss Thusa's Spinning Wheel; A Novel* (Philadelphia: A. Hart, 1853) were set in the North.

the one that depended most on the connection between friendship and regional identity was *Eoline, or Magnolia Vale* (1852). *Eoline* clearly drew from Hentz's experiences, especially her teaching, for much of the action transpired at Magnolia Vale, a school for girls. The novel traced the quest for happiness of its young southern heroine, Eoline. Hentz dedicated the novel to "MRS. OCTAVIA W. LEVERT" as a "token of sincere friendship and admiration." It was evidence, for her readers, of her southern friendships.[37]

But, in *Eoline*, northern friends reformed Hentz's southern heroine, and the novel implied serious flaws in Hentz's adopted society. Like Smith's *The Uses of Solitude*, *Eoline* dramatized the way individuals benefitted from discussing their differences with good friends. Eoline was the beautiful, talented, and loving, but also spoiled and impulsive, planter's daughter. After refusing to marry the man of her father's choice, she chose to become a music teacher at Magnolia Vale. The pampered girl suffered from the loss of her usual luxuries until her two northern colleagues tutored her in restraint, discipline, and unselfishness. The more important of Eoline's two friends was Louisa More, a gentle Christian whose "friendship" was "a balm for all the wounds" that Eoline felt.[38] Raised in a poor but respectable family, Louisa taught Eoline charity and humility – virtues that the proud southern heroine badly needed.

Eoline's northern friends also taught her another virtue: work. The strongest influence in this regard was the school's young headmistress, whom the students nicknamed "Colonel" Manly. Miss Manly's masculine bearing hid innate kindness. She rigorously drilled her students and demanded that Eoline work. When an annoyed Eoline responded impulsively to the Colonel, the humble Louisa urged restraint. Eoline quickly saw that she should imitate her friend, asking Louisa: "Why cannot I be as gentle and lowly minded as thou art?" Eventually, Eoline realized that Miss Manly's discipline helped her, and she and the headmistress became good friends. In the kind of happy ending that Hentz favored, Louisa returned to New England, where she married; Eoline was reunited with her father, her wealth, and a husband; and the Colonel embraced a "nobler, more exalted sphere" of teaching as a single woman in the South.[39] Although Eoline was redeemed, the author stressed the character defects bred by her heroine's wealth and made the values of northern friends essential to her ultimate fulfillment.

[37] *Eoline; or, Magnolia Vale* (Philadelphia: T. B. Peterson, 1852), [3]. The spelling that Le Vert preferred separated the parts of the name, but many variants appeared and other family members used Levert. In the dedication, the spelling was entirely in caps, with no space.
[38] More's friendship, *ibid.*, 7.
[39] Question to More, 64; "exalted sphere," 260 in *ibid*. I am omitting any discussion here of the complicated romantic plot of the novel. Mary Ann Wimsatt has discussed the significance of Eoline's New England friendships in "Caroline Hentz's Balancing Act," in Carol Manning, ed., *The Female Tradition in Southern Literature* (Urbana: University of Illinois Press, 1993), 161–175. A full discussion of Hentz's attempt at sectional balance in *Eoline* is in Elizabeth Moss, *Domestic Novelists in the Old South: Defenders of Southern Culture* (Baton Rouge: Louisiana State University Press, 1992), 82–88, where she argues that the novel ultimately affirms a mainly southern perspective.

Hentz suggested that too much wealth was harmful, but she certainly did not embrace the lower classes. She made the refinement of education compensate for Louisa's poverty, and she wrote cruelly about a little commoner who attended Magnolia Vale. When Miss Manly required Eoline to share her room with Jerusha, a "vulgar and low bred" child, the heroine resisted. Jerusha was strictly southern, bragging that her father was "as rich as any body, and has got as many niggers, too." Displaying none of her usual sentimentality, Hentz made Jerusha a comic character, mocking her language and her manners. Although Louisa sympathized with the dreadful child and persuaded Eoline to try and teach her, Jerusha was "too animalized" to be fully salvaged.[40] Hentz's identification with the South was based on friendship with respectable people, and the boundaries of that status were not merely sectional.

The opening pages of *Marcus Warland, or The Long Moss Spring; a tale of the South* (1852) bore witness to how Hentz's educated and refined southern friends were affecting her work. Dedicating her novel to "Dr. Wildman" as a "testimony of gratitude and esteem" for his "encouragement and inspiration," Hentz did not mention that the man was her husband's physician and her advisor about publishing. Rather, after the dedication, Hentz proclaimed her "affections strongly clinging" to both sections of the nation and explained her indebtedness to her "intelligent and literary friends" in Columbus. They had listened to her reading of the manuscript "during its progress," and they had given her "frank and hearty encouragement." No wonder *Marcus Warland* portrayed slavery in a positive light.[41] And as that

[40] *Eoline*, 124, 122, 136.
[41] *Marcus Warland; or, The Long Moss Spring. A Tale of the South* (Philadelphia: A. Hart, 1852), 7–8. Dr. Wildman's role in Hentz's business relations is detailed in her letter to Abraham Hart, November 13, 1851, HSP. In the same place, she quotes Wildman's praise for the book as a good representation of the South. An early discussion of Hentz's tangled relationship with the commercial market is Mary Kelley's *Private Women, Public Stage: Literary Domesticity in Nineteenth-Century America* (New York: Oxford University Press, 1984), but see also Johanna Nicol Shields, "Writers in the Old Southwest and the Commercialization of American Letters," *Journal of the Early Republic* 27 (2007): 471–505. Charles Hentz identifies Dr. F. H. Wildman's role as his father's physician in *Diary and Autobiography*, 526, where he calls him "a great friend of our family" and describes his daily dose of morphine, which the doctor "weighed out always, a lot of doses ahead & ready – with the utmost care." Edward E. Baptist, in *Creating an Old South: Middle Florida's Plantation Frontier before the Civil War* (Chapel Hill: University of North Carolina Press, 2002), 257–258, makes *Marcus Warland* a fable about the settlement of the Florida Panhandle. He has Hentz moving to Florida in 1848, when she was actually living in Columbus, Georgia, but visiting her son Charles, who lived in Florida. Nicholas and Caroline moved to Florida in 1852, living first with a daughter and then, separately, with both children until their deaths in 1856; a useful chronology is provided by Stowe, in *Diary and Autobiography*, 45–47, even though it focuses on Charles. Baptist places *Marcus Warland* by reference to the Chattahoochee River, which flows by Columbus before it enters Florida. Columbus is in the southeastern corner of Georgia, close to both the Alabama and Florida borders, and it seems prudent to classify Hentz's settings as generally southwestern rather than fixing them on a particular location, given the family's constant movement and the absence of a comprehensive biography that tracks it carefully.

novel hit the market in 1852, she began planning for her more ambitious proslavery novel, *The Planter's Northern Bride*, which would tell the "*truth*" about the "noble-hearted people" of the South.[42]

Proslavery fiction identified Caroline Hentz with the South, regardless of her "affections strongly clinging" to all parts of the nation. Alexander Meek, the ceaseless promoter of southern literature, claimed her in his poem "Bird of the South," subtitled "An Allegory: for Mrs. Caroline Lee Hentz." While the poem praised Hentz's beauty and her grace, Meek insisted that he admired her "not for these charms" but for her "music excelling / All melody ever rapt fancy had dreamed!" Having dispelled any suggestion that his attraction was based on Hentz's sex, Meek called his friend "bird of the distance," then "Fair Bird of the South," and, to underscore their affinity, "Bird of my-own-land." The land they shared merged slavery and a southern past with values shared by middle-class people around the nation, among whom were the distant readers of Hentz's popular novels and Meek's *Songs and Poems of the South*.[43]

A fitting testament to Hentz's mixed loyalties was a notice of her death in 1856 in the *New England Genealogical and Historical Register*, which paid tribute to the woman who "filled so high a place in the social and literary world." First describing Hentz's New England connections, the eulogy called *The Planter's Northern Bride* "high evidence of her fascinating and gifted powers," with no mention of its proslavery dogma. The eulogy also quoted two paragraphs from an unnamed "distinguished and elegant person" who had praised Hentz earlier – Octavia Le Vert – and her selection placed Hentz's talents in an international rather than an American or southern context. Finally, the eulogy's anonymous author equivocated about Hentz's regional loyalties: "Although living and dying in the land of the orange and the magnolia blossoms, she never forgot, in the admiration bestowed upon her in Southern homes, the graceful elms which wave over the birthplace of her ancestors and kindred, nor the winding river whose rippling music found an echo in her youthful heart."[44]

The singular "social and literary world" evoked by a northern eulogist was made of white men and women who belonged to educated, town-dwelling elites. Such folk might live anywhere in the transatlantic world, and Hentz's southern friends were among them. Her gradual identification with southern

---

[42] Hentz to Abraham Hart, "*truth*" emphasized in her letter of December 16, 1852, HEH; "noble-hearted" in her letter of November 18, 1852, Woolman Library, Barnard College, New York. Both letters show how deliberately Hentz was designing a book that met the interests of the market as well as her avowed intention of vindicating slaveholding southerners. On the role of Dr. Wildman in encouraging her work, see Hentz to Abraham Hart, November 13, 1851, January 17, and June 24, 1852, HSP.

[43] Meek, "Bird of the South," in *Songs and Poems of the South*, 21–22.

[44] *New England Historical and Genealogical Register* 10 (January 1856): 194–195; Almost exactly the same passage by Le Vert was quoted in Mary Forrest, *Women of the South Distinguished in Literature* (New York: Derby and Jackson, 1861), 265–266, where Le Vert was identified as Hentz's "intimate friend."

people had not come easily, and self-interest and sympathy mixed in the process. Friendships encouraged enrollments in the Hentzes' schools. They compensated for the shortcomings of her marriage, and they became increasingly important when she faced new responsibilities as Nicholas declined. Because Caroline relied on local audiences and personal friends to review her literary efforts, she could hardly avoid identifying that work with "genial" white southerners. From the perspective of the twenty-first century, it is hard to understand how Hentz avoided seeing that enslaved black people suffered far more than she, despite her "hypochondriac fits" and the travails of teaching. Yet the popularity of her books suggests that many readers in the North as well as the South had the same blinders.

No writer of her generation portrayed the emotional experiences of respectable women with more sympathy than Hentz did, and her understanding of how friends supported one another resonated across regional boundaries. Her last novel, the autobiographical *Ernest Linwood*, showed how friendships helped a woman endure marriage to an irrational husband, and it was reprinted in Leipzig, Germany, as well as Boston, New York, Philadelphia, and Cleveland. Hentz sincerely tried to make the "literary and social world" a political reality by appealing to national, even international, ethical standards associated with the middle classes. She thought the regions could be reconciled, but she also thought the South was becoming gracefully modern, based on her experience in southwestern towns. Her hope was badly misplaced, but it was also the hope of Le Vert and Meek, among many others. By the time they were proved wrong, Hentz had died, sparing her the spectacle of her friends trying to kill one another.[45]

THE TANGLED FRIENDSHIPS OF A CONTROVERSIAL MAN

More often than not, middle-class friendships joined similar people, but some American writers imagined voluntary ties connecting radically different people. To take famous examples, both James Fenimore Cooper and Herman Melville challenged convention by depicting transracial friendships: Cooper with Natty Bumpo and Chingachgook in *The Last of the Mohicans* and Melville with Ishmael and Queequeg in *Moby-Dick*. Jeremiah Clemens experimented similarly in one novel set on the "outskirts of civilization," and his hero befriended Mexicans – people of mixed Spanish and Indian descent.[46] Clemens began writing fiction after a bitter conflict with powerful friends – people more like

---

[45] A partial listing from World Cat (http://www.worldcat.org) includes: a number of printings by J. P. Jewett & Co of Boston (1856 ff.); New York: Sheldon, Blakeman Co., 1856; numerous editions by T. B. Peterson, which issued her complete works in 1856; Cleveland: Proctor & Lovithington, 1856; Leipzig: W. Einhorn, 1856.

[46] James Fenimore Cooper, *The Last of the Mohicans. A Narrative of 1757* (Philadelphia: H. C. Carey and I. Lea, 1826), Herman Melville, *Moby-Dick; or, the Whale* (New York: Harper & Brothers, 1851), Jeremiah Clemens, *Mustang Gray, A Romance* (Philadelphia: D. Appleton, 1858). An 1859 edition of Cooper's novel (New York: W. A. Townsend, 1859)

him than not. Consistently, his fiction described true friendships between troubled heroes and loyal comrades. Clemens was as complicated as any fictional character. Seeming a difficult scion of the aristocracy – proud, impulsive, and much too fond of liquor – he was in fact the talented son of a self-made, northern-born man. Friendship and ambition mixed poorly, and when Clemens's friendship collided with power, it lost. The controversy suggests why the powerful might resist the spread of middle-class values.

Clemens enjoyed material comfort most of his life, but he was not well-born. A native of Pennsylvania, Jere's father James had moved to Kentucky at sixteen to join his older brother Jeremiah (the great-grandfather of Samuel Clemens, or Mark Twain). With his family's help, James became a merchant, acquired some property in Kentucky, and, in 1813, married Minerva Mills. They came to Huntsville, where James opened a store then slowly accumulated land and slaves. Despite prosperity, the family had difficulties. Three of Minerva's seven children died in the four years before her death in 1826. In 1834, Jere's adolescent sister Nancy married over the opposition of her father, who refused to allow the man in his house and disinherited her. Jere's only surviving brother died in 1850, and another sister died three years later. James Clemens lived until he was eighty. Even as he aged and grew blind, however, his ambitious son lived at home only intermittently, pursuing first one and then another occupation.[47]

Because his father had joined the respectable classes, Jere grew up a friend to the sons of the state's best families. The prosperous town of Huntsville had been founded just before the War of 1812 by men like LeRoy Pope, the town's "father," and his son-in-law, John Williams Walker, members of a

---

was illustrated by Felix Darley, who did the illustrations for *Adventures of Simon Suggs*, suggesting the overlap between humor and other forms of fiction and the homogenizing influence of the market for popular books.

[47] Property records in the Clemens family file, Huntsville-Madison County Public Library; family history found in Raymond Martin Bell and Harriet Cates Hardaway, "James Clemens of Washington County, Pennsylvania, 1734–1795 and His Family. Great-Great Uncle of Mark Twain," typed manuscript in the same file Jere and Samuel Clemens were third cousins. Nancy and W. S. Turner named their oldest child Jeremiah, which may suggest that Jere did not share his father's feelings toward his sister. James Clemens was described in terms that could never have been used for Jere: "He was a man of sound judgment, fine business capacity and imposing appearance, though somewhat reserved in manner, his success was due more to native talent and thrift than to personal popularity," in Judge Thomas Jones Taylor (1829–1894), *A History of Madison County and Incidentally of North Alabama, 1732–1840*, ed. with an intro. by W. Stanley Hoole and Addie S. Hoole (Tuscaloosa: Confederate Publishing Company, 1976), 76. Jeremiah never appeared in the census with property. In 1850 (when he was in the Senate) he was listed in the residence at James's residence, and Mary was listed with her father's household. After James Clemens's death in 1860, Jere and Mary lived with her father in town, although he did at that point apparently become involved in plantation management, and may have been doing so for several years during his father's declining health. See his letter to his daughter Mary, September 5, 1862, in the Jeremiah Clemens Papers, USAHI. I thank William Stubno for providing me with copies of the Mexican War letters from Carlisle Barracks. There has never been a scholarly biography of Clemens.

The Voluntary Bonds of Friendship   117

Virginia-based clan that had spread across the South. Politically powerful even before they brought Alabama into the Union, the group learned from popular disapproval to pursue its interests covertly, making alliances with other planters and with middle-class townspeople. Jeremiah Clemens's friends included Pope's grandsons (Walker's sons), among them Pope Walker, who would marry Albert Pickett's niece. Jere's better friends, however, were the members of another large family, that of Clement Comer Clay. Although they had excellent southern connections, the Clays did not belong to Huntsville's powerful "cousinry," and they were sometimes allies, sometimes competitors of the Walker family.[48] The Walker and Clay sons reached maturity along with Clemens, and several of them had their eyes on political office. There was not room in the town for all of them to succeed.

Jeremiah had advantages like the Clay and Walker boys, for James Clemens could afford to buy his talented son a college education. But, from a young age, Jere's temperament caused him problems. At eighteen, he was earning a reputation for wildness. The second Clay son, Jones Withers, wrote his brother Clement, Jr., reporting on a religious revival that had converted some of the young men in town, including Pope Walker. Jere, it seems, had "abandoned his religion already, having gone to the races at Florence, he won (it is said) a pretty large sum of money."[49] For a time, Jere and Clement attended different colleges: Jere, Transylvania College in Kentucky; Clement, the University in Tuscaloosa. Jere kept in touch. After he wrote Susannah Withers Clay, Clement's mother, she informed her son about it. "I really do love him," she explained, adding that Jere referred to Clement and Withers "with much affection."[50] Perhaps she felt sympathy for the motherless boy.

---

[48] For the power of the Clay and Walker families and the Broad River group in Huntsville, see Dupre, *Transforming the Cotton Frontier*, esp. 25–32, and J. Mills Thornton III, *Politics and Power in a Slave Society, Alabama 1800–1860* (Baton Rouge: Louisiana State University Press, 1978), esp. 10–17. Three of the four Walker grandsons of LeRoy Pope achieved political prominence, although to do so they had to migrate around the state. Between them they served eleven terms in the state legislature. Percy was a member of the U.S. House of Representatives, 1855–1857, Richard (Dick) was Speaker of the Alabama House of Representatives and member of the Provisional Congress and the Senate of the Confederacy; and Eliza Pickett's husband LeRoy Pope (called Pope) was the first Secretary of War of the Confederacy; see Thomas McAdory Owen and Marie Bankhead Owen, *Dictionary of Alabama Biography*, 4 vols. (Chicago: S. J. Clarke Publishing Co., 1921), 4: 1717–1718. On the sometimes friendly, sometimes not, rivalry between the Clays and the Walkers, see Ruth Ketring Nuermberger, *The Clays of Alabama: A Planter-Lawyer-Politician Family* (Lexington: University of Kentucky Press, 1958), esp. 164. She concludes that the Walkers outdid the Clays in law and the Clays outdid the Walkers in politics. See also Hugh C. Bailey, *John Williams Walker: A Study in the Political, Social, and Cultural Life of the Old Southwest* (Tuscaloosa: University of Alabama Press, 1964).

[49] Jones Withers Clay to Clement Clay, Jr., November 22, 1833, in *ibid*. Withers went on to gossip about the competition between the Walkers and the Clays.

[50] Susannah Clay to Clement Clay, Jr., February 1, 1834, in Clay Family Papers, DUL. I am grateful to Dan Dupre and the late Frances Roberts for helping me locate some of the references to Clemens in the large body of the Clay Papers.

Jere was often too much ruled by his emotions. At eighteen, he fell in love with Mary Read, the daughter of his father's partner. Apparently, Mary was as lovely as Alex Meek had observed when he rejected her for lack of wealth, which did not matter to Jere. In a poem he wrote for her in 1833, he confessed that he had trouble sorting out his feelings. He claimed that her love could "cheer him in the rugged paths of fame" and "point the way which leads to Heaven above." He also admitted that his intense feelings might "be passion – love – I know not what." It was not uncommon for a young man to confuse ambition with fate and love with passion. But Clemens's feelings stayed too near the surface for his own good.

This temperament marred his friendship with Clement Clay, in whom Jeremiah confided. Writing Clement one winter Sunday in 1833, Jere addressed him as "Dear Friend," while his language showed that competition and a passionate nature already ruffled their friendship. After joking edgily about Clement's failure to correspond, Jere plunged into an emotional reflection about the mood produced by a rainy day. "My spirits have imbibed a portion of the day's melancholy and gloom," he wrote poetically, but "I like such days." Adding an ironic touch – Clement knew Jere lacked religion – Jere wrote: "Strange as it may seem to you, I love the Sabbath." The day invited him to abandon "the fierceness of hate & the burning eagerness of Revenge" that marked a man of honor. Again, he was conflating religion with his feeling for Mary, for he claimed that he felt the healing influence of her "matchless and immaculate soul" on his more passionate self. He freely shared his feelings about Mary, sure that Clement understood them because he knew "all that she *was* and *is* & all that I esteem her to be.[51]

Friendship was muddled with a touchy honor in what followed, as Jeremiah confided less romantic, but equally personal, thoughts about manly achievement. He bragged about a speech he had given and implicitly asked Clement to share his pride, repeating the praise of one impressed observer who had commented: "'I never was so much mistaken in a man (meaning me) in my life.'" The observer had known that Clemens was "'tolerable smart,'" but now he saw Jere was "'already a great man.'" Jere admitted liking the attention: "Believe me Clement the applauses of a crowd are more than acceptable, let philosophers say what they will." Perhaps this admission focused Jere's thoughts on his future, for he returned to the subject of Mary, whom he wanted to marry. He knew that "some of the good people of Huntsville," had been telling Mary he was "too wild as ever to render her happy." He promised he would identify the gossipers "& may the God of Heaven desert me in the hour of my greatest need if I do not make them repent a repetition of such conduct."[52] Jere may have suspected that the Clays were warning Mary about him, but he trusted his friend enough to share feelings that

---

[51] Clemens to Clay, Jr., January 19, 1834, in *ibid*. Jere was at Transylvania and Clement apparently in Tuscaloosa.

[52] *Ibid*.

would have been an embarrassment if revealed to Clement's classmates in Tuscaloosa.

Nonetheless, there was gossip about Jere among the Clays. Later that same year, two of them described the wedding of Jeremiah and Mary Read. Withers wrote an aunt that "all of our family were invited except Grandmama, *myself*, and the *children*." Repeating what he had heard, Withers commented rudely that "Old Mr. Clemens sat by his daughter-in-law at table, and Jeremiah wished Mother to sit by him, thereby performing the part of his Mother." Another relative wrote that "the party was quite pleasant but almost too crowded." She cattily observed that "the bride looked very unconcerned and indifferent" and that the groom was "agitated and all the evening restless and I thought in a very bad humour." She hinted at scandal, claiming that Jere "would willingly have gotten off if there had been any possible means of escape – but Major Read seemed bent and determined on it." She feared "poor Mary" would "not be as happy as she deserves to be."[53] Clemens's friendship with the Clays was shaky.

If it was the case that a forced marriage added to Clemens's personal difficulties, it did not change his shortcomings, for he was reluctant to let them go. Four years after his wedding, he wrote Mary's sister-in-law an "Air" that described how "woe and pain" had changed him, without specifying the source of either. "Misery's fire," he said, had given his heart "a flinty hardness" and a "Tiger's fierceness." But Clemens's poem claimed that both "fate and vice" had scarred his life, half-dodging responsibility for his problems. In any case, he would not abandon the "rugged paths of fame," and his ambition grew along with his hardened heart.[54]

---

[53] Withers to Ann Eliza Withers, December 6, 1834, and Mary Withers to Ann Eliza Withers, in the Levert Family Papers, UNC. Withers also commented on the scandal about Nancy Clemens Turner's marriage: "Mrs. Turner went to her father on that night [of her brother's wedding], and spoke to him, he told her 'she was welcome at all times to his house, and might yet consider it her home, but that he never could receive her husband.'" Susannah Withers Clay was sister to Ann Eliza, who would marry Francis John Levert, of the same wealthy family as Octavia Walton Le Vert. Marked "private," Mary Withers's letter described the attendees and participants in the wedding party, who included her sister Maria, which indicated a close friendship between the family and Mary Read. Mary's father John was James Clemens's first partner in a mercantile business in early Huntsville.

[54] "To Mary," dated 1833, and "Air – Tis said that absence conquers love," in Mrs. Certain Papers, ADAH, Montgomery. My thanks to Christine Dee for sharing information about these poems. Clemens's descendents apparently burned most of his papers out of concern for his reputation. Among the few that are preserved, a letter from a grandson acknowledges that Clemens "drank heavily, and Mother [Clemens's daughter] attributed his failure to reach the highest political posts to that habit – probably it was a contributing cause to his death at only 50 years"; W. H. Townsend to his niece May, August 24, 1937, Clemens Papers, USAHI. No family genealogies or records preserve the date of Clemens's daughter's birth. Virginia Clay (Clement's wife) suggests that Clemens's marriage did not preclude his eye for pretty women, and, although she describes him as "the personification of manly beauty," (13) her disapproval is patent, and an anecdote about his flirtation with her is full of carefully couched, but damning details; *Belle of the Fifties*, 13–15.

As it did, Clemens's friendship with the Clay family was crucial. Over the long haul, the Clays would block his political ambitions to achieve their own, but this development was not initially clear to Jere, who found his friends useful. The *pater familias*, Clement Comer Clay, had been a U.S. congressman, and he was elected governor of Alabama the year Jere turned twenty-one. Jere was made a federal district attorney, probably due to the senior Clay's influence, and, in 1839, he became a law partner with the father and son. He helped to manage their family's business, and he was elected to the state legislature for the first of five terms with their support. He and young Clement wrote occasionally for the Huntsville *Southern Democrat*, which spoke for the Clay family. The law partnership was reorganized in 1841, and Clemens left it. By then, the political ambitions of Clement, Jr., had surfaced, and he won a legislative seat in 1842. The following year, however, Jere was reelected, and in 1844 the two friends served together. Clemens was a successful legislator, garnering a statewide reputation for his poise and intellect. Dark-haired, handsome, and dashing as well as talented, he seemed destined for greatness.[55]

The state legislature was a place where able young men made friends and formed alliances that served for life. Clemens came to know William Smith and Alexander Meek, and he enjoyed masculine conviviality. On Christmas Day 1841, Clemens introduced a resolution about a "Joint Song" for the two houses of the legislature. The poem made fun of dozing legislators and "half bent" senators, and it called for adjournment to celebrate the day with "eggs [i.e., eggnog] and game." Smith had written the poem, and Clemens boldly read it, whereupon the body promptly adjourned.[56] There was camaraderie in Tuscaloosa, but the place was also serious. Those who wanted higher office found that there were fewer spots than there were aspirants, and competition was fierce. This did not augur well for Clemens, for his potential rivals – three Clay and four Walker sons – had very good family connections, and he did not.

---

[55] All three of the Clay sons practiced in the family firm in the 1840s, and the reasons Clemens left the practice are not clear. The Clay family biographer comments that Clemens's "love of adventure, dissipated living, hostility to secession, and ultimate unionism progressively antagonized the highly moral and strictly state-rights Clays"; Nuermberger, *The Clays*, 77–78. But not all of that was apparent in 1841. Clay family letters during this period make only routine remarks about Jere in connection with the legal business of the firm. See Clay, Sr., to Clay, Jr., February 4, 1840; Clay, Jr., to Clay, Sr., February 6, June 19, and August 4, 1841; Withers to Clay, Jr., August 8, 1842, in Clay papers, DUL. Clement, Jr., wrote his father that an opposing newspaper criticized the junior editor of the *Democrat*, but he did not know whether that meant him or Clemens; Clay, Jr., to his father; August 4, 1841. Two years later, the *Democrat* carried an advertisement for Clemens's new practice (with Sam Moseley); the following year, Clement, Jr., still junior editor of the paper, reported from Tuscaloosa on his activities and those of Clemens; *Democrat*, May 4, 1843, and December 14, 1844. On Clemens's appearance, see Willis Brewer, *Alabama, Her History, Resources, War Record, and Public Men, from 1540 to 1872* (Spartanburg, SC: Reprint Co., 1975, c.1872), 363.

[56] "Joint Song," quoted in Easby-Smith, 40–41.

The Voluntary Bonds of Friendship 121

At this juncture in his career, Clemens served in the Mexican War, which permanently shaped his friendships and provided material for his writing. Clemens's vision for the South was expansionist, and he met northerners who shared his enthusiasm. Serving as an officer in Zachary Taylor's army with the Ninth Infantry Regiment, he made northern friends such as Franklin Pierce of New Hampshire. Although Jere hoped for martial honor, he could not portray himself as a hero because he saw little if any action. Still, his letters to Mary, as well as the ones printed in local newspapers – the *Democrat* and the *Whig Advocate* – glorified American valor and praised the beauty of the far West. Although he made friends among the "best part" of the Mexican population and sympathized with their humiliation in a losing war, he scorned the majority, whom he described as "Proud, Ignorant, and Conceited."[57]

Clemens's letters did not mention it, but the war may have increased his drinking. In the fall of 1847, Lawson Clay (the third son) reported from Vera Cruz to his mother with criticism and friendship in equal parts: "Lt. Col. Clemens has taken to brandy & water within a few weeks past & seems to have little regard for or great faith in the strength of his constitution. He has been and is very kind & civil to me, and I esteem him very much because of it."[58] While the family would continue to watch Clemens's drinking habits, they were apparently not yet suspicious about his northern friends, and Susannah Clay's brother, Jones Withers (one of her sons bore the same name), was Jeremiah's commander and could observe him. Lawson's letter indicated that the friendship between Clemens and the Clays was still intact.

If Clemens sensed the danger his ambitions presented to his friendship with the Clay family when he returned from war in 1848, he ignored it. He quickly learned, however, that there was a difference between sharing friendship and sharing power. Making political capital from his service, Clemens ran for Congress as a Democrat. Unsuccessful, he set his sights higher in 1849. In a misstep from which he never recovered, he crossed his friends when the state legislature chose him to fill the unexpired senatorial term of the deceased Black Belt Democrat Dixon Hall Lewis. Clemens won by appealing to Whigs and defeating the leading Democratic candidate, Benjamin Fitzpatrick, a former governor and Lewis's brother-in-law (one of the Walkers was a less popular candidate). Fitzpatrick had powerful friends and relatives in southern Alabama (and South Carolina) and allies in northern Alabama, including the Clays.[59]

---

[57] "Best part," Clemens to Mary Read Clemens, December 10, 1847; derogatory comments about Mexicans in Clemens to "My dear daughter," May 3, 1848, in Clemens Papers, USAHI.

[58] Lawson Clay to Susannah Clay, October 13, 1847, Clay papers DUL. For examples of Clemens's newspaper letters, see the Huntsville *Southern Advocate*, June 3, 1848, and the *Democrat*, June 14, 1848.

[59] As part of his campaign, Clemens took a temperance stand. See approving comments in the Huntsville *Southern Advocate* (Whig), which also printed one of his speeches on drink; January 12 and 19, 1849. For a description of the senatorial election that places it in the context of partisan and regional rivalries in Alabama, see Thornton, *Politics and Power*,

Now edited by Withers Clay, the Huntsville *Democrat* pounced on Clemens. The Clays and their allies deployed their power to ruin Clemens politically, and his erratic conduct gave them an easy target. Clemens served in the Senate during the controversy over slavery that led to the Compromise of 1850, and he first opposed, then supported, the Compromise. On the floor of the Senate, Robert Barnwell Rhett of South Carolina, a relative of the Fitzpatrick group, attacked Clemens for his political treachery, and an outraged Clemens threatened a duel. *Harper's* printed a cartoon of the affair, making Clemens a national joke. The public assaults in the *Democrat* became uglier, calling Clemens "Lucifer" and calling one of his speeches "trash, trash, trash."[60] Southern-rights newspapers across the state joined in the attacks. For all of his talent and ambitions, Clemens could not overcome his opponents. Despite his bad habits, his friendship with the Clays was acceptable until he showed his independence. With or without a drinking problem, he was outmanned by the family and its strong allies.

Behind the scenes, the conflict was personal, for Clement attacked Jeremiah with a ruthlessness born of his own ambitions. The junior Clay relayed to his father caustic gossip that showed no sympathy for his former friend. In 1851, he had heard that "Jeremiah Clemens had become so puffed up that his clothes could hardly hold him & that he swallows not less than a quart of liquor daily & is growing as contemptible in public opinion as he deserves to be."[61] Not surprisingly, two years later the younger Clay was elected to the Senate over Clemens (and another one of the Walker sons). Probably the Clays had, all along, seen Jeremiah as a kind of client for their patronage and found his ambitions an affront. Certainly his drinking was excessive. But Clement Clay's cutting words suggested that the family's friendship had once been genuine and now he had to convince his father that Jere was unworthy of trust.

In office, Clement feared a resurgence of his former friend's influence. From Washington, Clay sent his father a long, secondhand account of a tavern brawl

---

182–183. The alliance between the Clays and the Black Belt Democrats was in place as early as 1841. See the letter of Congressman Dixon Hall Lewis to Benjamin Fitzpatrick, in which he assesses the prospects of the party in the state at the request of Clay, Sr.; letter of January 19, 1841, in Benjamin Fitzpatrick Papers, Southern Historical Collection, UNC, Chapel Hill.

[60] These intemperate attacks and many others are quoted in Clyde Drummond, "Biography of Jeremiah Clemens: A Personal, Political, Military and Literary Sketch of His Life" (unpublished M.A. thesis, Alabama Polytechnic Institute [later Auburn University], 1932; passages quoted from the *Democrat* and other newspapers, 47, 49. South Carolina's literary figure Paul Hamilton Hayne wrote his wife about Rhett's "disagreeable dilemma," reporting that Clemens had called him a "coward" and a "liar" (both of which were unforgiveable by even minimal standards of honor). Hayne said that he hoped to hear that Rhett had "blown out his [Clemens's] brains," Paul H. Hayne Papers, DUL. On Clemens's erratic course, see *ibid.*, 201–203. See also Wallace Hettle, *The Peculiar Democracy: Southern Democrats in Peace and Civil War* (Athens: University of Georgia Press, 2001), which focuses on Clemens's aggrieved sense of honor in a chapter called "Curing the Sir Walter Disease – The Politics and Fiction of Jeremiah Clemens," 122–141.

[61] Clement Clay, Jr., to Clement Clay, Sr., February 16, 1851, Clay Papers, DUL.

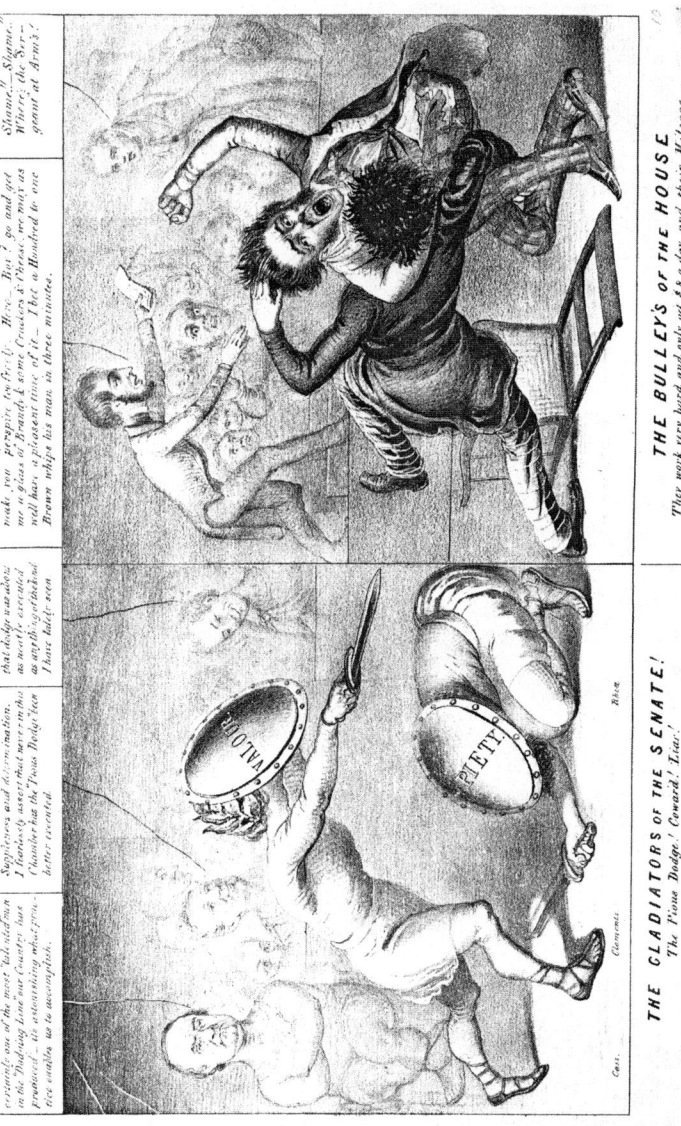

FIGURE 4.2. "Gladiators of the Senate; Bulley's of the House."
This political cartoon derides the strife in the U.S. Senate (left panel) and the House of Representatives (right panel) during the sectional controversy of 1850–1851. The left panel shows Jeremiah Clemens attacking Robert Barnwell Rhett of South Carolina, and it followed a debate between them that threatened to precipitate a duel. Courtesy of the Library of Congress.

between Clemens and a Mississippi congressman. He repeated other news of Clemens's drinking: "He is, as I understand, boarded at the national Hotel & provided with wines, liquors & other appliances for corrupting Congress, – all at the expense of his clients. He gives dinners, suppers, treats, gambles, &c &c. He looks very rubicund & bloated." The *Democrat* questioned Clemens's friendship with President Pierce. Privately, Clay wrote his father of rumors that Pierce would place Clemens in his cabinet, urging that good Democrats like Fitzpatrick and the senior Clay speak to Pierce and block the "reckless and unprincipled man." Jeremiah failed in an attempt to win a congressional seat in 1854, and the *Democrat* exulted.[62]

Clemens's career was wrecked, thanks in part to his former friends. The *Democrat's* sentiments were echoed in a short piece written by Alexander Meek, a loyal partisan. Headed "How the mighty are fallen," Meek claimed that Clemens was once "applauded by his friends and admired by the State of Alabama as one of her most gifted sons." He became an "important lesson" because he was "swayed by every breeze" when he broke with party leaders. But, unlike Clay, Meek acknowledged Clemens's "splendid intellect" and "superior talents," which suggested some sympathy for his former friend. With the Democrats at his heels and the Whigs a permanent minority, Clemens never again held public office. Clay, Jr., served a decade in the U.S. and Confederate Senates. Clemens lingered in Washington, using his influence to make a living.[63] He also worked for a time as an editor for the Memphis *Daily Eagle*.

[62] Clement Clay, Jr., to Clement Clay, Sr., March 14, 1854, *ibid*. See also Clement Clay, Sr., to Clement Clay, Jr., January 9, 1854, *ibid*., for more comments on Clemens's ambitions, wondering if the president is "not fully informed of the character and conduct of that reckless and unprincipled man," and asking him to make sure that Fitzpatrick or some other reputable Alabamian inform him fully, for "to appoint Jere to any high office would be, in effect, to offer a premium for political treachery." In the first letter, Clay enclosed his wife's letter, which commented on Clemens's health. See also Clay, Jr.'s, long confidential letter to southern Alabama party leader Bolling Hall, in which he discredited Clemens and offered himself as a senatorial candidate, seeking support; Clay, Jr., to Bolling Hall, September 30, 1853, in Bolling Hall papers, ADAH; in the same letter Clay speculates that Pope Walker would be a candidate again, not anticipating that this time the Walker family's candidate would be Richard. The election is recounted in Nuermberger, *The Clays*, 116–118; in Thornton, *Politics and Power*, 333–334; and in Lewy Dorman, *Party Politics in Alabama from 1850 through 1860* (Tuscaloosa: University of Alabama Press, 1935), 93–95.

[63] Clay, Jr., to Clay, Sr., January 8, 1854, Clay Papers, DUL. Fragment of an essay about Clemens in Meek Papers, MDAH. Mistrust of Clemens was not simply partisan. Prominent Whig attorney Thomas Judge wrote from Montgomery to a young political ally in Washington that Clemens was determined to profit improperly from a small role in settling claims for the state of Alabama: "Have any sort of a difficulty with Clemens before you permit him to extort from you. At all hazards do not pay him more than the $5,000 – that is too much. But do not say to Clemens I have written thus"; see Judge to Jefferson Franklin Jackson, March 15, 1855, in Jefferson Franklin Jackson papers, ADAH. For examples of the consistency and persistence of the Huntsville *Democrat*'s assaults, see Nov. 7, 1850, July 24, 1851, and November 15, 1855. For comments within the Democratic party elite, see many letters to the powerful planter Bolling Hall throughout the early 1850s; for examples, see John Gill Shorter to Hall, August 26, 1853, and John Bragg to Hall, September 8, 1853, in which he says that Clemens

Then, in the late 1850s, Clemens began publishing novels that evinced his sense of betrayal and the alienation of a man who did not fully accept his mistakes. Two of the novels were western adventure stories, set partly in the Mexican War, and they featured violent and sensual heroes. Like the early poem that blamed "fate and vice" for his misery, Clemens's novels alternately blamed the heroes' problems on an indifferent universe and their own moral flaws. Although his stories were sensational, they used middle-class standards of friendship to show the good in thoroughly hardened men. Almost existential in its portrayal of action in the face of uncertainty, Clemens's fiction revealed his personal distress. Nonetheless, it aimed at the popular market, and it was published by J. B. Lippincott of Philadelphia.

Clemens's use of friendship in his first novel revealed his persistent desire for the acceptance of respectable people. He dedicated *Bernard Lile; An Historical Romance Embracing the Periods of the Texas Revolution and the Mexican War* (1856) to a comrade from Huntsville: "play-mate and class-mate of my childhood and boyhood – the zealous and unwavering friend of a manhood which the shadow has darkened as often as the sunshine has gladdened." Following this undisguised reminder that Clemens still had friends, his preface claimed to draw from experience. His story had "no plan, for human life has none." Neither did it "paint the author's ideal of a perfect man," for "in all the 'busy, bitter scenes' through which I have passed, I have met no such character, and believe not in its existence." Clemens argued, however, that human imperfections demanded sympathy, for no man was "so free from errors" that he could afford to be "uncharitable to the sins of others."[64] Like Hentz's *Eoline*, *Bernard Lile* paired friends who were from different regions of the country: a hardened New Englander with a likeable, albeit crude, southwesterner who shared his confidence and his exploits. A murderer and outcast, Lile prospered as a soldier of fortune, but he eventually repented and joined the Texas wars as a patriot. Wounded in battle, the reformed sinner died with his loyal friend at his side.

Friendship played an even greater role in Clemens's next work, *Mustang Gray: A Romance* (1858). This novel, too, was dedicated to an "unwavering

was "unhorsed everywhere" (and also takes sides against the Walker family of Huntsville, Pickett's relatives-in-law.); Hall Papers, ADAH.

[64] The dedication to George Neal, which was a full paragraph rather than the usual line or two, unpaged; Preface, quoted passage ix–x; *Bernard Lile* (Philadelphia: J. B. Lippencott & Co., 1856). On the influence of the war on American ideas about manhood, see Amy S. Greenberg, *Manifest Manhood and Antebellum American Empire* (Cambridge: Cambridge University Press, 2005). Clemens's novels were genre-bending, combining stories of war with what was emerging as a Western, and they warrant more attention than they have received. Useful discussions of the early Western that help put Clemens's fiction in perspective (but do not discuss it) are William T. Pilkington, *Critical Essays on the Western American Novel* (Boston: G. K. Hall, 1980); Richard W. Etulain, *Telling Western Stories: From Buffalo Bill to Larry McMurtry* (Albuquerque: University of New Mexico Press, 1999); and the more theoretically informed Nathaniel Lewis, *Unsettling the Literary West: Authenticity and Authorship* (Lincoln: University of Nebraska Press, 2003).

friend," who had served under Clemens in the Mexican War and supported him "through all the less manly and more bitter struggles of parties and of politics." Although Clemens's preface warned that, without "a merciful God," all men follow their innate "evil tendency," it also insisted that men could not control fate, and the main character destroyed himself.[65] Mabry Gray was born into a middle-class family in North Carolina, but, once orphaned, he let passion overwhelm him. Spurned by the girl he wooed, he shot her lover. Fleeing to Texas, the heart-broken murderer became "Mustang," a desperado among Mexican outlaws who smuggled slaves and luxuries to American settlers. Eventually he became a Texas Ranger. Patriotism led him to fight the Mexicans without changing his character. Gray finally regretted his first murder, but he resumed his bloody deeds at the war's end. Once again, however, Clemens reminded his readers of the virtue of charity; thus he gave Mustang Gray friends who loved him whatever he did.[66]

Gray's first friend was a fellow southerner, John Allison. Clemens idealized their friendship to reflect perfect trust, equality, and sympathy. As adolescents, Allison and Gray were opposites who learned from each other. Allison was the son of a rich patriarch, as cautious as Gray was reckless. Brother to the girl Gray loved, he tried in vain to plead Mabry's case with his sister. After Gray murdered her seducer, Allison abandoned his privileged life and followed the fugitive to Texas. Although John avoided Mustang's crimes, they protected each other. John never judged his errant friend, and he was at Gray's bedside when he died.[67] Like the novel's dedication, John Allison reflected Clemens's problems, for Allison was to Mabry Gray everything Clement Clay was not to Jere Clemens. From beginning to end, John was a true friend.

Clemens's expanded his characterization of friendship with Gray's Mexican friends. They did not qualify as the "best part" of the population – educated people of Spanish descent – Clemens had described to his wife. The first of Mustang's friendships was with an American trader's middle-aged wife, Josefa, who gave Gray domestic comfort in the unstable Southwest. Drawn

---

[65] *Mustang Gray* (Philadelphia: J. B. Lippencott & Co., 1858), dedication, iii; quoted passage from preface, vi. There is no reliable critical analysis of *Mustang Gray*.

[66] The theme of Christian charity is repeated frequently, and, near the end of his book, Clemens concluded that "before we anticipate the fiat of his Maker upon his [Gray's] misdeeds, let us turn to the 13th chapter of Paul's Epistle to the Corinthians, and impress upon our memories the estimation in which Charity was held by the great Apostle," 293. See J. Frank Dobie, "Mustang Gray: Fact, Tradition, and Song," for a summary of the legend of the real Gray, including references to Clemens's novel, which is the only extended treatment of Gray; reprinted from *Publications of the Texas Folk-Lore Society*, 10 (1932), c. Texas Folk-Lore Society, Austin, TX, 1932.

[67] Clemens sketched the benefits of the friendship for Mabry's youthful development, insisting that "both profited, but Gray the most" from the exchanges between Mabry and John. Mabry not only learned of the "world without" but also "to appreciate his own powers by comparison," and feeling "the gloom his solitary existence had imparted to his character melted away before the ringing, joyous laugh of his light-hearted associate," 16–17. Mustang's last words were to John; *Mustang Gray*, 295.

to Mustang's almost feminine grace, Josefa loved him as a friend from the moment she saw him. She lived just on the edge of honesty, and she threatened violence with an ease that betrayed Clemens's prejudice. She was fat rather than beautiful. But Josefa did not lack a woman's virtues. Candid about her affection, she nurtured Gray with food, clothing, and shelter. Josefa loved Gray more than her villainous brother, whom she threatened to kill if he harmed her friend. And Gray understood that Josefa's friendship "influenced him in a great degree" from the time he met her until he died.[68]

Josefa's male counterpart was Pedro, a grizzled older man whom Gray instantly befriended. In contrast to Allison, the peasant was uncivilized, and his friendship derived partly from the comradeship of war. Although Mustang chose Pedro as a friend when he proved his courage in battle, the men were similar because each had been betrayed by "false-hearted" friends. Pedro taught Mustang about horses, smuggling, and Indian warfare, and the brave pair dispatched dozens of Mexicans and Comanche Indians. Even so, their friendship was based on sympathy and trust. Pedro instinctively knew that the two men had "kindred natures" – a sure sign of true friendship. Moreover, Gray's "low, sweet voice, the gentle demeanor, the beaming countenance, beautiful as that of a woman" touched "the heart of the Mexican." The pair shared reflective moments, discussing the beauty of the prairies, their favorite music, and the meaning of manhood. Although Mustang sometimes called Mexicans "Greasers," he discussed their traits with Pedro, and the two friends compared their judgments.[69] On the prairies of Texas, Mustang and Pedro were equals, not just partners in violence.

Conscious of the various forms of friendship, Clemens contrasted male bonding and ethical friendship in the events surrounding a dinner Gray gave for the Texas Rangers at Josefa's ranch. Expecting a drunken feast, Mustang asked Josefa to remove herself, her children, John Allison, and even the furniture from the great hall where it would occur. Clemens explained that Gray owned a huge supply of liquors, "the largest, perhaps in Texas," and that Mustang was addicted to alcohol – "it mattered little to him what it was" – because it blotted out despair. At the dinner, then, Gray and his violent comrades drank themselves stupid. They bragged about gambling, sang "The Last Rose of Summer" and "The Star Spangled Banner," and toasted their friends. A special toast was reserved for the absent John Allison – "Kindhearted as a woman, in danger's hour no man ever yet knew his blood to run cold or slow." Finally, some of the men "were leaning their foreheads on the table." Others "had fallen from their seats, and were snoring on the dirt floor." One announced "I'm drunk. Drunk as hell. There's no doubt about it."[70]

Clemens quickly turned, however, from the jolly debauchery to a better form of friendship, underscoring the points he made by separating Josefa and

---

[68] *Ibid.*, quoted passage, in the context of a description of Josefa, 75.
[69] *Ibid.*, 102–103.
[70] *Ibid.*, Mustang's drinking habits, 239–240; toast to John, 251; drunken Rangers, 252.

John from the drinking scene and by noting John's womanly heart. The evening after the party, Gray played on the floor with Josefa's three children, who tickled him, pulled his hair, and played "ride horse" on his arm. For a full page, Clemens moralized that Gray was not purely murderous, wild, or kind, but all of these traits in one complex man.[71] Gray deserved the reader's charity, Clemens advised. And, virtuous or not, he had friends.

From beginning to end, Clemens's story dramatized the imperatives of friendship. He claimed to know the real Gray – a man who would become a legend. "With all his faults," Clemens wrote, he "was one 'who loved me, and whom I loved long ago.'"[72] Clemens's novel pushed the conventional limits of friendship, yet it also reflected his moral confusion. He had the intellect to think deeply, and he was driven by irrational impulses. He taught ethical lessons about human conduct, and he never fully confronted his own weaknesses. Although Clemens's dedications reflected his public shame and his appeals to charity suggested his guilt, neither Clemens nor his hero abjured ambition and its material rewards. Clemens wanted friends who were "unwavering," and Mustang Gray's friends sustained both his heroism and his criminal exploits. In showing the value of friendship, Clemens suggested its moral ambiguity.

Wanting badly to make himself, Jeremiah challenged the power of a family that had ascended more successfully than he ever would. And, having done so, the Clays took advantage of blood ties and pragmatic friendships to secure their place within the ranks of elite slaveholders across the state and South. To the Clays, alliances with men like Clemens were useful, but they did not expect to compromise their privilege for anyone's talent, and they did not have to. Clemens's passionate nature and his drinking caused him serious problems, if hardly unique ones among politicians. Nonetheless, he made friendship a symbol of the relations free men should form, and his imagination reflected his own frustrated efforts at self-determination. The characters of John Allison, Josefa, and Pedro demonstrated that Clemens believed in ideal friendship. But, in actuality, his alienation had begun, and it would grow. If friendship could create bonds to southern people, its failure could also break them.

* * *

Alexander Meek, William Smith, Caroline Hentz, and Jeremiah Clemens revealed the inevitable dissonance between ideals about friendship and the various forms it assumed in the rising South. For them, there was no clean separation between ideas in print and ordinary experience. Actual friendships mixed lofty intentions and sincere affection with self-interested, sometimes irrational habits based on honor and hierarchy, competition and prejudice. But friendships that affirmed the power of sympathy, the possibility of equality, the necessity of trust, and the rewards of communication showed that writers possessed the

---

[71] *Ibid.*, play with children, 254.
[72] *Ibid.*, preface, vii.

roughly democratic ethics of other educated Americans. In theory, friendships made people responsible for one another without reducing anyone's individual freedom. After all, John Allison willingly left his home to follow Mabry Gray into exile. Nonetheless, the individualistic core of friendship too easily masked self-aggrandizement. From Gray's perspective, Allison's friendship was an abiding source of comfort in a life of shame. From Allison's perspective – which Clemens casually neglected – friendship had less obvious rewards. In fact, friendships were a mixed blessing, even if they lasted a lifetime.

Despite that, the rising South's writers believed that true friendship would make their society better, and they were not entirely wrong. Choosing friends was an act of self-determination that affected the future. Friends like Smith and Meek, or Evans and Lyons helped each other grow as individuals, using persuasion to encourage self-awareness. And, while effecting individual improvement, friendship promoted social harmony. It did not do as much as writers claimed to mitigate inequality. In their idealizations, writers showed friendships between rich and poor, men and women, southerners and northerners, and even between Americans and Mexicans, and they overstated. It goes without saying, moreover, that these idealizations of friendship neglected slaves (without articulating racial exclusiveness). Nonetheless, because friends tolerated their differences and cared for each other, true friendship had the potential to improve the Southwest and, for that matter, America.

The usefulness of friendship was illustrated in the experiences of Meek, Smith, Hentz, and Clemens. Southern-born men like Meek and Smith created a mutually advantageous literary alliance, and the New England-born Hentz integrated herself into the life of successive small towns by making friends. Consciously or not, Clemens used the Clays to attach himself more firmly to Huntsville's elite. The ethics of individual striving implied social instability, which contained both opportunities and threats. As adults, most of Alabama's writers enjoyed upward mobility, which convinced them they were self-made. Some – certainly Smith, Evans, and Hooper – had seen their families decline, and this made them acutely aware of the need for self-reliance within all relations. The voluntary bonds of friendship smoothed out the rough spots in an uncertain environment and promised that good people would help one another along.

But that society contained a pecking order, and it was reflected in friendships. Regardless of their wealth, or lack of it, writers were able to make friends with such people as the Walkers, Coffees, and Le Verts. Mrs. Coffee opened her home to the Hentz family as they left Florence, and she patronized their school. These were more than helpful gestures, though they did not appreciably alter the Hentz's economic status. Hentz's dedication of *Eoline* to Octavia Le Vert suggested sympathy between women of different classes, but the dedication also noted Hentz's "admiration" for her social superior. Wealthy friends did not often transfer material resources to nonrelatives, nor did they willingly share power, as Clemens painfully learned. When Pickett's niece married Pope Walker, the historian fretted that the family's collective power might "ruin" his father's estate. And, although Pickett counted the

Hoopers as friends, he described George only as "respectable." At one time or another, Meek dedicated a song lyric to Hooper's wife, addressed a poem to Hentz, dedicated a section of a book to Smith, and wrote a poem for Smith's wife. These were public tributes to the firm friendships that middle-class people made among themselves.

Like the process of self-making and the efforts of middle-class families, friendships encouraged incremental social change. Because every sizeable town in Alabama depended on the cotton-planting hinterland around it, the tensions between middle-class values and the hierarchical habits of slavery rarely produced conflict. Like most other townspeople, writers did not challenge the planters who dominated the region's cash economy and influenced its politics. Instead, through individual initiative and through their cooperation with friends and family, writers used a free society's opportunities to achieve personal success. They expected some planters to be among the educated people who led the South forward. But they thought persuasion was the only legitimate means of producing change, because commands and coercion applied to slaves. Although Pickett had a planter's wealth and the prerogatives of a patriarch, he understood this distinction. When he addressed his wife and his readers, his language demonstrated how a middle-class ethics of freedom was permeating the respectable society of the rising South.

In trying to apply the ethics of self-determination to a slave society, Alabama's writers faced internal and external challenges. Within the Southwest, they spoke for an emerging class of prosperous townspeople who constituted a strong minority – but a minority, nonetheless. And their success in pursuing a middle-class agenda depended, in part, on whether men like Pickett would restrict their dominating habits to their slaves or would try and control other whites. After the Mexican War, moreover, the growing popularity of antislavery ideas in the North threatened to block the South's expansion. The struggle between northern and southern middle-class people about slavery in the nation's future was fought not only in politics but in print. There, Alabama's writers sought readers who would accept their ideas. And, there, they could not completely suppress the tension between the ethics of self-determination and slavery.

PART TWO

WRITING FREEDOM, WITH SLAVES

To its writers, the freedom for white people to make themselves was crucial to the rising South. When they described self-making, or family, or friends, they depicted middle-class southwesterners as similar to other Americans, and they were expressing what they believed to be true. But these literary men and women could not always avoid the divisive subject of slavery, which hid beneath their optimism. And, after the Mexican War, debates about the expansion of slavery increasingly polarized middle-class Americans. For southwesterners in a commercial literary market, this development produced a dilemma. If they openly defended slavery, they offended northern readers; if they did not, they risked their southern reputations. When they addressed the subject, most of Alabama's writers proceeded carefully. But, when they wrote their region's histories and created black characters in fiction, they began to bare the ethical contradictions middle-class southwesterners lived with on a daily basis.

5

Southwestern Histories for a Divided Market

> [Ovid Bolus] had a great contempt for history and historians. He thought them tame and timid cobblers ... borrowers of and acknowledged debtors for others' chattels, got without skill ... barren and unprofitable non-producers in the intellectual vineyard – *nati consumere fruges.*
> Joseph Baldwin, *The Flush Times of Alabama and Mississippi*

Joseph Baldwin opened *Flush Times* with "Ovid Bolus, Esq.," a story about a splendid liar whose tall tales improved on history, for which he had "great contempt." By making fun of the "tame and timid cobblers" who wrote history, Baldwin invited readers to laugh at his comic version of the southwestern past. He was like serious historians, however, in worrying about the reception of his work. To sell more than a handful of books to local people, would-be historians had to think broadly about their region, and they wrote amidst escalating sectional conflict. Inevitably, then, a pervasive tension marked what they wrote and how they marketed their histories. Publishing during the 1850s, they celebrated the past but more quietly suggested the threat of conflict with the North and the subtle strains that slavery produced in the rising South.[1]

Alabama's authors grasped the relationship between their personal ambitions and the economic opportunities of a free and modernizing society. As Baldwin began his comic sketches, the story of Ovid Bolus cleverly exposed his anxieties. Like Johnson Hooper's Simon Suggs, Baldwin's Ovid was overly self-determined, constantly reinvented by lies that liberated him from "dry and common-place" facts. If Ovid lied because of his "genius," he also knew how "to turn an abstract idea into cash." Nonetheless, Ovid declined to publish his lies, for "to betray authorship in the present barbaric, moral and intellectual condition of the world is fatal." Still, Baldwin noted, famous authors

---

[1] Originally published in New York: D. Appleton, 1853; quotes from the convenient paperback (Baton Rouge: Louisiana State University Press, 1987), 3–4. The quote from the Roman satirist Horace, "born to consume the fruit of the earth," is from his *Epistles*, Book 1, Epistle 2. It referred to useless people who only ate what farmers labored to produce. The passage was familiar to educated readers.

like Charles Dickens "can do as much lying, for money, too, as they choose." Without missing a beat in his sketch, Baldwin related authorship to the free market in which *Flush Times* was published. As he suggested, it gave talented men artistic license. They could mix imagination with history, demonstrate genius, and make money, so long as they did not make the "fatal" mistake of too much self-promotion.[2]

Baldwin understood that writing comic history placed him squarely in the public arena, for, by the 1850s, Alabamians shared a national zeal for celebrating the past. Northern historians like George Bancroft and Richard Hildreth and southerners like Charles Gayarré and William Gilmore Simms wrote ground-breaking works, while middle-class citizens across the country organized to preserve local and state histories. Through the initiative of University President Basil Manly, Alabamians created a historical society in 1850. The next year, Albert Pickett published the state's first complete history. *Flush Times* appeared in 1853; and Alexander Meek's *Romantic Passages in Southwestern History* came out in 1857. In 1859, Johnson Hooper edited and published the response of an eccentric pioneer, Thomas Woodward, to Pickett's history. As historical writing flourished across the United States, southwesterners commemorated their ascent out of the wilderness. Because historians addressed a popular topic, Alabama's newspapers and regional journals watched their endeavors.[3]

Like most other American historians, Alabama's writers made the problem of slavery marginal to their interpretations, which touted the progress of free white people. American military and diplomatic activities had established

---

[2] *Flush Times*, "facts," 3; "cash," 5; "lying" for money, 17. For a brilliant discussion of the trials and opportunities of publishing books, see Michael O'Brien, *Conjectures of Order: Intellectual Life and the American South, 1810–1860*, 2 vols. (Chapel Hill: University of North Carolina Press, 2004), ch. 13, "The Honors of Authorship."

[3] On the Alabama Historical Society, see A. James Fuller, *Chaplain to the Confederacy: Basil Manly and Baptist Life in the Old South* (Baton Rouge: Louisiana State University Press, 2000), 145–149. Albert James Pickett, *History of Alabama and Incidentally of Georgia and Mississippi*, 2 vols. (Charleston: Walker & James, 1851; reprinted in one volume, Tuscaloosa: Willo Publishing Company, 1962). Alexander Meek, *Romantic Passages in Southwestern History* (New York: S. F. Goetzel & Co., 1857; repr. Spartanburg, SC: The Reprint Company, 1973). Hooper's publication was Thomas S. Woodward, *Woodward's Reminiscences of the Creek, or Muscogee Indians* (Montgomery: Barrett & Wimbish, 1859). Excellent discussions of Southerners' enthusiasm for their own history are in Elizabeth Fox-Genovese and Eugene D. Genovese, *The Mind of the Master Class: History and Faith in the Southern Slaveholders' Worldview* (Cambridge: Cambridge University Press, 2005), ch. 5, "The Slaveholders' Quest for a History of the Common People," 170–200, which briefly refers to the comic histories, and O'Brien, *Conjectures of Order*, "The Shape of a History," 2: 591–777, which briefly discusses Pickett, Meek, and the comic historians. Benjamin Buford Williams briefly lists or describes early histories, including local ones and Pickett's, in *A Literary History of Alabama: The Nineteenth Century* (Rutherford, NJ: Fairleigh Dickinson University Press, 1979), 142–149. On U.S. history generally, a good survey is George H. Callcott, *History in the United States, 1800–1860* (Baltimore: Johns Hopkins University Press, 1970).

the Southwest, and federal land sales and monetary policy had influenced its economic development. To be reasonably accurate and attractive to readers, therefore, historians had to blend regional and national developments. But writers could not entirely ignore slavery, which had created the region's riches, as Meek had reminded readers of the *Southron* in 1839.[4]

In point of fact, these writers varied in showing slavery's effect. Always thinking of land, the planter Pickett described a Southwest created by conquest in which blacks participated, willingly and not. Preoccupied with the law, Baldwin spoofed ambitious attorneys who made incidental profits from insignificant slaves. In the spirit of Romanticism, Meek claimed that slavery united white men through race pride while making some wealthy. And the rough-hewn Woodward suggested that a man's conduct toward slaves reflected his character more than did his class. Beneath a general consensus that slavery mattered in some way, however, lay the more troubling reality that slavery influenced whites unequally. As if to avoid this fact, all four historians neglected plantation slavery and traced the rise of a civilization that was united, democratic, and very much like the rest of the American West.

Although history was popular, writing it was a competitive business that required authors to think like capitalists and assess the relationship between creative production and sales. To acquire the money and fame that only many readers could award, writers had to consider how a provincial subject matter could be made attractive; in this respect, the traits they shared with northerners enabled middle-class authors to relate to potential readers. In addition, the free market for books diminished the competitive edge of rich men, indirectly abetting the talents of men like Baldwin, Meek, Hooper, and Woodward. That same middle-class market required a planter like Pickett to address the reading public without too much presumption. His wealth helped him become Alabama's first historian, but it did not eliminate a feisty competition.

But the allure of the commercial market was problematic for southern authors in any popular genre. Because mass-produced books from northern firms came at prices and a quality that small-town presses could not match, historians bent on sales preferred to use publishers in New York or Philadelphia. Yet some southerners felt threatened by the centralization of publishing in the Northeast. Especially after antislavery writers like Harriet Beecher Stowe and Frederick Douglass exploited the national market, some of the South's self-appointed defenders demanded southern books from southern presses. Augusta Evans, for one, claimed that healthy competition improved

---

[4] Still useful is Thomas P. Abernethy, *The Formative Period in Alabama, 1815–1828* (Tuscaloosa: University of Alabama Press, 1965, c. 1923). Daniel S. Dupre gives an excellent portrayal of one part of northern Alabama in *Transforming the Cotton Frontier: Madison County, Alabama, 1800–1840* (Baton Rouge: Louisiana State University Press, 1997). The early period is discussed in Adam Rothman, *Slave Country: American Expansion and the Origins of the Deep South* (Cambridge, MA: Harvard University Press, 2005), which does not mention Pickett in the text but quotes him (without attribution), uses his papers, and mentions Meek; Pickett quote, 127; Meek quote, 219.

the South's writers and that northern sales demonstrated the South's intellectual strengths. And, in fact, with weak copyright laws, writers could publish at home, or in the North, or both at once.[5]

In the 1850s, then, publishing history involved political as well as economic choices. Defenses of slavery invited controversy rather than enlightened discourse, and the market encouraged caution, no matter where an author published. Middle-class readers could pick and choose among many books, and their preferences were hard to predict. If northerners and southerners heartily disagreed about slavery's future, southern readers did not agree among themselves about how, practically, to protect their peculiar institution. It is no wonder that Alabama's historians avoided raising the subject directly. Their focus on white folks' accomplishments came from a genuine belief that, given freedom, individual initiative caused progress. Nevertheless, their reflections about a common American past may have focused writers' anxieties about a future they could not control.

The rising South's histories reflected these crosscurrents. Bent on pleasing southern readers, Pickett used a publisher in Charleston for his *History*, and the wealthy planter tried to persuade his readers that he and his kind represented their interests. Baldwin first aimed at a regional audience, then put *Flush Times* with a New York press, increasingly attracted to the fast track. Meek first published in Alabama's towns but eventually tried to publish in New York, hoping that readers in a decentralized nation would accept a democratic South with slavery. Even while Hooper published his own work in the North, he printed Woodward's history on his local newspaper's press. Countering Pickett, it suggested a more open society than the one the planter preferred.

In sum, the early historians of the Southwest faced challenges on many fronts. Their subject matter required them to relate southern slavery and American freedom. They operated in competitive markets and appealed to divided middle classes. They could chase money and national fame, but their neighbors might prefer gentility and regional loyalty. They emphasized the harmony of their society while feeling its internal stress. Educated southwesterners cared about their past, for they thought it placed them in the forefront of civilization. That meant that historians, comic or serious, got plenty of public notice. In a divided society, literary self-determination was even trickier than "Ovid Bolus, Esq." made it seem.

AN ANXIOUS PLANTER'S HISTORY

Albert Pickett saw history as a planter whose land and slaves determined his status. He increased an ample inheritance with a good marriage and attention

---

[5] I have discussed the tension between the market and southern loyalties at greater length in "Writers in the Old Southwest and the Commercialization of American Letters," *Journal of the Early Republic* 27 (Fall 2007): 471–505. An earlier discussion of this problem was in John

to farming, and he never wrote for a living. He denied crass motives, yet the stirring narrative in his *History* reflected his materialistic view of self-determination. Pickett's *History* displayed the martial spirit of his Democratic Party's founder, Andrew Jackson. And, like Jackson's, Pickett's assertive will had roots in slavery and in honor. Equating his welfare with that of his state, Pickett feared for the security of slavery, and he was willing to compromise the freedom of ordinary whites to protect it. His anxieties led him to aim his *History* at the readers of the South, where his status carried weight, but he also eyed the larger market of the North. His chronicle warned readers – wherever they were – that touchy southern men would brook no meddling with their freedom or their land.

Early on, Pickett exhibited his desire to unite the public behind slavery and his propensity for violent rhetoric by writing, in his twenties, about politics for his brother-in-law's Montgomery newspaper and for the local *Planter's Gazette*. In the wake of Nat Turner's 1831 revolt, Pickett authored a grand jury report that was carefully pitched to his audience in Montgomery. Wishing to solidify the "enlightened public opinion" of "a moderate, reflecting, and intelligent people," he taunted the abolitionists that "the slave whom you instigate to our massacre, whom you goad on and inflame with savage ferocity can never effect any thing like a general rebellion." Slaves were so controlled that they might slay "a whole community of women and children, but they cannot extend the bloody work." Suddenly, however, he called for tighter controls not only over slaves but also local white critics of slavery.[6] With a planter's eyes, Pickett saw that free speech might endanger his interests.

McCardell, *The Idea of a Southern Nation: Southern Nationalists and Southern Nationalism, 1830–1860* (New York: W. W. Norton, 1979), ch. 4, "A Southern Republic of Letters."

[6] *Ibid.* Typescript in the Pickett Papers, ADAH, under the heading "Presentment Against the Abolitionists," with Pickett's note that he was the author. The Grand Jury's brief recommendations to the legislature treated the real issues beneath Pickett's assault on moralizing northerners: that magistrates "continue vigilant and watchful"; that slave patrols be "strictly observed"; that laws prohibiting the immigration of free blacks be enforced; and that "additions be made to the Criminal Code, providing for the immediate removal of all such persons upon whom suspicion may rest." An illuminating discussion of the *History* is Philip Beidler, *First Books: The Printed Word and Cultural Formation in Early Alabama* (Tuscaloosa: University of Alabama Press, 1999), "Antebellum Alabama History in the Planter Style: The Example of Albert Pickett," 63–75. See also Michael O'Brien, "On the Writing of History in the Old South," in Lothar Hönnighausen and Valeria Gennaro Lerda, eds., *Rewriting the South: History and Fiction* (Tübingen, Germany: A. Francke, 1993), 144–146. Copies of many of Pickett's newspaper articles are in his Pickett Papers, ADAH. For the political power of Pickett's friends, see J. Mills Thornton, *Politics and Power in a Slave Society: Alabama, 1810–1860* (Baton Rouge: Louisiana State University Press, 1978), 210, which places Pickett's history in the context of rising sectionalism. Pickett's neighbors in Autauga County, across the Alabama River from Montgomery, were politically ambitious Democratic planters, including Crawford and Absalom Jackson, Bolling Hall, and Benjamin Fitzpatrick, and in this instance and others he seems to have spoken for them. For a particularly clear statement of his eagerness to support them politically, see Pickett to Bolling Hall, October 19, 1853, in Bolling Hall Papers, ADAH.

In 1845, Pickett wrote a second grand jury report that more openly advocated restrictions on the freedom of white men. The report proposed taxing itinerant peddlers out of existence, arguing that their "cheap and worthless wares" hurt all "classes" of people. Pickett's class bias showed, however, when he began with the harm peddlers did to planters, whose slaves were lured into "insurrection," and to merchants, who could not compete by roaming the country. Even less tactfully, Pickett lumped together "inexperienced white people" and "ignorant negroes," who should, presumably, be saved from their own poor judgment about cheap goods. The most controversial proposal, however, called for a ban on interstate slave traders. And Pickett's first reason revealed his self-interest: "The State literally swarms with an immense negro population increasing every year the quantity of cotton and bringing down its price."[7]

Although Pickett did not mention that the "immense" supply affected the value of slaves, too, his reasoning attracted unwanted attention. While few newspapers responded favorably, Johnson Hooper, writing in the Wetumpka *Whig*, approved restrictions because eastern slaves had "ideas and a degree of intelligence, which is it not prudent should be communicated to the black population of the Southwest." But others assaulted Pickett, who was sufficiently piqued to respond. He revealed his wounded pride to the Mobile *Herald and Tribune:* not only had the paper misrepresented him, it had "associated my *name* with that of *another family!*" In the Hayneville *Chronicle*, the planter claimed that he had written "for the good of the State, independent of all *Political Parties, Cliques, or Intrigues*" and also "without fear, or the hope of reward." But the *Herald and Tribune* had charged that Pickett acted as a rich man, and the Eufaula *Democrat* pronounced his proposal "not only untenable, but perfectly ridiculous, anti-republican and aristocratic."[8] These charges contained more than a grain of truth. By this time, Pickett and his family owned close to two hundred slaves and several thousand acres of land and were, by their own standards, "aristocratic."[9]

---

[7] Second grand jury report, typescript in the Pickett Papers, ADAH, under the heading "Presentment of the Grand Jury," with Pickett's notation of his authorship.

[8] All from clippings in Pickett Papers, ADAH. See also *A Reply to the Objections Urged Against a Prohibitory Law in Relation to the Introduction of Negroes* (Wetumpka, AL: Printed by Charles Yancey, 1845). On the interstate slave trade, see Michael Tadman, *Speculators and Slaves: Masters, Traders, and Slaves in the Old South* (Madison: University of Wisconsin Press, 1989), Walter Johnson, *Soul by Soul: Life inside the Antebellum Slave Market* (Cambridge, MA: Harvard University Press, 1999), and Stephen Deyle, *Carry Me Back: The Domestic Slave Trade in American Life* (New York: Oxford University Press, 2005), which is especially strong on the divisive effects of the trade within the South.

[9] In 1831, Pickett's sister-in-law had written home that her husband had little to do with townspeople because "you must know he is very aristocratic and that of itself would render us unpopular"; Eliza Pickett to her sister Jane Keely, November 27, 1831, in Pickett Papers, ADAH. Because Pickett's holdings (and his father's) in land and slaves were scattered in Montgomery and Autauga Counties, it is difficult to determine exactly how much they owned. The census of 1850 lists 103 slaves for his father and 90, at two places in Montgomery County, for Albert; U.S. Census for 1850, Montgomery and Autauga County. Although it has less information

In the wake of this controversy, Pickett abandoned the tactics of direct public advocacy about slavery – a wise decision because he was temperamentally unsuited for the give-and-take of debates. His proprietary attitude notwithstanding, Pickett really did want to make contributions to his state, and he could do that by writing history. His wealth and leisure allowed him to gather information that might otherwise disappear in time. Moreover, by writing the history of Alabama when it was still a territory, Pickett could make slavery appear essential. His history would be a public service and also serve the interests of slaveholders. He was about to discover, however, that dignified authorship did not protect a man from competition or controversy.

By 1846, Pickett was laying the groundwork for his *History* through subtle advertising that exploited his status and connections. After writing articles for the Alabama *Journal*, Pickett assembled a pamphlet called *Eight Days in New Orleans*. It combined travelogue, history, and puffery, predicting that the "Queen City" would become "the largest city on the continent of America, and perhaps in the world." His sketch of Jackson's defense of New Orleans called his hero "the most extraordinary man that ever lived in any age or country." Pickett mailed the pamphlet to prominent men, asking them to send materials for his larger history. Respondents wished him success: Alabama politicians like Supreme Court Associate Justice John A. Campbell and Senator William R. King; regional figures like journalist J. D. B. DeBow and historians J. F. H. Claiborne and Charles Gayarré. Charleston's *Southern Quarterly Review* noted the pamphlet, calling its opening "too ambitious" but commending Pickett's mind and his "good eye for observation." Auspiciously, the editor anticipated a larger "work that will be a valuable contribution to the literature of the country."[10]

Pickett's opening strategy invited controversy, however, because his potential rivals had friends, and newspapers buzzed about the historical competition. The Mobile *Herald* hoped that Alexander Meek "would before this have gone further" into his history. In a positive letter about Pickett in the *Alabama Journal*, Hooper called him "friend" but also printed a letter that reminded readers of his rivals. Noting that Meek (a real friend) had not finished his "splendid contributions," Hooper laughed that "like the spasmodic efforts of a dying giant we fear they are to cease." The editor of the Carrollton *Republican* sharply remarked that *Eight Days* was "only thrown out as a feeler by Mr. Pickett, to see how his proposed history of Alabama would be

---

about slaves than about land, see the useful discussion in Frank L. Owsley, Jr., "Albert J. Pickett: Planter-Historian of the Old South," *Louisiana Studies* (Summer 1969): 179–182.

[10] *Eight Days in New Orleans in February, 1847* (Montgomery: n.p., 1847), 33, 18, 13; *SQR* 12 (October 1847): 534. The articles originally appeared in the *Alabama Journal*, and it is likely that their press printed the pamphlet but Pickett made sure his readers knew that he "caused them to be embodied in the present form"; *Eight Days*, 4. Despite Pickett's boosterism, his pamphlet contained close descriptions and at least one random attack on abolitionists; *ibid.*, 10. Many responses from notable men to Pickett's mailing are in Pickett Papers, ADAH.

received by the public." In April, Samuel Townes, the editor of the Marion *News* and a local historian, suggested that Pickett should "confer with" Meek, omitting his name but insisting that Pickett would "doubtless know to whom we allude." Later, Townes claimed to be "not very sanguine" that Pickett's history would be completed and laughingly gave the planter only "'a year and a day'" to finish it.[11]

Pickett cleverly used Townes's engagement to gain more public support. In a letter to the editor, the planter emphasized his expenses: he had traveled the region "in search of manuscripts and oral information"; he had bought a "large number of books"; and he would go to Europe, if necessary, to find accurate facts. He called on gentlemen with "generosity and State pride" to help him. But, indicating his class awareness, he also asked "early settlers" to send him facts about ordinary people: "their modes of living, their journeys to the State, their privations and sufferings, their perils with the Indians, ... the appearance of the country, the soil, the climate, the rivers, and the establishment of forts and towns." And he asked for any material; "it makes no difference how ruff or rude." Pickett insisted that he would finish in a "year and a day" and added, with uncharacteristic public humor, that he should at least get credit for trying.[12]

Like newspaper editors, Pickett's private correspondents sometimes bruised the thin-skinned planter's ego. In a series of exchanges with Meek's friend Simms, Pickett sent a writing sample, asked the famous writer how to compose, and sought materials and names of people who might aid him. A little impatiently, Simms instructed the neophyte on style and warned him about plagiarism. He cautioned Pickett to avoid the ornate language of his sample and advised him to write and rewrite. He also recommended sources, suggesting names of books and telling Pickett where to get them. After reading *Eight Days*, Simms suggested "*en passant*" that Pickett had made "small grammatical errors." These "should be carefully avoided in things of more elaborate character."[13] With authority earned by fame, Simms tutored the amateur.

Unlike Simms, Pickett wanted mostly southern readers, and, after four years of work, he contracted with a Charleston publisher for his *History*. Still, a concern for quality led him to New York. Trusting no one, he stayed there

---

[11] Typescript of clippings, Pickett Papers, ADAH: Mobile *Herald*, March 29, 1847; Hooper comment to the Alabama *Journal* quoted in the Franklin (County) *Democrat*, April 7, 1847; comment from the *Journal* quoted in the Huntsville *Southern Advocate*, August 6, 1847; Carrollton *Republican*, July 28, 1847; Marion *News*, July 23, 1847.

[12] Marion *News*, August 13, 1847, *ibid*. During the years when he was writing, Pickett also published some of his work in pamphlet or periodical form. See, for example, *Invasion of the Territory of Alabama by One Thousand Spaniards under Ferdinand DeSoto in 1540* (Montgomery: Brittan & DeWolf, 1849).

[13] William Gilmore Simms to Pickett, advice on writing, March 18 [1847]; suggestions about books (which included reference to materials that Meek had gathered), April 14, 1847; "*en passant*," October 25, 1847; all in Pickett Papers, ADAH.

a month early in 1851 to oversee the "execution" of the maps and pictures for his book. He wrote his wife that he was "treated with much attention" and described the city's mechanical wonders as well as the luxurious Astor House. "New York is brilliant," he claimed: "Everybody looks cheerful & happy & the ladies are adorned with the richest & most elegant apparel." In contrast, Pickett carped to a neighbor about "the splendor, the meanness, the selfishness & the ridiculous moneyed aristocracy of the North on the one side, & the poverty distress & destitution of the lower classes on the other." He complained that "money is the god of these people. It will buy up the honor of the men & prostitute the virtue of the women." But he claimed to speak "from observation *alone*, for I have not entered the *market* to test the matter." His neighbors, he bragged, were "infinitely more virtuous, honest & and unselfish" than Yankees, and he rested his hopes for sales on people like them.[14]

However snide his comparison between northerners and southerners, Pickett knew that a Charleston publication limited his sales, and he was paying out of pocket for the northern engravings and the southern printing. He boasted to his friend that, except for illustrations, "the whole work will be *Southern*." But then he worried: "Will Southern people *buy* the book of a southern author & printed by a Southern House?" And he answered his own question with doubts: "*Nous verrons*." Although Pickett had chosen a substantial printer with a steam press, he hovered over the work in Charleston. Apparently, people there were properly attentive. Pickett wrote his wife that Arthur Hayne, brother of the late Senator Robert Hayne, gave him a dinner that the governor attended. He disliked his first hotel but moved to another where the owners fussed over him. Although he missed his family, he would not leave Charleston until the "disagreeable" supervision was done.[15] The planter wanted the best book a "Southern House" could produce, and he wanted it to sell.

For all of his hostility, Pickett cared about the northern market. In September of 1851, several months after the *History* appeared, he received a complimentary letter from Henry Schoolcraft, who had done pioneering work in northwestern history and Native American culture. The planter answered that he hoped the *History* "would meet the approbation of *other* learned & distinguished gentlemen at the North." He told Schoolcraft he was marketing books in the Northeast, using language that showed his continuing control: "I have sent 150 copies to Philadelphia to Thomas Cowperthwaite for sale & to G. Wilford New York" (both of whom Simms had recommended). But he had not heard from either. He told Schoolcraft that he hoped to appeal to "authors & libraries in those cities – if the *citizens* do not feel interested enough in a

---

[14] Pickett to Sarah Pickett, February 13, 1851; to his neighbor Absalom Jackson, March 7, 1851; both in *ibid*.
[15] Further remarks to Jackson, also in letter of March 7, 1851; "disagreeable job," May 15, 1851. He commented on his dinner with the governor and other prominent South Carolinians, Pickett to Sarah Pickett, April 12, 1851. All letters in *ibid*.

southern work to buy it."[16] Eager for attention from other elites, Pickett hoped to overcome his disadvantages without catering to northern opinion.

From its opening pages, the *History* revealed Pickett's aim at the South. Instead of a dedication to a single individual, Pickett listed a page-full of distinguished gentlemen: sixteen from Alabama; two each from Georgia, Mississippi, Florida, and Louisiana; one from Tennessee; and seven from South Carolina, including Simms and his dinner host, Arthur Hayne. Although some of the South's historians were there, the group was notable for its political stature. Pickett's "Preface" lamented the labor and expense of locating materials. He emphasized, however, that the *History* was his civic "duty," even though it was "the hardest work of my life." Pickett recognized Meek, the "accomplished writer," for his "condensed, but well written and graphic account" of the expedition of Hernando de Soto, and he pronounced it "correct." In further acknowledgments to "gentlemen of talents and distinction," Pickett even thanked a few northern historians.[17] But the strong southern emphasis in the front matter set the direction he would follow in the text.

Simms had sniped that a large book on a "small State only two hundred years old, is an absurdity," but Pickett's *History of Alabama* swept over two and a half centuries in two volumes.[18] The first volume began with de Soto's expedition in the sixteenth century, and the second ran through the War of 1812, with brief sketches of public men after statehood in 1819. Pickett lavished praise on the Southwest's natural beauty. His favorite topics were gory battles between the Indians and whites, but he also examined Native American cultures – clothing, architecture, politics, family relations, sports, and styles of warfare. He used all of the English-language sources he could find, including interviews. Pickett footnoted and compared his sources, often with long quotes, and he explained the credibility of oral statements. He tried to be transparent, but, because local readers could not consult a large library like his, he used his definitive tone, his reputation, and those of the eminent people in his dedication to establish his authority.

Throughout his *History*, Pickett played to his readers and connected Alabamians with their past. He included all types of people when he gave settlers' names and their kin. He recorded the intermarriage of Native American and Europeans like that of Abram Mordecai, a well-known Jewish settler, and his "half-breed" wife, who had black as well as Creek ancestry. He identified the contemporary locations of historic sites. After discussing the establishment of Fort Toulouse (not far from his plantations), Pickett asked the "citizens" of "Montgomery, Coosa, Tallapoosa, Macon and Russell" counties to reflect that "one hundred and thirty-seven years ago" the French had traded peacefully

---

[16] Pickett to Henry R. Schoolcroft, September 15, 1851, HEH.
[17] *History*, "Preface": "hardest work," 10; Meek, 13.
[18] William Gilmore Simms to Pickett, March 18, 1851, Pickett papers, ADAH. This advice was too late, for Pickett had already completed writing and was just months away from publication, but it seems unlikely he would have heeded it earlier.

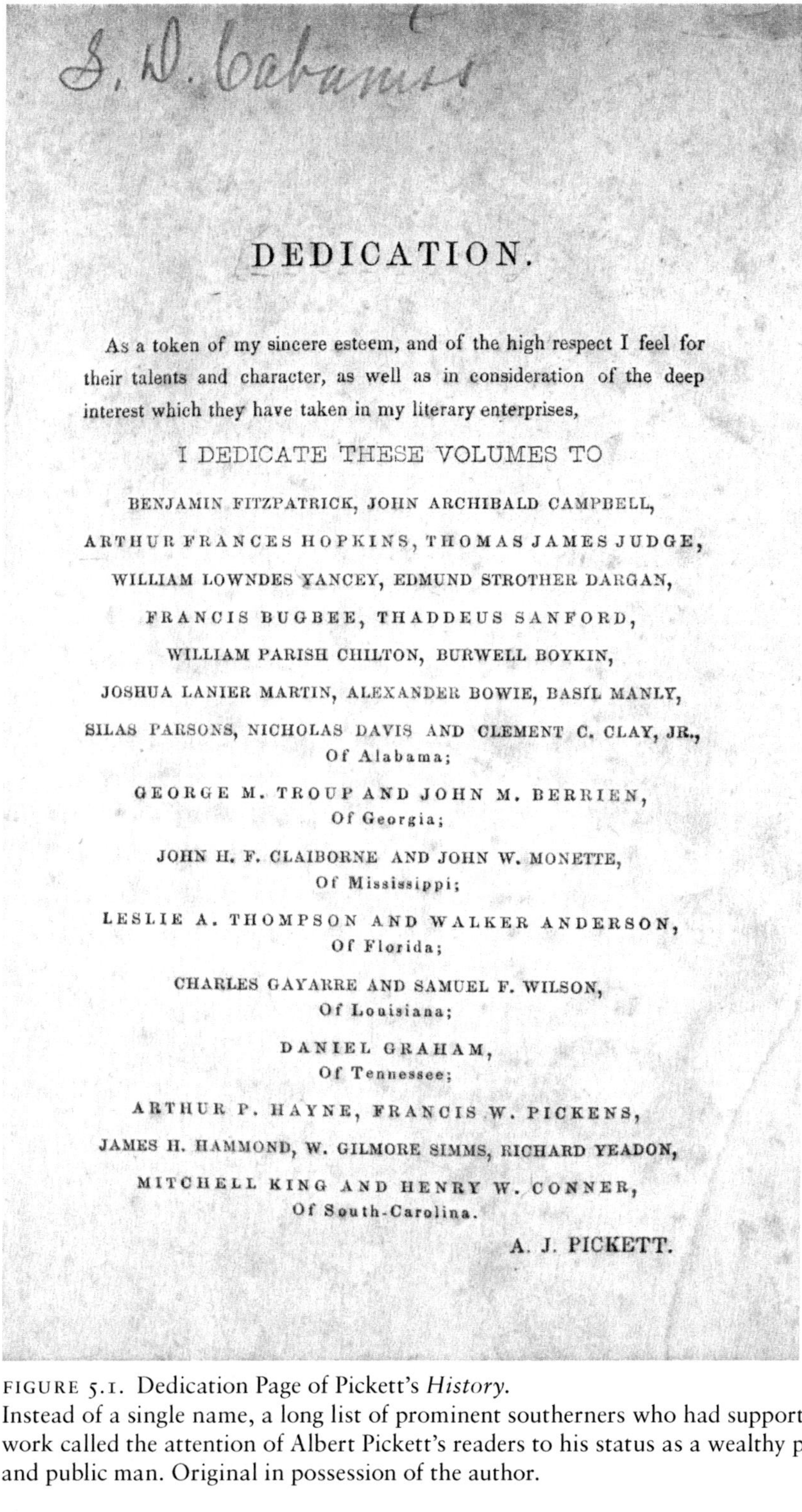

DEDICATION.

As a token of my sincere esteem, and of the high respect I feel for their talents and character, as well as in consideration of the deep interest which they have taken in my literary enterprises,

I DEDICATE THESE VOLUMES TO

BENJAMIN FITZPATRICK, JOHN ARCHIBALD CAMPBELL, ARTHUR FRANCES HOPKINS, THOMAS JAMES JUDGE, WILLIAM LOWNDES YANCEY, EDMUND STROTHER DARGAN, FRANCIS BUGBEE, THADDEUS SANFORD, WILLIAM PARISH CHILTON, BURWELL BOYKIN, JOSHUA LANIER MARTIN, ALEXANDER BOWIE, BASIL MANLY, SILAS PARSONS, NICHOLAS DAVIS AND CLEMENT C. CLAY, JR.,
Of Alabama;

GEORGE M. TROUP AND JOHN M. BERRIEN,
Of Georgia;

JOHN H. F. CLAIBORNE AND JOHN W. MONETTE,
Of Mississippi;

LESLIE A. THOMPSON AND WALKER ANDERSON,
Of Florida;

CHARLES GAYARRE AND SAMUEL F. WILSON,
Of Louisiana;

DANIEL GRAHAM,
Of Tennessee;

ARTHUR P. HAYNE, FRANCIS W. PICKENS, JAMES H. HAMMOND, W. GILMORE SIMMS, RICHARD YEADON, MITCHELL KING AND HENRY W. CONNER,
Of South-Carolina.

A. J. PICKETT.

FIGURE 5.1. Dedication Page of Pickett's *History*.
Instead of a single name, a long list of prominent southerners who had supported his work called the attention of Albert Pickett's readers to his status as a wealthy planter and public man. Original in possession of the author.

with the "rude inhabitants" of their area. He also detailed pioneers' harrowing struggles. An indomitable woman inspired the survival of her party; she was a Mrs. Dwight, from one of New England's "best families."[19] Pickett's varied cast of characters enhanced Alabama's importance, demonstrated the diversity within a slave society, and displayed an ostensibly democratic spirit.

Consciously or not, Pickett obscured causes and minimized the connection between national and regional histories by focusing on heroic individuals. Except for his important discussions of Native Americans, he neglected analysis and described wars, treaties, explorers, and generals. For example, while he detailed Jackson's battle at Horseshoe Bend with original illustrations, he ignored the reasons for expansion – perhaps because all of Pickett's plantations lay within the land the general took from the Creeks.[20] Pickett's approach suited an inexperienced historian, and his action-packed narrative fit his talents. The florid Romanticism of Bancroft's multivolume tribute to American freedom was yielding to a realism that Pickett preferred. Moreover, both his neglect of national events and his portrayals of individual action fit Pickett's story of self-determined people. Behind a history that hardly mentioned the United States lay the principle that individuals' decisions caused change. In that fundamental assumption, Pickett's narrative was as thoroughly American as Bancroft's.

But Pickett's *History* was also the narrative of a slave society, and he inserted slaves frequently in his accounts of individual action. He noticed that whites fled warring Indians with their "negroes" (his consistent usage); and he often reminded his readers that Creeks or "half-breeds" like Alexander McGillivary owned slaves, too. A few African Americans were brave. One slave named Hester encountered the Indians with her owner and survived a chest wound to tell white settlers about the event. In a legendary fight on the Alabama River, Caesar, the former slave of an Indian, held the Creeks' canoes alongside those of his white compatriots while they fought hand-to-hand. Unnamed "noble" slaves battled other Indians when they could have escaped from their masters.[21] Slaves disappeared after their heroics, however, and Pickett did not give their kin or residence. Like other writers' fiction, Pickett's *History* was primarily about white people.

---

[19] *History*, Mordecai's wife, 421; Ft. Toulouse, 196; Mrs. Dwight, 354.
[20] *Ibid.*, 510. The Treaty of Fort Jackson following the Battle of Horseshoe Bend (1813) had ceded most of the Creek lands in south central Alabama, and all of Pickett's properties lay within the cession. Following Pickett's service as aide to camp to Governor Clement Clay, the Huntsville politician sent with Pickett a letter of introduction to Andrew Jackson, whom the young planter visited at the Hermitage. Pickett returned with a portrait of Jackson, a gift from the former president and a visual reminder of the future historian's identification with the southern general who had done so much for the planters of the Southwest. Pickett's son-in-law commented on the portrait and on Pickett's "unadulterated" admiration of Jackson in M. L. Woods, "Personal Reminiscences of Col. Albert James Pickett," *Transactions of the Alabama Historical Society, 1891–1903*, vol. IV, ed. Thomas M. Owen (Montgomery: Printed for the Society, 1904), 615–616.
[21] *History*, "noble" slaves, 468–469; Hester, 536; Caesar's role in the canoe fight, 363–366.

Pickett used slaves to make some points. The ugliest example was his account of the 1813 battle at Fort Mims, where, in his estimate, a thousand of William Weatherford's Creek warriors destroyed roughly five hundred whites, loyal Indians, and black slaves. As eyewitnesses told Pickett, two slaves warned the fort's officers that Indians were massing in the woods. But, when no attack materialized, whites said the slaves had lied, and the officers immediately whipped one slave. They postponed the beating of the second at his master's insistence. When another slave glimpsed the Creeks, fear of whipping kept him silent, and they attacked by surprise. Pickett recounted the bloody assault – men shot and scalped; children swung against walls, their brains knocked out; babies cut from their mothers' wombs; and women mutilated "in a manner which neither decency nor language will permit me to describe." He closed by reminding readers of the slaves: of the "negro who was whipped, and of the other who was killed by the Indians while tied up, ready to receive the lash."[22] The beating of these slaves illustrated errors, and Pickett asked his readers to be alert for hidden danger.

Here and there, Pickett's anxieties about slavery intruded dramatically. When he briefly described the French empire, he put "SLAVERY" in capital letters. He detoured for a gruesome episode in which shipwrecked French sailors cannibalized their African companions. Then, gratuitously, he attacked hypocritical abolitionists: the French, who ate slaves, the English, who "captured them in Africa," and the Puritans, who "received them, paid for them, put them to hard labor, sold and re-sold them for many years." Pickett also threatened. After praising the Chickasaws, he appealed to Southwest's "young men" to remember how the "bravest race that ever lived" had "drenched the soil with the blood of the invaders." Then he asked: "Will you ever disgrace that soil, and the memory of its first occupants, by submitting to injustice and oppression, and finally to invasion?" And he answered, "'No – no – never!'"[23] The foreboding larger context was so clear that Pickett did not need to identify his imaginary invaders as Yankees.

Ending his narrative before Alabama's statehood, Pickett appended brief sketches of some of the men who led it into the national period. Here Pickett's upper-class bias, his loyalty to the Democracy, and his friendships in Autauga County affected his text. Without exception, he praised benevolent, public-spirited men of wealth, noting their successes and ignoring their many slaves. He insisted that this universally admired, working aristocracy served "all classes." Not by chance, Pickett had connections to most of his subjects, and most were prominent Democrats: John Williams Walker (his niece's father-in-law) and the senior Clement Clay from Huntsville; the first governor,

---

[22] Ibid., mutilation, 542; slave lashing, 543. Pickett devoted an entire chapter to the massacre at Fort Mims.
[23] Ibid., "SLAVERY," 215; attack on abolitionists, 225; question, 298. After posing a similar question in the context of the Creeks' bravery, he answered more equivocally: "Posterity may be able to reply," 611.

William Bibb, whose family linked Huntsville and Autauga County; Pickett's own father; and his family's friends in the South Carolina clique that ran the Democratic Party in the Black Belt. In his conclusion, as in his opening dedication, Pickett showed how much his understanding of history reflected his own elevated social position.

By ending in 1819, Pickett avoided the controversies around him. He offered only a mild note of declension to reinforce his idea that Alabama needed new heroes: he would leave more recent history to one "fonder than we are of the dry details of State legislation and fierce party spirit."[24] But this, the *History's* last line, may indicate that Pickett was exhausted from the "hardest work he had ever done." To a celebratory audience in Montgomery, he spoke as a perfect booster. Despite "enterprising" settlers, the town had once been "one of the most dissipated, wicked places I ever saw," but now it was a "highly refined, moral, & religious community." With a typical townsperson's pride, he cited "statistics," counting schools with their enrollments, bales of cotton, factory investments, hotels, railroads, steamboats, and plank roads.[25] Planter that he was, Pickett spoke for the rising South.

Although Pickett always claimed that the threats to the Southwest's future were external, the planter's mistrust extended to his fellow Alabamians. He shared the acquisitive individualism that propelled his society, but he disliked free competition when it applied too much to him. He published his *History* in the South, where he thought he could control the process. Although he wanted to combine freedom for white men with slavery for black people, he would restrict other white men's freedom to protect his own class interest. He was prepared to do battle like the Chickasaws before "submitting to injustice and oppression," but he wondered if other men would fight beside him. One of his neighbors recalled that Pickett, on his deathbed in 1858, "exhorted" his close friends not to secede from the Union for "light or trivial causes," but to do so "if our rights were wrested from us."[26] To Pickett, self-determination required slaves. While his *History* made freedom and slavery inseparable, he reflected the uneasy alignment of middle-class townspeople with planters. And he was not sure the alliance would hold.

---

[24] *Ibid.*, "dry details," 669. In his excellent discussion of the literary significance of Pickett's history, Philip Beidler argues that Pickett stopped the history largely because he wanted to avoid the subject of the growth of slavery; *First Books*, 74.

[25] "History of Montgomery," manuscript speech delivered at the laying of the cornerstone of a Baptist church, Pickett Papers, ADAH. Pickett refers to the ninety-two-mile West Point railroad, which means the speech was after 1850, though the date is uncertain. Privately, however, he told his wife that "any portion" of Texas was healthier than Montgomery and that the town was "the most extravagant" place he knew. His comment to his wife, December 5, 1856, was written from Texas, when he was clearly trying to persuade Sarah that migration would be a good idea; Pickett Papers, ADAH.

[26] Comment by Crawford Jackson, *Brief Biographical Sketch of the Late Col. Albert James Pickett* (Montgomery: Barrett & Wimbish, 1859), 14. This sketch was printed on Hooper's press, and its friendly references to Hooper suggest that the Autauga Democrats were courting Hooper for his influence with former Whig voters.

THE HISTORIAN OF UNFETTERED INTELLECT

"Not Found in Pickett's History" read the subtitle of the first sketch Joseph Baldwin published in the *Southern Literary Messenger* in 1852. With that line, Baldwin announced a comic alternative that celebrated a broader freedom than Pickett conceived. Baldwin was a pragmatist who saw ideas as instruments. "The best speaking and writing," he wrote his son, "is a strong sense with the point of wit on it: like an ax made of iron with the edge steeled."[27] And that activist conception of intellect defined Baldwin's history. Entranced by the creativity of law, he thought that free men perpetually remade their inherited institutions. If such thoughts raised questions about slavery's future, Baldwin was reluctant to ask them, and he defended the South. But he identified with the national future and marketed his work accordingly. His history drew an upward arc that followed the freedom of the rising South more than its slavery.

Baldwin had entered southwestern public life at a young age. After a brief stay in Mississippi, he moved in 1837 to the heart of Alabama's cotton country: first to Gainesville, a busy river port, and then to the Sumter County seat at Livingston. Plunging into politics, Baldwin wrote his fiancé Sidney White that the state's Democratic legislature embodied the familiar exclamation: "'Come, my son, and see with what little wisdom the world is governed.'" To correct that, the young Whig won election to the legislature in 1843. There he defended his planter constituents against the spokesmen for small farmers, who wanted to prevent the use in state apportionment of the federal (three-fifths) ratio for counting slaves as people. Baldwin argued for the ratio and suggested that his opponents leaned toward antislavery.[28] Although this position served Baldwin's wealthy constituents, ambition, not slavery, was the engine that drove him.

But he owned enslaved people. Never primarily a farmer, much less a planter like Pickett, Baldwin in 1840 owned three slaves. One of them was probably Camilla, who had belonged to Sidney's family, and the two others were perhaps her husband and daughter. Baldwin sold slaves more than once, and, in 1850, he accepted a mortgage on a carpenter named Davis (40), his wife Nancy (35), their daughter Betsy (12), and a man named Frank (26) to secure

---

[27] "Ovid Bolus, Esq., Attorney at Law and Solicitor in Chancery: A Fragment, Not Found in Pickett's History," *SLM* 18 (July 1852): 433; Baldwin's advice to his son Alexander, July 23, 1853, in Lester-Gray Collection.

[28] The quote is from Axel Oxenstiern (seventeenth-century Swedish statesman, whom Baldwin did not identify to Sidney), in Baldwin to Sidney White, December 11, 1839, in *ibid.*, from Tuscaloosa, where the legislature met and his brother Cyrus lived. Sidney's father, John White, was a Whig Judge, her brother Alexander would be a Whig member of Congress, 1851–1853 (and a post–Civil War Republican), Joe's cousin Alexander H. H. Stuart, with whom he had studied law, was a Whig Congressman, 1841–1843, and later Secretary of the Interior under Millard Fillmore (1850–1853) – to mention a few of Baldwin's excellent political connections. Mills Thornton notes that the white basis bill was a Democratic measure that the party defended as "democratic"; *Politics and Power in a Slave Society*, 114.

a debt the man owed him; Baldwin agreed to sell the slaves if the client could not pay. In 1850, Baldwin owned seven slaves – three men, three women, and a child. Slavery was, then, a part of Baldwin's personal history.[29]

Confident that the Constitution guarded slavery, Baldwin sought a national reputation. At the Whig convention of 1848, he supported Zachary Taylor. The next year, a "somewhat mortified" Baldwin lost a close congressional race. His ambition intact, he built his legal practice, then began writing. "Ovid Bolus, Esq.," his first sketch for Richmond's *Southern Literary Messenger*, was unsigned, but that reticence was short-lived. After more sketches in the regional journal, Baldwin determined to try the northern market. Perhaps he was inspired by Hooper, because one of Baldwin's stories was about "Simon Suggs, Jr.," and in it a northern editor advised Suggs that local repute was "ephemeral."[30] In search of national fame, Baldwin would publish his sketches as a book, minus the subtitle "not in Pickett's history." Baldwin was betting on a market where relatively few readers knew that Pickett had written history.

Baldwin approached New York without the hostility Pickett had evinced. In the manner of Hooper, who had relied on William Porter for his first publication, Baldwin had the help of John R. Thompson, editor of the *Messenger*. In the summer of 1853, he went to Richmond and met Thompson, who "made fun" of New York's "literary crowd" and reported that William Makepeace Thackeray, during a visit to Richmond, had called Baldwin's sketches "the right stuff." In early July, the pair of southerners went to New York, where Baldwin negotiated with publishers.[31] At once excited and overwhelmed by the city, Joe wrote Sidney a clever account of his altered self-awareness:

Whiz – fizz – buzz – bliz – sizz – rubadub – rumble tumble – racket, jar and jostle, Babel outBabelled, and confusion confounded. I've been trying to get myself in some

---

[29] U.S. Census for Sumter County, Alabama, 1840 and 1850. Sidney's mother wrote her that the family's "servants" sent Sidney their regards, and she sent her own to Camilla; April 16, 1840, in Lester-Gray Collection. If Camilla and her daughter were the two females Baldwin owned in 1840, it is possible that Camilla was the older woman Baldwin owned in 1850, but the daughter does not match the age of the two women in their twenties he owned in that year unless the approximate age given in 1840 (less than ten years old) was incorrect. The bills of sale, in the same Collection, were dated March 29, 1844, and January 12, 1846. Although they could have been records relating to Baldwin's clients, their inclusion in the family papers suggests that is not the case. Probate records in Sumter County do not indicate that Baldwin frequently bought and sold slaves, but of course such records do not account for all sales.

[30] Cornelius's recollection of his brother's mortification in his "Memoir" of Joe, in Lester-Gray Collection; "*Simon Suggs, Jr., Esq.*" first appeared in *SLM* 19 (February, 1853): 65 74, then in *Flush Times*, quoted passage, 115; see also Shields, "Writers in the Old Southwest," 471, for further comments on the borrowing of Hooper's character. Baldwin supported Taylor only after determining that his hero Henry Clay was not "electable"; quoted in Malcolm Macmillan, ed., "Joseph Glover Baldwin Reports on the Whig National Convention of 1848," in "Notes and Documents," *Journal of Southern History* 25 (1959): 366–382.

[31] All but the last quote, Baldwin to Sidney, written from Richmond, July 5, 1853; last quote, Baldwin to his son Alexander (called Sandy or Sandie), July 23, 1853; both in Lester-Gray Collection. Baldwin's first letter to Sidney from Richmond was dated July 4, and by the end of the month he was back in Virginia.

frame of self-consciousness, but can't do it. I've lost my identity – all sense of individuality is swallowed up in the seething mass of humanity that is boiling like a caldron around me.

He complained that his "brain got weak from a multitude of images on it," calling the city the Niagara of "all cataracts." Baldwin insisted, however, that it was no place to live.[32]

Baldwin's "individuality" rose to meet New York's opportunities as he bargained with publisher D. Appleton. He cautioned Sidney to expect little, because "from what I hear a first book never brings anything but dry fame to an author," but he planned "to get as much as I can." In fact, he got 10 percent, the "highest allowable" royalty of a first author. The "main thing," however, was to gain "a reputation" so he could "demand his *own terms with the craft.*" He understood that only sales mattered to the publishers: "Whatever may be the reputation of a writer as a mere magazine writer, that will *not command the booksellers, who only regard the author as a bookmaker.*" Although Baldwin quickly saw that authorship was only part of selling books, he was not intimidated. He expected to shape his future.[33]

Leaving New York, Baldwin reevaluated it and his prospects. From Winchester, Virginia, near his birthplace, he wrote Sidney that "you get mighty tired of the roar and rattle of New York, but you seem to miss them mightily when you get into the country again." In terms that did not bode well for his life in rural Alabama, he continued that "other places seem so little, solitary and insipid afterwards that you are pressed with a sense of loneliness and desolation." Baldwin praised his friends in Virginia but said he was equal in "native intellect" to "any of them," and he meant "to claim my place as modestly as becomes a diffident man, but firmly." The city had inspired him with a vision of literary greatness, and he would assert it as a gentleman should.[34]

In *Flush Times*, Baldwin asked his readers to see the Southwest as monumentally significant. Although Baldwin's book was immediately compared with Hooper's, his gentle satire distinguished it from the outrageous humor in *Simon Suggs* as well as from Pickett's serious history, and Baldwin was both narrator and a subject of his stories. Where Hooper had used American politics to broaden his scene, Baldwin made the intellectual heritage of the English-speaking world converge on the Southwest. Unlike Pickett, he liberally scattered allusions, from the Greek general Themistocles to the American huckster P. T. Barnum, and above all to British writers – often to Shakespeare, but also to contemporaries like Sir Walter Scott. He compared

---

[32] All quotes from Baldwin to Sidney, written from New York, from the St. Nicholas Hotel, July 12, 1853, in *ibid*.

[33] First quote, Baldwin to Sidney, remainder from Baldwin to his son, July 23, 1853; both in *ibid*.

[34] First two quotes, Baldwin to Sidney, July 30, 1853; second two from Baldwin to Sidney, August 3, 1853; both in *ibid*.

western lawyers to British statesmen and all sorts of Americans: popular entertainers, famous criminals, writers, and, most of all, politicians and other lawyers. More than name-dropping, Baldwin put himself and his colleagues on a vast stage.[35]

Baldwin established his intellectual themes with the opening sketch of the liar Ovid Bolus. One of the greatest Latin poets, the real Ovid (43 BCE–17 or 18 CE) had been a onetime lawyer and public official, and he had both celebrated and satirized the transformation of the Roman Republic into an Empire. Baldwin thought the Southwest could be as significant as Rome. As educated readers knew, the Latin poet's most famous work was the *Metamorphoses*, a poem that made humans into deities and Greek myths into Roman ones. Like the contemporary Romantics, the southwestern Ovid "asserted the Spiritual over the Material," raising "the spirit of man to its true and primeval dominion over things of sense and grosser matter." "Ovid Bolus" universalized Baldwin's work, but it also emphasized the power of ideas in free society. It made the sketches a form of intellectual history or, in a way, a southwestern mythology.[36]

Like Ovid, most of Baldwin's characters were self-made men. He contrasted Virginians with southwesterners to emphasize this point. Baldwin admired Virginians' sociability and integrity, but he thought them too stuck in the past to exploit their opportunities. Although migrating Virginians joined the speculative frenzy of flush times, they went bankrupt "by neighborhoods." In contrast, the freedom of the Southwest energized more intellectually alert, less scrupulous men. Showing scant respect for authority, Baldwin's wily lawyers manipulated facts, competed for honor, and, in the process, remade the law. But the best of his men were like the "gentleman of the Old School with the energy of the New" he featured in one approving sketch.[37] Clearly, his models were middle-class men who combined gentility, responsibility, ambition, and plain hard work. Just as clearly, the author was chief among them.

Unlike Pickett's bloody southern soil, Baldwin's frontier was American and progressive. The Southwest, he claimed, had produced lawyers equal

---

[35] There are excellent discussions of *Flush Times* in John Mayfield, *Counterfeit Gentlemen: Manhood and Humor in the Old South* (Gainesville: University Press of Florida, 2009), 60–66, in James Justus, *Fetching the Old Southwest: Humorous Writing from Longstreet to Twain* (Columbia: University of Missouri Press, 2004), *passim*, in Adam Tate, *Conservatism and Southern Intellectuals, 1789–1861* (Columbia: University of Missouri Press, 2005), chapters 7–9, and John M. Grammar, *Pastoral and Politics in the Old South* (Baton Rouge: Louisiana State University Press, 1996), chapter 5. My summary of *Flush Times* does not attempt a comprehensive account of his famous book.

[36] "Ovid Bolus, Esq.," 3–5, in *Flush Times*.

[37] *Ibid.*, on lawyers, 79, 94; "gentleman," in "The Hon. Francis Strother," 250. Strother was actually Francis Strother Lyon, a leading Alabama lawyer. Baldwin wrote his wife that "Frank Lyon and his family" were "pleased" with the sketch, which was Baldwin's most favorable depiction of a southwestern lawyer; Baldwin to Sidney, December 22, 1853, in Lester-Gray Collection.

FIGURE 5.2. Simon Suggs, Jr.
The frontispiece of Joseph Baldwin's *Flush Times in Alabama and Mississippi* (1853) depicted one of his characters, Simon Suggs, Jr., who was the putative son of Johnson Hooper's more famous fictional scoundrel. Although he wished for his work to be seen as more genteel than that of Hooper, Baldwin was not above exploiting his predecessor's fame. Courtesy of the W. S. Hoole Special Collections Library, The University of Alabama.

to those "in any other quarter of the Union." More seriously than usual, he explained in "The Bar of the South-West" why westerners achieved greatness. Because institutions were "built from the ground up," men started as equals, acted independently, and gained rewards. This West demanded self-determination. "Where can a man get this self-reliance so well as in a new country," Baldwin asked, "where he is thrown upon his own resources; where his only friends are his talents; where he sees energy leap at once into prominence; where those only are above him whose talents are above his; where there is no *prestige* of rank, or ancestry, or wealth, or past reputation – and no family influence, or dependants, or patrons ... [?]" Without "*surveillance*," the very "atmosphere" of new society "refreshes, vivifies and vitalizes thought, and gives freedom range and energy to action." This was the "law of liberty" in action. Lawyers, Baldwin asserted, were "a representative of the character of the people." Unfettered minds made his new country American.[38]

Still, Baldwin casually twisted slavery into his history. The opportunity to make money from conflict lured lawyers to the Southwest: contested claims to property, "an elegant assortment of frauds constructive and actual," "swindling Indians by the nation," and crimes – "what country could boast more largely of its crimes?" But "an important addition" to this morally dubious litigation was dispute over property in slaves. Slaves were bought and sold on worthless credit, fraudulently traded when they were "unsound." Like swindles and crimes, speculation in slaves tested men's ethics, and, although Baldwin claimed that those who emerged with morality intact were stronger for the effort, he knew that many men failed to improve. He implied that, as they did, slaves might no longer be commodities tossed from one soiled hand to another. For the moment, however, they were lost in the shuffle. Major Wormly, the helpless Virginian, "consoled himself" that the slaves he lost to debt would become healthy through hard work.[39] Few of Baldwin's other slaveholders gave their human property a thought.

Mostly, Baldwin's slaves were bystanders in the competition that brought progress. Some were servants like Jo in "The Earthquake Story." Some were farm workers. Uncle John Olive had "about fifteen negroes, of all sorts and sizes" and did not "succeed very well with them, either in governing them or making much of a crop." He asked Baldwin to defend his assault of a man who had been "whippin' my nigger, Remus – Remus told me so hisself." The "fifty or sixty negroes" of one "jolly Virginian" were like insurance, because the "occasional sale of a negro or two" could prevent "insolvency, until a green old age." But enslaved people were also pawns. Simon Suggs, Jr., married a woman for her property. He then divorced her, "magnanimously giving her one of the negroes, and a horse, saddle and bridle." Ovid Bolus lied that he had planned to marry a rich girl until her father told him to free his slaves.

---

[38] *Flush Times*, 224–229, 241.
[39] *Ibid.*, 237–238; Wormly reference, 104.

Ovid's "love for the 'peculiar institution' wouldn't stand it," and he left the girl.[40] For the most part, slaves appeared so briefly that laughing readers could easily overlook them – as Lincoln may have done.

Throughout *Flush Times*, Baldwin put white men's freedom in the foreground and kept slavery in the background of the rising South. But one story suggested his anxiety, and it linked slavery to the market for books. "Sam Hele, Esq." did not appear in the *Southern Literary Messenger*, which suggests that Baldwin wrote it for northern readers. It responded to *Uncle Tom's Cabin*, and the title character chased off a woman who tried to teach antislavery to southern children. Alabama readers recognized Hele as Sam Hale, a Black Belt lawyer and editor who was the brother of John Hale of New Hampshire, one of the first antislavery members of the United States Senate. Baldwin and Sam Hale were actually friends, and Baldwin "got acquainted" with the senator during his trip northward. With typical confidence, Baldwin privately pronounced Senator Hale "a good fellow, very entertaining and witty," who "seemed to take a fancy to me."[41] Nonetheless, "Sam Hele" implied that antislavery ideology was ludicrous.

Baldwin's Hele was a New Englander who accepted slavery, but, as his town's leading cynic, he was unduly fond of criticizing his fellow southwesterners. Sam "liked the most vigorous words, the working words of the language." He "tore the feathers off of a subject, as a wholesale cook at a restaurant does the plumage of a fowl." After a good-natured description of Sam, Baldwin nastily introduced another New Englander, Miss Charity Woodey: "the ugliest woman I ever saw" and a "bundle of prejudices." "Engaged in the police business of life," she came as a "missionary" to convert southern girls to "her narrow and precise system of manners and morals" and to her views of "the subject of slavery in particular." At a village party, tipsy townsmen persuaded Sam to "get her off." As one of them told Sam, "you've been snarling at every thing about you so long, suppose you just try your best this time, and let off all of your surplus bile at once, and give us some peace."[42] Sam obliged.

Thus Baldwin turned one northerner on another. Flattering Miss Woodey that they were both superior, Sam told dreadful stories about the town's residents, beginning with basic immorality and progressing through various crimes to their mistreatment of slaves. Two men bet on whether or not a powder-horn lit in his throat would "blow the top of the negro's head off, which it did." Infants were sold "in big hamper baskets ... by the dozen" when the price was right, and others were drowned "like blind puppies, in the creek."

[40] Ibid., "Uncle John Olive," 319–323; fifty slaves, 92; Simon Suggs, Jr., 140; Ovid, 10.
[41] Baldwin to Sidney Baldwin, July 30, 1853, in Lester-Gray Collection; in the same letter he noted that he had bought books for "all of us," mentioning "Thackery, Dickens, Hawthorne, Longfellow, and Fielding," a mixed bag of gentlemanly authors.
[42] *Flush Times*, Sam's language, 284–285; Miss Woodey's appearance and morality, 291–292; the plan, 293. For the identification of Hele, see H. D. Farish, "An Overlooked Personality in Southern Life," *North Carolina Historical Review* 12 (1935): 341–353.

To cap off his campaign, Sam told Miss Woodey that the townsmen tarred and feathered abolitionists. Immediately, she left for the North.[43] A caricature of Yankee meddling, she got her come-uppance from the brother of an antislavery politician.

Despite his ugly lines, Baldwin made fun of everyone involved, as if to laugh off southern and northern concerns. Baldwin disarmed his northern readers with a New England trickster. But he subtly turned Sam's jokes on southerners. Although Sam thought himself clever, Miss Woodey mailed his lies to "Mrs. Harriet S – – –," who put them in her "book of fictions, in which the slaveholders are handled with something less than feminine delicacy and something more than masculine unfairness." Furthermore, the school's director claimed he bought Miss Woodey's contract for $300 and paid her way home "to get rid of her." Ridiculing her parsimony, Baldwin claimed she would "live at ease" on the interest of the small sum. But the town had lost money, and Sam's outrageous tales had gotten into print. Baldwin criticized "a very popular fiction" – Stowe's work – in a book he began with a liar's tales.[44] Whatever Baldwin's morals, his tactics were ingenious. They denied the seriousness of slavery, and they sold books.

Like everything else from the pen of a southwestern author, *Flush Times* was about white people – their self-determination in the healthy chaos of freedom. Against "perversions of patriotism" – the claims to superiority of people in the old states – Baldwin offered "cosmopolitan views" that demonstrated the virtues of the new.[45] There was, however, a worrisome implication in the structure of *Flush Times*. Although it was clear that Baldwin believed civilization had arrived in the region, what was its fate as development slowed? Would men continue to think creatively? Or would Alabamians become like Virginians: attractive but irrelevant? Nearly all claims to American exceptionalism raised this problem, but it seemed especially crucial for a slave society, and Baldwin evaded it. In his personal history, however, he acted out an answer.

Baldwin had contemplated a fresh start for years (like Pickett, he had visited Texas), and the excitement of New York seems to have stimulated his ambitions. Shortly after his return, he moved to Mobile, the closest thing to a metropolis in Alabama. There, he assumed the legal practice of his friend Philip Phillips, recently elected to Congress; and, there, he eagerly awaited the appearance of *Flush Times*. Although Joe missed his family, he liked the limelight, and his spirits remained high as he mingled in the best society. When the New York "Journal of Commerce" favorably reviewed his book, he was annoyed because the publishers had not yet sent his copy, but, when it came, he pronounced it "a very good looking volume." Joe sent Sidney "favorable" reviews, frustrated that reviewers were anonymous. Nonetheless, Baldwin

---

[43] *Flush Times*, stories about slaves, 299–300.
[44] *Ibid.*, 303.
[45] "The Bar of the South-West," 224, in *ibid*.

began "to think I stand a chance of being enrolled with the writers of the land."⁴⁶

Life in Mobile whetted Baldwin's appetite for fame. Although, like Augusta Evans, he was disgusted by the city's ostentatious display, he carefully measured local reaction to his book and reveled in its being "the town talk." When he wrote Sidney that "I am like a lion – at least like a cat," he further guarded his ego by claiming to "have been treated with a hospitality quite distressing." Georgia's famous Senator Robert Toombs gave him "a lot of attention," as did the ladies. Baldwin claimed that his book was "more appreciated as the reader is more intelligent." One gentleman compared him to Charles Lamb and Washington Irving, whom Baldwin particularly admired. "You would be surprised," he wrote, "at the surprise which seems to be felt at the tone of the book, and the polish of the style, the ripeness of the scholarship (!!!)." People acted "as if all at once an author had jumped forth into life like the fellow from Jupiter's brow."⁴⁷ He knew, on the contrary, that writing was serious work, even if the results were funny.

Baldwin was no less anxious than Pickett to have his public image match his aspirations. Although he had invited readers to compare him with Hooper by writing "Simon Suggs, Jr., Esq.," he boasted to Sidney that the "notices of the book do not speak of it as a Suggs-like affair but as gentlemanly authorship." In telling terms, he bragged that he stood "a great deal better as a man of genius than ever I stood before." Like other writers, Baldwin was uncomfortable about marketing himself. However "gratified" he was with his book's reception, he assured his wife that he was being "perfectly quiet, not doing anything to puff or be puffed – not even making the acquaintance of the writers for the press." After Hooper reviewed *Flush Times,* Baldwin was happy that he put "it up to the highest notch" and gave it "*a permanent place in literature.*" Despite wanting to be known for his "gentlemanly authorship," he wrote his fellow humorist a note of thanks.⁴⁸

---

⁴⁶ Annoyance, followed by note that he got the book, Baldwin to Sidney, December 11, 1853; "enrolled with writers," Baldwin to Sidney, December 22, 1853; both in Lester-Gray Collection. Baldwin had written his wife in late November that he recognized the move to Mobile was a mistake and that he was trying to get out of the arrangement with Phillips; November 26, 1853, in *ibid.* In addition to Baldwin's wife and children, his household included his sister Cornelia and seven slaves. Baldwin by now had a small farm in Livingston, the Sumter County seat, and the census value on the property was $2,300; U.S. Census, Sumter County, 1850.

⁴⁷ All quotes, Baldwin to Sidney, December 30, 1853, in Lester-Gray Collection.

⁴⁸ First quote, Baldwin to Sidney, December 22, 1953; remaining quotes in Baldwin to Sidney, December 30, 1853; note to Hooper, June 10, 1854; all in *ibid.* Baldwin's anxieties about how readers perceived him were common among authors. Among works that deal with male anxieties (mostly northern) about authorship in a market economy are Michael Newbury, *Figuring Authorship in Antebellum America* (Stanford: Stanford University Press, 1997), Grantland S. Rice, *The Transformation of Authorship in America* (Chicago: University of Chicago Press, 1997), and David Leverenz, *Manhood and the American Renaissance* (Ithaca: Cornell University Press, 1989).

By now, however, Baldwin had fixed his gentlemanly ambitions on the world beyond Alabama. *Flush Times* was a success in the market, with more than twenty thousand copies printed in the first year; by 1854, Appleton had issued at least nine printings, including two in London. The *Southern Quarterly Review* called it "full of fun and spirit" but "not all fun," commending the "really brilliant sketches" and "excellent analysis of character." Indeed, Baldwin had already announced plans for a more serious history to "show the people that I am not a mere joker." He intended to allay sectional tensions, he wrote his Virginia cousin, Secretary of the Interior Alexander Stuart, so the nation could grow. Hoping that his new book would do "some good" in that respect, he joked that he could "at least ... make some reputation by it." In his thank you note, he had promised Hooper a copy of the new history as soon as it was published.[49] But he also told Hooper that he was emigrating. Having coined a name for the boom years of southwestern history, Baldwin left the region behind in 1854.

Baldwin's destination was San Francisco, where a wide-open legal frontier offered his ambitions free play. As he reflected from California to Sidney about his decision to leave the Southwest, he suggested that its history had not played out as he expected, and, if its future was not bright, neither was his. As he wrote, he had been "burning daylight" because "the dull tame routine of Alabama life was not suited to my disposition, aims, ambitions." He had decided "that a man of genius (as my few friends thought) had no business playing big cards at a picayune game and wasting life energy and talents at a small retail trade, where local distinction and backwoods triumphs only are to be won." Baldwin did not identify slavery as a problem or suggest that the plantations of the Black Belt made it "dull." It is not clear what became of Baldwin's slaves, but he opted for a free society, hoping that the future was his "to be won."[50]

In addition to the royalties he earned on thousands of copies of *Flush Times*, Baldwin's comic history helped him make himself. Although he stopped writing "for a while" to focus on building a legal practice, he wrote Sidney that he would one day create "something worthy of my talents and the expectations of my friends." Baldwin was proud that his reputation had preceded him: "I meet men every day who speak of my works as things long familiar to them." More amazingly, he was admired "not only among the refined and

---

[49] *SQR* 9 (April 1854): 555. "Joker," Baldwin to Alexander H. H. Stuart, April 15, 1852; "let us grow," Baldwin to Stuart, November 21, 1853; "nationality," Baldwin to Stuart, April 16, 1852; reputation, November 21, 1853, all in Alexander H. H. Stuart Papers, UVA. Hooper letter cited in n. 48. The *Messenger* estimated that *Flush Times* sold twenty thousand copies in six months; *SLM* 20 (February 1854): 125.

[50] Baldwin to Sidney, February 22, 1855, Lester-Gray Collection. The probate records of Sumter County do not show any sales of his slaves when he left. They do show the disposition of his real property by Sidney and his former law partner, Thomas Wetmore. It is possible that Baldwin sold or transferred the slaves within his family or Sidney's. Deed Books for Baldwin's years in Sumter County are in the Court House, Livingston, Alabama.

Southwestern Histories for a Divided Market 157

intellectual, but rough men from the mountains. This is as near fame as a man can get." While he identified his ambitions with his new home, however, he was still southern. When "that Yankee fellow, Putman" failed to give his newest book "high praise," Baldwin griped that the man had "turned Abolitionist and tries to disparage anything Southern." And he told Sidney that disputes about slavery were perhaps worse than they were in the East.[51] Although the conflict he tried to joke away had followed him, Baldwin's personal history would match the upward arc he traced in *Flush Times*. Within four years of his arrival, he was elected to the Supreme Court of California, where he could actively remake American freedom.

ONE ROMANTIC, TWO SKEPTICS, AND THE AFTERMATH OF PICKETT'S *HISTORY*

Alexander Meek was not happy with Pickett's *History*. And he was too disgruntled to joke in public about it, as Baldwin did. In 1847, when the planter had publicized his intentions, Meek offered his services, then returned to work on his own manuscript. Unlike Pickett, Meek wrote philosophical history aimed at geographically diverse audiences. Like Baldwin, he believed that the combination of freedom and intellect created progress. But Meek idealized southern culture more than either Pickett or Baldwin. As these men marketed their works, their ideas became matters of public concern. By the time Meek's *Romantic Passages in Southwestern History* appeared in 1857, Pickett's work had been debated for years. And in 1859, Johnson Hooper – friend to all three historians – sponsored a quirky challenge to Pickett by General Thomas Woodward.[52] Alabama's writers agreed that slavery was important but differed in subtle ways about its relationship to freedom. Writing for middle-class audiences, they competed to define what the rising South was all about.

Meek's historical writing was published in regional periodicals and pamphlets from the 1830s forward, but Pickett's competition stimulated the handsome "giant" to produce a book. Within months of Pickett's public announcement, Meek wrote William Gilmore Simms that he had an unfinished manuscript "on his hands," but it was too long and he lacked evidence to "fill up" some periods. He complained that the "want of connection with publishers and ignorance of their usages" had "discouraged" him and made

---

[51] First quote, Baldwin to Sidney, February 22, 1855; second, Baldwin to Sidney, November 11, 1854; in Lester-Gray Collection.
[52] Meek to Pickett, June 8, 1847, in Pickett Papers, ADAH. Meek shared some information about sources for de Soto's route with Pickett, telling him that the best account was his own, published in 1839 in *The Southron*; he expressed his regrets that Benjamin Porter had given up his "enterprise"; and he said he hoped to "issue" his history, which he had been working on for "some years" in a "few months." Porter had written Pickett the month before that he once gave up his work in "deference to Meek" but resumed it when Meek was so slow. Now, "I most freely and unhesitatingly give up the field to you, if you desire it"; Porter to Pickett, May 1, 1847, Pickett Papers, ADAH.

him "procrastinate." He fussed that Pickett lacked "sufficient ability" as a historian. Yet Meek thought the market could judge, claiming that "the best work will alone succeed" in competition, "and if mine should not be the best it ought not to succeed." He admitted that while his "sympathies" were "all literary," his "habits" were "anything else." He expected to improve, however, assuring Simms that "I have got the God of my nature down, now, and I think I will strangle him before he can rise."[53]

Instead, his habits persisted. In 1850, after returning from the Eastern Shore of Mobile Bay, Meek confessed to his brother Sam that he had visited the resort to "complete" his history but yielded to "the crowd of company, the fashionable attractions of the place (our Southern Newport)" and the lassitude of summer. Joking that his pen was "well nigh oxidized from disuse" and his manuscript "'hung fire,'" he would finish "by writing it nightly" after working at the Mobile *Register*. Meek claimed that reports of Pickett's progress were "humbug," hoping to beat his rival to press.[54] When he failed to do so, Meek saw that Pickett had gained a competitive advantage. In November of 1851, after Pickett's *History* was printed, Meek wrote Simms that "mine must lie upon the shelf until his has run its career." He wryly acknowledged that he would like to point out Pickett's "errors, blunders, fictions, and shortcomings – but it would be attributed to jealousy; so I let the acid vinegar remain uncorked." Meek again excused himself: editing left him so "fagged out with leaders, paragraphs, and items" that he could not write history.[55] Pickett's advantages in diligence, determination, and wealth had prevailed.

Meek was not Pickett's only critic, for state and regional periodicals proudly greeted the *History of Alabama* but observed its flaws and debated details. Among the South's premiere periodicals, the *Southern Literary Messenger* ignored Pickett's work, *DeBow's Review* in New Orleans discussed it within a description of Alabama, and only the *Southern Quarterly Review* in Charleston gave it comprehensive coverage. Unfortunately for Pickett, however, the author of the latter review was Simms, who had already cautioned the planter about his writing and who shared his friend Meek's Romantic conception of history. Although Simms's review did not really contain "acid vinegar," it was not the kind of response the planter-historian sought.[56] Pickett

---

[53] Meek to Simms, May 18, 1847, in Meek Papers, ADAH. Meek estimated his manuscript would run 600–800 pages, and he never completed it.
[54] Alexander to Samuel M. Meek, October 3, 1850, in Meek Papers, MDAH.
[55] Meek to Simms, November 23, 1851, in ibid.
[56] The first notice in *DBR* praised a work done by "southern hands," and said the style was "neither finished nor elaborate, but clear, perspicuous, and simple," 11 (December 1851): 687–688; two longer discussions followed: 12 (January 1852): 55–66, and 12 (February 1852): 148–169. *DeBow's* first discussion commented on the "simplicity" of Pickett's "truthful and minute narrative" in a somewhat more positive vein than Simms. *DeBow's* also quoted one of Pickett's passages asking for southern resistance to antislavery. Although the reviewer criticized Pickett's handling of his sources, his main complaint was that Pickett had stopped his work too soon. Simms's review was unsigned, *SQR* 9 (January 1852): 182–209, but the text

had written to gain regional reputation, but he wanted to be taken as a serious author.

In fact, Simms praised Pickett's use of a southern press. The editor reminded readers of his frequent laments about southerners' dependence on northern books (his complaints were like picking "the half scarred sore which no medicament can ever heal"). Decrying the South's failure to engage in "honorable competition" with the "history-manufacturer" of the North, Simms urged state legislatures to require that all textbooks be southern and noted that Pickett's *History* was "beautifully printed."

In other respects, Simms was much more critical. Pickett's simple style was "uneven," neither "unique" nor "coherent." But, much worse, his conception of history was grievously flawed. His mere "chronicle" neglected what was important: "the career of a people; showing their moral standards, their mental powers, the character of their genius, their passion and tastes, the deeds they have done, and those events which have shaped, or, in any way, influenced their destiny." Simms quoted copiously, found some facts useful but others in error, and suggested an uncritical reliance on out-of-date sources. In the end, he credited the "patriotic" historian for a book with which southerners could "gratefully identify," and he asked for its "ample patronage."[57] For Simms, even a flawed book, if made from native materials, served the South.

Too proud to respond directly, Pickett indirectly answered Simms's criticism that Pickett misunderstood the nature of history. In 1854, the planter addressed the Historical Society of Alabama on "The Origins and Progress of History in the Eastern Hemisphere." In his paper, he posed as the defender of democratic history. Pickett insisted that history must be "popular" and "benefit all classes." It must focus on facts, for "philosophical disquisitions" misled "the public." Granting that even a "perfect historian" would offer some opinion, Pickett asserted that "pure narrators" were the "most delightful." The planter's address was never printed, however, and he continued to suffer criticism with quiet reserve.[58]

The Historical Society dignified the competition among historians by inviting Meek to speak the following year. In advance, Hooper puffed the event in the Montgomery *Mail* with implicit comparison to Pickett. "No man in the State," he wrote, "has given more attention to the investigation of its history" than Meek, and "certainly" none had done so with "an equal amount of scholarship, mental power, and that peculiar combination of judgment, taste, and imagination required to set historic details in an attractive light before the reader or hearer." Hooper added that he hoped Meek's oration would prompt his friends to call for the completion of his "long-promised history of Alabama." In the event, Meek's address, *The Claims and Characteristics of*

---

implicitly identifies him. My thanks to David Moltke-Hansen for confirming that Simms was the author.
[57] Quoted phrases, in order: 187, 187, 188, 191, 191, 195, 193, 209, in *ibid*.
[58] Typed manuscript copy of the address in Pickett Papers, ADAH.

Alabama History, made not the slightest reference to Pickett or his *History*. And, conscious that he was behind his rival, Meek published his elegant address as a pamphlet.[59] Ambitious middle-class men had access to print that wealth could not completely outweigh.

For two decades, Meek had exploited his friendships, had taken advantage of his role as a popular editor, and had issued short publications in numerous venues. He had also pursued his version of a progressive political agenda. Elected to the Alabama legislature in 1853, he authored the bill establishing the state's first system of public education. In 1856, he finally realized his long-standing hopes for a favorable marriage with an alliance that connected him to slave-based wealth for the first time in his life. His marriage to Eliza Slatter, the widow of prominent slave trader Hope Hull Slatter, cemented the position Meek had gained on his own in Mobile. Although Eliza no longer had large numbers of slaves, Alexander assumed the legal management of her extensive urban property. With his famous sociability unabated by marriage, he befriended young women writers, including Augusta Evans. He encouraged his friend Octavia Le Vert, Mobile's leading socialite, to write an account of her travels in Europe, and he wrote the preface to her *Souvenirs of Travel* himself.[60] All of this kept Meek before the public.

By the mid-1850s Meek had achieved a regional reputation, and he wanted more. Shortly before his marriage, Meek produced his only major publication with a northern firm, *Red Eagle*. This epic-style poem wove three strands around the character of William Weatherford, or Red Eagle, the Creek leader: his romance with a half-white girl, events from Alabama's history, and Weatherford's martial feats. Issued by D. Appleton of New York and dedicated to Simms, *Red Eagle* had been a long time "in its nest," for Meek had told Simms as early as 1843 that the poem was near completion, and Simms had published part of it in 1845. Nonetheless, Meek was excited by the finished poem's reception. He sent his brother Sam specially

---

[59] Montgomery *Mail*, July 12, 1855; *The Claims and Characteristics of Alabama History. An Address Before the Historical Society of that State, At its Anniversary at Tuscaloosa, July 9, 1855* (Tuscaloosa: Printed by J. F. Warren, *Observer* Office, 1855).

[60] A brief overview of the education act is in William Warren Rogers et al., *Alabama: The History of a Deep South State* (Tuscaloosa: University of Alabama Press, 1994), 118–120. Thornton makes elite support of a state system of public education a sign of their alienation from the common people, who preferred local control; *Politics and Power*, esp. 293–295, 300–302. Robert Eno Hunt, in "Organizing a New South: Education Reformers in Antebellum Alabama, 1840–1860" (Ph.D. dissertation, University of Missouri–Columbia, 1988), also depicts reformers as modernizers. Mobile historian Peter Hamilton, among others, commented on Meek's friendship with women, and with Evans in particular, in his essay in the *Library of Southern Literature*, Edwin Anderson Alderman, Joel Chandler Harris, et al., eds., 16 vols. (New Orleans, Atlanta, etc., Martin & Hoyt, 1913), 8: 3602, 3604. For an example of Meek's helpfulness to young women writers, see Julia Mildred [?] to Meek, May 3, 1850; Meek told his brother about Le Vert's preface, Alexander to Samuel Meek, September 13, 1857, both in Meek Papers, MDAH. For a discussion of Meek's marriage and its economic consequences, see Shields, "A Social History of Antebellum Alabama Writers," *AR* (July 1989): 180–181.

bound presentation copies, bragging that "the Knickerbocker, the So. Lit. Messenger, the N.O. Delta, Harper, N.Y. Tribune, The Churchman, and numerous others" had praised him "to my heart's content," and that most of Alabama's newspapers had, too. But he was annoyed that the editor of Mobile's *Evening News* had refused to review *Red Eagle*, a "simply ridiculous" move that exposed the man's "ignorance, folly, and malevolence."[61] Plainly, Meek wanted reputation in the North and the South.

Enjoying wealth and leisure in his new marriage, Meek determined to construct books for the popular market from his older, miscellaneous writings. He selected a publisher with offices in Alabama and New York to issue two more books – *Romantic Passages in Southwestern History* and *Songs and Poems of the South*. S. H. Goetzel, an Austrian printer who had been in Mobile since 1853, now employed the editor's brother Ben. Goetzel was opening a New York office, and Meek had expected that Le Vert's book and his own would be issued there. Ben wrote Sam Meek in September of 1857 that Alex was at the Astor House, "busy reading the proofs of his books, both of which are being published by the Northern Branch of the House with which I am doing business," and that they would be out in a month. Meek himself wrote Sam, ebullient about his prospects and excited by the city. His publisher had chosen the name for *Romantic Passages*, which contained only a small portion of Meek's "super-abundance of materials." The author told Sam that Le Vert's *Souvenirs* was "selling 'like hot cakes'" and was applauded in the New York presses, hopeful that his books would meet the same fate.[62] Using Goetzel seemed a perfect strategy to reach otherwise incompatible goals: using a southern press and reaching northern readers.

---

[61] "In its nest" is a phrase Meek repeated several times to Simms about his poem; see, for example, Meek to Simms, November 23, 1851; other quotes, Alexander to Sam, December 22, 1855, in Meek Papers, MDAH. *The Red Eagle* (New York: D. Appleton & Co., 1855); the poem was dedicated to Simms. By far the best discussion of the long poem is in Beidler, chapter 6, "A.B. Meek's Great American Epic Poem of 1855; or, The Curious Career of *The Red Eagle*," which also describes its generally favorable reception in the North and South. Although Beidler asserts that *Red Eagle* was published in New York and Mobile, Ellison, *Check List of Alabama Imprints*, lists no Alabama publication, and neither does WorldCat. Simms had published a section of the poem in his *Southern and Western Magazine and Review* 2 (1845): 119–120. As early as 1843, however, Meek had written Simms that he expected to have the poem, which "still lingers with one wing unfinished," completed soon, and that a local printer would "put it to press, in the winter," Meek to Simms, October 20, 1843, HSP. Meek knew himself when he said he procrastinated.

[62] Quotes, Ben to Sam, September 20, 1857; Alexander to Sam, September 13, 1857, in Meek Papers, MDAH. On the Goetzel firm, see John Tebbel, *A History of Book Publishing in the United States, Volume I: The Creation of an Industry, 1630–1865* (New York & London: R. R. Bowker, 1972), 465–467. While in New York, Meek presided at the first American Chess Congress; see the account in Daniel Willard Fiske, *The Book of the First American Chess Congress* (New York: Rudd & Carlton, 1859), esp. 97–99, for his address at the final banquet. See also Johanna Shields, "Delusions's Carnival of Death: A Different War Poetry for the South," in David Moltke-Hansen, ed., *The Transformation of War in the Writing of William Gilmore Simms* (Columbia: University of South Carolina Press, forthcoming).

The strategy initially failed. In November Meek and his wife were back in Mobile, and he sent Sam his two books, neither of which was published in New York because of the "heavy financial pressures" of 1857. Disappointed, he wrote that "no copies were given to the Editors there, and consequently there are no Notices in the Northern papers." With the financial crisis felt less in the South, Goetzel issued the books in Mobile "to raise ready money." Meek was resigned to his fate, for "*new books are, everywhere* suffering from the *pressures* and mine must share this push." In any case, Meek was cheered that *Frank Leslie's Magazine* had published a "Biographical Sketch" about him, written by well-known humorous writer Thomas Bangs Thorpe, accompanied by a "'counterfeit presentment,'" about which he joked, tickled with the publicity.[63] Goetzel could later issue the new books in the North, and, for now, Meek had published three southwestern books – two of poetry and one of the region's history.

Although *Romantic Passages in Southwestern History* was drawn mostly from two decades worth of orations, including the one for the Alabama Historical Society, Meek's preface assured his readers that it contained authentic history. In treating, like Pickett, the conquest of Native Americans by Europeans and Americans, Meek covered similar subjects: de Soto's journey, earliest settlements, the battle at Fort Mims, and other conflicts with the Creeks. He more or less invited comparisons. Meek was "gratified" that writers like George Bancroft, Pickett, and Simms had used his research in their "more capacious and dignified performances," and he insisted that he was already writing a "more elaborate work" rather than this one for the "general reader." While his publishers had "suggested" his title, he wanted readers to know that the term "romantic" applied to his dramatic style rather than any lack of "authenticity," for his work was based on "years of labor and research." Meek spoke for his "section of our country" – a pairing that suggested regional history with national meaning.[64]

Romantic Passages gave a southern flavor to ideas that were shared by many educated Americans. A Romantic like both Bancroft and Simms, Meek had a democratic spirit as close to that of the northerner as that of his southern friend. Unlike Pickett, who rejected "philosophical disquisitions," Meek reconciled regional and national history through a Romantic concept of culture. Culture included morality, manners, and intellect; it reflected nature; and it reflected

---

[63] Alexander to Sam, November 15, 1857, in Meek Papers, MDAH. "Counterfeit presentment" is from Shakespeare's *Hamlet* (III, iv), and it was popularly used to refer to pictorial images in the press, which is Meek's meaning here. Meek identified Thorpe as T. "Bee-Hunter" Thorpe, after the humorist's popular book *The Hive of the Bee Hunter, A Repository of Sketches, Including Peculiar American Character, Scenery, and Rural Sports* (New York: D. Appleton, 1854), although Thorpe is best known as the author of "The Big Bear of Arkansas," which appeared in William T. Porter's anthology, *The Big Bear of Arkansas and Other Sketches, Illustrative of Characters and Incidents in the South and Southwest* (Philadelphia: T. B. Peterson, 1843).

[64] *Romantic Passages*, "Preface," iii–iv.

and influenced history and government. In Meek's view, nature gave the races different abilities, and the natural environment shaped history, which meant that the world's cultures varied enormously. Given freedom, variations created nations, and, within the large American continent, they made sovereign states. Because a decentralized government allowed diversity among its sovereign states, competition and emulation led to national progress.[65] In Meek's vision, freedom allowed the Southwest to complement an American destiny.

Within that freedom, slavery could thrive. Meek opened *Romantic Passages* with an 1839 oration that explained the "distinctive" character of the Southwest. He claimed that nature fostered agriculture, which made southwesterners industrious, practical, and self-reliant, while warfare encouraged independence and patriotism. In peace, rural life required sociability. All of these traits were American and southern; but slavery made the region peculiar. "By producing two broad and distinct classes [i.e., races] in society," it created "a spirit of superiority and self-esteem, a certain aristocracy of feeling, and a pride and chivalry of character, which do not elsewhere so generally exist." Slavery made some men rich, but the wealthy did not dominate society. Instead, plain people were "not only the bones and sinews" of the region but "its veins, its arteries, which conduct the regular and healthful currents of pure vitality through the whole body politic." To know the Southwest was to know its "yeomen" rather than "planters who rule over large numbers of slaves."[66] Meek argued, then, that racial slavery unified the white people of the Southwest instead of dividing them.

Together, freedom and genius moved Meek's agrarian utopia forward. He insisted that ideas flourished only in free societies, where the "man of genius, however obscure his parentage, or humble his condition" rose and where great minds cooperated with ordinary ones. Although the "muscularity of intellect" belonging to common men was the "best hope" of the "national mind," Meek thought that genius gave ideas their highest form, and the interaction between genius and popular culture was constant in free society. In the United States, the "pillars" of the nation were "freedom of conscience, freedom of thought, freedom of speech, and freedom of the press," and the same guarantees made Alabama's constitution "distinguished above all others." Just as American government – by promoting the "unrestrained exercise of mind" and the "progress of intelligence" – ensured the nation's destiny, Alabama's charter of freedoms assured its future greatness.[67]

[65] "Philosophical disquisitions," Pickett's phrase, see n. 58. Anyone interested in southern romanticism should begin with Michael O'Brien's essay "The Lineaments of Antebellum Southern Romanticism," in *Rethinking the South: Essays in Intellectual History* (Baltimore: Johns Hopkins University Press, 1988), 38–56.
[66] "The Southwest; Its History, Character and Prospects: An Oration Before the Erosophic Society of the University of Alabama, December 7, 1839)," in *Romantic Passages*, 57–59. The oration was originally published by Meek's friend, Joseph Baldwin's brother Cyrus (Tuscaloosa: C. B. Baldwin, 1839).
[67] All quoted passages except reference to Alabama's constitution from "Americanism in Literature: An Oration Before the Phi Kappa and Demosthenian Societies of the University

Crucially, that freedom was for white men only. Without discussing African Americans, Meek claimed that slavery was "naturally, morally, and politically right and beneficial," but his discussion of Native Americans revealed his racialism. Meek called the Indian "ignorant, superstitious, cruel, bestial and obscene" and pronounced him "unsusceptible of civilization, and unfitted, by the instincts of his nature, for the higher, or even the lower, degrees of intellectual and social culture." Because Native Americans had no vocabulary for "abstract" or "spiritual" concepts like "Peace" and "Virtue," they could not reason about civilization. The historian explained how Weatherford became a "great orator" by manipulating his people with "circumlocutions and comparisons drawn from the physical world." Meek's point: "a master spirit may ever assert its superiority among an ignorant and barbarous people."[68] Perhaps a ray of doubt appeared in his admiring sketch of Red Eagle, as well as in the short story "The Fawn of Pascagoula," which featured a lawyer's infatuation with an Indian maiden. As in the poem *Red Eagle*, Meek equivocated about the issue of interracial relations, while justifying the subordination of Native Americans and African Americans by equating race with culture.

Meek traced the upward path of southwestern history within the framework of these Romantic concepts. His narratives were better organized but factually similar to Pickett's. Meek's essays about de Soto's expedition and the Fort Mims "massacre," for example, featured bravery, drama, and bloodshed, albeit with fewer scalpings and mutilations than Pickett's. Meek placed whipped slaves at Fort Mims with less detail and moralizing about white men's mistakes, and he had the slave Caesar fasten battling canoes together on the Alabama River. Less often than Pickett, he connected settlers' experiences to contemporary people and places, but he, too, linked Alabamians with their "sanguinary" past. Unlike Pickett, however, Meek emphasized the negative results of a violent history. It had given men "roughness of manner" and "an improper haughtiness of spirit," taught "a disregard of the laws and of any restraint," produced "neglect of the charities and courtesies of social life" and, most seriously, engendered "a general deterioration of the moral feelings."[69] This was a past to be escaped.

---

of Georgia, at Athens, August 8, 1844," in *Romantic Passages*, 122–127. In his 1855 oration to Alabama's Historical Society, Meek repeated his earlier claim that the constitution of Alabama was "distinguished above all others for its guarantees to freedom of conscience, freedom of thought, freedom of speech, and freedom of individual action," *ibid.*, 79.

[68] *Ibid.*, slavery beneficial, "The Southwest," 58; characterizations of Indians, "Sketch of Weatherford, or the Red Eagle, the Great Chief of the Creeks in the War against General Jackson; with Incidental Accounts of Many of the Leading Chiefs and Warriors of the Muscogee Indians," 260, 268–269. Meek portrayed Weatherford as exceptional (perhaps because he was of mixed blood), but he insisted that he was not literate, as Pickett had said; 267.

[69] *Ibid.*, "The Massacre at Fort Mims; with a Historical Sketch of the First Settlements in Alabama, the Battle of Burnt Corn, and the other Events that led to the Creek War of 1813–1814," "sanguinary" on the first page of the essay (233) and frequently thereafter; criticisms of early settlers in "The Southwest," 52.

Meek insisted, in fact, that such crudeness disappeared as civilization deepened, and the critical developments were schools and newspapers – the marks of middle-class, town-based life. "The flight of the honey-bee is said to mark the progress of the Anglo-American race," he wrote, "but the presence of the printing press is a surer index of its growth in intelligence and refinement." Again, this was a national phenomenon with a sectional bent. When intellectual life is concentrated in one metropolis, he argued, it stifles inspiration, and, "instead of being the large, fresh, oak-like growth of the heart of the whole people," it "becomes the dwarfed and noxious vegetation of a hotbed of vice and effeminacy." If the country would be great, genius cannot be "compelled to languish in obscurity in the provinces." By spreading education into every township in the state of Alabama, Meek would unite the ideas of towns with rural virtues.[70]

Over and over, Meek equated the progress of the Southwest and the nation. In an 1848 oration that ignored the raging controversy over slavery's extension, he insisted that the Mexican War proved the "great destiny of including the whole North American continent in one mighty brotherhood of free and flourishing States, that shall ever stand, a Pharos of Freedom, to illuminate and guide the world." Meek's history was as optimistic as any in America. The "great law" of humanity, he wrote, is "progress to the infinite, the eternal, the omniscient, the perfect. Ever onward, never attaining! All things, when aright, move upward, unceasingly, (by a great spiral revolution,) to the unattainable throne of God!"[71] These "philosophical disquisitions" (to use Pickett's terms) distinguished Meek's history from the planter's action-filled chronicle and placed the Southwest in a grand design for human improvement.

Meek believed this vision would sell books, and apparently it did, for Goetzel issued *Romantic Passages* five times in 1857 (including twice in New York), but sales did not meet Meek's expectations. *DeBow's Review* briefly noted his "long since established" reputation "as one of the most gifted and

---

[70] *Ibid.*, flight of the bee, in "Claims and Characteristics," 103; stifling urban effect, in "Americanism in Literature," 131. John Mack Faragher comments that the bees beloved by white pioneers in Illinois were called by the Kickapoos "'white people's flies,'" and were seen as "harbingers of the hated settlers"; *Sugar Creek: Life on the Illinois Prairie* (New Haven: Yale University Press, 1986), 75.

[71] *Romantic Passages*, "Pharos of freedom," in "National Welcome to the Soldiers Returning from Mexico: An Oration Delivered by Appointment, at Mobile, Alabama, July 4, 1848"; "spiral" in "Americanism in Literature," 113. The Pharos was the lighthouse at Alexandria, one of the seven wonders of the ancient world. Meek's soaring enthusiasm prompted the reviewer in the *SQR* (probably Simms) to observe that he had "boldness, nerve, originality, passion, – too much, perhaps, for cold criticism to tolerate" – which seems fair; from a one-page review of the original oration, which was published in Charleston by Burges & James in 1844; *SQR* 7 (January 1845): 257–258. The review began by comparing Hugh Legaré's restrained interpretation of the influence of America on politics and law to Meek's effusion, which had suggested that the American influence was "every where." But the reviewer conceded that Meek "has so warmed us up with his subject, and his beautiful method of treating it, that we really have no heart to dissent," 257.

accomplished of the literary men of the South," adding that the Meek would soon complete "the most complete and valuable history of the State that has yet appeared." The *Southern Literary Messenger* gave *Romantic Passages* a single line after an editorial about the "never-to-be-sufficiently decried" problems of southern literature. Ironically, the editor illustrated his theme with the "mirth-provoking and thoroughly original papers, brimful of fun," *Flush Times*. "When published in book form," *Flush Times* gained "a popularity almost unprecedented in our literature"; but only then was it "praised" in the South, where it had first gotten "scarce a line of commendation."[72] National popularity was one thing, a long-established reputation in the South another, and the tension between them was chronic.

Pickett, Baldwin, and Meek managed that tension with different emphases, but all of them hoped for recognition at home and in the North, and they described the history of the rising South as a triumph of self-determination. The next entry into the region's history was strictly a local publication, a nostalgic collection of memories that only incidentally analyzed social change. General Thomas S. Woodward's *Reminiscences of the Creek, or Muscogee Indians* appeared early in 1859 from the struggling press of Johnson Hooper, who did not pretend to be a scholar. Woodward's *Reminiscences* had first appeared as letters in Hooper's Montgomery *Mail*. Published now in book form, Woodward's letters attacked heroic history, and Hooper wrote an approving introduction. In it, he explained his admiration for Woodward and took credit for bringing his recollections to the public. The *Reminiscences* involved Hooper in the competition over southwestern history, and Woodward's eccentric perspective resembled that of the middle-class editor.

Hooper was in bad shape in 1859, and his publication of the *Reminiscences* was likely a bid for support. The *Mail* had begun in 1854 as a Know-Nothing paper dedicated to southern rights, but it stayed in financial trouble, caught between the capital's older, more orthodox papers (the Democratic Montgomery *Advertiser* and the Whiggish *Alabama Journal*). Hooper reminded readers of his poor health. His other writing remained popular: between 1855 and 1860, northern firms issued four new printings of Hooper's two humorous collections. In 1856, moreover, a New York agricultural press published his *Dog and Gun*, a rambling description of southerners' hunting skills, and two more northern firms reprinted it within three years. But Hooper feared for the rising South. He bitterly mistrusted the Democratic planters of Autauga County,

---

[72] *DBR* 22 (June 1857), 715; *SLM* 25 (December 1857), 473; single line on 476, after a full paragraph about *Songs and Poems of the South*. *DeBow's* writer promised to say more about Meek's historical work in a later article on Alabama – perhaps hoping that the "complete" work would been published, but, when the article appeared a few months later, Meek got only one line for his "beautiful and intelligent" collection; *DBR* 26 (February 1859): 232. *SLM* accurately assessed Meek's poetry when it observed that the "reader is never deeply moved by the thoughts expressed even in his more serious compositions," but praised Meek's southern "patriotism," 25 (December 187), 476.

even though Pickett was a family friend.[73] And he suspected that his long-time Whiggish allies lacked the backbone to protect slavery. Increasingly radical, he urged united southerners to confront the North with an ultimatum: respect our institution or we fight. Worried that he lacked supporters, Hooper probably published Woodward's history to increase his influence.

Hooper claimed sponsorship of Woodward's book even as he politely distanced himself from its rough style. Addressed to "a large class of readers" who cared about Alabama's "early history," Hooper's introduction linked his initiative with the public interest. An old Indian fighter, former Whig, and grandson of a Native American woman, the general had quickly attracted attention with his letters to the *Mail*. Embarrassed by his "want of early education and the inaccuracy of his style," he only "yielded" to Hooper's insistence that the letters make up a book. Hooper explained these circumstances to disarm "the hypercritical," who might be "severe" about Woodward's "homely but effective phraseology." He emphasized Woodward's "indomitable will," "sturdy self-reliance," great intelligence, and kind heart. But the editor also warned that Woodward "mercilessly flayed" men who were "presuming or pretentious" "with a biting sarcasm." The book's purpose was "the correction of several popular errors." As it turned out, those errors belonged to Albert Pickett.[74]

Woodward's *Reminiscences* corrected Pickett about matters small and large. The general began deferentially. Pickett misplaced a town – "a matter of no importance." Pickett "must have been misinformed" by a source who was "not very reliable." Pickett's education showed in his work, but Woodward was "better acquainted with Indian history." As he progressed, Woodward grew sarcastic. When he reached the canoe fight, he admitted that his version might "be censured by some." But he did not care because Pickett was "utterly incorrect." Either the planter "has a very fruitful imagination, or has been most egregiously imposed upon, or perhaps both." His exaggerations "would do for a novel, but not history." Historians like Pickett "who wish to deal a little in the marvelous for the amusement of readers" should consult men like Woodward.[75]

The crotchety general deflated most of Pickett's heroes by suggesting that they were mere braggarts. In one campaign of 1817–1818, friendly Indians carried the fighting for whites, "unless a stray shot from one of our guns killed an Indian or a negro." "To speak the honest truth," he wrote, "there have not been as many warriors in the Creek and Seminole Nations, in my time" as white men claim to have killed. He quipped that "history is a thing often exaggerated, and by none so much as the official reports of these little Indian

---

[73] Pickett had long been associated with the Democratic Party and was, in the 1850s, actively involved in the inner circle of the local elite; see, for example, Pickett to Bolling Hall about party matters, October 13 and 19, 1853, in Bolling Hall Papers, ADAH, Montgomery.
[74] All quoted passages in Hooper's "Introduction," *Woodward's Reminiscences*, 3–5.
[75] *Reminiscences*, 13, 14, 17, 72–73, 76.

fights." Woodward was candid about his bias. His friend "Billy" Weatherford had given him an explanation for the events at Fort Mims, and Woodward let him argue his case. Woodward illustrated Andrew Jackson's character with a conflict between himself and the famous hero. Mostly, he debunked: "If the firing of a few guns and occasionally killing an Indian or two, can be considered fights, I have seen many," he wrote; "but as I did not think proper to detail them at a time, when perhaps a little capital might have been made of them, I will dispense with it now."[76] "A little capital" showed that Woodward knew the utility of glorifying the past, even if he did not do it.

Unlike Pickett and Meek, and much more rudely than Baldwin, Woodward mocked Alabama's elite. He made it plain that he was neither rich nor powerful, and he did not cater to men who were either. In one episode, he demonstrated the mass confusion of Indian wars when whites fired round after round at nonexistent opponents. The shooters were planters – Pickett's neighbors. In another tale, Woodward stopped "sons of the first families about Nashville" from harassing plain men. While completing his letters, Woodward heard of Pickett's death. He paid tribute to the "intelligent, sensible, practical" men who were Pickett's friends in Autauga County, and he called Pickett a "high-toned gentleman." Then his letter returned to Alabama's brawling and drinking elite, ending with a story about a man who forcibly stopped the flogging of negroes for bringing whiskey into a military camp. The "good and brave" man knew that "white men were to blame."[77] Focused more on character than class, Woodward's social standards were at least unconventional.

Woodward's ideas about race were even less orthodox. Detailing his own mixed ancestry, he speculated about a transracial future when "Americans shall all be Americans." He also argued that Indians and blacks had excellent memories because they did not rely on paper. More surprisingly, Woodward used "negro history," although he knew that "the ignorant and unobserving" would "laugh." Fittingly, then, he provided genealogy for blacks and Indians. The slave Caesar, of canoe fight fame, had parents – Tabby and Bob (without last names, but he named their owners). Another famous warrior, Siro, was the son of Polly Perryman, "the most remarkable negro that I have known in my time." "As intelligent as negroes ever get to be," Polly lived to be 115, and Woodward cared for her. Most significantly, Woodward told the story of Ketch, a slave whose extensive mixed-race ancestry included one of Pickett's supposedly white witnesses to history. Obviously, Woodward's curiosity about race had narrow limits, and he owned some of the slaves he named, but,

---

[76] Ibid., 148.
[77] Ibid., Nashville's families, 139; Autauga planters and Pickett, 102–103; flogging, 108. In his description of the firing at nonexistent Indians, Woodward noticed the kin ties among the families of Bolling Hall, Dixon H. Lewis, and Benjamin Fitzpatrick, all Hooper's Democratic opponents (135). He had also, however, called Hall an "American gentleman" (60), and a certain amount of his ridicule was in the manner of an old man telling stories of his youth, mixing with other rowdy young men who were now dignified leaders even though they were his political opponents.

within white men's history, he remembered Billy Weatherford, Polly, Ketch, and their families.[78]

In publishing Woodward's work, Hooper became a contrary participant in the construction of public memory. Like Pickett, the humorist wanted white men united behind slavery, but not behind rich planters. Woodward's history suggested that rank did not matter to brave men, who would treat all people as they deserved to be treated. In *Simon Suggs*, Hooper had told readers that the "breed" of African Americans was "devilishly mixed," and he had written critical stories about whippings. Although Hooper wrote as a gentleman in his introduction to Woodward's history, he wanted "hypercritical" people, who misunderstood rough language for foolishness or refined writing for truth, to know their errors.[79] When he entered the contest over Alabama's history, he spoke for self-determination and slavery on his own unusual terms.

Hooper wisely printed Woodward's letters for local readers only, for the recollections were too particular to amuse people outside of the Southwest. Even so, they probably shocked genteel citizens. Woodward wrote that, as a young man of mixed ancestry, he was "tempted ... to quit what the world terms civilized and christian man," and his standards were still marginal to polite society. The proud and ailing Pickett had been unwilling to challenge this rough adversary in public, but, just before his death, he took steps to correct the record. Through one of his Democratic friends, he arranged for the posthumous printing of a letter from a very distinguished gentleman who defended Pickett's interpretation. Without Pickett's presumptions, however, Woodward's stories also addressed a self-reliant people. And, when Hooper published the *Reminiscences* for southwestern readers, he wanted to make them one – whether to stand down or fight with their northern critics. The late, lamented Pickett would have approved of that.[80]

* * *

Examining the recent past is a bit like looking into a mirror, and that was certainly the case for these early historians. The wealthy planter Pickett

---

[78] *Ibid*., speaking English and Americans, 21; "ignorant and unobserving," 94; Polly, 93. Woodward was illustrating his claim about the reliability of "negro history" with the convoluted story of the slave Ketch, who had belonged to famous Indian trader and land speculator George Galphin. Galphin had many mixed-race descendents, and Woodward's sketch was clearly designed to show that one of the men Pickett had relied on for historical information was perhaps the grandson of a slave, though he passed as white, while Woodward had relied on Ketch, a supposedly honest black slave. But, perhaps because Pickett's witness had friends and family, Woodward did not say that he was of mixed race. Instead, he said that a mixed-blood woman was married to the man's father and had "raised" him.

[79] *Suggs*, 142; *Reminiscences*, 3.

[80] *Reminiscences*, 125. Hooper had been friends with Pickett for two decades and had frequently praised him in his newspapers. Why he chose to publish a frontal assault on the planter's credibility is perplexing. Perhaps Hooper wanted to become part of the process by which gentlemen preserved the state's past, because he was sensitive about his own lack of higher

saw southwestern history as a battleground for land; the energetic lawyer Baldwin recalled flush times as a contest where practical intelligence produced order; the sociable editor Meek imagined a democratic and agrarian South led by an intellectual elite; and the irreverent, tough-minded Woodward glimpsed the beginnings of a society organized by character rather than rank – a conception Hooper implicitly endorsed.

Such personal idiosyncrasies marked histories published within an impersonal market, for these writers saw a modernizing economy at the further end of the progress that began with settlement. Alabama's past and the market seemed to be connected, over time, through countless, unmediated choices by free people. But marketing choices suggested these writers' differences about the rising South. Pickett saw competition as combat and northerners as threat, and he published close to home. Baldwin began with a southern publication but expected the northern market to bring him fame. Touting intellectual freedom, Meek believed that competition would unify Americans, so he entered both the national and regional markets at once. Because Hooper had realized by 1856 that book sales did not indicate northern sympathy for slavery, he published about guns and hunting in the North and aimed Woodward's history at Alabama's readers. These writers knew that success rested on their ability to persuade. Their confidence, or lack of it, was a measure of whom they trusted with slavery and freedom.

Without much ideological flourish, each of these historians paired slavery with freedom. In Pickett's heroic history, slaves belonging to all sorts of people made land worth fighting for. Among Baldwin's lawyers, slaves were incidental to the main action, and the ignorant or idle whites gave way to those whose creativity moved society forward. Meek's yeomen were satisfied to let intellectuals lead them, while racial slavery gave white men common identity. And Woodward described people sorted by merit, implying that racial inferiority warranted a benign slavery. Whether slavery existed to make land productive,

---

education. He had long engaged in bitter partisan warfare with Pickett's Democratic friends, and he was no doubt amused that Woodward made fun of prominent Democratic politicians. If Hooper had an ax to grind, his introduction gave him some distance from the process, but the planter's death probably shortened public controversy. Nonetheless, Michael Woods, Pickett's son-in-law, explained in his "Reminiscences" that after Woodward had "ridiculed" Pickett's interpretation of Alexander McGillivery as educated, Associate Justice John Campbell ("aware of what had been published in Alabama"), Woods himself, and Mississippian J. F. H. Claiborne entered the fray in Pickett's behalf; "Personal Reminiscences of Colonel Albert James Pickett," *Transactions of the Alabama Historical Society, 1899–1903* IV (1904): 609–610; clipping of Claiborne's article in J. F. H. Claiborne Papers, UNC. Hooper was not mentioned in Woods's account of the controversy, but Pickett's friend Crawford Jackson quoted at length from Hooper's promotion of Pickett's efforts (just before his death) to write a "History of the South-West," Jackson called Hooper Pickett's "intimate and personal friend," and Jackson used Hooper's press to print his sketch of Pickett's life: *Brief Biographical Sketch of the Late Col. Albert James Pickett of Alabama* (Montgomery: Barrett and Wimbish, 1859), 9–11. By this time, both Hooper and the Montgomery Democrats were at sea, politically, and searching for allies in any quarter.

keep the underclass out of trouble, unite white men, or reinforce the order of nature (or all of these), Alabama's historians thought it necessary.

But the self-determination of free people was a much more prominent theme in all of these histories than was slavery. These writers shaped their histories to show a society in which white men proved their worth with action. Little in them sanctioned aristocratic values. Baldwin explained self-reliance in the new country by the absence of the "*prestige* of rank, or ancestry, or wealth," but that idea was implicit in every history.[81] Even Pickett, not known for his democratic views, emphasized that Alabama was led by a working gentry and self-made men. All of these writers testified to the presence of inequality, but they made wealth a result of initiative, intelligence, or character, and they did not scorn the poor.

And while, in different ways, each writer distinguished lower from upper classes, they meant their histories to be democratic. Hooper cautioned against evaluating a historian by his polish, Baldwin treasured the admiration of rough men, and Pickett claimed that philosophy obscured history for ordinary people. Meek and Woodward even implied that self-making might benefit non-whites, but only Woodward offered the radical suggestion that, someday, all Americans would be one.

Nonetheless, the competition over the early history of the Southwest revealed some strains within the respectable classes. It let Alabama's middle-class writers and their friends flex their muscles, through a print medium they dominated. Pickett's pleading for historical materials (no matter how rough or rude) and quietly accepting public criticism is instructive. It suggests limitations to upper-class power in Alabama, where being seen as aristocratic and anti-Republican was a handicap. To be sure, Pickett's pitches for his history advertised his status, but he wrote for newspapers, where middle-class people were his readers, and, while he referred to his wealth, he also stressed his work. The competition between Pickett and his fellow historians was notably restrained compared to political battles. No one slandered anyone. The planter's *History* eventually became the established history of Alabama, and Meek never published his *magnum opus*. But the contest was unresolved when Pickett died. In the nation, more readers were entertained by Baldwin than by Pickett. And, if the editor of the *Southern Literary Messenger* was right, his "unprecedented" national reputation gave Baldwin the edge at home.[82]

The agreement within these diverse histories was significant, in any case. All of these historians saw a past in which freedom was uneven but essential, for it was making white men the best that they could be. Nowhere in these histories was there much concern for black people who failed to advance themselves, for they were thought incapable of self-determination. Nowhere was

---

[81] *Flush Times*, 228.
[82] Indeed, an ad in the Tuscaloosa *Independent Monitor* (Whig), claimed that Baldwin had been established as "among the first writers of the age," December 14, 1854.

there a hint that enslaving black people was a choice white southwesterners made, for the choice was identified with men who lived centuries before. These writers saw opportunities everywhere for self-reliant men, but they expected progress to require constant effort. Despite the presence of slavery, these were American histories about a world in which people worked to better themselves materially and prove themselves socially. Tragically, self-determination for the white men of the rising South meant that slavery would endure until they chose to end it, and no one saw that in the cards.

6

Slave Characters and the Problem of Human Nature

> There is not a man in the South owning a hundred negroes who knows scarcely any more of the names of the slave children than I do.... [H]e would not know anything about that until the children had reached the age of twelve or fourteen.
>
> Jeremiah Clemens, Congressional Globe

When he addressed the United States Senate in April of 1850, Jeremiah Clemens posed as a planter who owned too many slave children to know their names. The "hundred negroes" actually belonged to his father, and Clemens's exaggeration was as typical as it was callous. But his boast projected false confidence, and his hopes for the rising South contained anxieties no swagger could hide. Like Clemens, Johnson Hooper, Caroline Hentz, and Augusta Evans spoke to both northerners and southerners. Understandably, they, too, were loath to admit doubts.[1] In middle-class homes, however, self-determination and slavery lived side by side, and that created irrepressible anxieties. While these writers wanted to think that the differences between white and black

---

[1] *Congressional Globe*, 31st. Congress, 1st Session, 673. The best recent discussions of southern intellectuals and slavery are Michael O'Brien, *Conjectures of Order: Intellectual Life and the American South, 1810–1860*, 2 vols. (Chapel Hill: University of North Carolina Press, 2004), esp. ch. 18, "Our Slavery Question," 2: 938–992, and the analyses of Elizabeth Fox-Genovese and Eugene D. Genovese, especially *The Mind of the Master Class: History and Faith in the Southern Slaveholders' Worldview* (Cambridge: Cambridge University Press, 2005), and *Slavery in White and Black: Class and Race in the Southern Slaveholders' New World Order* (Cambridge: Cambridge University Press, 2008). A succinct and thoughtful discussion of the theoretical conflict between the progress of civilization and slavery is Eugene D. Genovese, *The Slaveholders' Dilemma: Freedom and Progress in Southern Conservative Thought, 1820–1860* (Columbia: University of South Carolina Press, 1992). Lacy K. Ford, *Deliver Us from Evil: The Slavery Question in the Old South* (Oxford: Oxford University Press, 2009), traces the evolution of proslavery ideology to about 1840 and finds the differences between paternalism and racist ideology waning. See also James Oakes, *Slavery and Freedom: An Interpretation of the Old South* (New York: Alfred A. Knopf, 1990).

people justified slavery, they saw similarities as well. The daily relations of slavery bred uncertainty about the basic nature of human beings, with toxic effect.

Clemens spoke during a debate over recording the names of slaves in the constitutionally mandated census. Posturing aside, Clemens portrayed slaves as property more than people, even though the infamous three-fifths clause referred to "Persons." Writers were unable to reconcile the tensions associated with the dual status of slaves as persons and property, but they did not ignore those tensions, as Clemens seemed to do. As chattel, or moveable property, enslaved people were uniquely vulnerable to the transformative changes of the nineteenth century. So, for example, both *Flush Times* and *Simon Suggs* satirized the way southerners turned slaves into commodities when the market expanded. For all of its admitted ills, southerners found the internal slave trade essential, and, by the 1850s, some propagandists talked of resuming the international slave trade as well. In the context of such discussions, property trumped humanity.[2]

Still, the fact that slaves were valuable property did not fully obscure their humanity. Indeed, Clemens's claim that planters did not know their slave children's names implied that small slaveholders did know them. Until 1860, when Clemens's father died, Pickett was the only major slaveholder among Alabama's writers, most of whom owned fewer than five slaves, if any. Like Pickett and Clemens, who each inherited dozens of slaves, Baldwin, Hooper, William Smith, and perhaps Evans owned some people because of inheritance or gifts. In an odd sense, slavery was familial for these white owners. It is impossible to know whether any of these writers sold people they were given – at least in part because names of slaves were not, in fact, recorded in the census.[3] Whatever the case, most writers could easily name their human property. Clemens's suggestion that slaves were anonymous did not apply consistently.

Instead of expressing hardened views like Clemens's, most writers of the rising South avoided the ethical dilemmas associated with slavery. One way or another, they had opted into slavery, and they were unwilling to consider its essential evils. They were not systematic thinkers, and they wanted to sell books. So, although southern ideologues had articulated a comprehensive defense of slavery by the 1840s, most of Alabama's writers used proslavery ideas only briefly, or indirectly, in their popular writing. In a divided market, the safest literary strategy was a tight focus on white people.

---

[2] Among the many studies of the legal foundations and implications of slavery, three general studies are especially useful: Mark Tushnet, *The American Law of Slavery, 1810–1860: Considerations of Humanity and Interest* (Princeton: Princeton University Press, 1981), Thomas D. Morris, *Southern Slavery and the Law, 1619–1860* (Chapel Hill: University of North Carolina Press, 1996), and the essays in Paul Finkelman, ed., *Slavery and the Law* (Madison, WI: Madison House, 1997).

[3] I traced slaveholding using censuses, probate records, letters, and diaries, but such records are woefully incomplete, as examples in this chapter show.

Evans suggested as much in 1859, not long after the appearance of her novel *Beulah*. In a series of anonymous articles for the Mobile *Daily Advertiser*, she criticized northern writers for elevating the "low and sensual African" into roles that his "physical inferiority and mental incapacity" did not warrant. But Evans urged southern writers not to respond with "recrimination," and she opposed the crusade for a "southern" literature. Readers and critics who indiscriminately praised everything southern, she warned, condemned the region's authors to inferiority. She asked southern writers to compete throughout the English-speaking world, promoting values that applied to (white) society generally. She believed that well-written, conservative books could make the southern case indirectly – which *Beulah* was doing, even as Evans wrote.[4]

Beulah also showed, however, that Evans wanted to improve her South, and she believed that many middle-class readers were sympathetic to her goals. She was positive that such readers populated the lyceums, churches, charities, and social circles in Alabama's towns. Although she was proud that southern reformers were more conservative than their northern counterparts, she and other advocates for the rising South agreed with them in wanting a society filled with self-controlled, reasonable, and sympathetic people.[5] As meliorists, moreover, Evans and her fellow writers expected the ethics associated with a progressive conception of freedom to apply to slavery – not to end it, but to make it secure. Therein lay problems they could not solve.

At its foundation, of course, slavery violated the ethics of self-determination by preventing enslaved people from choosing how to live. Claiming it suited the "low and sensual Africans," masters regularly made choices for their slaves about work, families, and friends. That much denial of self-determination seemed reasonable to writers and most other white southerners. But claims that slaves were mentally and physically inferior could only go so far, especially in the case of household servants. A planter who needed slave labor to

---

[4] Mobile *Daily Advertiser*, quoted passages from October 16 and November 6, 1859; the four articles – the first two called "Northern Literature" and the last two called "Southern Literature" – appeared October 16, 23, 30, and November 6, 1859, and they deserve more discussion than space permits here. Evans hinted that her essays responded to one that appeared (anonymously) in August in *Russell's Magazine*. It was by Henry Timrod, called "Literature of the South," and it is reprinted in *The Essays of Henry Timrod*, ed. Edd Winfield Parks (Athens: University of Georgia Press, 1942). As I have suggested elsewhere, these articles made Evans a defender of the South and yet justified her use of a northern publisher; see "Writers in the Old Southwest and the Commercialization of American Letters," *JER* 27 (Fall 2007): 499. The articles are discussed in Elizabeth Moss, *Domestic Novelists in the Old South: Defenders of Southern Culture* (Baton Rouge: Louisiana State University Press, 1992), 163–166, and, with somewhat better balance, in Naomi Sofer, *Making the "America of Art:" Cultural Nationalism and Nineteenth-Century Women Writers* (Columbus: Ohio State University Press, 2005), 69–72.

[5] A major point in John W. Quist, *Restless Visionaries: The Social Roots of Antebellum Reform in Alabama and Michigan* (Baton Rouge: Louisiana State University Press, 1998), which also finds slaveholding planters in Tuscaloosa sympathetic to reforms along Whiggish lines.

extract wealth from the soil might claim that African Americans only had physical strengths. Middle-class people could make no such claim.

In fact, the ethics of self-determination virtually required the recognition of slaves' humanity, because to deny it would reflect badly on white owners. In essence, writers could deny simple reason and morality to black people only by suggesting that southern whites lacked them. Town slaves cleaned, cooked, and cared for children. No self-determined people could rely constantly on unthinking creatures in their homes. If only for their own self-esteem, writers had to believe that black people were capable of making many good choices about everyday life. Therefore, while they claimed that racial inferiority decreed slavery, generalizations about the character of African Americans carried troublesome implications. The ethical standards of self-determination could not be easily satisfied with a color line.[6]

Proslavery ideology did not resolve this ethical dilemma. Hooper, Hentz, and Evans sometimes referred to its general sentiments. By their time, an ancient Christian paternalism had been updated with sentimental depictions of happy slaves who, like immature children, required the protection of fatherly masters. Because paternalism required masters to display Christian charity, however, it set a demanding standard. A pre-Darwinian, scientific racism appeared in the Southwest in the early 1840s, adding a more rational and modern aura to proslavery ideas, with far less sentimentality. In work that won him international repute, Mobile's Dr. Josiah Nott explained physical differences between blacks and whites.[7] In 1846, Hooper's press published a book by a Mississippi physician who summarized religious and secular defenses. But no extant proslavery ideology justified brutality or indifference toward the humanity of slaves, even while it sanctioned their exploitation.

Instead, relying on the ethics of self-determination, writers implied, or even admitted, that masters conducted themselves poorly. In the late antebellum period, some southerners discussed modest reforms: how to mitigate such evils as the destruction of families or the reliance on physical punishment instead

---

[6] The conjunction of relatively liberal political ideology with racism has been a persistent theme in recent scholarship about both the North and the South. See, for example, James B. Stewart, "The Emergence of Racial Modernity and the Rise of the White North, 1790–1840," *JER* 18 (Summer 1998): 181–217, and Lacy K. Ford, "Making the 'White Man's Country' White: Race, Slavery and State Building in the Jacksonian South," *JER* 19 (Winter 1999): 713–737. Taking such arguments further, Arthur Riss has argued in *Race, Slavery, and Liberalism in Nineteenth-Century American Literature* (Cambridge: Cambridge University Press, 2006), that northern writers were redefining liberal personhood so as to exclude black people. For all of their racism, Alabama's writers did not deny the humanity of enslaved people.

[7] A study that demonstrates the significance of Nott in scientific circles as well as the depth of his racial prejudice is Reginald Horsman, *Josiah Nott of Mobile: Southerner, Physician, and Racial Theorist* (Baton Rouge: Louisiana State University Press, 1987). The tensions between the conservative theology of paternalism and scientific racism (which argued for polygenesis and thus denied the parentage of Adam and Eve) are discussed in the studies of proslavery thought in n. 1.

of incentives, routine, and persuasion. Challenging slavery's legitimacy was absolutely taboo in Alabama, but quiet suggestions for improvement were not.[8] For slavery to meet the ethical standards of self-determination, masters had to be reasonable and sympathetic, and writers occasionally observed that some masters were neither.

Behind these writers' concerns lay a middle-class, town-based slavery that was unlike plantation slavery in important ways, legal similarities notwithstanding. More than one writer suggested that household slavery was like the arrangements of bourgeois people in the North (or England), where domestic servants lived in employees' homes. Clearly, writers thought that household slaves were better fed, clothed, and sheltered than poor whites. And they knew that, while domestic slaves labored long hours, they performed fewer backbreaking tasks than poor white farmers, much less black field hands. Town society was most writers' model for the human relations of a rising South, and it connected white and black people differently than in the countryside.[9] There were not many slaves in these writers' books, but there were even fewer plantations.

Committed to a progressive South, Hooper, Hentz, and Evans typically wrote about white people in towns, and they usually neglected the enslaved. In private, they noticed individual services they gained, as if labor, not ownership, defined slavery. Hentz wrote that "Uncle Young" had found a spider of a "new species" for her husband's collection, that the same man ploughed the garden, and that he had white-washed their home. When her son Charles laughed that the "authoress" baked her own biscuits, he noted that her "good cook" (as Caroline called her) had the night off; and neither Hentz named the black woman.[10] In letters or diaries, these writers emphasized their kind, not the men and women who served them.

---

[8] Although there were firm limits to the willingness of southerners to reform slavery, a number of scholars have demonstrated that reforms were proposed. For some important examples, see Mitchell Snay, *Gospel of Disunion: Religion and Separatism in the Antebellum South* (Cambridge: Cambridge University Press, 1993), esp. 78–98, Ford, *Deliver Us from Evil*, 527–532, and O'Brien, *Conjectures of Order*, 2: 965–991.

[9] There are two standard studies of urban slavery: Richard C. Wade, *Slavery in the Cities: The South, 1820–1860* (New York: Oxford University Press, 1964), and Claudia Dale Goldin, *Urban Slavery in the American South, 1820–1860* (Chicago: University of Chicago Press, 1976). But few studies describe slavery in towns. For the Southwest, the best is Lisa Tolbert, *Constructing Townscapes: Space and Society in Antebellum Tennessee* (Chapel Hill: University of North Carolina Press, 1999), and see her discussion of the neglect of town studies, 6. For an exhaustively researched analysis of enslaved people in a little town not far from Alabama, see David E. Peterson, "Slavery, Slaves, and Cash in a Georgia Village, 1825–1865," *JSH* 75 (November 2009): 879–930. Peterson found that "masters, by recognizing bondpeople's natural desire for autonomy, by incorporating autonomy into their personalized plans for mastery, and by selectively ignoring inconvenient legal restraints" made slavery more profitable without having to use "the unrealistic and unpleasant application of unrelenting physical force," 929.

[10] Hentz Diary for February 19, March 16, April 23, 1836, Hentz Family Papers, UNC; Hentz to Maria Stafford, June 2, 1846 [?], *ibid.*; Charles's comment quoted previously in Chapter 2, n. 45.

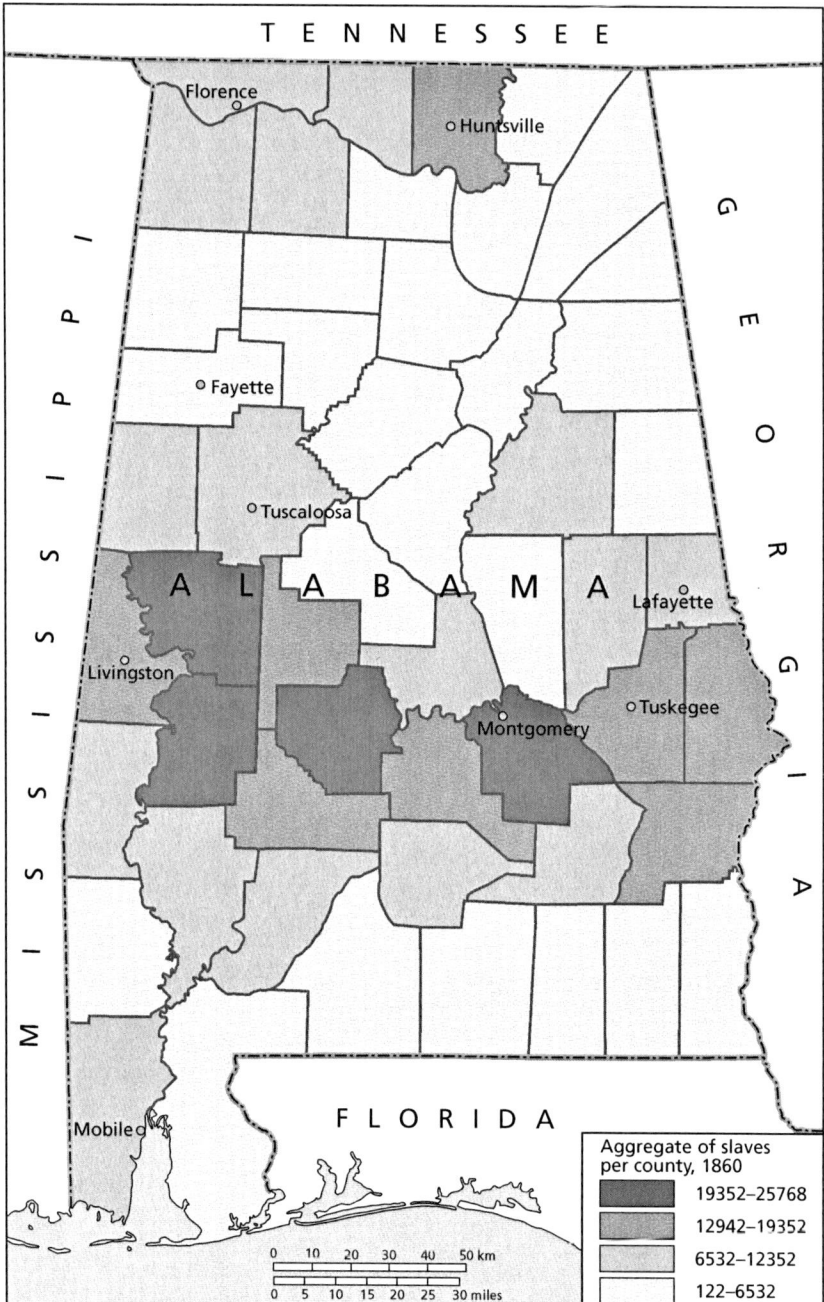

FIGURE 6.1. Distribution of slaves in Alabama, 1860.
The map shows the importance of slavery in the Black Belt of the state but also the significance of the Tennessee River Valley, where Caroline Hentz lived for a time and Jeremiah Clemens was born and died. This skewed distribution of slaves was determined by the presence of large farms and plantations, rather than the towns where writers lived. Map by Cox Cartographic, Ltd.

The same was true for fiction, which, except in Hentz's case, rarely portrayed slaves interacting with whites, much less other blacks. Writers inserted slaves – calling them servants – into scenes where they might be expected, as in the hotel in Baldwin's "Cave Burton, Esq." If they gave slaves a rare bit of dialogue, they made it a dialect that reflected the stereotypes of minstrelsy. Such linguistic stereotyping was extremely common. In *Uncle Tom's Cabin*, common slaves spoke crudely, while Stowe's major black characters spoke more refined English. As she demonstrated, however, giving speech to slaves underscored their humanity, and that was asking for trouble, from a southern writer's perspective.[11]

Giving dialogue to slaves obliged the writers of the rising South to imagine the minds of black people, and only the most determined author ventured into that territory. Hooper, Hentz, and Evans wrote some speaking parts for slaves. With his usual audacity, Hooper twice described slaves' attempts to resist whippings. With her usual sentiment, Hentz made slaves childlike, obedient or not. With her usual confidence, Evans gave one willful slave the moral message of her novel *Beulah*. All three writers gave blacks relatively minor roles. They only obliquely suggested that masters could improve slavery, and they implied that it was not so bad, anyway. But writing dialogue for black characters produced ambiguous results.

The ambiguity came from the attempt to fit slavery into the ethics of self-determination, where it did not belong. Hooper implied that masters should exercise power reasonably, while showing they did not. Hentz suggested that masters made voluntary contracts with slaves, but her hero relied on threats. And Evans portrayed a strong-willed slave who challenged her heroine and foiled a white female villain. Each writer blurred the lines between black and white characters. Instead of reason and sympathy, masters used force, manipulation, and deceit. Slaves resisted their masters. Most problematically, they showed reason and sympathy, and they judged white people. The black characters of Hooper, Hentz, and Evans represented a puzzling human nature, imperfectly sorted by race.

When they discussed slavery as an institution, these writers referred to proslavery ideas; but when they imagined slave characters, ideology faltered and anxieties appeared. All three writers accepted slavery as one of many inequalities. They discriminated between the educated and the illiterate, the rich and the poor, the civilized and the barbaric, and they thought they were the better sort. They did not feel guilty about slavery. They knew, however, that it distinguished them from northerners, who might share their racial prejudice. Their

---

[11] Stowe's use of dialect is a long-standing controversy, and, because the topic is related to her racial ideology, there is now a large and lively literature about it. For a sampling, see two collections: Mason Lowance, Jr., Ellen E. Westbrook, and R. C. De Prospo, eds., *The Stowe Debate* (Amherst: University of Massachusetts Press, 1994) and Eric Sundquist, ed., *New Essays on Uncle Tom's Cabin* (Cambridge: Cambridge University Press, 1986). There is an excellent Web site that directs students to a variety of historical and literary sources about *Uncle Tom's Cabin*: http://utc.iath.virginia.edu.

depictions of slaves reflected their desire to fit their South into a middle-class America. But when they created conversations between black and white characters, these writers' uncertainties about the human foundations of the rising South emerged, with profound implications for its future.

THE DARKEST KIND OF HUMOR

Johnson Hooper thought a blunt version of truth lay behind his sometimes shocking stories. Each of his collections – *Adventures of Simon Suggs* and *The Widow Rugby's Husband* – held a story about a master whipping his slave, and Hooper made humor from the events. In these stories, Hooper imagined African Americans speaking, and they showed native wit and a morality sufficient to judge their masters. Hooper knew, firsthand, the difficulty of controlling impulses, but he thought it essential, and he frequently satirized white people who lacked self-control. Still, he thought they had sufficient rationality to better themselves and to behave properly toward slaves. Although he showed human nature at its worst, he saw the grim combination of white power and slave labor as necessary to the rising South.[12]

For Hooper personally, lack of self-control was a chronic problem. His family's decline in the port of Wilmington, North Carolina, had scarred his adolescent pride, with unfortunate results. His mother Charlotte explained that "poor Johnson" was humiliated about his lack of education: "He don't wish to continue at school without any hope of going to college & says if he is to be a clerk, let him go at once." His father, she wrote, was "deeply disappointed" in their son. Brother George, who had some success controlling the boy, wrote De Berniere that their younger brother Johnson was "lazy" and ran around at night.[13] Charlotte explained that he was "easily led into evil" and was "completely governed" by the "low company" he kept. Johnson's faults were "many and inexcusable," she wrote, but he had "good principles." While she worried about his lack of faith and his failure to obey his conscience, he was

---

[12] Hooper, *Some Adventures of Captain Simon Suggs, Late of the Tallapoosa Volunteers; Together with "Taking the Census" and Other Alabama Sketches* (Philadelphia: Carey and Hart, 1845), and *The Widow Rugby's Husband; a Night at the Ugly Man's and Other Tales of Alabama* (Philadelphia: A. Hart, 1851).

[13] "Poor Johnson" or a similar phrase appears most frequently in Charlotte Hooper's letters about Johnson, but the same phrase also appears in Louisa Hooper (sister) to De Berniere, August 29, 1834, and A. M. Hooper (father) to De Berniere, March 31, 1836; John De Berniere Hooper Papers, UNC. Charlotte was still referring to Johnson in those terms after he was a notable public figure; see her to De Berniere, March 22, 1851, bemoaning "poor" Johnson's "utter indifference to religion," and her to De Berniere's wife Mary, May 6, 1854. Johnson's unhappiness about his schooling, Charlotte to De Berniere, Dec. 30, 1833; A. M. to De Berniere about his view, July 11, 1835; what to do with the "poor fellow," Charlotte to De Berniere August 22, 1832 [?]; George's comments on Johnson, George to De Berniere, February 3, 1833, in which he also noted that Johnson and his father worked for the same printer, the elder Hooper doing make-work to keep him busy as his eyesight failed, the teenager working for wages that might reach $1.00 per day. All of these letters in JDBH Papers, UNC.

"always penitent." "If kept out of the way of bad examples," she concluded, "he will become a good man."[14] But Johnson was slow to change, and his mistrust of human nature reflected that fact.

As the Hoopers struggled to avoid real poverty, slavery was part of their strategy. Johnson's father had once inherited some wealth: he owned ten slaves in 1830 and still had seven in 1840. But he had sold one to benefit George, who studied law while living "on the proceeds of the sale of Henry," and perhaps he sold others to help support his family. Fears of a slave uprising in Wilmington had frightened Charlotte, who wanted to migrate to a free state, but she understood that the men preferred the South. "Tempted by the glowing narrative" of prosperity, George had migrated to Alabama and Johnson had followed. The older brother began to practice law and farm, and, by 1840, he owned six slaves. Johnson's ambitions were different. His mother had long hoped he would become a "respectable Editor," and, as Johnson belatedly matured, his ambition was to move minds.[15] Never able to accumulate wealth, Hooper was committed to slavery without owning a single person on his own. He sold a woman for his mother-in-law, fretting over the price. By 1850, his household held his wife's one slave, a gift from her father; and, soon after, their sons inherited three family slaves from Johnson's parents.[16]

Too few copies of Hooper's first newspaper survive to reveal his serious thoughts about slavery, but his humor showed his concerns. Written first for local readers, then a national audience, Hooper's humor made slavery part of the tumultuous process by which the Southwest was being civilized. Although his joking may have distressed some northerners, Hooper's generic crudeness effectively excluded humanitarians from his readership. He aimed at worldly readers, and his methods were like those of minstrel shows, which made black

[14] Charlotte's summation of Johnson's character, Charlotte to De Berniere, March 29, 1833 in *ibid*.

[15] George's enthusiasm, George to De Berniere, February 3, 1833; his mother's hopes, Charlotte to De Berniere, August 22, 1832 [?]; further comments on Johnson's ambitions, A. M. to De Berniere, June 12, 1833 [?]; A. M.'s slaves, U.S. Censuses of 1830 and 1840 for Chatham County, NC. Charlotte's fears were expressed in letters to De Berniere, September 20, 1831 [?] and June 10, 1830 [?]. All family correspondence in JDBH Papers, UNC. George's slaves, U.S. Census of 1840 for Russell County, Alabama.

[16] Living on Henry, George Hooper to D. B., April 21, 1833, in JDBH Papers, UNC; selling a female slave, Johnson Hooper to Mrs. T. B. Heard (his sister-in-law), August 22, 1850, reproduced in Edgar E. Thompson, "The Literary Career of Johnson Hooper: A Bibliographical Study of Primary and Secondary Material (With a Collection of Hooper's Letters)" (M.A. thesis, Mississippi State University, 1971), 83; will of Greene Brantley, in "Inventory of County Archives, Wills: Verbatim Copy of Wills, Chambers County," 304–305, will dated December 3, 1849, with Hooper given some authority to manage the business of the estate but the slave property to belong to Brantley's daughters only; reference to the slaves of Hooper's parents in George M. Hooper to Caroline M. Hooper, February 6, 1857, in Caroline Mallett Hooper Papers, UNC. A full account of how the trade in slaves permeated the southern landscape, compromising the morality of white people and damaging the lives of black people, is Stephen Deyle, *Carry Me Back: The Domestic Slave Trade in American Life* (New York: Oxford University Press, 2005).

people comically inferior but oddly human. Giving slaves dialogue, Hooper made them ignorant and helpless yet aware of their plight.[17]

Crudity notwithstanding, there was a reformist hook in Hooper's humor, and he ridiculed people who oppressed their slaves. In *Simon Suggs*, Hooper admitted some of slavery's evils: that the races were "devilishly mixed," that white people made commodities of black ones, and that masters meanly whipped slaves.[18] His black characters were not cavorting like those in minstrel shows, for they recognized their oppression and their lack of power. Hooper made his scenes realistic enough to be believable but sufficiently exaggerated to let his readers feel superior to the comic characters. And the most frequent targets of his satire were selfish white men who should have been responsible – men like bankers, preachers, and state legislators. Armed with instinctive self-knowledge and formidable self-control, Suggs conned these villains. He meted out a rough kind of social justice while enjoying his creative power.

Hooper connected Suggs's perverse justice with slavery in his phony biography's opening scene, which explained how young Simon began to control his own fate. The scene contained three characters: the boy Suggs, a precocious trickster; his father Jedediah, a "'hard-shell' Baptist preacher"; and Jedediah's slave Bill, Suggs's playmate. The skeleton of Hooper's plot was simple: Jedediah caught Simon and Bill gambling; he whipped Bill; but Suggs outwitted his father and escaped the beating. Jedediah epitomized the harsh patriarchy of the Southwest, both as a father and a master. Hooper made Jedediah a tyrant, good for nothing to boys except to "beat 'em and work 'em," so Simon had to escape him. But Suggs's "sable friend" could not escape.[19] Hooper's story ridiculed Jedediah's attempt at mastery and Bill's efforts to assert himself. It emphasized Simon Suggs's ability to best both his father and the slave. But unlike Jedediah, who was completely bamboozled, Bill was a knowing victim. He saw the force that trapped him, but his wit was insufficient to gain the freedom that Simon Suggs easily won.

At every point in this story, Hooper's decision to give Bill a voice emphasized the hard necessity of slavery. Jedediah was a greedy man whose inapt biblical quotes showed his stupidity. Nonetheless, when he spied Suggs and Bill playing in the field instead of working, he knew they were up to no good.

---

[17] Nancy Snell Griffith found evidence that the first of Hooper's stories about slavery appeared in the *East Alabamian* in the winter of 1844–1845, then in the *Spirit*. She also cites copies appearing in the Baltimore *Republican and Daily Argus* and the Columbus (Georgia) *Times* in February of 1845; *Humor of the Old Southwest: An Annotated Bibliography of Primary and Secondary Sources* (Westport, CT: Greenwood Press, 1989), 119. It would be impossible, however, to trace the number of other, no longer extant, southern newspapers in which the stories also appeared, although the complete computerization of nineteenth-century papers will eventually improve our knowledge of how widespread the reprintings were.

[18] Race-mixing and commodification, *Simon Suggs*, 142–147; whippings, see n. 20.

[19] *Ibid.*, "Hard shell," 13; "beat em," 10; "sable friend," 20, but earlier the narrator identifies Bill as a "negro boy" (14) and Jedediah calls him "that nigger," even though he also refers to the two boys as "youngsters" (15), while Simon calls Bill by his name.

As Jedediah approached, Suggs scrambled to hide the fact that he and Bill were gambling. First, he pocketed the "small coins" that were "the stake." Sensibly, Bill objected: "But, mass Simon, ... half dat money's mine. Ain't you gwine to lemme hab em?" Suggs insisted he was just about to win (he was cheating with a hidden card). Bill retorted, "Well, but mass Simon, we nebber finish de game, and de rule – ," only to be interrupted by Simon with "Go to an orful h — l with your rule." The narrator observed that "Bill was perforce compelled to submit to this inequitable adjustment of his claim," emphasizing that Bill's knowledge did him no good.[20] Even for a young "mass," compulsion worked, and Suggs kept the coins.

Hooper reemphasized Jedediah's tyranny and Bill's futile knowledge as the episode unfolded. Trying to fool his father, Suggs insisted that the boys were playing "mumble-peg." Jedediah demanded a demonstration: "So you git *upon your knees*, do you, to pull up that nasty little stick! You'd better git upon 'em to ask mercy for your sinful souls and for a dyin' world." Quickly grasping his father's purpose, Suggs insisted that Bill assume the vulnerable posture since he was "the best hand." Bill was not fooled by Simon's "modesty," and he wanted Simon to become the victim. But Jedediah impatiently gestured for the black boy to bend over. As both boys expected, Jedediah used his "longest hickory, with both hands" to give Bill a hard lick. Just then, Suggs accidentally dropped his hidden card. With that, the truth tumbled out, and a wrathful Jedediah hauled the boys away to a "formal" whipping at the customary site.[21]

Now Hooper silenced Bill to highlight Suggs's self-control. The narrator recited Simon's thoughts: his "wits, in view of the anticipated flogging, were dashing, springing, bounding, darting about, in hot chase" of a means of escape. Hooper made time for Simon's mind to work as Jedediah strung Bill up and whipped him. He focused carefully on Suggs's reaction. Suggs's "eye followed every movement of his father's arm; and as each blow descended upon the bare shoulders of his sable friend, his own body writhed and 'wriggled' in involuntary sympathy." While Simon's body responded to Bill's pain, however, his mind was on himself. As Jedediah untied Bill, Suggs devised a trick. Using the preacher's greed and his ignorance about playing cards, Simon enticed the old man to bet. Promptly, he cheated Jedediah into giving him a horse and the right to leave home. Bill's whipping was a diversion that let the trickster find opportunity. As Suggs rode away, he reminisced briefly about his "frolics" with Bill.[22] With this gesture to childhood, Hooper minimized the whipping. It had freed Simon, at Bill's expense.

---

[20] Ibid., 15–16.
[21] Ibid., first blow, 16; the whipping was at "the scene of all formal punishment administered during work hours in the field," 18. Here, by implication, the white boy and the black boy are both being used by the mean-spirited father to cultivate his fields, which, one presumes, were not very extensive.
[22] Ibid., 17–18; Simon recalls his "frolics with Bill and Ben," Simon's brother, as part of a very brief, "half melancholy" mood at his departure, 30.

Despite this appalling story, *Simon Suggs* was a popular book. Hooper made Bill intelligent enough to see what Jedediah and Suggs were doing to him. He ridiculed Jedediah's immorality and asked readers to laugh at Simon's triumph. He meant for Bill's dialect to be funny, too, but, by giving Bill a voice, Hooper complicated his plot. He linked black slavery with white freedom, while acknowledging that slavery was not always benevolent. And he gave Bill the capacity to judge white people. Hooper, in effect, admitted that slavery involved particular wrongs – witness Simon's "involuntary sympathy" – but he made it inevitable. While his humor was at Bill's expense, it was not really about Bill. It was about white people who should be better: a grown man who was beyond redemption, and a boy who had a future to make his own.

Hooper suggested Simon's kinship with the black boy and showed absolutely no sympathy for Suggs's tyrannical father. And Jedediah was one of many such white characters in *Simon Suggs*. Hooper called Suggs a "beast of prey," but predators like Jedediah were his favorite victims. In Hooper's view, blacks were secure only when whites were responsible, for a free Bill could not survive among the predators of the Southwest. At bottom, Hooper's story was more about the southwestern future than Simon Suggs's past, for it was a kind of truth-telling that might cause reform. Although Hooper aimed his satire hardest at lower-class men like Jedediah, he targeted upper-class people, too, as when one pompous character assured Suggs he could "comprehend the difference between the conduct of an insolent official, and that of the high-bred, gentlemanly, public functionary." Suggs knew there rarely was a difference.[23] He found the worst men the easiest to fool. Hooper showed false paternalists like Jedediah abusing victims of all races and classes, and Suggs gleefully brought them down.

Hooper was slowly improving himself as he wrote about Suggs, and slavery was part of his effort. With his ambitions spurred by success, Hooper in 1846 moved to Montgomery to become co-owner and editor of the Whig *Alabama Journal*. With his venture mortgaged, Hooper took risks. He and his partner expanded circulation to three times weekly, extended their indebtedness, and began publishing books. The ill-fated experiment produced only two volumes, both of which demonstrated Hooper's commitment to slavery. The first was Dr. Matthew Estes's *A Defence of Negro Slavery as it Exists in the United States*, which summarized proslavery arguments from religion to the new racial science, and the second was *The Catechetical Instructor*, a drill book for religion, "especially for the Oral Instruction of the Colored Population." But Hooper's frail credit structure collapsed, and Estes could not pay him for the proslavery book.[24] It was one thing to advocate slavery and quite another to sell the idea.

---

[23] *Ibid.*, Nature made Simon a "beast of prey" but "did not refine the cruelty by denying him the fangs and claws," 13; the "public functionary" passage appeared in the mouth of a would-be bank director bent on bribing Suggs, who was posing as a legislator, 48.

[24] Matthew Estes, *A Defence of Negro Slavery As It Exists in the United States* (Montgomery: Bates and Hooper, 1846), and *The Catechetical Instructor* (Montgomery: Bates and Hooper,

Hooper's bad habits probably hastened his failure, for his problem with self-control was showing again. And once again, he saw his flaws, now in the context of an increasingly civilized slave society. On a business trip to Mobile, Hooper lost money at poker. Penitent, he wrote a creditor friend: "To say that I am ashamed of myself expresses nothing of my feelings." Then he generalized with customary humor: "that a man in debt as I am, and afraid almost to stay about home on that account, should have been guilty of the meanness of losing $50 at poker ... is not only disgraceful to myself, but humiliating to human nature in general." He "felt so mean and sick about it, that I dared not face white people in Mobile." And he closed, "yours in sackcloth and ashes."[25] Hooper's funny apology distinguished between his penitent self and Mobile's white people and implied that black people could not judge him. But "human nature" related Hooper's faults to those of people everywhere – just as constant, just as much to be regretted, just as much to be forgiven, and just as much to be improved.

Hooper put this skeptical ethic to use when he assaulted his political opponents, and his humor crackled with resentment at upper-class people who pretended to be better than he. Writing in the *Journal* in 1847, he attacked "Aveneg," a spokesman for the well-connected Autauga County Democratic clan. Hooper dripped derision:

We know that he [Aveneg] is connected with great people, Governors, U.S. Senators, and other "big bugs." We know that he is of the "chivalry," "the purest aristocracy in the world." We know all this; but we see no reason why his being of the "upper ten" should necessarily induce enmity to a poor "worm of the dust" – a Whig editor. We have a proper respect for the aristocracy – we have never got between the "wind" and "Aveneg's" nobility. Not we. We know our place better.... But while we are willing, and stand always ready, to uncover whenever any scion of any of the "first family" heaves in sight, we must still insist on our right to live on the same earth with them – nay in the same city.

Feigning deference while his wounded pride cut hard, Hooper spoke a language of class as plain as the vernacular of Simon Suggs.[26] Even with slavery behind it, presumption galled the poor editor.

1847). For a more complete discussion of Hooper's venture into regional publishing, with a picture of Estes's frontispiece, see Johanna Shields, "Writers in the Old Southwest and the Commercialization of American Letters," *JER* 27 (Fall 2007): 486–490. For comments in a Black Belt paper on the Estes volume, see the Greensboro *Alabama Beacon*, January 2 and March 13, 1847, where the editor describes the book as "well got up and written with a proper spirit." I am indebted to G. Ward Hubbs for copies of these notices; see his assessment of Estes's book in *Guarding Greensboro: A Confederate Company in the Making of a Southern Community* (Athens: University of Georgia Press, 2003), 71–72.

[25] Hooper to E. Sanford Sayre, [undated but probably winter 1846], Bates and Hooper records in the Sayre file, Thomas Watts papers, ADAH.

[26] Montgomery *Tri-Weekly Alabama Journal*, September 20, 1847. Hooper was referring to members of the powerful coalition of planters that included Benjamin Fitzpatrick, the ally of the Clay family whom Jeremiah Clemens crossed; their connections ran from the Black Belt northward in Alabama and across the South to South Carolina. For a discussion of the role

Hooper's compulsion to satirize kept him in hot water. In January of 1848, he wrote an outrageous piece for the *Journal*, mightily offending the proper citizens of Montgomery, and especially Democrats. When a legislator had a coming-out party for his daughter, Hooper parodied it with a comic portrayal of a "Nigger Ball." One young Democrat observed in his diary that it had created "considerable excitement" – probably an understatement. Racist humor often ridiculed African Americans' social customs, mocking such celebrations as slave weddings for their putative misuse of white people's rituals. Here, Hooper reversed the familiar pattern, using the sociability of slaves to make fun of whites.[27] His sketch cut too close to the truth he saw – that humans constantly deluded themselves when they put on airs, regardless of their race.

Hooper's skepticism about human potential deepened when his business collapsed. To escape the "thralldom of debt," Hooper practiced law when his friends in the legislature made him a circuit solicitor. Back in Lafayette, he intermittently edited a paper, writing stories in which the solicitor exchanged trickery with backwoods people. In 1849, Hooper published a new collection with a press in Tuscaloosa. Two years later, an altered version appeared in Philadelphia as *The Widow Rugby's Husband* (dedicated to Alexander Meek). Although some of the stories were excellent, some were no better than the nonsense that appeared in newspapers everywhere, and many of them evinced a new bitterness. The collection contained one awful story, "Captain Stick and Toney," about the whipping of a slave. Hooper made his slave character speak, and the choice revealed more of his doubts about human nature – black and white.[28]

This story satirized an educated man. Captain Stick was a "remarkably precise old gentleman," "conscientiously just," and "methodical in his habits." But he was no wiser than Jedediah Suggs, and he was meaner. He enjoyed whipping his slave Tony, and he had rigged a system of debits and credits to tally his lashes. So precise that he "adjusted his tortoise-shell spectacles with great exactness," Stick kept the week's bookkeeping for the cruelty his name suggested in a small account book. After one week's reckoning, the Captain took Tony to the stable, "drew his cow-hide and remarked – 'Now, Tony, you

---

of these planters, later known as the "Montgomery Regency," see J. Mills Thornton, *Politics and Power in a Slave Society, Alabama, 1800–1860* (Baton Rouge: Louisiana State University Press, 1978). Hooper's enmity to this group ran deep, and it seems to have taken an edge from his sense that they slighted him despite his very good Carolina connections.

[27] Unfortunately, I have been unable to find the original of Hooper's article. For a brief comment, including the quoted passage, see the diary entry of Matthew Blue for January 7, 1848, in Matthew Blue Papers, ADAH.

[28] The phrase "thralldom of debt" appears in a letter from Hooper to his sister-in-law, Mrs. Thomas Heard, August 22, 1850, which appears in Thompson, "Literary Career," 85. Hooper later referred to work as an editor as that of a "galley slave," and both casual references suggest that he felt his poverty reduced him to an unacceptably slave-like status; see Hooper to De Berniere, August 15, 1855, in JDBH Papers, UNC. The Tuscaloosa collection was originally entitled *A Ride with Old Kit Kuncker and Other Sketches and Scenes of Alabama* (Tuscaloosa: M. J. D. Slade, 1849).

black scamp, what say you, you lazy villain, why I shouldn't give you fifteen lashes across your back.'" Whatever the number, the lashes would be "as hard as I can draw" – evidence, for Hooper's readers, of Stick's ugly nature.

The story then related Tony's futile efforts to escape punishment. He pled, "Gor a mity, massa, don't hit yet" and rolled his eyes in terror while trying to find offsetting credits for his fifteen debits. After getting five credits for "scourin' ob de floor," Tony remembered the perfect good deed: he had tattled to his mistress about a white boy's abuse of Stick's duckling. Tony knew Stick's anger at the white child would divert him, and, sure enough, the master forgot his tally. Stick harshly said, "I wish you had brought him to *me*" and promised Tony ten more credits. As Stick inspected his little book to "settle the balance," Tony grinned and said, "Bress de Lord, ole massa, ... *dats all*," pleased that he had calculated faster than Stick. When the master lost self-control, he lost control of Tony, but the slave's wit did him no good because Stick did not care about numbers. He debited Tony ten extra "stripes" as "judgment for costs" of the transaction and whipped him, "chuckling" at his "ingenuity as well as the perfect justice of the sentence."[29] Whatever Stick represented, it was not justice.

Hooper thought that justice demanded better masters, for slaves could not avoid errors. Hooper made Tony servile, but he showed no sympathy at all for Stick, who was not like the stupid preacher Jedediah Suggs. Despite his cruelty, Stick was civilized, like Hooper's readers. Perhaps some southern readers grimaced at the kind of misdeed they knew occurred, and perhaps some laughed. It is unlikely, however, that many northern readers did so, and, in fact, this second collection of stories never achieved the popularity of *Simon Suggs*.[30] Hooper's caricature of an accountant in Captain Stick was less about rationality than about how cruelty overwhelmed it. Because he believed white men could control themselves, given constant efforts at self-improvement, Hooper thought that freedom gave the Southwest its future.

He expected it to be built on a peculiar combination of capitalism and slavery. In an 1851 letter to De Berniere, who contemplated joining his brothers in Alabama, Hooper's hopes for a modernizing Southwest jumped off the page as he sketched De Berniere's options. One possibility was the area in east Alabama near Talladega, which had "fine" lands and teemed with "iron, marble, slate &c." With a plank road opening to Montgomery, the society, now

---

[29] All quotes from this story, "Captain Stick and Toney," in *Widow Rugby's Husband*, 32–34. "Toney" is spelled differently in the title and the text of the story.

[30] *Ibid.*, 34. It is impossible to ascertain exactly how many reprintings of the same edition occurred in a single year, but the Suggs stories were republished by four publishers (Carey and Hart, T. B. Peterson, Getz and Buck, and H. C. Baird) at least ten times between 1845 and the Civil War, and it is certain that Carey and Hart (later A. Hart) issued more than one printing in the first year or two of the publication; T. B. Peterson and Carey and Hart also published *Widow Rugby's Husband*, both in 1851, and Peterson, which specialized in inexpensive books, issued it in 1855 as well. Peterson also published a combined edition of both books in 1858.

good "*in spots*," would become better "in all respects." Because a railroad connected Talladega to the river, it would soon have "permanently valuable" mills. In fact, "mechanical pursuits" already thrived. Perhaps a better choice would be locating near the planned rail link between Mobile and the Ohio River. This spot had "all the prominent advantages of city and sea-shore residence with the cheapness and health of an up-country one." It would develop a mixed economy of "milling and farming," because Mobile was a "near & good market." The Southwest was only civilized "in spots," but Hooper's confidence prevailed.[31] With slaves providing industrial labor, free men could rise, even in the east Alabama home of Simon Suggs.

Hooper saw his writing as part of the process by which white men would improve themselves. He suggested as much in response to questions posed to him in 1853 by an advocate of the "Alabama law," which would permit localities to prohibit the sale of liquor. Hooper, the solicitor, offered the number and cost of crimes caused by drunkenness in his circuit. His "conservative" estimates blamed liquor for many murders, assaults, and other crimes. He claimed that violations for selling liquor without license and "selling liquor illicitly to slaves" accounted for "*ten per cent*" of all grand jury indictments. Nonetheless, Hooper flatly opposed banning liquor sales to white men. It "would add to the amount of law breaking" – they would not accept control (and he intended to drink). He wanted "judicious" legislation to aid "an enlightened public opinion," not laws to force morality on free people. As he later wrote, he hoped that a "steady, well-regulated public sentiment" would "direct and correct in every department of life."[32] Hooper would use persuasion on everyone capable of self-control.

Controlling black people was a different matter. While Hooper thought there were right and wrong ways to control slaves, his support for the institution never flagged. In the spring of 1854, when "respectable citizens" took a slave from jail to burn him, Hooper disapproved of the "high-handed measure," for "while we have laws we should abide by them." But he later justified a similar event on the grounds of "self-preservation" and noted that the perpetrators had "made up the value of the slave ($850) to the family." Hooper's racism was intractable. As he wrote in 1857, "In time of crisis, there are only two classes of Alabamians: white Southern men and black slaves."[33]

That overstated his case, for Hooper contrasted a "worm" with the "upper ten." Nonetheless, he genuinely hoped that the Suggses of the world would improve themselves, and he believed that progress depended on the combination of freedom and slavery. Hooper's hopes depended on rational, morally

---

[31] Johnson to De Berniere, March 29, 1851, in JDBH Papers, UNC.

[32] Hooper to John M. Taylor, Corresponding Secretary, Alabama State Reform League, July 3, 1853, in Governor's Papers, ADAH. "Steady" in Montgomery *Weekly Mail*, August 31, 1854. An important account of temperance is in Quist, *Restless Visionaries*, 155–234, which connects the movement in Tuscaloosa with "individuals closely linked to the nation's material development," 234.

[33] Montgomery *Mail*, May 31, 1854, August 31, 1854, January 30, 1857.

alert men who controlled themselves and shared their knowledge, just as Hooper thought he did. This was his prescription for the best civilization human nature could realize, anywhere. Hooper's racial opinions were the kind of self-serving morality he distrusted, and perhaps he sometimes sensed that they were no more reliable than the pieties of Jedediah or the calculations of Stick. Even with the limits Hooper assigned them, however, Bill and Tony saw white men as they were – not terribly good.

A SENTIMENTAL VIEW OF SLAVERY

Hooper's stories showed white men losing self-control as they tried to dominate other people, and his fears were not unique. Despite her northern upbringing, Caroline Hentz thought that the near-term future of America required a paternalistic southern slavery. She was slightly more optimistic than Hooper about white people's self-control and somewhat more hopeful about African Americans' potential. But she infused her writing with doubts that were not unlike his. Hentz saw men's tyrannical impulses from the perspective of a woman with a domineering – in the end, mentally unbalanced – husband. Resigned, she idealized marriage in much of her fiction. She idealized slavery, too, but she feared that the violence in human nature threatened it. Even as she defended white southerners, the voices of black characters revealed her doubts.

Hentz brought mixed feelings about slavery to the South. En route to Chapel Hill in 1826, she wrote her family with her impressions: "You see such a swarm of greasy negroes filling the houses and streets. It is enough to put one out of conceit with everything." But she described the "wonderful" nurse she had acquired for her fourteen-month-old son, failing to mention the race of the "daughter of a most respectable mother," herself a nurse for "the best families of the city." Hentz gave Nicholas credit, asking her family to "feel as grateful to my husband as I do, for his solicitude to obtain this indulgence." Although her first-born died accidentally in 1828, by the time she left Chapel Hill Caroline had three children, and a fourth was born in Cincinnati.[34] Given her gratitude for help with one child, her adjustment to slavery was probably foreordained.

Still, racial prejudice had not convinced Hentz that slavery was right. In Chapel Hill she aided the "colored bard" of North Carolina, George Moses

---

[34] Caroline to her family, November 5, 1826; letter transcribed and inserted in the manuscript autobiography of Charles A. Hentz, Hentz Papers, UNC. Charles describes the death of Marcellus and the birth of other siblings in *Diary and Autobiography*, 405. The infant climbed up the back of a chair in which either Caroline or Nicholas – Charles did not record which – was sitting, and when the adult got up, unaware of Marcellus's presence, the chair tipped over and he suffered a brain concussion. The event is also related briefly in Kemp P. Battle, *History of the University of North Carolina: Vol. 1: From its Beginning to the Death of President Swain, 1789–1868*, 2 vols. (Raleigh, NC: Edwards & Broughton Printing Co., 1907) 1: 420, who notes that the child was buried in the garden of another faculty member; online copy available at http://docsouth.unc.edu/nc/battle1/battle1.html.

Horton, who gratefully wrote in an 1845 sketch that Hentz corrected his "many poetical errors." Unable to write, Horton spoke his poems while Hentz transcribed. He recalled that she sometimes wept, perhaps from grief, for among Horton's earliest poems was a "dirge" about her small child's death. "Unequivocally anxious to announce" her pupil's talent, Hentz had his antislavery poem "On Liberty and Slavery" published in her hometown's Lancaster (Massachusetts) *Gazette* in 1829. And she wrote the newspaper supporting Horton's attempt to emancipate himself. Horton recalled that white men also patronized his work, but *The Poetical Works of George Moses Horton* (1845) paid special tribute to Hentz for her efforts to "supply and augment the stock of servile genius."[35] And Hentz seems not to have forgotten Horton.

During her first year in Alabama, further removed from her family and alienated from Nicholas, Caroline grew more dependent on slave labor. As Locust Dell gained students, Caroline taught and managed the domestic side of the boarding school and household. Slaves cooked, cleaned, and did laundry. Her son Charles later recalled the comfortable brick buildings that housed family and students, with servant's quarters next to the backyard kitchen. Uncle Young and Aunt Judy, hired slaves, worked at home and at the family's small farm several miles away, and Hentz occasionally mentioned them in her diary. Despite their labor, Caroline, too, worked hard. With humor, she complained to her diary: "Oh! What a life it is – Oh woes [sic] me. This weary world! I am often tempted to say," checking the thought: "Man is doomed to earn his subsistence by the sweat of the brow & the fire of his brain & why not woman also?"[36] Still, the working mother could write, in part, because of Uncle Young, Aunt Judy, and other hired slaves.

While her accommodation to slavery was practical, Hentz worried about men who controlled other people and not themselves. On the one hand, she feared the force of passions in black and white people, and she respected authority, deferring to her husband even if she doubted his wisdom. When

---

[35] *The Poetical Works of George M. Horton, the Colored Bard of North Carolina, to Which is Prefixed The Life of the Author, Written by Himself*; Electronic Edition at http://docsouth.unc.edu/fpn/hortonpoem/hortonpoem.html, xvii–xviii; original publication Hillsborough, NC: D. Heartt, 1845. The poem's text is reprinted in Horton's *The Hope of Liberty, Containing a Number of Poetical Pieces;* Electronic Edition at http://docsouth.unc.edu/southlit/horton/horton.html, 8; original publication Raleigh, NC: K. Gales & Son, 1829. Horton's poem condemned slaveholders: "Say unto foul oppression, Cease: / Ye tyrants rage no more, / And let the joyful trump of peace, / Now bid the vassal soar." Hentz's patronage of Horton is explained in the context of changing modes of publication in Leon Jackson, *The Business of Letters: Authorial Economies in Antebellum America* (Stanford: Stanford University Press, 2008), 54–66, and Jackson also discusses Horton's efforts to free himself through publishing poetry.

[36] May 30, 1836, Diary, Hentz Papers, UNC. Charles describes the school in *Diary and Autobiography*, 412–413, with additional comments on Aunt Judy and Uncle Young, 414, and recollections of a barbecue that show how fully he accepted post-war idealization of "happy darkies," 418.

she noted with some surprise that Nicholas had boxed the ears of a misbehaving student, she added that the "big girl" and other culprits "deserved a sound whipping." On the other hand, irrepressible anxiety about unchecked emotions marked Hentz's diary. One day she described a happy shopping trip with her daughter but ended with darker thoughts. Hearing "piercing shrieks" from the house of a "free black man, who was abusing his wife and family," Hentz moralized: "How many horrid and revolting forms does human passion assume." If she thought of Nicholas, she did not mention it then, but the next day she recorded her misery at his continuing anger about her "one transgression" – her friendship with another man in Cincinnati.[37]

Hentz's fear of passions weighed heavily in her conflict with Nicholas, and she was quick to blame her own. She felt some guilt about her former friendship, and she wanted "unwavering faith" to banish her troubles. Struggling with her feelings, she hoped that "the waves of human hopes & passion might roll in vain over the erring, but repentant heart." Her son Charles recalled that any polite gentleman's attention produced a "stormy ordeal" for Caroline, and he did not say that the storms became violent. Still, they must have impressed Caroline with the need for obedience. She longed "for indifference – Let principle remain – but let feeling be taken away."[38] All too ready to accept her husband's paternalistic authority, Hentz embraced self-control as a remedy for the disorder of strong feelings.

Ideally, however, paternalism reflected sympathy, which came from the heart, as did passions. Hentz's affirmation of the heart's feelings showed in "Wild Jack, or the Stolen Child," a long story written right after Hentz left Alabama. Although "Wild Jack" drew on tales about thieves who kidnapped slaves for sale, it explored the sympathy that "unites the great brotherhood of mankind." When white citizens rescued the stolen child of a mulatto woman, Hentz claimed they acted from "divine philanthropy" instead of "self-interest." They helped a free black woman, whose "child was her own property" and whose "loss impoverished no one but herself." But while Hentz stressed the citizens' paternalism, she dramatized the feelings of the mulatto mother, and she quoted a poem that asked her readers to "Think not the heart in ebon mould / To nature's softest touch is cold."[39] At about the same time Hentz wrote her story, Harriet Beecher Stowe made sympathetic black characters show slavery's evil. Written to defend white southerners, "Wild Jack" let an emotional black woman judge whites.

---

[37] Ear boxing, May 15; "piercing shrieks," March 5; "one transgression," March 6, 1836; all in Diary, Hentz Papers, UNC.
[38] "Unwavering faith," April 27, 1836, Diary, Hentz Papers, UNC; Charles's comments on his father's temper, *Autobiography and Diary*, 406; "indifference," Diary, August 12, 1836, Hentz Papers, UNC.
[39] *Wild Jack; or The Stolen Child: and Other Stories* (Philadelphia: A. Hart, 1852); "brotherhood" and "philanthropy" in citizens' action, 55; poem, 47. Like many others, this collection was reissued several times both by Hart and by T. B. Peterson, with some variations in contents.

Hentz built "Wild Jack" around African American motherhood, cautiously probing popular assumptions about black families. The mother-child bond was a contested issue in pro- and antislavery ideology, and Hentz's choice of topics suggested her lingering qualms about slavery. The story's two central characters – a white mother, Mrs. Elliott, and a black one, Dilsy – gained moral insight from each other. Mrs. Elliott evaluated Dilsy's feeling toward children because the mulatto was a wet nurse for little Bessy Elliot and Dilsy brought her toddler, Jim, to her workplace. Mrs. Elliott had decided that Dilsy was "deficient in sensibility" because she neither "lavished" on Bessy the "endearing caresses" servants usually bestowed on their masters' children nor showed "tenderness" for Jim. Hentz made the women's dialogue crucial. Mrs. Elliott quizzed Dilsy: "You are not overly fond of children, are you?" Dilsy responded that she did not care about "hugging and kissing 'em as some does," but "I thinks and feels." Based on that, Mrs. Elliott decided that Dilsy had good principles without much feeling.[40]

But Dilsy did have feelings, and she expressed them. When Wild Jack, a local ne'er-do-well, kidnapped Jim, Dilsy turned to her employers to rescue her child. Dilsy poured out her gratitude to Mr. Elliott for his willingness to help, saying "God Almighty bless you, master." Hentz suggested that Dilsy had been guarding her feelings because she mistrusted white people. The black mother cried, "I thought nobody care for little negro – free, too. Oh, Lordy! Jimmy – little Jimmy!" And Dilsy shouted for "her Jim, her baby, her child, in the most piteous and heart-rending accents." With that, Mrs. Elliott realized that she had wrongly "accused her of not *feeling*" and reflected "how little we can know of what is passing in the heart." Halfway through her story, Hentz denied that black mothers were indifferent to their children.[41]

Although Hentz defended paternalism with the Elliotts's concern for Dilsy, she equivocated. Because Wild Jack sold Jim to a slave trader, the townsmen's first efforts to recover the child failed. As Dilsy's doubts about whites returned, Mrs. Elliott preached. "You are wrong to give up to despair, Dilsy," she counseled: "You've told me sometimes that you had no friends – that a poor mulatto couldn't have any. You see, you are mistaken." She assured Dilsy that the townsmen would not have tried harder to recover Bessy Elliott, had she been stolen. Dilsy was unconvinced. With irrefutable logic, she argued: "Nobody would think of stealing your baby. Nobody would buy a white baby." And Mrs. Elliott flushed at the truth. Agreeing that white children were not stolen for sale, she urged Dilsy to put her trust in God, "if not in man." Hentz completed her story with the townsmen recovering Jim, but the conclusion did not erase the words Hentz had given Dilsy.[42] The black mother's voice questioned an institution that put black babies at risk, and Hentz let that problem stand.

---

[40] *Ibid.*, Dilsy's sensibilities, 49–50, 52.
[41] *Ibid.*, Dilsy's emotional excitement and Mrs. Elliott's response, 55.
[42] *Ibid.*, 59–60.

Hentz suppressed her questions as she became more attached to the South. When Nicholas grew enfeebled, she needed money, and she wrote furiously. In December of 1852, Hentz, now living in the panhandle of Florida, wrote her Philadelphia publisher Abraham Hart with ideas for a book to correct *Uncle Tom's Cabin*. Promising that the "cement" of her book would be "*truth*, ... nothing but *truth*," she recalled an episode from Chapel Hill in the 1820s. Hentz wrote that an "agent of abolitionism" posing as a minister got permission to preach to the slaves, giving them "tracts, which some of them could read." The citizens thought theirs were the most "contented, happy set of slaves" in existence until a "faithful negro" reported that the outsider was "kindling the fires of insurrection." Ignoring the slaves' fate when the "plot" was revealed, Hentz emphasized her fear, telling Hart that she would "never forget the agonies I suffered." Sure enough, she wove her memories into *The Planter's Northern Bride*, a defense of the "noble" southern people.[43] It revealed that the "agonies" of her fear lay deeper than she knew.

In *The Planter's Northern Bride*, Hentz dramatized proslavery arguments. To focus on slavery rather than a woman's feelings – her usual concern – she made a man her central character and resolved her romantic theme with a marriage very early in the two-volume work. To show why the humble-born northern bride, Eulalia Moreland, loved the South, Hentz filled her novel with affectionate slaves who constantly talked with white people. Hentz made her hero, Russell Moreland, the epitome of southern chivalry and a paragon of paternalism. In addition to his speeches, she inserted authorial arguments that Africans' inferiority required slavery. Acknowledging a few evil masters, she insisted that Moreland's benevolence was typical. And she claimed that white southerners Christianized and civilized Africans better than any foreign missionary could. Hentz argued that slavery would end "in God's good time." In the interim, if abolitionists duped the slaves into rebellion, they would destroy the nation. Hentz explained that she was trying to prevent that dreadful development.[44]

---

[43] Hentz to Hart, December 14, 1852, HEH. *The Planter's Northern Bride*, 2 vols. (Philadelphia: A. Hart, 1854), 2:182.

[44] *The Planter's Northern Bride*, 1: 109. *The Planter's Northern Bride* has received extensive commentary – far more than Hentz's other works – in scholarship pertaining to women's fiction and to slavery. See Joy Jordan-Lake, *Whitewashing Uncle Tom's Cabin: Nineteenth-Century Women Novelists Respond to Stowe* (Nashville: Vanderbilt University Press, 2005), 83–89; Nina Baym, *Woman's Fiction: A Guide to Novels by and about Women in American, 1820–1870*; 2nd ed. with new Introduction and Supplementary Bibliography (Urbana: University of Illinois Press, 1993), 137; Moss, *Domestic Novelists*, 109–118; Cindy Weinstein, *Family, Kinship, and Sympathy in Nineteenth-Century American Literature* (Cambridge: Cambridge University Press, 2004), 76–85; Philip D. Beidler, *First Books: The Printed Word and Cultural Formation in Early Alabama* (Tuscaloosa: University of Alabama Press, 1999); and Michael O'Brien, *Conjectures of Order*, 2: 770–774. Among these, Baym, Moss, and Beidler especially place the response to Stowe in the context of Hentz's other work. Few discussions of *The Planter's Northern Bride* quote at length from the black characters, and, unfortunately, without extensive quoting it is impossible for a modern reader to imagine the extent of Hentz's terribly crude racial stereotyping.

FIGURE 6.2. Mr. and Mrs. Moreland and Albert, from *The Planter's Northern Bride* (1854).
This illustration from Caroline Hentz's famous proslavery novel shows a humble slave prostrating himself before his benevolent master and mistress. Hentz was answering Harriet Beecher Stowe's novel, *Uncle Tom's Cabin* (1852). Courtesy of the W. S. Hoole Special Collections Library, The University of Alabama.

Predictably, Hentz's defense of the South involved race. Moreland's only "fear" for his northern bride concerned her "repugnance to the African race," but he knew that she would learn to love slaves and slavery in the South. Intending to rebut Stowe with black characters, Hentz made them stereotypical but essentially human. While she called racial mixing a violation of divine law, she claimed it improved black people, and her most important slave character was Moreland's mulatto valet, Albert. Albert accompanied his master to Massachusetts, where the planter found his bride. Albert confused the color line, but Hentz tried to make him more black than white. Although she claimed he spoke without the "almost unintelligible jargon which delineators of the sable character put into their lips," she made fun of Albert's speech.[45]

Hentz ran into trouble, however, when she used Albert to compare free and slave labor, for her middle-class prejudice showed. Like proslavery ideologues, she claimed that northern servants were more exploited than slaves. But then she made slaves more refined than white domestics. This move badly muddied her claim that only white people deserved freedom, which she called a "glorious

---

[45] *Planter's Northern Bride*, Moreland's "fear," 1: 203; Albert's dialect and Hentz's humor at his expense, 1: 14–16. Eulalia's fear was the result of her encounter with a fugitive slave her father had sheltered. She and Moreland discuss her attitude in a dialogue Hentz used to explain her theory of divinely ordained racial differences; *ibid.*, 1: 202–205.

possession" to those with the right "character." Albert alternately lorded over and assisted working-class whites, noticing how hard they worked. He formed a special bond with Betsy, an Irish cook, who admired his "aristocratic mode of living." Betsy grumbled, "I'm ten times more of a slave" than Albert, who agreed, "that's the truth, Miss Betsy." Betsy knew she was outclassed. When the Morelands invited her to return South with them, Betsy declined: "your fine niggers don't make fun of me here," in the kitchen, "but let me stick up as a lady's maid and go among 'em, I'd be the biggest laughing-stock under the sun!" "Betsy was right," Hentz added, confirming the servant's views.[46]

Hentz had even more difficulty separating the humanity of black and white people with another mulatto slave, Chrissy. While pushing her white servants in the direction of slavery, Hentz moved this slave toward bourgeois, sentimental ideals. Like Stowe's characters, Hentz's formed voluntary attachments: romantic love, devotion to children, and loyalty to their masters. Pushing that idea to its extreme, Hentz made slavery a kind of contract that slaves freely chose. Moreland called it a "covenant," suggesting both religious and legal ties. Hentz gave slaves, then, a degree of self-determination, but she tried to limit it.[47] With Chrissy, the personal servant of Moreland's sister Ildegerte, Hentz suggested that slaves' inferiority distorted (but did not destroy) their morality. Perhaps recalling Uncle Young and Aunt Judy, Hentz treated slave marriage as normal; less honestly, she also showed it strained by a slave's choice rather than a master's. She made Chrissy sympathetic but too weak to manage freedom.

Hentz linked Chrissy's traits with middle-class values.[48] Unlike other slaves, Chrissy avoided ostentatious display. She had "unusual prudence and forethought," so she was always alert, unlike the typical black who could sleep anywhere – "on the ridge-pole of a house, or the apex of a church dome." Hentz gave Chrissy proper sympathies. She loved her husband, Jim, and her children, but she was also devoted to her mistress, who trusted the slave. Ildegerte took Chrissy to the North, despite warnings that the slave might be lured away. The mistress insisted that Chrissy loved her even more than Albert loved Moreland. But she added pragmatically: "She has a husband and children, too." Hentz showed Chrissy's pain at her departure from home but limited it through religious resignation. Chrissy said to Ildegerte, "I hates to leave my old man and the little children," but concluded: "Never mind Jim and the children. Leave 'em to Lord Almighty. He knows what's best."[49]

---

[46] *Planter's Northern Bride*: "glorious possession," 1: 294; Betsy's comments on the difference between Albert and herself, 1: 174; Betsy's response to moving South, 2: 277–278.

[47] *Ibid.*, 2: 57.

[48] Hentz had Chrissy show that she was self-conscious about her light color, insisting that "all the colored people ain't black," to which her friend Judy responded "I'd heap sooner see 'em black, than gray or yellow. It's more 'spectable," *ibid.*, 1: 268. Judy also described her own "great, big, thick, ugly lips" and more, 1: 267, contrasting them with Chrissy's appearance.

[49] *Ibid.*, Chrissy's character, 1: 224; Ildegerte's comments, 1: 219; Chrissy's willingness to trust her family to "Lord Almighty," 1: 222.

Finally, however, Hentz made Chrissy unreliable and, therefore, unable to control her own fate. All along, Chrissy vacillated about returning home. When Ildegerte promised her eventual freedom, Chrissy protested that she could not care for herself and "Jim 'most a fool," so he could not be counted on either. Yet she was enticed into running away by northerners. Chrissy lacked the force of reason behind her feelings – her love of Jim, her children, and her owners – and she yielded to a white person's cunning. Soon, Chrissy found freedom intolerable and returned to the plantation, forgiven by her mistress.[50] Hentz made Chrissy loving but insufficiently firm to cling steadfastly to her mistress and her husband. Not smart enough to resist a white man's wiles, Chrissy fled her home; too intelligent to accept the limited freedom she found in the North, she reenslaved herself. She knew she could not be self-determined.

Chrissy typified Hentz's belief that slaves could not be fully civilized. And this problem led to her novel's lurid climax: the story of an abolitionist-inspired insurrection that she had intended to tell from the start of her plans for *The Planter's Northern Bride*. Like the man she said she recalled from her stay in Chapel Hill, Hentz's villain, the evil abolitionist Brainerd, pretended to be a minister, and he fooled both masters and slaves. Unable to resist Brainerd's cunning, Moreland's slaves accepted his plan for rebellion, although Moreland and his slaves had solemnly pledged mutual ties. By breaking their covenant, Hentz's slaves demonstrated that they were incapable of handling freedom.

Nonetheless, the climax to Hentz's novel dramatized her difficulty in distinguishing between black and white people. Moreover, it revealed that the covenant between masters and slaves rested on force and the passions she feared. Hentz voiced this awareness first through two black characters: Jerry and Jack, who had been led by Brainerd to commit robbery. Caught, they were thrown in jail, where the jailer's wife overheard them arguing about the plot. A frightened Jack thought Brainerd had lied. The abolitionist had said that "the Lord gwine to fight for us, with great big flaming sword!" Jack thought not: "Don't much believe he got any!" Jerry called Jack a "great big fool of a nigger," and he warned that Jack would "swing up by that black neck of yourn, way up yonder on the pine tree," if he confessed. The jailer's brave wife confronted the slaves. After trying persuasion, she threatened that they would "both swing from the scaffold into flames hotter than your Christmas bonfires." Terrified, Jerry and Jack revealed the plot.[51] But Hentz had decimated the notion that voluntary covenants secured slavery.

Hentz's jailhouse drama prefaced a larger, more emotional confrontation on Moreland's plantation – a rare scene in Alabama's literary depictions of

---

[50] *Ibid.*, 1: 250. Chrissy's flight, just as Ildegerte's husband died, was designed to show Chrissy's thoughtlessness in the face of her mistress's grief and also to emphasize Ildegerte's kindness in forgiving the runaway when she returned. Jim was "broken-hearted" at Chrissy's "desertion, though he, too, forgave her; 2: 63.

[51] The confrontation between the jailer's wife and two slaves, *ibid.*, 2: 183–190, contains all quoted passages.

slavery, for it pictured many blacks massed, outdoors, around a few whites. In heightened images of light and dark, Hentz evoked a war between rational order and human passion. Moreland dominated the crowd with his iron will. Barely repressing his anger, he cajoled and threatened. Reminding his slaves of their covenant, he asked if they did not deserve "the severest punishment, for treachery and ingratitude to a master as kind and forbearing as I have been?" When Paul, the black apostle to Moreland's slaves, blamed Brainerd, Moreland softened toward the "poor, deluded creatures." He read a letter from a freed slave who now petitioned for his family to be reenslaved. With that, Paul kneeled and begged Moreland's forgiveness: "don't send us away," he pled. "Trust us once more." And all but one of the slaves "prostrated" themselves, begging to be kept as slaves.[52]

But Hentz's docile slaves lacked self-control, and Moreland tamed them with threats, not a covenant. When the blacksmith Vulcan challenged him, Moreland warned harshly: "Dare to resist me, and you shall feel the full weight of my indignation." The defiant slave responded, "'I ain't gwine to let no man set his feet on my neck' ... and he shook his iron hand over the throng, and rolled his bloodshot eyes, like a tiger ready to spring from its lair." Still more ominously, Moreland responded: "There is but one master here. Submit to his authority, or tremble for the consequence." Like an animal, Vulcan lunged. Now the preacher Paul struck Vulcan, shouting, "Let me kill 'em, massa – let me kill 'em." But a calmer Moreland stopped the slaves who were ready to beat Vulcan "to jelly." As the master forgave Paul, Hentz nailed her point. A sobbing Paul explained that his "heart" was good but he had a "mighty poor head." Finally, Moreland reaffirmed the covenant his slaves had violated and quieted them.[53] Against animalistic blacks, "submit" or "tremble" seemed right to Hentz, although it hardly evoked a covenant.

Finally, moreover, Moreland lost his self-control. In the last chapter of *The Planter's Northern Bride*, Brainerd and Vulcan had fled to Massachusetts where, improbably, the hero met them before another crowd. With Albert's help, Moreland convinced the white northerners that the rebels were evil and that northern hostility to slavery was misplaced. Suddenly, however, Moreland yielded to his simmering anger and assaulted Brainerd, with a blow "instantaneous as lightning." As Vulcan cowered, Hentz restored Moreland's self-mastery. The blacksmith, who "had one of those surly, animal natures that grow affectionate and yielding under a stern, controlling will," begged to be reenslaved. Now Moreland renounced his ownership: "I have always said that the moment one of my slaves became rebellious in feeling to me, they might go." Benevolent again, he promised to "relieve" the blacksmith if he got in trouble, "but the relation of master and servant must exist no longer."[54] With

---

[52] *Ibid.*, Moreland's first threat, 2: 203; Paul's begging, 2: 207.
[53] *Ibid.*, 2: 208–210.
[54] *Ibid.*, Moreland's assault on Brainerd, 2: 267; his exchange with Vulcan, 2: 275.

this, Hentz reaffirmed the concept of slavery as a voluntary covenant, in spite of its obvious basis in force.

Appropriately, then, Hentz closed her novel with more violent imagery. Despite their "exalted and refined" minds and "steadfast and true" hearts, northerners underestimated the dangers with which southerners – with their "noble, generous hearts" and "ingenuous and lofty minds" – lived. She wrote, not from "the expectation of honour or profits," but to enter "the lists as a champion of the South." And her last line invoked the violence Hentz's chivalric self-image suggested: "Should the burning lava of anarchy and servile war roll over the plains of the South, and bury, under its fiery waves, its social and domestic institutions, it will not suffer alone." As if recalling Moreland's "lightning" blow, she warned that the "lightning bolt that shivers" the South, "must scorch and wither" the North.[55] This apocalyptic vision bared Hentz's fears, and her sentimental slavery paled by comparison.

Knowing full well that slavery was not a covenant, white southerners appreciated Hentz's effort. In fact, the town of Columbus, Georgia, awarded her a cash prize for *The Planter's Northern Bride*.[56] Perhaps she convinced some northern readers of the danger of rebellion. *Godey's Lady's Book* published a long eulogy in 1856, praising Hentz's "true and noble patriotism" and her "entire truthfulness." The editor merely noted *The Planter's Northern Bride* and failed to mention slavery. To northern readers who feared a slave-based aristocracy, however, Hentz's fiction inadvertently struck a familiar theme. Despite making black characters praise servitude, Hentz transformed her hero into a warrior looking for a fight and turned her book into a threat of passionate action.

Ultimately, Hentz saw an uncertain human nature, whether it belonged to whites or blacks, men or women, upper- or lower-class characters. She sympathized with some black characters even as she stressed the animalism of others. As much as she tried to refute Stowe, her mulatto characters suggested the sexual exploitation in *Uncle Tom's Cabin*. And her white hero barely controlled his will to power. Always frightened by irrationality, Hentz could hardly be secure. Significantly, her last novel, *Ernest Linwood*, portrayed a marriage between a writer and her insanely jealous husband, who repented only after driving her to the brink of madness. But the wife remained wary when her husband reformed, for "the passions, though chained as vassals by the victor hand of religion, will sometimes clank their fetters and threaten to resume their lost dominion." In the end, Hentz doubted that men could control themselves, and the language of slavery betrayed her fear.[57]

---

[55] Ibid., 2: 280–281.
[56] In addition to a prize of $200, the city gave her a piece of jewelry; see one of the earliest studies of women's fiction, Helen Waite Papashvily, *All the Happy Endings: A Study of the Domestic Novel in America, the Women Who Wrote It, the Women Who Read It, In the Nineteenth Century* (New York: Harper & Brothers, 1956), 87.
[57] Hentz, *Ernest Linwood* (Boston: John P. Jewett & Co., 1856), 466–467; Godey's quote from "Editor's Table," *Godey's Lady's Book*, August, 1856, available at http://www.uttyler.edu/

THE MYSTERIOUS SLAVE

In contrast to Caroline Hentz, Augusta Evans never wrote a novel about slavery. Like Hooper and Hentz before her, Evans was confident she could command national audiences, and she did so with her 1859 novel *Beulah*. This novel of a young woman's torturous self-discovery focused on Evans's white heroine. Although most of the slaves around Beulah were barely noticeable, Evans gave one black character, the slave Harriet, an important role. As Evans's heroine tried to avoid submission to the man she loved, the author put her own advice in this slave's mouth. Evans's novel suggested that psychological self-determination and essential inequality were compatible for both white and black women. But Harriet represented the mystery of human nature from her first to her last appearance in *Beulah*. Through the strong will Evans gave her, Harriet retained a moral stature that could neither be denied nor explained.

Slavery was imbedded in Evans's personal history. Although her seriously indebted father had mortgaged his thirty-six slaves when she was a small child, he kept most of them with him when he first moved to Alabama. When he moved to Texas, he sold some slaves and perhaps left others with his brother-in-law, Seaborn Jones, who held Matt Evans's mortgages. By 1850, when the Evanses were back in Alabama, Matt owned two men, two women, and one child. Although slaves did not relieve Augusta of all responsibilities, they reduced the manual labor of the ten white family members. When rising early to make breakfast, one slave, Minervy, discovered Augusta's writing. She helped the adolescent hide the manuscript of *Inez* from her father – Minervy's master. As Rachel Lyons Heustis later told the story – replete with dialect – Minervy took the secret to Augusta's mother, who helped hide it until Augusta gave her father the finished product for Christmas.[58] But Evans's earlier letters to Rachel barely noticed the household's slaves. Only her sociability suggested the freedom they gave the young author.

---

vbetts/godeys%201856%20July-Dec.htm. Many of Hentz's books are available at the excellent collection of Wright American Fiction: http://www.letrs.indiana.edu/web/w/wright2/, where some fiction from most of these writers appears.

[58] U.S. Census, 1840, Russell County, Alabama, lists Evans with thirty-three slaves in his household; U.S. Census, 1850, Slave Schedule, Mobile County, Alabama, lists five slaves in his household. William Perry Fidler, Evans's only biographer, has little to say about slavery; he notes that Matt Evans's thirty-six slaves were mortgaged in 1839 to Seaborn Jones and speculates that the "worldly goods were sold at public auction"; Fidler, *Augusta Evans Wilson, 1835–1909: A Biography*, paperback reissue of the original (Tuscaloosa: University of Alabama Press, 1951), 19. Fidler relates the story of Minervy and the manuscript, 40–41, quoting a letter from Lyons that appeared in Evans's obituary in the Mobile *Register*, May 10, 1909, 2. Evans wrote her friend and minister Walter C. Harriss, in April of 1856, that she had been "nursing a sick servant," one of the rare references to slaves in her extant correspondence; see Sara S. Frear, "'You My Brother Will Be Glad With Me': The Letters of Augusta Jane Evans to Walter Clopton Harriss, January 29, 1856, to October 29, 185[8?]," *AR* (April 2007): 111–141, quoted passage 131.

Evans's family made her southern, but she knew the larger world through books by the time she wrote *Beulah*. Freely borrowing, she explored her heroine's intellectual quest through reference to works her better-educated readers knew. For example, she compared Beulah's search for truth to that of Herr Teufelsdrockh in Thomas Carlyle's *Sartor Resartus*, although she made it a contrast. *Beulah*'s romantic plot, however, selectively borrowed from Charlotte Brontë's enormously popular *Jane Eyre*, without naming it. Although Jane did not suffer Beulah's intellectual angst, both heroines were poor girls thrust into upper-class society. The orphaned Jane became a governess and eventually married her older, aristocratic employer, Edward Rochester. Beulah, Evans's orphan, became a teacher and author before marrying Guy Hartwell, the wealthy guardian twice her age. Evans addressed middle-class readers everywhere – "people who speak the English language," she put it.[59] Like masculine adventure stories, romances were a kind of escapist fiction that appealed to thousands of readers, and Evans knew her market well.

Like Brontë's best-seller, *Beulah* reconciled self-determination with woman's inequality, and *Jane Eyre* – brimming with useful servants – may have prompted Evans to give a black woman agency in her story. Both Jane and Beulah were welcomed into the homes of their benefactors by lower-ranking women. Rochester's housekeeper, Mrs. Fitzhugh, and Hartwell's slave, Harriet, helped the orphans cope with aristocrats. Like Rochester, the morosely irreligious Hartwell was ill-equipped to care for the young girl he sheltered in his home. And Hartwell's sister, May Chilton, who lived with him, was wholly unfit for nurture. Thus, a "negro woman" became Beulah's "special guardian and friend."[60] Harriet bluntly expressed Evans's ideas. Accepting her place as

[59] Mobile *Register*, Oct. 30, 1859. The fullest reference to Carlyle's book is in *Beulah*, 210–211. Among others, Elizabeth Fox-Genovese discussed the reliance on *Jane Eyre* in her excellent introduction to the paperback edition of *Beulah* (Baton Rouge: Louisiana State University Press, 1992), xxiii, arguing that Evans relied more fully for her themes on Samuel Taylor Coleridge, Thomas Carlyle, and William Hamilton. There are many outstanding discussions of *Beulah*. Among the best are those by Fox-Genovese and that by Anne Godwin Jones, *Tomorrow Is Another Day: The Woman Writer in the South, 1859–1936* (Baton Rouge: Louisiana State University Press, 1981), 51–91. Both Phillip Beidler and Michael O'Brien emphasize Evans's originality, with Beidler placing greater emphasis on her literary accomplishment in the context of American and British literature and O'Brien on the philosophical implications and relevance to Southern thought; Beidler, *First Books*, 114–126; O'Brien, *Conjectures of Order*, 2: 1162–1170. O'Brien calls Evans's novel "a work of such high intellectual and abstract seriousness that it is impossible to find its companion in antebellum American literature"; *ibid.*, 1163. Interestingly, no scholar to date has evaluated the significance of Harriet.

[60] *Beulah*, "negro," 46; "special guardian," 199; all quoted passages are from the modern paperback edition by LSU; full citation in n. 59. Mrs. Fitzhugh calls herself a "housekeeper," Charlotte Brontë, *Jane Eyre*, Norton Critical Edition edited by Richard J. Dunn, 2nd ed. (New York: W. W. Norton & Co., 1987), 87. Among other interesting plot parallels are the master's dogs (Pilot, in *Jane Eyre*, and Charon, the mythical ferryman across the river Styx, in *Beulah*), and the presence in the heroes' past of an insane wife, although in Brontë's novel the wife was not (at first) dead, while in Evans's she was. Evans's novel was, however, more

a slave, she advised Beulah to appreciate Hartwell's supervision and rely on God. Through Harriet, therefore, Evans indirectly put proslavery ideas in her romance.

From the moment she introduced Harriet, however, Evans revealed her own uncertainty about human nature. The slave who justified inequality was mysterious: she had no size or shape, only a face that was "leathern." She had neither a black family nor black friends, and she had no domestic space of her own. Yet she was irreducibly human. With steady purpose, Evans gave Harriet a strong will, unshakeable self-confidence, a warm heart, instinctive knowledge, a moral sense, and significant independence, despite her obedience to Hartwell's orders. Harriet judged May Chilton and acted bravely on her judgment. She judged Beulah. She told her master unpleasant truths. Harriet was both self-determined and a slave. She represented inexplicable, perhaps unknowable, facts of existence. Like the servants in *Jane Eyre*, Harriet inhabited the margins of Evans's novel, quietly slipping in and out, as a good servant should. But her few words and her deliberate actions carried part of the plot.[61]

Evans consistently made Harriet a foil to May Chilton. Hentz had suggested that lower-class whites and blacks were similar and that slaves were like family. Evans went further, making a slave better than an upper-class white family member. A vapid socialite dependent on her brother, May instinctively feared that Guy might divert his fortune from her and her daughter Pauline to Beulah. Evans contrasted Harriet's sympathetic mothering with May's hostility. When Hartwell brought Beulah, sick with grief from her sister's death, to his home, Harriet was "surprised, at the advent of the simply clad orphan." But the slave displayed an "impenetrable countenance." Harriet undressed the "poor mourner" and put her to bed as Mrs. Chilton watched. Speaking for their common superior, Harriet instructed the white woman: "Miss May, master says you need not trouble about the medicine. I am to sleep in the room and take care of this little girl." May needlessly asserted her authority: "See that she is properly attended to, as my brother directed." Evans deftly signaled May's selfishness when she whined, "My head aches miserably, or I should remain myself," leaving the slave to nurse the bereaved girl.[62]

---

orthodox in its views of women and religion than Brontë's. A useful discussion that makes clear how familiar Evans's model was is Cree LeFavour, "'Jane Eyre Fever:' Deciphering the Astonishing Popular Success of Charlotte Brontë in Antebellum America," *Book History* 7 (2004): 113–141.

[61] *Beulah*, 60.

[62] *Ibid.*, 47. It seems unlikely that Evans meant for May to echo Stowe's Marie St. Claire, who "always had a head-ache on hand for any conversation that did not exactly suit her," and refused to care for her dying child Eva because of her own imaginary illnesses, but the resemblance is notable; quoted passage, *Uncle Tom's Cabin*, Norton Critical Edition: edited by Elizabeth Ammons (New York W. W. Norton & Co., 1994), 230. On the other hand, Evans did not shrink from judging useless Southern women unfavorably, either in private or in her fiction, and she certainly intended here to make May epitomize all she thought wrong with them. After the opening scene, May decided to please her brother by offering to replace

Beginning with this introductory scene, Evans gave Harriet independent feelings. She made Harriet responsive to Beulah's needs but aloof from white people, even the master she obeyed. Harriet's "face softened" as she asked Beulah what made her cry. To Beulah's complaint that God had not let her die with her sister, Harriet offered "philosophic" advice: "It's a bad plan to fly in the Almighty's face, that way, and tell him what He shall do, and what He shan't." Although she was moved to say more, Harriet hushed when Hartwell appeared, and she silently obeyed his instruction to bring Beulah a glass of water. In a scene of less than three pages, Evans neatly sketched her conservative order: the master, who commanded servant, orphan, and sister; the slave, who affirmed a divine plan and, implicitly, her place in it. But Evans imparted mystery to the slave with the "impenetrable countenance."[63]

Even as she counseled obedience, the enigmatic slave offered friendship and began to undermine May. Because Hartwell had ordered Harriet to "nurse and take charge of" Beulah, the slave told the tearful child to obey her. Beulah acquiesced as the slave washed her face and hands, puffed her pillows, and put a cup of tea to her "quivering lips." When Beulah refused to eat, Harriet reminded her it was Hartwell's wish "so you might as well do it at once." And when Beulah ate, Harriet "praised her obedient spirit." Then, however, Harriet suggested there was danger about: "If you knew as much about this family as I do, you would cry, sure enough." But she comforted Beulah, too: "My master says he has adopted you, and since he has said it, everything will work for good to you." Finally, Evans had the slave speak for herself, warning Beulah that "there will come times when you need a friend besides master, and be sure you come to me when you do." Refusing to say more, Harried urged Beulah to "remember what I tell you when you get into trouble." At Hartwell's approach, Harriet fell silent again.[64]

Obviously, Harriet gave Evans's plot dramatic tension, so the writer reemphasized the slave's mysterious nature each time she reappeared. As Beulah recovered her self-reliance, Evans created a contest of wills between orphan and slave. While expressing gratitude, Beulah insisted, "I have not been accustomed to have some one always waiting on me, and in the future I shall not want you." "Wondering" at Beulah's "independent spirit," Harriet warned her again about unseen danger: "Take care how you begin to countermand his orders, for I tell you now there are some in this house who will soon make it a handle to turn you out into the world again." Without naming Mrs. Chilton, Evans underlined Harriet's inexplicable self-confidence, as the slave urged Beulah to "mind what I say," said "keep your eyes open," and "vanished" in a "dark passage" of the house.[65]

Harriet as nurse, and his response was to ask "can I trust you?" It was no surprise to the reader, therefore, that May drank the medicine she was to give Beulah and lied to her brother about it; *Beulah*, 53–54.

[63] Ibid., 46–48.
[64] Ibid., 57–58.
[65] Ibid., 65.

Finally, Harriet acted decisively to spoil May Chilton's scheming. Observing from a window Mrs. Chilton's abuse of Beulah, Harriet fulfilled her promise to be the orphan's friend. She told Hartwell about his sister's malevolence. At first, Hartwell seemed impatient, but Harriet insisted that he listen to her or he would "never get at the truth," and that got Hartwell's attention. Harriet told him that Beulah had overheard Mrs. Chilton calling her a "miserable beggar." With "towering rage," Beulah had confronted the woman, then she "got every rag of her old clothes, and left the house" in tears. Amazed but not displeased at Beulah's audacity, Harriet told her master: "If you had only been here to hear that child talk to Miss May. Good Lord, how her big eyes did blaze when she told her she could earn a living." As Hartwell hurried away to fetch Beulah, Harriet again disappeared "by a circuitous route."[66] Although Evans's slave had temporarily thwarted Beulah's growing self-reliance, she did so by insistently revealing the evil in a wholly dependent, aristocratic woman. Harriet's was hardly slavish behavior.

If, in a way, Harriet's willing obedience was like that of Hentz's black characters, her stubborn will and quiet prescience elevated her above Dilsy or Chrissy. When Beulah grew up, Harriet's warning against the heroine's independence failed. As Beulah prepared to leave Hartwell's home, Harriet appeared, with a "steady, wondering gaze" that upset the young woman. Evans launched the slave into another round of advice. If Hartwell spent his money on Beulah, it was "nobody's business but his own." Angrily judging the willful heroine, the slave said, "you are mighty simple, I can tell you, if you don't stay here" to accept Hartwell's largesse. Evans reminded her readers of Harriet's status when Beulah retorted, "that will do, Harriet." But Harriet persisted. And she quoted the Bible: "Take care, child. Remember, 'Pride goeth before a fall.'" Evans again emphasized Harriet's status by noting that Beulah "ill brooked Harriet's plain speech," but that the orphan's gratitude "checked the severe rebuke" she contemplated. Harriet left the scene "with anything but a placid countenance," and Beulah departed to make her way in the world. In this contest of wills, the immediate outcome was inevitable. Nonetheless, Evans's intention was to prove Harriet right and Beulah wrong.[67]

Evans dropped Harriet from her novel as she charted her heroine's attempt at independence. Beulah taught, gained fame as a writer, and rejected Hartwell's proposal of marriage. She exhausted herself pondering contemporary literature and philosophy, which led her to doubt God. Her willfulness made her miserable until she finally accepted the divine plan, as Harriet had advised. Evans's portrayal of Beulah's inner turmoil, however, consumed most of her novel. And, before she was done, Evans developed social themes that paralleled Beulah's psychological struggles. She had quietly suggested such themes with May Chilton's character, and now she made them explicit. Harriet had disappeared, but slavery was profoundly implicated in Evans's ideas.

[66] Ibid., 95–96.
[67] Ibid., 149.

Through *Beulah*, Evans attempted to reconcile the bourgeois ethics of self-determination with slavery, and the effort produced tensions she could not resolve. Ethical confusion about the relationship between work and its material rewards were rife in nineteenth-century America, as household production diminished and economic consumption grew among middle-class townspeople.[68] Influenced by Romantic and Christian opposition to materialism, as well as her family's position, Evans insisted on the virtue of work but frowned on extravagance. Like many other writers, she criticized frivolous women and dissipated men; and she made selfish aristocrats like May the special target of her scorn. If conscientious people had to work, however, slaveholders faced obstacles to virtue, and their conspicuous consumption increased the problem. Even though she sensed it, Evans would not admit that slavery made the tension between work and materialism even more intractable than it was in the bourgeois ethos she adapted.

Evans identified the reluctance to work as a problem southerners shared with other Americans, and she made women responsible for reform. Describing a snobbish southern socialite, Evans complained about "this fine-ladyism, this ignoring of labor." And she argued that "this false-effeminacy ... is the unyielding lock on the wheels of social reform and advancement." In a similar diatribe, she insisted that progress required women to "sever the fetters" that "fashion, wealth, and worldliness have bound about you." When, she asked, would women stop fluttering "moth-like, round the consuming flame of fashion?" Their neglect of duty drove their men "into the world, reckless and depraved, with callous hearts, irrevocably laid on the altars of Mammon." Evans prayed: "God hold the women of America" to "true womanly instincts."[69] By choosing to labor at home, women could lose their "fetters" and change the world.

But at the center of white southerners' homes were the Harriets of the region, and they appeared everywhere in Evans's fictional city, just as they did in Mobile. In *Beulah*, slaves variously answered the doors, ran errands, cared for pets, drove carriages, waited on children, nursed the sick, cooked for white families, and dressed their mistresses. Their service was woven into the lives of white families. Evans noted that Hartwell owned a plantation, but she set no scenes there, and she stressed his occupation as a nurturing physician.

---

[68] In one of many authorial intrusions about metaphysical issues, Evans laments the "frightened denials" of people who so much fear materialism that they deny the aesthetic truths of nature, unable to find a way between "gross materialism" and "subtle pantheism"; and she asks "Oh! why has humanity so fierce a hatred of medium paths?" *Ibid.*, 225–226. The best brief discussion of proslavery advocates' ambivalence about work and materialism is Eugene D. Genovese, *The Slaveholder's Dilemma: Freedom and Progress in Southern Conservative Thought, 1820–1860* (Columbia: University of South Carolina Press, 1992). A sensitive treatment of the way in which concerns about work and materialism intersected in mid-century northern and southern people's lives is Anne C. Rose, *Victorian America and the Civil War* (Cambridge: Cambridge University Press, 1992), ch. 2, "Work," 68–108.

[69] *Beulah*, first comments, 33; longer diatribe, 373.

With these moves, Evans handily separated the economic basis of the upper class from its social existence and put hard labor, the slave trade, whippings, and fragmented black families aside. In a way, the literary separation was realistic: Mobile thrived as a cotton port for Alabama's rich plantation region, upriver.[70] Yet Matt Evans worked in the trade that was funneled through the city, and Augusta knew the urban economy rested on the plantation slavery she set offstage. Keeping Hartwell in town, caring for his patients, was a slight of hand that did not quite work, as Harriet showed.

When Evans banished Harriet from her story, then, she obscured a real problem. Early on, she had dramatized the conflict between Beulah's independence and her reliance on Harriet, and she severed the heroine's dependence when she moved her out of Hartwell's home. But Evans backtracked. As Beulah earned money, she set up housekeeping in the "pigeon box of a house" she rented with a friend. Although she worked hard and lived simply, when asked if she would "play cook" in the cottage, the heroine retorted "No, indeed!" for her companion was going to find a "good servant." Evans insisted that May Chilton's daughter Pauline found happiness when she learned to cook, clean, and serve in her husband's humble household. Nonetheless, the author never put Beulah near a boiling pot or a broom.[71]

On the contrary, as Evans concluded her heroine's quest, she restored Beulah to a big house with slaves. Evans stressed romance when she put Beulah back within Hartwell's mansion, with a "costly diamond" on her finger, but she noted Beulah's material gains. Hartwell, she wrote, "had hastened the marriage," eager to claim his bride, and, in the same sentence, the author slid into the passive voice: his mansion "had been thoroughly repaired and refurnished." Hartwell, of course, had not picked up a hammer, moved a chair, or hung a drape, any more than Beulah cooked her meals or swept her floors. Servants did the hard work out of sight, as Evans and her readers understood. Beulah was now destined only for the "holy work" of saving her husband's soul.[72] With slaves creating wealth and leisure for women, Evans's civilization had serious flaws. Harriet had told Beulah she was "mighty simple" not to take Hartwell's money. How could a self-determined woman "sever" these attractive "fetters"?

---

[70] A study of Mobile's economy is Harriet E. Amos, *Cotton City: Urban Development in Antebellum Mobile* (Tuscaloosa: University of Alabama Press, 1985).

[71] *Beulah*, experiment in housekeeping, with quoted passages, 298–301. When her mother May visited and called her a "drudge," Pauline read her "those famous remarks of Lady Mary Montagu, in which all domestic pursuits, even cooking, is [sic] dignified as a labor of love," 390. The phrase "even cooking" suggests Evans's distaste for household work. In fact, she made fun of Montagu's strictures after the war, suggesting that they seemed "quite *comme il faut*, when penned from the luxurious depths of her ladyships delightful *boudoir*," but not in the hot summer of Mobile; Evans to J. L. M. Curry, October 7, 1865, in *A Southern Woman of Letters: The Correspondence of Augusta Jane Evans Wilson*, ed. by Rebecca Grant Sexton (Columbia: University of South Carolina Press, 2002), 107.

[72] *Beulah*, wedding plans, 416; "holy work," 420.

Evans did not know, for she was deeply committed to slavery. Evans's literary success supplemented her father's salary, and her family increased their reliance on slavery. By 1860, the twenty-five-year-old unmarried writer, still living with her parents, owned slave "property": a woman exactly her age and three small children. Since Matt Evans's slaveholdings had increased to eight, there were more black than white people in the household. Perhaps these were the children and grandchildren of slaves who remained from Matt's original holdings, people who had been shuttled back and forth from Seaborn Jones's plantation as the Evans family moved about. Certainly Augusta recognized her family's indebtedness to the Joneses, for she dedicated *Beulah* to her aunt, "as a feeble tribute of affection and gratitude."[73] Perhaps, however, Evans's earnings paid for new human property. However she got them, slaves were helping to assure Evans's future – or so it seemed in 1860.

In the short term, Evans's ambitions expanded. While insisting to Lyons that her writing was not "*mere gratified ambition*," but "*God's work*," Evans planned to enjoy the profits from *Beulah* before they were fully realized. She joked with her friend that "Fame don't pay. Well, I take that back." If her joke suggested some discomfort, she accepted it. After visiting New York to arrange the publication of *Beulah*, she enthusiastically wrote a northern literary friend about their dinners at Delmonico's – hardly the site of restrained domesticity. How she envied him, she wrote, for his "circle of gifted, humorous friends where the icy fetters of formal etiquette are severed and congenial spirits meet." And she gushed about her "bright dream" of travel, hoping to spend the winter in Rome and Florence and the summer in Germany. A homebound woman who wished to grow was making more materialistic "fetters" to be "severed."[74]

Like *Beulah*, Evans's hopes identified her with an international intelligentsia that often acquired the time for writing through the strenuous labor of others. The tale that described a slave hiding Evans's first manuscript appreciated Minervy's deception. But the story did not suggest that Minervy shared Evans's gains, for "God's work" gratified Evans's ambitions rather than the needs of her slaves. And in that, she resembled authors with servants on both

---

[73] Evans wrote that she had lost her "property (negroes and Confederate bonds)" in the above letter (n. 71) to Curry, Oct. 7, 1865, in *Correspondence*, 107; *Beulah*, frontispiece. U.S. Census, 1860, Slave Schedule, Mobile County, Alabama. The children of Augusta's slave woman were seven, four, and two months. Seaborn Jones, a prominent Georgian, had several plantations. His son John had accompanied Evans on her trip to New York to market *Inez*; see Fidler, 68–69, and J. C. Derby, *Fifty Years Among Authors, Books, and Publishers* (New York: G. W. Carleton & Co., 1884), 391. For more comments on the relationship of Jones to Evans's interest in slavery, see Chapter 3, n. 55.

[74] First three quotes, Evans to Lyons, July 30, 1860, in *Correspondence*, 18; second two, Evans to William A. Seaver (an editor of *Harper's*), July 30, 1860, in *ibid.*, 5. It seems only fair to point out that, at twenty-five, Evans was hardly settled in her plans for her life; she was eager to realize some of her hopes, and she was excited by her first major success. Her reliance on slavery shaped her existence, but it probably did not contribute much to her enthusiasm about European travel.

sides of the Atlantic. By making Harriet a humble and nurturing slave in a splendid home, Evans assured her middle-class readers that southern slavery was an acceptable form of domestic labor.

Still, Harriet demonstrated Evans's psychological as well as material dependence on slavery, for Evans had quite deliberately made Harriet's message her own. As she wrote her friend Rachel, an author should plan her plot carefully: "Trace clearly to the end, your grand leading aim, before you write a line and then you will find no trouble, I think, in weaving the details."[75] In Harriet's case, however, the details revealed more than Evans intended. Practically speaking, Harriet resisted the dehumanizing effects of slavery by being enigmatic. And Evans gave the slave a knowledge Beulah lacked. Harriet warned the heroine about her pride, quoting the Bible and claiming a truth that transcended civilizations. She knew the value of service from doing, not from the reading that led Beulah astray. The slave nurtured, while Beulah obsessed about herself. By engaging Harriet and Beulah in a mission that preached women's subordination and "God's plan," Evans made both characters labor under the same truth. When Evans imposed her imagination on Harriet, she made the slave neither fully bound nor fully free. If Evans's readers thought seriously about Harriet, they may have wondered why the strong woman was enslaved.

Regardless, Evans made the subordination of her black slave and her white heroine strangely good, and the writer's romantic plot further showed her psychological indebtedness to slavery. If all servants were expected to obey, only slaves were supposed to have masters who controlled home, food, family, friends, and faith. The power conferred by slavery distorted the selfhood of masters and slaves alike. And *Beulah*'s conclusion showed the result. As Beulah married, banishing all thoughts of an independent career, she planned Hartwell's future and determined to teach him faith. She became "conscious of the power she wielded" over him in the "holy work of love."[76] But Evans placed a psychological trap in her romantic ending by making Hartwell's very soul dependent on Beulah and blurring the boundaries between them. This suggests a slaveholder's moral snare: the projection of her ego onto the selfhood of another through the "power she wielded." The logic of slavery had shaped Evans's plot.

The mysteries Evans sensed were too profound for her to manage, and they touched the foundations of southern civilization. Harriet was the product of Evans's fertile mind, and something of Harriet's resistance came from Evans's confidence that a deferential woman could be self-determined. Harriet was also, however, an unconscious tribute to women like Minervy, who found space in slavery to act for themselves. In proslavery ideology and household realities, gender and racial inequality reinforced each other. Trying to exclude slavery from northern interference, southerners called it their domestic institution,

[75] Evans to Lyons, November 15, 1860, in *Correspondence*, 21.
[76] *Ibid.*, 418, 420.

and slavery had profound significance within middle-class homes. Outside of slavery's reach, however, the problematic character of self-determination challenged other middle-class homes, where inequalities shifted over time and affection vied with exploitation. *Beulah's* success confirmed that many readers worried about women's self-determination. When she calculated her earnings, Evans probably thought she and the South had a marvelous future. Her enigmatic slave character Harriet suggested that was not the case.

* * *

Like Hooper's black characters – Bill and Tony – and Hentz's – Dilsy, Albert, Chrissy, Vulcan, and Paul – Evans's Harriet had no last name, the symbol of free people's self-possession. Although these African Americans figured marginally in the stories of white people like Simon Suggs, Russell Moreland, and Beulah Benton, they were not incidental to the authors' purposes. For white southerners to give voice to black characters was both daring and presumptuous. A common shortcut through difference, stereotyping suggested the failure of imagination in an age of inequality. Hooper leaned heavily on stereotypes of black people, looking for racist laughs; Hentz twisted many of her types from Stowe's work. Evans's decision to use racial stereotypes sparingly had striking results, not all of which she intended. Even as stereotypes without last names, however, black characters exposed the rotting foundations of the rising South.

Behind these black characters stood enslaved human beings whom Hooper, Hentz, and Evans knew – people who had agency, intelligence, and morality. They yielded capital when their owners needed it, as when Hooper's family sold Henry to pay for George's education. They provided services, as when Uncle Young whitewashed the Hentz's fence and their "good cook" made biscuits (or left Caroline to make them herself). They kept family secrets, as when Minervy hid Augusta's manuscript from the adolescent's father. These writers expected to determine the lives of slaves, and they wanted to see their actions as good, but they also saw power's limits and its dubious results. Fictional black characters revealed uncertainties about the relationship between slaves and masters, and these uncertainties came, in part, from writers' homes.

Hooper, Hentz, and Evans used black characters to illustrate how white people could control their destinies. It was Hooper's white rascal who cleverly gained his freedom, it was Hentz's white Morelands who embodied benevolence, and it was Evans's white heroine who planned to save her rich husband's soul. Bill, Toney, Albert, Chrissy, Paul, Vulcan, and Harriet had to live with their status, while white people could hope for better. White people seeking self-improvement were a stock in trade of popular fiction, and characters like Simon, Russell, and Beulah reflected aspirations all middle-class readers could appreciate, wherever they lived. These white characters lived with slaves, however, and Hooper, Hentz, and Evans tried to make that good. Hooper's black characters displayed their helplessness, but it highlighted white men's power and freedom. Hentz measured the nobility of white southerners by their restrained

Slave Characters and the Problem of Human Nature 209

conduct toward brutish slaves. And Evans connected slavery with the nurture and well-being of white people in their homes. Whether or not they relied on race, all three writers affirmed the importance of slavery for white people.

Nonetheless, Hooper, Hentz, and Evans revealed at least some of slavery's wrongs through their black characters. Hooper's Bill saw Jedediah intended to strike him; his Tony knew Stick was cruel; and the author ridiculed the white masters. Hentz's Dilsy saw that black babies, not white ones, were kidnapped; her Jerry and Jack feared the rope; and Dilsy's mistress and the jail-keeper's wife acknowledged these harsh realities. Evans's Harriet slipped about her master's house, trusting no one, and Evans contrasted her nurture with the meanness of an aristocrat. In these ways and others, the dialogue of all three writers revealed the negative effects of slavery. While Hooper and Hentz relied on racial prejudice to justify slavery, neither they nor Evans attempted to justify cruelty, greed, violence, or deception. Their black characters revealed those evils and more. Antislavery writers showed wrongs to attack slavery itself, but that was clearly not the purpose of Hooper, Hentz, and Evans. Had they not thought slavery's abuses were correctible, they would not have mentioned them, for they addressed readers in the North and South.

All three of these writers thought that the ethical standards of the middle class were going to improve their society, including its slavery, and they made the reason and sympathy of self-determined individuals the key to social progress. Hooper's humor implied that the absence of those traits disfigured Jedediah Suggs (who lacked reason) and Captain Stick (who lacked sympathy). Although Hentz insisted that her aristocratic hero was reasonable and sympathetic, she revealed her fears when he used threats and coercion to control people – as in the plantation scene where he subdued rebellious slaves or in the northern meeting where he confronted abolitionists. Like Evans, who condemned the materialism, dissipation, and frivolity of the wealthy, and Hooper, who mocked the "purest aristocracy in the world," Hentz seemed to have inexpressible doubts about the character of rich men and women. And none of Alabama's writers expected a great deal from the uneducated classes beneath them. Firmly committed to middle-class values, most of them suspected that neither great wealth nor abject poverty engendered good conduct.

Such suspicions created anxiety about their society, where wealth and slaves were unevenly distributed and the middle classes were a minority. It would take time to convert thousands of poor white farmers into a bourgeois class, and, in the interim, they might be unreliable, perhaps not much better than blacks. And, as the model of Moreland suggested, it might be hard to persuade men who ruled slaves that they were not entitled to command white people. In an inegalitarian society, the conduct of masters toward slaves was a constant brake on trust. It suggested a human nature that was inconsistently reliable. Hentz's claim that slavery would disappear in "God's time" was unique among Alabama's writers. But her uncertainties about human nature were not unique. Fears mixed with middle-class hopes for a rising South.

One reviewer dimly perceived the paradoxical result. In October of 1860, just before the fateful presidential election of that year, the *Southern Literary Messenger* tackled Evans's *Beulah*. It hailed this "modern novel" as a "herald" of a great literature emerging from the "heart" of the South. But the reviewer was puzzled. He or she was glad that Beulah accepted religious faith and a woman's proper place but found that the novel had flaws. Evans too quickly dismissed minor characters (not surprisingly, the reviewer failed to notice Harriet); she did not name her southern setting; and she displayed too much erudition. But the "chief error" in the book was Guy Hartwell, its putative hero. Although Evans described him as "magnificent," the reviewer saw that Guy emitted an "invidious mist": "In all that he does and says Dr. Hartwell is not so very wonderful at last." The reviewer realized Hartwell's weakness, but he or she did not see that, in the shadows of the master's household, an enigmatic slave helped him out. Harriet's strength and her master's "invidious mist" represented fears Evans would not admit, and could not hide. And they were, indeed, in the "heart" of the South.[77]

For all of their hopes, then, Evans and her peers were not optimistic about wholesale reforms. Slavery did not block, but it did retard the faith in progress that had grown in Western civilization since the Renaissance. Just as Evans criticized materialism without questioning the economics of slavery, writers separated evils done by individuals from the system that made them possible. They expected gradual progress through individual effort but thought that human nature prohibited radical change. Writers did not have a dim view of human nature because they wanted to protect slavery, although they did want to protect it. As their dark characters' voices suggested, they saw many weaknesses in humans because they lived with slavery. With a kind of narcissism bred by dependence, these writers projected irrational impulses onto black people and used them to justify slavery. And, more directly, slavery represented white people's capacity for violence, self-aggrandizement, and deception. Ironically, black characters not only testified to white people's failings, they showed that slavery limited the imagination and diminished the opportunities of freedom.

Still, Hooper, Hentz, and Evans reached national audiences. In their racism, these three writers reflected widespread assumptions among middle-class Americans about the differences between the civilized and uncivilized people of the world. Slavery seemed to them a logical, even inevitable, solution to racial inequality, and – as Hentz observed in her recital of pro-slavery arguments – they had inherited the institution and had to make the best of it. Because otherwise decent white southerners believed slavery had to be, writers hoped that northerners would see it, too. It was important, however, that a belief in self-determination connected Hooper, Hentz, and Evans with other Americans, for they gained a wide readership for their

---

[77] "Beulah," *SLM* 35 (October, 1860): 241–248; quoted passages: "modern novel" as "herald," 243; "heart" of South, 242; problems with Hartwell, 245.

views of enslaved African Americans by fusing their depictions with more positive values.

Surrounded by people who shared their views, none of these writers felt guilty about slavery. An irreligious Hooper blamed wrongs on "human nature in general"; Hentz implied slavery was wrong but called its presence "divine mystery"; and Evans suggested that it was part of "God's work." These differences mattered little to the enslaved, for they were accompanied by a shared commitment to securing slavery. Johnson Hooper's cruel humor, Caroline Hentz's racist sentimentality, and Augusta Evans's escapist romance reflected three faces of the same self-doubt that locked middle-class southerners into the fatal grip of slavery. Nothing – certainly no amount of force – could release these people from the damage they did to themselves, and little – in the absence of force – could prevent the harm they inflicted on black people. Other Americans, however, had greater faith in human potential, and some of them applied that faith to black as well as white people. Evans claimed that readers would approve if southerners wrote for all English-speaking people, and the sale of her books gave rise to her hopes. When it came to slavery, however, it mattered who was persuaded and who was not. Alabama's writers wanted American progress with southern slavery, but they could only estimate the numbers and location of their sympathetic readers and only guess what future was in their minds.

PART THREE

THE CRISIS OF THE RISING SOUTH

Alabama's writers were public figures, inherently political whether or not they held office. Because they represented a middle class that benefited from American progress, they balked at early southern nationalism. Nonetheless, they shared common political worries. They believed that ambitious politicians across the United States were threatening self-government. They feared that uninformed voters were becoming puppets to tyrants who used democracy to mask malevolent goals. And they linked these fears to the master-slave relationship. By the time of Lincoln's election, these writers hotly disagreed about how to secure a viable future for their slave society. When war came, therefore, they led in different directions, but they described similar signs that despots were at work around them. Before the fighting ended, Alabama's surviving writers realized that their individual freedom mattered far more than the enslavement of black people. With renewed intensity, they wrote to determine their lives.

7

Slavery and Political Trust

> There is no stopping place in the descent from liberty to slavery.... [S]ecurity is abandoned, whenever a minority succeed in controlling a popular election by threatened violence.... If we yield ... we will soon be drifting upon the waves of anarchy, slaves where we sought to be masters.
>
> Jeremiah Clemens, speech in 1860

The strains that appeared in the history and literature of the 1850s riddled the acrimonious political debates of the decade. The writers of the rising South always claimed to defend freedom. Using stark contrasts, Jeremiah Clemens warned Alabamians in 1860 of "the descent from liberty to slavery," and he begged voters not to enslave themselves to a secessionist minority. The men he addressed were not directly coerced, but he wanted them to think and vote more independently.[1] Writers with different political views shared Clemens's concerns. Joseph Baldwin, William Smith, and Johnson Hooper also warned about politicians who endangered self-determination and weakened democracy at its roots. But, as these writers tried to provide crucial leadership, slavery's pernicious influence blighted their efforts.

Slavery gave wretched vitality to a fear of power dating from the American Revolution, when patriots predicted disaster in a politics that elevated power-hungry British aristocrats above impoverished masses. Ben Franklin had famously written of the poor that "it is hard for an empty bag to stand upright," and Alabama's writers shared the widespread idealization of American voters as productive freeholders. They supposedly resembled the sturdy yeomen who fought the Revolutionary War rather than the landless poor of European nations. Like their fellow citizens, Baldwin, Smith, and Hooper thought that self-determined Americans managed their lives, politically, through self-government. Like many other activists, these men espied corruption when money and power came together, and they sometimes hurled accusations at

---

[1] Speech at Huntsville, August 6, 1860, from a typescript copy of the speech printed in the Montgomery *Weekly Post*, September 5, 1860, in the Jeremiah Clemens folder, ADAH.

their opponents about bribery and manipulation of voters. More generally, they worried that voters could easily be corrupted if they were not self-sufficient.[2]

In the nineteenth century, however, the ideal of self-sufficiency acquired more psychological dimensions, without ever losing its economic foundations. As household production diminished in importance and the professional classes grew, ideas about the nature of property and work slowly shifted. In the middle class, homes did not necessarily produce income, and brainpower counted for more than physical labor. Baldwin, Smith, and Hooper believed that self-government required voters with economic autonomy, but their insistence on self-control made political independence a function of inner character, too. They thought that people who lacked mental independence could no more govern themselves than they could improve their lives or contribute to social progress. Idealizing reason and sympathy, these writers made voluntary relations, achieved through persuasion, as critical in politics as they were in family, friendship, and community.[3] This model made democracy safe.

This model, however, seemed in constant jeopardy from something that resembled slavery. Although slavery was the opposite of freedom because force prevented a slave's self-determination, slavery's more subtle mechanisms of control gave it special relevance to democratic politics. These writers knew that masters often used deception, manipulation, or threats, and they saw

---

[2] The continuing importance of republican ideas about autonomy is a major theme in J. Mills Thornton, *Politics and Power in a Slave Society: Alabama, 1800–1860* (Baton Rouge: Louisiana State University Press, 1978). He emphasizes the fears of yeomen and suspects that antebellum politicians manipulated them. Without disagreeing, I emphasize that politicians had their own reasons to fear the loss of autonomy. Among the many influential historians who have treated the centrality of republican ideas, Gordon Wood's series of books have perhaps been most important; see esp. his monumental work *The Creation of the American Republic, 1776–1787* (Chapel Hill: Published for the Institute of Early American History and Culture by University of North Carolina Press, 1969). Joyce O. Appleby has emphasized the fit between American politics and liberal capitalism in such works as *Capitalism and a New Social Order: The Republican Vision of the 1790s* (New York: New York University Press, 1984) and, more recently, in the broader interpretation of *The Relentless Revolution: A History of Capitalism* (New York: W. W. Norton, 2010). An important early study that helped identify the tension between southern concerns about slavery and republican ideas is Drew M. McCoy, *The Elusive Republic: Political Economy in Jeffersonian America* (New York: W. W. Norton, 1980).

[3] I have been influenced here by Lawrence F. Kohl, *The Politics of Individualism* (New York: Oxford University Press, 1989), which focuses on the partisan divisions fostered by differing understandings of individualism, and by my conversations with the author. From a very different perspective, I found useful the post-Marxist argument of Jürgen Habermas, *The Structural Transformation of the Public Sphere: An Inquiry into a Category of Bourgeois Society* (Cambridge, MA: MIT Press, 1989), who sees the psychological turn as early evidence of the invasion of capitalism into all of Western life. Following Habermas, John L. Brooke argues for more attention to his analysis of the role of persuasion, "Consent, Civil Society, and the Public Sphere in the Age of Revolution and the Early American Republic," in *Beyond the Founders: New Approaches to the Political History of the Early American Republic*, ed. Jeffrey L. Pasley, Andrew W. Robertson, and David Waldstreicher (Chapel Hill: University of North Carolina Press, 2004), 207–250.

some owners abuse their power under cover of law. More viscerally than any revolutionary precedent, the model of slavery suggested to Baldwin, Smith, and Hooper that subtle domination and silent submission were fundamental patterns in human nature. "Daily exercised in tyranny," as Thomas Jefferson had written, they saw its shadow when one white man controlled another. These writers feared that powerful men, their patriotism warped by ambition, would tyrannize an irrational electorate that sustained them. With leaders yoked to voters, and vice versa, writers saw the reflection of slavery: a narcissistic relationship in which masters rested their identities so much on bondsmen that neither was fully free.[4]

In the 1850s, these writers perceived this frightening dynamic in the democracy they practiced. They understood the intricacies of political manipulation because they employed it in pursuit of ambition. They knew from experience that office seekers kept quiet about the advantages of the power, claiming to advance the common good. Because political parties concentrated power, they seemed to pose special threats to a nation of independent citizens. Thoroughly entangled with parties, Baldwin, Smith, and Hooper criticized the way they limited autonomy, as when "wire-workers" (the common epithet) engineered nominations, for example, or legislative caucuses enforced decisions made in secret. Perhaps more importantly, writers worried that parties deliberately spread misinformation. As editors and authors, these men knew that parties ran newspapers and controlled the flow of print, and they knew exactly how much publications cost. They could not see how to combat lies in print except, possibly, with more print. In the political press, new patterns of organization

---

[4] Query XVIII, in *Notes on the State of Virginia*, in Thomas Jefferson, *Writings* (New York: Library of America, Viking Press, 1984), 288. The most important studies of the relationship between American political ideas and slavery are those of David Brion Davis, especially *The Problem of Slavery in the Age of Revolution* (Ithaca: Cornell University Press, 1975), but there are many others. All scholars recognize slavery's influence on southern politics, but they differ about how it was important. Most recent scholarship emphasizes the conservative influence, in part as a result of the breadth and force of the interpretations of Eugene Genovese and Elizabeth Fox-Genovese. Links between racism and a more democratic, *herrenvolk* ideology of the plain folk have long been argued by scholars such as George Frederickson, *The Black Image in the White Mind: The Debate on Afro-American Character and Destiny, 1817–1914* (New York: Harper & Row, 1971). More recently, Lacy K. Ford has argued that the two influences were reconciled by 1840 in *Deliver Us from Evil: The Slavery Question in the Old South* (Oxford: Oxford University Press, 2009), 505–534. In focusing on the middle-classes, I suggest a relationship between the fairly inegalitarian but liberal capitalism of an international bourgeoisie. More generally, I am persuaded that slavery was psychological poison to people who valued autonomy, and here I am influenced by a theoretical argument that began with Hegel's discussion of lordship and bondage. The ur-source is Georg Friedrich Wilhelm Hegel, *Phenomenology of Spirit*, trans. A. V. Miller (Oxford: Clarendon Press, 1977). My thanks to Susan V. Donaldson for calling my attention to the contention of Susan Buck-Morss that Hegel was influenced by Caribbean slavery (rather than the European class struggle) – an argument that philosophers will debate but which seems, at least, historically plausible; Buck-Morss, "Hegel and Haiti," *Critical Inquiry* 26 (Summer 2000): 821–865; later expanded as *Hegel, Haiti, and Universal History* (Pittsburgh: University of Pittsburgh Press, 2009). The article, which comprises most of the book, is available at http://www.jstor.org.

met modern technology. As the power of print expanded, so did these writers' anxieties about its potential for its abuse and its impact on individual autonomy.[5]

Only some of these anxieties grew from fears of a northern political majority against slavery. Convinced of similarities within the American middle class, these writers tried to persuade readers that the Southwest was progressive, and they believed it was.[6] Because they could not admit that slavery was immoral, they blithely blamed northern politicians for opposition to its expansion. But they competed for leadership within the South, and these three men also exposed slavery's hidden influence when they wrote about their fellow southerners. As they sought simultaneously to protect slavery and promote the town-dwelling middle class, writers knew that both wealthy planters and poor farmers sometimes resisted change. Given their ambitions, they did not criticize either group directly. But, when Baldwin, Smith, and Hooper suggested that politicians misled an uninformed southern public, they revealed subterranean cracks in the social foundations of the rising South.[7]

Baldwin, Smith, and Hooper were not simply spokesmen for the interests of an emerging middle class or a slave society. Grounded in their daily lives, the ideal of self-determination was also a core value that shaped their identities. Deviations from that ideal, either by domineering leaders or passive voters, seemed truly dangerous to democracy. And such danger made these intelligent men wary about their own ambitions. As writers, they manipulated language to gain readers; as politicians, they used the new political machinery to win office. Most importantly, as masters, they controlled slaves, and while

---

[5] These generalizations are based on my reading of the texts. Thornton, *Politics and Power*, however, has a masterful analysis of the way newspaper editors fit into the machinery of politics in Alabama, 128–131. He notices that their role in "party governance" is "infrequently noticed" (128), and, despite the efforts of the newest political historians (n. 3, *supra*), that is still too true for the antebellum South.

[6] I concur with Jonathan D. Wells's conclusion that the middle class had few constructive alternatives to secession, although most of them did not embrace it willingly, but his assessment that "the southern middle class ... had largely abandoned partisan politics to the planter class in the 1850s" seems not to fit Alabama; *The Origins of the Southern Middle Class, 1800–1861* (Chapel Hill: University of North Carolina Press, 2004), 224. Thornton found that Alabama's leading fire-eaters were townsmen, but he does not define their social class; *Politics and Power*, 241–242.

[7] Although there continues to be serious disagreement among historians about the extent of social unity in the Old South, I am persuaded by William Freehling's interpretation of the constant interaction between secessionists and less radical southerners in the political dynamic. I do not suggest that class differences caused secession – and this is not a book about the causes of the Civil War – but I do argue that concerns rooted in class affected the way these people (along with some of their readers and supporters) saw the political conflict. Most relevant here is Freehling's second volume, *The Road to Disunion. Vol. 2, Secessionists Triumphant: 1854–1861* (New York: Oxford University Press, 2007). A recent major interpretation that emphasizes the fundamental difference between North and South rather than differences within the South is John Ashworth, *Slavery, Capitalism, and Politics in the Antebellum Republic. Volume 2, The Coming of the Civil War, 1850–1861* (Cambridge: Cambridge University Press, 2007).

they probably employed persuasion, they likely used deceit, menace, or coercion as well. No matter how much they justified themselves, their self-doubt emerged. The confluence of slavery with mass-based politics fostered mistrust. Self-determination seemed all the more essential and dreadfully elusive.

Unconsciously and not, then, Baldwin, Smith, and Hooper illustrated the influence of slavery on political ideas that were basically American. It produced perceptive critiques of modern politics, but it also created blind spots and magnified fears. Baldwin analyzed the nation's history in *Party Leaders*. Lauding independence, he raised the specter of new forms of tyranny in a modernizing polity, and he made a southern planter represent the threat. Smith attacked politicians in his satiric fiction, *As It Is*, and his southern characters suggested a merging of political corruption and psychological dependence. Hooper's writing showed that economic dependence aggravated political anxieties and produced a rhetoric of hate.[8] Although their politics diverged – Baldwin left the South, Smith opposed secession, and Hooper became a fire-eater – their examples illustrate how slavery distorted the ideas and hampered the leadership of middle-class men. These men wrote in the *lingua franca* of Americans, but into it they loaded fears that words could not assuage. Voting required trust in particular men and in the representative system. When writers denied the morality of politicians and questioned the reliability of voters, they moved toward violence, well before the fighting began.

THE PSYCHOLOGY OF TYRANNY

Joseph Baldwin thought that American freedom promised progress if wise leaders guided the nation and ordinary people voted independently. He was, nonetheless, uncertain about the future. Although he never wrote – and seems not to have believed – that slavery was as necessary as freedom, he certainly knew that some southerners would fight to keep them joined. Baldwin wrote his second book, *Party Leaders*, during the brief truce produced by the congressional Compromise of 1850, which temporarily resolved the conflict over slavery's expansion. Despite the book's positive intentions, it signaled his mistrust. Baldwin wanted leaders to appeal to reason and sympathy rather than passion and prejudices. He doubted, however, that politicians would consistently repress their ambitions, and he questioned the rationality of the crowd. *Flush Times* had expressed Baldwin's optimism about Americans' capacity for self-improvement. *Party Leaders* revealed his fears that a modernizing polity hid new forms of slavery.

Baldwin's political ambition preceded *Flush Times* and *Party Leaders*, and he typically used humor to disguise it. In 1849, the year he failed to win election to Congress, Joe wrote his cousin Alexander Stuart, a prominent Virginia Whig, that he wished to go to California "backed by the influence and position

---

[8] Baldwin, *Party Leaders* (New York: D. Appleton and Co., 1854); Smith, *As It Is* (Albany, NY: Munsell & Rowland, 1860).

of an honorable and responsible office," and he asked "Sandy" to help him. In 1850, after President Millard Fillmore appointed Stuart Secretary of the Interior, Joe wrote a funny plea for his cousin's patronage. "If I might be so bold," he asked, "how do you feel way up there? Away up, with Bryant's duck 'in that thin, cold atmosphere'? Feel any ways dizzy in the head?" He urged Stuart to get rid of all Democratic office holders, "hoist" out any "Disunion Whigs," whose "flatulent politics come more from their guts than their brains," and replace them with family, although "I scarcely know what I want – the thing has come on me so sudden." "Generally," he added, "I can say as a physiological fact – that hard work don't agree with my peculiar constitution – good pay does."[9] Baldwin's joking took the edge off his ambitions and, perhaps, eased some discomfort about them.

Quite seriously, Baldwin believed – like Whigs everywhere – that independent men must often cooperate for progress. This view entailed active government, but he insisted – like other southern Whigs and many northern ones – that it did not warrant meddling with slavery. He thought that the Constitution was a contractual relationship among equal states and that good-faith contracts required voluntary self-restraint, not coercion. Maintaining balance among equals was difficult, but Baldwin believed it could be done, and he shared his cousin Stuart's desire to preserve the compromise achieved under Fillmore. In 1852, Baldwin supported the president's renomination, opposing Senator Daniel Webster because his opposition to slavery's expansion denied southern "equality." "I can stand a pretty strong odor of nationality," he wrote Stuart, "but that is a little too strong. It would dissolve the Union if practically carried out."[10]

Baldwin identified his ambitions with the nation and the South. In the spring of 1853, former president Fillmore visited Mobile, where Baldwin was basking in praise for *Flush Times*. Baldwin enjoyed "an excursion to the Bay" in which he shared the spotlight with "the X," laughing that Fillmore was "under the pleasant delusion that all this hullabaloo was for the dead President instead of for the live author." Baldwin had discussed the "nearly done" *Party Leaders* with "the X," and he thought to dedicate it to Fillmore. But he changed his mind and chose his uncle Briscoe Baldwin, who sat on the Virginia Court of Appeals until his death in 1852.[11] Whether he wished to avoid identifying with a northerner or claim his kin, Baldwin made a southerner's choice.

---

[9] Baldwin to Stuart, March 2, 1849, September 27, 1850, in A. H. H. Stuart Papers, UVA. Baldwin slightly misquoted William Cullen Bryant's famous poem "To a Waterfowl," which reads "cold thin atmosphere."

[10] Baldwin to Stuart, April 16, 1852, in A. H. H. Stuart Papers, UVA. Baldwin became a Democrat when his party collapsed, but he was always, intellectually, a Whig. The definitive study of the Whig Party is Michael F. Holt, *The Rise and Fall of the American Whig Party: Jacksonian Politics and the Onset of the Civil War* (New York: Oxford University Press, 1999), but also important for Whig thought is Daniel Walker Howe, *The Political Culture of the American Whigs* (Chicago: University of Chicago Press, 1979).

[11] Baldwin to Stuart, April 15, 1853, in A. H. H. Stuart Papers, UVA.

Southern loyalties complicated Baldwin's Whiggery. In 1853, the *Southern Literary Messenger* published part of *Party Leaders*: sketches of Andrew Jackson and Henry Clay called "Representative Men." Apparently, Stuart criticized Baldwin's interpretation because the author answered defensively that he "only *seemed*" to tilt toward Jackson. Even though Baldwin sided with Democrats about expansion, he protested Stuart's suggestion that he was "too progressive." Like other Whigs, he had "liberal" and "larger American ideas" about the economy. He had mistrusted the 1852 Whig presidential nominee, Winfield Scott, but he argued that if the general had advocated a transcontinental railroad and canals to connect America's coasts – had he "thrown out these measures 'like comets'" – the Whigs would have defeated Franklin Pierce. Baldwin insisted that Congress "must embrace great principles or the intellect of the country will be dormant and the intellect is Whig." He wanted the nation to "have peace" and "grow for 25 years."[12] If government fostered prosperity, the South would manage slavery.

Hopes for his future within a moderate nation motivated Baldwin to write *Party Leaders*, which D. Appleton of New York issued in 1854. Having written Stuart that he wanted to do "some good," Baldwin blended "interest with instruction," especially for "young men." In "familiar history," the book traveled from the Revolution to 1852, focusing on five leaders: Alexander Hamilton, Thomas Jefferson, John Randolph, Jackson, and Clay (all but one of whom was a slaveholder). Claiming to be nonpartisan, Baldwin wrote carefully about all party leaders. He made the founders models but would not treat them with "superstitious reverence," for the same misdeeds "that now degrade politics into the dirtiest of trades, *then* had sway, though, doubtless, in far fewer instances than in this age of their full-blown development." Unlike other judgmental historians, he claimed to consider men "made in the laboratory of nature," which mixed diverse traits "into one organized, composite mass, the whole of which is man."[13] By

---

[12] Baldwin to Stuart, November 21, 1853, in Stuart-Baldwin Papers UVA (this is a different collection than the one cited previously in n. 11). The *Messenger* published "Representative Men: Andrew Jackson and Henry Clay" while still using the "flush times" sketches; "Representative Men," part I, *SLM* 19 (September 1853): 521–530, part II, *SLM* 19 (October 1853): 585–598, with both essays being the lead article in their respective numbers. The preface to *Party Leaders* was dated July 1854, from Livingston, shortly before Baldwin's departure for California. His brother Cornelius managed the details of publication in New York while Joe was en route to the west coast.

[13] His purpose, Baldwin to Stuart, November 21, 1853, in Stuart-Baldwin Papers; method and audience, *Party Leaders*, 8; founding generation, 22; whole man, 139. Baldwin also commented in his preface that the original essays in the *SLM* had been well received by "gentlemen of high position and distinction," ibid., 10. Adam L. Tate, "From Humor to History: Joseph Glover Baldwin and *Party Leaders*," *AR* (April 2007): 83–110, reads the book as "a reflection upon what had gone wrong with political development in America and in Alabama," 97. Although I differ with both in stressing Baldwin's modernizing tendencies, the best discussions of Baldwin's political thought are John M. Grammer, *Pastoral and Politics in the Old South* (Baton Rouge: Louisiana State University Press, 1996), and Adam L. Tate,

applying principles of human nature to politics, Baldwin encouraged young men to work for the common good. Self-government did not have to be the "dirtiest of trades."

Baldwin's hopes for independent Americans enlivened *Party Leaders*, which he sprinkled with Whiggish assessments of the psychology of voters. The "essential general advantage" of "a free and popular government," Baldwin asserted," is that "*it elevates the masses.*" Without "external control," men had "individuality of will," which was "the distinctive attribute of freedom and of manhood." As free men gained "self-respect" and "the respect of others," acquired "more or less" information, and got involved in public affairs, "the currents of intelligence, which circulate over the country," further informed them. These competent men accumulated property and educated their children. In this way, the "masses" became middle-class citizens.

Baldwin expected the masses to elevate themselves slowly, but he thought it almost inevitable. As it transpired, the common folk would take care of themselves and trust men of the "higher class" to take care of government, for they knew that leaders had power only with votes. Baldwin allowed that by "restricting suffrage" in the short term, government might be more rational and efficient, but, he asked rhetorically, "is it wiser to have better laws or a better people?" And he answered his question with a bold affirmation: freedom awakened everyone "to energetic and independent action," so "the contagious influence of mind upon mind obtains; and the immense volume of its aggregate thought and enterprise, starting from its millions of streamlets, pours forth its material objects." Independence brought not only prosperity but "higher mental reach and attainment" for everyone.[14] A middle-class nation could have secure and steady freedom.

Thus far, Baldwin was an optimist. Like most Whigs, however, he qualified, repeating the common claim that the masses of other countries had a limited capacity to govern themselves. Uniquely, American history had assured self-government by encouraging "individuality of will." And, because Americans could satisfy their own "few and simple wants," they needed little from government. Scattered across a continent in "homogeneous communities," they had "practical equality." But Baldwin thought these advantages were at risk if property became scarce and men crowded in cities, "in the Northern States especially." Linking expansion with independence, he insisted that the vast continent promised a healthy future for popular government.[15]

Conservatism and Southern Intellectuals, 1789–1861: Liberty, Tradition, and the Good Society (Columbia: University of Missouri Press, 2005).

[14] Quotes in this paragraph and the preceding one from *Party Leaders*, 82–85.

[15] *Party Leaders*, general characterization, 74–75; "Northern States," 85. Baldwin critically wrote about the French Revolution that "virtuous liberty" required "self-respect" and "self-control." Men could not suddenly become capable of self-government, for "the yell of slaves, drunk with blood and license," was not the "shout of freedom," 46. In this context, the "slaves" were white Frenchmen.

Baldwin also argued that political parties were inevitable in a free country, grounding his analysis in human nature. He claimed that contrasting ideologies produced parties everywhere. Progressives liked change, action, the future, and war, while conservatives were devoted to stability, caution, the past, and peace. But American parties also grew from petty disagreements and personal ambitions, which came from human nature, too. Free men always formed parties, not only because the "exaggerated" claims of office seekers aroused them but also because "we are all partisans – men, women, and children." Partisanship grew from both "combativeness" and "sympathy," or, to put it differently, from the "selfish and social passions." And, like mixed human nature, parties could be constructive.[16]

But Baldwin feared that parties might diminish psychological autonomy. When men take sides, he wrote, "mind acts on mind," and collective mentality overwhelms individual morality. The effect of a crowd on individuals "swells their importance," and "gives them a sense of power," while the "most ignorant" are "drawn by clamor, like bees, as by an instinct." Lured by flattery, men "become identified" with the "common enterprise" rather than thinking independently. Despite parties' disturbing impact on individuality, Baldwin thought their excitements were "the safety-valves that let off the discontent, and the surplus energies" of Americans. Like theater in France or bullfighting in Spain, much of the hubbub was for "fun": with "the steam being unconfined, the fiercest explosions of wrath are only the bursting of rockets in the upper air." After this mildly anxious analysis, Baldwin concluded that "we must take the evil with the good."[17]

Nonetheless, the potential defects in popular government made wise leadership imperative, and Baldwin explored it by assessing each of his party leaders. Always pragmatic, he led his readers to consider what conduct was useful and what was not. His five subjects were all patriotic, intelligent, and independent. Baldwin variously praised bourgeois traits like self-discipline, self-knowledge, and individuality, aspects of honor like courage and magnanimity, and religious principles like charity and tolerance. If his leaders had a common flaw, it was ambition, which reduced their ability to cooperate.[18] Throughout, Baldwin stressed communication, which reflected a leader's

---

[16] *Ibid.*, Baldwin's discussion of progressive and conservative tendencies and parties, 71–72; his summary of their nature and influence, 277–280.

[17] *Ibid.*, 71–72. Historians who have emphasized southerners' antipathy to party include Kenneth S. Greenberg, *Masters and Statesmen: The Political Culture of American Slavery* (Baltimore: Johns Hopkins University Press, 1985); George C. Rable, *The Confederate Republic: A Revolution Against Politics* (Chapel Hill: University of North Carolina Press, 1994).

[18] The closest Baldwin came to summarizing the traits of good leadership was in his assessment of why John Randolph was not a good party leader. Randolph "had not the coolness, the tact, the knowledge of men, the compromising disposition, the forbearance, the conciliation, the sympathy, the power of making friends of the many, of drawing to himself the confidence and respect of others, the sober gravity and weight of character which befit" a leader in a party system; *Party Leaders*, 178.

character, influenced his success, and affected the independence of the voters he addressed.

Baldwin analyzed speeches, letters, and documents, measuring the ways in which class and culture shaped ideas. For each leader, he evaluated vocabulary and style as well as the intellectual content of their communications, showing that what worked in speech was not effective in print, and vice versa. For Jefferson, Hamilton, and Randolph – well-born men dealing with a restricted suffrage – gentlemanly skills sufficed; for Clay and Jackson – men with middling origins, addressing all white men – they did not. Moving from the first parties to later ones, Baldwin evaluated the changes in communication required by a modernizing polity. So, for example, Whigs failed to defend their bank against Jackson because "the unlearned man of the backwoods knew the American people better than the erudite scholar of the refined metropolis." Wise leaders should encourage independence.[19] Baldwin's logic implied that skillful communicators with bad character might foster voters' weaknesses, not their strengths.

Baldwin's anxieties about independence bled profusely into his analyses of Jackson and Clay. Both southwesterners were first elected by voters who were so "independent in spirit" that candidates had to address their "robust common sense" and "unsophisticated feelings." They could not be fooled by "elaborate tricks and tinsel, the prettinesses of expression, the balanced sentences and glittering periods of oratory, much less the artful dodges and the slippery equivocations of a tricksy politician." Face-to-face, a candidate's character was readily observed and measured. When Clay and Jackson occupied a national stage, however, communications and character had a troubling relationship. Baldwin began with Jackson, using the material Stuart had disliked in the *Literary Messenger*. He recognized the leader's effectiveness: "if we measure power by success," he wrote, "the palm must be awarded to Jackson."[20] But Baldwin's symbolism showed his fear that the great Democrat might control voters in a new, modern way.

By evoking industrial power, Baldwin suggested that Jackson amassed unprecedented energies. The process began with Jackson's will: "His faculties did not sweep a large circle, but they worked like a steam engine within that circle." He transmitted his energy partly through patronage – that "most effective engine of Party," which "establishes communication all over the country" – and partly through "the most powerful press that ever supported an administration." His Washington *Globe* "was a whole troop of cavalry and a pack of flying artillery besides." Jackson's force was "centrifugal," because he gathered the "terrible might" of "freemen" and their "great individuality of will ... into a single and common effort." It was "centripetal," because his

---

[19] *Ibid.*, Jackson as unlearned, 335; laws and people, 84. Randolph, wrote Baldwin, "gave a new value to the quoted sentence," 267.
[20] *Ibid.*, characterization of southwestern voters, quote, 286, full discussion 284–286; power and success, 300.

"administration was a highly-charged galvanic battery, and the office-holders and aspiring politicians were the media ... by which the electric current flowed out upon the people." Jackson transmitted "the electric influence that arouses and animates a brave people," standing "pictorially" before them. As their "warlike and aggressive" nature responded to Jackson's will, Democrats moved in eerie unity.[21]

Clay, in contrast, demonstrated the cooperation among independent men. Baldwin's tense language vanished when he considered the Whig, whom he called the greatest American since Washington. He stressed Clay's gentlemanly skills in Congress. The beauty of his character lay in its "harmonious proportions," combining courage, will, and intelligence – "the physical, moral, and intellectual" – in near perfect balance. Clay spoke not to the "prejudices" or "passions of the masses," but to "reason," the "moral sense," and "generous sensibilities." With imagery that suggested the voluntary ties of sympathy, Baldwin described Clay's persuasive skills: "transfusing himself into others; now in the closet, now at the mess table, now in the committee room, in the drive, on the street, everywhere." Clay attracted voters by projecting "his character upon the imaginations and hearts of his generation." He represented a sound approach to a modernizing polity.[22]

Writing for a national audience, Baldwin tip-toed around slavery, but it subtly informed his discussion. He suggested that, while Clay's overweening ambition hurt his chances for the presidency, he was also blocked by Virginians too eager to defend slavery. Like the Virginians in *Flush Times*, they defended abstract principles and lived in the past. Baldwin admired the Virginians' states-rights principles, but he saw they would lose in contests "with the impulsive and eager utilitarianism and impatient wishes of the people." Privately, he argued that only a pragmatic, compromising politics could protect both slavery and the Union. As he wrote a friend, opposition to slavery's extension was so "popular" in the North that "politicians on both sides betray a very natural desire to get on the Sunny side of it." Given

---

[21] *Ibid.*, "Steam engine," 300; patronage as "engine," 318; press, 299; centrifugal and centripetal, 296; "terrible might," 65; administration as "battery," 318; nerves as "electric," 65; "pictorially," 293; "warlike and aggressive," 65, and often thereafter. Two brilliant older studies of the literature and politics of the Jacksonian era have influenced my reading here: Leo Marx, *The Machine in the Garden: Technology and the Pastoral Ideal in America* (New York: Oxford University Press, 1964); John William Ward, *Andrew Jackson, Symbol for an Age* (New York: Oxford University Press, 1955).

[22] *Party Leaders*, "Harmonious," 363; balanced character, 367; appeal to reason, 309; "transfusing," etc., 356; "projecting his character," 367. Little of Baldwin's admiration for Clay had appeared in the *Messenger*, where the emphasis on Jackson's power had apparently disconcerted Stuart. Baldwin frequently discussed Clay's failure to reach the White House. Ironically, he called the aging Kentuckian's failure to get the Whig nomination of 1848 his "last chance" (*Party Leaders*, 352), but Baldwin had been a member of the convention and had refused to support Clay; see Malcolm C. McMillan, "Joseph Glover Baldwin Reports on the Whig National Convention of 1848," *JSH* 25 (August, 1959): 366–382, which contains a letter explaining that he could not support Clay because he was unelectable.

that, it was foolish for southerners to demand abstract commitments about slavery's future.[23] When they opposed economic development, moreover, slaveholders thwarted those Whiggish northerners who would buy prosperity by leaving slavery alone. Despite Clay's ambitions, the Kentuckian's practicality seemed wise, and Baldwin thought that slaveholders ignored it at their peril.

Baldwin declined to deal directly with slavery. He granted that the "half-healed, half-covered sore of the slavery question" contained "inherent difficulties" but did not explain what they were. He equivocated about whether the institution was temporary or permanent. He criticized the foreign slave trade, and he called Randolph's manumission of his slaves a sign of the "noblest elements of character" (though kinder than it was wise). He approved Randolph's strictures against abolitionists who disregarded the "interests of the slave" and set back for years the "'cause of humanity to these unfortunates,'" implying that slaves deserved decent lives but agitation was wrong. Baldwin gingerly linked Virginia's decline with slavery, as he had done in *Flush Times*. While slavery encouraged "the pride, the individuality," the sociability, and the manners of Virginians, it had "other and worse effects," for masters lived in "luxury and elegance." Dependent on slaves, they had delusions of nobility instead of practical self-reliance. Even so, Baldwin dodged.[24] He called the "slavery question," not slavery itself, a "sore," but he could not say how to heal a "half-covered" wound.

Nonetheless, the model of slavery shaped Baldwin's analysis. Throughout, Baldwin made "individuality of will" the defining characteristic of Americans, and he never mentioned the denial of slaves' self-determination. But Jackson's dominance of the Democrats resembled slavery, although it was produced by free speech instead of a whip. To be sure, Baldwin portrayed Jackson both as a benevolent slaveholder and a patriotic leader. The president always claimed to act "in the name of freedom." But Baldwin cautioned: "Liberty is a very indefinite term, and conveys a very vague meaning." It can be "invaded in the small beginnings – in the cautious encroachments of tyranny, feeling its

---

[23] *Ibid.*, state rights, 87; popularity of antislavery, 373–374. Baldwin believed that the states retained their sovereignty and the right to secede "in order to escape from an unconstitutional law" (109), but he also thought these doctrines were not especially useful. Jackson, he said, "struck down the doctrine of State Rights" and substituted more popular "national doctrines" (348). Halfway through the Civil War, Baldwin wrote an unpublished fragment about California in which he satirized antebellum southerners' propensity for defending abstractions and their failure to consider concrete gains and losses; see Richard E. Amacher and George W. Polhemus, eds., *The Flush Times of California* (Athens: University of Georgia Press, 1966), 33.

[24] *Party Leaders*, "sore," 355; Randolph's slaves, 238–239; slavery in Virginia, 153–54. After Baldwin's death, his brother Cornelius wrote Alexander Stuart that Joe aspired to be a "backwoods Lord Braugham, as he would have expressed it." The British Whig statesman and founder of the *Edinburgh Review* was an ironic model, because he was well-known for his role in outlawing slavery in the British Empire. See Cornelius Baldwin to Stuart, January 14, 1867, in Stuart-Baldwin Papers, UVA.

way gradually to ungranted and unlawful dominion." That creeping tyranny "requires sharper acumen than the masses possess, to see at the right time." Jackson led men to obey rather than act for themselves.[25] At every turn, *Party Leaders* revealed Baldwin's fear that a man like Jackson might virtually enslave free men.

Baldwin's analysis aimed at Jackson, but he also attributed voters' submission to human nature. Jackson's popularity rested on the "HEROIC ELEMENT." Focusing on the psychology of crowds, Baldwin claimed that it was "the nature of men to side with the strong." He argued that "the crowd must look up to a man before they will applaud him," much less "be governed by him," and they will only look up to men "they fear, or, at least, whose qualities they fear." Because men feared him, Jackson had a hypnotic quality that "works more powerfully upon men than virtue or intellect." It was "a fascination of the eye which charms like the serpent."

Aware that this analysis contradicted his emphasis on Americans' individuality, Baldwin temporized. "Love wins," he asserted, and "power commands." But love comes from "personal relation" and "proximity," and the "man of a nation" is only an "ideal" figure – "the hero of the crowd." Without personal connections, Jackson's power rested on fear. Indeed, Baldwin suggested, frightened men would vote for Satan if he had "human form."[26] When power commanded fear, independence vanished, and, with it, the security of popular government. The martial language with which Baldwin concluded his book left little doubt that violent conflict was in his mind.[27]

Despite his effort at objectivity in *Party Leaders*, Baldwin's immediate fears focused on slavery. In an 1848 letter to a fellow Alabamian, he had exposed his concerns about a degraded democracy's impact on slavery, with his own ambitions no doubt in mind. New York politicians were the "fishiest, and most mercenary & predatory in the Union." And, "on the skirts of all parties, in the large cities," men lived on the spoils. Southerners could not "pander our interests to their cupidity." If individuality was protected by "equality of condition," as he wrote in *Party Leaders*, poor men in northern cities might obey leaders less attached to slavery than was Andrew Jackson. Writing Stuart in 1852, Baldwin had warned that if northerners blocked slavery's extension, the

---

[25] "individuality," see n. 15; vagueness of freedom, *Party Leaders*, 332–333. In his account of Patrick Henry, the "almost perfect orator," Baldwin also noted that Henry's speeches could destroy "individuality and selfhood in the masses under his spell" and make them "seem but as one man," 166 (once again, the art of mass persuasion practiced by a southerner).

[26] Ibid., 294–295. The reference to Satan was specifically to John Milton's Satan from *Paradise Lost*, and Baldwin wrote that he would get more votes in France "at least" than François Fenelon, the seventeenth-century religious thinker.

[27] When Baldwin shifted his focus from Jackson to Clay, as his book drew to a close, Baldwin wrote that he turned from the "man of War" to the "man of Peace," but his style did not make that shift. Instead, martial imagery colored his entire account of political competition. Probably the greatest number of references are to medieval jousting and Sir Walter Scott's *Ivanhoe*; see, for example, the comparison of John Randolph to Scott's character Brian De Bois-Guilbert, 323.

Union would collapse. He repeatedly suggested that cooperation and economic development could avert the crisis. But frightened men thought poorly. When fearful southerners jettisoned compromise, they encouraged the Republican Party in the North. As Baldwin's hopes waned, he removed his family to the safety – and his ambition to the possibilities – of California, and *Party Leaders* was lost in the politics of slavery.[28]

MASTERY AND SELF-MASTERY

William Smith merged his fears about slavery and political self-determination into some of the strangest writing that came from the antebellum South. Like Baldwin, Smith thought self-government demanded independent leaders and voters; he, too, wanted Whiggish nationalism to mix with protection for slavery; and he reached similar sticking points. But Smith lacked Baldwin's confidence. While Baldwin analyzed the social psychology of mass-based politics with an instinctive poise, Smith probed inward, agonizing about who he was. If Baldwin's irony masked reservations about American politics, Smith's dark humor revealed much greater forebodings. Rife with the author's self-doubts, it found painful tensions between the ethics of self-determination and political ambition. Especially in his bizarre satire *As It Is*, Smith showed the corrosive influence of slavery's presence in the rising South.

Smith saw political ambition as a legitimate expression of self-determination. Yet, like other educated Americans, he believed that extreme ambition was a publically dangerous and privately debilitating appetite. Like all aspects of self-determination, ambition needed self-control. Smith had learned independence the hard way: orphaned before he was eight, he grew up in Tuscaloosa with the help of struggling siblings, the oldest of whom – a beloved brother – was killed by the Mexicans at Goliad in 1836. Recurrent setbacks taught Smith that self-determination required ceaseless effort. His mother, he said, had inscribed "the word *ambition* on my heart," and he constantly ran for office. For thirty years, he pursued acclaim while questioning his need for it. He once asked on the floor of Congress: "What would life be worth without ambition?"[29] Not knowing, he organized his ideas around a problematic mixture of desires and aversions.

Smith's earliest writing showed him connecting slavery, autonomy, and ambition. Late in 1836, while the twenty-one-year-old was editing *Bachelor's Button*, he wrote "The Whig, or the Diary of a Young Candidate," a little satire. Like the peculiar "Memoirs of an Ambitious Man," which recalled his troubled childhood and his blinding of a slave, "The Whig" carried

---

[28] "Fishiest," quoted in McMillan, ed., "Baldwin Reports on the Whig National Convention," 374; "pander," 375.
[29] Mother and ambition, "The Memoirs of an Ambitious Man," *Bachelor's Button* (January, 1837): 2: 24; life without ambition, *Congressional Globe, Appendix*, 32nd Congress, 2nd Session (January 5, 1852), 57.

personal freight. It described a young "man of feeling," who repressed his nature to run for office: "why should my MIND be enchained in this perplexing bondage?" the candidate mused. He approached voters with "DECEIT" and "Hypocrisy" instead of the "sympathy" he showed friends. The candidate's reflections about his lost "liberty" were broken by a slave who sought a favor for his master. Reluctant to alienate a voter, the Whig granted the master's request but resolved to leave politics rather than lose his "dear, sweet independence."[30]

Ambition triumphed, however, and, with it, more tension. The Whig stifled his emotions to woo three voters: an overseer, a woodman, and a wagonman. The overseer's "fierce dog" – "the best nigger dog in all these parts" – frightened the candidate, who suppressed his fear to befriend the man's wife and caress their baby. The woodman had yeoman-like virtue and claimed hope for his son's future but not the "withering" anxiety of personal ambition. Although the Whig thought such a distinction might be "untenable," he admired the woodman's "ennobling philosophy" and preferred his vote to "every other vote in the county" – until he met his next potential voter, the wagonman. Because he carried gin "just for such fellows," the Whig got drunk with the rude man, who was clearly of the lowest sort.[31]

After his trying search for votes, the Whig relaxed with his feelings, but the contrast between slavery and freedom preyed on his mind as he reflected about his affections for a young girl. When he tried to cage a wild bird for her, he waxed sentimental about "liberty": "Lives there a creature who doats not on thee as its dearest gift!" Although the candidate had barely noticed the slave bearing his master's message, the young man sympathized with a bird and chafed at the self-imposed bondage of ambition.[32] He was not independent like the woodman he admired.

Continuing to pursue office in spite of his discontent, Smith's Whig became cynical about liberty. He practiced his "first harangue," hoping it would lift him "to the very pinnacle of Fame." But when the time came to speak, he panicked and fled to a nearby hotel. From there, he heard his opponent speak and the crowd roar its approval. Recovering his senses, the Whig returned to the waiting voters and delivered a speech about "FREEDOM" and "LIBERTY." By saying "'Liberty – liberty – liberty,'" he could "gain every ear and excite every mind," for the word had "magic in it." After he worked his magic, however, the Whig celebrated and got drunk. As he sobered up and staggered into the street, he fell into a mud hole where his "face was buried in slime" – the odd story's last words.[33] The physical humor underscored the candidate's shame. Enslaved by ambition, he had deceived voters and damaged his

---

[30] "The Whig, Or the Diary of a Young Candidate. By a Man of Feeling" appeared in *Bachelor's Button* (December, 1836): 1:13–28 and (January, 1837): 2: 7–14; quoted passages, 1: 13–14.
[31] Ibid., dog, 1: 18; hope and anxiety, 1: 23–24; gin, 1: 26.
[32] Ibid., 1: 21.
[33] "The Whig," preparation, 2: 7; listening to opponent, 2: 11; liberty, 2: 13; slime, 2: 14. The slime-covered face may be interpreted as a reference to the loss of honor from public

self-respect. At twenty-one, Smith had defined problems he could neither evade nor resolve.

Smith's little satire addressed anxieties he planned to live with. He began editing the capital city's Whig newspaper, the Tuscaloosa *Independent Monitor*, and he was elected mayor in 1839. He served two terms in the legislature. At Christmas in 1841, when Smith wrote and his friend Jere Clemens read a poem asking the speaker to adjourn, he joked about the "House of Asses" who should "bray no more." Smith was learning to enjoy the comradeship of other ambitious men. Two years later, he broke with the Whigs, left politics for the law, married, and began a family. When his wife died, Smith moved to the nearby small town of Fayette, where he married again in 1847, built a second legal practice, and became a militia general. As his ambitions reawakened, Smith tested his political ideas anonymously in an essay for Simms's *Southern Quarterly Review* in 1848. "War and its Incidents" compared the Mexican War to the wars between Rome and Numidia in the second century BCE.[34] Once again, Smith's subject was ambition, and this time he considered its impact on the electorate.

Smith's essay warned that American voters could become supine dependents of "military chieftains." Concerned that a general was about to become president, he suggested that the United States could evolve, like Rome, from an agrarian republic into an empire. With recurrent images of dominance and submission, Smith explained how war bred "imperious" men, who misled voters with tales of their heroism. A Roman general gave "a speech for the mob": "a regular democratic affair, with quite enough of the demagogue in it to modernize it." Rome's example prompted "irritating reflections" about Andrew Jackson's dominance of men who were "born to be controlled" – "like women." Smith praised sturdy yeomen but claimed that war made some of them "idle, dissolute and lazy." And war encouraged men's violent tendencies. Predicting the candidacy of Zachary Taylor, Smith admired the general's

---

humiliation, but Smith insisted that the candidate was concerned about both his inner sense of worth and what others thought of him. In Bertram Wyatt-Brown's terms, Smith's conflict is between shame and guilt, and his ambivalence resembles that the author finds in Nathaniel Hawthorne's story "My Kinsman, Major Molineaux," with which *Southern Honor* begins; *Southern Honor: Ethics and Behavior in the Old South* (New York: Oxford University Press, 1982), 3–24.

[34] The anecdote about Smith and Clemens, along with the text of the poetic resolution, is in Anne Easby-Smith, *William Russell Smith of Alabama* (Philadelphia: Dolphin Press, 1931), 40–41. Tuscaloosa was an important center of Whiggery in Alabama, and Smith's elections were due in part to the support of Whigs. Smith, "War and Its Incidents," *SQR* 25 (January 1848): 1–54. See Michael O'Brien's comments on authors' anonymity in "On the Mind of the Old South and Its Accessibility," in *Rethinking the South: Essays in Intellectual History* (Baltimore: Johns Hopkins University Press, 1988), 22–23, and, more particularly about the *Southern Quarterly Review*, in *Conjectures of Order: Intellectual Life and the American South, 1810–1860*, 2 vols. (Chapel Hill: University of North Carolina Press, 2004), 1: 558–562. "The Whig" was unsigned but, because all of Smith's readers knew he was the main writer for his magazine, and his style was odd enough to be instantly recognized, it could hardly have been anonymous to local readers.

pledges to break the "shackles" of party but warned that republics fall from "*success* in war."³⁵

Like Baldwin, Smith used parties but found them disconcerting. Even though he had become a Democrat, "Incidents of War" echoed Whig assaults on Jackson. In the brief lull after the Compromise of 1850, Smith successfully ran for Congress as a Unionist, defeating a Southern Rights Democrat. In 1853, he was reelected as a Union Democrat, defeating both a Whig and a Southern Rights Democrat. Two years after that, he won again over the same Southern Rights man, but now Smith ran as a member of the American or Know-Nothing Party, which represented the remnants of Whiggery. Ambition caused Smith's changing affiliations, for parties were in flux. Geographically diverse, his district included poor farmers in Fayette County, townsmen in Tuscaloosa, and wealthy planters in its Black Belt counties.³⁶ Parties connected him to voters, but Smith mistrusted them and saw himself as independent.

Smith's six-year experience in the House increased his anxieties without tempering his ambition. Like Baldwin, he wanted to ignore slavery and attend to issues that might unite North and South. While a Democrat, Smith supported the "Young America" movement and called for economic growth, continental expansion, and restraint abroad. Young Americans, he said, were self-determined men: "all those intellectual persons who entered life with a laudable ambition to make themselves *men*" and ascended "by the force and power of genius and learning." Smith claimed to speak for the plain people, too. He advocated a homestead bill because it would create "*social independence*" by

---

[35] "War and its Incidents," "chieftans," 5; "imperious," 36; "relying on disasters," 11; the general's speech, 37; "irritating reflections," 39; born for control, 36; impact of war on many men, 3; Taylor as "brilliant contrast," who relied on people not party, 41; fall of republics, 51. Smith opposed both Generals Scott and Taylor in 1848 and supported Michigan Democrat Lewis Cass for the presidency. Smith's comparison of late republican Rome and the contemporary United States showed his preference for the patrician general Sulla over the "new man" Marius, but, as his political position suggests, he blamed both military men (and the Roman Senate as well) for the collapse of the republic. Marius was the demagogue who prompted Smith's reflections on Jackson. Smith's attitude to war was probably also affected by the loss of his father and brother. "War and its Incidents" contained a "digression" (46) on the "melancholy thought that FAME belongs to those who survive the battle and not to those who fall!" (44). Smith insisted that "the historian seems to have nothing to do with the dead! not even to count them with accuracy!" (45).

[36] Smith commented on the floor of the House: "I have never coalesced with any faction.... I had to fight my way back to Washington through both the Democratic and Whig parties," *Congressional Globe, Appendix*, 33nd Congress, 1st Session, January 18, 1854, 74. He won elections largely due to his majorities in Fayette and Tuscaloosa County, both of which had been his residences. See Lewy Dorman, *Party Politics in Alabama from 1850 through 1860* (Tuscaloosa: University of Alabama Press, repr. 1955, c. 1935), 184–185, for election returns, by county and district. Smith's district incorporated some of the richest plantation regions of the state as well as one of the poorest counties – Fayette. When Joseph Baldwin ran for Congress in this district in 1849, his extremely poor showing in Fayette cost him the election; Smith's ability to carry both the poor county and the town was critical. By 1853, however, Smith was courting the Democratic party leadership, as he was "*looking ahead*," Smith to party leader Bolling Hall, October 20, 1853, in Hall Papers, ADAH.

granting citizens land – unlike profligate spending that fostered an "order of nabobs." But Smith attacked immigrants and Catholics, and, like Baldwin, he insisted that urban spoilsmen fooled the ignorant and used ill-gotten power to attack slavery.[37] Not fitting any party, he claimed to be his own man.

Smith walked a fine line. On the floor of the House, he had denounced "secession in all its phases – in all its aims, and even in all its abstractions," and he had proclaimed his intention to "live and die" with that position. Although he belittled antislavery northerners, he also criticized southern aggression. In 1856, he attended the American Party convention, supported Fillmore, and was briefly considered for the vice presidential slot. But in 1857, after Republicans absorbed most northern Whigs, Smith lost to the Southern Rights congressional candidate he had once trounced.[38] He only carried Tuscaloosa County. Ambition and independence seemed irreconcilable.

While ensnarled in political controversy, Smith met personal challenges that turned his attention to literature. After his second wife died in 1853, leaving Smith with four small children, he met Wilhemine Easby, who was visiting Fillmore's daughter at the White House, and the next year he married

[37] "Young America" explained in "The Census Printing – Presidential Candidates: Speech of Hon. W. R. Smith of Alabama, in the House of Representatives, March 18, 1852," in *Congressional Globe, Appendix*, 32d Congress, 1st Session, 370; "social independence" explained in "The Homestead Bill: Speech of Hon. W. R. Smith, of Alabama, in the House of Representatives, April 27, 1852," in *Congressional Globe, Appendix*, 32d Congress, 1st Session, 514. Smith commented on his independence in supporting a bill proposed by his friend, Jeremiah Clemens ("whose genius has made him a peer among Senators"); see "Lieutenant General, Speech of Mr. Smith, of Alabama in the House of Representatives, January 5, 1853," *Congressional Globe, Appendix*, 32nd Congress, 1st Session, 58. Smith's daughter covers some of his political career, but it is best followed through the pages of the *Congressional Globe*, which also illustrates Smith's off-beat humor in action. For his attack on New York Democrats and urban spoilsmen, see "'Hards' and 'Softs,' Speech of Hon. W. R. Smith, of Alabama, in the House of Representatives, January 18, 1854," *Congressional Globe, Appendix*, 33nd Congress, 1st Session, 72–76; the worst assault on Catholics and immigrants was in "The Naturalization Laws – Policy of the Roman Catholic Church, Speech of Hon. W. R. Smith, of Alabama, in the House of Representatives, January 15, 1853," in *Congressional Globe, Appendix*, 33nd Congress, 2d Session, 94–103. Like many other of his speeches, Smith had these printed for distribution. During his service, Smith also published an illustrated poem opposing the recognition given to Hungarian revolutionary Louis Kossuth; see *Kossuth Coppered, or the Banquet at the Capital of Laputa, containing Gulliver's Great Speech* (New York: T. Frere, 1852). Although neither mentions Smith, the best accounts of the congressional politics during the period of his service are in Holt, *Rise and Fall of the Whigs*, and both volumes of Freehling's *The Road to Disunion*. A recent study of Young America is Yonatan Eyal, *The Young American Movement and the Transformation of the Democratic Party, 1828–1861* (Cambridge: Cambridge University Press, 2007), which emphasizes the moderate antislavery views of the movement and slights southern participation.

[38] Quoted in "'Hards' and 'Softs,'" 75. Easby-Smith describes Smith's participation in the American Party convention of 1856, drawing from contemporary newspapers, and she also notes his nomination for the vice presidential slot; *William Russell Smith*, 79–81. According to Dorman, Smith was defeated in 1857 on the basis of his congressional record, when his opponents claimed that he had "voted to censure Preston Brooks for caning Sumner" and opposed filibustering expeditions into Kansas; *Party Politics in Alabama*, 140.

the nineteen-year-old. She quickly bore three children, and, after his defeat, Smith resumed legal practice in Tuscaloosa. When the third child died at three months of age, her parents consoled themselves with books. William tutored Wilhemine in Greek and published legal works.

Following another election loss in 1859, a shaken but still ambitious Smith produced two major literary works in 1860. Aimed at different audiences, their themes were related. The long poem *The Uses of Solitude* was published in Tuscaloosa, and the satiric novel *As It Is* was published in Albany, New York. Smith's Phi Beta Kappa poem had preached self-reliance to young men and their friends. Hoping to discourage secession, Smith told them to muster "the power to be / Still in the uproar, deaf to all the shouts / of angered multitudes"; and he cited leaders from Cicero to Daniel Boone who were inspired to greatness by solitude.[39] In contrast to his poem about constructive leaders, Smith's strange novel *As It Is* speared politicians who failed to think for themselves. And its place of publication, timing, and content suggested Smith's wish to persuade northern voters to reform politics instead of slavery. Seeing secession and war on the horizon, Smith wrote from fear, but he acted, nonetheless.

Published anonymously, *As It Is* showed Smith's distrust of the nation's political elite. It featured both northern and southern politicians too mired in corruption to be independent. Smith's tale centered on the misadventures of Jack Sterling, a freshman congressman who was unable resist the dissipation of the "Federal City." Smith ridiculed Washington's politicos by giving them comic names like Pustleponch, Blunderbuss, and Clodhead, saving positive names for Sterling and for Belvedere, the only statesman in a miserable lot. In addition to detailing the futile attempt by Sterling and other "conservative" men to elect Belvedere Speaker of the House, Smith ridiculed the capital's corruption: whoring, gambling, drinking, infidelity, influence-peddling, bribery, deceit, and plunder of the public treasury.[40] It was wise to omit his name on the title page.

In treating an ambitious congressman's quest for selfhood and success, *As It Is* exposed Smith's long-standing anxieties. Something of a mishmash, the novel mixed satire and romance, and Smith's flawed hero represented American,

---

[39] Lines from *The Uses of Solitude* (Tuscaloosa: Printed for the Alabama Alpha of the Phi Beta Kappa Society of the University at Tuscaloosa, 1860), 33. Easby-Smith briefly describes her father's first marriages, *William Russell Smith*, 44, noting that one daughter from his second marriage died "in early youth." She dates the death of Smith's second wife in 1853 and relates the story about Smith's meeting his next wife (the author's mother) at the White House. Because Fillmore stepped down in early 1853, Smith either met Wilhemine before his wife died or immediately thereafter. Easby-Smith also describes the Smiths's "great grief" on the death of their third child and attributes his tutoring of his wife to an effort "to divert her mind," 87–88. Unless Easby-Smith's chronology is flawed, Wilhemine had three babies in the first four years of her marriage. *As It Is* (Albany, NY: Munsell & Rowland, 1860).

[40] *As It Is*, "Federal City," 35; "conservative," 88–89. Smith called Sterling "General" as the book opened but eventually dropped the title. Smith was himself a militia general by this time. Smith described his hero as a "thin, tall man" (10), perhaps to avoid comparison in the event readers knew his authorship. Smith was short and stocky.

southern, and universal themes. Sterling was a vaguely southern politician with literary interests. He lacked self-control, a weakness highlighted when he fell in love with a married woman as the book began. She was Beatrice Curtis, a "perfect woman" named after Dante Alighieri's famous heroine. Far too vain and hungry for approval to be self-reliant, Sterling carried a copy of the *Divine Comedy* with "numerous pencilings and marginal notes," and he preened when people "peered into the book – of course, it was respectable to read Dante." The congressman had a good mind and a kind heart, but he was impulsive. Unlike his friend Belvedere, who wisely "gathered briars for the pleasure of plucking away the thorns," Sterling "pulled flowers by the way" and "expected" to rise in the world without "patience" or "industry."[41]

Nevertheless, Sterling's conduct toward the orphan Lily (a pretty flower) suggested an outside chance for his improvement. Smith made his hero half benevolent by borrowing, like Evans, from popular fiction in which orphans and their patriarchal guardians had romantic bonds. On his first day in the Federal City, Sterling was taken to a fancy brothel by Senator Burton, "the great king-key-keeper of all the secret luxuries of the city." Sterling was shocked at the "den of pollution," the "girls," and their madam, but he was charmed by the madam's ward Lily, "a mere child ten or twelve years of age." When he pulled Lily onto his lap, one of the "girls" chided her, and Lily retorted, "I am sure you sit in gentlemen's laps," insisting that Sterling was a "good man." Predictably, he "kidnapped" Lily, hiding her in a hotel room next to his, where politicians gathered. Disguising Lily as a boy named Ernest, Sterling got her a job as a congressional page. But, to get her appointment, he agreed to vote for the election of one Vereprompt as doorkeeper and manager of pages.[42] Smith gave Sterling good intentions even as he acted on impulse, bent the law, placed Lily in new jeopardy, and compromised his integrity.

Smith seems to have aimed at portraying legitimate mastery and grateful submission, with mere hints of romance, but doubts about Sterling's benevolence surfaced from the moment he put Lily on his lap. Smith marked Lily's sexuality. Sterling called his disguised ward "my little Ganymede" and compared her to Rosalind, the cross-dressing heroine who called herself Ganymede in Shakespeare's comedy *As You Like It*. In one scene, Belvedere burst into the room where Ernest/Lily stood in the bathtub, "but the towel had a happy

---

[41] Ibid., "perfect" Beatrice, 14; *Divine Comedy*, 15; Belvedere and Sterling compared, 152. Smith assessed Sterling's personality with tongue in cheek. "With all his fine qualities and his intellectual capacities," the hero was "given to habits of affectation," and he had an "air of conceit," 15.

[42] Ibid., Burton's title, 37; Lily's age, 45; "girls," 41; Lily's retort, 46; "den of pollution," 57; "kidnapped," 99. The brothel scene featured a dance-floor brawl between one of the girls and a senator, which resulted in a police raid. While Smith avoided risqué language, he explained that the girls' affections were a "marketable commodity," 44. He drew attention to Sterling's flawed character even as he rescued the orphan. When Lily had a convulsion from excitement, Sterling was "wild with apprehension, not so much for the life of the frail creature before him, as for his own personal honor," 60.

location, and she sank down into the water!" In another, Lily "wrapped herself" in Sterling's robe, kissed his pillow, and dreamed that he was kissing her.[43] Although Smith made Lily more child than woman and Sterling more father than lover, his ambivalence was striking. *As You Like It*, Shakespeare's playful comedy, became *As It Is*, a satire of modern social relations.

Like Sterling's relationship with Lily, his illicit pursuit of Beatrice connected mastery and self-mastery, and it linked Smith's plot with slavery. Beatrice's doting father was a sugar planter who gave her slaves so she would not rely on "white servants." And Beatrice was "beloved" by her slaves. On the other hand, the planter's money corrupted her husband. A self-made man, Curtis had been a dedicated physician and devoted husband until Beatrice's father gave him $20,000. With unearned wealth, Curtis disintegrated. As he chased the "high life," drank to excess, and gambled, Sterling's flirtation with Beatrice aroused his suspicions. Losing all self-control, the jealous husband abused his wife, seduced another woman, and, in his most depraved moment, fondled his thirteen-year-old sister-in-law's breast as she slept.[44] The absolute antithesis of self-determination, Curtis destroyed himself, and Sterling only contributed to his ruin. A tangled plot obscured the connection between slaves, wealth, and decadence, however, and Smith made Beatrice mostly good and her father well-intentioned.

More obviously, Smith's Washington teemed with slaves to ambition, and Sterling's political autonomy was as shaky as his morality. His maneuvers showed his struggle to be independent – and his failure. When he wangled Lily/Ernest's appointment as a page, Sterling qualified his commitment to Vereprompt by noting that all party members voted "under the control of our leaders." And, when he sought Belvedere's election as Speaker, Sterling resisted his party but used its tactics. Clodhead, the leading candidate, declaimed on "the sublime beauty of partisan faith," while Belvedere

---

[43] *Ibid.*, Ganymede/Rosalind, 83; bathtub scene, 158; Lily's love for Sterling, 135–136; women as objects of control, n. 35, *supra*. The advertisement placed by the madam after Lily's disappearance was headed "kidnapped or seduced away," 99. Although, for the most part, Smith emphasized that Sterling was thoughtless rather than evil, it is also possible that Smith subconsciously drew here on his family history to suggest pedophilia. He claimed to be a cousin to Wade Hampton of South Carolina, whose young daughter had been molested by wealthy planter and former congressman, James Henry Hammond. (Smith's mother was a Hampton, but I have been unable to find any close blood relationship in genealogy sources.) The facts about the Hampton scandal are in Drew Faust, *James Henry Hammond and the Old South: A Design for Mastery* (Baton Rouge: Louisiana State University Press, 1982), 241–245. To these suggestive passages, Smith added homoeroticism. Ernest/Lily carelessly led his/her spinster music teacher into infatuation and mischievously flirted with another young girl. On the relevance of sexual scenes for the larger culture, see Elizabeth Barnes, *States of Sympathy: Seduction and Democracy in the American Novel* (New York: Columbia University Press, 1997).

[44] *As It Is*, servants, 61; "beloved," 69; "high life," 72. Smith expounded at length on Curtis's ruination by wealth, summarizing: "He was no longer the same man. The fixed attention, the staid gravity of appearance, so inseparable from the energetic pursuit of business, had given way to feverish restlessness. A vague pleasure-hunting look disfigured his once resolute countenance," 74.

complained that "politicians" foolishly made partisanship "the touch-stone of integrity." Belvedere lost to party discipline, despite Sterling's attempt to corral votes.[45] Independent enough to challenge his party, Sterling was too ambitious to abjure it.

After his failure to win Belvedere's election, Sterling opted for self-gratification, yielding to temptations he had felt all along. Instead of rising in the world, he fell. He attended showy parties where Washingtonians swapped favors, and he drifted further into immorality by indiscreetly wooing Beatrice. When he gave her a copy of Johann Wolfgang von Goethe's *Wilhelm Meister*, a popular *bildungsroman*, the couple privately discussed its merits until "the timidity of guilt" silenced them. And Sterling stroked his vanity with other flirtation. At one lavish dance, he met a Dr. Thimblerigg, who sought a $200,000 congressional appropriation for a soap-making machine. Thimblerigg asked his wife to feign Sterling's seduction and win his vote, and Sterling enjoyed the "game" she played.[46] Sterling's desire for acceptance by men and by women was leading him badly astray. His weak ego could not withstand corruption.

[45] Ibid., "southern," 76; NY Democrat, 91; "control," 84; Clodhead's faith, 87; Belvedere's sarcasm, 98. Smith's account of Belvedere's attempt at election drew from his role in the contested speakership election of 1855, a matter his northern readers would have understood. During that contest, Smith and roughly thirty men, mostly former Whigs from border states, refused to support either the Republican or Democratic candidates and helped to freeze the business of the House for weeks. The group Smith voted with originally contained members from twelve states, and it was primarily composed of inexperienced congressmen. In *As It Is*, Smith makes Sterling's coalition contain thirty members, one from each state, with most of them new members, and the group meets in his room, under his leadership (100–105). He also makes the coalition a revolt against the Democrats, but Smith's Alabama colleague Percy Walker (Pope Walker's brother) explained that the actual rebels opposed both southern (Democratic) and northern (Republican) extremists, a view echoed by Humphrey Marshall (former Whig) of Kentucky, who received the group's first vote; *Congressional Globe*, 34th Congress, 1st Session, 37, 47. For overviews of the controversy, see Holt, *Rise and Fall of the Whigs*, 961–963, and William E. Gienapp, *The Origins of the Republican Party, 1852–1856* (New York: Oxford University Press, 1987), 240–246. Gienapp emphasizes the significance of the election for the Republicans' plans to absorb northern Know-Nothings. Holt observes that some southern Know-Nothings scattered their votes rather than vote for a Democrat, but Smith was not among them. He voted for William Aiken, Democrat of South Carolina, on the final roll call, with "great reluctance"; *Congressional Globe*, 34th Congress, 1st Session, 341. Holt incidentally confirms Smith's claim that congressional patronage, including the doorkeeper's position, was involved in the dispute; *Rise and Fall of the Whigs*, 962.

[46] *As It Is*, "timidity," 164; Thimblerigg's "game," 201. Sterling admires Goethe as a "true man as well as a great genius," who loved nature and the "genius in man," 163. Johann Wolfgang von Goethe's *bildungsroman* was popular in the South, although southerners resisted the perfectionist implications of his Romanticism; see Fox-Genovese and Genovese, *Mind of the Master Class*, 577–578. There were many English editions of Goethe's most popular works; one of the most common was Thomas Carlyle's translation, *Wilhelm Meister's Apprenticeship and Travels*, 2 vols., rev. ed. (Boston: Ticknor, Reed, and Fields, 1851). By putting his positive evaluations of Goethe in the mouth of Sterling, whose morality was suspect, Smith may have criticized the Romantic author, but the perfect Beatrice also admired Goethe. Sterling responded with a "throb of passion" (204) to Mrs. Thimblerigg's flirtation, and her husband urged her to "Cultivate him, my love, cultivate him: *and do it up brown, at that*" (205). The

As his hero stumbled about, Smith suddenly reintroduced slavery into his already awkward plot. And the new twist showed Smith's concerns about antislavery partisans' use of print. When Congress had convened in 1859, organization of the House was delayed while Republicans struggled to find a candidate for the speakership who had not signed a promotional publication for Hinton Helper's *The Impending Crisis of the South*. Helper's book had alarmed southern congressmen by urging white farmers to revolt against slavery, and Republicans could not elect a Speaker without a southern vote. After cloakroom maneuvering and heated speeches, Republicans finally found a candidate who had not endorsed Helper's book. *As It Is* substituted a poem called "Ignipotence Abroad" for Helper's book, but readers surely recognized Smith's allusion when the dissipated Senator Burton received the manuscript poem with a note requesting his endorsement – to help the poet find a "respectable publisher."⁴⁷ Like Helper's book, the poem warned of an impending crisis. Would Burton – the man who took Sterling to a brothel on his first day in Washington – endorse it?

Before resolving the issue, Smith reproduced an incredible seventeen pages of "Ignipotence Abroad" to show that politicians were driving the Union into hell, watched by the devil himself. Monstrous in a comic sort of way, Smith's devil has sins like those of the men in *As It Is*. He is a vain womanizer, a gambler, and a power-hungry politician of mythic proportions. As the poem opens, the devil discusses with his "favorite" wife his upcoming visit to Washington, which adjoins "the hot precincts of hell." Eager to enlarge his empire, he will investigate reports that "several of the sovereign states / Are soon to be annexed to my dominion." While he obsessively dresses, hiding his tail in his pants, the dandy devil describes Washington's politicians to his wife.

The devil's preferences explain who is most diabolical in the Federal City, and, not surprisingly, his favorites are northern antislavery men. He claims that "G——s [Joshua Giddings, Republican of Ohio] would wade through sulphureous flames / To liberate all sooty colored dames." Indeed, the devil has "a fellow feeling" for the whole state of "O – – o," which is "good at negro-stealing": "At negro-killing, she is even better, / And substitutes *starvation* for

---

best account of congressional corruption is Mark W. Sommers, *The Plundering Generation: Corruption and the Crisis of the Union, 1849–1861* (Oxford: Oxford University Press, 1987), which makes it clear that Smith's satire did not exaggerate.

⁴⁷ All quotes, *As It Is*, 214. Freehling discusses the significance of the contested speakership election of 1859 from the perspective of alarmed southerners in *Road to Disunion: Secessionists Triumphant*, 246–256, 265–266. Smith made the author of "Ignipotence Abroad" southern, too; he had inherited a plantation and forty slaves but had recklessly gambled them away. Burton had loaned him $500 to cover a risky gamble, extracting a promise from the poet that he would never gamble again if he lost. He won, and later sent Burton the poem, hoping he would give him still more money. Episode with the southern gambler-poet and Burton, 117–119. Ignipotence was not a word commonly used in the nineteenth-century, but Smith probably adapted it from Alexander Pope's translation of the *Iliad*, where "power ignipotent" belonged to Vulcan.

the *fetter*." More briefly, the devil admires proslavery politicians like "W ––e" (Henry Wise, Democrat of Virginia) for their quixotic tilting at windmills. Like Baldwin, Smith thought the pursuit of abstract protections for slavery was counterproductive, but he did not linger over southern sins. Although the devil plans to take the northern and southern states "one by one," he indicates his satanic affection for northerners and suggests a racist rationale for slavery.[48]

As the devil sets out on his journey to Washington, "Ignipotence Abroad" anticipates the catastrophe of civil war. He comes upon a railroad where two Irishmen and a German have maliciously removed a rail. Pleased at their wickedness, the devil watches an apocalyptic train wreck. Thrilled at mangled corpses and survivors, he is delighted that the perpetrators are also crushed by a runaway car. Through most of *As It Is*, Smith blamed politicians for their own corruption; in "Ignipotence Abroad," he made foreign voters cause the wreck of the Union.[49] Senator Burton refused to endorse "Ignipotence Abroad." He "thought well" of it and sent the author $400 to help him find a publisher, but he declined to have his name used "in any way." The corrupt politician valued ambition too much to take a principled stand with voters, who might prefer to ignore the impending crisis.

Smith's exposé was too self-reflexive to have a satisfactory ending, and he left his jumbled plot hanging fire. Within the book's last pages, Sterling yielded to his passions and expressed them to Beatrice, who sent him packing. Her dissolute husband was shot to death by a crooked gambler. While Smith hinted that the new widow or a grown-up Lily could help Sterling improve, he gave no clue about how. On the back leaf of his book, Smith promised that a sequel named "Love's Apprenticeship" was "in press"; if it was, however, the Civil War prevented its appearance.[50] By publishing *As It is* anonymously in Albany, Smith consigned it to literary oblivion. It is ironic, however, that he did not attach his name to his work. Independence was hard in 1860, especially for an ambitious Unionist trapped in the politics of slavery.

Although the wild plot of *As It Is* grew from Smith's experience, his readers may have missed its southern roots. He made his characters vaguely southern, often by indirection, and he evaluated them by standards that belonged

---

[48] All quotes, *As It Is*, 218–220. Smith suggested that Wise, specifically, was like Don Quixote by placing him on "Rosinante's ghost" and "storm / All of hell's windmills." Rosinante was Quixote's horse. Smith included other politicians with his customary blanks, and some were southern but more of his poetic satire was about northerners like Giddings and Salmon Chase, Ohio Republican and potential nominee for the presidency in 1860.

[49] *Ibid.*, 230. The immigrants appeared as "two sons of the boggy isle, / And a Hessian from the southern wars, / Crouching behind a rock!" 321.

[50] Sterling's revelation of his feelings and Beatrice's proper response, *ibid.*, 253–254. The title Smith projected for his second volume may refer to Goethe's *Wilhelm Meister's Apprenticeship*, or, conceivably, to Shakespeare's *Love's Labors Lost*, another romantic comedy. Smith left behind no explanation of what happened to the second volume.

to middle-class townspeople everywhere.[51] Believing that independence was a psychological state, he hung Sterling's problems on his inability to control himself. And, as he had done in his poetic sketch of Alexander Meek, Smith connected Sterling's need for approval with a fatal lack of self-reliance. But, all along, slavery had led Smith to suspect that attempts at mastery destroyed self-mastery. However imperfectly, he sensed that the psychology of dominance produced dependence for superior and subordinate alike, and he glimpsed the problem in himself. Propelled by ambition, Smith would not confront his self-doubt. He hoped that free men would continue voting rather than going to war, but he feared, quite correctly, that they would not.

THE FAILURE OF SELF-DETERMINATION
AND THE POLITICS OF HATE

Baldwin and Smith worried about the quality of American leaders and voters, the two essential components of self-government. Similar concerns warped Johnson Hooper's late writing. Hooper made no effort to persuade northerners about politics in the 1850s. Instead, he promoted radical ideas in southern newspapers like his own Montgomery *Mail*. Like Baldwin and Smith, Hooper thought independence the *sine qua non* of white men's civilization. Sadly, his personal autonomy required not only talent, which he had, but a self-discipline that was sporadic, at best. Moreover, he suffered from the weakness of Alabama's developing middle class. In a society where land and slaves bespoke power, Hooper felt disadvantaged. Without the emotional balance of Baldwin or the anxious self-reliance of Smith, Hooper spun into a downward spiral in the late 1850s. In the *Mail*, Hooper taught the politics of hate and helped propel Alabama into secession.

Although Hooper's psychology was uniquely his, social influences helped transform him from a popular humorist to a fire-eater. Whether they wrote for newspapers, magazines, or books, most American writers produced for a commercial market, which made their talent a commodity. And sales rarely produced a livable income. Authors' worries about autonomy shaped literature as different as Thoreau's *Walden* and Hooper's *Simon Suggs*. Although dependence on markets typified middle-class professionals in many places, slavery displayed the shame of permanent inferiority only to southerners, and their typically small local markets hurt them, too.[52] Hooper found dependence

[51] For example, Burton, an old friend of Sterling, had introduced Sterling and Beatrice as they traveled to the city from the South. Belvedere's name suggests aristocracy, and it was the name of a notable Virginia plantation. Lily was from Baltimore. Beatrice's planter father had known Curtis before Beatrice married him, which suggests that the doctor, too, was southern.

[52] Hooper noted that he had received a copy of *Walden* but did not have time to review it; Montgomery *Mail*, Sept. 7, 1854. The reliance of these writers on limited markets is developed more fully in my "Writers in the Old Southwest and the Commercialization of American Letters," *JER* 27 (Fall 2007): 471–503. Among other many useful works on the reaction of

humiliating and inferiority intolerable. The more he failed at self-determination, the more he doubted himself and resented his critics. By choosing to write for a living, Hooper infected himself with an incurable malaise.

As a hopeful young author, Hooper had found political machinations comical, if mildly worrisome. By acknowledging that freedom let some men be predators, his popular humor tapped broad American anxieties. Hooper's concern about the dangers of mastery first appeared in the stories of Simon Suggs. Using only his mother wit, Suggs specialized in duping those men who used power to harm people they were supposed to help – men like his overbearing father, Jedediah. *Simon Suggs* satirized demagoguery in general and newspaper editors in particular, and Hooper wrote for Whiggish readers who shared his skepticism but hoped for progress. He exposed untoward mastery but suggested that free society would correct its defects.

These hopes and doubts occurred again in a clever little story from Hooper's second collection, the same one that had contained the awful tale of Captain Stick and Tony. "Jim Wilkins and the Editor" made fun of a naïve voter who confused a friendly competition between newspaper editors with actual conflict.[53] Written in the late 1840s, this story suggested that partisanship was a game among gentlemen, but, like *Simon Suggs*, it questioned the motives of political journalists. It raised issues that became more troublesome for Hooper in the 1850s: that drinking was an occupational hazard; that an editor might not be honest, or honorable; and that voters might easily be deceived.

In Hooper's story, two editors – a Democrat and a Whig – regularly swapped insults in print but got "gloriously fuddled together" every Saturday. After one "spicy week," they walked into a bar "lovingly," toasted the "*Freedom of the Press*," and adjourned to a back room for a game of billiards, closing the door behind them. As their play began, a tipsy Whig named Jim Wilkins entered the bar, overheard the game's competitive banter, and mistook it for a serious fight. Through the closed door, Wilkins cheered for the Whig while the bartender told him to "keep still, you jackass." Finally, Wilkins heard the Whig say, "I give in – whipped! – let's liquor!" and the two players reentered the bar. Incensed that his fellow partisan had quit, Jim cancelled his subscription to the Whig paper. In language that revealed his class, Jim explained why: "In the fust and fomost place, you let that feller ... whip you like a —————! In the second place you hollered like a dog, and then you treated to git friends

---

writers to the market, see Michael T. Gilmore, *American Romanticism and the Marketplace* (Chicago: University of Chicago Press, 1985), and Grantland S. Rice, *The Transformation of Authorship in America* (Chicago: University of Chicago Press, 1997). Hooper openly acknowledged his dependence on sales. As he wrote in the *Mail*, asking for subscribers, "we have no others means of support" than the newspaper, and while he personally could ignore "the question of soup," his family had to eat; September 28, 1854.

[53] "Jim Wilkins and the Editors" first appeared in *A Ride with Old Kit Kuncker and Other Sketches and Scenes of Alabama* (Tuscaloosa: M. D. J. Slade, 1849) and then in the almost identical collection, *The Widow Rugby's Husband; a Night at the Ugly Man's and Other Tales of Alabama* (Philadelphia: T. B. Peterson, 1851); quotes from the latter version, 97–101.

again." As he stalked out, Wilkins said he would read nothing written by "sich a cowardly, no count, sow-pig of an eddytur." Unfazed, the two editors got really drunk, ending Hooper's story.[54]

In spite of its humor, "Jim Wilkins and the Editors" revealed Hooper's self-doubts. Although he ridiculed Wilkins, features of his own life underlay this story. Hooper described drunkenness as a man who knew how good it felt to let go. He made Wilkins tipsy but the editors drunk, and Hooper excused them with a joke: they "do better now, but *then!* ah the headaches!" Hooper also made fun of honor in a way that showed an editor's sensitivity. Because Wilkins assumed that opposing journalists were enemies, he thought his Whig should never surrender, and Hooper spoofed his own occupation by making the editors close friends despite their politics. But Wilkins's comparison of the Whig to a whipped " ------ " denoted a black man's submission, the ultimate dishonor.[55] With this funny story, Hooper suggested dissonance between the editors' private and public identities. Such dissonance was not quite honest or honorable.

Sales of Hooper's first two books surely encouraged his self-confidence and probably led him to think that many readers accepted slavery. Like other racist jokes in Hooper's stories, his sly reference to a whipped " ------ " in "Jim Wilkins and the Editors" testified to his belief that many gentlemen shared his prejudice. In fact, Hooper's works were frequently reprinted by northern presses, and he even had gained international readers, for the popular British journal *Bentley's Miscellany* had published one of his stories in 1850.

In 1856, Hooper took a slightly new direction with *Dog and Gun*, a how-to manual that compared southern birds, guns, and shot with those in other parts of the sporting world. Without much of his typical humor, it asserted southerners' skill with weapons – perhaps because Hooper thought it relevant to the times. *Dog and Gun* was published by New York firms, although Hooper's steam press in Montgomery could easily have printed the slim book. Hooper wanted to make money anywhere, however, for his advertisements aimed at southwestern readers, too. And he dedicated *Dog and Gun* to Hilary William Herbert, the most famous sporting author in America. An expatriate British aristocrat, Herbert lived in New Jersey and had never met Hooper.[56] Like the dedication of *Simon Suggs* to a New York editor, the dedication of *Dog and Gun* reflected Hooper's broad ambitions.

[54] Ibid.
[55] Ibid.
[56] "How Simon Suggs 'Raised Jack'" appeared in a collection issued by *Bentley's Miscellany*, Vol. XXVII (London, 1850); the same issue contained Herman Melville's "White Jacket." See Milton Rickels, "The Humorists of the Old Southwest in the London Bentley's Miscellany," *AL* 27 (1956): 557–560; Louis Fraiberg, "The Westminster Review and American Literature, 1824–1885," *AL* 24 (1952–1953): 310–329. German translations of *Simon Suggs* appeared in 1852 and 1853 in a three-volume work called *Nordamerikanisches Volksleben* (Leipzig: C. E. Kollman, 1852, 1853), but Hooper may not have known about this recognition of his work. *Dog and Gun: A Few Loose Chapters on Shooting* was first printed by the agricultural press of Orange and Judd (New York, 1856) and by C. M. Saxton (New York, 1856), soon

Nonetheless, 1856 was a crucial turning point for Hooper. The near victory of the Republican Party in the presidential election convinced Hooper that only a bold confrontation by united southerners could deflect antislavery politics. Despite several reissues, *Dog and Gun* did not make Hooper an internationally known sporting writer, and it was the last of his efforts to reach a national audience. At the same time, the collapse of the Whig Party deprived Hooper of a solid foundation for a newspaper, and he had to scramble for subscribers. His ability to make a living was seriously undermined. Taken together, these changes destroyed Hooper's self-confidence. With that, in a nation at risk, his humor became nastier and his politics outrageously radical.

Like *Dog and Gun*, Hooper's newspaper, the Montgomery *Mail*, had originally demonstrated his hopes for a national alliance of conservative gentlemen and his continuing ambitions as a writer. Despite the fact that his previous venture in the state's capital had produced the "thraldom of debt," Hooper had still believed he could prove his worth. Too poor to move his wife and children from Lafayette, where he had lived during his financial recovery, Hooper had borrowed money again and established the *Mail* in 1854 with business partners who let him do most of the writing.

Over the next six years, Hooper expanded the paper, going from a weekly to a tri-weekly and then a daily printing, and he published books like Woodward's *Reminiscences* from his firm's press. Consistently defending the "Rights of the South," he boosted his city, the state, and the South, touting progress in everything from copper mines to drama. He puffed the bookstore of a friend, insisting that planters demonstrated their intellects by buying books from around the world. He reviewed the sermons of local preachers, suggesting a religiosity he never had.[57] He was a perfect southern Whig, except that his party was on the brink of extinction.

---

afterward by A. O. Moore (New York, 1858), and a fourth time by C. M. Saxton with Barker and Co. (New York, 1860). It was still being reprinted, by northern firms, during the Civil War. Philip D. Beidler has provided an excellent introduction to a modern paperback edition (Tuscaloosa: University of Alabama Press, 1992). Hooper noted the arrival in Montgomery of the Saxton printing, *Mail*, January 22, 1857, and printed a friendly review by an anonymous reader.

[57] "Thraldom of debt," Hooper to his sister-in-law, Mrs. Thomas Heard, August 22, 1850; letter reproduced in Edgar E. Thompson, "The Literary Career of Johnson Hooper: A Bibliographical Study of Primary and Secondary Material (With a Collection of Hooper's Letters)" (M.A. thesis, Mississippi State University, 1971), 85. "Rights of the South" was part of the title to an article attacking "party combinations for the spoils, which ... lessen the power and degrade the political condition of the slaveholder," *Mail*, May 3, 1854. Detailed summaries with profuse quotes of Hooper's writing in the *Mail* are in Marion Kelley, "The Life and Writings of Johnson Hones Hooper" (M.A. thesis, Auburn University, 1934), and Hoole, *Alias Simon Suggs*, but they must be used with caution. Both authors shared Hooper's enthusiasm for southern rights; they neglected his racism and his Whiggish principles, and they implicitly endorsed his violent rhetoric. Because there are long continuous runs of the *Mail* on microfilm, many historians have relied on Hooper's journalism, and his influence on Alabama's secession is explored in Thornton, *Politics and Power*.

At first, Hooper sought readers who wanted another Whiggish alliance and attached his paper to the Know-Nothing Party, while labeling himself an "independent outsider." When that party failed, Hooper urged readers to forget parties and unite behind slavery. He ferociously attacked Democrats in Alabama and Republicans in the North. But he had to scratch frantically for readers when more Alabamians than not became Democrats.[58] All along, he had known that people doubted the sincerity of partisan editors, and he had made fun of them himself. Now he had boxed himself in. As a Whig, he had no party; if he joined the Democrats, he could seem dishonest or dishonorable, or both. His laughing doubts about political journalism had become serious problems.

In truth, Hooper genuinely disliked leading Democrats, and his fears of mastery showed most clearly in the vitriol he poured on them. Hooper's animus reflected his understanding of freedom as self-determination. He consistently attacked the planters who led the local party as spoilsmen who impeded the modernization of slave society. Believing that government should provide a broad foundation for economic improvement, Hooper thought their laissez-faire ideology was harmful. Living along a fine river system, with ample access to credit and education, Democratic planters needed little help from government. Unlike equally wealthy Whigs, who wanted the state to promote progress, the rich Democrats and their "party drones" pandered to uneducated men for the sake of power. Hooper's newspaper advocated education, and, in the face of Democratic opposition to railroads, corporations, and manufacturing, it supported "state aid."[59] In Hooper's view, the Democrats condemned the Southwest to economic inferiority and weakened its only chance to protect slavery through a united stand.

Hooper's vision of progress was modern in a dreadful sort of way, anticipating later imperialism in its racialist assumptions. But Hooper's investment

[58] "Independent outsider," *Mail*, March 22, 1854. Hooper insisted that the American party was the only hope for slavery within the Union; he supported the party's goal of curbing the influence of immigrants but differed with its anti-Catholicism; *Mail*, October 13, 1855. Two years later, claiming that there was no longer a "National party," he promised to join one if it appeared, but "we put our face against any party, call it by what name you will, that does not act out, as well as profess the Southern doctrine on slavery," *ibid*., October 18, 1857.

[59] "Party drones," *Mail*, Jan 21, 1857, in a comment approving a fire-eating Democrat who thought "that a reasonable share of intellect ought to be made a prerequisite for distinguished official position." "State aid" was a phrase used in Alabama politics for public support of infrastructure development; on the controversy's significance, see Thornton, *Politics and Power*. Of the powerful Montgomery Regency, Hooper wrote sarcastically that "the Senatorial family is a tree with wide-spread roots. Many people sit under its branches, repose it its shade, and eat of its fruit," *Mail*, June 7, 1854. He called it "Senatorial" because its leading figure was Senator Benjamin Fitzpatrick. For an example of Hooper's advocacy of "internal improvements" and the "promotion of Alabama's interests," see the *Mail*, August 24, 1854. Hooper attended at least one of the annual conventions that promoted southern economic diversity without challenging the significance of agricultural wealth; on their role, see Vicki Vaughn Johnson, *The Men and the Vision of the Southern Commercial Conventions, 1845–1871* (Columbia: University of Missouri Press, 1992).

in slavery was much more psychological and ideological than economic. He had promoted scientific racism from its emergence in the early 1840s, and he was paternalistic in the sense that he wanted benevolent masters to show the discipline necessary to advance civilization. Allowing for differences among southerners about particular aspects of slavery, he revolted at suggestions it could disappear. The *Mail* supported reopening the foreign slave trade, forbidding voluntary emancipations, exporting free blacks, and punishing anyone who threatened the racial status quo. Hooper eventually used race to appeal to ordinary voters, and, because he knew they were skeptical about an active state, he reluctantly agreed to defer "state-aid" to win their support. When he thought Democrats agitated slavery issues for mere partisan advantage, however, he asked "can the people of the South ever trust the Democracy after this?" He called politicians who opposed his radicalism traitors, for his mistrust was deep.[60]

Hooper's stinging humor revealed the social foundations of his extremism. Chronically in debt, Hooper worried that men thought him a hireling. Covering his embarrassment with self-deprecation, Hooper joked about his poverty, but he hinted that he was better than men whose only asset was wealth. In a book review, Hooper praised the Roman satirists Juvenal and Horace as "those dashing fellows who so delighted in lashing snobs," and then he quoted Juvenal: "Nil habet infelix paupertas durius in se quam quod rediculos homines facit." The sour Roman patrician's observation – that the most unbearable thing about poverty was how it exposed a man to ridicule – fit Hooper's situation all too well. He joked about the improved reputation of journalism, which the "masses" no longer regarded as "a sort of tolerated loaferism," and quipped that "with this change in social footing" there came no money. At the same time, he bragged that his great-uncle signed the Declaration of Independence and that he owned a copy of the signer's college degree.[61] Hooper's insecurity was painfully apparent.

And it had political significance. Partisan editors constantly ran the risk of insulting a touchy man, and Hooper often crossed the line. He not only derided Democrats' politics, he ridiculed them. Hooper ruthlessly pursued wireworkers like William Garrett, former speaker of the state House and one of the "drones" who pulled wires for the Democratic planter elite. Under the headline "STARTLING POLITICAL FACT! EX-SPEAKER GARRETT

---

[60] Quoted passage, *Mail*, January 22, 1857, in regard to Kansas. On Hooper's cooperation with Yancey in the movement to reopen the trade, see Eric H. Walther, *William Lowndes Yancey and the Coming of the Civil War* (Chapel Hill: University of North Carolina Press, 2006), 216–219. Opposition to emancipation and deportation of free blacks, *Mail*, January 30, 1857; deferring the issue of state aid, February 3, 1857 (article may have been written by Hooper's partner, who wrote that he spoke for the "editors, as *individuals*").

[61] Juvenal quote, *Mail*, March 29, 1854; "tolerated loaferism," August 10, 1854; comment on the signer, September 28, 1854. A closer translation of the passage from Juvenal is "the misfortunes of poverty carry with them nothing harder to bear than that it exposes men to ridicule." My thanks to my colleague Richard A. Gerberding for help with the translation.

BEHEADED," Hooper gloated at the man's defeat for a legislative seat: "That's the last of laughing William ... he can never be governor now." In 1857, Hooper's exchanges with Noah Cloud, editor of the Democratic Montgomery *Advertiser*, got so heated that Hooper called Cloud out. Cloud refused to "fight a duel," and Hooper printed their exchange of notes in the *Mail*.[62] As his fears about his future grew, Hooper's amused tolerance for political warfare vanished.

Indeed, by now Hooper believed that most partisan politicians were personally corrupt. Anticipating the inauguration of Democrat James Buchanan in 1857, Hooper lambasted the "Federal city" as "the hot-bed of corruption and impurity for both sexes." The inauguration would feature "office-seekers, bribe mongers, Congressmen, fashion-seekers, mere adventurers, women with characters cracked, and women with characters to *be* cracked by this visit; the pure and the impure; all huddled together promiscuously." The devil, he insisted, should visit Washington "to take notes of the progress of republican luxury, vice and corruption."[63] Hooper's satire retained some of his former humor, but his point was obviously serious. Like William Smith a few years later, he equated personal dissipation with political ambition and made both satanic.

Hooper's letters showed the pathology of his extremism: its peculiar combination of hopes for self-determination and fears derived from slavery. In 1855, Johnson wrote his brother De Berniere that he was nothing but a "galley slave" – a pun that was not very funny, for he had "a nervous prostration" after the last political campaign. Three years later, he promised to visit D. B. in North Carolina but could not say when, for he relied on "free passes" to "save expenses." As the election of 1860 approached, Hooper wrote in his paper that opponents were trying to "beat down" the *Mail*. He confided to D. B. that "the business is such that we can't pay current expenses," and he faced "absolute pecuniary ruin." Depressed, he complained that "work begins to fog me down again; & I must work harder than I have ever done, with less of spirit, hope or money." And then, remarkably, Hooper wrote that

---

[62] Garrett "beheaded," *Mail*, June 16, 1857; Cloud dispute, June 23, 1857. The "beheaded" headline was a play on a well-known satiric pamphlet Hooper had written about the spoils-driven coalition between the Democrats and former Whigs; see *Proceedings of the Democratic and Anti-Know Nothing Party, In Caucus; or the Guillotine at Work* (Montgomery: Barrett & Wimbish, 1855). Garrett got his revenge in his reminiscences, which condemned Hooper for his drinking and his vulgar writing. See William Garrett, *Reminiscences of Public Men in Alabama for Thirty Years* (Atlanta: Plantation Publishing Company's Press, 1872), 528–529. Cloud was a former Whig, and he and Hooper had once been friendly. Their dispute was about Kansas: Hooper blamed Democrats for reopening the slavery issue in 1854 without gaining anything concrete for the South, and he predicted that Kansas would become a free state. His position on Kansas was similar to that of William Smith and Jeremiah Clemens, who were much less radical, the critical difference being that Hooper abandoned hope of cooperation with any northerners and the others continued to hope that some allies could be found.

[63] *Mail*, February 11, 1857.

if southerners accepted a Republican victory, he would "struggle to get away to California or perhaps towards the North." But, he added, he was so poor "that I may not be able to do anything."⁶⁴

In unexpected ideas like migration to a free state, Hooper acknowledged that self-determination was crucial to any prospects he had. But his self-control was woefully inadequate, and he did not acknowledge his bad habits to his brother. As a matter of principle, Hooper accepted the importance of self-control. He wrote a young relative that it was necessary to "control your temper ... so that there is no internal corrosion of the affections, no impairment of the tone of mind." And he recommended "cold water" to sooth "morbidly irritable nerves – tho' Lord knows I get little enough of it here." In truth, however, Hooper drank too much liquor, and he was prone to the "temptations of dissipation." Laziness and dissipation, he later warned his son, were "the sirens which destroy the promise of hundreds of brilliant young men." Nonetheless, while his health was failing and his business collapsing, Hooper traveled around the South attending the races – there was a popular horse named after him – and such entertainments were no way at all to avoid temptations.⁶⁵

As he frequented the races, Hooper probably tried to recruit sporting gentlemen to his radical cause, for his mistrust of politicians was complete. In the spring of 1860, Hooper had admitted that the Democratic Party held the "fate of the Slave States" in its hand, and he begged southern Democrats to stand firm and guarantee the future of slavery. Even so, Hooper's willingness to support Democrats was minimal; they were still "mere political plunderers, to whom the aggrandizement or the ruin of States is as nothing, compared with the success or failure of personal schemes." His only hope was that they would have "*fear* of the *Southern masses*." Hooper would support Democrats only as a "free and independent" journalist, and "only so far, and so long as, advocacy of them is advocacy of the South."⁶⁶ Refusing to follow some former Whigs in supporting a unionist ticket, Hooper insisted that Lincoln's election was sufficient cause for immediate, unilateral secession. He suspected that other southerners might retreat.

Fears about mastery and fears for slavery had merged in Hooper's mind, and his alienation was complete. As the presidential election approached, Hooper urged the *Mail's* readers to vote for John Breckinridge, the nominee

---

⁶⁴ Hooper to De Berniere, August 15, 1855, March 6, 1858, and August 14, 1860, all in John De Berniere Hooper Papers, UNC. "Galley" was a reference to the process of printing as well as to the naval slaves of the ancient Mediterranean.

⁶⁵ Hooper to Sarah J. Brantley, April 9, 1854, quoted in Kelley, 327; Hooper to William De Berniere Hooper, October 21, 1861, reprinted in Thompson, 103. Hoole tracks some of Hooper's visits to races through notes in the *Mail*; *Alias Simon Suggs*, 121–128.

⁶⁶ Hooper's comments on the Democratic convention, April 21, 1860. On the previous day, Hooper's notes from a trip to New Orleans reported on the races in several articles that were sandwiched in between comments on the upcoming presidential election and southern economic development; *Mail*, April 20, 1860.

Slavery and Political Trust

of the southern Democrats. And, in a revealing mental slip, he claimed that he personally would vote for the "rights of slaveholders, even if we intended – which we do not – to remove to a free State so soon as *the danger* comes."[67] The "which we do not" was not exactly false: he had told De Berniere he would flee to a free state if the South submitted, not when "*the danger*" arrived. He saw himself standing bravely, and he feared that other southerners might "submit" to the results of an election rather than fight. If they did, he would not live among them, but he lacked the courage to admit his despair to his readers.

In his effort to create backbone where he perceived cowardice, Hooper bared the worst of his personal fears. Just before the election, he addressed "Slaveholders and NonSlaveholders of the South" and proclaimed the harmony of unequal white men. Abolition, he insisted, would ruin poor whites because "the rich – the sagacious" would leave the South, and a "war of races – a war of extermination" would occur. He fantasized briefly that instead of "antagonism between the two races," "harmony and identification" might take place. Then, "*amalgamation* must be the result." He hastily dismissed these nightmares, insisting that all white men would stand together to create a "powerful and prosperous confederation of commonwealths, controlling the welfare and destiny of other nations, but controlled by none."[68] By his own lights, Hooper was no demagogue because he wrote the truth. But even as he embraced slavery, it had destroyed his confidence. If the "rich" and "sagacious" might migrate, leaving the poor to a "war of extermination" or "*amalgamation*," neither masters nor common whites could be trusted.

Hooper's mistrust poisoned him, through and through. On the night of the election for Alabama's secession convention, Hooper wrote D. B. a letter that revealed once more how he confused his personal failings, his economic dependence, and his fears about slavery. If D. B. had worried that Johnson was "bitter, perhaps too bitter," his brother's response could not have reassured him. Predicting secession, Johnson attacked compromisers: "it would be the height of folly, cowardice, and disloyalty" for anyone to hesitate. He reported "insurrectionary plots, instigated by the North," among the "servile race." With even more vitriol than usual, he proclaimed his hatred of the "fanatical portion of the North" and regretted that he could not "help to destroy them." He ranted: "I hate them instinctively – I hate the race and the blood from which they spring.... I hate them more than I do any thing in this world, or than I can hate in that which is to come." Expecting to die soon, he would advise his sons "to leave a despoiled and degraded" South if the North should "subjugate us."[69]

---

[67] "Which we do not," *Mail*, October 31, 1860. Hooper's comment to his brother that he might migrate had been made ten weeks before this editorial comment, and he repeated similar sentiments to D. B. eight weeks later; Hooper to De Berniere, December 25, 1860, in JDBH Papers, UNC.

[68] *Mail*, November 2, 1860.

[69] Hooper to De Berniere, December 25, 1860, in JDBH Papers, UNC.

Realizing his lack of self-control, Hooper calmed himself instead of pursuing this violent "train of thought." But he shifted to family matters and to his business in a way that surely confirmed D. B.'s anxiety about his brother's mental state. He reported that his partner at the *Mail* was about to die, which would be "a sad blow, every way, but it will fall most heavily on me, who wished to sell to pay debts." He once more complained about his health, bitter that no one realized his exhaustion. "People here do not consider me at all worn – you know no one ever suspects the failing of the old hack until he tumbles down in his harness," he wrote, derogating himself with a slight touch of humor. He was, however, "worn out and without a hope," except that his sons would start as "honest men," even if it were in the North. In terms that indicate how harshly he judged himself, Hooper admitted his self-pity: "I feel ashamed both of my weakness and egotism. With more delicate health and harder work, you have fought the world even longer than I – and without whining."[70] This language was as compelling as Hooper's incantation of hatred. Aware that he could not master himself, he was consumed with fear that "the world" would master him.

Hooper was such a wreck by 1860 that his brother may have known he was beyond help. In some ways a caricature of a hot-headed man of honor, Johnson had the pride, aggression, and sensitivity to shame associated with the familiar stereotype. What damaged him most, however, was his failure to meet his own standards for self-determination. His gentlemanly aspirations notwithstanding, Hooper was much more a middle-class professional than a cavalier. He preached self-control, hard work, and improvement but he was intemperate, inconsistent, and perpetually in the "thralldom of debt." From his youth, bad habits hampered his efforts to achieve independence. His disappointment became self-loathing, then hatred of people who bested him. But Hooper's immense hatreds carried weight. The *Mail* was among the strongest of Alabama's secessionist papers, agitating in terms that were hard to counter with reason.[71] After Lincoln's election, Hooper issued calls to arms and adorned his paper with printed guns and cannons. He was destroying himself, and he would no longer be alone.

* * *

Baldwin, Smith, and Hooper did not literally fear their own enslavement, despite their allusions to it. They knew, however, that slaves experienced punishment, intimidation, and deceit, and they noted those patterns when they recurred – as when Jim Wilkins compared the loser of a fight to a "whipped ------." As activists, Baldwin, Smith, and Hooper found electoral

---

[70] Ibid.
[71] Thornton credits the "Hooperites" for the defection of many former Whigs in the Black Belt to southern Democrat John C. Breckinridge, noting that Unionist John Bell ran well in other former Whig areas of the state; *Politics and Power*, 409. In Thornton's account, Hooper was a main spokesman for the radical former Whigs who steadily pushed Yancey and other Democrats toward extreme positions. The extraordinary violence of Hooper's prose can fully be appreciated only by reading it.

politics and partisan competition like slavery when ambitious men tricked the uninformed through hidden means, or when the powerful sought to "beat down" legitimate opposition, not when gentlemen cooperated voluntarily. The signs of mastery alarmed writers, and they knew the impulse firsthand.

For Hooper, the attempt to reconcile self-determination for white men and enslavement for black people had destructive results. And the mistrust that fed his radicalism weakened more cautious writers. In the face of belligerent secessionists, a unionist like Smith stalled. He could hardly counsel faith in Republicans, whom he thought corrupt. He had publicly proclaimed his mistrust of fire-eaters, too. Without northern allies, how could he urge distressed citizens to follow him? A confident master – an imaginary one like Caroline Hentz's Moreland, or a real one like Andrew Jackson – might confront a crowd and impose his will on fearful men. Imbued with middle-class values, Smith was not a fearless master but a man who sought to master himself. Knowing secession was wrong, he saw no clear alternatives. For Smith, as for Hooper, doubts in other men and self-doubt came from the same poisonous source.

Like Smith, Jeremiah Clemens opposed secession, and he displayed the debilitating effects of similar fears in a brilliant speech to voters in Huntsville in the late summer of 1860. Clemens targeted devious southern Democrats, whom he had personal reasons to mistrust. He warned that they had used "the negro" as "a cloak for every ambitious design, and an excuse for every departure from democratic principle." And they made "denunciation" of the North "an all sufficient atonement" for their own sins: "for broken faith, tyrannical usurpation and degrading corruptions." Tracing the history of proslavery politics, Clemens blamed radicals for many evils. They had made it seem "plausible" for northerners to charge southerners "with a design to convert the government into a grand slavery propagandism." Democrats had "taught" southern men to "distrust one another," and now they used "inflammatory" propaganda to "blind the popular judgment, and incense to madness the popular heart." To prove his point, Clemens quoted Hooper's incendiary *Mail*. It had deliberately spread rumors of invasion, hoping "'that the last excuse is about to be bayoneted out of every Southern man, who has refused to believe that the fighting men of the North are all our enemies.'"[72] Hooper was Clemens's former Know-Nothing ally, not a Democrat, but he was now a villain.

Clemens found no one to trust. While he excoriated secessionists and praised American freedom, he did not defend northerners. Calling secession a "fatal delusion," he warned that self-government itself was at stake. "Do not be deceived," he begged his listeners. Regardless of their promises, the fire-eaters would lead voters "down into the bloody mire of a brutal and inhuman revolution." Clemens did not explain how a rising South would be safe in the Union. He wanted to preserve slavery in peace, like Smith, who soon refused to sign Alabama's ordinance of secession because it was "*the tocsin*

---

[72] Clemens, Speech at Huntsville, August 6, 1860, in Clemens Folder, ADAH.

of war and the death knell of slavery." Aware that his options were narrow, Clemens preached fear to a frightened people. "There is no stopping place in the descent from liberty to slavery," he told them. If Alabamians allowed fire-eaters to determine their fate, they would "soon be drifting upon the waves of anarchy, slaves where we should be masters."[73] Self-government required a measure of trust, but Clemens had next to none.

The ominous model of slavery distorted Clemens's assessment of politics, and he no more saw the sources of his fear than any other writer. In fact, he saw it not at all, for, as Joe Baldwin wrote in *Party Leaders*, "deception comes most effectually from a man himself deceived."[74] So close to slavery that they saw its ills, writers were too dependent to imagine its alternatives. But their commitment to the American form of self-government, with all of its inequalities, was equally fierce and almost equally blind. Writers treasured voluntary ties that men and women freely chose, and no one thought of defining sympathy, or friendship, or love, as compulsory. But there were compulsions in any government, even self-government. Baldwin, Smith, and Hooper sensed that free men did not always make free choices, for they knew the power of words. As they groped to find how freedom and inequality mingled in modern politics, the ugly model of slavery corrupted them. When they acted, they were not fully free.

---

[73] Ibid., Smith quote, *Reminiscences of a Long Life; Historical, Political, Personal and Literary* (Washington, DC: W. R. Smith, Sr., 1889), 306.
[74] *Party Leaders*, 95.

8

Self-Determination and Slavery in Conflict

> [B]eyond this bloody baptism open vistas of life-long usefulness.
>
> Augusta Evans, *Macaria*

Although the rising South had a violent birth, its writers looked for peaceful growth, and the Civil War shattered their hopes. Having believed that slavery and freedom must coexist, they saw both endangered. Before the war, individual opportunity and economic growth had sustained these authors' secular faith. Overlooking their dependence on others, they thought that personal choices and voluntary relations were a safe and sufficient basis for social progress. During the war, however, their individualism clashed with the need for collective action. When writers disagreed with families, friends, or communities, as they often did, they tested the strength of self-determination. In 1864, Augusta Evans predicted that the postwar peace would "open vistas of life-long usefulness" for white men and women.[1] But, more realistically, she and other writers found their ability to act limited. As their society collapsed, they were haunted by images of slavery – ghosts that gave new life to old fears. In the end, without slavery, they avowed a tragic kind of freedom.

Only three of Alabama's authors created significant war literature. Before war began, Caroline Hentz and Albert Pickett had died, and Joseph Baldwin had left the South. Johnson Hooper died in Richmond while Union armies threatened in 1862; and Alexander Meek tended a dying wife, quickly remarried another rich widow, and awaited the war's end at her home in Mississippi. But Evans, William Smith, and Jeremiah Clemens penned conflicting interpretations of the Civil War. Evans dedicated to the Confederate armies a passionate plea for women to sacrifice their men in battle. After opposing secession, Smith served in the Confederate Congress and published a nasty satire about Abraham Lincoln. And Clemens slowly turned Unionist, supported Lincoln's reelection, and wrote an anti-Confederate novel just before the war was over.

---

[1] Augusta Jane Evans, *Macaria; or Altars of Sacrifice*, ed. with an intro. by Drew Gilpin Faust (Baton Rouge: Louisiana State University Press, 1992), 414.

Ironically, the South's crisis created new literary opportunities.[2] For these three authors, writing remained a primary mode of self-determination: a means of expressing themselves, fathoming their world, giving order to their lives, and, once again, making a little money.

In crucial respects, however, the war reordered their immediate priorities, and their vision of a middle-class Southwest yielded primacy to a more elemental desire for their society's survival. Despite a bedrock individualism, Evans, Smith, and Clemens saw that collective action was essential. And this was true regardless of how they wanted a rising South to persist: in a triumphant Confederacy, a reunited nation with slavery, or a reconstructed region without it. With new priorities, these writers found class differences less important than social harmony. They could see that neither town nor countryside escaped the hardships of war, and that both rich and poor whites suffered. Racial solidarity among whites and nearly universal resentment of antislavery Yankees mitigated other differences, and middle-class interests were briefly eclipsed by each writer's desire for southerners to unite, in or outside the Union.[3]

Yet each writer was alarmed by rifts that appeared in white society as the war ground on. Perhaps dissent over such issues as food shortages and conscription suggested to these slave-owning writers that nonslaveholders would turn against slavery. But this fear was unspoken, if it existed. Instead, Evans, Smith, and Clemens recurred to the fateful dynamic suggested by slavery. They saw tyrannical leaders deceiving, manipulating, and even coercing the masses. While differing in many respects, all three authors – a fire-eating woman, an unhappy congressman, and a vacillating Unionist – fixed some disapproval on Jefferson Davis, the planter who was president of the Confederate States of

---

[2] A recent study of popular war writing is Alice Fahs, *The Imagined Civil War: Popular Literature of the North and South, 1861–1865* (Chapel Hill: University of North Carolina Press, 2001). Fahs treats Evans as an exceptional southern woman writer and does not mention Clemens or Smith, and she finds many similarities between northern and southern popular writers with differences primarily in the degree of inequality they espoused. Older, very influential studies of Civil War literature are Edmund Wilson, *Patriotic Gore: Studies in the Literature of the American Civil War* (New York: Oxford University Press, 1962), and George M. Frederickson, *The Inner Civil War: Northern Intellectuals and the Crisis of the Union* (New York: Harper and Row, 1965). The most thoughtful treatment of middle-class culture during the war is Anne C. Rose, *Victorian America and the Civil War* (Cambridge: Cambridge University Press, 1992).

[3] Perhaps because there were no major battles in Alabama outside of the 1864 campaign to capture Mobile, there are few accounts of Civil War Alabama. The older study by Walter Lynwood Fleming, *Civil War and Reconstruction in Alabama* (New York: Columbia University Press, 1905) is the only comprehensive study, and its Confederate bias is notable. Useful for overviews are two chapters on the war in William Warren Rogers et al., *Alabama: The History of a Deep South State* (Tuscaloosa: University of Alabama Press, 1994), and the sketches of Civil War governors in Samuel L. Webb and Margaret E. Armbrester, eds., *Alabama Governors: A Political History of the State* (Tuscaloosa: University of Alabama Press, 2001). Among the many short histories of the Civil War, still the most readable of those that focus on the South is Emory Thomas, *The Confederate Nation, 1861–1865* (New York: Harper and Row, 1979).

America.⁴ They identified danger with both mastery and slavery, with a presumptuous ruler and gravely weakened whites.

Evans, Smith, and Clemens reacted to the disintegration of slavery in ways that were both different and similar. Without facing the inevitable until the last hour, Evans decided that white women might be healthier without slaves. Smith became so gloomy about the weakness of human nature that he imagined slaves dominating white men. And Clemens, now thoroughly alienated from respectable society, depicted a slave who would fight for his freedom. For all three, war literature continued a focus on white men and women. Nonetheless, each realized – if they had not before – that slaves had some measure of self-determination. Smith and Clemens more readily accepted slavery's ending, perhaps because they both predicted the war would bring it on. But they, like Evans, expected the long-term subordination of black people.⁵

Perhaps, however, the efforts of enslaved people to liberate themselves affected these three writers, for their anxieties about autonomy grew. Even as they sought public approval, they announced their independence and integrity. Both Evans and Clemens portrayed heroic wartime characters who maintained self-reliance against the odds. Smith's satire had no heroes, for he found independence even more tenuous than before the war. Significantly, all three writers created characters who were narcissists: dangerous men who dominated their dependents but required their approval. Shades of such mastery appeared in Evans's dictatorial father, in *Macaria*; in Smith's autocratic Lincoln, in *The Royal Ape*; and in Clemens's ruthless Parson, in *Tobias Wilson*. And all of these tyrannical figures met bad ends.

In obvious ways and subtle ones, war eroded these writers' faith in self-determination. Clearly, war made it hard to predict the results of their choices, for they lived, as Smith wrote, with "controlling and uncontrollable circumstances."⁶ Still committed to persuasion, they sought leadership through writing and other means. Both Smith and Clemens pursued high

---

⁴ For the internal conflict in Alabama during the war, see Malcolm C. McMillan, *The Disintegration of a Confederate State: Three Governors and Alabama's Wartime Home Front, 1861–1865* (Macon, GA: Mercer University Press, 1986), and Margaret Storey, *Loyalty and Loss: Alabama's Unionists in the Civil War and Reconstruction* (Baton Rouge: Louisiana State University Press, 2004). The modern controversy over the extent to which the Confederacy suffered from internal dissent was renewed by the publication of the exhaustive study by Richard E. Beringer, Herman Hattaway, Archer Jones, and William N. Still, Jr., *Why the South Lost the Civil War* (Athens: University of Georgia Press, 1986); a recent study that finds nationalism persistent through the war is Anne S. Rubin, *A Shattered Nation: The Rise and Fall of the Confederacy, 1861–1868* (Chapel Hill: University of North Carolina Press, 2005); and popular divisions are stressed in Stephanie McCurry, *Confederate Reckoning: Power and Politics in the Civil War South* (Cambridge, MA: Harvard University Press, 2010), and she notes Evans's reaction to them, 196.
⁵ There is no modern study of slavery or its ending in Alabama. It is treated along with the rest of the South in Leon F. Litwack, *Been in the Storm So Long: The Aftermath of Slavery* (New York: Alfred A. Knopf, 1979).
⁶ Smith to Wilhemine Easby-Smith, January 14, 1861, in Easby-Smith Papers, LC.

office, and Evans dispensed advice to Confederate officials. But war made moral certainty elusive. And all three writers portrayed substantial challenges to the ideal of self-determination, especially when they merged personal and political themes. Drawing directly from wartime experience, they described men and women making fateful, often flawed decisions. With new awareness of their limitations, Evans, Smith, and Clemens reevaluated the meaning of independence.

Northerners like Lincoln saw the Civil War as a conflict between slavery and freedom, but these authors had hoped that slavery and freedom were complementary. All along, when they had seen human traits that seemed to defy customary social categories, they had suppressed their anxieties. And when they had seen shades of slavery in the domination of one free person by another, they had refused to face slavery's evil influence. As the war wore on and their options for action narrowed, they doubted the quality of freedom. Attempting what they saw as principled conduct, under great stress, they concluded that human nature was too indeterminate and the world too uncertain for real confidence in the results of individuals' decisions.

Despite those reservations, Evans, Smith, and Clemens argued that women and men must aggressively act or passively lose their freedom. And they found the resolve to follow their convictions, whether or not they were sure about right and wrong. Impelled by fear that the world was a brutish place where the strong preyed on the weak, they urged that self-determined individuals guide those who could not help themselves. Because they were unable to think that all humans might, finally, be equal, they asserted a modern ethics of uneven freedom.[7]

FATE AND FREEDOM

Unwed in her mid-twenties, Augusta Evans identified her destiny with that of the Confederacy. During the war, her growing desire for autonomy and influence mixed with anxiety about a proper woman's freedom. The result was *Macaria*, which attached Confederate propaganda to a romantic story. Like her previous novels, *Macaria* forced into aesthetic coherence the tension between women's self-determination and their dependence. Now, however, she located that tension within the larger issue of whether humans were free to determine their lives or fated to live without meaningful choices. This issue especially disturbed Evans because she believed that nature decreed her subordination. Despite her uncertainty about the scope of self-determination, Evans acted on her principles. Bolstered by faith, nationalism, and admiring friends,

---

[7] Both Frederickson, *Inner Civil War*, and Wilson, *Patriotic Gore*, see a decrease in optimism as a result of the war, but Louis Menand, *The Metaphysical Club* (New York: Farrar, Straus and Giroux, 2001), has traced the constructive intellectual consequences of the destruction of prewar certainties. I have tried to suggest here that something of both phenomenon occurred among these writers.

she claimed greater freedom for white women – so they could meliorate and sustain inequality.[8]

On the eve of war, a personal crisis forced Evans to make a difficult choice. During her 1859 visit to New York, she met James Spaulding, a conservative Christian journalist fourteen years her senior, and they became "conditionally" engaged. Intellectually, Spaulding was a perfect match. Believing that God destined women for marriage, he also thought them equal in intelligence and approved of women authors' "share in public life." But Spaulding was a Republican, and Evans severed the relationship after he visited her family in the summer of 1860. Although the particulars are unclear, she defiantly wrote Rachel Lyons: "I shall *live* and *die, Augusta Evans.*" "Literary women" might not be as "happy" as wives and mothers, but they felt "deep peace and satisfaction," and they were "crowned with a glory such as marriage never gave." Twisting the Christian admonition that "no man can serve two masters" (God and materialism), she claimed that it was impossible to "serve two Masters; Fame and Love." Choosing her vocation and the fame it brought, Evans hid any disappointment she felt.[9]

Evans revealed her feelings, however, when rumors of her engagement threatened her fame. In November, she wrote her "dear aunt" Mary Jones in Columbus, Georgia, that she had a "sad heart" because there was ugly talk about her in the Georgia capital. A friend had written that "'it is *now reported all over town* that Miss Augusta is *married to the Editor of the* [*New York*] *World*.'" Evans complained that she had "tried to shield the whole matter from the public," and now Spaulding was branded a "'Black Republican.'" Dismayed to have "*my name*" misused, Evans blamed her aunt's son-in-law, secessionist politician Henry Benning. He "might as well have put it in the newspapers at once" as initiate the gossip.[10] By now, at least, Augusta did not regret her broken engagement. She cared too much for her reputation.

---

[8] All textual references to *Macaria* are from the LSU edition, cited in n. 1. The original publication was issued by Richmond: West and Johnson, 1864.

[9] "Conditionally" is Evans's phrase in the letter to her aunt that is discussed in the next paragraph and cited in footnote 10; Evans to "My dear Aunt" [Mary Jones], November 26, 1860, in *A Southern Woman of Letters: The Correspondence of Augusta Jane Evans Wilson*, Rebecca Grant Sexton, ed. (Columbia: University of South Carolina Press, 2002), 18–19; Spaulding quote from *The True Idea of Female Education. An Address Delivered at Pittsfield, Mass., Before the Young Ladies Institute* (New York: John F. Trow, Printer, 1855); Evans to Lyons, July 30, 1960, in Evans, *Correspondence*, 23. Fidler describes the engagement, based partly on family tradition, partly on the account of Evans's publisher J. C. Derby, which may not be reliable. Fidler writes that Evans broke the engagement late in 1860, and he traces Spaulding's views on secession through his newspaper writing, but Evans's July 30 letter to Rachel implicitly dates the broken engagement before the end of July. Fidler's account is in *Augusta Evans Wilson, 1835–1909* (Tuscaloosa: University of Alabama Press, 1951), 74–82. The quote from the "Sermon on the Mount" is rendered, in the King James version of the Bible that Evans knew, "No man can serve two masters: for either he will hate the one, and love the other; or else he will hold to the one, and despise the other. Ye cannot serve God and mammon," Matthew 6:24.

[10] All quotes but the last, Evans to her "dear aunt," November 26, 1860; "newspapers," Evans to her aunt, December 4, 1860, Evans, *Correspondence*, 23, 26. Editor Sexton identifies the

Evans soon displayed her ardent southern nationalism. When a female editor asked her to endorse a petition against secession, she angrily refused. Sending Henry Benning a copy of her response, Evans asked him to read it to the Georgia convention if the Unionist woman claimed her support. With false modestly, she assured Benning that "of course" if the woman omitted Evan's name he should do so, too, for she had no wish "to have my name alluded to at all." As the Confederate government formed in Montgomery, she visited with leading politicians. Influential Georgian Thomas R. R. Cobb called her "very young-looking, though not pretty and very loquacious and sensible." She began to form a network of male leaders like her "noble, peerless friend," William Yancey, Congressman Jabez Curry, and General P. T. Beauregard. Evans wrote unsigned newspaper articles, sending copies to her friends to claim her authorship.[11]

Evans used her male friendships to try and influence public decisions. Her audacity disguised, she wrote Beauregard that she could not fight but that her "feeble, womanly pen could contribute to the consummation of our freedom." She quizzed him about military issues and forwarded to him her correspondence from Yancey. She talked strategy with other generals in Mobile and bitterly criticized the Davis administration for not heeding Beauregard's plans for the war. She lobbied Curry for a Confederate copyright law and suggested other reforms. She wanted him to curb radicalism and narrow the suffrage (a "delicate matter"), and she thought the lower class should be "trained and elevated to a higher standpoint" before it could participate fully in government. Evans nursed the sick and wounded – a womanly act that extended the customary sphere of genteel women. She more directly entered the world of men by visiting fortifications and making speeches to soldiers.[12]

aunt as "probably" Mrs. Jones and identifies "the Bennings" as "old friends and distant relatives" of Evans, but it is clear that Evans refers to Henry Benning, who was a long-time secessionist and prominent, if controversial, politician and jurist, and Mary Jones's son-in-law. These connections are explained by the Columbus State University Archives, which holds the Henry Benning-Seaborn Jones Collection, on its Web site, http://archives.colstate.edu/findingaids/mc6.php. Benning was later a Confederate general, for whom, ironically, Fort Benning, Georgia, is named.

[11] Letter to female editor, Evans to Mrs. V. L. French, January 13, 1861, and to Benning, same date, quoted passages in Evans, *Correspondence*, 28, 27. Cobb is quoted in Fidler, 89; reference to Yancey as "noble," Evans to Gen. Beauregard, August 19, 1863; commenting on Yancey's death, in Evans, *Correspondence*, 74. For examples of articles sent to friends, see Evans to Lyons, August 21, 1861, in *ibid.*, 35–36, to Beauregard, August 4, 1862, in *ibid.*, 41–43, and to Curry, Nov. 10, 1862, in *ibid.*, 47. Curry was a well-placed young politician at the time, having already served in the U.S. Congress and now a member of the Confederate Congress. He was a friend of Octavia Le Vert and Basil Manly, which suggests a prudent tolerance of different kinds of literary and political opinions. For Evans's friends, see Jessie Pearl Rice, *J.L.M. Curry, Southerner, Statesman and Educator* (New York: King's Crown Press, 1949); Eric H. Walther, *William Lowndes Yancey and the Coming of the Civil War* (Chapel Hill: University of North Carolina Press, 2006); T. Harry Williams, *P.G.T. Beauregard: Napoleon in Gray* (Baton Rouge: Louisiana State University Press, 1955).

[12] "Feeble pen," Evans to Beauregard, August 4, 1862, in *Correspondence*, 42; first quotes on suffrage, Evans to Curry, July 15, 1863, in *ibid.*, 67. When Curry was defeated for reelection,

Even as Evans acted, however, she admitted fears. When the poet Henry Timrod, a friend of Rachel's, visited Augusta in 1862, she was distracted by "many fears" for her brother, who was at the battle of Shiloh. She was "afraid," therefore, that Timrod did not recognize her intellect, that he would "consider me very hopelessly *stupid*." She wrote Beuregard that, although she was "reluctant to transcend the proper sphere of womanhood," she would not be "deterred" from her duty "by fear of the ridicule or wrath of those who contend that women have no interest in manners appertaining to Government errors." Although she would avoid "unnecessary notoriety," she was not "*afraid* to *avow*" her opinions.[13] Yet she was fearful that her status as a woman diminished her effectiveness.

In *Beulah*, Evans had considered women's freedom from a conservative social perspective, and the popular novel was filled with contradictions. A writer, Beulah tried to forego dependence on a wealthy man but yielded to love and abandoned literary fame. The enigmatic slave Harriet had expressed Evans's belief that women and slaves shared a God-ordained subordination, yet the black woman had remarkable autonomy. Evans had bitterly criticized frivolous women and her materialistic society, and she had insisted on the value of work. But her novel ended with Beulah ensconced in a mansion. During the war, as women in North and South assumed greater roles – fundraising, managing farms and businesses, participating in public events, and writing war poetry, fiction, and songs – Evans seized the opportunity to assert herself. Not surprisingly, the contradictions of *Beulah* reappeared.

Evans had barely hinted in *Beulah* that slavery hampered women's self-determination, but she began to examine the problem directly during the war. When Jabez Curry wrote that he was contemplating a speech on slavery's benefits for women, Evans asked him to drop the subject. She argued that slavery harmed white women because servants did work that would make their owners healthy. She insisted that this problem could, theoretically, be "counterbalanced" by greater leisure for women to develop their minds and their "womanly accomplishments," but that in fact was not the case. Instead, she lamented, "thoroughly educated women are deplorably rare among us; we have thousands who are graceful, pretty, witty, and pleasant companions for a promenade or pic-nic, but their information is painfully scanty;

---

she lamented to him that it was the fault of "Universal Suffrage," which she called "an effete theory of Utopian origin," inappropriate for this "sternly real, rushing, explosive 19th century"; Evans to Curry, October 16, 1863, in *ibid.*, 77–78. Evans forwarded Yancey's correspondence to Beauregard, September 23, 1862, in *ibid.*, 45; quizzed him about battles and told of lobbying with generals, March 17, 1863, in *ibid.*, 54–57; criticized Davis (one example among many), Evans to Curry, December 10, 1862, in *ibid.*, 48–51; and wrote him about copyright, July 15, 1863, in *ibid.*, 65. Melissa Homestead treats Evans's copyright efforts in *American Women Authors and Literary Property, 1822–1869* (Cambridge: Cambridge University Press, 2005). On Evans's wartime activities, see, for examples, Evans to Rachel Lyons, June 26, 1861, and Jan 22, 1862, in *Correspondence*, 33–34, 39.

[13] On Timrod, Evans to Lyons, May 31, 1862, 40; to Beauregard, August 19, 1863, 72; both in *ibid.*

their judgment defective, their reasoning faculties dwarfed, their aspirations weak and frivolous." Evans had derided such vapid women in *Beulah* without mentioning slavery. Now, when she scanned women's history, she found "no examples worth adducing in favor of slavery." Assuring Curry that this negative pattern was not an "inexorable necessity," she left the subject behind.[14] Nothing in her letter recognized slavery's evils for black women.

When she wrote Curry, Evans had already completed a Confederate novel that displayed her idea of *"perfect womanhood,"* complete with slaves. In August of 1861, Evans wrote Lyons that she had sent her "precious MS" to her northern publisher, J. C. Derby, probably referring to an early version of *Macaria; or Altars of Sacrifice*. Eighteen months later, however, she wrote Lyons that she was "copying the *MS* of a new Novel," which she would publish as soon as it was finished. Whatever changes she had made in her manuscript, Evans had already negotiated terms with Richmond publishers West and Johnson for "$1000 cash, and ten percent on every copy published." At about the same time, moreover, Evans quietly made arrangements to have the work published in New York. *Macaria* glorified the Confederacy, and it won Evans money and fame by asserting autonomy for women within a conservative social order.[15]

Macaria combined propaganda about the wartime sacrifices of Confederate women with a love story. After its dedication to the Confederate armies, however, the novel ignored the war for two hundred pages, and most of its inflammatory language was confined to the last several chapters. This structure may suggest that Evans altered the romance she had sent Derby in 1861. In any case, Evans's views of the Confederacy were less prominent than her concerns about women's self-determination. While her heroine promoted Confederate nationalism and begged other women to do the same, *Macaria* grew from Evans's continued preoccupation with her own future. It made women crucial figures in a public struggle, yet promised them intense emotional lives without husbands. No wonder it appealed to many readers, North and South.

Like Evans's earlier novels, *Macaria* proclaimed women's right to choose their lives within a conservative society. Evan's heroine, Irene Huntingdon,

---

[14] Evans to Curry, July 15, 1863, in *ibid.*, 66–67.
[15] "Perfect womanhood," Evans to Lyons, June 14, 1864, 104; her "precious" manuscript, Evans to Lyons, August 20, 1861, 35; her copying efforts, Evans to Lyons, March 20, 1863, 59; negotiations with publishers, Evans to Messrs. West & Johnson, February 22, 1863, 53; all in *ibid.* An enlightening account of the publication of *Macaria* is Melissa Homestead, "The Publishing History of Augusta Jane Evans's Confederate Novel *Macaria*: Unwriting Some Lost Cause Myths," *MissQ* 58 (Summer-Fall 2005): 665–702. Homestead demonstrates that, contrary to earlier accounts, there was no 1863 publication of the novel and that Evans was herself involved in the northern publication of her book. Excellent discussions of *Macaria* are in the first chapter of Sarah E. Gardner, *Blood and Irony Southern White Women's Narratives of the Civil War, 1861–1937* (Chapel Hill: University of North Carolina Press, 2006), and Drew Gilpin Faust, *Mothers of Invention: Women of the Slaveholding South in the American Civil War* (Chapel Hill: University of North Carolina Press, 1996), some but not all of which repeats her fine introduction to *Macaria*.

gained significant autonomy at great cost. She sacrificed her father and her lover on battlefields and, in an obvious parallel with Evans, decided to "live and die, Irene Huntingdon." Although Evans wrote Curry that *Macaria* contained "less philosophic lore" than *Beulah,* it was as intellectually ambitious. Evans tried to show that Irene's choices, like those of the South, reflected God's will, but troubling questions about freedom intruded into her complex plot.[16] Even as Evans defended women's right to be self-determined, under God, she feared that an indifferent fate ruled humankind.

Evans's perfect woman, Irene, had to fight for autonomy because she was the child of a despotic aristocrat, a master as much as a father. To consolidate his fortunes, Mr. Huntingdon tried to marry his only child to her self-indulgent cousin Hugh. With Irene's mother long dead, her father's "*surveillance*" dictated everything from Irene's splendid wardrobe to her friendships. Irene resented his materialism and snobbery and hated being watched, but she mostly obeyed. To offset him, Evans gave Irene a surrogate family: the poor widow Amy Aubrey, her son Russell, and her niece Electra Gray. Irene leaned on Mrs. Aubrey, a model of motherly piety; she loved Russell, a brilliant, diligent, and alarmingly handsome young man; and she befriended the artistic Electra. But Mrs. Aubrey had once spurned Irene's father, so he forbade Irene to see the family. By barring Irene from nurture, love, and friendship, he impeded her self-determination.[17] She spent her nights gazing at the heavens from atop her father's mansion, and she wrote anonymous articles about astronomy. Irene's intellect was free.

Evans made Irene's plight resemble slavery. At first, Irene deceived her father and saw the Aubreys. When he demanded that she marry Hugh, however, she openly defied him. Threatening a "whipping," the tyrant "shook her violently," promised to have his way, and banished the fifteen-year-old girl to boarding school. At nineteen, Irene returned home and denounced her father's plans for her marriage as materialistic and "loathsome," proclaiming herself a "free-born American." Then she rejoiced that "she had burst the fetters; she was free."[18] But she loved the father who required her obedience, so, while she would not marry Hugh, she hid her love for Russell – even from Russell, until he left for war. Evans neither bent Irene to her father's will nor gave her

---

[16] "Live and die," *Macaria,* 317; "less philosophical lore," Evans to Jabez Curry, July 15, 1863, in Evans, *Correspondence,* 68.

[17] "Surveillance," 60, 158, in *Macaria.* Irene, Evans wrote, "was allowed no margin for the exercise of judgment or inclination; her associates were selected, thrust upon her; her occupations decided without reference to her wishes," and "she determined to resist," 158, *ibid.* Evans emphasized that Irene disliked the fashionable clothing and jewelry her father insisted she wear and that she resented having to socialize with prominent and mindless upper-class people.

[18] "Whipping," 58; "ignoble," "loathsome," and "free-born," 200; "fetters," 202, *ibid.* Mr. Huntingdon intended to break his daughter's will when he banished her: "How will you relish getting up before day, kindling your own fire, if you have any, making your own bed, and living on bread and water?" he asked her, suggesting the life of a hard-worked slave, 58, *ibid.*

to Russell, for she would not choose between them. Instead, Evans freed her heroine from both men.

Evans indirectly justified Irene's autonomy in an authorial reflection that cautiously probed the status of women. Drawing from emerging evolutionary ideas, she argued that human nature was not fully knowable even though its development obeyed "rigid laws." Although the "various relations" of particular individuals explained their character, she wrote, those relations were unpredictable. Only "the bloody seal of Experience" taught truth. Assuring her readers that "the variety of emotional and intellectual types is even greater than the physical," Evans said that no one could know the "mysteries" of human nature. Both men and women were constantly evaluated by social conventions, and yet they could "neither be lopped off nor elongated to meet the established measure." "We shade our eyes, and pass into the dim unknown," she argued, "from breath to breath, from step to step, from hour to hour."[19]

However limited human knowledge was, Evans made a slave understand her heroine's predicament, just as Harriet had done in *Beulah*. *Macaria* contained many devoted servants, and the leading one, "aunt" Nellie, was a much lesser figure than Harriet. Still, she tried to protect Irene, for she saw that Mr. Huntingdon would harm his child. Despite the blindness of age, Nellie glimpsed Irene's future: "Oh, my baby! my baby! there is trouble and sorrow thickening for you; I know it. I have had a warning of it." The "oracular" nurse had seen "awful signs" when there was an eclipse on the day of Irene's birth and the "chickens went to roost." Although Irene smiled at Nellie's "superstition," she later admitted that the sun's eclipse foretold the shadow on her life. "I am not superstitious," she said (marking her difference from Nellie) "but I can not be blind to the striking analogy – the sombre symbolism." Like the nearly blind slave, Irene saw the shadow of fate; but it only increased her determination to be free.[20]

With increasingly complex symbolism, Evans returned again and again to the idea of fate. The "chilling voice of destiny" spoke to Irene; she was caught in the "unyielding web of human destiny"; she knew that within the "loom of destiny" ran "dark alien threads" in her life. Her heroine, Evans wrote, had a "merciless destiny," which was "cold, grim, Sphinx-like." But the monstrous Sphinx – half woman, half beast – symbolized not only fate but its defiance. The ancient Sphinx had devoured men unable to answer her riddle about human existence until the king Oedipus succeeded; then she died. Could men control their destiny? Russell seemed to alter his "fate" through ambition and

---

[19] "Rigid laws" and "various relations," 62; "bloody seal," 66; "variety of types" through "elements lopped off," 124–125; "shade our eyes," 135; all in *ibid*. Evans certainly did not dispute all inequality. Reflecting on the age of the universe, she had "not a doubt" about sentient beings on other planets. Humans "stood as one small family circle amid clustering worlds" but "earthly races" contained "distinct, unalterable types," 179, *ibid*.

[20] Nellie's advice, 167; Irene's agreement, 235; in *ibid*. Evans was fond of comparing the sadness in Irene's life to a shadow; see her friend Harvey's observation that her "shadow has spread," 233, *ibid*., just preceding Irene's use of the eclipse as a metaphor for her dark future.

hard work. Evans wrote that Confederates saw "the historic Sphinx must find an Oedipus, or Democratic Republican Liberty would be devoured," for they refused to believe "that Americans could live and not be free." But Russell could not be Oedipus because Evans had planned his death.[21] At least figuratively, the Sphinx would die by Irene's hands when Evans freed her heroine.

Evans began liberating Irene in a crucial chapter that opened with philosophical speculation about freedom. She questioned the controversial theory of Englishman Thomas Henry Buckle, who theorized that statistical tendencies rather than individual decisions explained the destiny of nations. Was his "theory of immutable cycles correct," Evans asked; "is the throbbing, surging world of human emotions and passions" nothing but an "arithmetical problem?" In a sudden, peculiar turn, Evans deflected her question by quoting the Roman poet Terence: "'*Davus sum non Oedipus*'" – I am Davus, not Oedipus. Davus was a stereotyped character of a male slave in classical comedy, and Terence's well-known line contrasted the slave's inability to answer existential questions with Oedipus's solution to the Sphinx's riddle. After this puzzling identification with a slave, Evans, without a pause, shifted to stories of famous wartime heroines. Whether or not Irene knew the meaning of existence, she would be free to act heroically, and the chapter ended with Mr. Huntingdon's death in battle.[22]

Evans was not freeing Irene into a cold world, for she contrasted the confining relations women had in families with the voluntary ties of friendship. With near perfect consistency, Evans had Irene choose friends who allowed her to practice freedom: sharing her feelings, testing her ideas, and advancing her self-knowledge. Evans defined her ideal of friendship extravagantly. "When a truly honest, noble soul meets an equal," she wrote, "barriers of position and age melt like snow-flakes in sunshine, all extraneous circumstances fall away, and, divested of pomp or rags, as the case may be, the full, undimmed majesty of spirit greets spirit, and clear-eyed sympathy, soaring above the dross and dust of worldly conventionalities, knits them in bonds lasting as time." In effect, Evans claimed that friendships transcended social class by forgetting "pomp" and "rags." Friends afforded both freedom and

---

[21] "Chilling voice," 69; "unyielding web," 115; "loom" with "dark threads," 191; "merciless," 68; Russell defies his "fate," 9; Confederacy needs an Oedipus, 308, *ibid*. Evans wrote Lyons that to write a novel one must "elaborate your plot, trace clearly to the end, your grand leading aim, before you write a line," November 15, 1860, in *Correspondence*, 21. Even if Evans had modified her original plot, she would surely have decided on Russell's death when she began her revisions.

[22] Quotes about Buckle and Davus, *Macaria*, 331. The line is from Terence, *Andria*, line 194. Although Evans may or may not have read Buckle's history, it was widely written about. The *SLM* carried a hostile review (originally in the *National Intelligencer*) that explained the ideas Evans refers to here and elsewhere; *SLM* 27 (October 1858): 268–283. The U.S. edition was Thomas Henry Buckle, *History of Civilization in England*, vol. 1 (New York: D. Appleton, 1858). Irene fainted and then grieved for her father at the end of this chapter, but on her very next appearance she expressed her belief that the "agency of its daughters" would help save the Confederacy, *Macaria*, 368.

intimacy. And, unlike women's subordination in families, friendship promised equality.²³

Two of her friends – Mrs. Aubrey and the saintly northern missionary, Harvey – led Irene to a God who freed her from religious convention and made her spiritually self-determined. Evans also gave Irene two older male friends – both of them indifferent to religion – and they helped her recast the southern tradition of female deference. The first, Dr. Arnold, was a misanthropic physician, and the second, Irene's uncle Eric, was her studious but sickly companion. Both men were better guides than Mr. Huntingdon, and they encouraged her assertiveness with banter. Irene probed their friendly oversight. When Eric teased Irene about her reluctance to discuss Russell, she asked: "Do you recognize no difference between a parasitic clinging and an affectionate friendship, a valued companionship based on congenial tastes and sympathies?"²⁴ Unlike her father, her friends accepted Irene's self-reliance.

With wealth she inherited from her selfish father, a maturing Irene adopted a new kind of southern paternalism. Evans steered between the models of anti-slavery reformers and southerners who rejected modern reform. In their scrappy conversations, Dr. Arnold mocked Irene as "Lady Bountiful" and laughed that she was "inaugurating a new system," one that thrust women into public for "self-glorification." Irene defended women's leadership in "judiciously-conducted" charities, which did public good by "systematizing" work and "inducing punctuality." But Evans also gave Irene lower-class white people to nurture personally. Although Evans sermonized about the beneficial lessons of poverty, she argued that poor whites should be elevated through education. Ambivalent about the significance of class, Evans envisioned a culture that blended personal benevolence with bureaucratic charity – tradition with modernity.²⁵

Evans suggested culture overcame class by paralleling Irene's story with that of the poor artist Electra, whose imperfections clarified the ideal of "*perfect womanhood*." Electra was a passionate religious skeptic; Irene told her that she needed self-control and faith. Electra was a genius who painted from inspiration, while Irene used system and logic and encouraged Electra to be rational. Electra bravely ran the blockade with Confederate secrets, but she consistently deferred to Irene's more disciplined strength. When both women became Confederate nurses, Electra grew ill from exhaustion while Irene drew strength from adversity. Throughout the novel, as Evans showed Electra's shortcomings, she implied that her readers should imitate Irene.²⁶

---

[23] *Macaria*, 36. I have explored the significance of these friendships in more depth in "The Dynamics of Southern Friendship in the Civil War Novels of Augusta Evans and Jeremiah Clemens," *MissQ* 60 (Spring 2007): 303–333.

[24] 182, *ibid*.

[25] "Lady Bountiful," 273; "new system," 260; her rejoinders, 261–262, *ibid*. Evans addresses the benefits of poverty, which teaches hard work and discipline, 42; a typical visit of Irene to the poor, 255–259, *ibid*.

[26] By making Electra an artist and Irene a scientist, Evans was asserting roles for women in male-dominated fields. See Nina Baym, *American Women of Letters and the Nineteenth-Century*

Self-Determination and Slavery in Conflict 263

The two women drew together in Evans's melodramatic conclusion, where the final violence necessary to Irene's liberation occurred. Evans justified the violence with long passages of propaganda. She attacked northern abolitionism, atheism, and materialism and praised the freedom-loving South. She dramatized battles, suffering, and death, as the women nursed the wounded in the spring of 1862. Using ideas she had tested with Beauregard and Curry, Evans made the Confederacy the world's best hope for a conservative form of self-government. And she made "Christian women" the "safeguards" of her nation's "liberties and purity." Her propaganda fully deployed, Evans ended *Macaria*. Irene's male friends gathered around her: Dr. Aubrey caring for the wounded; Harvey ministering to soldiers; and Eric acting as Irene's guardian. As the three men watched, Russell died in Irene's arms from battlefield wounds. With that, Irene gained autonomy and new intimacy in the voluntary ties of friendship.[27]

Finally, having released Irene from love's mastery, Evans added final lines that ordained her "life-work." Unlike Beulah, whose work was saving her husband, Irene claimed "the hallowed work" of social benevolence. She was no longer "vexed" by a "baffling Sphinx" – the impossible choice between love and duty. Her inheritance would support a women's school, which Electra would manage. It would educate poor women for "industrial pursuits" so they could earn more "remuneration." With Electra leaning on her, Irene embraced single womanhood: the friends would be "social evangels," loving all "suffering" humans. Irene reminded Electra, however, that Eric, Dr. Arnold, and Harvey would share their lives. Bound only by friendship, Evans's southerners were free in the midst of war.[28]

Sciences: Styles of Affiliation (New Brunswick, NJ: Rutgers University Press, 2001), 161–166, where she contrasts the feminine style of Electra with Irene's masculine pursuits, which are, nonetheless, "amateurish." On Electra as a serious artist, see the chapter on Evans in Naomi Z. Sofer, *Making the "America of Art:" Cultural Nationalism and Nineteenth-Century Women Writers* (Columbus: Ohio State University Press, 2005), 66–104; on *Macaria* especially, 77–87. Sofer links Evans's views of art with those of influential English critic John Ruskin, who modified Romantic aesthetics by requiring art and architecture to display moral truth.

[27] Women as "safeguards," *Macaria*, 368–369; shortly after delivering this speech, Irene told Electra her work showed too much "morbid melancholy," a criticism that caused a "quiver" on the weaker friend's face, 369, *ibid*. Upon Russell's death, Irene embraced Harvey, with a "wintry smile" flitting over a "mouth that had seemed frozen" (405), which indicated a slight thaw in the strong heroine's reserve. Irene's repression of her love for Russell may reflect Evans's attempt to hide her feelings about James Spaulding.

[28] For Irene, religious benevolence unlocked the Oedipus to the "baffling Sphinx that had so long vexed her," *ibid*., 255; women's pay and opportunities, 410; single women as evangels, 413; "hallowed work," 414. Evans closed her novel with a long passage from Elizabeth Barrett Browning's well-known poem "A Drama of Exile," which recounted the expulsion of Eve from the garden of Eden and had Adam urge her to a life of service. Evans probably knew of Browning's antislavery poetry, and perhaps she believed that using the Englishwoman to conclude the novel demonstrated the breadth of her conservative ideas, slavery notwithstanding. On single women, see Jennifer Lynn Gross, "'Lonely Lives are not Necessarily Joyless:' Augusta Jane Evans *Macaria* and the Creation of a Place of Single Womanhood

When Evans completed *Macaria* early in 1863, she could imagine that her South was still rising and that its deficiencies would be addressed with middle-class values rather than revolutionary change. Even as Irene outlined women's future, however, she appealed to planters, as a "class," to sponsor an "American Renaissance," for she expected their leadership, too. When the Confederacy lost ground, she blamed Davis's administration and wondered why he ignored superior generals like Beauregard: "This is a Sphinx, of which I can not prove the Oedipus," she wrote. As 1864 opened, she complained to Jabez Curry that southerners were "willing to glide unhesitatingly into a dictatorship," motivated by "hatred of Lincoln" rather than principles of liberty they once espoused.[29] Still unwilling to abandon slavery, she had seen its negative image behind Irene's subordination to her father, and she saw it again in southerners' submission to Davis. But she could not imagine that her South would die.

In point of fact, Evans's personal life steadily improved. Her letters to Lyons said little about politics but reported on her writing and chatted about the attention she won from men. Mobile remained in Confederate hands until the war's final days, and Evans still had slaves. In 1864, Evans wrote Lyons that she constantly heard a servant announce: "'Miss Gusta somebody is coming up the walk.'" Evans gossiped about flirting, while fantasizing that she deserved a literary biographer like James Boswell, who served the famous British author Samuel Johnson. Two officers helped her in the garden all day, "transplanting flowers, tying up vines, and saying brilliant things! Which alas! For want of a Boswell! will not be preserved for the kind and tender public." With her new status as a Confederate heroine, fame and love may have seemed compatible.[30]

Despite its propaganda, *Macaria* urged roles that middle-class women in the North and South were adopting, and it reconciled freedom and inequality in ways that seemed responsible to many white readers. Irene made ethical choices amidst differences that Evans thought permanent, like race, or mysterious, like gender, or temporary, like class. As Evans saw it, "bloody Experience" required adaptation and action, and she used friends to mediate between womanly deference and self-assertion. By focusing on her short-term gains, however, Evans finessed the question that haunted *Macaria*: was all self-determination controlled by an overriding fate? Blinded by her reliance on slavery, she could not imagine how free a person could be.

---

in the Postwar South," *American Nineteenth-Century History* 2.1 (2001): 33–52, and, more generally, Christine Jacobson, *Southern Single Blessedness: Unmarried Women in the Urban South* (Urbana: University of Illinois Press, 2006), which focuses on Charleston and Savannah.

[29] *Macaria*, 409; Evans to Beauregard, December 14, 1863, in Evans, *Correspondence*, 82; Evans to Curry, January 27, 1864, in *ibid.*, 92. In the same letter, she suspected that "Buckle's social and political cycles seem to some extent reproduced in the curious phrases of popular opinion" in the Confederacy as it moved from democracy toward centralization; *ibid.*, 91.

[30] Evans to Lyons, March 14, 1864, in *ibid.*, 99–100.

Self-Determination and Slavery in Conflict

FIGURE 8.1. Georgia Cottage, the home of Augusta Evans during the Civil War. This graceful cottage was on the outskirts of Mobile, where businessmen like Augusta Evans's father lived, commuting into the mercantile district downtown. This modern photograph features magnificent live oak trees that were less imposing, if they were there at all, when the Evans family lived in the house. Courtesy of the Library of Congress.

INDEPENDENCE AND THE POLITICS OF WAR

William Smith had none of Evans's confidence in the Confederacy. Still, he exploited the opportunities it afforded his ambitions. Although his third marriage had eased his chronic loneliness, William spent much of the war away from Wilhemine, brooding in her absence. When he served as a delegate to Alabama's secession convention and a member of the Confederate Congress, his letters to her examined his feelings and justified his public conduct. With its affectionate inequality, Smith's marriage seemed to exemplify satisfying relations between free people, and it increasingly anchored him in an unstable world. He sensed a contradiction between men's independence and their ambitions, including his own, but he could not fully understand it. In ways he never explained, and probably could not, he thought that men's political conduct somehow reflected their relations with women. Although he questioned his motives, Smith did not see how anxieties about mastery shaped his thought. Plagued during the war by terrifying uncertainties, he advocated freedom and feared its loss.

In several ways, Smith epitomized the problems of the middle class in a slave society. Through hard work and three favorable marriages, he had achieved comfort. He lived most of his life in Tuscaloosa, where middle-class people thrived, but his congressional district ran from the ordinary farming county of Fayette, where he once lived, to the rich plantation areas in the Black Belt. He relied on large majorities in Tuscaloosa but, necessarily, he appealed to all classes of white men. His writing interpreted the difficulties of self-determination in terms that blended psychology, politics, and class. Smith's story "The Memoirs of an Ambitious Man" had criticized the self-indulgence of a wealthy planter's child, who eventually reformed himself. "The Candidate" had bared the tensions bred by ambition and critically portrayed both an overseer with a "nigger dog" and a drunken poor man. And *As It Is* satirized the weak self-control of a southern congressman and the decadence of the nation's capital. Consistently, Smith's images revealed the inner doubts of a middle-class man who sought self-determination and acceptance in a slave society.

As Alabama approached secession, Smith wrote his 1860 Phi Beta Kappa poem *The Uses of Solitude*. Written partly to combat the popular rage for secession, it was an extended call for independence, and most of it explained how solitude led to greatness. In its darker passages, however, Smith conceded that "solitary toil" could create "melancholy" and "minds unstrung." He insisted that "stubborn and superior" men made loneliness "a slave" to higher purposes, because geniuses used it to explore the "mazes of mysterious reason." The conclusion to Smith's poem, however, made solitude much less appealing, for it described the certainty of lonely death. In his stark imagery, a man's "nearest friend withdraws his kindred grasp" and "drops" his "icy body" into a "yawning gulf / Whose shadowy waves no beaches find to lave." Having urged self-reliance to the men of Phi Beta Kappa, Smith warned them of the death "all must reach" and "go alone." In the contest of the political crisis, however, this apparent contradiction makes sense, for he feared the dire consequences of reckless collective decisions.[31] For Smith, the "yawning gulf" of death was an existential reality that gave urgency to human choices. The "slave," melancholy, had taught this philosophy to a "stubborn and superior" man.

Smith's politics assured his isolation, for Unionists faced a "prejudging and unrelenting majority" ready to secede on Lincoln's election. Although towns harbored opposition to secession, divisions within the state were complex, and there was widespread hatred and fear of Republicans. Only months after he wrote *The Uses of Solitude*, his district sent Smith to the secession convention at Montgomery, where he opposed disunion. But he also defended slavery, and he wrestled with narrowing choices as Alabama left the Union. While crowds celebrated in the streets, a "trembling" Smith wrote his wife that "the holiday feeling is fraught with the demons of dissolution. The country is destroyed – unless God in his kindness should roll back the tide of this disastrous Revolution," and he did not expect deliverance. Acutely lonely, he

---

[31] *The Uses of Solitude* (Tuscaloosa: Printed for the Alabama Alpha of the Phi Beta Kappa Society of the University at Tuscaloosa, 1860), 22–23, 45.

told Wilhemine that the time away from her seemed "like years." Not just his "solitary nights" but the "momentous character" of secession had "spread out the time so indefinitely."[32]

With the weight of unwelcome choices upon him, Smith defended his independence to his wife but also showed his need for approval. Before the final vote on secession, he made two pleas for Union, for which he was "heartily congratulated," and, afterward, he was "entirely satisfied" with his opposing vote. Distressed by the "anarchy" around him, he questioned the fire-eaters' morality, but he erased the line because there were "honest and patriotic men" among them. He clarified his options for Wilhemine. He could oppose the convention's decision and "array the people of the state, one against the other in a desperate Civil War," or he could "surrender" his "scruples" and help them unite. Smith did not admit that continued Unionism would wreck his career. He defended his decision to "share the state's destiny."[33]

Unsure that his Unionist wife agreed with his choice, William justified himself by emphasizing their inequality. As a woman, she could not "imagine" his delicate position. He was bound to the majority's decision, which might require him to fight, while she would enjoy "larger liberties." He had "learned by experience" that "tears *will indeed 'make the head ache,'*" but she would "weep *tonight*." Smith did not disdain, for he respected his wife. In the convention, he had quoted a poem about the American flag she wrote during the election of 1860. It had "brought down the House and galleries most tremendously," and he promised to acknowledge her authorship "in some delicate way." Nonetheless, he feared that public disclosure of her opinions would create problems for them. And he warned Wilhemine: "*Word* your letters cautiously."[34] Custom limited her freedom and he approved, in the face of growing southern nationalism.

Realizing how much he depended on Wilhemine, William praised her abilities and frequently expressed his love. He knew she could "manage" the

---

[32] With a very shaky hand, Smith wrote a brief note at 3:00 on January 11, saying that he was "trembling" at the passage of the ordinance and the rejoicing people; the following day he wrote a longer letter, still agitated, about the "demons of dissolution" and "disastrous Revolution"; "solitary nights," from the same letter. William Smith to Wilhemine Smith, January 11 and 12, 1861, in Easby-Smith Papers, LC.

[33] The note at 3:00, January 11, contained the information that his speech had been "heartily congratulated"; "anarchy," comments that were erased, and his choices; William to Wilhemine, January 12, 1861, in *ibid*.

[34] The contrast between their positions and his use of her writing, William to Wilhemine, January 12, 1861; advice on cautious wording, William to Wilhemine, January 20, 1861; both in *ibid*. In the latter letter, he also suggested she write on "domestic and not political subjects," and said he would keep her letter but "hide it carefully – from other eyes." Someone, perhaps a family member, sent Millard Fillmore a copy of Wilhemine's speech; he praised her effort and said he remembered her as a young girl; Millard Fillmore to Wilhemine Easby-Smith, October 17, 1860; *ibid*. There are a few letters from Wilhemine to William Smith in the Easby-Smith Papers, UNC, but the most important Civil War correspondence is at LC. Unfortunately, some of it is indecipherable.

household "better than I could do it myself." Wilhemine's competence freed William to act independently, and their intimacy comforted him. He wrote her about how well he slept (or not), what he ate, and how he felt. He promised he had not drunk "a tumbler full" of wine during his absence – a precision that suggests she watched his consumption. He described his love. Her "arms" were "the *gates of Paradise*," appending a pun: "(will the *figure* do?)." Her letters, he wrote, "always lift me out of the company and business in which I may happen to be."[35] He felt more complete because of her.

Just beneath the surface of his marriage, however, household slavery also increased Smith's freedom of action, and he reminded Wilhemine of his authority by directing the slaves through her. The Smith household had five slaves: two adult women, a young adult man, and two children. Wilhemine probably relied on all but the youngest. The Smiths' garden helped feed the family, and William sent Wilhemine instructions about its planting throughout the January convention. Just before secession, he wrote that she should "not fail to plant peas early" and "have" the asparagus planted with a little manure. She should "tell Buck" to buy cotton seed. A few weeks later, he gave more instructions about what she should "have" done: "have" the "little box-hot-bed" moved to hold early lettuce; "have" the celery transplanted in rows near the turnips; "have the spade run down between the celery rows." Wilhemine's job was to "manage," and William usually did not name the slaves who would labor at her command.[36] He directed a team of subordinates from a distance, confident that they would function without his physical presence, because Wilhemine knew his wishes.

Smith had significant anxieties about mastery, however, and his letters sometimes exposed them. He had asked Wilhemine to read Boswell's life of Johnson so their "minds" would "be running on the same themes" – "the great phases of human life." His reading prompted the solitary writer to self-criticism, and, only half seriously, he wrote "My Darling" about his odd daydreams. His weary mind had created, "out of the shadowy realm of vacancy," images with the "absolute necessity of reality," but he knew that the images were not real. It was a "happy man," he claimed, who can imagine a world and then "contemplate with real sadness the downfall of his own creation fragment by fragment." He may have remembered his poem about the

[35] She could "manage," William to Wilhemine, January 12, 1861; comment about wine, January 15, 1861; arms like Paradise, January 12, 1861; her letters lifting him up, January 20, 1861; all in Easby-Smith Papers, LC.

[36] Comments on peas and asparagus, with note about Buck and the cotton seed, January 10, 1861; further instructions on planting, January 20, 1861, when he did "not feel so gloomy as I did a week ago"; both, William to Wilhemine, *ibid*. Another letter in early spring sent instructions to Buck about the livestock and more planting that she was to "have" done, although some of these instructions were more direct: "Sow lettuce ... sow the balance of turnips ... and the rest of the green beans – and another bed of peas." It seems evident that William was customarily in charge of the garden, and he wrote that he would "expect a great vegetable dinner" when he got home; William to Wilhemine, April 12, 1861, *ibid*. For the ages of slaves, see U.S. Census, 1860, slave schedules, Tuscaloosa County.

solitary dreams of ambitious men when he granted that such fantasies could be "dangerous," though there were "no days in dreams."[37] Watching ambitious Confederates turn a fantasy into frightening reality, Smith's thoughts repeatedly turned inward.

And, in this same letter, Smith reflected again about the relationship between independence and mastery. He offered Wilhemine a little mock-biography in which he claimed that his innately good "disposition" as a boy had been overwhelmed by arrogance and the "sweeping habiliments of ambition." Becoming morose and selfish, he had "nursed" the "diseases of solitude." Taught by his mother the "single idea of his superiority," he used his "marvelous mind" to imagine companions, but he saw they were no substitute for real friends. More than two decades earlier, the autobiographical sketch "Memoirs of an Ambitious Man" had connected Smith's mother, who made him a "little Caesar," with his mastery over slaves. This time, Smith ignored slavery as he admitted that his sense of superiority isolated him from other free men.[38] Still confident that he had been right to oppose secession, he felt alienated and alone.

Whatever his anxieties, Smith's ambitions were intact, and he was already involved in his latest project: *The History and Debates of the Convention of the People of Alabama, January 1861*. It would preserve Smith's words, but he did not expect it to boost his literary reputation because it contained other men's speeches, too. If critics believed it was "*my* duty to supply brains to the book," he joked, "I shall be terribly flagellated." But he would be happy if it made money. As the Confederacy formed in Montgomery, Smith readied his book. He assessed the cost of printing in different towns, gathered transcripts of speeches, and lobbied the Alabama legislature to subscribe to the publication. Aware of his market, he calculated that if the state bought three hundred copies at $5.00 each, he would earn enough to print abundant copies for sale. He wrote his wife that he felt "comfort in the prospective profit" he could make without risk.[39]

Despite his fears about an impending war, Smith was cheered by his return to writing. A trip to Atlanta to supervise his book's printing suggested literary prospects in the Confederacy. Atlanta was "peculiarly" suited for "a great publishing house, as books can be hence disseminated with the greatest facility." He wrote Wilhemine that the speeches in his book would not be "as dull" as he had feared. Reading Boswell had reminded him of the "difficulties and annoyances which the great men of the earth have encountered, particularly

---

[37] Request that she read Boswell, April 12, 1861; the reflections, April 15, 1861; William to Wilhemine, Easby-Smith Papers, LC.
[38] *Ibid.* For the earlier autobiography, see *supra*, Chapter 3, 84–87, where quoted phrases are cited.
[39] William to Wilhemine, January 14 and February 13, *ibid*. William Russell Smith, ed., *The History and Debates of the Convention of the People of Alabama ... on the Seventh day of January, 1861* ... (Montgomery: White, Pfister & Co.; Atlanta: Wood, Hanleiter, Rice & Co.; Tuscaloosa: D. Woodruff, 1861; Spartanburg, SC: Reprint Co., 1975).

those who had to write for their bread and butter." Half in jest, he compared himself to "intellectual giants" and hoped that future readers would "reward and celebrate him with praises."[40]

To no one's surprise, Smith played a starring role in *The History and Debates*. Also unsurprisingly, he had second thoughts about his political independence, or lack of it, as he recorded the convention's proceedings. He wrote Wilhemine that he almost regretted not making a major speech against secession, for his views had been "perfectly matured." A full explanation would probably have given him "character" before the public but also "a hostility that would have been unrelenting." Although Smith's speeches had briefly defended slavery, they also explained his loyalty to the Union, his hopes for rapid reconstruction, and his insistence that the will of the people must be obeyed. While making him appear a thoughtful leader, Smith's book highlighted his willingness to adjust his ambitions in an unpredictable setting.[41]

Privately, Smith saw himself as a responsible man among irresponsible Confederates. Initially unsure how to "shoulder the troubles of the state," he raised recruits and was commissioned a colonel. He immediately resigned, however, to seek election to the House of Representatives, where he served two terms. Smith's hopes for the Confederacy waxed and waned, but he lent it lukewarm support. Having accepted it because of "controlling and uncontrollable circumstances," he feared that war would bring devastation and the end of slavery, and he urged peaceful reunion. Early on, he warned Wilhemine that a "long war" would produce a "dictatorship" by the "stubborn" leaders of the Confederacy. The country would fill with "beggars – bullies – and thieves." In every town a "blustering corporal" would organize common men "demoralized" by "poverty" into "squads" of pillagers.[42] From the war's start, he imagined a society ruined by mastery and degradation.

Smith's personal mastery diminished with war, as Wilhemine acted more independently. He reminded her in the spring of 1862 that he had "the utmost confidence in her ability to take care of herself," and she did.[43] When Wilhemine

---

[40] William to Wilhemine, April 12, 1861, Easby-Smith Papers, LC. Several months earlier he had hoped that "the South will be more profitable than formerly," writing specifically about publishing his book and, in general, about their financial difficulties; William to Wilhemine, January 20, 1861, *ibid*.

[41] William to Wilhemine, January 14, 1861, *ibid*.; he quipped that he thought he had "let a bird go" when he decided not to make the speech. His fullest speech on popular government was an argument that the Confederate Constitution should be submitted to the people for a vote; *History and Debates*, esp. 347–348.

[42] "Shoulder the troubles" and "controlling ... circumstances," William to Wilhemine, January 14, 1861; characterization of a "long war," July 23, 1861; both in Easby-Smith Papers, LC. The best source for following Smith's movements during the war is Anne Easby-Smith, *William Russell Smith of Alabama; His Life and Works, Including the Entire Text of the Uses of Solitude* (Philadelphia: Dolphin Press, 1931); on his military recruitment, see 134–137, 141.

[43] "Utmost confidence," William to Wilhemine, May 6, 1982, in Easby-Smith Papers, LC. In 1861, sixteen-year-old Sidney joined the army and Smith's older children went to live with his

unexpectedly demonstrated her independence by becoming a Roman Catholic, William quietly acquiesced. He was a casual Christian who saw her as his best link with the divine, but he had, in Congress, attacked Catholicism and said that he wanted to "teach American wives that their husbands are their only confessors." Years later, Wilhemine described the news of her conversion as "the most severe blow that ever befell" William. Because of an inheritance, she had been "utterly independent," but she was unsure "whether he would bid me take my children and go – or what." But he accepted her decision, and she remembered his self-control – the "battle he must have fought with himself" – and his "great and abiding love and respect for me."[44] From her perspective, his willingness to accept her religious autonomy strengthened their marriage.

While many Confederates, like Evans, found comfort in God and nationalism, Smith had only his wife. From Richmond in 1862, when Union armies occupied the Virginia peninsula, William described his continued isolation. He had never before "realized so sensibly the solitariness of my nature," he wrote Wilhemine. His "hundreds of acquaintances" were like "total strangers." His solace was that it made her his "only refuge, and secures to you the heart more completely." He vented his political opinions to her. When the fall's Confederate offensive produced the bloody battle at Antietam and the preliminary Emancipation Proclamation, Smith raged at Lincoln for provoking slave insurrection and predicted that emancipation would prevent British aid to the South. But he was angrier at southerners who had planned the invasion of the North. He fumed that Davis and his supporters would never negotiate, and even "the slaughter of the women and children of the entire South would not change their stubbornness."[45]

In February of 1863, Smith wrote his wife a letter that showed the depth of his fears. His fiction had loosely connected political mastery with the domination of women and slavery. Now he completely merged them in a nightmarish vision of an America with white slaves. Writing from the empty hall of the

---

second wife's family in a rural part of the state. William and Wilhemine's daughter Mamie was sent to school in Washington, under the care of Wilhemine's mother (and the protection of federal armies). Wilhemine and the younger children stayed sometimes in Tuscaloosa, on one occasion in a Mobile boarding house, and often they traveled about. Wilhemine went to New Orleans and, late in the war, to Washington, to care for family business. At least one black member of the household traveled with her as a nurse.

[44] Smith's most thorough speech against Catholicism, *Congressional Globe*, 33nd Congress, 2nd Session, *Appendix*, 94–103, quote, 103; conversion episode is described in Easby-Smith with a great deal of editorial commentary; the letter containing the quoted passage (undated), 138–139, quote 139. Easby-Smith also says that her father had "for many years drifted from religious practice," at the time of this event, 138. Anne C. Rose discusses the conversion and the Smith's family's management of religious differences in the context of Protestant-Catholic marriages in *Beloved Strangers: Interfaith Families in Nineteenth-Century America* (Cambridge, M.A: Harvard University Press, 2001), 98–109.

[45] His loneliness, William to Wilhemine, July 21, 1862; comments on Antietam and its results, William to Wilhemine, September 26 and October 21, 1861, Easby-Smith Papers, LC.

House of Representatives, where he was opposing the centralization of war power, Smith indicted South and North. Both parts of "our great continent," he groaned, were approaching something "infinitely worse than anarchy." He foresaw the strong ruling the weak, with "brutal war" becoming "the trade of men and servility, degradation, and wretchedness, the fate of women." Anglo-Americans had long been known as a "great race of men," but soon they would be "superior" only in "physical ability, brutality of habit and stubbornness of resolution."[46] The negative model of slavery defined Smith's fears.

Smith doubted that "popular government" could survive the war. With the southern people seething like a "human volcano" under strain, their leaders had decided that only "a centralizing tyranny" could "check and control" the "demon spirits" at work. Considering that awful possibility in familiar images, Smith found it "hard to give up our cradled ideas of human liberty." It was "hard to surrender" the notion that America was the world's home for "Freedom," but liberty was "a frail figure" that must be "protected and supported by law and order." Even if the South won, its "very success" would produce the power "which resides only in a single arm." Wondering if Americans had misjudged human nature, he bitterly described his century's political philosophy in the phrase "*man must have a master*."[47] Although he would not abandon hope, Smith feared that freedom would yield to universal slavery.

As usual, however, Smith was treating his melancholy by writing Wilhemine, and he allayed it further by composing a satiric drama. Perhaps with an eye on the fall's elections, Smith created propaganda, but he also intended to wring money from Confederate readers. He wrote Wilhemine that the "grotesqueness" of *The Royal Ape* satirized the "facts" about Lincoln, and its name reflected widespread caricatures of the president in the press. Late in February, Smith sketched its five acts; a month later, he asked Wilhemine to criticize the manuscript. He urged her not to "fear of ever offending me," although she might "seriously object" to its "flirtatious" parts, which he thought would amuse men. Smith vacillated about having his play performed. He bragged that "gentlemen of taste and literary ability" had pronounced its "excellence – surpassing *any thing of the day*," but he ruefully admitted that was "not much to say for it." In the end, he decided to have *The Royal Ape* printed instead of staged and planned to ask "some of the best publishing houses to push it," hoping for sales.[48]

The Royal Ape projected all of Smith's dread of universal slavery onto northerners. Set during the first battle at Manassas, it opened with a drunken melee in the Capitol just before the battle, and it concluded farcically with the Lincoln family's attempt to flee Washington after the Union defeat. To

[46] William to Wilhemine, February 5, 1863, *ibid*.
[47] *Ibid*.
[48] Outline with comments on "grotesqueness" and "facts," William to Wilhemine, February 23, 1863; "not to fear" making critical comments, March 5, 1863; he knew she would "seriously object," March 29, 1863; response of "gentlemen" and plans for publication, April 18, 1863; all in *ibid*.

ridicule "Yankees," Smith put much of their dialogue in silly rhymed couplets. Drawing on the traditions of carnival, in which low people took high rank and upturned moral standards, Smith made women and slaves rule. And he figuratively crowned Lincoln as the lord of misrule, a jester who became king.[49] Echoing rumors circulated by Lincoln's opponents, Smith depicted the president as a coward and a tyrant. Even while he ridiculed northern politicians, however, Smith's satire revealed deeper fears he had repeatedly expressed.

Rather like Congressman Sterling in *As It Is*, Smith's Lincoln displayed his weakness through dependence on women. Smith's treatment of the president's marriage inverted the author's ideal: emotional union between relative equals, with men fondly dominant. A simpering idiot, Smith's Mary Lincoln spurred the ambitions of her husband and her son Robert, and she ignored their faults instead of bolstering their morality. In the "flirtatious" passages, Robert seduced the servants and joked crudely about his sexual exploits, and the bumbling president made passes at the same girls. After the battle, as the family scrambled to flee, the maids disguised Robert as a girl. At his wife's bidding, the president donned a scotch cap and striped pants – a reference to rumors of his disguise traveling through Baltimore before his inauguration. As they fled, Mrs. Lincoln stuffed into their clothing copies of her husband's youthful poetry – mostly sentimental tributes to her. Lincoln meekly thanked his wife: "I am ruled by you, / And would be ever led by one so true."[50]

Smith designed this line for a laugh, but it was rooted in serious concerns. Both Lincoln's subordination to his wife and his flirtations reflected Smith's anxiety that men could not be fully autonomous because they needed women. In satirizing Lincoln's poetry, moreover, Smith hinted at himself. One of his first publications was the romantic poem *The Bridal Eve*, and he wrote love sonnets to Wilhemine from Richmond, joking that the poems might immortalize them.[51] Smith accepted his wife's relative independence and sensed his

---

[49] *The Royal Ape: A Dramatic Poem* (Richmond: West & Johnson, 1863) did not carry Smith's name, and it was printed in Columbia, South Carolina, by the South Carolinian Book and Job Office (which also printed Evans's *Macaria* at about the same time). Smith had southerners call northerners "Yankees" throughout the play. A rare literary analysis of *The Royal Ape* is in Elizabeth Young, *Disarming the Nation: Women's Writing and the Civil War* (Chicago: University of Chicago Press, 1999), 50–54, which argues that the play "suggests the wartime rhetoric of national masculinity turned topsy-turvy in both racial and sexual terms," 50. Perhaps Smith chose Manassas as a means of combating his depression, for he had written Wilhemine following the battle: "I shall not again despair," July 23, 1861, in Easby-Smith Papers, LC.

[50] Lincoln's comment to his wife, 76, *Royal Ape*. Lincoln asks his wife to gather his manuscripts so that, if he is remembered as a "tyrant," people will still "link me with gentler memories," 74. The bundle of poetry contains five hundred sonnets about "Mrs. Lincoln's young perfections," with such names as "The Western Goddess" and "Diana's Sister." Other poems include "The Magic Touch of Whiskers," and there is one "five act tragedy" called "The Bloody Plot"; titles, 75. Smith wrote a five-act tragedy about Aaron Burr when he was in Mobile in 1836, although only a fragment survives.

[51] Smith's daughter wrote that her father always wrote sonnets to his wife on her birthday. William wrote Wilhemine that "these sonnets will live long after we have passed away."

own dependence. Mary Lincoln represented Smith's fear that, if men "must have a master," women would take the role.

Slaves also sought mastery in *The Royal Ape*. Twenty-five years earlier, Smith had written that slavery encouraged a child to be an autocrat, and now that negative paradigm infected his play. Smith placed its climax at Manassas. After brief scenes of southerners' bravery, two slaves – Sambo and Hercules – in "grotesque" Confederate uniforms captured two Republican politicians who had come to watch the battle. With gun pointed, Sambo ordered one of the men to "shed" his clothes: "You am dis darkee's *prisoner*. S'render at screshun, or I'll blow you clean away to Bosting." When the politician protested "I am the colored man's friend. I come here to assist you," Sambo retorted, "Well den, just gib me a good suit ob close!" Suddenly producing a hidden gun, the Yankee shot Sambo, proclaiming "so perish all the South, both black and white." But Sambo was only stunned, and, after a "terrible struggle," the slave pinned the politician to the ground. Smith ended his climactic act with mastery turned upside down.[52]

Smith's doubts about human nature showed in his racial imagery. In his depiction, Sambo saw through the Yankee's claim of friendship, and the cowardly politicians lied, while the slaves' actions matched their words. Despite their rude diction and comical clothing, Smith's slaves were anything but docile. As Sambo marched his "contraband" back to the Confederate camp, he announced his motive: "ebery nigger dat captivates a Yankee is to be free." Although Sambo was deceived in that, his line revealed Smith's knowledge that slaves wanted freedom.[53] Like the woman who ruled her husband, Sambo and Hercules reflected Smith's fears of a universal desire for mastery.

But the most compelling projection of Smith's fears was his "melancholy" Lincoln, and the northern president was strikingly like the author. Smith gave the president two modes of speech: that of a tragic hero and that of a buffoon. Before the battle, the president declined to "play the jester" in "the solumn grandeur of this hour, / When death makes ready for its carnival." And Lincoln soliloquized in earnest, his language full of Smith's convictions:

> I saw the glittering columns in their march,
> And felt an honest pride in the display;
> While, in the murmurs and confused sounds
> That came up from the marshal'd multitude,
> I recognized too well the mingled jest

He specifically compared her to Petrarch's Laura but did not claim he was the equal of the famous Italian poet. He later submitted several sonnets to her for criticism and promised to change the "lines" she had suggested he revise; letters quoted in Easby-Smith, *William Russell Smith*, 147.

[52] Quoted passages all from *Royal Ape*, act III, scene IV, 46–51.

[53] "ebery nigger," *ibid.*, 47. My interpretation linking Smith's worries about women and slaves parallel Young, *Disarming the Nation*, 50–54, although she does not refer to the author's personal life.

> And merry laugh of men unused to war.
> Resolves on victory or death are solemn,
> And nurse themselves in silent meditation.

Like the "trembling" Smith in Montgomery, Lincoln decried premature celebration: "I do not like this merriment; it tells / Of shallow half resolves; betrays impatience, / An empty eagerness to win the fight, / Anticipating victory as of course."[54] Smith's deliberate use of blank verse gave a tragic stature to his "royal ape" that no satire could completely undo.

Smith's Lincoln was no more paralyzed by his fear than was the melancholy author. Instead, the president sought mastery, in terms that echoed Smith's frightened letter to Wilhemine. Lincoln believed that "a state of war is one of despotism. / There should be, to control it, but one will; / And that must be untrammel'd. Tyranny, / Brutal, remorseless tyranny is needful / To bring successes." With unrelenting ambition, Smith's Lincoln planned to blame the "babbling Senators" for defeat – to make himself the "star / And centre of this desolating war." Once more, after Manassas, the president spoke Smith's fears of "the beginning of the deadliest strife / That ever mark'd the animosities / Of those God-imaged monsters we call men." By controlling those monsters, Lincoln enacted Smith's bitter observation about his century's philosophy: that "*man must have a master.*"[55]

Smith's dénouement made the president a carnival figure, but, like a tragic hero, Lincoln's desire for mastery doomed him. And this Lincoln saw his fate, even as he spoke in silly rhymes. Like the "ancient king transformed into an ass," he would "go forth" as "the jeer'd of every fool whose idiot eyes may glow / With merry glances at my overthrow." Smith's Lincoln ended the drama playing the "*ape.*"[56] Although Smith wanted Confederates to laugh at their foe's humiliation, his play revealed the author's inner fear. As his daydream about the pleasure in destroying an imaginary world "fragment by fragment" suggested, Smith feared his own potential for tyranny, and, in too many ways, the president who was both tragic and comic was like the ambitious southerner. The carnival spirit of *The Royal Ape* bespoke a nightmare, and, despite his ridicule of Yankees, Smith did not say where order rightly lay.

Indeed, for all of its propaganda, Smith's play asked Confederate readers to think as well as laugh at their opponents. Hamstrung by ambitions that joined his fate to that of the South, Smith could not be truly independent. He was,

---

[54] Robert Lincoln calls his father "melancholy" in a long conversation with his mother about whether Lincoln's depressed state indicates that he is mad or great, 18–21; jester at carnival, 24; soliloquy, 21; all in *Royal Ape*. Most of Lincoln's observations occur in the context of conversations with General Winfield Scott. For a creative discussion of Lincoln's tendency to depression see Joshua Wolf Shenk, *Lincoln's Melancholy: How Depression Challenged a President and Fueled his Greatness* (Boston: Houghton Mifflin, 2005). Whether Smith knew much about Lincoln's melancholy or not, it seems clear that the commonly depressed southerner felt some underlying similarity with the northern president, as he understood him.

[55] "Despotism" through "star and centre," 31; "monsters," 66; both in *Royal Ape*.

[56] "Ancient king," 76; "ape," 85; *Royal Ape*.

after all, up for reelection in 1863. But he denied lofty principles to the few white southerners in *The Royal Ape*. The brave and (once more) "stubborn" Confederate leaders who briefly appeared in the climax urged rebel soldiers to victory without a single word about liberty, or any other political ideal. Smith satirized the North, but his Confederacy did not symbolize human freedom, and he may have thought of stubborn southerners when he wrote that "every fool" would jeer at Lincoln's "overthrow."[57] Because Smith himself felt the impulse to mastery – he was the "stubborn and superior" man in *The Uses of Solitude* – he worried that "God-imaged monsters" reflected universal human nature. He hoped for a middle-class world in which white people prospered through self-reliance, but slavery defaced his dreams. Believing he acted responsibly, Smith voiced the profound uncertainties of a class that had trapped itself.

THE LESSONS OF WAR

Like William Smith, Jeremiah Clemens thought secession was disastrous, and he believed he represented ordinary people. Clemens was widely regarded as a brilliant man, but he was self-obsessed, ambitious, and, by 1860, weakened from longtime alcohol abuse. Although his loyalties shifted, Clemens eventually cooperated with the Lincoln administration. In 1865, he published *Tobias Wilson: A Tale of the Great Rebellion*, a novel that staked his claim to office in a postwar South.[58] Clemens idealized friendship in his fictional society of humble Unionists, as he had in his earlier fiction, and his idealizations seemed even more self-referential than before. But Clemens also wrote from his heart. With real sympathy, he assigned middle-class values to plain farmers who fought the Confederacy. No longer committed to slavery, Clemens saw its reflection in the murderous impulses of white men. He refused to glorify war, although he admired its more heroic moments. Like Evans and Smith, Clemens had come to believe that people must act independently in an unpredictable world, never sure that they were right.

After his controversial term in the Senate ended in 1853, Clemens had not held political office. In the late fifties, his three novels had been published with one of the largest American firms, J. B. Lippincott. The second, *Mustang*

[57] "Stubborn" characterization comes from General P. T. Beauregard's oration to his soldiers during the battle, 39, in the climatic act III, *ibid*. Beauregard's speeches concentrate on heroics; one closes by telling the soldiers: "Let him be a laggard who would be a slave!" 36. Jefferson Davis appears briefly on the battlefield, but Smith could not go so far as to give the Confederate president any words. Perhaps significantly, Smith's only serious reference to freedom comes in the words of a northern citizen who insists on "freedom of speech" and the Constitution because he wants to shout for Davis and the Confederacy, and a crowd would shut him up, 57; all in *ibid*.

[58] (Philadelphia: J. B. Lippencott & Co., 1865). The best analysis of the novel is in Wallace Hettle, "'Curing the Sir Walter Disease': The Politics and Fiction of Jeremiah Clemens," in *The Peculiar Democracy: Southern Democrats in War and Peace* (Athens: University of Georgia Press, 2001): 122–141. Less useful because of its author's pro-Confederate bias is William Stanley Hoole, "Jeremiah Clemens, Novelist," *AR* 18 (January 1965): 5–36.

Gray, even found its way into German translation, and, according to *DeBow's Review*, its sales were "immense." All of Clemens's novels featured sympathetic outcasts who reflected his resentment at the political elite that scorned him.[59] Ironically, however, the man who never felt accepted by Huntsville's upper class achieved wealth just before his human property vanished. With his elderly father's death in 1860, Clemens inherited one-third of an estate that included two plantations, an elegant town house (where he would live), and more than 125 slaves. Not long thereafter, John Read, Jere's father-in-law, also died, leaving Mary Clemens one-fourth of his smaller estate. By specifying that Jere could "in no way" use her inheritance, Read guarded his child from her erratic husband.[60]

As the election of 1860 neared, Clemens reentered politics, campaigning for John Bell, the former Whig who opposed secession. Despite his alarm, Clemens moved carefully. After Lincoln was elected, Clemens wrote John Crittenden, the Unionist senator from Kentucky, that Alabama's Unionists had a "difficult and dangerous game to play" but must gain *"time."* Sorry that Lincoln won, he thought the election "strictly legal and constitutional" and not as bad as the refusal of northerners to return fugitive slaves. He denied any *"right* of secession," and he said he would not be dragged "into treason," but he did "not pretend" to see his way "clearly" out of the crisis. In an equivocal letter to the Huntsville *Advocate*, Clemens blamed secessionists' lies and northerners' "hypocritical cant." He wanted slavery's security but thought southerners should unite only to protect it, "not to plunge into revolution." Still, he promised to cooperate if secessionists prevailed, for "if they wreck themselves," they would "wreck me and my neighbors also."[61] At odds with the majority, Clemens thought independence futile.

[59] *DeBow's* claimed to be quoting the "New-York Journal of Commerce" (but did not use quotation marks) to the effect that *Mustang Grey* had an "immense sale," 28 (September 1860): 352. The same passage also claimed that Evans's *Beulah* "had passed through fifteen editions in three months." *Mustang Gray: A Romance* (Philadelphia: J. B. Lippincott & Co., 1858) was copyrighted in 1857 but issued by that firm at least twice in 1858 (with the same text but different advertisements in the back of the volume) and again in 1859; the German printing was issued as *Mustang Gray: Eine Erzählung aus Texas*, translated by Wilhelm Eduard Drugulin (Leipzig: Verlag von Christian Ernst Kollmann, 1859). *Bernard Lile* (Philadelphia: J. B. Lippincott & Co., 1856), Clemens's first novel, was reprinted in 1858 and again in 1869. *The Rivals* (Philadelphia: J. B. Lippincott, 1859) was reissued in 1860 by the same firm. WorldCat, the source for the printing years, does not identify multiple printings of the same edition in any given year, and there is no reliable way to determine how many copies of these books sold, lacking extensive records from Lippincott.
[60] Will of James Clemens, Madison County (AL) Will Book 1, p. 299, dated September 14, 1855, with a codicil providing for keeping the estate intact until the eldest reached 21, placing the estate under Jere's control, and freeing four slaves, 300. In January of 1861, Clemens and the other executors declined to serve, 301. Will of John Read, Book 1, 257, probated April 22, 1861. A complete listing of the Clemens estate is in Bell and Hardaway, "James Clemens of Washington County, Pennsylvania ...," Jeremiah Clemens folder, Huntsville Heritage Room, Huntsville-Madison County Public Library.
[61] Clemens to John Crittenden, November 26, 1860, in Crittenden Papers, LC, Washington, DC; Clemens to Hon. H. B. Wood, printed in the Huntsville *Advocate*, December 5, 1860.

Clemens could not stand on solid ground. Elected to the secession convention, he pledged to Crittenden that he would "cling to the Union though it leads me to the *gibbet*," but only if slavery was protected. At the convention, he opposed secession but voted for the final ordinance. After secession, Clemens became major general in the state militia but resigned after the Confederate government was formed. He wanted higher office – eyeing the new Senate seat – but he was widely mistrusted. One Democrat wrote that Clemens was "as dead as a stinking & putrifying mackerel" and should not get a single vote. In the spring of 1862, when federal troops occupied Huntsville, Clemens returned to Unionism. With his former friend Clement Clay now a Confederate senator and most of upper-class Huntsville supporting the Confederacy, Clemens associated with Union officers and egregiously offended his neighbors. One local diarist recorded with disgust that Mrs. Clemens "dashed by" en route to an outing with Union officers' wives "right in front of the funeral procession" of a Confederate soldier. Behind the scenes, Clemens negotiated with the Lincoln administration.[62] By mid-war, the man who would not be dragged into treason was called a traitor.

The best of men could not have navigated these shoals well, and Clemens foundered. In the fall of 1862, he defended himself to his daughter Mary, the wife of a Confederate officer. He reminded her that he "never pretended to any extravagant love" for the Confederacy. He had been "forced into" it, despite his fear that it would end in "military despotism." Clemens made principled claims: "I pity the man whose actions are governed by his feelings," he wrote, "or who can not contemplate the possibility of doing right because it is right." Still, he admitted that he had entertained northerners in his home. Some of them were friends from the Mexican War, who were simply doing their duty. He insisted that no civilized person should "abstain from social intercourse" with "old friends."[63] Hoping his daughter would forgive him, Clemens claimed that he was true to his principles under duress.

---

[62] Clemens to Crittenden, December 25, 1860 (the day after the secession convention election), in Crittenden Papers, LC; the unidentified Democrat was writing former U.S. Congressman George Smith Houston, November 6, 1861, in Houston Papers, DUL; Mary Chadick quoted in *Incidents of the War: The Civil War Journal of Mary Jane Chadick*, edited and annotated by Nancy Rohr (Huntsville, AL: Huntsville-Madison County Historical Society, 2005), entry for July 5, 1862, 69. Rohr's annotations helpfully track the events that transpired in Huntsville during the war. William S. Hoole claims that "distrusted, disillusioned, and disgusted, the sick, sensitive former senator and soldier, no doubt seeing himself as some kind of martyr," went back to Huntsville after his "enemies" prevented his influence in the Confederacy, with no evidence for any of these statements. Hoole's Confederate sympathies are revealed in his claim that the occupied territory around Huntsville was a "center of refuge" for Unionist "traitors, deserters, renegades, mossbacks, and marauding outlaws who terrorized the countryside, destroying property, raping, murdering and committing other atrocious crimes"; Hoole, "Jeremiah Clemens, Novelist," 26. Clemens's attempt to negotiate is described in a letter from Gen. O. M. Mitchel at Huntsville to the Secretary of War, in May of 1862; *War of the Rebellion: A Complication of the Official Records of the Union and Confederate Armies* (Washington, DC, 1880–1892): 1, X, 167.

[63] Clemens to "my dear daughter," September 5, 1862, in Jeremiah Clemens Papers, USAHI.

More honestly, however, Clemens explained that he acted to protect himself, his family, and his friends. Union officers were the only law in town, and Clemens used them. One officer had protected "mine & your Mother's property and had protected Clemens's wounded nephew without exacting a promise that the young man would not "rejoin the army." For these favors, Clemens invited the officer's wife to stay in his home. Another officer protected the family against people filling their "back yard, kitchen, & servants rooms" – "nurses, free negroes, convalescing, & straggling soldiers," who were disorderly. That officer would "lend no countenance to the business of enticing or stealing negroes," and Clemens also invited this man's wife to visit. These associations let Clemens help "such of our citizens as might get into trouble" and gained his family "a complete & perfect protection against insult or injury." Now, he wrote, the federals were gone, and he wanted to leave town so he would not be harassed.[64]

At this point, Clemens's hopes seemed minimal. He knew slavery was weakened, and he did not expect to live through the war. He wrote to his daughter that "Charles ran away with the Federals," that "Archy" was probably gone, too, and that five plantation slaves left "of their own accord & one was pressed & carried off with his wagon & team." Unhappy with his losses, he added that "the occupation of this County has been a costly business to us." "Perhaps" she might think that his "gloomy" letter came from "sick fancies," for he was bleeding from the stomach, and doctors suspected cancer. But he had the same morose convictions he "entertained before the war," and there was nothing to be done but suffer with "firmness." Clemens was so ill that he made a will in June of 1863, "being feeble in body." He left his daughter's husband his Mexican War pistol and saber, the "relics of a war not half so murderous as that in which he has himself borne so gallant a part."[65] Clemens's will reminded his family that he, too, had courage.

Nonetheless, only with the Union army's return to Huntsville in the winter of 1863–1864 did Clemens make a final break from the Confederacy. In January, Withers Clay reported to his brother Clement that Clemens gave an "oyster dinner" to celebrate the return of his friends. With the army at his back, Clemens presided over public meetings advocating reconstruction, but, in early April, he and his wife left Huntsville for Philadelphia. A Confederate diarist cheerfully commented that it was "a good sign for us." In October of 1864, Lippincott printed a letter from Clemens asking Alabamians to surrender their "delusions." Having lost their liberties to the "soulless tyranny" of the Davis administration, they should secede from the Confederacy, support Lincoln's reelection, and seek restoration of the Union. Shortly before the election, the "refugee" spoke at a Philadelphia Union League meeting to oppose

[64] *Ibid.*
[65] *Ibid.*; Will of Jeremiah Clemens, Madison County (AL) Will Book 1, p. 312, dated June 2, 1863.

the "enemies" of the nation.[66] With the Confederacy collapsing and slavery all but gone, Clemens made a firm choice.

Now Clemens's ambitions resurfaced to join politics and literature. Probably Clemens was writing a manuscript before he left Huntsville, for the final events of his novel *Tobias Wilson* took place in the fall of 1863, and its preface was dated January 9, 1865. Maybe he hoped his novel would sell in the South, but it aimed at northern readers, too, and perhaps one in particular. Shortly after finishing the book, Clemens wrote Lincoln with a plan to restore Alabama to the Union and the author to office. He described politics in northern Alabama, arguing that the state needed a loyal governor to repeal secession and abolish slavery. Clemens claimed that he had been "again and again urged" to apply for the position. After observing that an unsuccessful application would handicap his "usefulness" to the cause of reconstruction, he assured the president he would serve if needed.[67] In light of Clemens's ambitions, his novel would be useful.

To be fair, *Tobias Wilson* put the best possible face on Clemens's conduct without making him a hero. The author appeared in his novel only briefly, as a visitor to a rural home not long after secession. There he insisted that reckless opposition to the Confederacy would only "endanger" Unionists without promoting peace. Their wisest course was patience until "*action* promises to be useful." War was a "terrible agent," but it would destroy the "putrefying sores and loathsome cancers" that were "eating" the life from the Union. Clemens admitted that he referred to slavery with these gruesome images. Still, he counseled, "it would not be prudent" to broadcast such ideas "from the housetops."[68] Clemens wanted readers to believe that popular support for the Confederacy justified his caution and that his inaction was constructive.

To dramatize the hard choices Unionists faced in Alabama, *Tobias Wilson* portrayed a society torn from within. Clemens did not confront the divisions in his own town, where he was a pariah. Instead, he set his novel in mountainous Jackson County, just east of Huntsville, where most residents were small farmers, slaves were scattered, and Unionists were more numerous. From 1862 on, rival forces had roamed the region sweeping up supplies and recruits. War, Clemens wrote, had destroyed "the foundation of the social system." After secession, "love, friendship, natural affection, kindness, toleration, and charity, all died." Clearly referring to himself, he claimed that "he who refused to become a traitor had only the alternative of becoming an outcast." One of Clemens's plain-spoken characters connected the economic and moral results of war. It was "making men who were tolerably well off,

---

[66] Clay's comments in J. Withers Clay to Clement Clay, Jr., January 7, 1864, in Clay Family Papers, DUL; observation of the Clemens's departure by Chadick in *Incidents of the War*, 148; *Letter from the Hon. Jere. Clemens* (Philadelphia: J. B. Lippencott & Co., 1864), dated October 4, 1864; Clemens to J. H. Orne, October 26, 1864, in Gratz Collection, HSP, quoted passages 3, 13.

[67] Clemens to Abraham Lincoln, January 21, 1865, in Lincoln Papers, LC.

[68] *Tobias Wilson*, 25–26.

poor, and poor men, beggars; making honest men, thieves, and kind-hearted human beings, blood-thirsty panthers."[69] In Clemens's war-torn society, men lost their moral bearings.

The simple plot of *Tobias Wilson* allowed Clemens to focus his attention on his characters' ethical dilemmas. His hero Tobias, an earnest young Unionist, entered the conflict after Confederate predators murdered his beloved grandfather. Tobias (or Toby) loved and married Sophy Rogers, a poor, uneducated, but virtuous neighbor, whose warm-blooded brother Thomas was Toby's best friend. At Sophy's insistence, Tobias declined to seek revenge for his grandfather's murder and her brother took up the bloody task. As fighting escalated, the two men made different choices. Tobias joined the Union army in nearby Chattanooga, and Thomas became a ruthless partisan. Although Clemens's female characters gave men moral guidance, his novel centered on Tobias and Thomas, who were fully responsible for their decisions.

Clemens placed Tobias and Thomas within the remnants of a rural society devastated by war, and his fiction reflected his reduced hopes for the rising South. It contained hard-working, self-reliant farming people who cared nothing for slavery. They ploughed fields, tended livestock, cooked meals, and celebrated a marriage together. Hardy men explored caves, drank water from streams or liquor from flasks, and constantly explained themselves in good-natured, down-to-earth speech. Although Clemens was less talented than his younger cousin Samuel, or Mark Twain, *Tobias Wilson* anticipated Twain's later work in his candid portrayal of ordinary Americans. His animated, sometimes comic, dialogue made plain folk appealing despite their rough manners and lack of education. Like Twain, Jeremiah was ambivalent about respectable society, and he was clearly disillusioned with the ruling classes of the South. Minimizing invidious distinctions between men and women or well-born and humble, his Unionists treated one another with equality and respect.[70]

---

[69] *Tobias Wilson*, 168, 84. Nearly the entire novel takes place in Jackson County, near the headwaters of the Paint Rock River, which is near the Tennessee-Alabama border. Clemens's geographic and demographic descriptions were very specific, for he wanted his readers to understand that he was writing about the plainest Alabamians. In 1860, Jackson County contained 14,878 white people, of whom 482 were slaveholders. If the average white family contained five people, roughly 16 percent of the population lived in slaveholding households, and most of those would have been located near the Paint Rock or Tennessee Rivers, not in the tiny, isolated coves Clemens describes in graphic detail. The best account of Unionism in northern Alabama is Storey, *Loyalty and Loss*, although she does not deal with Clemens because she only treats men who never supported the Confederacy, which he briefly did.

[70] There has been no modern literary scholarship connecting Twain to his third cousin. Samuel did know of Jeremiah's existence; see his letter to his mother and sister, written from Honolulu, HI, noting that he had conversed with Anson Burlingame, U.S. Minister to China, who told him a "good deal" about Jeremiah, http://www.marktwainproject.org/xtf/view?docId=letters/uccl00101.xml;style=letter. Hettle draws attention to the sentimental style Clemens used in his earlier fiction and overlooks his use of vernacular and the treatment of plain characters in *Tobias Wilson*, in an otherwise helpful discussion of the significance of Clemens's movement away from traditional conceptions of honor; *Peculiar Democracy*, 137.

Clemens's hero Tobias clearly stood for middle-class values. Toby had been born in town to a comfortable family, but his father's speculations, and then his death, changed Toby's life. Clemens described how Tobias's grandfather liquidated the estate and emancipated all of the family's slaves, providing them with support, and moved Tobias and his mother to Jackson County. There, they worked hard and lived without regret for what they had lost. Tobias learned self-control, reason, and sympathy from his mother and grandfather, who gave him formal education and taught him to be "gentle and good." Although the boys at muster day called Toby "Miss Nancy" because he refused to fight his peers, the dutiful adolescent rejected the demands of competitive honor. The "single ray" of light in Tobias's "solitary boyhood" was his friendship with Thomas. Tobias and Thomas guided each other by discussing their differences, and they acted as equals, despite Tobias's relative refinement. Through their warm friendship, Clemens idealized the voluntary relations of a democratic society.[71]

That said, Clemens deepened his novel by making the friends represent competing ethical values in the Unionist South. Their moral dilemma was not whether but *how* a man should oppose the Confederacy – Clemens's own dilemma, as he saw it. With some sympathy for both, Clemens contrasted Thomas's middle-class ethics with Tobias's traditional ethos of honor. The standard of Tobias, Sophy, his mother, and his grandfather prohibited violence, envy, greed, and pride. Based in a simple religious faith, it extolled love, fellowship, humility, and equality, which made it the antithesis of a slave society. Thomas's standard called for competition, bravery, and revenge – a plain man's version of southern honor. Tobias rejected some, but not all, of Thomas's standard, for he applied religious ideals to martial honor in a Christian warrior's code that required defense of home and family. The two men shared an egalitarian outlook as well as honesty, intelligence, and self-reliance. Tobias and Thomas represented differences that war exposed within the South. And Tobias was the better man.

Clemens first exposed the ethical differences between the friends through Thomas's decision to seek revenge for Toby's grandfather's death. Acting in secret, Thomas coolly plotted the murder of the men who killed Mr. Wilson. When he encountered one of the villains in the mountains, Thomas gave him "three minutes" to pray, then shot the man from his saddle as he fled. "There would have been no excuse for missing a wild pigeon at that distance," Thomas mused. But the villain was only wounded, and Thomas worried about killing him off. "It is hard to *finish* a man in this fix; and yet if I do not, I put my own life and that of my friends in fearful jeopardy." So, he concluded, "I *must* put an end" to him, and he threw the body off a huge cliff, leaving the

---

[71] *Tobias Wilson*, "gentle and good," and "Miss Nancy," 45; "single ray," 117. Clemens did not suggest that Tobias's grandfather gave the former slaves land but that he had a "piece of ground reserved for their support," 114, *ibid*. I discussed the significance of these friendships in more detail in "Dynamics of Friendship."

scene "without casting one look at the mangled form." Thomas was "born for a partisan leader." He knew murder was wrong, but he justified it. And Clemens made Thomas mostly good in spite of the murderous ways that war provoked.[72]

Clemens offset Thomas's violent code of honor with Toby's gentler ethics, which the author identified with religion and with women. Although Tobias's mother was "masculine" in appearance and intelligence, she had what Thomas called "strait-laced religion," and she and Sophy persuaded Tobias to forego revenge. A pure and delicate beauty, Sophy represented both romantic and divine love. When Thomas wondered if it was wrong "to make an earthly idol" and "mingle veneration of the CREATOR with adoration of the creature," he concluded that it was not, for Sophy represented the love of a "merciful Redeemer."[73] Clemens explained that the law of love had replaced a sterner code of obedience because God knew men were too weak to obey. By loving Sophy, Tobias was saved from the sin of revenge. Clemens expressed conventional views when he made women represent morality, but Sophy's religion did not control his novel. Like William Smith, Clemens did not find God's will manifested in the war.

Clemens claimed spiritual faith but denied that religion controlled men's choices. Refusing to wholly condemn Thomas's murders, Clemens insisted that the "feeble and flickering lamp of human reason" contained "so much of doubt and uncertainty – so little to guide us aright" that men could not count on divine guidance. "Why speculate upon what we can never know with certainty?" he wrote (as he speculated). More bleakly, he insisted that "there is a stern and pitiless Deity, who follows us by day and reposes by our side at night, forever watching what golden thread he can break, what joy he can poison, and what hope he can extinguish forever!" This deity was not Sophy's "merciful Redeemer" but a cruel master.[74] Men made choices, in the dark about a distant God.

With this uncertainty, Clemens struggled to make the Civil War a conflict between good and evil. Although he called the Confederacy "wicked," he feared that a deity "whose purposes we cannot comprehend" might not sustain his judgment. Secessionists destroyed the Union "upon a hellish pretext that, at some distant and uncertain day in the future, the right of one man to hold his fellow-man in bondage might be denied by the General Government." Still, he admitted, history might find them right. Needing to justify himself, Clemens hoped a "fearful and dread retribution" would overtake the Confederate leaders. As one of his common men put it, he wished Confederate

---

[72] *Tobias Wilson*, account of the shooting, with quoted passages, 50–153; "born for a partisan leader," 156. Hettle, 140, argues that Clemens "was not quite comfortable" with his decision to make Tobias rather than Thomas his hero, which seems like a reasonable conclusion.

[73] *Ibid.*, "masculine," 9; "strait-laced," 325; Sophy as "idol," 123. Clemens more specifically wrote that Mrs. Wilson had a "strong and masculine intellect," *ibid.*, 111.

[74] *Ibid.*, "flickering lamp," 201; "why speculate," 123; "demon of revenge ... rattlesnake," 246; "stern and pitiless Deity," 325–326.

leaders "were in the bottom of hell, and Jeff Davis the lowest of the lot."[75] But, while the character sketches in his novel judged his enemies instead of leaving revenge to God, Clemens was unsure what was right, and his doubts rested largely on the influence of slavery.

Like Evans and Smith, Clemens knew slavery too well to have confidence in human nature. He was certain that the dominating spirit of slavery corrupted Confederates. Detailing their predations, he attacked men like the "popinjay general" Joseph Wheeler, who recruited good men and turned them into brigands. Clemens focused more of his anger on one Captain Sykes, who pretended to be a gentleman but was a heartless partisan and a malevolent seducer of young girls. And he scathingly condemned Parson Williams, a "bigoted, intolerant, and unforgiving" Baptist preacher "held up as a pattern for the rising generation by every gray-haired fool in the neighborhood."[76] These deceitful men only pretended to be benevolent leaders. The Captain and the Parson deserved the deaths Clemens gave them.

And Clemens went out of his way to identify Parson Williams with slavery. Thomas planned the Parson's execution because Williams had organized the murder of Tobias's grandfather. When he met the preacher's slave Isham in the woods, Thomas decided to use the black man's knowledge of his master's daily routine to facilitate the killing. Clemens offered his views of slavery through the exchange between Thomas and Isham. Thomas thought Isham would help him because the Parson "treated his servants badly": he gave them adequate food and clothing but "whipped them unmercifully for the least fault, and made even the women and children work before day, and after dark, in the worst weather." But such a life had affected the slave. When Thomas sympathized that Isham did not "love" the preacher, Isham responded with mistrust. He warily asked if "Massa Rogers" was "foolin' dis nigger?" Thomas insisted that he never misused anyone, especially "a negro who has no friends to take up for him," and Isham believed him. He admitted that he "couldn't" love his master "if I tried. But I never tried."[77] From Clemens's perspective, slavery revealed the Baptist master's inhumanity. The problem was that it also diminished the slave's moral capacity. Like war, slavery altered men's ability to be good.

Isham's story revealed how slavery and race complicated Clemens's views of human nature. On the one hand, he made Isham dismayed about cooperating in his master's death, and he explained it with a racialist argument. The "negro," Clemens wrote, "is very far from being cruel or blood-thirsty by nature." Slaves had accepted "treatment" that was, "in many cases, the reverse of humane." On the other, Clemens claimed that the "first saturnalia" of freedom might make black men vengeful. The saturnalia was a Roman carnival in which slaves and masters exchanged roles, and Clemens's reference, like Smith's carnival of death, was a tacit admission of slavery's influence on

---

[75] Ibid., 201–202, 84.
[76] Ibid., "popinjay," 175; "bigoted," 52–53.
[77] All quotes from the encounter between Isham and Thomas, 182–184, *ibid*.

his understanding of human nature. Thomas hoped that the "new and strange aspirings for freedom" would lead Isham to help him. And, indeed, Isham cooperated so that Thomas could exact revenge. But also Isham planned to join the Yankee army.[78] His freedom would let Isham kill, just like the vengeful white man he assisted in a murder.

Clemens used the interaction between his hero Tobias and a second black man, Jake, to suggest that inequality might be good. In desperate flight from Captain Sykes's Confederates, Tobias encountered Jake fishing near a gristmill. Despite the usual comic stereotyping, Clemens gave Jake deliberate agency, for he immediately helped the hero. Jake warned that there were "secess" men at the mill "wid guns," and he offered to get Tobias some food. As he left to get the meal, Jake, "with his hat in one hand, slowly scratching his head with the other," worked out a "difficult problem": how to warn Tobias if the Confederates discovered his presence. Jake decided he would be "singin', or makin' some kind of a fuss" if Tobias needed to run. As it turned out, Jake safely returned with food, and a grateful Tobias tried to give him money. The slave refused it, saying "Nebber mind, sir, you can help me some ob dese times, and den we'll be eben. I don't want no pay for helping a man who is fightin' for President Linkum." Evincing his superiority with his gratitude, Tobias paid Jake and continued his flight, fed and rested. Clemens did not mention Jake's bravery, and the black and white men pursued a common goal without becoming equal.[79] Clemens did not make Jake and Tobias "eben."

All of Clemens's uncertainties prevented a triumphant ending to his novel. After detailing the battlefield death of the wicked Captain Sykes, Clemens left his two main characters at war, hinting they, too, would die. They had made different choices: Tobias was serving as a general's aide at Chattanooga; Thomas was pursuing rebels in the mountains. In the novel's closing scene, however, Thomas recognized the superiority of the hero Tobias. "He is better, and braver, and more gifted than any of us," Thomas said. And he reaffirmed the bond of friendship among unequal men: "Though I miss him sorely, I would not have his genius fettered by such a career as suits me, and which I must follow until peace returns to bless our land, or this body makes a feast for wolves and vultures."[80] Recognizing their difference, Thomas chose to put Tobias before him, achieving a rugged heroism in spite of his dubious morality. In the anarchy of guerrilla war, killing was a virtue and the ultimate expression of mastery; perhaps, in that indeterminate context, it, too, was good.

Clemens retained this grim ambivalence in his novel's final paragraph. Tobias, he wrote, would soon march into "one of those terrible scenes of carnage, in which our little ambition so often prompts us to seek *glory* at the risk of a *grave*." "It would be unjust," he quickly added, to "ascribe such motives"

---

[78] *Ibid*. Thomas warned Isham that the Yankees would not take him unless he wanted to be a soldier.
[79] All quotes from the encounter between Jake and Tobias, 222–224, *ibid*.
[80] *Ibid.*, 327.

to most soldiers. And he offered a qualified endorsement: that "higher impulses and more noble aspirations" moved most men, and that their "heroism" might "almost be claimed as the offspring of religion." Just as "almost" marked Clemens's unwillingness to merge war and religion completely, "our little ambition" for "*glory*" acknowledged his persistent fear of men's desire to be superior.[81] Endlessly ambitious and fully involved in the wrong of slavery, Clemens was hardly heroic. Because his novel was a bid for leadership in a postwar South, it implied a new harmony between upper-class, middle-class, and plain folk, and between blacks and whites. It did not glorify the Union, or war. Clemens thought men occupied an uncertain world, with right beyond their ken, and *Tobias Wilson* showed the terrible results.

Clemens's Unionists wrestled with the demands of self-determination. They helped each other make hard choices and lived or died with the consequences. They shared Clemens's dilemmas, although he never fought or killed. When Clemens finally chose sides, he yielded slavery but not racism, much less ambition. By setting *Tobias Wilson* in Jackson County, he avoided a direct assault on Huntsville's elite. He knew, however, that he would never be welcome in his hometown, and he returned only to die in May of 1865. Vilified by his neighbors and frustrated in his ambitions, Clemens had dedicated *Tobias Wilson* to his wife Mary, his "comfort and support." He would not predict their future because "life is a Pandora's box from which strange and fearful things are forever winging their flight." At his death, Mary placed on his tombstone the words of Clemens's "merciful Redeemer": "Come unto me all ye that labor and are heavy laden, and I will give you rest."[82] She hoped he would find peace in death.

* * *

Evans, Smith, and Clemens watched the Confederacy fall and, with it, their longstanding desire for slavery to support white people's freedom. Smith and Clemens had warned that a war would destroy slavery. Smith supported war reluctantly and gradually turned defeatist. His satire revealed a deep outrage at anyone, northern or southern, who relished a needless war. Only Clemens supported the North – and then only when the Union Army protected him. In their belief that a Republican victory in 1860 was insufficient cause for war, Clemens and Smith differed with Evans, who thought it better for everyone in the South to die than accept Republican rule. To the end, she equated slavery with individual liberty. Somewhere along the way, Smith and Clemens decided that white freedom far outweighed black slavery.

---

[81] *Ibid.*, 328. As Hettle observes, "Clemens seems to make a decisive step away from southern honor, yet the language he uses indicates some uncertainty about his new archetype of heroism," *Peculiar Democracy*, 140.

[82] *Tobias Wilson*, Dedication, iii. The tombstone inscription is in Diane Robey, Dorothy Scott Johnson, John Rison Jones, Jr., and Frances C, Roberts, *Maple Hill Cemetery, Phase One* (Huntsville, AL: Huntsville-Madison County Historical Society, 1995), which also shows that Mary Clemens placed the stone. She could have acted in compliance with Jeremiah's wishes, because his death was not sudden.

At first, defeat "crushed" Evans. After losing her human "property," she joked about the unpleasant realities of cooking for her family in Mobile's heat. Nonetheless, she continued to write, partly to earn money, partly to show her talent, and partly to express her convictions. In 1866, she produced *St. Elmo*, one of the best-selling novels of the nineteenth century. Another southern woman's tale, and another with a northern publisher, it preached self-determination and inequality as if a terrible war and the end of slavery hardly mattered. Still pondering fate, Evans hoped God would ultimately sustain her ideals, but she intended to act in the interim. As she wrote Beauregard in 1867, "If the Buckle theory of historic cycles be true (and can we doubt it?)," she hoped for an upward "*spiral*" of conservative freedom.[83] Marrying a rich, much older man in 1868, Evans enjoyed the new public role for conservative women: eulogizing the Lost Cause. She lived into the twentieth century, publishing novels from time to time. Her income, plus her husband's wealth, ensured that she spent little time in the kitchen of their beautiful home, and she learned that freed people would work hard, for just a little money.

Peace brought Smith renewed hope. Relieved at the war's end, he applied for a presidential pardon, claiming that his choices in 1861 had been "to leave the country, be mobbed, or take part" in the Confederacy. With his ambitions alive, he ran for governor in 1865. Unusually sanguine, he praised the "Christian moderation" of the victors "after the slaughter" and asked Alabama's voters to accept their "duty" to the freed slaves.[84] He urged citizens not to fixate on how "idle, lazy, and thievish" the freedmen were – it was true, he claimed, but it did not have to matter. In effect, he asked whites to use sympathy and reason in order to make their broken society better. They should see that "a new joy" was "infused" in African Americans. He posed a question: "Suppose you had been a slave yesterday ... would you not feel like going on a spree?" And he insisted that "these creatures have human instincts and frailties." To them, "the word LIBERTY has a charm in its sound and in the combination of its letters, even to the most ignorant." Smith made unequal freedom an idea for action, and he asked white men to make it work.[85] In retrospect, it seems hardly surprising that he failed to win election.

---

[83] "Crushed," used repeatedly, but see Evans to Curry, October 7, 1865, which also contains the reference to her lost "property"; in *Correspondence*, 109, 107; reference to Buckle, Evans to Beauregard, March 30, [1867], in *ibid.*, 139. Evans's letter to Curry of January 27, 1864, also suspected that "Buckle's social and political cycles seem to some extent reproduced in the curious phrases of popular opinion" in the Confederacy as it moved from democracy toward centralization; *ibid.*, 91.

[84] "Leave the country," quoted in Thomas B. Alexander and Richard E. Beringer, *The Anatomy of the Confederate Congress: A Study of the Influences of Member Characteristics on Legislative Voting Behavior, 1861–1865* (Nashville: Vanderbilt University Press, 1972), 40. Speech quoted in Easby-Smith, *William Russell Smith*, 166–168.

[85] Quotes, *ibid.*, 168; all three candidates for the governorship in 1865 were former Unionists who had supported the Confederacy; see the brief discussion of the election in Rogers et al., *Alabama: The History of a Deep South State*, 332–233.

Smith's friend Meek had always been more explicitly southern, and far more optimistic. As a secular Romantic, Meek had seen some vaguely transcendent spirit behind the rising South. He had attended the national Democratic convention in 1860, supported his friend William Yancey, and walked out when southern demands went unmet. But, as Smith observed, Meek reluctantly supported secession, and the poet/historian saddened during the war. He kept a list of "dead friends," including his rival Albert Pickett and his true friends Caroline Hentz and Johnson Hooper. Never seriously religious, he wrote paraphrases of Psalms, as if seeking consolation. Apparently, he planned another collection of his poetry, for he wrote an introductory poem not long before his death in November of 1865. His draft "Proem" had many crossed-out lines. Confessing his literary sins, Meek expressed remorse at providing "vain and vapid Visions" to support the South.[86] Humbled, he asked readers to heed his repentance and hear his hopes for a renewed freedom.

Meek understood the nature of his errors, although he was confused about Biblical details – he made southerners like Adam and Eve leaving the paradise of Eden and like the Israelites leaving the bondage of Egypt. Regardless, he knew secession was a mistake, and there was no kind of Confederate heaven. Now southerners stood "before the thundering Sinai" to "sue for peace and pardon." Symbolically "flinging" his poems before the "altars of the Land," Meek called them "Dreams of a Delusion," showing only the "follies, vagaries, and crime" of rebellion. He wanted his old poems to "prove a lesson / To all our States in after years, / To shun the vortex of Secession, / The maelstrom gulf of blood and tears." And he called for an "endless Union," in which people would be "linked in a grand communion / Of Law and Liberty and Life!"[87]

Meek's "Proem" was a total reversal for the ailing poet. From the time he first praised the Southwest, Meek had believed that the "unrestrained exercise of mind" would produce a great civilization based on slavery, which he had proclaimed "naturally, morally, and politically right and beneficial." As he wrote in *Romantic Passages in Southwestern History*, he expected "progress to the infinite, the eternal, the omniscient, the perfect." Now, he made no mention of slavery when he described how, "fired by hopes of earth's perfections," he and his friends had sought a "weird Utopia." After first writing "man's perfections," he scratched through "man's" and substituted "earth's," as if reminded that perfection was not human.[88] Surely slavery explained, however, his startling phrase "weird Utopia," for he saw that Confederates were deluded. Perhaps the best

---

[86] "Dead friends" list in Alexander B. Meek Papers, ADAH; "Proem," in A. B. Meek Papers, DUL. It is subtitled "Prelude," reinforcing the notion expressed in the poem that it was intended as an introduction. In a long and genuinely appreciative funeral oration, Meek's long-time friend, the Rev. Phillip P. Neely, said that Meek had regretted his youthful attitude to religion but that he was also unwilling to profess his faith because he was uncertain he was fully prepared; *Address Delivered at the Funeral of Hon. Alexander B. Meek* (Columbus, MS: Printed at the Sentinel Job Office, 1866), 3.

[87] "Proem."

[88] Quotations on slavery, Chapter 5, *supra* 196; remaining quotes, "Proem."

image the effusive poet ever created, "Weird Utopia" perfectly mirrored Meek's regrets. His rising South had vanished in the humility of defeat.

With varying degrees of optimism, Meek's fellow writers had once shared his vision for a progressive slave society, and success in the market had helped convince them it was possible in the American nation. Sometimes they had freighted slavery discreetly into stories of white freedom, and sometimes they flaunted the South's peculiar institution, but it was always there, creating inexpressible fears. Even when slavery was disappearing, the Southwest's writers spoke for a conception of freedom that contained substantial inequality, and in that they were much like the Americans who read their books. If it seems fitting, to twenty-first-century readers, that *The Royal Ape* never found many buyers, it is less reassuring that Evans's *Macaria* sold many thousands. The rising South's writers had wrongly expected northern Americans to accept slavery, but they rightly understood that mixing freedom with inequality was a popular creed. By the standards of a market serving middle-class people, these writers understood the culture of freedom remarkably well. As she collected royalties from *Macaria*'s northern sales, Evans must have smiled at her success.[89]

Over a span of some thirty-odd years, the writers of the rising South moved from the universalism of the Enlightenment and the hopeful side of Romanticism toward a somber view of an indeterminate humanity in an uncertain world. They began with great hopes for their slave society, but their optimism was always shadowed by the realities they lived with. Instead of realizing that people who valued their own freedom and denied it to others would always be afraid, they saw a "poor, weak human nature" obtaining everywhere. If slavery taught them fear, however, freedom created their activism, for as much as these writers doubted that humans could know truth, they insisted on independent conduct. Convinced that white people should choose their homes, jobs, husbands or wives, friends, and leaders, they expected improvement as well as errors. Although slavery blighted their ideas about freedom, writers learned those ideas in homes and communities where inequalities seemed right and good. For these men and women, writing was – to borrow Thoreau's phrase – "action from principle," a way to address readers who could accept or reject their ideas at will.[90] With and without slavery, they avowed an ethos of freedom that left their minds in chains; and that was a uniquely American tragedy.

[89] As Melissa Homestead has written, in a nice turn of phrase, Evans was "reoccupying the Northern market" immediately after the war; "Publishing History of Macaria," 692; and Homestead tracks the publications of the novel, observing that, unfortunately, we do not know exactly how many copies were sold.

[90] "Poor, weak human nature," is Evans's phrase in *Macaria*, 262, but, with less sentimentality, most writers would have agreed with the characterization; "action from principle," "Resistance to Civil Government," in Henry David Thoreau, *Walden and Resistance to Civil Government*, ed. William Rossi (New York: W. W. Norton, 1992), 232. Thoreau, of course, intended action to represent a pure morality that would separate the "diabolical" from the "divine" in man – something Alabama's writers would have thought impossible (or irrelevant) – but he defined it also as "the perception and performance of right," which was a main tenet of their ideas.

Epilogue

The Remains of a Rising South

> Let every man achieve his own renown,
> Nor wait for Fortune: multitudes may shout
> O'er small deserts, and give elated Hope
> Deceitful promises; Posterity
> Will not be thus betrayed; who waits on others
> Loses his time and dies without a name.
> William Russell Smith, *Uses of Solitude*

As winter ended in 1889, William Smith added a short postscript to his *Reminiscences*. Now seventy-four, he lived with his beloved Wilhemine in a large, rambling house at 122 East Capitol Street in Washington, DC. The three-story home, once the property of Smith's father-in-law, was the oldest on the block. When Smith stepped off his porch and headed west, he faced the looming dome of the Capitol, just across the street. Because Smith had served in Congress and his wife had been raised in Washington, the city was familiar when the family arrived there in 1879. Nonetheless, Smith had fixed on Alabama as he finished drafting his recollections from the piles of papers he had gathered over a long public life. His concluding note, dated March 27, 1889, proposed that another volume might bring interested readers closer to the "present day," but, as they stood, Smith's *Reminiscences* covered a time before the Civil War and a now-distant place, his home town of Tuscaloosa.[1]

---

[1] Poetry from *The Uses of Solitude* (Tuscaloosa: Printed for the Alabama Alpha of the Phi Beta Kappa Society of the University at Tuscaloosa, 1860), 6; William Russell Smith, *Reminiscences of a Long Life; Historical, Political, Personal, and Literary* (Washington, DC: W. R. Smith, Sr., 1889), 376. Anne Easby-Smith's biography of her father is filled with details about the family's life in the house on East Capitol, which was actually two houses connected. A picture of the home is at http://genealogytrails.com/washdc/bio_easby_w.html, which also reprints William Easby's will. Illuminating comments of Wilhemine Easby-Smith about her father's property and connections are in "Personal Recollections of Early Washington and a Sketch of the Life of Captain William Easby, delivered before the Association of the Oldest Inhabitants of the District of Columbia, May 3, 1913," at http://memory.loc.gov. For the curious, Google Earth provides an eye-level perspective of the Capitol from the 100 block of East Capitol

The *Reminiscences* were stories of the rising South. Nostalgically but not uncritically, Smith recalled the promising society that had inspired his ambitions. He told anecdotes about many inhabitants, even thieves who had prowled the infant town. More than anything, however, he spun stories of men who prospered through their own talent and initiative – men like him. He created categories for these townsmen and gave each a chapter: editors, lawyers, doctors, merchants, poets, and university men. Smith had no category for farmers, but he did recall one friend who suffered the "misfortune" of being born into a planter's family. Brought up rich, this bright fellow did not know how to work, so he failed to gain "enduring fame." Smith suggested a benign town slavery with stories of the "sable bard" Adam, an affable "genius" who composed spontaneous poems at the request of white townspeople. Fittingly, Smith framed his *Reminiscences* with references to print: first, Tuscaloosa's newspapers; last, its poetry and, tacked onto the final page, his plans to write another book for the shelf-full he had already published. Smith would not die "without a name" for any lack of effort on his part.[2]

The town that Smith remembered seemed to have promise, like the young man who had lived there. Although Smith's model for a self-made man was himself, his *Reminiscences* did not dwell on his orphaned childhood. He skimmed over his futile efforts to prevent secession and his miserable service in Richmond. And he omitted the embarrassments of Reconstruction, when he could not get elected to public office and served a short year as president of the university, resigning when he was labeled a Republican collaborator. During the postwar years, Smith had gone on writing: he translated the fifth book of the *Iliad*, published by D. Appleton in New York, and he edited a local newspaper, to which his wife and children contributed. Eventually, however, he and his family left Tuscaloosa. Because of his wife's property, Smith lived comfortably in Washington, practiced law, and continued to write. Back home, middle-class people were embracing an exploitative capitalism they wrapped in plantation legends and the mythology of a Lost Cause.[3] But Smith

---

Street, requiring only imagination to remove renovations, cars, and recent landscaping and see roughly what William Smith saw.
[2] The friend with the "misfortune" to be a planter's son was Burwell Boykin, *Reminiscences*, 262; quote for Adam, 178, but he is described, with quotes from his poems, 178–184. Smith compared Adam to Terence (creator of the slave Davus to whom Evans referred in *Macaria*), and to Aesop, with the comment that their "color" was unknown and "posterity" does not care what it was; 178. Smith observed that Adam often composed satire, and his examples bear out the comment. Whether Smith realized it or not, his quotations from Adam's poems showed that the slave judged white townspeople, not always kindly.
[3] Easby-Smith's biography omits none of the unhappy aspects of Smith's life; *William Russell Smith of Alabama: His Life and Works* (Philadelphia: Dolphin Press, 1931). Smith also published a guide for studying the *Iliad*. See Homer and William Russell Smith, *Diomede: From the Iliad of Homer* (New York and London: D. Appleton & Co., 1869); William Russell Smith, *Key to the Iliad of Homer for the Use of Schools, Academies, and Colleges* (Philadelphia: Claxton, Remsen and Affelfinger, 1871). Basic studies of the relationship between Old South mythology and postwar ideas are Gaines M. Foster, *Ghosts of the Confederacy: Defeat, the Lost Cause*

now had the leisure to resurrect a community he wanted readers to know, and it was not a land of cotton.

Despite the fact that Smith had been a politician throughout his years in Alabama, literary themes got more space than politics in the *Reminiscences*. The long sketch about Tuscaloosa's poets featured Alexander Meek, barely mentioning the political arena the two close friends had occupied for decades. Smith briefly claimed that Meek had greeted secession with the "gloomy reluctance of a sagacious patriot," but he omitted the fact that Meek had stood defiantly with William Yancey at the 1860 Democratic convention. Instead, Smith detailed Meek's sociability, generosity, and genius, offering an extended critique of his friend's writing. Meek, Smith admitted candidly, was not a profound poet. He rhymed too much and rarely wrote in blank verse, which Smith thought a higher form. Smith said that he wrote about his friend "*con amore*," and that seems true, but he was also using Meek. His criticisms let Smith display his favorite theories – and explain his own lack of fame. Meek, he complained, would only be recognized for his true genius when the "ruling high priests" of literary criticism "cast off their sectional prejudices."[4]

With that remark, Smith's literary conclusions assumed political import. Already, he had quietly reminded his readers that the South he had loved was not the one they read about in the literature of the Lost Cause. The fire-eating Yancey, for example, had brought "ruin and desolation to the happiest and most prosperous people on the globe" (one might think Smith included the "sable bard"). And Smith recalled that he opposed secession as the "*tocsin of war and the death knell of slavery*" (one might think they were equally regrettable). Finally, he reprinted, in its entirety, the *Uses of Solitude*, the fifty-page blank-verse poem he had written for a Tuscaloosa audience just before Lincoln's election in 1860. The poem was an extended plea for self-reliance, but its conclusion warned the young men of Phi Beta Kappa:

> There is one Solitude that all must reach,
> And go alone! Must edge a precipice –
> Edge it alone – for on its crumbling brink
> The nearest friend withdraws the kindred grasp,
> And drops, impatiently – reluctant drops
> The icy form into the yawning gulf
> Whose shadowy waves no beaches find to lave.

When he wrote those haunting lines, Smith had glimpsed a catastrophic death for the rising South, and he feared it would be self-inflicted.[5] Now this bleak

---

and the Emergence of the New South, 1865–1913 (New York: Oxford University Press, 1987), and Charles Reagan Wilson, *Baptized in Blood: The Religion of the Lost Cause, 1865–1920* (Athens: University of Georgia Press, 1980). A useful collection of essays that treats the broader issue of memory is Fitzhugh Brundage, ed., *Where These Memories Grow: History, Memory, and Southern Identity* (Chapel Hill: University of North Carolina Press, 2000).

[4] *Reminiscences*, "Sagacious patriot," 340; "*con amore*," 324; "high priests," 343.
[5] *Ibid.*, Yancey, 222; "tocsin," 306; conclusion to poem, 375.

vision concluded his *Reminiscences*. It showed at once his political prescience and his literary skill.

Smith's dour line about the "sectional prejudices" against authors like Meek excused the low status of southern writing, including his, but it discounted the popularity of his peers. If we measure influence by books in print, which at least suggests readership, some of Alabama's writers were still successful when Smith wrote his recollections. T. B. Peterson of Philadelphia, the noted publisher of affordable books, was issuing those of Caroline Hentz and Johnson Hooper in the 1880s. After his death in 1864, Joseph Baldwin's *Flush Times* was reprinted over and over again until century's end, selling many thousands. Just after the turn of the century, Augusta Evans told a fan that the sales of her novels, "irrespective of foreign imprints," had surpassed 425,000 copies. And, as the only full account of any secession convention, Smith's *History and Debates* shaped historical memory. In the late twentieth and twenty-first centuries, scholars trace the literary influence of the comic writers, Hooper and Baldwin, and the women authors, Evans and Hentz, on the literature of the South and nation.[6] When Smith died in February of 1896, the beautiful new building of the Library of Congress (now the Jefferson Building) was nearing completion, just beyond his front windows. One imagines the book lover watching the construction with interest, in hope that his books and those of his friends would be preserved there.

From his vantage point on Capitol Street, moreover, Smith must have seen that his fellow writers' ideas were still at work in the politics of the nation. Three months after Smith's death, the Supreme Court, still meeting in the Capitol across the street, handed down its decision in *Plessy v. Ferguson*. Formally sanctioning segregation, the court spoke for a white majority convinced that "the voluntary consent of individuals" precluded real equality for a race that was inferior by "nature."[7] Although many pens encouraged

---

[6] Evans to Mildred Rutherford, October 12, [1905], in *A Southern Woman of Letters: The Correspondence of Augusta Jane Evans Wilson*, ed. by Rebecca Grant Sexton (Columbia: University of South Carolina Press, 2002), 186. General publication information from WorldCat, http://worldcat.org. Some publishers of Baldwin's work listed the number of copies already printed. Among the many studies of women's fiction that see ongoing significance for Evans or Hentz are Carol S. Manning, *The Female Tradition in Southern Literature* (Urbana: University of Illinois Press, 1993); Nina Baym, *Women's Fiction: A Guide to Novels by and About Women in America, 1820–1870* (Ithaca: Cornell University Press, 1978). Twentieth-century critics who specialized in humor praised the contributions of what they commonly called the "frontier" humorists; the first major study of the relationship between them and later major writers was Kenneth S. Lynn, *Mark Twain and Southwestern Humor* (Boston: Little, Brown, 1960) which contrasted Twain's humanism with the proslavery writing of men like Baldwin and Hooper and did not mention Clemens. Other studies that emphasize continuity, with less attention to slavery, are M. Thomas Inge, *The Frontier Humorists: Critical Views* (Hamden, CT: Archon Books, 1975); Bertram Wyatt-Brown, *Hearts of Darkness: Wellsprings of a Southern Literary Tradition* (Baton Rouge: Louisiana State University Press, 2003); David S. Reynolds, *Beneath the American Renaissance: The Subversive Imagination in the Age of Emerson and Melville* (New York: Alfred A. Knopf, 1988).

[7] Quote taken from the text of the decision at http://caselaw.lp.Findlaw.com.

Epilogue

FIGURE E.1. William Russell Smith.
Unlike the other male authors he knew in Alabama before the Civil War, William Russell Smith lived to an old age, and he continued to write until shortly before his death in 1896. Courtesy of the W. S. Hoole Special Collections Library, The University of Alabama.

racism among northerners who rarely saw a black person, the writers of the rising South played an early part. Their stories about respectable slaveowners encouraged white readers to smile harmlessly at characters like Smith's "sable bard" or Baldwin's "servant," Jo, never to imagine them as equals. By making racial politics subordinate to the larger theme of American freedom, the writers of the rising South anticipated a middle-class consensus that prevailed long after *Plessy*.

Forty years after William Smith concluded the *Reminiscences*, his daughter Anne Easby-Smith used his large collection of papers to compose his biography. Her angle of vision was very different from his. She covered his whole life, from the dreadful childhood through his death, and she explained (as well as justified) his politics. As a Roman Catholic nun, Anne stressed the role of faith in the family's history, praising her mother's strength and gratefully recalling her father's deathbed conversion. Even as she wrote, her old neighborhood was changing again: their house on East Capitol was razed to make a site for a splendid new Supreme Court Building. Easby-Smith paused during her writing to visit the Library of Congress in search of one of her father's books. *As It Is*, she told her readers, was not on the shelves, so she could not describe her father's satire of national politics.[8] Of the two major works he published in 1860, she only presented one, ending her biography, in fact, with the *Uses of Solitude* – the very same conclusion Smith had chosen for his *Reminiscences*.

But *As It Is* was hardly irrelevant to the American scene in the 1930s, when Easby-Smith wrote. Was her neglect of *As It Is* an insignificant omission or a convenient literary erasure? Maybe William Smith had no copy of his racy satire, or another of his children had removed it; perhaps the Library had temporarily misplaced the copy it owned. Easby-Smith had, to be sure, an abundance of superb material to work from, and she quoted profusely from Smith's public papers, other books, and letters. Nevertheless, it is hard to see how a devout nun could have praised *As It Is*, with its brothel and whores, gambling, and sexual misconduct. And how would a proud daughter treat her father's revelations of corruption, for he had implicated the South with the Congress in a national scandal? From the lobbyist Dr. Thimblerigg, who asked his wife to seduce a young congressman, to the flamboyant Senator Burton, who knew the capital's "secret luxuries," Smith showed that politicians sold their votes, ignored their responsibilities, and used violence, bribery, and extortion. Yet he was one of them. Had Anne Easby-Smith located *As It Is*, she would not have known what to write about it any more than her father, the politician, knew how to conclude its thorny, tangled plot.

In *As It Is*, Smith imagined American society both from perspective of the rising South and the nation, and he did not want them separated, no matter how they disagreed about slavery. Perennially skeptical, Smith thought corruption was as likely in Washington, DC, or Montgomery, Alabama, or Richmond, Virginia, as it had been in ancient Rome. Although any history is full of coincidences, it was not chance that prompted an ambitious southerner to write about the "federal city," nor a fluke that the "royal ape" sounded like him, nor accident that drew him to East Capitol Street. Despite the deep moral divisions between northerners and southerners, men and women from the towns of Alabama wrote for middle-class Americans, and Smith's personal and public histories represent the forces that brought them together in fateful tension. Like the comic tales that attracted Abraham Lincoln to *Flush Times*, Smith's stories asked recognition for a rising South that was largely

---

[8] Easby-Smith acknowledged that the work was in the catalog but said "it has been 'off the shelves' for some time and it has been impossible to obtain any data regarding it"; *William Russell Smith*, 90. But then she also claimed that his only political mistake was in supporting the American Party, *ibid.*, 83 – the sentiment of a Catholic daughter, all the more remarkable because of the many controversies in which Smith was involved.

American. Believing that freedom existed so that white people could better themselves, all of these writers taught that individuals created progress, and that inequality was unavoidable. This flawed conception of freedom was not born in the rising South, but it had lived very well in the region's towns, and it did not end with slavery and the Civil War. It was perfectly at home on the Capitol Hill where William Smith concluded his life.

Index

"Aaron Burr" (Smith), 72
Adam (slave), 292
Adventures of Captain Simon Suggs (Hooper)
  civilization in, 59
  class in, 184
  contents of, 51–52, 57
  dedication in, 241
  demagoguery satirized in, 240
  excerpts from, 25, 53–54
  Joseph Baldwin's *Flush Times* compared to, 149
  journalists satirized in, 240
  nature of humor in, 149
  persuasion in, 56
  popularity of, 57, 187
  publication of, 51
  racism in, 56
  self-determination in, 239
  slaves and slavery in, 58, 169, 174, 180, 182–184
  undercurrents of fear in, 70
Advertiser (Montgomery, AL), 166, 245
Advocate (Huntsville, AL), 121, 277
African Americans.
  Augusta Evans on, 175
  after Civil War, 287
  free, 191, 244
  and freedom, 19
  and racial prejudice, 20
  and self-determination, 20, 171
  Thomas Woodward on, 168
  and white middle classes, 19
  See also slaves
"Air" (Clemens), 120
Alabama
  capitals of, 57
  changes in, 3
  compared to Illinois, 15
  constitution of, 163
  Democrats in, 243
  economy of, 2, 4, 7, 26
  education in, 12, 14, 25, 27, 29
  growth of towns in, 8
  intellectual life of, 29
  legislature of, 147, 269, 270
  libraries in, 14
  magazines in, 44
  middle class in, 2, 8
  Native American population of, 4, 25
  natural resources in, 4
  newspapers in, 12, 248
  poetry about, 103
  politics in, 7, 77, 117, 266
  print culture in, 2, 13–15, 30
  publishing in, 12, 161
  rivers in, 4
  secession in, 247, 249, 265, 266
  self-improvement in, 28
  slave population of, 3, 7, 25
  Unionists in, 277
  upper classes in, 171
  white population of, 4
Alabama Female Institute, 46
Alabama Journal (Montgomery, AL)
  Albert Pickett's works in, 78, 139
  Johnson Hooper and, 139, 184, 185–186
  as Whig publication, 57, 166, 184
Alabama River, 164
Albany, NY, 233, 238
Alston, Philip, 44
"Americanism in Literature" (Meek), 15
American Party, 232
American Revolution, 215

"American Scholar, The" (Emerson), 15, 27
American Tract Society, 13
Antietam, MD, 271
Appleton, D. 149, 156, 160, 221, 292
Archy (slave), 279
Aristidean, 57
As It Is (Smith), 219, 228, 233–239, 266, 273, 296
Astor House, 161
As You Like It (Shakespeare), 234
Atlanta, GA, 269
Aunt Judy (slave), 190, 195
Aunt Patty's Scrap-Bag (Hentz), 111
Autauga County, AL, 145, 146, 166, 168, 185

Bachelor's Button: A Monthly Museum of Southern Literature, 31, 44, 72, 101, 228
Baldwin, Briscoe, 65, 220
Baldwin, Cornelia, 66, 68
Baldwin, Cornelius, 65, 68
Baldwin, Cyrus, 14, 65, 67, 100, 101
Baldwin, Joseph
  and Alexander Meek, 100
  ambitions of, 70, 147, 148, 149, 155, 156–157, 166, 170, 218
  on arrival in Southwest, 92
  books purchased by, 14
  childhood and education of, 65
  and class, 168, 171
  and competition, 98, 218
  and concept of family, 63
  and concept of migration, 63
  death of, 294
  and democracy, 216–218
  early adulthood of, 65
  and freedom, 2, 15, 17
  and friendship, 98
  and humor, 67
  idealization of southern culture by, 157
  on intellect, 147
  and John Hale, 153
  and Johnson Hooper, 155, 156, 157
  legacy of, 294
  legal career of, 9, 66, 148, 154, 156
  and literary market, 135
  and Millard Fillmore, 220
  on Mobile, AL, 155
  and patriarchy, 69
  personality of, 67, 154
  physical characteristics of, 67
  political career of, 7, 147, 148, 157, 219–220
  political views of, 217–218, 221, 223
  and property, 16, 17, 222
  and publication of *Flush Times*, 14
  relocations by, 11, 147, 154, 156, 219, 228, 251
  and Sam Hale, 153
  and self-determination, 218–219
  and self-sufficiency, 216
  and slavery, 7, 11, 20, 66, 71, 148, 156, 174, 218
  social life of, 154
  status of, 98
  on U.S. expansion, 222
  and wealth, 65, 66
Baldwin, Joseph, family of
  brother-in-law, 68
  children, 66–67, 147
  contribution of, to Baldwin's success, 65, 68
  cooperation among, 67
  cousin Alexander Stuart, 156, 219–220, 221, 227–228
  father, 65, 67, 68, 92
  father-in-law, 66, 67, 92
  gender roles in, 67
  lessons learned from, 62
  mother, 65, 66, 94
  mother-in-law, 67
  and self-determination, 71
  separations from, 70, 154
  siblings, 14, 65, 66, 67, 68, 92, 100
  uncle, 65, 220
  and wealth, 65
  wife, 66–68, 70, 94, 149, 155, 156–157
Baldwin, Joseph, works by
  characteristics of, 93
  critiques of, 97
  earnings from, 156
  families in, 93
  as popular fiction, 93
  publication of, 148–149, 153
  reception of, 133
  reviews of, 157
  slavery in, 135
  See also individual works by Baldwin
Baldwin, Sidney White
  correspondence with, 66, 67–68, 70, 147, 149, 155, 156–157
  extended family of, 67
  father of, 66, 67
  and husband's absences, 70
  mother of, 67
  relocation by, 11
  role of, in marriage, 66, 67
  and slavery, 11, 67, 147
  Virginia background of, 66
Baltimore, MD, 273

Bancroft, George, 134, 144, 162
"Bar of the South-West, The" (Baldwin), 152
Barnard, Frederick A. P., 34, 36, 38
Barnum, P. T., 149
Battle of New Orleans, 139
Beauregard, P. T., 256, 257, 263, 264, 287
Bell, John, 277
Benning, Henry, 255, 256
Bentley's Miscellany, 51, 241
Bernard Lile (Clemens), 125
Betsy (slave), 147
Beulah (Evans)
  audiences for, 90, 91
  characters in, 199
  dedication in, 206
  domesticity in, 205
  elements of Brontë's *Jane Eyre* in, 200
  elements of Carlyle's *Sartor Resartus* in, 200
  excerpt from, 95
  friend's critique of, 97
  gender in, 208
  impetus for writing, 90
  inequality in, 200
  main character of, as orphan, 92
  messages in, 207
  "philosophic lore" in, 259
  plot of, 90–91, 200–203, 207, 263
  proslavery ideas in, 201
  publication of, 90, 175, 206
  purpose of, 175
  religion in, 90
  reviews of, 210
  self-determination in, 90, 200, 204, 208
  slaves and slavery in, 179, 200–209, 257, 260
  southern viewpoint in, 175
  success of, 90–91, 208
  women depicted in, 258
  women's roles in, 257
Bibb, William, 146
Big Bear of Arkansas, The, 56
Black Belt, 3, 4, 7
Black Hawk War, 4
Black Warrior River, 100
Bob (slave), 168
books, 12, 13, 14
Boone, Daniel, 61, 64
Boston, MA, 25
Boswell, James, 264, 268, 269
Brantley, Mary. *See* Hooper, Mary Brantley
Breckinridge, John, 246
Bridal Eve, The (Smith), 102, 273

Buchanan, James, 245
Buck (slave), 268
Buckle, Thomas Henry, 261, 287

Caesar (slave), 144, 164, 168
California, 156, 157, 219, 228, 246
Camilla (slave), 147
Campbell, John A., 139
"Captain Stick and Toney" (Hooper), 186–187
Carey and Hart, 51
Catholics and Catholicism, 85, 86, 90, 232, 271, 295
Chambers County, AL, 9
Chapel Hill, NC, 40, 43, 189, 193, 196
Charles (slave), 279
Charleston, SC
  1860 Democratic national convention in, 1
  Albert Pickett in, 78, 79, 80, 136, 141
  conservatism in, 35
  intellectual life of, 25
  Johnson Hooper in, 48, 49
  publishing in, 139, 140, 158
  upper classes in, 35
  William Gilmore Simms in, 32
Chickasaw Indians, 145
Chronicle (Hayneville, AL), 138
Churchman, 161
Cincinnati, OH, 40, 41, 107, 110, 189, 191
Civil War
  Abraham Lincoln and, 15, 254
  Alabama writers and, 251
  Alexander Meek and, 288
  Augusta Evans and, 253–254, 286
  conscription during, 252
  food shortages during, 252
  Jeremiah Clemens and, 253–254, 286
  literary opportunities presented by, 252
  lower classes and, 252
  southern countryside and, 252
  southern towns and, 252
  and southern unity, 252
  upper classes and, 252
  William Russell Smith and, 253–254, 286
  women and, 257
Claiborne, J. F. H., 139
Claims and Characteristics of Alabama History, The (Meek), 159–160
class. *See* middle classes
Clay, Clement Comer, 117, 120, 122, 124, 145
Clay, Clement, Jr., 117, 118–119, 120, 122–124, 126, 278
Clay, Henry, 103, 221, 224, 225, 226
Clay, Jones Withers, 117, 119, 122
Clay, Lawson, 121

Clay, Susannah Withers, 117, 119, 121
Clemens, James, 10, 116, 117, 119, 173, 174, 277
Clemens, Jeremiah (author)
  and Abraham Lincoln, 279, 280
  and Alexander Meek, 120, 124
  ambitions of, 116
  career of, as newspaper editor, 124
  childhood and early adulthood of, 116, 117
  and Civil War, 252–254, 286
  and class, 99, 252
  and Confederacy, 278–280, 282, 283–284
  death of, 286
  drinking habits of, 122–124, 128, 276
  finances of, 63, 116
  and friendship, 99, 116, 128–129
  health of, 279
  impetus of, for writing, 116
  and Johnson Hooper, 249
  legal career of, 10, 120
  and Lincoln administration, 276, 278
  and Mexicans, 121
  military career of, 121, 126, 278, 279
  personality of, 116, 117, 118, 128, 276, 277, 286
  physical characteristics of, 120, 122, 124
  political career of, 21, 120, 121–124, 173, 174, 253, 276, 278, 280
  political views of, 249–250, 251
  property of, 10, 277, 279
  and public acceptance, 125
  public opinion on, 276
  relationship of, with Clay family, 117–124, 126, 128, 129
  and religion, 118, 283
  relocations by, 279, 280
  and secession, 215, 249–250, 276, 277–278, 283
  and self-determination, 128, 253–254
  and slavery, 7, 21, 173, 174, 249, 253, 276, 277, 279, 284, 286
  and society, 99, 253, 277, 280
  tombstone of, 286
  and Union officers, 278–279
  vision of, for South, 121
  on white enslavement, 22
  and William Russell Smith, 120, 230
  on women and morality, 283
Clemens, Jeremiah (author), family of
  daughter, 278, 279
  father, 10, 63, 116, 117, 119, 173, 174, 277
  father-in-law, 277
  mother, 116
  nephew, 279
  siblings, 116
  son-in-law, 279
  wife, 63, 118, 119
Clemens, Jeremiah (author), works by
  audiences for, 125, 173, 280
  betrayal depicted in, 125
  during Civil War, 251, 253
  early poetry, 125
  friendship depicted in, 99, 115–116, 125–128
  See also individual works by Clemens
Clemens, Jeremiah (uncle), 116
Clemens, Mary Read
  and Alexander Meek, 100, 118
  correspondence with, 121
  courtship of, 118
  father of, 119
  and husband's tombstone, 286
  inheritance of, 277
  marriage of, 119
  property of, 279
  relocation by, 279
  sister-in-law of, 119
  Tobias Wilson dedicated to, 286
Clemens, Minerva Mills, 116
Clemens, Nancy, 116
Clemens, Samuel ("Mark Twain"), 116, 281
Cloud, Noah, 245
Cobb, Thomas R. R., 256
Cochrane, John, 101
Coffee, John, 43
Coffee, Mrs. John, 107, 108, 129
College Musings (Smith), 72
Columbia, SC, 30
Columbus, GA, 83, 111, 113, 198, 255
competition in southwestern society, 98, 101, 102, 106, 108
Compromise of 1850, 122, 219, 220, 231
Confederacy
  Augusta Evans and, 263, 264
  Jefferson Davis as president of, 253
  Jeremiah Clemens and, 278–280, 282, 283–284
  legislature of, 251, 265
  literary opportunities in, 269
  William Russell Smith and, 270, 276, 292
Congress, U.S., 21, 75, 122, 153, 173, 237, 276
Congressional Globe, 173
consumer goods and consumerism, 8–9, 17, 39, 98, 204
Cooper, James Fenimore, 28, 61, 115
Coosa County, AL, 142
Covington, KY, 40

Creek Indians
  Andrew Jackson's defeat of, 52
  at Horseshoe Bend, 144
  depicted in Meek's *Red Eagle*, 160
  depicted in Meek's *Romantic Passages in Southwestern History*, 162
  depicted in Pickett's *History of Alabama*, 81, 82, 142, 144, 145
  and slavery, 144
  trade with, 76
  See also Reminiscences of the Creek, or Muscogee Indians (Woodward)
Creek War of 1836, 4, 30, 42, 53, 72, 117
Crittenden, John, 277, 278
Curry, Jabez, 256, 257–258, 263

Dadeville, AL, 49
Daily Advertiser (Mobile, AL), 175
Daily Eagle (Memphis, TN), 124
Dante Alighieri, 234
Darley, F. O. C., 56
Davis (slave), 147
Davis, Jefferson, 252, 256, 264, 271, 279
Davus (literary character), 261
De Lara; or, The Moorish Bride (Hentz), 46
DeBow, J. D. B., 139
DeBow's Review, 158, 165
Declaration of Independence, 48, 244
Delta (New Orleans, LA), 161
Democrat (Eufaula, AL), 138
Democrat (Huntsville, AL), 121, 122, 124
Democrats and Democratic Party
  1860 convention of, 288, 293
  and 1860 presidential election, 247
  in Alabama legislature, 147
  Alabama writers and, 7
  Albert Pickett and, 137
  Andrew Jackson and, 137
  economic policies of, 7
  Jeremiah Clemens and, 121, 249, 278
  Johnson Hooper and, 57, 243, 246
  leaders of, 146, 243
  predominance of, 243
  satirization of, 51
  small farmers and, 7
Depression of 1837, 83
Derby, J. C., 258
Dickens, Charles, 134
Divine Comedy (Dante), 234
Dog and Gun (Hooper), 166, 241, 242
Douglass, Frederick, 135
Drake, Elizabeth, 107
Dwight, Mrs., 144

"*Earthquake Story, The*" (Baldwin), 7, 152
Easby (father of Wilhemine Easby Smith), 291
Easby, Wilhemine. *See* Smith, Wilhemine Easby
Easby-Smith, Anne, 72, 74, 75, 296
East Alabamian (Lafayette, AL), 12, 49, 50, 51, 56, 57, 58, 60
Eight Days in New Orleans (Pickett), 139–140
Emancipation Proclamation, 271
Emerson, Ralph Waldo, 15, 27
Enlightenment, 17, 18, 289
Eoline, or Magnolia Vale (Hentz), 112–113, 125, 129
Ernest Linwood (Hentz), 115, 198
Evans, Augusta
  activities of, 88, 92
  on African Americans, 175
  and Alexander Meek, 15, 160
  ambitions of, 89–90, 206, 254
  and change, 3
  childhood and early adulthood of, 83–84, 88, 91, 92
  and Civil War, 251, 252–254, 256, 257, 264, 286
  and class, 209, 252, 262
  and competition, 98
  and concept of family, 63
  and concept of work, 204
  and Confederate leaders, 256, 257, 259, 263, 264, 287
  fame of, 258, 264
  finances of, 90, 287
  on freedom, 2, 258–261
  and friendship, 95, 106, 129, 261–262
  and gender roles, 83, 84, 91, 264
  and inequality, 91, 92
  landholdings of, 91–92
  legacy of, 294
  life of, after Civil War, 287
  and literary success, 90, 91
  and marriage, 88, 90, 91, 97, 254, 255, 287
  and materialism, 209, 210
  on Mobile, AL, 155
  on northern publishing, 135
  on options available to women, 91
  personality of, 88, 256
  physical characteristics of, 88, 256
  on plotlines, 207
  and proslavery ideology, 176
  and Rachel Lyons, 91, 97, 129, 199, 207, 255, 258, 264
  and racism, 210
  and reform, 204
  and religion, 89–90

Evans, Augusta (*cont.*)
  and secession, 256
  and self-determination, 83, 84, 87, 88, 90, 92, 129, 210–211, 253–255, 258
  on Shakespeare, 90
  as slaveholder, 206, 264
  and slavery, 87, 91, 174, 175, 211, 253, 257–258, 264, 286
  and social status, 88
  on southern literature, 175
  and southern progress, 175
  and wealth, 10, 88, 90, 91
  writing habits of, 93
Evans, Augusta, family of
  aunt, 206, 255
  literary inspiration provided by, 93
  mother, 83, 84, 88, 199
  parents, 63
  siblings, 84, 88, 257
  troubles in, 62
  uncle, 206
  See also Evans, Matthew R.
Evans, Augusta, works by
  anonymous newspaper articles, 175, 256
  audiences for, 173, 199, 200, 209, 210–211, 258, 289
  characteristics of, 93
  critiques of, 97
  depictions of women in, 83
  during Civil War, 251, 253
  earnings from, 206, 208, 258, 289
  gender roles in, 84
  marriage in, 86
  persuasion in, 90
  religion in, 85–86, 90
  self-determination in, 85, 86
  slaves and slavery in, 87, 177, 179
  success of, 294
  See also individual works by Evans
Evans, Matthew R.
  Augusta Evans on, 88
  and Augusta's writing, 84, 93
  career of, 10, 83, 84, 205
  finances of, 10, 83, 199, 206
  health of, 83–84
  marriage of, 83
  property of, 10, 83, 91–92
  relocations by, 83, 84, 199, 206
  risks taken by, 83, 88, 91
  slaves owned by, 10, 83, 87, 88, 91, 199, 206
Evans, Sarah Howard, 83, 84, 88, 199
Evening News (Mobile, AL), 161

"*Fair Bird of the South*" (Meek), 114
family (concept)
  Alabama writers and, 62–64
  gender roles in, 63, 64
  importance of, to self-determination, 61–64
  and inequality, 83, 93
  middle classes and, 62, 63, 64
  and migration, 63
  and persuasion, 93
  and self-determination, 65, 92, 93
  and slavery, 64
"Farewell to Florence" (Hentz), 108
farmers
  activities of, 177
  Alabama writers and, 26
  Alexander Meek and, 58
  Caroline Hentz and, 58
  and change, 218
  improvement of, 209
  Johnson Hooper and, 58
  and literacy, 25
  literary depictions of, 281
  and slavery, 147
  Thomas Jefferson on, 16
  as William Russell Smith's constituents, 231
"Fawn of Pascagoula, The" (Meek), 164
Fayette, AL, 230, 266
Fayette County, AL, 231
Fillmore, Millard, 220, 232
fire-eaters, 105, 219, 239, 249, 250, 252, 267, 293
Fitzpatrick, Benjamin, 35, 121, 124
Florence, AL
  Alabama writers in, 26
  Andrew Jackson in, 43
  Caroline Hentz in, 9, 40, 41, 46, 107, 108
  and Creek War of 42
  Hentz family in, 129
  Jeremiah Clemens in, 117
  literary club in, 9
  population of, 41
  publishing in, 43
  schools near, 32
  social leaders in, 43
Florida, 3, 193
Flush Times of Alabama and Mississippi, The (Baldwin)
  Abraham Lincoln and, 15, 153, 296
  audiences for, 136, 171
  characters in, 68, 150
  and class, 171
  compared to Hooper's *Adventures of Captain Simon Suggs*, 149

compared to Pickett's *History of Alabama*, 149
contents of, 16, 65, 68, 149–150
evidence of civiliation in, 154
excerpts from, 133
family in, 68, 69
focus of, 154
freedom/liberty described in, 2
historical perspective in, 169
lawyers depicted in, 9
marketing of, 70
postwar reprints of, 294
publication of, 14, 68, 134, 136, 156
purposes for writing, 68
reviews of, 154, 155, 156
and self-determination, 71, 152, 154
self-determination in
significance of Southwest in, 149, 150
slavery in, 152–153, 154, 170, 174
Southern Literary Messenger on, 166
success of, 70, 156, 220
Fort Mims, 145, 162, 164, 168
Fort Toulouse, 142
Frank (slave), 147
Frank Leslie's Magazine, 162
Franklin, Benjamin, 28, 74, 215
free labor, 19
freedom
 Abraham Lincoln on, 15
 Alabama writers and, 16, 289, 295, 297
 and class, 16, 17, 19
 early American republicanism on, 17
 historical changes underlying, 2
 impact of, on literature, 15
 and inequality, 289
 intellectual and psychological bases for, 17
 as literary topic, 15
 northern definition of, 15
 and persuasion, 27
 and progress, 65, 147, 175
 and property, 16–17
 and race, 1, 15, 19, 22, 163–164, 171, 194, 295
 and self-determination, 18–19
 and self-improvement, 16, 17–18
 Simon Suggs as example of, 52
 and slavery, 2, 157, 163, 170, 188, 289
 southern definition of, 15
 See also individual writers and works
friendship
 Alabama writers and, 95
 and class, 98
 and competition, 101, 102, 106

functions of, 97, 129
and gender, 107, 110, 111
history of, 96
impact of, 95
and inequality, 129
middle classes and, 95, 97, 99, 106, 130
problems with, 99
qualities of, 96–97
and race, 115
and self-determination, 95, 96, 99, 129
and social change, 130
and social harmony, 129
and social status and power, 129
See also individual writers and works
Furman University, 48

Gainesville, Ala., 66, 147
Garber, Alexander, 65, 68
Garrett, William, 244–245
Gayarré, Charles, 134, 139
Gazette (Lancaster, MA), 190
Georgia, 3, 91, 94, 103, 107, 256
Georgia Scenes (Longstreet), 37, 50
Giddings, Joshua, 237
Gindrat, John, 80
Glen Alpine, 47
Globe (Washington, D. C.), 224
Godey's Lady's Book, 13, 14, 46, 198
Goethe, Johann Wolfgang von, 74, 236
Goetzel, S. H., 12, 161–162, 165
Goliad, TX, 72, 228
Greensboro, AL, 72
Gulf of Mexico, 3, 4

Hale, John, *153*
Hale, Sam, *153*
Hamilton, Alexander, 221, 224
Harper's Magazine, 13, 122
Harriet (slave, literary character), 200–203, 207, 208, 209, 257, 260
Harris, Sarah Alston. *See* Pickett, Sarah Alston Harris
Hart, Abraham, 193
Hawthorne, Nathaniel, 14, 70
Hayne, Arthur, 141, 142
Hayne, Robert, 141
Henry (slave), 181, 208
Henry, Patrick, 37
Hentz, Caroline
 activities of, 41, 42, 47, 190, 191
 and Alexander Meek, 14, 32, 100, 108, 109, 110, 114, 130, 288
 anxiety felt by, 44

Hentz, Caroline (*cont.*)
  childhood of, 62
  and civilization, 59–60
  and class, 58, 113, 209
  and condescension, 28
  and Creek War of 1836, 42–43
  death of, 251
  early career of, 26–27, 28
  and early days in Florence, AL, 41
  eulogies for, 114, 198
  fears of, toward unrestrained emotions, 190, 191, 198
  finances of, 47, 111
  and friendship, 98, 99, 112, 114–115, 128–129
  and George Moses Horton, 189–190
  and Harriet Beecher Stowe, 40
  legacy of, 294
  and literary clubs, 9, 40, 107
  and Maria Stafford, 108, 109, 110
  marriage of, 40, 41–42, 107, 110, 111, 189, 190, 191
  and Mrs. John Coffee, 129
  New England background of, 29, 32, 39, 58, 107, 111, 114, 129, 189
  and North-South relations, 115
  and Octavia Le Vert, 109–110, 112, 114, 129
  personality of, 43, 107
  and print culture, 59
  and proslavery ideology, 176
  and public, 59
  and race, 58, 209, 210
  and religion, 108
  relocations by, 40, 41, 46, 47, 107, 108, 109, 110, 189, 191, 193
  as schoolmistress, 41, 42, 46, 47, 108
  and self-determination, 58, 210–211
  and slavery, 7, 42, 107, 109, 115, 177, 189–190, 193–198, 209, 210, 211
  as social critic, 45, 112
  and social status, 108
  and society, 43, 46
  and success, 29, 40, 42, 43, 46, 47
  and voluntary societies, 108
  and wealth, 58, 112, 113, 129
Hentz, Caroline, family of, 189, 191
  See also Hentz, Charles; *See* Hentz, Nicholas
Hentz, Caroline, works by
  audiences for, 60, 114, 173, 198, 199, 209, 210–211
  earnings from, 47, 111, 193
  magazines published in, 32, 46, 72
  marriage in, 189
  New England settings for, 111
  poetry, 41, 42, 43, 44, 46
  popularity of, 84, 111, 114, 115
  postwar publication of, 294
  race in, 201
  slaves and slavery in, 58, 113–114, 177, 179, 189, 193–198, 201
  southern character of, 111
  See also individual works by Hentz
Hentz, Charles
  as adult, 109
  on father, 40
  on Hentz family's stay on Coffees' plantation, 108
  on life in Florence, AL, 108, 190
  on life in Tuscaloosa, AL, 46
  and Meek family, 108
  on men's attention to his mother, 191
  on mother's activities, 47, 177
Hentz, Nicholas
  acquaintances of, 108
  activities of, 41–42
  and Alexander Meek, 108
  finances of, 47
  as immigrant, 95
  marriage of, 107, 110, 111, 190, 191
  mental state of, 47, 107, 110, 111, 191, 193
  and religion, 108
  relocations by, 40, 41, 46, 47, 107, 108, 109, 110
  as schoolmaster, 41, 43, 46, 47, 108, 190–191
  and slavery, 189
  and society, 43, 46
Hentz, Thaddeus, 109
Herald and Tribune (Mobile, AL), 138, 139
Herbert, Hilary William, 241
Hester (slave), 144
Heustis, Rachel Lyons. *See* Lyons, Rachel
Hildreth, Richard, 134
Historical Society of Alabama, 9, 134, 159, 162
History and Debates of the Convention of the People of Alabama, January 1861, The (Smith), 269–270, 294
History of Alabama (Pickett)
  as Alabama's first full history, 134
  Alexander Meek and, 157, 158
  audiences for, 137, 140, 141–142, 171
  and class, 171
  contents of, 142–146, 164, 165, 171
  message of, 137

Index 307

motives for writing, 158–159
publication of, 78, 80, 81–82, 136, 140–141, 146, 158, 170
research and writing of, 78, 140–141, 142, 162, 171
responses to, 134, 158–159, 167, 171
self-determination in, 144
as serious endeavor, 149
slavery in, 170
Hooper, Charlotte, 180–181
Hooper, De Berniere
brothers of, 44
career of, 48
and Caroline and Nicholas Hentz, 43
correspondence with, 187–188, 245, 247–248
health of, 248
Hooper, George
and Albert Pickett, 76, 98, 129–130
and brothers, 63, 180
and class, 98
and education, 181, 208
and legal career, 76, 181
and relocations, 44, 49, 181
and slavery, 181
and William Dickson Pickett, 97
Hooper, Johnson
and 1856 presidential election, 242
as advocate for southern literature, 48
and Albert Pickett, 98, 157, 167
and Alexander Meek, 28, 139, 157, 159, 288
ambitions of, 181, 218
on *Blackwood's* magazine, 14
career of, as newspaper editor, 12, 14, 49, 50–51, 57, 184, 186, 239, 242–243, 245, 248
career of, as publisher, 12, 57, 134, 136, 166, 170, 176, 184, 241, 242
childhood and early adulthood of, 26–27, 28, 48, 49, 180–181
and civilization, 57, 59–60, 189
and class, 58, 98, 171, 248
and competition, 218
and condescension, 28
death of, 251
and democracy, 216–218
dependence of, 239–240
drinking habits of, 57, 240, 241, 246
finances of, 166, 184–185, 186, 242, 244, 245–246, 247, 248
health of, 166, 246, 248
on human nature, 211
and humor, 49, 52
influence of, 248
and Jeremiah Clemens, 249
and Joseph Baldwin, 155, 156, 157
late 30s and early 40s of, 239
legacy of, 294
legal career of, 9, 64, 186, 188
and literary market, 135
as Mason, 9
mental state of, 247, 248
and migration, 63, 246, 247
personality of, 48, 49, 52, 180–181, 185, 239, 242, 244, 246, 248
and persuasion, 29, 59, 188
physical characteristics of, 49
on Pickett's *Eight Days*, 139
and planters, 166, 169
political views of, 7, 51, 138, 217–218, 219, 242, 243, 245, 246–247, 249
and print culture, 59
and proslavery ideology, 176
and public, 59
and race, 58, 188, 189, 209, 210, 244
racehorse named after, 246
and religion, 242
relocations by, 44, 49, 181, 184
reputation of, 48
review of *Flush Times* by, 155
and secession, 239
and self-determination, 58, 129, 169, 210–211, 218–219, 239, 243, 245, 246, 248
and self-sufficiency, 216
and slavery, 7, 166, 167, 169, 170, 174, 181, 182–184, 186–187, 218, 243–244
society envisioned by, 57
and success, 29, 184
and wealth, 58, 64, 181
and Woodward's *Reminiscences*, 157, 166, 167, 169, 170
writers read by, 14
Hooper, Johnson, family of
children, 181, 242, 246
cousins, 48
father, 48, 180, 181
father-in-law, 181
great-uncle, 48, 244
mother, 180–181
mother-in-law, 181
and slaves, 181, 208
wife, 63, 181, 242
Hooper, Johnson, works by
audiences for, 60, 173, 181, 187, 199, 209, 210–211, 239, 240, 241, 242
class in, 185

Hooper, Johnson, works by (*cont.*)
  compared to minstrel shows, 181
  consumer goods in, 8–9
  later, 239, 242
  literary style in, 51
  political, 185–186
  popularity of, 166, 241
  publication of, 12, 56, 136, 148, 294
  and self-sufficiency, 219
  slaves and slavery in, 58, 177, 179, 180, 181, 182–184, 186–187, 189
  and society's improvement, 188
  See also individual works by Hooper
Hooper, Mary Brantley, 49, 64, 130, 181
Hooper, William, 48
Horseshoe Bend, 4, 52, 144
Horton, George Moses, 189–190
House of Representatives, U.S., 237
Houston, TX, 84
Howard, Sarah. *See* Evans, Sarah Howard
"How the Times Served the Virginians" (Baldwin), 69–70
Huntsville, AL
  Bibb family in, 146
  booksellers in, 14
  Clay family in, 129, 145
  Clemens family in, 116
  founding of, 116
  Haydn Society in, 9
  Jeremiah Clemens in, 9, 129, 249, 277, 278, 279, 280, 286
  leaders in, 117
  manufacturing in, 8
  prosperity in, 116
  Smith family in, 94
  support for Confederacy in, 278
  Union occupation of, 278, 279
  upper classes in, 278
  Walker family in, 77

Iliad, 292
Illinois
  Abraham Lincoln in, 94
  compared to Alabama, 15
  education in, 25
  Indian population of, 20
  libraries in, 14
  middle classes in, 9
  and migration, 94
  newspapers in, 12
  schools in, 12, 14
  slavery in, 94
  and statehood, 4

  voluntary associations in, 9
  white literacy in, 12
  white population of, 12
Impending Crisis of the South, The (Helper), 237
Independent Monitor (Tuscaloosa, AL), 35, 36, 39, 230
Indians. *See* Creek Indians; Native Americans; *Reminiscences of the Creek, or Muscogee Indians* (Woodward); Seminole Indians
inequality
  Alabama writers and, 98, 171, 297
  and class, 98
  and competition, 98
  families and, 83, 93
  and freedom, 289
  and friendship, 129
  and gender, 64, 93, 110, 207
  literary depictions of, 93
  and progress, 209
  and race, 207, 294
  and self-government, 250
  and slavery, 93, 207, 210
  See also entries for individual writers
Inez: A Tale of the Alamo (Evans), 84–87, 88, 89, 90, 92, 199
Irving, Washington, 155

J.B. Lippincott, 125, 276, 279
Jackson County, AL, 280
Jackson, Andrew
  Alabama writers and, 27
  and Creek Indians, 4
  in Florida, 3
  as founder of Democratic Party, 137
  at Horseshoe Bend, 51, 52, 144
  leadership of, 249
  literary depictions of, 51, 52, 103, 144, 168, 221, 224–225, 226–227, 230
  and War of 1812, 139
  wife and friends of, 43
Jackson, Rachel, 43
Jane Eyre (Brontë), 200
Jefferson Building (Library of Congress), 294
Jefferson, Thomas, 3, 17, 217, 221, 224
"Jim Wilkins and the Editors" (Hooper), 240–241, 248
Johnson, Samuel, 264, 268
"Joint Song" (Smith), 120, 230
Jones, Mary, 255
Jones, Seaborn, 199, 206
"Journal of Commerce," 154

Index

Kendall, Amos, 51, 59
Kentucky, 71, 75, 94, 116, 277
Ketch (slave), 168, 169
King, William R., 139
Knickerbocker, 161
Know-Nothing Party, 243, 249

La Fayette Society, 60
La Grange College, 32, 46
Lafayette, AL
  Johnson Hooper in, 49, 51, 60, 186, 242
  newspapers in, 12
Lafayette, Marquis de, 46
Lamar, Mirabeau, 103
Lamb, Charles, 155
Last of the Mohicans, The (Cooper), 115
lawyers, 8, 9, 16, 26, 97, 150, 152
Le Vert, Octavia Walton, 98, 109–110, 112, 114, 115, 129, 160
"Legend of the Silver Wave, A" (Hentz), 45–46
Lewis, Dixon Hall, 121
liberty. *See* freedom
Library of Congress, 294, 296
Lincoln, Abraham
  ambitions of, 63
  and African American self-determination, 20
  and Civil War, 15, 254
  education of, 25
  election of, 248, 266, 277, 293
  and *Flush Times*, 7, 15, 153, 296
  and free labor theory, 19
  on freedom, 15
  and friendship, 97
  "House Divided" speech by, 19
  Jeremiah Clemens and, 251, 279, 280
  Johnson Hooper and, 246
  legal career of, 9, 97
  marriage of, 63, 97
  military career of, 4
  and property rights, 16
  relocations by, 94, 273
  and self-determination, 18
  and servants, 10
  and slavery, 2, 22
  upward mobility of, 10
  as Whig, 7
  William Russell Smith and, 271
  See also Royal Ape, The (Smith)
Lincoln, Mary Todd, 11, 63, 273, 274
Lincoln, Robert, 273
Linda; or, The Pilot of the Belle Creole (Hentz), 111
literary magazines. *See* magazines
literary societies, 28

Livingston, AL, 147
Locke, John, 17
Locust Dell, 41, 42, 43, 190
London, England, 156
Longfellow, Henry Wadsworth, 14, 70
Longstreet, Augustus Baldwin, 37, 50
Lost Cause, 287, 292, 293
Louisiana Purchase, 3
Lovell's Folly (Hentz), 40
Lyell, Charles, 4
Lyons, Rachel
  and Augusta Evans, 91, 97, 129, 199, 207, 255, 258, 264
  and Henry Timrod, 257

Macaria (Evans), 2, 251, 253, 254, 258–264, 289
Macon County, AL, 142
magazines, 12, 13, 14, 28, 63, 134
Magnolia, The, 32, 38
Mail (Montgomery, AL)
  audiences for, 243
  book reviews in, 14
  establishment of, 166, 242
  finances of, 166, 245, 248
  Jeremiah Clemens and, 249
  Johnson Hooper as editor of, 166, 239, 242–243
  political content in, 243, 244–245, 246–247, 248
  Thomas Woodward and, 166, 167
Manassas, VA, 272, 274
Manly, Basil, 33–34, 35, 36, 37, 38, 48, 58, 134
Marcus Warland (Hentz), 113
marriage (concept), 63, 64
  See also family (concept)
Martin, Joshua, 108
Massachusetts, 15, 111
McGillivray, Alexander, 144
Meek, Alexander
  and 1860 Democratic national convention, 1
  as advocate for southern literature, 30, 31, 33, 102, 114
  and Albert Pickett, 158, 159, 288
  ambitions of, 160, 161, 166
  and Augusta Evans, 15, 160
  and Basil Manly, 33–34, 38
  biographical sketch of, 162
  career of, as editor, 30, 32, 45, 50, 59, 102, 158, 160
  career of, as historian, 82
  and Caroline Hentz, 14, 32, 100, 108, 109, 110, 114, 130, 288

Meek, Alexander (cont.)
  childhood and early adulthood of, 26–27, 28, 30, 100–101
  and Civil War, 251, 288
  and civilization, 59–60
  and class, 33, 37, 58
  and condescension, 28
  and Cyrus Baldwin, 14, 65, 100, 101
  death and funeral of, 99, 288
  drinking habits of, 9
  on education, 165
  and elites, 168
  and fame, 160, 162
  finances of, 30, 63, 102, 161
  and freedom, 2, 162–164
  friends of, 97
  and friendship, 98–99, 102, 103, 104, 106, 128–129, 160
  health of, 288
  idealization of southern culture by, 157
  and Jeremiah Clemens, 120, 124
  and Johnson Hooper, 28, 139, 157, 159, 186, 288
  and Joseph Baldwin, 100
  legal career of, 30
  library of, 14
  and literary market, 135
  on literature and culture, 36
  and marriage, 63, 97, 100
  and Mary Brantley Hooper, 130
  and Mary Read, 100, 118
  military career of, 30, 53
  in Mobile, 1
  and New York City, 161
  on newspaper editors, 39
  and Nicholas Hentz, 108
  and North-South relations, 115
  and Octavia Le Vert, 160
  as orator, 15, 30, 33, 101
  on patriarchy, 35
  personality of, 30, 34, 99, 104, 107, 158, 160, 293
  and persuasion, 31–32, 33
  physical characteristics of, 30, 31
  and Pickett's *History of Alabama*, 157, 158
  political career of, 1, 8, 30, 102, 124, 160, 288, 293
  and politics, 100
  and popularity, 106
  and print culture, 59
  and progress, 157, 163, 165
  pseudonyms for, 31
  and public, 39, 59
  and race, 58, 164, 171
  and religion, 288
  as Romantic, 162
  on rural life, 36
  and secession, 105, 288, 293
  and self-determination, 29, 58
  and self-protection, 101
  and slavery, 7, 93, 105, 135, 163–164
  as social critic, 27, 33
  social life of, 100–101, 158
  and social status, 29, 160
  society envisioned by, 1, 170, 288
  and success, 29
  and upper classes, 33
  and voluntary associations, 9, 34, 100
  and Wilhemine Easby Smith, 130
  and William Gilmore Simms, 32, 34, 36–38, 140, 157–158
  and William Lowndes Yancey, 105
  and William Russell Smith, 14, 31, 97, 98–106, 129, 130, 239, 293
  and women, 30, 100–101, 160
  writing skills of, 101
Meek, Alexander, family of
  first wife, 102, 160, 161, 251
  father, 13, 30
  lessons learned from, 62
  mother, 103
  second wife, 251
  siblings, 63, 64, 108, 158, 160, 161
Meek, Alexander, works by
  audiences for, 60, 161
  histories, 30, 32, 139, 140, 142, 157–158
  magazines published in, 72
  poetry, 30
  popularity of, 103
  publication of, 136, 160, 162
  slavery in, 58, 135
  Southron statement of principle, 31
  unfinished, 171
  William Gilmore Simms and, 162
  William Russell Smith on, 293
  See also individual works by Meek
Meek, Ben, 161
Meek, Eliza Slatter, 160
Meek, Samuel (brother), 63, 64, 158, 160, 161
Meek, Samuel (father), 13, 30
Melville, Herman, 115
"Memoirs of an Ambitious Man, The" (Smith), 75, 87, 93, 228, 266, 269
Messenger, 70
Metamorphoses (Ovid), 150
Mexican War
  Alexander Meek and, 165
  Evans family and, 84

Index

fiction set during, 125
growth of antislavery movement after, 123, 130
Jeremiah Clemens and, 121, 126, 278, 279
William Russell Smith and, 230
Mexicans, 99, 115, 121, 126–127, 228
middle classes
  and African Americans, 19
  Alabama writers and, 123, 296
  and concept of family, 62, 63, 64
  and consumerism, 8, 17, 204
  dependence of, 239
  development of, 2, 8, 26–27, 216
  and domestic values, 82
  and education, 28
  ethics of, 18
  and free labor, 19
  and freedom, 16, 17
  and friendship, 95, 97, 99, 106, 130
  and government, 9
  homes of, 17
  and immigrants, 19
  and lower classes, 19, 28
  and marriage, 66
  as minority, 209
  and Native Americans, 19
  and paternalism, 130
  and persuasion, 58
  and planters, 146
  and print culture, 12, 14–15, 171
  and progress, 64, 209
  and property ownership, 16–17
  and race, 210, 295
  and reading, 29
  scholarship on, 18
  and self-determination, 27, 58, 60, 64, 92, 99, 173
  and self-improvement, 17–18, 28–29
  and servants, 11
  and slavery, 16–17, 130, 173, 176, 208
  and towns, 218
  and voluntary associations, 9, 134
  and work ethic, 216
Miller, Stephen, 39
Mills, Minerva. *See* Clemens, Minerva Mills
Minervy (slave), 199, 206, 207, 208
Mississippi, 3, 65, 147, 251
Mississippi River, 4
Mississippi Territory, 4
Mobile, AL.
  Alexander Meek in, 1, 98, 160
  Augusta Evans in, 88, 155, 256, 287
  Caroline Hentz in, 109
  characteristics of, 154, 188
  during Civil War, 264
  Confederate leaders in, 256
  economy of, 205
  Evans family in, 84, 88
  Johnson Hooper in, 185
  Joseph Baldwin in, 98, 154, 155, 220
  nativism in, 85
  population of, 8
  publishing in, 12, 44, 102, 161
  railroad connections to, 188
  society in, 88, 109, 160
  wealth in, 88
  William Russell Smith in, 72
Mobile Bay, 4, 158, 220
Moby Dick (Melville), 115
Montgomery County, AL, 13, 142
Montgomery, AL
  Albert Pickett and, 76, 137, 146
  booksellers in, 14
  Confederate government in, 256, 269
  Democrats in, 186
  Johnson Hooper in, 57, 184, 186
  newspapers in, 78, 137
  population of, 8
  publishing in, 241
  roads to, 187
  secessionist convention in, 266
  society in, 186
  state Capitol in, 57
  William Russell Smith in, 275
Mordecai, Abram, 142
Mustang Gray: A Romance (Clemens), 125–129, 277

Nancy (slave), 147
Nat Turner's Rebellion, 137
Native Americans
  activities of, 4
  Alexander Meek and, 32
  and freedom, 19
  and lack of citizenship, 25
  literary depictions of, 16, 45, 142, 144, 145, 152, 162, 164
  and slavery, 144
  and whites, 4, 16, 17, 19
New England Genealogical and Historical Register, 114
New Orleans, LA, 3, 139, 158
New York, NY
  Albert Pickett in, 78, 80, 140–141, 148
  Alexander Meek in, 161
  Augusta Evans in, 206, 255
  John R. Thompson and, 148
  Joseph Baldwin in, 14, 70, 148, 149, 154

New York, NY (*cont.*)
  publishing in, 12, 84, 90, 102, 135, 136, 140, 160, 161, 165, 221, 241, 258, 292
News (Marion, AL), 140
newspapers
  Alabama writers and, 36, 38, 39, 43
  Alexander Meek on, 165
  contents of, 12, 28, 39, 43, 50, 134
  contributors to, 36
  idealization of family in, 63
  impact of, 43
  market for, 12
  origins of, 13
  partisan, 12, 39, 224
  and persuasion, 39
  political parties and, 217
  struggles of, 28
"Nice Sense of Honor, A" (Hentz), 45
9th Infantry Regiment, 121
North Carolina, 48, 75, 76
Nott, Josiah, 176

Ohio, 237
Ohio River, 4, 188
"On Liberty and Slavery" (Horton), 190
Ovid, 150
"Ovid Bolus, Esq." (Baldwin), 133, 147, 148, 150, 152–153

Panic of 10, 41, 117
Parkman, Francis, 61
Party Leaders (Baldwin), 219, 221–228, 250
Perryman, Polly, 168, 169
persuasion
  Alabama writers and, 27, 39, 130
  bases for, 52
  and childrearing, 63
  and democracy, 216
  early American legacy of, 28
  Emerson and, 27
  families and, 93
  impact of, 38
  in marriage, 64
  Johnson Hooper and, 57, 59, 188
  middle classes and, 58
  newspapers and, 39
  and patriarchy, 78
  and social change, 130
  social dynamics of, 48
  toasting as form of, 37
  as Whig tactic, 52
Peterson, T. B., 294
Philadelphia, PA
Philadelphia Union League, 279

1848 Whig convention in, 7
  Jeremiah Clemens in, 279
  newspapers from, 41
  publishing in, 125, 135, 186, 193, 294
  self-improvement in, 28
Phillips, Philip, 154
Pickett, Albert (author, father)
  absences of, from home, 92
  and Alexander Meek, 157, 288
  ambitions of, 155, 166
  attitude of, toward powerful families, 10
  in Charleston, SC, 141
  and class, 98, 168
  and competition, 146
  and concept of family, 63
  death of, 251
  finances of, 62, 75, 81, 82, 92, 93, 130, 135, 136–137, 158
  and freedom, 130
  and friendship, 98
  and gender roles, 79, 92
  and George Hooper, 129–130
  idealization of southern culture by, 157
  and Johnson Hooper, 157, 167
  landholdings of, 10, 76, 78, 82, 136, 138, 144
  and migration, 82
  in Montgomery, AL, 146
  in New York, 140–141
  and patriarchy, 130
  personality of, 76, 78–79, 80, 81, 82, 139, 140, 146, 158, 169
  physical characteristics of, 80
  as planter, 81, 146
  political views of, 78, 137–138, 146
  response of, to criticisms of *History of Alabama*, 159
  and secession, 146
  and self-determination, 82, 146
  and slavery, 7, 64, 76, 79, 82, 93, 136, 137, 138, 169, 174
  and social status, 146
  Thomas Woodward and, 168
  and voluntary associations, 9
  and Walker family, 129
  and William Gilmore Simms, 140, 158
  and Woodward's *Reminiscences*, 169
Pickett, Albert (author, father), family of
  brother-in-law, 78
  children, 78, 79, 82, 83, 93
  correspondence with, 93
  father, 62, 75–76, 78, 146
  grandson, 82
  inequalities in, 64

Index 313

niece, 76–78, 94, 117, 129
siblings, 76, 78
wife, 64, 76, 78–79, 80–81, 93, 136, 141
Pickett, Albert (author, father), works by, 78, 135, 171
See also individual works by Pickett
Pickett, Albert (grandson), 82
Pickett, Albert (son), 79
Pickett, Lida, 79
Pickett, Sarah Alston Harris
correspondence with, 78, 79, 80–81, 82, 141
family of, 76
health of, 80
and husband's absences, 79, 80, 92
husband's concerns for, 93
inheritance of, 76
marriage of, 78, 79, 80–81, 93, 130
role of, 79
and slavery, 76
Pickett, Sooky, 79
Pickett, William Dickson, 76, 97
Pickett, William R., 75–76, 78, 81
Pickett's Springs, AL, 76
Pierce, Franklin, 121, 124, 221
Planter's Gazette, 137
Planter's Northern Bride, The (Hentz), 114, 193–198
planters
Alabama writers and, 58, 130
Alexander Meek and, 58, 163
Augusta Evans and, 264
Caroline Hentz and, 58
and change, 218
as Democrats, 166, 243
Johnson Hooper and, 58, 166, 169, 243
as leaders, 35, 77, 130
literary depictions of, 92, 168
and middle classes, 146
and persuasion, 58
and self-determination, 92
and slavery, 147
townspeople and, 130
William Gilmore Simms on, 35
William Russell Smith and, 231
Plessy v. Ferguson, 294, 295
Poe, Edgar Allan, 57
Poetical Works of George Moses Horton, The (Horton), 190
Poor Richard's Almanac, 33
Pope, LeRoy, 116, 117
Porter, William T., 51, 54, 56
print culture
Alexander Meek and, 59
Caroline Hentz and, 59

competition in, 135
impact of, 2, 14–15
Johnson Hooper and, 59
middle classes and, 14–15, 171
and northern publishing, 135–136
and politics, 218
reform organizations and, 204
religious organizations and, 13, 14
and slavery, 130
and wealth, 28
See also magazines; *see* newspapers
"Proem" (Meek), 1, 288–289
progress, 172, 188, 209, 210, 243
Protestantism, 84, 85

Randolph, John, 221, 224, 226
Read, John, 277
Read, Major, 119
Read, Mary. *See* Clemens, Mary Read
Reconstruction, 292
Red Eagle (Meek), 164.
See also Weatherford, William ("Red Eagle")
Register (Mobile, AL), 102, 158
Reminiscences (Smith), 291–294, 295, 296
Reminiscences of the Creek, or Muscogee Indians (Woodward)
audiences for, 169
contents of, 167–169, 170, 171
introduction to, 167, 169
perspective of, 166
publication of, 134, 169, 242
as response to Pickett's *History of Alabama*, 134, 157
slavery in, 135, 170
Renaissance, 210
"Representative Men" (Baldwin), 221
Republican (Carrollton, AL), 139
Republicans and Republican Party
and 1856 presidential election, 242
and 1859 Speaker of the House election, 237
and 1860 presidential election, 286
Alabamians and, 266
forces strengthening, 228
Johnson Hooper and, 243
northern, 243
on slavery's impact, 2
Whigs and, 232
William Russell Smith and, 249
Rhett, Robert Barnwell, 122
Richard Hurdis (Simms), 35
Richmond, VA
Johnson Hooper in, 251

Richmond, VA (*cont.*)
  Joseph Baldwin in, 70, 148
  publishing in, 68, 258
  Union Army encroachments on, 251
  William Makepeace Thackeray in, 148
  William Russell Smith in, 271, 273, 292
Rocky Mountains, 3
Romantic Passages in Southwestern History
    (Meek), 134, 157, 161, 162, 163–166,
    170, 288
Romantics and Romanticism, 18, 150, 289
Royal Ape, The (Smith), 251, 253, 272–276,
    289, 296
Russell County, AL, 83, 142

"Sam Hele, Esq." (Baldwin), 153–154
San Antonio, TX, 84
San Francisco, CA, 156
Santa Anna, Antonio López de, 72
Sartor Resartus (Carlyle), 200
Schlegel, Frederick von, 33
Scott, Walter, 149
Scott, Winfield, 221
secession
  Alexander Meek and, 288, 293
  Augusta Evans and, 256
  Jeremiah Clemens and, 215, 249–250, 276,
    277–278, 283
  Johnson Hooper and, 246
  Lincoln's election as trigger for, 246, 266
  Whigs and, 277
  William Russell Smith and, 219, 249, 251,
    266–267, 270, 292, 293
Second Treatise of Civil Government
    (Locke), 17
self-determination
  Alabama writers and, 29, 123, 129, 136,
    289, 297
  Albert Pickett and, 146
  Augusta Evans and, 253–254, 258
  and class, 171
  concept of family and, 62, 65, 92, 93
  and democracy, 215–216
  and friendship, 95, 96, 99, 129
  literary depictions of, 136, 144, 152, 154
  literary orphans and, 92
  middle classes and, 27, 58, 60, 92, 99, 173
  as national ideal, 60
  and older traditions, 99
  planters and, 92
  and political ambition, 228
  and progress, 209
  and race, 171–172, 176
  and self-control, 228
  and slavery, 65, 130, 146, 171–172, 176, 207
  threats to, 215
  and wealth, 92
  writing as means of, 252
  See also freedom. *See* individual writers
self-government, 250
self-sufficiency, 216
Seminole Indians, 167
  See also Creek Indians; Native Americans
Senate, U.S., 21, 122, 153, 173, 276
"Sex of the Soul, The" (Hentz), 110
Shakespeare, William, 96, 149, 234
Shenandoah Valley, 65
Shiloh, TN, 257
Simms, William Gilmore
  and Albert Pickett, 140, 158
  and Alexander Meek, 32, 34, 140, 157–158
  as author, 134
  banquet for, 36–38
  earnings of, 28
  on history's focus, 159
  on literature and culture, 36
  as magazine editor, 32
  and patriarchy, 58
  and Pickett's *History of Alabama*, 142,
    158–159
  as Romantic, 158, 162
  on rural life, 35
  as social leader, 36
  on southern publishing, 159
  and *Southern Quarterly Review*, 230
  and University of Alabama commencement,
    35
  and works by Alexander Meek, 160, 162
"Simon Suggs, Jr., Esq." (Baldwin), 148, 155
Siro (slave), 168
Slatter, Hope Hull, 160
slavery
  Alabama writers and, 93, 123, 133,
    134–135, 136, 174, 179, 250, 289
  arguments supporting, 193
  California and, 157
  compared to northern domestic service, 194
  and concept of family, 64
  Confederates and, 284
  coverage of, in histories, 134–135, 136
  criticism of, 27
  debates about, 123, 133
  defenses of, 20–21, 174, 176, 179
  end of, 253
  expansion of, 218, 219
  and freedom, 1, 2, 15, 57, 157, 163, 170,
    188, 289
  and gender, 207

and hierarchy, 130
and inequality, 93, 210
literary depictions of, 20, 152–153, 154, 197
and literary market, 136
as literary topic, 15
means of control in, 216
middle classes and, 17, 130, 173, 208
mother-child bond in, 192
northerners and, 115
and progress, 20, 188, 210
and race, 207, 244
reform of, 176–177
and self-determination, 65, 130, 146, 171–172, 176, 207
and slave trade, 21, 174
southerners and, 115
Thomas Woodward and, 135
urban, 176, 177
and wealth, 163
white fears of, 22
women and, 257–258
See also individual writers
slaves
activities of, 17, 21, 176, 177, 190, 199, 208
Alabama writers and, 21–22, 26
as assets, 7
compared to northern domestic servants, 177, 194
and education, 25
and farms, 7
forced migrations of, 21
and freedom, 253
hired, 190
humanity of, 174
literary depictions of, by Augusta Evans, 87
middle classes and, 16–17
monetary value of, 188
and patriarchy, 130
as property, 174
recording of, in U.S. census, 147, 174
and self-determination, 207, 216
as sources of capital, 208
urban, 17, 177
and white prosperity, 16
See also African Americans
slaves, literary depictions of
by Alabama writers, 7, 20, 22, 177, 179, 210
by Albert Pickett, 144–145
by Augusta Evans, 86–87, 199, 200–203, 204–205, 208–209, 260

by Caroline Hentz, 194, 198, 203, 208–209
by Jeremiah Clemens, 284–285
by Johnson Hooper, 182–184, 186–187, 189, 208–209
by Joseph Baldwin, 7, 16, 152, 295
by Terence, 261
by William Russell Smith, 274, 295
Smith, Anne. *See* Easby-Smith, Anne
Smith, Elizabeth, 71, 74, 269
Smith, Sidney, 72
Smith, Wilhemine Easby
and Alexander Meek, 130
childhood of, 291
children of, 75, 233
conversion of, to Catholicism, 270–271
correspondence with, 266–272, 273, 275
daughter Anne on, 296
husband's absences from, 265
life of, after Civil War, 291
love sonnets for, 273
management of slaves and household by, 268
marriage of, 75, 232
newspaper contributions by, 292
personality of, 75
poetry by, 267
political beliefs of, 267
property owned by, 291, 292
relocations by, 291, 292
Smith, William Russell
activities of, during Civil War, 265
as advocate for southern literature, 102
and Alexander Meek, 14, 31, 97, 98–106, 129, 130, 293
ambitions of, 218, 239, 269, 275, 287
career of, as editor, 31, 44, 72, 230, 292
childhood and early adulthood of, 10, 64, 71–72, 75, 92, 93, 94, 228, 269
and Civil War, 251, 252–254, 286
and class, 252
and competition, 218
and concept of family, 63
and Confederacy, 270, 276, 292
daughter's biography of, 72, 74, 75, 296
death of, 294, 296, 297
and democracy, 216–218
drinking habits of, 268
earnings by, 269
and fame, 293
finances of, 266
and friendship, 98–99, 106, 128–129
and gender, 273–274
and Jeremiah Clemens, 120, 230
legal career of, 10, 230, 233, 292
life of, after Civil War, 287, 291, 292–293

Smith, William Russell (*cont.*)
  and literary success, 72
  military career of, 72, 230, 270
  as orator, 101–102
  personality of, 71, 72, 75, 99–100, 104, 228, 249, 265, 269, 271, 274, 276
  on political ambition, 228
  political career of, 11, 75, 102, 228, 230, 231–232, 233, 251, 253, 265, 266–267, 270, 271, 276, 287, 291, 292, 293
  political views of, 102, 217–218, 228, 231, 245, 249, 266, 270, 271–272
  and popularity, 106
  and print culture, 11
  and religion, 271, 283, 296
  relocations by, 230, 291, 292, 296
  and secession, 105, 219, 233, 249, 251, 266–267, 270, 292, 293
  and self-determination, 64, 75, 106, 107, 129, 218–219, 253–254, 275
  and self-sufficiency, 216
  and slavery, 7, 71, 105, 174, 218, 253, 266, 268, 286
  and wealth, 10, 71, 72
  and William Lowndes Yancey, 105
  writing skills of, 101
Smith, William Russell, family of
  first wife, 230
  children, 72, 74, 75, 232, 233, 292, 296
  father, 71, 74
  literary inspiration from, 93
  mother, 71, 74, 75, 269
  relocations by, 292
  second wife, 230, 232
  siblings, 72, 74, 75, 92, 228
  third wife, 75, 232–233, 265, 266–272, 273, 275, 291, 292
  troubles in, 62
Smith, William Russell, works by
  Alexander Meek on, 102
  audiences for, 275
  characteristics of, 93, 228
  during Civil War, 253
  love sonnets for third wife, 273
  as popular fiction, 93
  sketch of Alexander Meek, 239
  slavery in, 93
  slaves and slavery depicted in, 74
  translation of *Iliad*, 292
  See also individual works by Smith
Social Principle: The Source of National Permanence, The (Simms), 35
Songs and Poems of the South (Meek), 102–103, 114, 161

Soto, Hernando de, 142, 162, 164
South Carolina, 32, 35, 83, 121, 122, 146
South Carolina College, 48
Southern Democrat, 120
Southern Literary Messenger
  Alexander Meek's works mentioned in, 161, 166
  editor of, 148
  Joseph Baldwin's works in, 147, 148, 153, 166, 171, 221, 224
  Pickett's *History of Alabama* ignored by, 158
  review of Evans's *Beulah* in, 210
  Richmond, Va., publication of, 68, 148
Southern Quarterly Review, 139, 156, 158, 230
Southern Rights, 232
Southron, The, 31–32, 45, 59, 101, 135
Souvenirs of Travel (Le Vert), 160, 161
Spaulding, James, 255
Speed, Joshua, 97
Spirit of the Times, 51, 54, 56, 57
Springfield, IL, 10, 28
St. Elmo (Evans), 287
Stafford, Maria, 108, 109, 110
Stafford, Samuel, 108
Stowe, Harriet Beecher, 40, 135, 154
Stuart, Alexander H. H.
  correspondence with, 156, 219–220, 221, 227–228
  criticism of Baldwin's work by, 221, 224
  Flush Times dedicated to, 65
  political career of, 65, 156, 219, 220
Suggs, Simon (literary character)
  and audience, 53
  characteristics of, 52, 133
  on education, 25
  first appearances of, 51
  motto of, 26
  and persuasion, 56, 59
  popularity of, 48
  and public, 59, 60
  as representative of middle-class aspirations, 208
  success of work presented in, 29
  as vehicle for social criticism, 52
Sumter County, AL, 147
Supreme Court, U.S., 294, 296

Tabby (slave), 168
"Taking the Census" (Hooper), 51
Talladega, AL, 66, 187–188
Tallapoosa County, AL, 142
Tallapoosa River, 52, 81
Taylor, Zachary, 121, 148, 230

Index

Temperance Society, 30
Tennessee, 43
Tennessee River, 4
Tennessee Valley, 41
Texas, 82, 83, 84, 103, 199
Texas War for Independence, 72
Thackeray, William Makepeace, 70, 148
Thompson, John R., 148
Thoreau, Henry David, 289
Thorpe, Thomas Bangs, 162
Timrod, Henry, 257
Tobias Wilson: A Tale of the Great Rebellion (Clemens), 253, 276, 280–283, 284–286
Toombs, Robert, 155
Townes, Samuel, 140
towns
  activities in, 17
  Alabama writers and, 26, 296
  antisecessionists in, 266
  and Civil War, 252
  consumer goods in, 17
  economy of, 205
  literary societies in, 25
  property ownership in, 16–17
  publishing in, 28
  slaves in, 17
  wealth in, 130
  See also individual towns
Transcendentalists 15
Transylvania College, 117
Tribune (Harper, NY), 161
Tuscaloosa County, 232
Tuscaloosa, AL
  Alabama writers in, 26
  Alexander Meek in, , 1, 9, 29, 30, 63, 99, 100, 102
  booksellers in, 14
  Caroline Hentz in, 46, 108
  Charles Hentz in, 109
  Clement Clay, Jr., in, 117
  Cyrus Baldwin in, 65
  depicted in fiction, 8
  historical society in, 9
  Jeremiah Clemens in, 119
  Johnson Hooper in, 9, 49
  manufacturing in, 8
  middle classes in, 266
  population of, 8
  print culture in, 292
  publishing in, 11, 31, 39, 186, 233
  schools in, 29
  state Capitol in, 29
  temperance society in, 9
  Thaddeus Hentz in, 109
  University of Alabama in, 34, 108
  William Gilmore Simms in, 58, 103
  William Russell Smith in, 11, 71, 72, 99, 228, 233, 266, 291, 292
  William Russell Smith's constituents in, 231, 266
Tuskegee, AL, 47, 109, 110
Twain, Mark. *See* Clemens, Samuel ("Mark Twain")

Uncle Tom's Cabin (Stowe), 153, 154, 179, 191, 193, 198, 208
Uncle Young (slave), 177, 190, 195, 208
University of Alabama
  Alexander Meek and, 30
  Clement Clay, Jr., at, 117
  establishment of, 30
  literary societies at, 46
  literature chair for, 34
  presidents of, 34, 292
  and relocation of state capital, 109
  William Gilmore Simms at, 35
  William Russell Smith and, 72, 292
University of North Carolina, 40, 48
Uses of Solitude, The (Smith)
  contents of, 61, 104–106, 112, 233, 266
  Daniel Boone's wife in, 61, 64
  included in Smith's biography, 296
  publication of, 233
  quotations from, 61, 64, 104–106, 266, 291, 293
  reprinted in Smith's *Reminiscences*, 293, 296
  Smith's self-depiction in, 276

Virginia and Virginians, 65, 77, 94, 225, 226, 238, 271
Virginia Court of Appeals, 220

Wake Forest University, 48
Walden (Thoreau), 14, 239
Walker family, 94, 117, 129
Walker, Eliza Pickett, 76–78, 94, 117, 129, 145
Walker, John Williams, 116, 117, 145
Walker, Leroy Pope, 77, 117, 129
War and Its Incidents (Smith), 230–231
War of 1812, 4, 116, 142
Washington, DC, 124, 245, 291, 292, 294, 296, 297
Weatherford, William ("Red Eagle"), 145, 160, 164, 168, 169
Webster, Daniel, 103, 220
West and Johnson, 258
"Whig, or the Diary of a Young Candidate, The" (Smith), 228–230, 266

Whig (Wetumpka, AL), 138
Whigs and Whig Party
  and 1860 presidential election, 246
  Alabama writers and, 7
  collapse of, 242
  commercial farmers and, 7
  economic policies of, 7
  Jeremiah Clemens and, 121
  Joseph Baldwin on, 224
  as minority, 124
  northern, 232
  and progress, 243
  and secession, 277
  urbanites and, 7
  use of persuasion by, 52
  and wealth, 243
Widow Rugby's Husband, The (Hooper), 180, 186–187
Wilde, Richard, 103
"Wild Jack, or the Stolen Child" (Hentz), 191–192
Wildman, Dr., 113
Wilhelm Meister (Goethe), 74, 236
Willard, Mr. and Mrs., 111
Wilmington, NC, 48, 49, 180, 181
Winchester, VA, 149
Wirt, William, 37
Wise, Henry, 237
Withers, Jones, 121
women, 83, 204, 257–258, 287
  See also individual writers and individual works
Woodward, Thomas, 135, 167, 168, *See also Reminiscences of the Creek, or Muscogee Indians*
work ethic, 204, 216

Yancey, William Lowndes, 105, 256, 288, 293
Young America movement, 231